FUNDAMENTAL RIGHTS IN EU INTERNAL MARKET LEGISLATION

This book attempts to systematise the present interrelationship between fundamental rights and the EU internal market in the field of positive integration. Its intention is simple: to examine the way in which, and the extent to which, fundamental rights protection is realised through EU internal market legislation. To that end, the analysis is conducted around four rights or sets of rights: data protection, freedom of expression, fundamental labour rights and the right to health. The book assesses not only what substantive level of protection is achieved for these fundamental rights, but it also estimates whether there is a 'fundamental rights culture' that informs current legislative practice. Finally, it asks the overarching question whether the current state of harmonisation amounts to a 'fundamental rights policy'.

The book offers a much more varied picture of the EU's fundamental rights policy in and through the EU internal market than perhaps initially expected. Moreover, it builds the case for a more conscious approach to dealing with and enhancing fundamental rights protection in and through internal market legislation, and advocates a leading role for the legislature in the establishment of an internal market that is firmly based on respect for fundamental rights.

Volume 58 in the Series Modern Studies in European Law

Modern Studies in European Law
Recent titles in this series:

EU Liability and International Economic Law
Armin Steinbach

The EU and Nanotechnologies: A Critical Analysis
Tanja Ehnert

Human Rights Between Law and Politics: The Margin of Appreciation in Post-National Contexts
Edited by Petr Agha

The European Union and Social Security Law
Jaan Paju

The Rule of Law in the European Union: The Internal Dimension
Theodore Konstadinides

The Division of Competences between the EU and the Member States: Reflections on the Past, the Present and the Future
Edited by Sacha Garben and Inge Govaere

Unity in Adversity: EU Citizenship, Social Justice and the Cautionary Tale of the UK
Charlotte O'Brien

The Use of Force and Article 2 of the ECHR in Light of European Conflicts
Hannah Russell

Environmental Crime in Europe
Edited by Andrew Farmer, Michael Faure and Grazia Maria Vagliasindi

Questioning EU Citizenship: Judges and the Limits of Free Movement and Solidarity in the EU
Edited by Daniel Thym

The European Union under Transnational Law: A Pluralist Appraisal
Matej Avbelj

Illegally Staying in the EU: An Analysis of Illegality in EU Migration Law
Benedita Menezes Queiroz

Social Legitimacy in the Internal Market: A Dialogue of Mutual Responsiveness
Jotte Mulder

The EU Better Regulation Agenda: A Critical Assessment
Edited by Sacha Garben and Inge Govaere

For the complete list of titles in this series, see
'Modern Studies in European Law' link at
www.bloomsburyprofessional.com/uk/series/modern-studies-in-european-law

Fundamental Rights in EU Internal Market Legislation

Vasiliki Kosta

• HART •
PUBLISHING
OXFORD AND PORTLAND, OREGON
2018

Hart Publishing
An imprint of Bloomsbury Publishing Plc

Hart Publishing Ltd
Kemp House
Chawley Park
Cumnor Hill
Oxford OX2 9PH
UK

Bloomsbury Publishing Plc
50 Bedford Square
London
WC1B 3DP
UK

www.hartpub.co.uk
www.bloomsbury.com

Published in North America (US and Canada) by
Hart Publishing
c/o International Specialized Book Services
920 NE 58th Avenue, Suite 300
Portland, OR 97213-3786
USA

www.isbs.com

First published in hardback, 2015
Paperback edition, 2018

British Library Cataloguing-in-Publication Data
A catalogue record for this book is available from the British Library.

ISBN: PB: 978-1-50992-000-6
HB: 978-1-84946-711-7

Typeset by Compuscript Ltd, Shannon
Printed and bound in Great Britain by
Lightning Source UK Ltd

Foreword by Bruno de Witte

Traditionally, and still today, the question of fundamental rights protection in the EU legal order has been seen as a matter for courts. In particular, the stories of how the Court of Justice of the European Union developed a doctrine of fundamental rights protection based on general principles of EU law, and of the relation between that Court's case law and its counterparts at international (ECHR) and national (constitutional court) level, have often been told, and new developments keep rekindling the scholarly interest in those themes.

The role of the EU's political institutions, and of EU legislative and administrative action, in protecting fundamental rights has recently been examined more extensively, although principally with respect to anti-discrimination law, and the area of freedom, security and justice. Vasiliki Kosta's book puts the spotlight on another field of EU law-making, namely internal market law.

The protection and promotion of fundamental rights is now also a firm duty for the internal market legislator. That duty is imposed by Article 51(1) of the EU Charter of Fundamental Rights which requires the EU institutions not only to respect the rights contained in the Charter but also to *promote their application* in the exercise of their competences. Further mainstreaming clauses were added or confirmed by the Lisbon Treaty. They are all prominently located in the TFEU and make it an obligation for the EU institutions to consider, in all their policies and activities (including, therefore, in the internal market domain), the values and objectives of gender equality, non-discrimination generally, social protection and animal welfare. More broadly speaking, all the mandatory requirements that the CJEU has recognised over the course of time as being able to limit trade or mobility in the internal market (these form, as is well known, a long and open-ended list) may, by logical extension, also form the object of internal market laws. If the member states are allowed to maintain restrictions on the free movement of goods or services when justified for the protection of their constitutional rights (as the CJEU recognised they could), then the European Union may address those same concerns when adopting harmonisation measures designed to eliminate the restrictions. And the fact that Article 114 TFEU, the principal legal basis for internal market legislation, expressly refers to only some non-market concerns, namely public health and safety and environmental protection, does not prevent fundamental rights concerns from being addressed through internal market legislation.

Internal market legislation, to be constitutionally valid, must satisfy a specific internal market test, in the sense that the Union legislator must make a plausible case that the act either helps to remove disparities between national provisions that hinder the free movement of goods, services or persons, or helps to remove disparities that cause distorted conditions of competition. However, these need not be, and cannot logically be, the only purposes of internal market legislation. Such legislation also invariably and legitimately pursues other public policy objectives. Internal market legislation is always also 'about something else', and that something else may be the protection, or regulation, of fundamental rights.

In the innovative analysis proposed in her book, Vasiliki Kosta starts by discussing this competence issue, namely whether the Union is entitled to address fundamental rights issues in internal market legislation, and on the basis of her positive answer to that question, she tackles the main rights which have thus been addressed in internal market legislation, namely data protection, freedom of expression, labour rights and the right to health. Some of the issues analysed in those chapters are among the most controversial parts of internal market law, such as the regulation of tobacco advertising, of posted workers, and of data retention. The analysis of these discrete subject areas is complemented by a chapter analysing in great detail the institutional mechanisms that were developed over the course of years, to help build a 'fundamental rights culture' in the EU's policy process.

This book gives a fascinating insight into EU fundamental rights law as it develops 'outside the court room', although the relevant Court judgments are, of course, duly examined. It offers an original, thoroughly researched and elegantly written account of an increasingly important domain of EU law.

Acknowledgements

This book started as a doctoral thesis at the European University Institute, Florence in 2007 under the supervision of Bruno de Witte. I thank him for his constant guidance, encouragement and support throughout the research and writing process. He has very much influenced the way I think about law and I am most grateful to him for everything he has taught me. It was a great privilege to work with him.

I would also like to thank my examining board, Hans-Wolfgang Micklitz, Niamh Nic Shuibhne and Clemens Ladenburger, for their most valuable comments on this work.

My thanks also go to the Greek National Scholarship authority, IKY, whose grant made this research possible.

I am grateful for having been given the opportunity to discuss aspects of this book with people from several EU institutions. I thank Kieran Bradley, Koen Lenaerts, Alvaro Oliveira, Martin Selmayr, Joze Strus, Gabriel Toggenburg and the staff of the EU Fundamental Rights Agency. I am also thankful to John Morijn, who reminded me to pay attention to the practical relevance of aspects of this book, and to Marise Cremona for her interest in the development of this project throughout the years.

Parts of this book were written during a stay in London, which Alison McDonnell helped to realise. I am most thankful to the British Institute of International and Comparative Law for hosting me and to Melody Cheng for more than her kind hospitality during that time.

I thank my colleagues at the Europa Institute of Leiden University, and especially Stefaan Van den Bogaert and Jorrit Rijpma, for their exceptional patience and support during the finalisation process of both the doctoral thesis and this book.

I spent my 'legal formative' years at King's College London, where the first ideas of this book emerged. I was very fortunate to receive the support of Andrea Biondi there, who encouraged me to pursue this research. I thank him very much for that.

I owe a large debt of gratitude to Ravi Mehta, who has been reading, debating with me and editing drafts for this book since the very beginning, and to Marios Iacovides and Anna Pitaraki, who helped with formatting and adapting the text to the publisher's housestyle. Without their invaluable help and generosity, I would have not been able to finish this manuscript in time.

Finally, warm thanks to the staff of Hart Publishing, who have made this publication possible.

This book is dedicated to my family. *Στο Λευτέρη, τη Ρόζα και την Αντωνία.*

Florence–Vienna–London–Leiden VK
March 2015

Table of Contents

Table of Cases

European Court of First Instance

European Court of Justice

European Court of Human Rights

European Committee of Social Rights

National Courts

Australia

Austria

Canada

Cyprus

Czechoslovakia

Germany

Romania

Slovenia

United Kingdom

United States

Table of Legislation

European Union

Conventions, Treaties, Agreements and Charters

Directives

Regulations

Decisions

National Legislation

Australia

Czechoslovakia

Finland

Germany

Greece

United Kingdom

United States

International Material

Table of Institutional Documents

EUROPEAN COMMISSION

Commission Proposals

Commission Green Papers

Commission White Papers

Commission Communications

Commission Recommendations

Commission Staff Working Documents

EUROPEAN PARLIAMENT

European Parliament Preparatory Legislative Documents

European Parliament Resolutions

European Parliament Decisions

European Parliament Working Documents

COUNCIL OF THE EUROPEAN UNION

Council Preparatory Legislative Documents

Council Conclusions

Council Guidelines

Council Discussion Documents

Council Presidency Documents

Council Resolutions

1

Introduction

I. SETTING THE SCENE: A FUNDAMENTAL RIGHTS POLICY IN THE INTERNAL MARKET?

THIS BOOK EXAMINES the relationship between one of the 'foundations' of the European Union (EU),[1] fundamental rights protection and its driving force, also considered the 'cornerstone of Europe's integration', the internal market.[2]

It focuses on the critical but neglected point where the two meet in the EU's *positive* integration process. This process is characterised by the active adoption of measures by the political institutions in order to pursue the objective of integration. It contrasts with the process of *negative* integration, through which the Court of Justice of the European Union (the Court) plays a central role in interpreting, applying and enforcing legal prohibitions set out by the Treaties.[3]

Fundamental rights and the internal market not only share their central position in the EU integration project, but also a further characteristic: their respective evolutions are typically described as stories of overall success. The narratives of success differ, however, in their respective fields.

For the internal market project, success was crucially dependent on complementing the operation of the free movement provisions with the pursuit of a rigid and defined policy involving the adoption of positive measures and institutional re-arrangements to facilitate implementation. In other words, the appropriate combination of negative and positive integration had to be achieved. The following is the conventional narrative.

The internal market project underwent a remarkable development from the initial steps in the European Economic Community (EEC) to abolish quotas and tariffs in the trading of goods, to the landmark jurisprudence of the Court of Justice boosting market-making by providing a very wide definition of quantitative restrictions.[4] Subsequently, the now-renamed EU overcame the stagnant period of the 1980s with the famous White Paper 1992[5] programme, which could be successfully pursued after adoption of the Single European Act. At the time, a pivotal provision was introduced—Article 100a of the EEC Treaty—today's Article 114 of the Treaty on the Functioning of the European Union (TFEU).

[1] Articles 6 and 7 TEU.

[2] M Monti, 'A New Strategy for the Single Market', Report to the President of the European Commission (9 May 2010) (hereinafter 'Monti Report').

[3] JHH Weiler, 'The Transformation of Europe' (1991) 100 *Yale Law Journal* 2403; and F Scharpf, *Governing in Europe. Effective and Democratic?* (Oxford, Oxford University Press, 1999).

[4] In particular, Case 8/74 *Procureur du Roi v Benoit and Gustave Dassonville* [1974] ECR 837.

[5] White Paper from the Commission to the European Council, 'Completing the Internal Market' (14 June 1985), COM(85) 310.

Decision-making at the EU level was facilitated by providing a legal basis for the adoption of harmonising measures by qualified majority voting (as opposed to the previously required unanimity). The adoption of a vast amount of legislation followed between 1986 and 1992,[6] so that today, the Commission is in a position to say that by 1993 the 'single market bec[ame] a reality'.[7] At the same time, on the occasion of the anniversary of the 1992 date which the White Paper set for completing the Internal Market, the Commission made efforts in order to address the ongoing shortcomings.[8] It adopted the Single Market Act I in order to 'boost growth and strengthen confidence'.[9] This item was kept high on the agenda, as is evidenced by the adoption of the Single Market Act II, which complements the list of key legislative actions contained in the former.[10] The political route therefore continues to be key for European trade integration.

The narrative of EU fundamental rights, in contrast, focuses on limits to EU activity—the classic negative function of fundamental rights as a 'shield', which contrasts to positive policy-making. This is not surprising, especially when bearing in mind that the watershed moment in the narrative was the introduction of fundamental rights protection in EU law by the Court.

Fundamental rights played a pivotal role in crucial moments of the evolution of the European legal order.[11] They constitute a measure for the legality of the EU's acts, as well as for that of its Member States when they are implementing those acts and when acting more broadly within the scope of EU law. Under Article 7 TEU, Member States may also lose some of their rights under the Treaties if a serious breach on their part of fundamental rights is established. In its external relations, the EU is sending the unequivocal message that it aims at 'exporting' the principle for respect of fundamental human rights,[12] thereby pursuing an *external* human rights policy. With the entry into force of the Lisbon Treaty, the EU now even has its own legally binding catalogue of fundamental rights[13] and finally established a legal basis mandating EU accession to the European Convention on Human Rights (ECHR).[14]

[6] According to the Commission, this included over 280 items. See http://ec.europa.eu/internal_market/top_layer/historical_overview/index_en.htm

[7] ibid.

[8] Interestingly, Monti identifies one of the three key challenges today as being the false sense that 'the single market had been really completed and could thus be put to rest as a political priority'. See Monti Report, above n 2, 6.

[9] Communication from the Commission to the European Parliament, the Council, the Economic and Social Committee and the Committee of the Regions, 'Single Market Act—Twelve Levers to Boost Growth and Strengthen Confidence "Working Together to Create New Growth"' COM(2011) 0206 final (hereinafter 'Single Market Act I').

[10] Communication from the Commission to the European Parliament, the Council, the Economic and Social Committee and the Committee of the Regions, 'Single Market Act II Together for New Growth' COM(2012) 573 final.

[11] As is very well known, the protection of such rights at the EU level constituted the precondition for the Member States' acceptance of the (constitutional) doctrines of supremacy and direct effect.

[12] Through means such as the 'conditionality clauses' in international agreements or the requirement imposed on a candidate country to fulfil a high standard of protection for human rights in order to be eligible for accession to the EU (the so-called 'Helsinki criteria').

[13] Charter of Fundamental Rights [2010] OJ C83/389.

[14] Article 6(2) TFEU. At the time of writing, the CJEU has declared that the draft agreement on the accession of the EU to the ECHR is not compatible with Art 6(2) TEU or with Protocol (No 8) relating to Art 6(2) TEU. See CJEU, Opinion 2/13 of the Court (18 December 2014). The direct consequence is that re-negotiations based on the Court's findings have to take place in order to go ahead with the accession process under the current Treaties. Considering how difficult it was to reach agreement on the draft under the Court's scrutiny, this is likely to prove a very difficult and drawn-out process.

A shift in attention to an EU *internal* fundamental rights *policy* also occurred, and it did so long before the Lisbon Treaty. The landmark moment was the 'turn of the millennium', when the search for 'a Human Rights Agenda for the year 2000' was announced.[15] The report that followed was compiled by Professors Alston and Weiler.[16,17] The authors forcefully identified an inherent paradox in EU fundamental rights protection, which had to be remedied: 'On the one hand, the Union is a staunch defender of human rights in both its internal and external affairs. On the other hand, it lacks a comprehensive or coherent policy at either level.'[18] This was of course not to deny that single instances of positive action did exist; gender equality is one important example,[19] and data protection and intellectual property are others.

In order to build a comprehensive and coherent fundamental rights policy, the authors put forward important proposals for institutional reform. Some of these have materialised today, such as the creation of Directorate General (DG) Justice and a separate Commissioner responsible for fundamental rights,[20] as well as the creation of the Fundamental Rights Agency (FRA).[21]

Interestingly, one of the arguments justifying the need for a comprehensive or coherent policy was the analogy drawn with the internal market: just as the EU internal market could only be completed by complementing negative integration with positive integration, so—it was said—comprehensive fundamental rights protection also required a complementary 'legal prohibition on violation with positive measures and a pro-active human rights policy'.[22]

It should be emphasised, however, that the analogy drawn between the two areas in this integration-inspired paradigm is asymmetrical in the following sense: in internal market law, at the core of the distinction between negative and positive integration stands the question of Member State impact; in other words, whether EU law will only strike down single instances of obstacles to trade on a case-by-case basis or whether it will take away the regulatory autonomy of Member States entirely and replace the national with a EU-wide harmonised standard. The choice between negative and positive integration therefore primarily concerns the vertical relationship between Member States and the EU.

In contrast, the distinction between the negative and positive role of fundamental rights is one that first and foremost concerns the actions and interaction of EU institutions and is

[15] *Leading by Example: A Human Rights Agenda for the Year 2000*, Vienna (9–10 October 1998), adopted by a *Comité des Sages*.

[16] P Alston and JHH Weiler, 'The European Union and Human Rights: Final Project Report on an Agenda for the Year 2000', in *Leading by Example: A Human Rights Agenda for the European Union for the Year 2000: Agenda of the Comité des Sages and Final Project Report* (1998) Academy of European Law, EUI, Florence; and P Alston and JHH Weiler, 'An Ever Closer Union in Need of a Human Rights Policy' (1998) 9 *European Journal of International Law* 658.

[17] The authors clearly acknowledge that similar proposals to some of those contained in the Report had been already made earlier in time: see Alston and Weiler, 'An Ever Closer Union', above n 16, 659.

[18] Alston and Weiler, 'An Ever Closer Union', above n 16, 661.

[19] Also acknowledged by the authors Alston and Weiler (ibid 666).

[20] The first Commissioner to hold this post was V Reding, Commissioner for Justice, Fundamental Rights and Citizenship (2010–14). Under the Juncker Commission, fundamental rights fall under a new portfolio on 'Better Regulation, Inter-institutional Relations, the Rule of Law and the Charter of Fundamental Rights', which is held by F Timmermans.

[21] Council Regulation (EC) No 168/2007 establishing a European Union Agency for Fundamental Rights [2007] OJ L53/1.

[22] Alston and Weiler, above n 16, 666.

therefore horizontal in perspective. Thus, the question of the nature of positive integration in the fundamental rights context is about two different types of EU institutional duties: the abstention of institutions from acting in violation of fundamental rights and a positive duty to *act* incumbent on the political institutions in order to protect and promote fundamental rights.

The arguments in favour of such an approach are not novel: judicial fundamental rights protection presupposes that a violation has already occurred, that the applicant had the means to access a court and that a judicial remedy is appropriate in the given situation, and ultimately accepts that justice is done only in an individual case. The subject matter of the present book is, crucially, at the intersection of these two (vertical and horizontal) paradigms.

Attention to the question of the position that fundamental rights assume in the internal market was triggered by the negative integration process that also occurred in the 2000s (although after the report of Alston and Weiler). A new line of case law emerged,[23] with the *Schmidberger*,[24] *Omega*,[25] *Viking*[26] and *Laval*[27] cases featuring particularly prominently. In this case law, the possibility of a direct collision between fundamental rights and internal market freedoms became starkly evident for the first time. This collision is complicated by the fact that both interests carry the epithet 'fundamental'. Unsurprisingly, there was an avalanche of academic commentary on fundamental rights in the process of negative market integration more generally.[28]

It is this conflict that triggered the examination conducted in this book as there appears to be an opportunity to address the tension emerging out of the process of negative integration through the mechanism of positive integration.

[23] J Morijn, 'Balancing Fundamental Rights and Common Market Freedoms in Union Law: Schmidberger and Omega in the Light of the European Constitution' (2006) 12 *European Law Journal* 15, 16–17; Case C-112/00 *Eugen Schmidberger Internationale Transporte und Planzüge v Republic of Austria* [2003] ECR I-5659, Opinion of Advocate General Jacobs at [89]; Case C-36/02 *Omega Spielhallen-und Automatenaufstellungs-GmbH v Oberbürgermeisterin der Bundesstadt Bonn* [2004] ECR I-9609, Opinion of Advocate General Stix-Hackl at [44].

[24] Schmidberger, above n 23.

[25] Omega, above n 23.

[26] Case C-438/05 *The International Transport Workers' Federation and the Finnish Seamen's Union v Viking Lince ABP and OU Viking Line Eestt* [2007] ECR I-10779.

[27] Case C-341/05 *Laval un Partneri Ltd v Svenska Byggnadsarbetareförbundet and others* [2007] ECR I-11767.

[28] See, eg, A Biondi, 'Free Trade, a Mountain Road and the Right to Protest: European Economic Freedoms and Fundamental Individual Rights' (2004) 1 *European Human Rights Law Review* 52; F Ronkes Agerbeeck, 'Freedom of Expression and Free Movement in the Brenner Corridor: The Schmidberger Case' (2004) 29 *European Law Review* 255; A Alemanno, 'Fundamental Common Market Freedoms v Fundamental Individual Rights in the EU; What Role for the ECJ after Omega?' (2005) *EU Focus* 2; Morijn, above n 23; V Skouris, 'Fundamental Rights and Fundamental Freedoms: The Challenge of Striking a Delicate Balance' (2006) 17 *European Business Law Review* 225; B Bercusson, 'The Trade Union Movement and the European Union: Judgment Day' (2007) 13 *European Law Journal* 279; T Blanke, 'Die Entscheidungen des EuGH in den Fällen Viking, Laval und Rueffert—Domestizierung des Streikrechts und europaweite Nivellierung der industriellen Bezieungen', Oldeburger Studien zur Europäisierung und zur transnationalen Regulierung Nr 18/2008; ACL Davies, 'One Step Forwards, Two Steps Back? The Viking and Laval Cases in the ECJ' (2008) 37 *Industrial Law Journal* 126; N Reich, 'Free Movement v Social Rights in an Enlarged Union—The *Laval* and *Viking* Cases before the ECJ (2008) 2 *German Law Journal* 125; C Joerges and F Roedl, 'Informal Politics, Formalised Law and "the Social Deficit" of European Integration: Reflections after the Judgments of the ECJ *Viking* and *Laval*' (2009) 15 *European Law Journal* 1; SA de Vries et al, 'The Protection of Fundamental Rights within Europe's Internal Market after Lisbon—An Endeavour for Harmony' in De Vries et al (eds), *The Protection of Fundamental Rights in the EU After Lisbon* (Oxford, Hart Publishing, 2013) 59.

The essential thesis is simple. Since the rules of the market clearly interfere with fundamental human rights protection, as guaranteed at the national level, the balancing of fundamental human rights on the one hand and market freedoms on the other hand is to a certain extent transferred to the European level. Thus, Member States lose a certain degree of their autonomy.[29] This 'loss of autonomy' not only occurs where the CJEU decides against the lawfulness of a national rule that causes fragmentation of the internal market, but also by the very fact that national rules are caught by free movement rules in the first place. This is particularly evident when taking account of the fact that the EU legislature enjoys the competence 'to harmonise laws in pursuit of market-building ends'[30] (and, it should be added, market-correcting ends) where 'rules vary between states yet cause *lawful* obstacles to trade integration' (emphasis added).[31] It should also not be forgotten that national autonomy can be indirectly constrained by regulatory competition between Member States.[32]

The reason for the utility of positive integration as a tool for calibrating the relationship between market freedoms and fundamental rights is that the balancing of the two interests can be addressed *in a conscious manner by the legislator*, instead of remaining 'a functional result of the degree of negative market integration and its system of competition among rules'.[33] Two features of EU legislative involvement serve to compensate in a way (even if not fully) for the loss of national autonomy in the name of the market. One reason is that there is Member State involvement in defining the appropriate balance (through the Council of Ministers), as well as participation of the only democratically elected institution of the EU, the European Parliament. The other reason is that the operation of the free movement rules is in its essence concerned with market-making, whereas positive integration is a powerful tool for market correction and has been to a large extent used as such.[34]

There is also another point mandating the examination conducted in this book. Ever since the Charter of Fundamental Rights (the Charter) became legally binding, there is also a clear obligation imposed on the EU institutions to promote fundamental rights within the powers and tasks of the EU.[35] Thus, these institutions are required to mainstream fundamental rights considerations in each and every legislative and non-legislative initiative. This clearly includes the positive market integration process, it being immaterial whether the national laws that are sought to be harmonised are concerned with fundamental rights regulation or another subject matter.

[29] MP Maduro articulates this idea when discussing the effects of negative market integration on efficiency enhancing versus redistributive (social) policies in 'Europe's Social Self: "The Sickness unto Death"' in J Shaw (ed), *Social Law and Policy in an Evolving Union* (Oxford, Hart Publishing, 2000) 331.

[30] S Weatherill, 'The Internal Market' in S Peers and A Ward (eds), *The EU Charter of Fundamental Rights: Politics, Law and Policy* (Oxford, Hart Publishing, 2004) 191.

[31] ibid.

[32] O de Schutter, 'A New Direction for the Fundamental Rights Policy of the EU', Working Paper Series: REFGOV-FR-33 (2010) 11.

[33] Maduro, above n 29. One might add that the balance struck in negative integration is also a result of the particular case that happens to come before the Court.

[34] Scharpf, above n 3; and W Wagner, 'Positive and Negative Integration in EU Criminal Law Cooperation', Paper prepared for presentation at ECPR's 5th Pan-European Conference on EU Politics (Porto, 24–26 June 2010) 2 with reference to Scharpf.

[35] Article 51(1) CFR.

Against this normative background, an evaluation of the fundamental rights policy in the internal market becomes necessary, and the following questions arise in that respect:

First, does the legislator consciously and expressly pursue an internal market fundamental rights policy? Does internal market legislation refer to, incorporate or address fundamental rights issues?

Second, when viewed from a fundamental rights perspective, what is the state of existing internal market harmonisation practice on fundamental rights? Is it considerable or negligible? Did it start only with the Charter or did it pre-exist that document?

Finally, what is the substantive level of fundamental rights protection achieved through the ongoing interplay between the Court and the legislator?

So far, this theme has not been extensively studied in a systematic way. Academic debates examining the relationship between fundamental rights and economic freedoms in the internal market have mainly focused on the tension between the two interests as it arises in the negative market integration process. Their relationship in the positive integration process has largely been neglected,[36] and the present book aims to fill this lacuna.

II. METHODOLOGY

The main part of this study consists of an examination of the existing harmonisation practice and its eventual legislative output. However, two inquiries had to precede this analysis.

First, this exercise presupposes an affirmative answer to a question, which is of vital importance in the daily policy-making process in the EU: as in all things, the EU lawmaker must first overcome the hurdle of establishing its competence to act—the EU is a creature of circumscribed competences. Therefore, at the outset, we must identify and explore whether and to what extent internal market competences can be used to deal with fundamental rights.

Second, ever since the 2000s, when the Charter was proclaimed, new mechanisms for fundamental rights protection outside the courts have emerged in the EU. These mechanisms were introduced to build a fundamental rights culture inside the EU institutions. The existence of such a fundamental rights culture was considered likely to decisively influence the EU's legislative output (in and beyond the area of the internal market). Therefore, an empirical examination of these mechanisms precedes any research into the presence or absence of an institutional culture. The starting point for assessing whether the *ex ante* fundamental rights scrutiny tools in place are operating to a satisfactory degree was therefore to screen legislation, pre-legislative and legislative history for fundamental rights language. Preliminary conclusions were subsequently tested in semi-structured interviews with EU officials. The results were fed into the analytical discussion below, primarily taking an EU institutional and constitutional law perspective, but also drawing on and comparing national practices, to the extent that it was deemed useful for informing the EU debate.

The main part of the book has been organised according to four fundamental rights protected by the Charter: data protection, freedom of expression, fundamental labour rights (the right to take collective action and the right to fair and just working conditions) as

[36] See A Bailleux, *Les interactions entre libre circulation et droits fondamentaux dans la jurisprudence communautaire. Essai sur la figure du juge traducteur* (Brussels, Bruylant-Publications des FUSL, 2009), who examines this relationship in both integration processes. See also de Schutter, above n 32, 11 et seq.

well as the right to health. In defining these rights, however, other instruments on which the relevant Charter provisions were based have also been taken into account, as can be discerned from the Explanations to the Charter.[37] First, this includes the ECHR as interpreted in the case law of the European Court of Human Rights (ECtHR) in Strasbourg. Its special significance was acknowledged in early CJEU jurisprudence[38] and has been given the following recognition in the Charter itself: according to Article 52(3) CFR, those rights contained in the Charter which correspond to rights guaranteed by the ECHR shall have at least the same meaning and scope as the latter (although EU law can always provide for a higher level of protection). Next are the other major conventions of the Council of Europe—including the European Social Charter. It should be noted that other international law instruments have also been taken into account alongside the EU's own (but not legally binding) social rights instrument: the Community Charter of Fundamental Social Rights of Workers.

The selection of, and examination according to, a limited number of rights chosen in this study keeps a sharp focus for the fundamental rights lens. It allows an analysis of a variety of legislation across different policy fields. It also reveals how different forms and levels of harmonisation can impact on the same right, but on different dimensions of that right.

The choice of the specific rights examined is motivated by three reasons. First, and most obviously, *the existence of legislation* that has been adopted on an internal market legal basis, which appears to have either a strong objective aimed at protecting those fundamental human rights—be that an exclusive, parallel or secondary objective of the legislation—or to have adverse implications on a fundamental right. This reflects the predominant approach taken in this study in analysing the harmonisation practice and legislative output, which is bottom-up or one of inductive reasoning. This means that the research commenced with specific observations and then progressed to detect patterns in order to be able to reach some general conclusions.

Second, a conscious choice has been made to cover rights that are, according to the traditional typology, understood to belong to different categories: civil and political rights on the one hand (data protection and freedom of expression, which are placed in the Charter's Chapter on 'Freedoms') and social and economic rights on the other (the right to collective bargaining, including the right to strike, the right to fair and just working conditions, and the right to health(care) which are contained in the Charter's Chapter on 'Solidarity'). This approach allowed an investigation into whether legislators adopt a different approach based on the generation of the right and, if so, how. This is a particularly interesting enquiry in view of the lauded indivisibility of the two types of rights in the Charter, which is not organised along those traditional lines, but is rather ordered in a 'transverse systematic' way.[39]

Finally, the rights chosen are among the most important in terms of their direct impact on human life, as opposed to economic activity,[40] which can also be expressed in fundamental

[37] Explanations Relating to the Charter of Fundamental Rights [2007] OJ C303/02.

[38] Case C 4/73 *Nold v Commission* [1974] ECR 491.

[39] S Sciarra, 'Diritti sociali fondamentali' in Baylos Grau et al, *Dizionario di Diritto Del Lavoro Comunitario* (Bologna, Monduzzi, 1996), cited in S Giubboni, *Social Rights and Market Freedom in the European Constitution—A Labour Law Perspective* (Cambridge, Cambridge University Press, 2006) 109.

[40] With the exception of commercial expression discussed in ch 5, 'Freedom of Expression'.

rights terms based on the Charter: the freedom to choose an occupation and the right to engage in work (Art 15 CFR), the freedom to conduct a business (Art 16 CFR) and the right to property (Art 17 CFR). Certainly, given the proximity of these rights to the economic freedoms, there is a considerable amount of legislation that could have been examined in this book—for an important example, consider the legislation on intellectual property.

III. ANALYSIS

A. The Internal Market Competence and Fundamental Rights

Chapter two establishes that there is an internal market competence to harmonise fundamental rights protection if certain conditions (as set out in the Court's legal basis case law) are met.[41] The precondition is that there are divergent national laws, which are liable to put the establishment and functioning of the internal market at risk or to distort competition. Importantly, once that is the case, the legislation is correctly founded on the basis of the internal market—whether it is of a market-making or a market-correcting nature and whatever the actual motives of the legislator. Such a measure can even *abolish* a specific market and cover purely internal situations, according to the Court's case law.

It should be noted that the above is true for regulation concerning all non-market values rather than only fundamental rights. In fact, there is a further commonality between fundamental rights and other non-market values. Both non-market policy objectives and fundamental rights have to be mainstreamed in the EU's action. The latter proposition means that irrespective of whether the subject matter of the laws harmonised is fundamental rights regulation, fundamental rights will be taken into account and further realised when harmonising.

As regards non-market objectives, a mainstreaming clause specifically for the internal market is to be found in Article 114(3) TFEU, but there are also the horizontal mainstreaming clauses in Articles 8–13 TFEU, including objectives such as consumer and environmental protection. As regards fundamental rights, the general mainstreaming obligation is contained in the Charter (in Art 51(1)), and a specific manifestation of this is the prohibition of discrimination (Art 10 TFEU). Fundamental rights as pursued in legislation can, however, still be distinguished from other non-market values, in that they constitute a foundational element of the EU, not merely an aspiration.

B. *Ex Ante* Fundamental Rights Tools

Chapter three is concerned with fundamental rights compliance, promotion and mainstreaming through non-judicial actors during the policy and law-making stages of

[41] Important literature on which this Chapter has drawn includes: JHH Weiler and SC Fries, 'A Human Rights Policy for the European Community and Union: The Question of Competences', Jean Monnet Working Paper 4/99; B de Witte, 'Non-market Values in Internal Market Legislation' in NN Shuibhne (ed), *Regulating the Internal Market* (Cheltenham, Edward Elgar, 2006); and F Scharpf, 'Negative and Positive Integration in the Political Economy of European Welfare States' in G Marks et al (eds), *Governance in the European Union* (London, Sage, 1996).

legislation. While this theme is not new in the academic literature of national legal orders (beyond Europe), for the specific EU context, the literature is limited.[42]

The chapter traces the gradual evolution of *ex ante* fundamental rights protection in the EU, setting out the tools that have been put in place at the different institutional levels and assessing their use.

What emerges is that although today all EU institutions have put procedures in place for conducting *ex ante* scrutiny, the European Commission still remains the primary actor in this process when it comes to the systematic and compulsory scrutiny of all legislation. However, at least up until the entry into force of the Lisbon Treaty, this *ex ante* process did not seem to perform adequately. A fundamental rights culture was apparently lacking. It is suggested that this is due to the absence of incentives and pressures from outside the administration. The Lisbon Treaty may serve to remedy this by providing judicial incentives (the increase in fundamental rights adjudication prompted by the Charter on the one hand and the envisaged EU accession to the ECHR—even if currently stalled[43]—on the other). One non-judicial incentive from within the EU legal order could be crucially provided by the FRA if it were granted an unconstrained mandate for legislative scrutiny. This is a matter that should be revisited in any re-negotiation of the body's founding regulation.

The EU combines almost all methods of *ex ante* scrutiny that can be found in national legal orders, which as a basic starting point appears promising. There is, however, considerable scope for improvement, both in terms of the current institutional/procedural foundations of the system and (if not more so) its operability. It is hoped that the increased attention to fundamental rights in the *post*-Lisbon era together with the new incentives provided therein will push forward the necessary advancements.

C. Data Protection

The examination of harmonisation practice, the concrete legislative output and the substantive level of fundamental rights protection therein commences with data protection in chapter four. The legislation in place[44] constitutes the prime example of *explicit* fundamental rights regulation based on the internal market and, as such, stands out from the rest of the legislation under examination. However, that is soon to change, given the introduction of a separate legal basis[45] for data protection, which has already been used for

[42] Notable exceptions on which this chapter has built include in particular those of P Alston and O de Schutter (eds), *Monitoring Fundamental Rights in the EU—The Contribution of the Fundamental Rights Agency* (Oxford, Hart Publishing, 2005) and the contributions therein; de Schutter, above n 32. See also more recently I Butler, 'Ensuring Compliance with the Charter of Fundamental Rights in Legislative Drafting: The Practice of the European Commission' (2012) 4 *European Law Review* 397; and O de Schutter, 'The Implementation of the Charter by the Institutions of the European Union' in S Peers, T Hervey, J Kenner and A Ward (eds), *The EU Charter of Fundamental Rights—A Commentary* (Oxford, Hart Publishing, 2014).

[43] See the analysis above in n 14.

[44] In particular, Directive 95/46/EC on the protection of individuals with regards to the processing of personal data and on the free movement of such data (DPD) [1995] OJ L281/31; and Directive 2002/58/EC concerning the processing of personal data and the protection of privacy in the electronic communications sector, [2002] OJ L201/37 (hereinafter the 'e-Privacy Directive').

[45] Article 16 TFEU.

proposing a new legislative package that is to replace the old data protection regime.[46] This shift from the market towards a specific fundamental rights legal basis is a noteworthy, albeit not novel phenomenon.[47] This development is indicative of the limits of pursuing fundamental rights protection through the door of a distinct competence such as that of the internal market (in this case, the legislator is prevented from adopting a coherent, comprehensive and overarching regime for the fundamental right pursued), but at the same time it also indicates the 'spill-over' potential when fundamental rights *are* pursued through the internal market.

Given that data protection is the most regulated fundamental right of the EU, the focus of this chapter is on the examination of the consequences of that fact: to what degree has the right gained a truly autonomous definition of its scope at EU level? At first sight, the answer seems to be that the degree is considerable. However, not only does empirical evidence suggest the contrary,[48] pointing to the fact that the instruments themselves allow degrees of variation in implementation, despite the choice of a maximum harmonisation approach, but also the CJEU's institutional deference when conflicting fundamental rights are at stake. Recent case law may suggest a changing approach. A further challenge has come from national constitutional courts as regards the Data Retention Directive,[49] through which the EU has delineated a restriction of the right to privacy. Interestingly, the challenge to the EU autonomous definition does not arise so much from national courts disagreeing with each other as to the definition of the right; rather, it seems to be a manifestation of common agreement that the EU standard, as set out in the Directive, is not a satisfactory one. In other words, it is not national constitutional diversity that clashes with EU interference here, but the fact that the EU standard as set out in the Directive seems to be falling short of those of the Member States. Finally, the European Data Protection supervisor and eventually the CJEU challenged the legislator's definition of restrictions to data protection when declaring the Data Retention Directive invalid.[50]

D. Freedom of Expression

Chapter five tackles freedom of expression. It takes three different dimensions of that right which the EU has attempted to regulate, or which it has actually regulated: media pluralism, the right to receive and impart information, and commercial expression. The instruments are organised according to the degree to which they are *expressly* conceptualised

[46] Commission Proposal for a Regulation on the protection of individuals with regards to the processing of personal data and on the free movement of such data, COM(2012) 11 final (hereinafter the 'General Data Protection Regulation').

[47] A comparison can be made with social policy, which was also initially (and still is to a certain extent) pursued through the internal market, before the insertion of a separate title in the Treaties.

[48] Communication from the Commission to the European Parliament, the Council, the European Economic and Social Committee and the Committee of the Regions, 'Safeguarding Privacy in a Connected World A European Data Protection Framework for the 21st Century' COM(2012) 09 final.

[49] Directive 2006/24/EC on the retention of data generated or processed in connection with the provision of publicly available electronic communications services or of public communications networks and amending Directive 2002/58/EC [2006] OJ L105/54.

[50] Joined Cases C-293/12 and C-594/12 *Digital Rights Ireland Ltd and Kärntner Landesregierung et al v Ireland* ECLI:EU:C:2014:238.

as fundamental rights legislation, starting from the legislation that is most expressly so conceived and progressing in descending order. Hence, the analysis commences with media pluralism. The discussion highlights the potential importance of an express fundamental rights conceptualisation not only in relation to the content of the legislation, but also in the politics of negotiation and lobbying. Consideration is also given to how the use of fundamental rights language may be employed to instrumentalise the competence argument. The demonstration of these points draws to a considerable extent on political science literature.

Next, the right to receive and impart information is regulated by the Audiovisual Media Services Directive,[51] the proposal of which Commissioner Reding had characterised as 'a harmonised implementation of the fundamental right of freedom of expression'.[52] Its origins[53] reveal a firm institutional belief that the instrument will ensure freedom of expression and promote democracy across Europe, and that rhetoric is still to be found in the Preamble of the current instrument. At the same time, the Directive can also be seen as restricting the freedom to provide and receive information, for example, to the extent that it imposes European quota rules, or restrictions on broadcasts for the protection of minors. These interests can also be conceptualised in fundamental rights terms, which means that the Directive is also an example of the European legislator striking a balance between conflicting rights.[54]

The fundamental rights rhetoric employed here did not provoke a challenge on competence grounds (from other policy actors). This is arguably because the right to receive and impart information coincides with the internal market freedom to provide and receive services (Art 49 TFEU). Furthermore, it is this trade lens that has coloured the greatest part of the substantive provisions adopted. It is clear that conceptualisation does matter for the content of a legislative instrument, which in this case turns out to be one of market liberalisation and increased commercialisation.

The final part of the analysis in chapter five turns to commercial expression, which as a concept is largely absent in the regulation of advertising—be that horizontal or sector-specific legislation. The vast majority of instruments considered here lack fundamental rights language both on the face of the text and in their legislative history. This is true irrespective of whether content-based or content-neutral rules are at stake. This finding seems to match the Court's approach of not conducting substantive review when legislation is challenged on the ground that the freedom of commercial expression is infringed. Hence, it appears that the presence of a fundamental rights approach would not have made a difference. It is suggested that the legislator's approach is justified, given the weak theoretical foundations on which recognition of that right rests.

[51] Directive 2010/13/EU of the European Parliament and of the Council of 10 March 2010 on the coordination of certain provisions laid down by law, regulation or administrative action in Member States concerning the provision of audovisual media services (Audiovisual Media Services Directive) [2010] OJ L95/1.

[52] V Reding's intervention in an European People's Party hearing on the scope of the Audiovisual Media Services Directive (29 June 2006).

[53] Commission Green Paper, 'Television without Frontiers—Green Paper on the Establishment of the Common Market for Broadcasting, especially by Satellite and Cable' COM(84) 300 final (14 June 1984).

[54] Pluralism, cultural identity and children's rights, the protection of human dignity and protection against hate speech, and the freedom to conduct a business. The latter is not mentioned in the instrument, but see Case C-283/11 *Sky Österreich GmbH v Österreichischer Rundfunk* ECLI:EU:C:2013:28.

E. Fundamental Labour Rights

The next chapters (six and seven) turn to fundamental social rights. Chapter six deals with two sets of fundamental labour rights: the right to fair and just working conditions, and the right to take collective action (including the right to strike), both of which were subjected to legislative intervention in response to Court-led negative integration.

The former is regulated in the Posted Workers Directive,[55] but it is not expressly acknowledged as such, even if the Directive was understood by the European Parliament as an instrument implementing the Community Charter of the Fundamental Social Rights of Workers, at least at an early stage of its negotiation. However, despite abandonment of that emphasis, the social dimension (and with it the fundamental rights dimension) could still outweigh the economic objective. This was reversed in later case law.[56] This in turn created a renewed momentum for a legislative response, leading to a proposal for a separate instrument.[57] The impact assessment of that instrument is permeated with fundamental rights language, as perhaps can be expected in the post-Lisbon era,[58] although this did not decisively affect the substantive outcome reached in the report (that the substance of the Posted Workers Directive[59] will not be re-opened) and also in the resulting final instrument.[60]

The right to take collective action has been dealt with by the legislator before and after the *Viking-Laval* line of case law through 'saving clauses'. These clauses served to exclude that right from the scope of application of the legislation at issue. Different types of 'saving clauses' have been produced in the instruments:[61] some in favour of national autonomy, others leaving the matter entirely to the CJEU, some equivocal and others seemingly unequivocal. Their potential (when unequivocal and in favour of national autonomy) to 'save' collective action from EU law could be seen as questionable, given that their application will be subject to the free movement rules of the Treaty. Yet they have a role in informing the Court of the weight that such rights should assume in the internal market. This function is crucial in the internal market where there is a need for both the Court and the legislator to work in tandem towards deeper integration.

[55] Directive 97/71/EC of the European Parliament and the Council of 16 December 1996 concerning the posting of workers in the framework of the provision of services [1997] OJ L18/1.

[56] Laval, above n 27.

[57] Commission Proposal for a Directive on the enforcement of Directive 96/71 concerning the posting of workers in the framework of the provision of services, COM(2012) 131 final.

[58] COM Communication, Strategy for the effective implementation of the Charter of Fundamental Rights by the European Union, COM(2010) 573/4 (19 October 2010).

[59] Directive 96/71/EC concerning the posting of workers in the framework of the provision of services [1997] OJ L18/1 (Posted Workers Directive).

[60] Directive 2014/67/EU of 15 May 2014 on the enforcement of Directive 96/71/EC concerning the posting of workers in the framework of the provision of services and amending Regulation (EU) No 1024/2012 on administrative cooperation through the Internal Market Information System [2014] OJ L159/11 ('the IMI Regulation').

[61] Directive 2006/123/EC on Services in the Internal Market [2006] OJ L376/36 (Services Directive); Posted Workers Directive, above n 59; Council Regulation (EC) No 2679/98 on the functioning of the internal market in relation to the free movement of goods among the Member States [1998] OJ L337/8 ('Monti I'); Commission Proposal for a Council Regulation on the exercise of the right to take collective action within the context of the freedom of establishment and the freedom to provide services, COM(2012) 130 final ('draft Monti II Regulation').

The chapter also examines the single legislative attempt to expressly regulate the right to take collective action at the EU level, the failed draft Monti II Regulation. However, this attempt—to the extent that one can make sense of the contradictory and hence poor legislative drafting—does not set out to expressly alter the Court's approach. In this sense, the approach seems similar to that taken with regard to the saving clauses enacted post-Lisbon.

Overall, the impression one gets is that the legislator opts for an 'abdication of political responsibility to the Court'[62] both in the use of saving clauses and in express regulation.

F. The Right to Health

Chapter seven tackles the right to health. Language naming the fundamental right to health is virtually absent in the internal market legislation and its legislative history, but the overall conclusion drawn is that such conceptualisation would have provided limited added value in this area. This can be explained partly by drawing on empirical arguments and partly by the nature of the right to health operating in a system of limited competences.

The arguments are the following. First, human health is among the values that rank very high in the internal market and it is pursued through a great amount of internal market legislation/regulation despite the absence of fundamental rights language. Second, this regulation is in fact in compliance with the fundamental right to health standards. Third, the strongest form of the right (its combination with the principle of non-discrimination: the 'negative dimension' of the right) is in the patient mobility context already guaranteed through the operation of the free movement rules. Fourth, in order to achieve the legislative aims, social mobilisation has not been facilitated by rights language. In fact, the types of civil society organisations involved in lobbying for EU health legislation are public health organisations, not human rights organisations, but tobacco lobbying groups did have recourse to the fundamental rights arguments in this context in order to oppose health legislation. It may be speculated that this has contributed to the introduction of fundamental rights language in the negotiations leading to the second Tobacco Products Directive.[63] Against this background, it can be maintained that linking health to fundamental rights can provide for a strong counter-argument when a proliferated use is made of other fundamental rights arguments (these would typically be fundamental rights relating to economic activity) in order to oppose health regulation. Finally, other areas where a fundamental rights approach could provide for added value is fundamental rights-compliant allocation and prioritisation of resources. However, there is no EU activity in this field due to competence constraints.

[62] T Novitz, 'Labour Rights as Human Rights: Implications for Employers' Free Movement in an Enlarged European Union' (2006–07) 9 *Cambridge Yearbook of European Legal Studies* 358, 371–75.

[63] Directive 2014/40/EU on the manufacture, presentation and sale of tobacco products [2014] OJ L127/1.

IV. CONCLUSION

The concluding chapter eight pulls together, reorganises and evaluates the findings of chapters two to seven in an attempt to answer the questions posed above and identified as central to this book. It reveals the prevalent type of conceptualisation of the legislation and identifies the determining factors that account for such a conceptualisation. Finally, it assesses the consequences of the adopted approaches both for the substantive content of legislation and for its judicial review. At the end of this assessment, we are left with a much more differentiated account of the EU's fundamental rights policy in and through the internal market than was perhaps initially expected.

2

Competence

I. INTRODUCTION

THE ASSERTION THAT internal market legislation can and does regulate fundamental rights may sound controversial at first sight. If it does so, the controversy will most certainly evolve around fears of competence creep. Two judgments will immediately spring to mind: the first one establishing that the EU does not enjoy a general power to regulate the internal market (*Tobacco Advertising I*) and the second one that EU (then the European Community (EC)) institutions do not have a general power to enact rules on human rights (*Opinion 2/94*).

This chapter will explain why, despite or in spite of these two cases, it is possible to pursue fundamental rights protection on the basis of the internal market. The discussion will focus on one of the most important and most controversial internal market provisions: Article 114 TFEU (ex Article 95 EC), even though internal market instruments can also be concerned with fundamental rights when adopted on the basis of the more specific internal market provisions (eg, on services, establishment).

First, the chapter will deal with the question whether there is a (horizontal) legislative fundamental human rights competence in the EU. Second, it will discuss Article 114 TFEU case law in order to analyse the conditions and the extent to which fundamental human rights protection can be harmonised under this provision.

In order to do so, initially it will lay out the basic principles of harmonisation under Article 114 TFEU. Subsequently, it will turn to the important inquiry of the scope of Article 114 TFEU, ie, when does secondary legislation fulfil the necessary functions stipulated in this provision so that it can be validly adopted on the basis of this article? The question that will be asked is when a measure improves the conditions for the establishment and functioning of the internal market.

II. HARMONISING FUNDAMENTAL RIGHTS UNDER ARTICLE 114 TFEU

The first important inquiry that must be undertaken concerns the question whether there is a fundamental human rights competence in the EU. This will be answered in the positive by dismissing the idea that *Opinion 2/94*[1] precludes such a proposition. Subsequently, we shall proceed to the arguments for such a competence, based on the case law of the Court, the current constitutional structure and the classic regulatory gap argument.

[1] *Opinion 2/94 Re Convention for the Protection of Human Rights and Fundamental Freedoms* [1996] ECR I-1759.

A. A Horizontal Fundamental Rights Competence

Opinion 2/94 is the first judicial authority that has to be dealt with when inquiring into whether there is a legislative fundamental human rights competence in the EU. The crucial assertion made in this Opinion is the following: 'No Treaty provision confers on the Community institutions any general power to enact rules on human rights.'[2] Whether this means that the EC legislator does not have under any circumstances the power to legislate on fundamental rights (when acting outside specific fundamental rights competences, such as that on anti-discrimination) can only be answered by taking a closer look at the Opinion.

The CJEU addressed the issue of whether accession to the ECHR is compatible with the EC Treaty. The first part of the request concerned the question whether such a power for accession was provided for in the EC Treaty. It commenced its reasoning on competences with reference to Article 5 EC and observed that the EC is bound to respect the principle of conferred powers.[3] Subsequently, after identifying the issue as one of external implied powers,[4] it made its famous statement and proceeded to note that in the absence of express or implied powers, it is necessary to examine whether accession by the EC to the ECHR may be based on Article 308 EC (now Art 352 TFEU).[5] After stressing the importance of respect for human rights, both as general principles of (then) Community law and as a condition for the legality of (then) EC acts, it held:

> Accession to the ECHR would entail [1] *a substantial change in the Community system* for the protection of human rights in that [2] *it would entail entry of the Community into a distinct international institutional system* as well as integration of all the provisions of the ECHR into the Community legal order. Such a [3] *modification of the system for the protection of human rights in the Community*, with equally [4] *institutional implications* for the Community and for the Member States, [5] *would be of constitutional significance* and would therefore be such as to go beyond the scope of [now] Art 308. It could be brought about only by way of Treaty amendment. (emphasis added)[6]

Although this chapter is not concerned with Article 352 TFEU, but with Article 114 TFEU, it is still important to scrutinise why the Court answered the question of competences in this case in the negative, since it is this Opinion that is habitually relied upon by those arguing against an EU fundamental rights competence.

The purpose of Article 352 TFEU (now ex Art 308 EC) is to function as a 'gap-filler' where action by the EU should prove necessary to attain one of its objectives and the Treaty has not provided the necessary powers. Yet the Court did not discuss at all whether human rights powers would fall within the scope of that provision, but rather turned to the essence of its argument that accession to the ECHR constitutes in substance a Treaty amendment.[7] That is why Article 308 EC could not be used as a legal basis for acceding to the ECHR, as

[2] ibid [27].

[3] ibid [24].

[4] It is settled case law that the EC (now EU) can enter into international commitments not only on the basis of express Treaty provisions, but also on the basis of implied powers which flow from other Treaty provisions. See especially Case 22/70 *Commission v Council* (*AETR/ERTA*) [1971] ECR 263.

[5] *Opinion 2/94*, above n 1, [31].

[6] ibid [34]–[35].

[7] See P Eeckhout, *External Relations of the European Union—Legal and Constitutional Foundations* (Oxford, Oxford University Press, 2004) 86.

that would mean that the relevant procedures that are necessary to bring about such an amendment would be circumvented.

The Court relied on five reasons, which precluded recourse to Article 308 EC[8] (now Art 352 TFEU), to arrive at its conclusion. On a closer look, it emerges that a special emphasis was placed upon the institutional consequences of accession to the ECHR. Accession would only entail a substantial change in the EC system because of the entry into a distinct international *institutional* system. Likewise, it is the *institutional implications* resulting out of accession that would be of constitutional significance. Consequently, it is not possible to discern from this judgment whether the EU has broader powers in the fundamental human rights field.[9]

Equally, it must be appreciated that the Court made the statement 'in the absence of express or implied power' without providing any substantial analysis on the existence of other Treaty provisions that might possibly confer implied powers with respect to fundamental human rights.[10] It merely inferred this from its critical declaration that no Treaty provision confers on the EC institutions any general power to enact rules on human rights.

The Lisbon Treaty gave an answer to the specific problem posed in *Opinion 2/94* and created a new legal basis for EU accession to the ECHR (Art 6(2) of the Treaty on European Union (TEU)). The suggestion made above that the Court was concerned about the institutional implications (most notably the implications for the CJEU itself) finds confirmation in the current negotiations for accession.

The new legal basis also provides that 'accession shall not affect the Union's competences as defined in the Treaties', suggesting that the competence created here is strictly limited to ECHR accession. Thus, if there is a fundamental human rights competence for the EU, it is to be found elsewhere.

Since respect for fundamental human rights is a condition for the legality of EU acts, as the Court reaffirmed in *Opinion 2/94* (something the ECtHR will also monitor following accession), certain institutional duties inevitably flow from this which make it impossible to conclude that there is no fundamental human rights competence whatsoever in the EU.

Having dismissed the view that *Opinion 2/94* excludes the possibility of any form of EU fundamental human rights competence, we shall proceed by discussing how a horizontal fundamental human rights competence *can* be considered to be existent on the basis of the CJEU's jurisprudence and the current constitutional structure.

Weiler and Fries[11] have argued very convincingly for a horizontal competence to address fundamental human rights questions. By analysing two instances of CJEU jurisprudence, they conclude that the Court has actually 'set … up a positive duty to take measures to ensure that certain [human] rights should not be compromised'[12] and that 'such a legislative competence is inherent in each and every field of legislative competence of the Community'.[13]

[8] It has been argued that insofar as recourse to (ex) Art 308 EC does not trigger these five effects, human rights promoting measures *can* be based on that provision. See especially JHH Weiler and SC Fries, 'A Human Rights Policy for the European Community and Union: The Question of Competences', Jean Monnet Working Paper 4/99, 19–20.

[9] Eeckhout, above n 7, 87.

[10] ibid 85.

[11] Weiler and Fries, above n 8, 10.

[12] ibid 13.

[13] ibid.

In *Commission v France*,[14] the Court found France to be in violation of its Treaty obligations for failure to take positive action to prevent individuals from obstructing the free movement of goods. Although acknowledging that fundamental freedoms (when they concern free movement) and fundamental human rights are *not* the same, since the former is an object of the Treaty, whereas the latter is a duty of the EU as a whole,[15] Weiler and Fries opine that a negative prohibition on free movement obstacles triggered a positive institutional[16] duty to ensure the freedom in question.[17,18] Thus, in the spirit of *Commission v France*, 'abstaining from taking action is … just as likely to cause an obstruction to fundamental human rights as would a positive violative act'.[19]

The second instance Weiler and Fries refer to is *T Port v Bundesanstalt für Ernährung*.[20] In the context of the transition from a national regime to the Community common organisation of the market at issue, the CJEU held that the Community Institutions are under a duty to act, in particular when the transition to the common market infringes certain human rights protected by Community law.[21] Hence, 'the Court is moving beyond the prohibition on measures which, in and of themselves, violate human rights and is setting up a positive duty' in order to ensure respect for those rights.[22] This institutional duty/obligation was also expressed in *Cinéthéque*, where it was held that: 'It is the duty of this Court to ensure the observance of fundamental rights in the field of Community law.'[23] Weiler and Fries submit that respect for fundamental human rights is an 'integral, inherent, transverse principle forming part of all objectives and powers of the Community', otherwise it would be questionable where the jurisdiction of the Court came from 'to ensure in the entire field of Community law the observance of fundamental rights'.[24]

With the entry into force of the Lisbon Treaty and the Charter gaining legally binding status, there is a further point to be made: that is, the obligation resting on the EU institutions and spelled out in Article 51(1) CFR to '*promote the application* [of the Charter] in accordance with their respective powers and respecting the limits of the powers of the Union as conferred on it in the Treaties' (emphasis added).[25]

[14] Case C-265/95 *Commission of the European Communities v French Republic* [1997] ECR I-6959.

[15] Weiler and Fries, above n 8, 12.

[16] The Court commented at [36] that the same considerations that applied to the Member States also applied to Council regulations on the organisation of the markets: *Commission v France*, above n 14, [36].

[17] Weiler and Fries, above n 8, 13.

[18] This seems to be the converse approach from that in the US with respect to the commerce clause (the equivalent to Art 114 TFEU), which grants a positive power to promote market integration. On the basis of this positive power, the Supreme Court imposed a negative obligation on the states not to interfere with interstate commerce—the (judge-made) doctrine of the 'dormant' commerce clause. See *Cooley v Board of Wardens of Port of Philadelphia ex rel Soc for Relief of Distressed Pilots*, 53 US 299 (1852) 318; *Robbins v Shelby County Taxing Dist rict*, 120 US 489 (1887) 493; *HP Hood & Sons Inc v Du Mond*, 336 US 525 (1949) 532; *Texas Industries, Inc v Radcliff Materials, Inc*, 451 US 630 (1981) 641.

[19] Weiler and Fries, above n 8, 10.

[20] Case 68/95 *T Port v Bundesanstalt für Ernährung* [1996] ECR 6065.

[21] ibid [40].

[22] Weiler and Fries, above n 8, 13.

[23] Joined Cases 60 and 61/84 *Cinéthèque v Fédération Nationale des Cinémas Français* [1985] ECR 2650 [26] cited in Weiler and Fries, above n 8, 14.

[24] Weiler and Fries, 'A Human Rights Policy', ibid.

[25] See also B De Witte, 'A Competence to Protect: The Pursuit of Non-market Aims through Internal Market Legislation' in P Syrpis (ed), *The Judiciary, the Legislature and the EU Internal Market* (Cambridge, Cambridge University Press, 2012) 32. See also P Eeckhout, 'The EU Charter of Fundamental Rights and the Federal Question' (2002) 39 *Common Market Law Review* 945, 980 (discussing the tension between Art 51(1) CFR and Art 51(2),

Beyond this, it should be noted that there is a further, more generally valid argument that is supportive of the submitted proposition—the regulatory gap argument.[26] It is in fact not limited to the question of the extent to which fundamental human rights can be regulated on the basis of the internal market, but applies to all non-market values equally.

The premise upon which it is based is a well-established doctrine: whenever there is positive harmonisation of a certain matter, derogations from the common market freedoms as regards that same matter are no longer permissible.[27] Thus, 'this doctrine presupposes that policy concerns underlying the Member State derogations have been addressed in the harmonisation measure or at least that the European legislator had the competence to do so',[28] for if this was not the case, an odd situation would arise: '[the] legislator could only harmonise away such disparate national requirements, but could not adopt EC-wide measures that give recognition to the common public policy values that underlie those disparate rules'.[29]

The considerations elaborated so far allow the conclusion that the EU legislator *does have* a certain competence to legislate on fundamental human rights within the scope of EU law. However, what has to be examined in further detail is the extent to which Article 114 TFEU can constitute an appropriate legal basis for such an action.

B. Article 114 TFEU and the Court's Case Law

i. Harmonisation Under Article 114 TFEU: Basic Principles

Before discussing the conditions and the extent to which it is possible to harmonise fundamental rights under Article 114 TFEU (ex Art 95 EC), it would be helpful to first lay out the basic principles. The named provision can be used as a legal basis if the measure adopted has as its object the 'establishment and functioning of the internal market' or is aimed at 'eliminating distortions of competition'.

In *Tobacco Advertising I*,[30] the Court ruled on the scope of the (then) Community legislature's competence under (then) Article 95 EC. The case concerned the validity of Directive 98/43/EC relating to the advertising and sponsorship of tobacco products. The Directive provided for the banning of all forms of tobacco advertising/sponsorship in the EC with some limited exceptions. Germany, concerned about 'creeping competences', argued that the Directive was in reality a measure for the protection of public health and that it was not a valid internal market measure because there was no significant inter-state trade in the services of the advertising media at issue.[31] Furthermore, the Directive constituted in

the latter stating that 'the Charter does not extend the field of application of Union law beyond the powers of the Union or establish any new power or task for the Union, or modify powers and tasks as defined in the Treaties').

[26] F Scharpf, 'Negative and Positive Integration in the Political Economy of European Welfare States' in G Marks et al (eds), *Governance in the European Union* (London, Sage, 1996).

[27] Case C-148/78 *Ministero Pubblico v Ratti* [1979] ECR 1629.

[28] B De Witte, 'Non-market Values in Internal Market Legislation' in NN Shuibhne (ed), *Regulating the Internal Market* (Cheltenham, Edward Elgar, 2006) 70.

[29] ibid.

[30] Case C-376/98 *Germany v Parliament and Council* [2000] ECR I-8419 (hereinafter *Tobacco Advertising I*). This was the first and so far the only case where the CJEU, annulled a measure based on Art 95 EC (now Art 114 TFEU) on the ground that the EC (now EU) institutions exceeded their competences.

[31] ibid, Opinion of Advocate General Fenelly, [37]–[38].

practice a total prohibition on tobacco advertising. Therefore, instead of promoting trade in advertising media for tobacco products and freedom to provide services, the Directive's effect, it was argued, was to negate those freedoms almost entirely.[32]

The Court found that (ex) Article 95 EC was an inadequate legal basis because various prohibitions were not justifiable by the freedom to provide services in the advertising sector or eliminating distortions of competition in this field, eg, the prohibition of advertising on posters, parasols, ashtrays, etc.[33] In other words, an outright ban was excessive and did not serve the internal market. In addition, the Directive did not ensure the free movement of products which were in conformity with its provisions[34] because Article 5 allowed the Member States to adopt stricter requirements concerning the advertising or sponsorship of tobacco products as they deemed necessary to guarantee the health protection of individuals.

The important principles[35] the Court set out in this leading case and in subsequent decisions were the following: Article 95 EC (now Art 114 TFEU) does not contain any general power to regulate the internal market.[36] The Court will therefore look at two conditions. First, whether the preconditions for harmonisation do exist, ie a real risk of obstacles to trade; the mere finding of disparities is insufficient.[37]

There must be either 'differences between national rules which are such as to obstruct fundamental freedoms and thus have a direct effect on the functioning of the internal market'[38] 'or to cause significant distortions of competition'.[39]

Harmonisation measures may also aim to prevent 'the emergence of such obstacles to trade resulting from the divergent development of national laws. However, the emergence of such obstacles must be likely and the measure in question must be designed to prevent them'.[40]

Where there is already a harmonising measure enacted, the legislator 'cannot be denied the possibility of adapting that act to any change in circumstances or development of knowledge having regard to its task of safeguarding the general interests recognised by the Treaty'.[41]

Second, the actual aim, purpose and effect of the measure. In looking at this issue, it will adopt a teleological interpretational approach and will thereby determine whether the measure 'in fact pursues the objectives stated by the Community [now EU] legislature'.[42]

[32] See JA Usher, Case Comment (2001) 38 *Common Market Law Review* 1519; *Tobacco Advertising I*, above n 30, [24].

[33] *Tobacco Advertising* I, above n 30, [99].

[34] ibid [101].

[35] See generally Case C-491/01 *R v Secretary of State for Health ex parte British American Tobacco (Investments) Ltd and Imperial Tobacco Ltd* [2002] ECR I-11453 (hereinafter *BAT*), Opinion of Advocate General Geelhoed (referring to *Tobacco Advertising I*) [18] (for an overview of the prerequisite conditions for Art 95 EC (now Art 114 TFEU) to be considered as the correct legal basis).

[36] *Tobacco Advertising I*, above n 30, [83].

[37] ibid [84].

[38] Case C-380/03 *Germany v Parliament and Council* [2006] ECR I-11573 [37] (hereinafter *Tobacco Advertising II*); Case C-58/08 *The Queen on the application of Vodafone Ltd and others v Secretary of State for Business, Enterprise and Regulatory Reform* ECR [2010] I-4999 [32] (hereinafter *Vodafone*).

[39] *Tobacco Advertising I*, above n 30, [84] and [106]. See also *Vodafone*, above n 38, 32.

[40] ibid [33] and the case law cited therein.

[41] ibid [34]. See also BAT, above n 35, [77], [78].

[42] *Tobacco Advertising I*, above n 30, [85].

At the same time, the legislature enjoys 'discretion, depending on the general context and the specific circumstances of the matter to be harmonised, as regards the method of approximation most appropriate for achieving the desired result, in particular in fields with complex technical features'.[43]

More generally, the CJEU established that the choice of the legal basis must rest on objective factors amenable to judicial review. Even if a measure pursues more than one aim, it should be based only on one legal basis—that which is reflective of the main aim of the measure ('centre of gravity test').[44] However, where there are multiple aims/purposes, which are inextricably linked, multiple legal bases can be used, provided that the relevant decision-making procedures are compatible.[45] All these principles have been confirmed in subsequent case law[46] and are well established.

It should be highlighted at this point that both the dicta on the 'main aim' of a measure as well as the reference to the 'centre of gravity', which are relied upon by the Court in all of its legal bases case law (beyond the internal market), are liable to lead to confusion when internal market legislation is at issue. The next section will demonstrate why that is so.

ii. Within the Scope of Article 114 TFEU (ex Art 95 EC): Improving the Conditions for the Establishment and Functioning of the Internal Market

The explicit wording of the Treaty provides that a legislative measure can be lawfully based on Article 114 TFEU (ex Art 95 EC) if it is intended to improve the conditions for the establishment and functioning of the internal market. As held in *Tobacco Advertising I*:

> [T]o construe this provision as meaning that it vests in the Community legislature a general power to regulate the internal market would not only be contrary to the express wording of the provision ... but would also be incompatible with the principle embodied in [now Article 5 EC] that the powers of the Community are limited to those conferred on it.[47]

Therefore, it is clear that Article 114 TFEU (ex Art 95 EC) can *only* be used in order to legislate on fundamental human rights if this legislation *in effect* improves the conditions for the 'establishment and functioning of the internal market'.

This then raises two questions. First, how does the necessary condition to improve the establishment and functioning of the internal market relate to another non-economic objective (and in our case specifically a fundamental rights objective) that a measure may pursue? Second, when will the necessary condition for having recourse to this legal basis be satisfied?

[43] Case C-217/04 *United Kingdom v Parliament and Council* [2006] ECR I-3771 [43].

[44] See, eg, Case C-155/91 *Commission v Council (Waste Directive)* [1993] ECR I-00939; Case C-187/93 *Parliament v Council (Transport for Waste)* [1994] ECR I-2857; and Case C-42/97 *Parliament v Council (Linguistic Diversity)* [1999] ECR I-869.

[45] See eg, Case C-300/89 *Commission v Council* [1991] ECR I-2867; Case C-211/01 *Commission v Council* [2003] ECR I-8913; Joined Cases C-164/97 and C-165/97 *Parliament v Council* [1999] ECR I-1139; and Case C-338/01 *Commission v Council* [2004] ECR I-4829.

[46] See eg, Case C-269/97 *Commission v Council* [2000] ECR I-2257 [43]; Case C-36/98 *Spain v Council* [2001] ECR I-779; *BAT*, above n 35; Joined Cases C-154/04 *The Queen on the application of Alliance for Natural Health Nutri-Link Ltd v Secretary of State for Health Nutri-Link Ltd* and Case C-155/04 *The Queen, on the application of National Association of Health Stores and Health Food Manufacturers Ltd v Secretary of State for Health and National Assembly for Wales* [2005] ECR I-6451.

[47] *Tobacco Advertising I*, above n 30, [83].

The first *Tobacco Advertising* case provides the initial clues for answering the first question. In this case, the Court began its reasoning with the assumption that the Directive at issue was a measure aimed to protect public health.[48] It seems that this conclusion was reached on the basis that 'the national measures affected are to a large extent inspired by public health policy objectives'.[49] However, the Court did also state:

> [P]rovided that the conditions for recourse to [now Article 114 TFEU] ... are fulfilled, the Community legislature cannot be prevented from relying on [Article 114 TFEU as a] ... legal basis on the ground that public health protection is a decisive factor in the choices to be made. (emphasis added)[50]

It becomes obvious that the Court did not truly engage in a discussion about which of the two aims that the measure pursues carried more weight, but rather held that as long as the conditions for recourse to (now) Article 114 TFEU are fulfilled, ie. as long as the measure improves the conditions for the establishment and functioning of the internal market, it is an appropriate legal basis, even if non-economic considerations were decisive for its adoption.

Advocate General Fenelly explicitly rejected application of the 'centre of gravity test' in order to assess whether the Community legislature acted within its powers in the situation at issue:

> *In the absence of a distinct Community harmonising competence* in respect of health protection, and *given the possibility of parallel pursuit* of health protection and internal-market aims, the question of whether the Community has acted within its powers cannot be determined by reference to a measure's putative centre of gravity as between these two incommensurable objectives. *The issue of competence must instead be resolved by assessing the Directive's compliance with the objective requirements of the internal market, having regard ... to the concrete internal-market benefits claimed for the measure.*[51]

This also seems to be supported by the *Biotechnological Inventions* judgment.[52] It emerges in this case that the essential purpose of a harmonising measure will be held to be improving the conditions for the establishment and functioning of the internal market if in pursuing an objective (in this case to promote research and genetic engineering in the EC) that falls within another Treaty provision (in this case Article 141 TFEU (ex Art 173 EC) and Article 179 TFEU (ex Art 163 EC)), it has the *effect* of removing 'legal obstacles within the single market that are brought about by differences in national legislation'.[53]

In *BAT*, Advocate General Geelhoed spelled out very clearly what this means:

> The issue boils down to the following: if a (potential) barrier to trade arises, the Community must be in a position to act. Such action must, as I construe the biotechnology judgment, consist in the removal of barriers. Art 95 EC creates the power to do so. No conclusive significance attaches in this connection to the issue whether the barrier to trade also constitutes the principal reason for action on the part of the Community legislature.[54]

[48] See T Hervey and J McHale, *Health Law and the European Union* (Cambridge, Cambridge University Press, 2006) 103.

[49] *Tobacco Advertising I*, above n 30, [76]. See also Hervey and McHale, above n 48.

[50] *Tobacco Advertising I*, above n 30, [88].

[51] *Tobacco Advertising I*, above n 30, Opinion of Advocate General Fenelly at [58].

[52] Case C-377/98 *The Netherlands v European Parliament and Council of the European Union* [2001] ECR I-7079.

[53] ibid [27]–[28].

[54] *BAT*, above n 35, Opinion of Advocate General Geelhoed at [100]–[101].

Two points are crucial here: first, the acknowledgment that internal market legislation can and, as institutional practice demonstrates,[55] most if not all of the time does pursue parallel objectives—the internal market objective and another non-economic objective. When it comes to health, safety, environmental protection and consumer protection, there is even a duty inscribed in Article 114(3) TFEU to pursue such objectives at a high level where the legislation concerns one of these aims. And when it comes to fundamental rights, the same type of duty results from Article 51(1) CFR, as already explained above.

Second, the 'centre of gravity' test is not applicable in this situation because, to repeat the words of Advocate General Fenelly, 'there is no distinct [EU] harmonising competence in respect of health protection'. The same is again true for fundamental rights, unless of course the measure seeks to address equal treatment or, ever since the entry into force of the Lisbon Treaty, data protection, because in these cases there is such distinct EU competence in place for these two rights.

Therefore, the main aim of the measure is in these circumstances immaterial, provided it contributes to 'the establishment and functioning of the internal market'. This leads us to the second question—namely, when will this requirement be satisfied?

At the outset, the wording of the Treaty will be noted. It does not speak of approximation measures, which shall have as their object the promotion of free trade in absolute and unconditional terms. The object is rather the establishment and functioning of the internal market. Now what type of market that is, ie, what type and degree of regulation is chosen in order to ensure other non-economic objectives, is for the legislator to decide.

Advocate General Fenelly has put the reason for this in the following terms:

> [T]he Community is not acting in a policy vacuum. In adopting approximating or coordinating measures, it substitutes Community-level rules for national rules which, whatever their restrictive effect on trade or distorting effect on competition, may have been motivated by entirely different substantive concerns ... Thus, in adopting legislative acts, the Community stands in the place of the Member States and *must give weight to national policy concerns which are not the subject of specific Community competence.* (emphasis added)[56]

Having established this, we shall now consider what characteristics of a measure will *not* impinge on its quality of being an instrument that contributes to the establishment and functioning of the internal market.

First, legislation can favour the non-economic over the economic objective to the extent that it can even be restrictive of trade and be correctly based on Article 114 TFEU. The idea of positive integration as a mirror image to negative integration is useful for understanding this proposition.

The adoption of harmonising measures inevitably involves weighing competing interests where clashes arise. This is exactly what is also reflected in the Treaty, which not only provides for free movement provisions but also for grounds to derogate[57] from those. The same type of balancing that is conducted by the Court when balancing free movement with

[55] See De Witte, above n 25.

[56] *Tobacco Advertising I*, above n 30, Opinion of Advocate General Fenelly at [65].

[57] Public health is expressly mentioned in Art 36 TFEU (ex Art 30 EC) and fundamental human rights have been accepted by the Court as constituting a ground of derogation. See, eg, Case C-112/00 *Eugen Schmidberger Internationale Transporte und Planzüge v Republic of Austria* [2003] ECR I-5659.

public policy considerations (as well as fundamental rights) must also be undertaken by the EU legislature when approximating national laws.

It emerges in the context of negative integration that the outcome of the balancing exercise can in certain circumstances be in favour of the non-market value, including when fundamental human rights are at stake,[58] and therefore sometimes even restrictive of free trade. On the assumption that the same balancing exercise must be undertaken with respect to positive integration, it must surely be possible for the EU legislature to adopt legislation that is reflective of the same type of outcome. Moreover, the legislature is not subject to the structural constraints of the Treaty, which construes free movement as the general rule, and the grounds of permissible derogations as narrow exceptions to that rule. This means that the legislature has even more scope to pursue the non-market interest.

Support for the above can be found in *Alliance for Natural Health.*[59] Even though the non-economic interest involved in this case was public health, it is still worth mentioning because it illustrates that certain non-economic interests can be actively mainstreamed into the process of harmonisation based on Article 114 TFEU (ex Art 95 EC) to the extent that free trade can even be restricted under certain circumstances.

The secondary legislation, which was challenged in this case on the ground that (then) Art 95 EC constituted an inadequate legal basis, was Directive 2002/46/EC. The Directive was aimed at approximating the laws of the Member States relating to food supplements and required that only those products that comply with it may move freely (Art 3). Article 4 provided that *only* those vitamins and minerals that are listed in the Directive could be used for the manufacture of food supplements and, consequently, only those food supplements could move freely. The applicants considered that the prohibition, which resulted out of the Directive, was aimed at protecting public health.[60] In addition, they argued that the Directive was restrictive of trade in that it was contrary to the principle of the free movement of goods.[61] The Court found that Article 95 EC was the correct legal basis because of the existence of different national regulations in respect to food supplements, which were liable to impede their free movement[62] (ie, because of actual/potential obstacles to trade).

Interestingly, certain passages in the judgment suggest that the Court considered that the non-economic interest (public health) was to be given equal consideration in the process of harmonisation as economic interests, and that is why a measure with provisions that are to a certain extent even restrictive of trade could be based on Article 95 EC. This can be derived from the fact that the Court based its analysis on the considerations that according to (then) Article 152(1) EC, 'a high level of human health protection is to be ensured in the definition and implementation of all Community policies'[63] and, according to Article 95(3) EC, 'in achieving harmonisation, a high level of protection of human health should be guaranteed'.[64] Furthermore, it noted that 'when there are obstacles to trade or it is likely that those will emerge … Art 95 EC authorises the Community legislature to

58 ibid.
59 See the case law mentioned above in n 46.
60 ibid [25].
61 ibid [26].
62 ibid [35]–[37].
63 ibid [31].
64 ibid.

intervene by adopting appropriate measures in compliance with Art 95(3) EC'.[65] These appropriate measures may even consist of an obligation to prohibit, provisionally or definitely, the marketing of a product or products.[66]

It results out of this that when adopting secondary legislation in order to improve the conditions for the establishment and functioning of the internal market, the EU legislature will have to take not only economic (free trade) but also certain non-economic (public health) considerations into account. Since both of these carry equal weight, when trying to achieve a balance between the two, the former can be restricted with a view to promoting the latter.

Therefore, it can be maintained that by analogy, the same considerations have to apply to harmonising measures, which are aimed at protecting fundamental human rights. In the context of harmonisation based on Article 114 TFEU (ex Art 95 EC), the EU legislature has to undertake a balancing exercise between economic and non-economic competing interests, which are not subject to an EU competence. The fact that this balancing exercise might have in certain circumstances an outcome that disfavours free trade does *not* mean that the legislation cannot still be classified as one adopted for the establishment and functioning of the internal market.

However, it is possible to assert that the considerations which allowed the Court in this case to arrive at its reasoning are simply non-existent with respect to fundamental human rights. There is neither a corresponding provision to Article 168(1) (ex Art 152(1)) EC in the fundamental human rights field nor a clause similar to Article 114(3) TFEU (ex Art 95(3)) EC that obliges the EU legislature to achieve a high level of fundamental human rights protection when approximating laws.

Nevertheless, the absence of those two provisions in the field of fundamental rights cannot alter the proposition established above. The fact that there is no specific title in the Treaty in order to promote fundamental human rights does not mean that this cannot be done *as far as possible within the scope of EU law and subject to the principle of subsidiarity*, in view of the fact that respect for fundamental rights is one of the principles upon which the EU is founded.

In addition, the absence of an express obligation similar to that spelled out in then Article 95(3) EC (now Art 114(3) TFEU) with respect to public health, ie, to guarantee a high level of protection of (in our case) fundamental human rights when approximating laws, does not discharge the EU legislature of this duty, as one would assume that this is inherent in the proposition that fundamental human rights constitute a measure of the legality of EU acts.

Moreover, as already noted above, with the legally binding provision Article 51(1) CFR, post-Lisbon it is beyond doubt that there rests a fundamental rights mainstreaming obligation on the (internal market) legislator.

The second characteristic that a measure can have and still be validly adopted on the basis of the internal market is that it can cover some situations, which are not linked to free movement. This can be illustrated based on Directive 95/46/EC on the protection of individuals with regard to the processing and free movement of personal data.[67] The instrument

[65] ibid [32].

[66] ibid [33].

[67] Directive 95/46/EC of 24 October 1995 on the protection of individuals with regard to the processing of personal data and on the free movement of such data [1995] OJ L281/31.

has been characterised as 'one of the most remarkable instruments that the European Community has adopted in the field of fundamental rights'[68] (and is extensively discussed in chapter four). Its *explicit purpose* is the 'protection of individuals'. This measure has the following dual aim: facilitating the free movement of personal data between Member States in order to promote cross-border economic activities *and* 'avoid[ing] the protection given to privacy by national regulations being gradually eroded under the pressure of these freedoms of movement'.[69]

Recourse to Article 114 TFEU (ex Art 95 EC) seems to be justified here in view of the different levels of protection of the right to privacy, which constitute obstacles to trade.[70]

The question whether this Directive has been lawfully adopted on the basis of (then) Article 95 EC arose indirectly in *Österreichischer Rundfunk*.[71] At issue was the right to privacy in relation to the processing of personal data. Directive 95/46/EC was invoked to challenge the power of the Austrian Court of Auditors to collect and make public details of salaries and pensions of employees of a number of public and local authorities, including the Austrian public broadcasting organisation.

The first issue the Court dealt with was applicability of the Directive. Article 3(2) of the Directive provides that it 'shall not apply to the processing of personal data in the course of an activity that falls outside the scope of Community law, such as … public security, defence, State security … and the activities of the State in areas of criminal law'. Nor shall it apply 'to the processing of personal data by a natural person in the course of a purely personal or household activity'.

According to Advocate General Tizzano, the situation fell outside the scope of EC law since there was no specific EC law governing this public audit activity, nor was the Austrian law intended to implement a Community obligation.[72] Arguments were put forward that there existed a link with EC law through Articles 39, 136, 137 and 141 EC and the 'Equal Treatment Directive' 76/207/EC. However, the Advocate General dismissed all of those as being strained. With respect to the free movement of workers, he stressed that the audit activity in question did not affect access by workers.[73] In relation to the rest, he observed that the references were made without any explanation and it was not obvious how such a link could be established.[74] He also dismissed the argument that the Austrian law which provided for disclosure of the salary data must be characterised as a provision implementing the Directive. It would be a circular argument to hold that any national provision requiring the processing of personal data is a provision transposing the Directive, 'and then from that premise, infer that every form of processing prescribed by a national provision

[68] EU Network of Independent Experts on Fundamental Rights (CFR-CDF), *Report on the Situation of Fundamental Rights in the European Union and its Member States* (2002) 15.

[69] ibid.

[70] Preamble to Directive 95/46/EC, recital 7: 'the difference in levels of protection of the rights and freedoms of individuals, notably the right to privacy, with regard to the processing of personal data afforded in the Member States may prevent the transmission of such data from the territory of one Member State to that of another Member State … this difference may therefore constitute an obstacle to the pursuit of a number of economic activities at Community level, distort competition and impede authorities in the discharge of their responsibilities under Community law'.

[71] Joined Cases C-465/00 *Rechnungshof v Österreichischer Rundfunk and others*, C-138/01 *Christa Neukomm* and C-139/01 *Joseph Lauermann v Österreichischer Rundfunk* [2003] ECR I-4989.

[72] *Österreichischer Rundfunk* (ibid) Opinion of Advocate General Tizzano, point 43.

[73] ibid [47].

[74] ibid [45].

is covered by the provisions of the Directive because, by definition, it is carried out in the course of an activity that falls within the scope of Community law'.[75]

The Advocate General then proceeded to 'the most intriguing part of his argumentation'.[76] He argued that the Directive could *not* be applied on the ground that it is intended 'to protect the fundamental rights and freedoms of natural persons, and in particular their right to privacy with respect to the processing of personal data'.[77] This was so because fundamental rights were not an independent objective of the Directive. To hold otherwise would be tantamount to accepting:

> [T]hat the Directive is intended to protect individuals with respect to the processing of personal data even quite apart from the objective of encouraging the free movement of such data, with the incongruous result that even forms of processing carried out in the course of activities entirely unrelated to the establishment and functioning of the internal market would also be brought within its scope.[78]

The Advocate General concluded that if one were to attach to the Directive this independent objective of protecting fundamental human rights, its legal basis would be inappropriate.[79]

The Court came to a different conclusion as regards the applicability of the Directive. It began its analysis by observing:

> Since any personal data can move between Member States, Directive 95/46 requires in principle compliance with the rules for protection of such data with respect to *any processing* of data as defined by Article 3. (emphasis added)[80]

It becomes obvious that the Court adopted a wide interpretation of the scope of the Directive and considered the processing at issue to fall prima facie within its scope. It then held:

> [R]ecourse to Article 100a of the Treaty as legal basis *does not presuppose the existence of an actual link with free movement* between Member States in *every situation referred to by the measure founded on that basis.* (emphasis added)[81]

Rather, what matters in order to justify recourse to Article 114 TFEU is that the measure must be intended to improve the conditions for the establishment and functioning of the internal market.[82] However, this matter was not subject to dispute before the Court.[83]

The Court concluded that in those circumstances, the applicability of the Directive could not depend on whether the situations at issue have a sufficient link with the exercise of the fundamental freedoms.[84] The fact that such a 'direct link'[85] was not necessary was also confirmed by the wording of Article 3 of the Directive, which defines its scope in broad terms

[75] ibid [48].
[76] A Knook, 'The Court, The Charter, and the Vertical Division of Powers in the European Union' (2005) 42 *Common Market Law Review* 367, 388.
[77] Art 1(1) of Directive 95/46/EC; *Österreichischer Rundfunk*, above n 72, Opinion of Advocate General Tizzano at [50].
[78] *Österreichischer Rundfunk*, above n 72, Opinion of Advocate General Tizzano, ibid at [53].
[79] ibid [54].
[80] ibid [40].
[81] ibid [41].
[82] ibid.
[83] ibid.
[84] ibid [42].
[85] ibid [43].

and does not make its applicability dependent on a link with the fundamental freedoms. In addition, the processing at issue did not fall within any of the exceptions listed in Article 3(1). As a result, the Directive applied.

Knook has commented that this outcome 'reveals a remarkable situation', namely, 'despite the fact that adoption of the Directive was probably incompatible with the Court's case law on the legal basis of Article 95 EC (now Art 114 TFEU), the principle of attribution of powers, and Opinion 2/94, the Court had apparently to apply it, simply because its legal basis was not contested'.[86]

It is true that the question of the legal basis was not subject to dispute in this case and, therefore, the Court had no choice but to apply the Directive in light of the fact that it considered that the situation at issue fell within its scope as defined in Article 3. It is thus necessary to analyse Knook's assertions as regards the Directive's legality, which were not examined by the Court, in order to defend the view that Directive 95/46/EC was lawfully adopted on the basis of (then) Article 95 EC.

The first assertion is that the Directive is incompatible with the Court's recent case law. It follows from the Court's jurisprudence that a measure is lawfully based on Article 114 TFEU (ex Art 95 EC) (ie, it improves the conditions for the establishment and functioning of the internal market) if it removes (actual or potential) obstacles to trade or eliminates distortions of competition. This is irrespective of whether this consideration was the legislature's primary reason to act and whether it also has the effect of promoting non-economic interests.

It clearly results out of the Preamble to the Directive that the different levels of protection with respect to the right to privacy across the EU are liable to impede the free movement of personal data. This may constitute obstacles in the pursuance of a number of economic activities and distort competition. Thus, it seems that the legislature was justified to act in these circumstances.

The next crucial issue is whether *the way in which* the legislature acted could be subject to criticism. It could be argued, along similar lines as Advocate General Tizzano, that the fact that the Directive is capable of bringing situations within its scope which are purely internal (according to the Court's interpretation of Article 3), such as that at issue in *Österreichischer Rundfunk*, means that Article 95 EC is an inappropriate basis for Directive 95/46/EC.

The Court, although not dealing with the question of the choice of legal basis, took a stance on this issue and held that recourse to Article 95 EC does not require an actual link with the free movement in every situation covered by the Directive. This was subsequently confirmed in *Tobacco Advertising II*.[87]

As a result, the fact that a measure with a dual aim (ie, trade and fundamental rights) is also capable of covering some situations where there is no link to free movement, and consequently no link to cross-border trade does not negate the measure's quality of improving the conditions for the establishment and functioning of the internal market. On the basis of this conclusion, Article 95 EC does not seem to be the wrong legal basis for this Directive on that ground either. As such, it is not obvious why the Directive is incompatible with the Court's case law.

[86] Knook, above n 76, 389.

[87] *Tobacco Advertising II*, above n 38, [80].

Since it has been concluded that Directive 95/46 EC is an internal market measure that has been validly adopted on the basis of Article 95 EC, it must also be concluded that the legislature did not exceed the powers which are assigned to it by the Treaty. The same must also apply to the assertion that it is incompatible with *Opinion 2/94*. This is so because adopting an *internal market measure* on the basis of Article 114 TFEU (ex Art 95 EC), which also has the characteristic of protecting fundamental human rights, does not suggest that that provision has been used as if it provided a general power to legislate on human rights.

Against the background of the Court's jurisprudence as analysed thus far, it can be concluded that Directive 95/46/EC has been lawfully adopted on the basis of Article 95 EC and, consequently, that it does not infringe the principle of attribution of powers or *Opinion 2/94*.

Having established what characteristics of a measure *do not* disqualify it from being one aimed at the establishment and functioning of the internal market, there remains the question what conditions *must* be satisfied. As already stated above, the Court has held that there must be divergent national rules that 'are such as to obstruct fundamental freedoms and thus have a direct effect on the functioning of the internal market'[88] 'or to cause significant distortions of competition'.[89] The difficult question is when will divergence of these measures be 'such' as to reach the necessary threshold requirement?

It is obvious that this is by and large an empirical question, which will have to be decided in each situation based on the facts of the case. It is also clear that the Court will rely in this respect to a great extent on the legislature's judgment, given the broad discretion that the latter enjoys in economic legislation where complex assessments and evaluations are to be undertaken.[90] However, this is not to say that the Court should rely exclusively on the stipulations of the legislature in the Preamble of the instrument—quite the contrary.[91] This is so because the drafters may merely copy the Court's phrases quoted above which constitute the constitutional tests for making a judgment on the vertical division of powers. Such an approach would run the risk of turning these tests into a 'drafting guide'.[92] At the same time, it is also clear that the Court cannot be required to conduct an in-depth empirical analysis, which may in certain cases be necessary, in order to conduct its assessment. Instead, it is sensible to direct its scrutiny to the Explanatory Memorandum and the Impact Assessment Report (IA),[93] which should provide sufficiently justificatory reasons why the threshold requirement has been met. Of course, the findings in the IA do not replace judicial review, nor should they be conclusive as to answering the legal basis question, especially given the fact that such a report is drafted at the very beginning of the drafting process by one institution (the Commission) before the measure is negotiated in the European Parliament and Council and eventually concluded.[94]

[88] ibid [37]; *Vodafone*, above n 38, [32].

[89] *Tobacco Advertising I*, above n 30, [84] and [106]; *Vodafone*, above n 38, [32].

[90] *Vodafone*, above n 38, [52]; *Tobacco Advertising II*, above n 38, [145].

[91] K Lenaerts, 'The European Court of Justice and Process-Oriented Review', College of Europe, Research Paper in Law 01/2012, www.coleurope.eu/sites/default/files/research-paper/researchpaper_1_2012_lenaerts_final.pdf, 7–8.

[92] Weatherill holds that this is already the case: S Weatherill, 'The Limits of Legislative Harmonization Ten Years after *Tobacco Advertising*: How the Court's Case Law Has Become a "Drafting Guide"' (2011) 12 *German Law Journal* 827.

[93] Lenaerts, above n 91.

[94] ibid 9.

However, be that as it may, what is important for present purposes is that once this threshold requirement has been met, the legislature can harmonise fundamental rights protection by having recourse to the internal market legal basis (subject to the principle of proportionality and subsidiarity).

III. CONCLUSION

This chapter has scrutinised the question of a legislative fundamental human rights competence in the EU.

The analysis of *Opinion 2/94* has revealed that the Court has not clarified this issue either with respect to Article 352 TFEU (ex Art 308 EC) or any other Treaty provision. Further considerations allowed the conclusion that there is a horizontal competence for addressing fundamental rights issues (per Weiler and Fries).

In the post-Lisbon Treaty situation, with the Charter gaining legally binding status, it is clear that the legislator has to fulfil the legal duty to protect and promote fundamental rights when acting within its competence (for our purposes, within the internal market). The conclusion finds further support by the more generally valid regulatory gap argument.

Against the background of the Court's case law, an attempt has been made to examine and illustrate how such a competence can be exercised on the basis of Article 114 TFEU (ex Art 95 EC).

To summarise, it has emerged that fundamental human rights standards can be harmonised on the basis of Article 114 TFEU when two conditions are met: first, there must be (excessively) different levels of fundamental human rights protection at the domestic level, which are liable to put the unity and therefore the establishment and functioning of the internal market at risk or distort competition (precondition for harmonisation).

Second, in order to prevent such a risk, harmonising measures can be adopted which need to remove those obstacles to trade in effect (and thus improve the conditions for the establishment and functioning of the internal market).

Third, harmonising measures may aim at preventing future obstacles to trade resulting from the divergent development of national law; however, such emergence must be likely and the measure in question must be designed to prevent them.

In terms of the relationship between the two aims of such measures, it can be maintained that, as long as the two conditions above are met, secondary legislation will be considered to be an internal market measure and the 'centre of gravity' test is of no significance in this area. This is so because this test will be only applicable when there is another more specific legal basis available for harmonisation, which in general is not the case for fundamental rights,[95] except for the areas of anti-discrimination and data protection.

Those measures can go so far as to even restrict free trade in certain circumstances, based on the ground that in the process of harmonisation, the EU legislature has to balance, similarly to the national legislators and the CJEU in the context of negative harmonisation, economic and non-economic interests. They can also cover some situations where there is no link to free movement as long as the two conditions above are met. This is indicative

[95] See also De Witte, above n 25, 35.

of the extent to which fundamental human rights standards can be harmonised under Article 114 TFEU.

Such harmonisation is, moreover, desirable because the legislator can pre-empt clashes between fundamental rights and market concerns. Such pre-emption could prove most valuable given that the legislator is not subject to the structural constraints in the treaties, which establish a certain bias towards the market concern (free movement is the general rule, and the non-market value, also fundamental rights, the exception to such rule).

The following chapters (chapters four to seven) will discuss the EU's legislative activity. They will illustrate that the European legislator has in fact given recognition to fundamental rights when regulating the internal market, sometimes explicitly in order to protect but also to restrict the right to data protection (chapter four), the right to strike (chapter six) and failed attempts in media pluralism (chapter five); fundamental rights are sometimes detectable in the legislative history but not so much in the text of the legislation (the right to receive and impart information (chapter five), the right to fair and just working conditions (chapter six)); and at other times without conceptualising the non-market value as a fundamental right at all (freedom of commercial expression (chapter five) and the right to health (chapter seven)).

Before doing so, however, it is necessary to examine a further question. This concerns *ex ante* protection of fundamental rights more broadly—in and beyond the internal market. The question is whether and to what extent the EU has managed to build a fundamental rights culture outside the courts (chapter three). The more generally valid findings to this broader question will allow a better understanding of the legislative output in the specific areas discussed.

3

New Mechanisms for Fundamental Rights Protection in EU Legislation: Building a Fundamental Rights Culture Outside the Courts

I. INTRODUCTION

THE FUNDAMENTAL ASSUMPTION on which this chapter is based is that robust protection of fundamental rights requires engagement not only with the judicial process (that is, post hoc fundamental rights review of legislation by courts) but also *ex ante* with the political/legislative process—by 'mainstreaming' fundamental rights into legislative action, legislative assessments of whether draft legislation is compatible with fundamental rights obligations and pursuing rights protection on the basis of legislation. Most of the attention in the EU fundamental rights discourse has focused on the Court of Justice of the EU (the Court) and the judicial process, even though the second dimension is at least of equal importance.

Assigning a protagonist role to the Court may seem natural since it was this institution that originally 'invented' fundamental rights protection for the EU legal order. Moreover, a certain philosophy underpinned this genesis. Fundamental rights protection in the EU has assumed a 'negative' or 'shield' function, in that it imposes limits on the EU institutions and on the Member States when acting within the scope of EU law.[1] For a long time at the EU level, fundamental rights had not been conceived as an objective to be achieved by the EU legislature, thereby excluding the potential conceptualisation of 'fundamental rights legislation'. Important exceptions to this were anti-discrimination legislation,[2] and within the scope of the internal market data protection rules discussed in chapter four. This limited perception is of course linked to the EU's limited competences and the institutional homage paid to anxious Member States that fundamental rights will not serve as a catalyst for competence expansion, something that is mirrored in Article 51(2) of the EU Charter of

[1] O de Schutter, 'A New Direction for the Fundamental Rights Policy of the EU', Working Paper series: REF-GOV-FR-33 (2010) 10.

[2] Directive 2000/43/EC implementing the principle of equal treatment between persons irrespective of racial or ethnic origin [2000] OJ L180/22; Directive 2000/78/EC establishing a general framework for equal treatment in employment and occupation [2000] OJ L303/16; Directive 2006/54/EC on the implementation of the principle of equal opportunities and equal treatment of men and women in matters of employment and occupation (recast) [2006] OJ L204/23.

Fundamental Rights (the Charter).[3] A combination of changes in the academic discourse commencing more than a decade ago,[4] as well as Treaty[5] and institutional[6] developments, have been accompanied by a change in institutional rhetoric today. Intentionally or not, the now legally binding Charter does serve as a catalyst for the use of fundamental rights language (and also by the Court), as is exemplified in the Commission Communication of 2010 and the 2011 Commission report on the Application of the Charter.[7]

The question of how to institutionalise fundamental human rights or 'the problem of guarding the guardians is as old as political philosophy itself'[8] and continues to be the subject of heated debate within the context of various legal orders. It is usually phrased in 'either ... or' terms and it is always possible to advance arguments against institutionalisation at one locus—judicial or legislative—rather than another.[9]

The following propositions are usually put forward against legislative institutionalisation. The first is the perception that the role of fundamental rights is to afford protection against constraints emanating from the state, ie, against executive and legislative powers. On that ground, it would be nonsensical to assign the task of fundamental rights protection precisely to the actor against whom rights are supposed to protect the individual in the first place. The second is that the resolution of conflicts involving fundamental rights is better left to the judiciary since 'judicial review places a higher priority on principled resolutions of conflicts than would otherwise be accorded by elected representatives'.[10]

In contrast, judicial institutionalisation has received a major challenge on democratic grounds. Two arguments, in particular, have strongly featured in the debates: first, the question whether democratic principle agrees with the fact that non-representative (judicial) institutions can quash the output of representative (legislative) processes;[11] and, second,

[3] 'This Charter does not establish any new power or task for the Community or the Union, or modify powers and tasks defined by the Treaties.'

[4] P Alston and JHH Weiler, 'The European Union and Human Rights: Final Project Report on an Agenda for the Year 2000' in *Leading by Example: A Human Rights Agenda for the European Union for the Year 2000: Agenda of the Comité des Sages and Final Project Report* (Academy of European Law, European University Institute, Florence, 1998); and P Alston and JHH Weiler, 'An Ever Closer Union in Need of a Human Rights Policy' (1998) 9 *European Journal of International Law* 658.

[5] Most notably, Art 6 TEU.

[6] The creation of a separate Directorate General Justice; a Commissioner for Fundamental Rights, Justice and Citizenship; and the establishment of the Fundamental Rights Agency, Council Regulation EC No 168/2007 establishing a European Union Agency for Fundamental Rights [2007] OJ L53/1 (hereinafter the 'FRA Founding Regulation').

[7] 'The development of individual policies concerning certain specific fundamental rights on the basis of the Treaties will continue, examples being protection of personal data, children's rights, gender equality, non-discrimination, intellectual property and freedom of movement.' See Commission Communication, 'Strategy for the effective implementation of the Charter of Fundamental Rights by the European Union' (19 October 2010), COM(2010) 573/4 (hereinafter the '2010 Commission Communication') 4; European Commission, 2011 Report on the Application of the EU Charter of Fundamental Rights (16 April 2012), COM(2012) 169 final.

[8] T Campbell, 'Human Rights: A Culture of Controversy', (1999) 26 *Journal of Law and Society* 6, 21.

[9] ibid.

[10] JL Hiebert, 'Interpreting a Bill of Rights: The Importance of Legislative Rights Review' (2005) 35 *British Journal of Political Science* 235, 237, with reference to one of the most prominent advocates of this position: R Dworkin, *Taking Rights Seriously* (Cambridge, MA, Harvard University Press, 1978); and R Dworkin, 'Constitutionalism and Democracy', (1995) 3 *European Journal of Philosophy* 4.

[11] S Evans, 'Improving Human Rights Analyses in the Legislative and Policy Processes' (2005) 29 *Melbourne University Law Review* 665, 667, with reference to J Waldron, *Law and Disagreement* (New York, Oxford University Press, 1999), 184–86, 285–94. This is of course a major concern of American constitutional thought—the so-called 'countermajoritarian difficulty'.

whether the institutional outlook of the judiciary—by its composition and procedures—is apt for fundamental rights protection.[12]

Nevertheless, there is one argument that explicitly supports a strong *ex ante* in addition to a post hoc *form* of protection[13]—an argument that can hardly be rebutted. This is the fact that *ex ante* mechanisms not only seek to further and realise fundamental rights, but also aim proactively to prevent violations from occurring.[14] This is fundamentally different from the *post hoc* judicial review of courts, which is by nature reactive and is only triggered once a violation has taken place in a concrete case. Indeed, when medicine uses both prophylactic and anaphylactic methods to cure illnesses, it is hard to see why policy specialists should only consider one of these when dealing with fundamental rights.

Furthermore, *ex ante* mechanisms are especially important in situations where the limits of judicial fundamental rights adjudication come most visibly to the fore. This is the case when complicated decisions regarding budgetary resource allocations are to be made,[15] as is more often the case with certain fundamental social rights, such as the right to accessing healthcare. When that typology of rights is at stake, many courts are—for good reason—deferential to the legislature. However, it is accordingly important that the legislator acts in compliance with its fundamental rights obligations. In other words: 'It is important that legislators realise that they are under a constitutional duty to treat the meeting of everyone's basic needs as an issue that has priority over other matters.'[16]

It appears from the above that maximum fundamental rights protection can only be achieved by taking a complementary approach. Some scepticism may be expressed as to the potential repercussions of the two systems on each other. In particular, an argument could be advanced that a strengthened *ex ante* review may lead to courts being (too) deferential towards the legislator and consequently not providing for serious judicial review,[17] and thus weakening one of the two forms of review. This may be less likely to occur in a system where judicial review (including on fundamental rights grounds) is deeply rooted, such as in the EU (or at the national level, such as in the UK). Furthermore, it is arguable that *ex ante* fundamental rights scrutiny of legislation is a 'constitutional tradition common to the Member States' since it exists in most national orders. In that light, the creation of such mechanisms at the EU level cannot be viewed as optional, but rather as a constitutional obligation.

In the EU, as in other legal orders, it was the advent of a bill of rights—the Charter—that shifted the focus to the legislative process. Indeed, the Charter's novelty did not concern the

[12] ibid.

[13] Also advocating a joint approach (ie, legislative *and* judicial) for fundamental rights protection, see Evans, above n 11.

[14] See also M Ryle, 'Pre-legislative Scrutiny: A Prophylactic Approach to Protection of Human Rights' [1994] *Public Law* 192.

[15] C Gearty, 'Against Judicial Enforcement' in C Gearty and V Mantouvalou, *Debating Social Rights* (Oxford, Hart Publishing, 2011).

[16] V Mantouvalou, 'In Support of Legalisation' in Gearty and Mantouvalou, above n 15, 132.

[17] National-level examples in respect to which these concerns could be raised are Finland and Sweden, where constitutionality control has traditionally been left in the first place (although not exclusively) in the hands of Parliament. See VP Hautamäki, 'Reasons for Saying No Thanks! Analysing the Discussion about the Necessity of a Constitutional Court in Sweden and Finland' (2006) 10 *Electronic Journal of Comparative Law*, available at: www.ejcl.org/101/art101-1.pdf.

Court's judicial review powers, which allow it to set aside laws that are incompatible with fundamental rights. These had already been assumed after it had established the respect for fundamental rights as a general principle of EU law. The real innovation is characteristic to all bills of rights, namely, 'the incentive and pressures it provides for those developing legislation to give more attention to how their decisions affect rights'[18] and 'to conceive of alternative and less restrictive ways to accomplish important social objectives and, where rights are adversely affected, to explain and justify the merits of legislative decisions'.[19] In other words, its real added value is that of fostering a fundamental rights culture among the lawmakers.

It is the task of this chapter to examine not only when and how such a fundamental rights culture has been sought after at the EU level, but also the extent to which it has been achieved. It will do so by tracing the evolution of this development at the outset (section II). It will then proceed with an in-depth analysis of the various tools that have been put in place (section III) in order to assess their performance and inquire into possible reasons for any identified malfunctioning. A comparison with *ex ante* tools of scrutiny, which exist at various national levels, will be provided where this would be useful for informing the EU debate. Finally, even though this chapter provides an account of *ex ante* scrutiny of EU legislation valid more generally, the examples of legislation examined are, as far as possible, those of the internal market.

II. EVOLUTION

Fundamental rights scrutiny of EU legislation during its drafting stage has been systematically applied after the adoption of the Charter of Fundamental Rights,[20] even though the legislator had demonstrated awareness of these issues at an earlier stage in time. For instance, certain earlier instruments included statements of compatibility with fundamental rights as guaranteed by the ECHR and/or as general principles of Community law.[21] Still, it is clear that the adoption of the Charter was a turning point in this process, despite its lack of legally binding force. A year after its proclamation, the then Commission President, Romano Prodi, and the Justice and Home Affairs Commissioner, António Vitorino, declared in a Decision of 13 March 2001[22] that all legislative proposals would be first scrutinised for compatibility with the Charter 'as part of the normal decision-making process'.[23] The decision was mainly 'internal' and not widely known (not even within the Commission itself).[24]

[18] Hiebert, above n 10, 242.

[19] ibid 243 with reference to PH Russels, 'The Political Purposes of the Canadian Charter of Rights and Freedoms' (1983) 61 *Canadian Bar Review* 30, 43.

[20] Charter of Fundamental Rights of the European Union [2002] OJ C364/1.

[21] Examples of internal market legislation include Directive 97/36/EC amending Council Directive 89/552/EEC regulating television broadcasting activities [1997] OJ L202/60, recital 15; Directive 95/46/EC on data protection [1995] OJ L281/31, recital 10; and Directive 98/44/EC on the legal protection of biothechnological inventions [1998] OJ L213/13, recital 43.

[22] Commission, Decision on the Application of the Charter of Fundamental Rights of the European Union. SEC (2001) 380/3.

[23] ibid. See also House of Lords, Select Committee on European Union, 'Human Rights Proofing EU Legislation', 16th Report (2005–06), 11, para 10.

[24] House of Lords, Select Committee on European Union, 16th Report, above n 23, 12.

It was replaced by a Commission Communication in 2005,[25] which did not in fact bring about any fundamental changes. Building on existing mechanisms, it sought to raise awareness by 'lock[ing] in *a culture of fundamental rights* in EU legislation' (emphasis added)[26] among all actors in the law-making process. 'The methodology' to achieve this included impact assessments prior to the preparation of a draft legislative text, explanatory memoranda accompanying Commission proposals, and recitals in the Preamble of the act as adopted, confirming that it respects the Charter. These tools will be discussed in detail below.

The 2005 Communication also foresaw that a report, prepared by the Legal Service, in agreement with (at the time) Directorate General Justice, Freedom and Security and the Secretariat-General would be submitted to the Group on Fundamental Rights, Anti-discrimination and Equal Opportunities[27] in 2007.[28] The aim of the report was to provide for a general appraisal of the workings of the internal monitoring since 2005. This report was delayed by two years in order to include two important developments: the establishment of the EU Fundamental Rights Agency (FRA)[29] and the 2009 revision of the Impact Assessment Guidelines.

The Commission finally published the report in 2009.[30] The appraisal commences with the finding, resulting out of the experience since 2005, 'that fundamental rights issues can arise in many disparate areas',[31] but that the area of legislative activity in which delicate assessments of possible fundamental rights limitations have to be made is Justice, Freedom and Security.[32] The main finding was as follows: 'The Commission believes that the standards of necessity and proportionality have been met in its proposals; its commitment to a culture of fundamental rights respect is real and of substance.'[33] However, it also acknowledged methodological shortcomings in light of suggestions made by the European Parliament in the Voggenhuber Report.[34] Four suggestions for improving the methodology were made: first, greater visibility for impact assessments, including its introduction

[25] Commission Communication, 'Compliance with the Charter of Fundamental Rights in Commission Legislative Proposals: methodology for systematic and rigorous monitoring' (27 April 2005), COM(2005)0172 (hereinafter the '2005 Commission Communication').

[26] President Barroso cited in Commission Press Releases IP/05/494.

[27] In December 2004, the Commission President issued a communication about the functioning and internal coordination of the Commission and set up five groups, one of which was attributed specific responsibility for fundamental rights compliance. This group was given the mandate to drive policy and ensure the coherence of Commission action in the areas of fundamental rights, anti-discrimination, equal opportunities and social integration of minority groups, and to ensure that gender equality is taken into account in Community policies and actions.

[28] 2005 Commission Communication, above n 25, 7.

[29] FRA Founding Regulation, above n 6.

[30] Commission Report, 'On the Practical Operation of the Methodology for a Systematic and Rigorous Monitoring of Compliance with the Charter of Fundamental Rights' (29 April 2009), COM(2009) 205 final (hereinafter the '2009 Commission Report').

[31] ibid 2. A notable example is Regulation (EC) No 1907/2006 concerning the Registration, Evaluation, Authorisation and Restriction of Chemicals (REACH), [2006] OJ L396/1, which raises data privacy issues.

[32] 2009 Commission Report, above n 30, 3.

[33] ibid 4.

[34] European Parliament, Report on compliance with the Charter of Fundamental Rights in the Commission's legislative proposals: methodology for systematic and rigorous monitoring, Committee on Civil Liberties, Justice and Home Affairs, Rapporteur: Johannes Voggenhuber (12 February 2007) (hereinafter the 'Voggenhuber Report').

in comitology, and possibly a separate Impact Assessment category for fundamental rights is desirable; second, better targeting of fundamental rights in recitals, and the consistent inclusion of a section explaining fundamental rights compatibility in Explanatory Memoranda; third, increased use of the expertise offered by the FRA in these processes, although it would not have a mandate to scrutinise the conformity of Commission proposals with fundamental rights; and, finally, ensuring through monitoring that fundamental rights are respected throughout the legislative process.

A further Communication in September 2010 adopted a strategy for the effective implementation of the Charter by the EU 'in the new legal environment existing since the entry into force of the Lisbon Treaty'.[35] In addition to the Charter becoming legally binding and the envisaged EU accession to the ECHR, the following developments were important for the Commission: 1) the fact that the European Parliament and the European Council have declared that promoting fundamental rights in the future area of justice, freedom and security is one of their priorities;[36] 2) the establishment of a Commissioner for Justice, Fundamental Rights and Citizenship; 3) the abolition of the pillar structure, the extension of the co-decision procedure and the extension of the Court's review powers in the area of freedom, security and justice, and the fact that members of the Commission have to promise, in a solemn undertaking before the Court of Justice, to uphold the Charter; 4) the confirmation of the importance of human rights protection in the EU's external action. Against this background, the Commission believes that 'all the components of an ambitious fundamental rights policy are present'.[37] This is an interesting statement, as the Commission for the first time speaks officially of an EU *policy*, which it intends to pursue in this field.

It is noteworthy that since the first 2001 Decision, none of these Communications has introduced any important change in methodology. Even the latest 2010 Communication (discussed in detail below) in essence repeats the methods and goals that have been expressed from 2001 to 2009, albeit with more detailed pronouncements. For example, a Fundamental Rights 'checklist' is presented, to be used by all instances involved in pre-legislative and legislative scrutiny, and certain new elements are aimed at refining and better implementing the existent methods, such as the development of 'operational guidance' aimed at assisting Commission departments to assess the impact of an initiative on fundamental rights in practice, for mainstreaming and impact assessment purposes.[38]

The 2010 Communication does, however, introduce one, albeit not very substantial, novelty, namely that the Commission will present an Annual Report on the application of the Charter.[39] The purpose of this mechanism is on the one hand stocktaking and on the other hand to provide for an opportunity for an exchange of views with the European Parliament and the Council. It is yet another instance of a recent trend—the proliferation of EU reports

[35] 2010 Commission Communication, above n 7, 2.

[36] European Council, The Stockholm Programme—An open and secure Europe serving and protecting citizens, [2010] OJ C115/1, 8 (note that the European Council also invited the EU Institutions and the Member States to ensure that legal initiatives are consistent with fundamental rights and remain so throughout the legislative process. Even more interestingly for the present purposes, the application of the methodology for a fundamental rights compliance check will be strengthened).

[37] 2010 Commission Communication, above n 7, 2.

[38] ibid 7.

[39] ibid 12–13.

on fundamental rights. Henceforth, all of the three institutions[40] as well as the FRA will be producing annual reports. Whether any follow-up steps are taken is another matter.

III. THE FUNDAMENTAL RIGHTS SCRUTINY TOOLS IN DETAIL

A. The Commission

As is clear from the evolutionary account presented above, the Commission has been the initiator and the driving force in elaborating a methodology for creating a fundamental rights culture in the EU institutional landscape. This role has included not only the task of ensuring that its own legislative proposals have been checked as to fundamental rights impacts and compatibility with the Charter, but also that rights standards are adhered to throughout the legislative process in the other institutions, as well as that Member States implement EU law in a fundamental rights-compliant way. This extended responsibility derives from the Commission's role as the 'guardian of the Treaties' and, by implication, as 'the guardian of fundamental rights'. In this light and in view of this distinctive role, it may be not surprising that so far, the Commission has been the only institution with a framework in place for a compulsory and *systematic* fundamental rights verification of *all* legislative proposals, and has situated itself as the *centrepiece* of 'the methodology'.

i. Pre-Legislative Scrutiny/Fundamental Rights Mainstreaming: Impact Assessments

The practice of subjecting all major Commission initiatives and EU legislation to a new method of Impact Assessments (IAs) commenced in 2002[41] and has been an important part of the Commission's programme for delivering 'Better Regulation'.[42] It was conceived as 'a tool to improve the quality and coherence of the policy development process'[43] and to 'complete the application of the subsidiarity and proportionality protocol annexed to the Amsterdam Treaty'.[44] The new IA method integrates all partial and sectoral assessments into one global instrument. It should be noted that the EU's IA system[45] includes various IA mechanisms, such as regulatory IAs and sustainable or sustainability IAs.[46] The latter involve the consideration of consequences of legislation on the economy, the environment and society as dimensions of sustainable development;[47] these types of IA are not only

[40] The European Parliament produces two annual reports: one by the LIBE Committee on EU Fundamental Rights (since 1993) and one by the Committee on Foreign Affairs on Human Rights in the World (since 1983).

[41] Communication from the Commission on Impact Assessment (5 June 2002), COM(2002) 276 final (hereinafter the 'COM IA Communication 2002').

[42] See Commission, Better Regulation Action Plan, COM(2002) 278 final.

[43] COM IA Communication 2002, above n 41, 2.

[44] ibid.

[45] Note that there are different types of IA systems across the world. See OECD Report on 'Sustainability in Impact Assessments—A review of Impact Assessment Systems in selected OECD countries and the European Commission', SG/SD(2011)6/FINAL (hereinafter the 'OECD Report 2011'), www.oecd.org/gov/regulatory-policy/Sustainability%20in%20impact%20assessment%20SG-SD(2011)6-FINAL.pdf.

[46] COM IA Communication 2002, above n 41, 2.

[47] Commission, Impact Assessment Guidelines, SEC(2009) 92 (15 January 2009) (hereinafter the '2009 IA Guidelines') 4.

concerned with minimising costs for business or regulatory burdens.[48] Thus, in theory at least, the economic component of IAs is not to be the predominant one in the EU.[49] At the same time, it appears that in practice, the quality of assessing non-economic impacts is still low in comparison with the economic impacts.[50] The methods employed in the EU 'integrated Impact Assessment approach' include cost-benefit analysis (CBA), cost-effectiveness analysis (CEA) and multi-criteria analysis (MCA).

Since its inception, the EU IA system has been subject to a series of reviews,[51] the latest culminating in the revised Impact Assessment Guidelines of 2009.[52] The Commission has also adopted the 'operational guidance' for taking account of fundamental rights in IA (hereinafter the '2011 Guidance'),[53] as foreseen in its 2010 Communication. This Guidance only complements (through further elaboration and the provision of examples) the 2009 IA Guidelines. The 2009 IA Guidelines laid out the standard methodological steps for IA and were already to a certain extent taking fundamental rights into account. The two documents will be therefore discussed together in what follows.

The discussion will commence with an explanation of what IAs are, what their purpose is and which actors are involved in this exercise. Subsequently, a step-by-step analysis of how IAs are conducted will be provided. This will explain and discuss the methodological steps taken in IAs, following which some suggestions on how the fundamental rights dimension in IAs could be strengthened will be put forward.

What are IAs? According to the 2009 IA Guidelines, their use is 'a process that prepares evidence for political decision-makers on the advantages and disadvantages of possible policy options by assessing their potential impacts'.[54]

It is the Secretariat General/Impact Assessment Board and the Commission departments concerned that decide each year which initiatives will need an IA.[55] Normally, all legislative proposals of the Commission's Legislative and Work Programme (CLWP) and all non-CLWP legislative proposals which clearly have economic, social and environmental impacts (except routine implementing legislation), as well as non-legislative initiatives defining future policies (eg, white papers, action plans and expenditure programmes), will be accompanied by an IA. This will also be the case for certain implementing acts ('comitology' items) that are 'likely to have significant impacts'.[56] The responsibility for the IA will lie with the lead service, which will need to involve relevant stakeholders. The lead service

[48] OECD Report 2011, above n 45, 5.

[49] A Alemanno, 'A Meeting of Minds on Impact Assessment—When Ex Ante Evaluation Meets Ex Post Judicial Control' (2011) 17(3) *European Public Law* 485, 488.

[50] See, for example, the Impact Assessment Board Report 2012 noting 'the need to strengthen the quality of the analysis for social impacts remains a concern', http://ec.europa.eu/smart-regulation/impact/key_docs/docs/iab_report_2012_en_final.pdf, 27.

[51] Commission report on 'Impact Assessment: Next steps—In support of competition and sustainable development (21 October 2004), SEC(2004) 1377; Commission, Impact Assessment Guidelines (15 June 2005) SEC(2005) 791 (updated in March 2006).

[52] For a discussion of these guidelines, see House of Lords, Select Committee on European Union, 'Impact Assessments in the EU: Room for Improvement?', 4th Report (2009–10).

[53] Commission Staff Working Paper, Operational Guidance on taking account of Fundamental Rights in Commission Impact Assessments (6 May 2011) SEC(2011) 567 final (hereinafter the '2011 Guidance').

[54] 2009 IA Guidelines, above n 47, 4.

[55] ibid 6.

[56] ibid point 1.4.

either undertakes the IA itself or it is contracted out, depending on whether there is a need for special expertise. Other Commission services are also involved through the IA steering groups[57] and inter-service consultation.

The Impact Assessment Board, which is composed of senior Commission officials, will control the quality of the IAs.[58] It is worth noting that IAs are only a support for decision-making, which the College of Commissioners will take into account; they cannot dictate anything as to the final decision on the content of a proposal, which remains a purely political decision.[59]

How are IAs conducted? The impacts are to be assessed through the answering of a series of questions by following *six key analytical steps*:[60] 1) identifying the problem; 2) defining the objectives; 3) developing main policy options; 4) analysing the impacts of the options; 5) comparing the options; 6) outlining policy monitoring and evaluation.

The 2011 Guidance stipulates that even before starting these steps, and ideally at the stage of drafting IA Roadmaps,[61] an initial screening should be conducted to assess whether fundamental rights are at issue. It should in the first place serve to check whether absolute or non-absolute right are likely to be affected. Absolute rights cannot be derogated from and therefore options and objectives violating them should be avoided. According to the '2009 IA Guidelines' this should also be taken into consideration when assessing an option.[62] If non-absolute rights are at stake, possible general interest objectives or rights and freedoms of others, which may be affected, are to be identified in the preliminary problem definition and policy options.[63] This initial identification of fundamental rights issues is generally speaking a welcome initiative; however, its limits should be acknowledged, namely the fact that any such assessment will be necessarily a very abstract exercise in view of the rudimentary stage of defining the problem and the objectives and developing policy options.

As regards *problem definition* (step 1), a major reason for public intervention is a 'discrepancy between the fundamental goals of the Union and the existing situation',[64] for example, protection of fundamental rights. In other words, since respect for fundamental rights is one of the EU's goals, inadequate protection (at the EU level) can be a reason for public intervention either in order to protect individuals against an interference with their fundamental rights or in order to promote a certain right.[65] The Guidelines do not specify

57 An Impact Assessment Steering Group must be set up for each IA at the beginning of the work. It should be involved in all phases (preparatory studies, consultation and drafting) and it should review the final draft of the IA report before it is submitted to the IA Board. The Steering Group (SG) should include 'the DGs whose policies are likely to be affected by or contribute to the objectives of [the] initiative, and the relevant policy coordination unit of the SG'. The expertise of other Directorates General should be fully used in order to assess impacts on, for example, fundamental rights. It is the 'best way for other services to ensure that their views are taken into account': 2009 IA Guidelines, above n 47, 8.

58 ibid 6.

59 ibid.

60 ibid 5.

61 IA Roadmaps will serve to integrate the IA in the Commission's annual Strategic Planning and Programming Cycle (SPP); they are prepared at the outset in order to plan the IA and 'include information on each of the analytical steps and the timing of the IA, or [have to] explain why an IA is not necessary'. See 2009 IA Guidelines, above n 47, 7–8.

62 2009 IA Guidelines, above n 47, 13.

63 2011 Guidance, above n 53, 11.

64 2009 IA Guidelines, above n 47, 21.

65 2011 Guidance, above n 53, 13.

this, but it is understood that this can only happen within existing EU competence. The other side of the coin is that fundamental rights 'can place legal limits on the Union's right to act'.[66] This is nothing more than the expression of the old pronouncement that fundamental rights constitute a measure for the legality of the EU's actions and therefore also a measure of verification as to whether the EU has a right to act at all.

It follows logically then that the *definition of the objectives* (step 2) should be coherent and consistent with respect for fundamental rights.[67] It is in fact one of the aims of the IA method to ensure consistency with this Treaty objective and to therefore assess such impacts.[68]

The Guidelines do not provide guidance as to how fundamental rights shall be taken into account at the stage of *developing main policy options* (step 3). The 2011 Guidance does make reference to step 3, stating first of all the obvious that 'policy options which would clearly violate fundamental rights should be discarded',[69] but also adding that if the options involve taking several measures, an assessment of a possible fundamental rights impact shall be taken for each of the individual measures (taking account of the principle of proportionality).[70]

At the *analytical step* (step 4), the likely economic, social and environmental impacts (intended and unintended) for each option have to be addressed. The 2011 Guidance points to the fact that it is difficult to quantify impacts on fundamental rights in most instances, in which case a qualitative assessment shall be conducted.[71]

Notably, there is no separate category to deal with fundamental rights. Any likely impact on that is to be examined within the three existing tables, ie, economic, environmental and social, although it is clear that most of the fundamental rights questions will be examined under the 'social impacts' category. However, one point is worth noting. The questions included within this table ('social impacts') target not only social fundamental rights (eg, the right of access to healthcare (Art 35 CFR),[72] workers' rights to information and consultation within the undertaking (Art 27 CFR)[73] and fair and just working conditions (Art 31 CFR)), but also civil and political rights (eg, respect for private and family life (Art 7 CFR), data protection (Art 8 CFR), access to justice (Art 47 CFR), the right to an effective remedy and to a fair trial, and gender equality (Art 23 CFR)).[74] Not creating a separate fundamental rights category, but instead subsuming the relevant assessment within the existing tables has been a deliberate choice. The Commission reasons that since 'fundamental rights of the Charter are diverse and cut across all sectors',[75] a separate fundamental rights category would lead to 'needless repetition by the assessing services instead of sharpening their focus

[66] 2009 IA Guidelines, above n 47, 22; and 2011 Guidance, above n 53, 13.

[67] 2009 IA Guidelines, above n 47, 5.

[68] ibid 6.

[69] 2011 Guidance, above n 53, 16.

[70] ibid 17 (the example of an option given is the 'option' of subjecting a Directive to five amendments).

[71] ibid.

[72] 2009 IA Guidelines, above n 47, 35 et seq, included in Table 2 under the heading 'Access to and effects on social protection, health and educational systems'.

[73] ibid under the heading 'Standards and rights related to job quality'.

[74] Property rights are examined under 'Economic Impacts' in Table 2 in ibid 34.

[75] 2005 Commission Communication, above n 25, 5, para 19.

on the practical impacts which might be relevant to those rights'.[76] The same assertions are again repeated in the 2011 Guidance.[77]

However, doubts have been expressed as to the validity of this argument.[78] The fear of duplication cannot prevail over the risk of a right being overlooked in certain cases where its inclusion in one of the existing categories is not obvious.[79] This argument holds strength when one considers that not all Charter rights are included as questions within the current impact assessment tables and that not all of them (in particular civil rights concerns arising in the area of Freedom Security and Justice) easily fit into that category.[80] These are all legitimate concerns that have been expressed since 2005, but this criticism is one that the Commission adamantly resists, and, unlike most of the other concerns raised in academic writing and in EU and national institutional reporting regarding application of 'the methodology', one it is not willing to acknowledge to date.

One could think of the following explanations for this: one is the question of resources,[81] even though it has not been put forward by the Commission as an issue at the time. An additional IA category on fundamental rights may increase the administrative and therefore also the financial burden for the assessing services—a cost that perhaps is viewed as not worth bearing. This would not necessarily imply that fundamental rights are not considered as equally important, or possibly even more important than the other objectives, but it could be explained by the Commission's view of the nature of the IA method. It is not a means of checking fundamental rights compliance.[82] This is a reasonable assessment considering the fact that a legal check on whether fundamental rights have been complied with can only happen on an actual text, a legislative proposal, which the IA Report is not. IA is, according to the Commission, rather a 'tool for preparing the factual material upon which such [legal] verification can take place'.[83] Even if a negative impact on a given fundamental right has not been identified during this process, so the argument goes, if there is a restriction of such a right, it is assumed that it will be identified at the legal scrutiny stage (this is discussed in detail below).

Another argument against a separate fundamental rights category is that a separate category may increase the framing of issues in fundamental rights terms, even where it would not be obvious that doing so would increase the added value. The result may be the 'banalisation' of fundamental rights arguments.

[76] ibid.

[77] 2011 IA Guidance, above n 53, 17.

[78] House of Lords, 16th Report, above n 23, 20–21, para 50; Voggenhuber Report, above n 34, 8, para 11; H Toner, 'Impact Assessment and Fundamental Rights in EU Law' (2006) 31 *European Law Review* 316, 325 ('the impression is that fundamental rights were and still remain tagged onto the impact assessment framework as a subsidiary concern'); ACM Meuwese, *Impact Assessment in EU Lawmaking* (The Hague, Kluwer Law International, 2008) 86.

[79] House of Lords, 16th Report, above n 23, 21; Voggenhuber Report, above n 34, 8.

[80] House of Lords, 16th Report, above n 23, 20, para 48.

[81] ibid 22, para 57, citing evidence of Commissioner Verheugen to the Select Committee during its inquiry into Better Regulation (Q 88); and House of Lords, Select Committee on European Union, 9th Report (2005–06), Paper 33.

[82] Dr Ladenburger for the Commission in House of Lords, 16th Report, above n 23, 19, para 43; and 2011 Guidance, above n 53, 10.

[83] 2011 Guidance, above n 53, 10.

On the other hand, de Schutter argues that the rejection of a separate IA category for fundamental rights results from the fact 'that the results of human rights impact assessments would be more difficult to ignore than if such results are part of a broader assessment, in which positive impacts at various levels (including eg effects on economic growth and social cohesion) can compensate for other, negative impacts (such as narrowing down of civil liberties or of the provision of certain public services)'.[84] The problem with this statement is that in the event that a violation of fundamental rights is at issue, this cannot be counterbalanced by other positive impacts (see the discussion on step 5 below).

However, de Schutter has also put forward another argument that may speak for a separate fundamental rights IA category. The argument is that IAs should do something more than what has been suggested above. IA should not merely prepare the subsequent fundamental rights compatibility assessment, but should in the first place serve to mainstream fundamental rights.[85] Mainstreaming requires:

> [T]hat we take into account, in the policy choices we make, the impact the different policy options we have at our disposal will produce on our capacity to further realise those rights. The realisation of rights is however an objective which, it is submitted, is better understood as a process than as an outcome, as a general direction in which to move, than as a target we either hit or miss.[86]

This is markedly different from a fundamental rights compatibility assessment, which will lead to a clear answer that 'either the proposal will be found to comply, or it will not'.[87] Therefore, the two processes should not be confused, especially since they may lead to different conclusions.[88]

De Schutter, while advocating this position, has provided for the following examples:

> [A] proposal made in the field of competition fails to contribute to the realisation of pluralism in the media as it does not offer safeguards against certain forms of concentration in that sector ... yet the same proposal may still be compatible with the requirements of freedom of expression, and even with the obligation imposed by the Charter that the pluralism of the media be 'respected'.
>
> Or we may note that a new information technology has not been designed in such a way as to minimise the impact on privacy and to facilitate the exercise by the individual concerned of the rights which safeguard from abuse in the processing of personal data (right of information, access and rectification, objection and appeal) ... and yet, find at the same time that such technology does not violate the requirements of Article 8 of the Charter of Fundamental Rights or the applicable legislation which develops its requirements.[89]

The distinction of the two processes does not emerge as a clear one when conceiving of this matter in practical terms and according to the above elaborations. What does it mean for a measure to 'fail to contribute to the realisation of media pluralism' or 'to minimise the

[84] O de Schutter, 'The Implementation of the Charter by the Institutions of the European Union' in S Peers, T Hervey, J Kenner and A Ward (eds), *The Commentary on the EU Charter of Fundamental Rights* (Oxford, Hart Publishing, 2013) 1646.

[85] O de Schutter, 'Mainstreaming Human Rights in the European Union' in P Alston and O de Schuter (eds), *Monitoring Fundamental Rights in the EU—The Contribution of the Fundamental Rights Agency* (Oxford, Hart Publishing, 2005) 37, 56.

[86] ibid 55–56.

[87] ibid 56.

[88] ibid.

[89] ibid.

impact on privacy' and still be in compliance with freedom of expression and the right to privacy as enshrined in the Charter?

It could be understood to mean that the process of mainstreaming entails a strive to go 'above', ie, to provide in legislation for a (optional) higher standard than that which is laid down in existing binding case law and legislation, and adherence to which would be compulsory for the legislative proposal to pass the compatibility assessment—hence why the emphasis is placed on 'further realisation'. If this is so, the distinction between the two processes becomes difficult in areas where no clearly applicable standard can be identified.

This can be the case due to a lacking judicial and/or legislative pronouncement on the matter. However, it is also true for rights, for which compliance cannot be established in the absence of progressive realisation. These are typically rights involving decisions about the allocation of resources and budgetary prioritisations. The larger the available resources in a given situation, the more expenditure for the purposes of furthering the right will be required, and this spending will have to be conducted in the most efficient way.[90] In a similar way to how it has been described above with respect to 'mainstreaming', 'compatibility' becomes here a process rather than a target, a process that should move towards full realisation. It is true that for these rights, minimum core obligations are normally set out in case law and binding legal instruments. Yet, it cannot be assumed that the mere meeting of these minimum core obligations would lead to a positive compatibility assessment, which would then be different from mainstreaming (that would require going above that minimal level). This is so because compatibility requires progressive realisation and minimum core obligations constitute merely the starting point on the 'continuum' of progressive realisation leading finally to full realisation.[91] In that sense, 'minimum core obligations are in fact [only] components of progressive realization'.[92] Failure to meet them will always mean failing the compatibility assessment. The converse is, however, not true, ie, meeting the minimum core obligations does not automatically lead to compliance with fundamental rights obligations. Nevertheless, in most cases, there will be no judicial pronouncement on the matter, as the question whether there is room to go beyond the minimum core obligations will typically be left to the discretion of the states.

In sum, when it comes to rights that require progressive realisation, the distinction between IAs and compatibility assessments as set out above fades. This is so because for these rights, progressive realisation (furtherance of the right as far as possible under the given circumstances) will be required for being in compliance with fundamental rights obligations.

However, another way in which 'further realisation' could be understood is not by providing for a more stringent standard, but rather by providing for more prescriptive measures in order to ensure that the implementation on the ground will occur in a fundamental rights-compliant way. One example is the Proposal for a Directive on minimum standards on procedures in Member States for granting and withdrawing international protection,

[90] This is known in international human rights law. See General Comment No 3 (9) of the UN Committee for Economic, Social and Cultural Rights, 5th Session (1990), which 'imposes an obligation to move as expeditiously and effectively as possible towards full realisation of the rights in question'.

[91] Jacobs, C, 'Demystifying the Progressive Realisation of Socio-economic Rights in South Africa' Paper presented to the Australia National University (October 2009)12.

[92] ibid 11.

where it was considered in the IA that the right to asylum and non-refoulement are better promoted by the option that 'implies a lesser margin for administrative error'.[93]

However one is to understand the process of mainstreaming, when defining the role of IA in relation to fundamental rights as one aiming for 'further realisation' of the right, the argument for a separate fundamental rights category certainly gains weight, as it clearly identifies the goal—the realisation of all fundamental rights—against which the impacts are supposed to be tested.

Regarding the stage of *comparing options* (step 5), the 2011 Guidance makes an important stipulation next to the again obvious remarks that the least intrusive measure or the measure with the highest positive impact should be chosen. That is, impacts of a different kind should not be added together or, in other words, negative impacts cannot be counterbalanced by positive impacts on other fundamental rights or by impacts of another kind.[94] This is not to be understood as excluding the classic balancing exercise that would entail precisely such counterbalancing when two fundamental rights clash, or when a restriction to a right is weighed against other interests in order to assess whether a violation has taken place. Instead, what it means (or should mean) is that a violation of one fundamental right cannot be counterbalanced by further protection of another one or a positive impact on another interest.

As regards the final stage of *monitoring and evaluation* (step 6), the 2011 Guidance draws attention to the fact that already the IA stage should consider 'what arrangements for monitoring and evaluating fundamental rights could be developed to match a given policy context',[95] especially because: 'In some cases, this will entail incorporating a specific obligation into the legislative proposal.'[96]

One important question that was under consideration during the preparation phase of the 2011 Impact Assessment Guidelines was whether the Commission Legal Service (and/or the Directorate General Justice) should join the Impact Assessment Board, and/or the IA steering groups that deal with sensitive issues. IAs have so far not been viewed as a process that should produce or involve legal advice, and there is a distinct lack of institutional willingness to convert them into such. This makes the option of involving the Commission Legal Service in this process contestable.

One motive for this reluctance is of a practical nature. It relates to the fact that legal advice is confidential, as opposed to IA reports, which are public. It is easy to comprehend that much of the successful 'brokering' of legislation in the Commission is dependent on this confidentiality, especially with regard to 'sensitive' legislative instruments (mainly in the Area of Freedom Security and Justice).[97]

Another practical argument against inclusion of the Legal Service on the Impact Assessment Board is based on the estimation that most of the time, the Legal Service's presence on these boards will be superfluous, either because the impact can be easily assessed without

[93] IA accompanying the Proposal for a Directive on minimum standards in procedures in Member States for granting and withdrawing international protection, SEC(2009) 1376, in 2011 Guidance, above n 53, 20.

[94] 2011 Guidance, above n 53, 20.

[95] ibid 22.

[96] ibid.

[97] See s D below. A similar argument has been advanced against an *ex officio* legislative scrutiny competence of the FRA.

the assistance of legal expertise or because fundamental rights issues will not arise in the first place. Therefore, a compromise solution is that the Legal Service and the Directorate General Justice do not join the Impact Assessment Board, but that it is at least guaranteed that they are consulted by it. No such compulsory consultation role of the Legal Service in the IA process is provided for in the 2011 IA Guidance, although it may be assumed that in practice, the Legal Service will become increasingly involved. The Guidance maintains that it is for the lead Directorate General to contact it as it sees fit.[98]

In addition to these practical arguments that could be put forward against involvement of the Legal Service in the Impact Assessment Board or IA steering groups, there remains the more general point, namely that IA, by its very nature, does not involve argumentation or deliberation of a legal nature. This task is reserved to the Legal Service when conducting the legal compliance check. Therefore, there is an argument that there is no need to involve the Legal Service at this preliminary stage of the law-making process.

However, there are good reasons for rebutting this assertion. Even though it is true that IAs, which measure and compare the impacts of available alternatives, are scientifically closer to an economic exercise than to a legal exercise, this does not mean that the exercise can be undertaken in the absence of legal expertise. The point can be illustrated when having regard to the new Fundamental Rights 'Check List'.[99] According to the Commission, this list would be covered in the (then) future operational guidelines on fundamental rights IAs:[100]

Fundamental Rights 'Check-List'

1. *What fundamental rights are affected?*
2. *Are the rights in question absolute rights (which may not be subject to limitations, examples being human dignity and the ban on torture)?*
3. *What is the impact of the various policy options under consideration on fundamental rights? Is the impact beneficial (promotion of fundamental rights) or negative (limitation of fundamental rights)?*
4. *Do the options have both a beneficial and a negative impact, depending on the fundamental rights concerned (for example, a negative impact on freedom of expression and a beneficial one on intellectual property)?*
5. *Would any limitation of fundamental rights be formulated in a clear and predictable manner?*
6. *Would any limitation of fundamental rights:*
    - *be necessary to achieve an objective of general interest or to protect the rights and freedoms of others (which)?*
    - *be proportionate to the desired aim?*
    - *preserve the essence of the fundamental rights concerned?*

[98] 2011 Guidance, above n 53, 10, fn 11.
[99] 2010 Commission Communication, above n 7, 5.
[100] The following table is reproduced verbatim from the 2010 Commission Communication, above n 7, 7.

Already the very first question proves the relevance of legal expertise. It is, on its face, a very simple enquiry about *what rights* are affected. One may assume that this is easily answered when consulting the newly legally binding EU list of rights—the Charter. However, it is immediately obvious (at least to any person of legal training) that in order to identify the rights that might be affected, one has to know the scope of the right involved. This is delineated not only by the fundamental rights catalogue, but also by examining implementing legislation and the Court's jurisprudence, which may define the scope autonomously for the purposes of EU law or may refer to the standard available in national, regional or international legal documents. Furthermore, since to the extent that the rights of the Charter overlap with those of the ECHR they shall have the same meaning and scope (even though higher protection is possible), one needs to have detailed knowledge of that catalogue and jurisprudence.

Similarly, the second point on the 'checklist' may be easily answered by a person trained in national and international fundamental/human rights law. The same cannot be said for non-lawyers, particularly since the Charter does not specify in the text itself which of the rights may be subject to limitation. Questions 3–4 require an assessment of the impacts on fundamental rights, which can only be answered in light of the answers given to the preceding enquiries.

The 2011 IA Guidance implicitly acknowledges both of these points. With respect to the former, it draws the attention of Commission staff that are to prepare the IA to various sources, such as the 'Explanations relating to the Charter of Fundamental Rights',[101] the Court of Justice of the EU and ECHR case law and Opinions and general comments of UN human rights monitoring committees. It is, however, questionable whether an Annex documenting the location of the sources can truly remedy the ignorance of non-lawyers/fundamental rights experts in this field, especially given the broad wording and reach of the Charter so that potentially any EU policy could fall within its scope. The establishment of the Fundamental Rights Unit (C.1) at the Directorate General Justice as a point of contact for further assistance seems to be a suggestion of greater practical use. However, this mechanism, as well as ensuring that members of that Unit are invited to the Impact Assessment Steering Group,[102] can and will only occur if the officials preparing the IA are aware of fundamental rights implications in the first place. Therefore, as a general rule, unless the IA is undertaken by officials with expertise that are routinely confronted with fundamental rights issues, or at least by an official with specialised training, it is more likely than not that fundamental rights issues are overlooked and that the IA becomes a mere 'box-ticking exercise'.

One option for addressing this problem is, as suggested above, to include the Legal Service in the IA steering group and/or the Impact Assessment Board. Another would be to ensure that at least one expert from the Fundamental Rights Unit at the Directorate General Justice is permanently part of the Impact Assessment Board. According to the current Rules of Procedure of the Impact Assessment Board, its members are composed of 'the Deputy Secretary General responsible for better regulation, acting as the Chair of the

[101] *Explanations Relating to the Charter of Fundamental Rights* [2007] OJ C303/17.

[102] 2011 Guidance, above n 53, 11.

Board, and two permanent officials at Director level from each of the following groups of Directorates-General: 1) Macroeconomic area of expertise: ECFIN, TAXUD, COMP, ESTA, TRADE …; 2) Microeconomic area of expertise: ENTR, MARKT, INFSO, MOVE, ENER …; 3) Environmental area of expertise: ENV, CLIMA, AGRI, MARE, REGIO …; 4) Social area of expertise: EMPL, HOME, JUST, SANCO, EAC …'[103]

In addition, there are four rotating members representing all four areas of expertise.[104] The current arrangement does not therefore ensure sufficient expertise in fundamental rights—in order for that to be achieved, it should be singled out as a separate matter of concern, even if considered within the existing categories. This would reflect their cross-cutting and horizontal nature.

A further measure aimed at avoiding the degeneration of the IA exercise into a 'box-ticking exercise' could be the introduction of a requirement that all officials responsible for an IA have to receive basic training on fundamental rights issues. The aim would not be to naïvely expect that such training could replace expertise; rather, it would be for the (perhaps still over-ambitious) aim of ensuring that non-expert officials could identify when they should seek further assistance.

The last point on the Commission's 'checklist' concerns the question of proportionality. One may raise the same concerns as above. The question of balancing a fundamental right with another interest or right can be characterised as a legal exercise, at least to the extent that the assessment needs to be in compliance with a bulk of precedent created by the Court on the application of this principle. On the other hand, however, there is an argument to be made that the balancing exercise encapsulated in this principle can also be approached from a non-legal (for instance, an economic, social or anthropological) point of view in setting out the available alternatives or, in other words, in 'the elaboration of a rule about possible priorities'.[105] Having in place such a thorough and rich assessment may be especially important with respect to economic legislation where the legislator enjoys a wide margin of appreciation. The legislator could thereby inform the judicial process on the question of proportionality. One situation where the Legal Service, when conducting legislative scrutiny, is already extensively relying on IAs is when conflicting fundamental rights are at issue. In the ideal situation, the IA identifies for example, what the practices are in the different Member States.

Having said that, the 'checklist' does not seem to be phrased in the most useful terms from a practical perspective, especially if it is to prepare the proportionality assessment—at most times the most crucial stage of fundamental rights analyses. As Morijn[106] has suggested, it appears more sensible to tailor the 'checklist' towards the specific needs of the IA

[103] *Rules of Procedure of the Impact Assessment Board*, Art 1, http://ec.europa.eu/governance/impact/iab/docs/iab_rules_of_procedure_final_en.pdf.

[104] ibid Art 5(4).

[105] Sir John Laws (as he then was), 'Is the High Court the Guardian of Fundamental Constitutional Rights?' [1993] *Public Law* 63, 74, as cited in K Syrett, 'Of Sources, Rationality and Rights: Emerging Trends of Judicial Review in Allocative Decisions' [2001] 1 *Web Journal of Current Legal Issues*.

[106] J Morijn has put forward two separate lists for a legal check and for IAs, both of which differ from that put forward by the Commission. See J Morijn, 'The EU Fundamental Rights Charter, the European Commission and the Council of Ministers: Checking the "Charter Checklists"' http://eutopialaw.com/2011/09/30/the-eu-fundamental-rights-charter-the-european-commission-and-the-council-of-ministers-checking-the-%e2%80%98charter-checklists%e2%80%99-part-2/.

process of choosing between different policy options, which should be different from those used for a legal assessment. Morijn's more appropriate list is the following:

> Prior questions:
>
> a. do policy options considered affect one or more rights laid down in the Charter? …
> b. what conditions need to be fulfilled with each of the policy options considered to avoid that an absolute right is affected and that the essence of possibly relevant non-absolute rights and freedoms are affected? …
> c. in case (a) non-absolute right(s) is concerned, is there any objective of general interest recognised by the Union that could justify the interference resulting from the policy options considered? …
>
> Main questions:
>
> d. what factual and/or statistical information or other evidence is available to substantiate the extent of the policy problem for which (each of) the policy option(s) considered (and involving interference with non-absolute rights) would offer a solution? …
> e. why would (a) policy option(s) that would not have the effect of interfering with a non-absolute Charter right, or to a lesser extent, not be capable of leading to the same policy outcome?

These questions, and the order in which they are posed, are evidently of greater use for preparing the IA. The 'main questions' properly prepare the ground for taking proportionality into account in the drafting and are not termed in a 'legal', but rather in 'policy-making' language. However, the need for legal/fundamental rights expertise is still apparent in order to answer them.

One way for bringing such expertise to the IA drafting is the involvement of the FRA in this process, with its in-house knowledge as well as its information collection abilities that are so central to the IA process. However, if such involvement was to be made contingent on the lead Directorate General requesting it, the necessary awareness of fundamental rights issues (the same problem as described above for involving the Directorate General Justice) and a willingness to engage an additional layer of administration would be prerequisites.

A final point to note on the question of knowledge and expertise is another option that would not specifically address legal expertise on fundamental rights, but which could mitigate any administrative or legislative knowledge gaps: the consultation of interested parties and stakeholders.[107] Next to the possibility of contracting-out substantive work for the IA,[108] this provides invaluable input. Under the current regime, public consultation is presented as an 'essential part' of the IA work. This is a positive approach not only in terms of good governance[109] (enhancing legitimacy and ensuring that policies are efficient and effective) but also from a fundamental rights point of view. Stakeholder participation has been considered to be a key element for a *human rights IA methodology/a rights-based IA*.[110]

[107] As foreseen in the 2009 IA Guidelines, above n 47, 18 et seq.

[108] But note that the IA report must be drafted by the responsible Commission service, which remains fully reponsible for it. See 2009 IA Guidelines, above n 47, 18.

[109] See European Commission White Paper on 'European Governance', COM(2001) 428 final, [2001] OJ C287.

[110] As expressed in the UNESCO-funded project, P Hunt and G MacNaughton, 'Impact Assessment, Poverty and Human Rights: A Case Study Using the Right to the Highest Attainable Standard of Health' Health and Human Rights Working Paper Series No 6, 33, www.who.int/hhr/Series_6_Impact%20Assessments_Hunt_MacNaughton1.pdf.

This methodology consists of six steps,[111] the fifth of which concerns the debating of options and foresees the engagement of stakeholders. At this step, it is foreseen that the IA report is circulated to all stakeholders so as to engage them in the debate of alternatives.[112] Importantly, civil society should also receive the draft, particularly in view of the fact that civil society often have access to information, ideas and views that may be difficult for the government—in our case the supranational lawmaker—to obtain. For example, it may be that the persons most likely to be affected are unlikely to participate as an interest group in the process (eg, undocumented migrant workers).[113] Under the 2009 IA Guidelines, the method for involving stakeholders and external parties is a flexible one, since it is considered that the need for external input will vary from IA to IA. So, for example, the Guidelines do not pin down at what stage which stakeholders should be engaged; instead, they emphasise the continuity of the process, encouraging early engagement and stipulating a series of minimum public consultation standards that have to be respected.[114]

As to who should be consulted, the Guidelines speak prophetically of 'those who will be affected by a new policy or initiative and those who will implement it as a Treaty obligation'.[115] At the institutional level, it may be sensible to involve the FRA in light of its ability to involve civil society through its Fundamental Rights Platform (FRP).[116] The 2011 Guidance identifies an optional role for the FRA and the Data Protection Supervisor during the consultation phase, which the wording ('you can also make use of')[117] seems to suggest would be ad hoc. However, a more systematic use seems more appropriate and could be, for example, introduced at the Impact Assessment Board level. Instead of giving the Board the possibility to consult external parties on, for example, horizontal issues,[118] one should consider making such consultation compulsory either when fundamental rights issues are in the draft report or when the Board considers that there are such possible implications.

To summarise, legal expertise may be crucial in assessing fundamental rights impacts, even if the nature of the IA is not on its face 'legal'. Therefore, involvement of the Commission Legal Service in the IA process should not be rejected from the outset on the basis of a 'division of tasks' argument. Furthermore, it should not be rejected because of confidentiality

[111] ibid. The six steps comprise: 1) Preliminary Check; 2) Assessment Plan; 3) Information Collection; 4) Rights Analysis; 5) Debate Options; and 6) Decision and Evaluation.

[112] ibid 42–43.

[113] ibid 43.

[114] 2009 IA Guidelines, above n 47, 19–20; and Commission Communication, 'Towards a reinforced culture of consultation and dialogue—General principles and minimum standards for consultation of interested parties by the Commission' (COM(2002) 704 final).

[115] 2009 IA Guidelines, above n 47, 19.

[116] See in this respect also European Parliament Resolution of 15 December 2010 on the situation of fundamental rights in the European Union—effective implementation after the entry into force of the Treaty of Lisbon (2009/2161(INI)), para 18 (recalls the Commission of its explicit task to involve parties concerned by broad consultations in order to ensure coherence and transparency in the EU's actions (Art 11(3) TEU) and underlines in this regard the importance of the FRA platform as a significant resource for fulfilling this task). The FRP is a cooperation network of composed of non-governmental organisations and institutions of civil society; it is a mechanism for the exchange of information and pooling of knowledge. See Art 10 of the FRA Founding Regulation, above n 6.

[117] 2011 Guidance, above n 53, 13.

[118] *Rules of Procedure of the Impact Assessment Board*, above n 104, Art 15.

concerns, as this is the very initial stage of lawmaking where no text is as yet formulated. For the same reason, involvement of the Legal Service may even be beneficial in terms of efficiency. It is better to have it involved in the preparation of the text than to produce legislation that will fail its test at a later stage. More generally, it should be remembered that the Legal Service's involvement is only one means of strengthening the fundamental rights dimension in IA; further ones include the presence of at least one fundamental rights expert member on every Impact Assessment Board and the provision of training of officials responsible for IAs. There is also the creation of a separate fundamental rights category (leading automatically to fulfilment of the proposed Impact Assessment Board requirement), which has and continues to be rejected. That is so despite its usefulness for the purpose of furthering fundamental rights during IAs. However, this may not be very surprising, considering the fact that there is currently (and regrettably) less awareness and emphasis on the 'mainstreaming' or 'furtherance' function of IA than on it as a means of preparing the material upon which the Legal Service may subsequently undertake a compatibility assessment. But, even so, if the IA is especially important for providing an informed account on the question of proportionality, the 'checklist' to be used in this process appears to be in need of revision. Finally, maximum involvement of stakeholders and interested parties should be ensured as well as involvement of an outside expert body, like the FRA.

ii. Legislative Scrutiny/Compatibility Assessments: Recitals and Explanatory Memoranda

The 2001 Commission Decision introduced the obligation that legislative proposals and draft instruments that 'have a specific link with fundamental rights' carry statements of Charter compatibility, which take the following standard form:

> This act respects the fundamental rights and observes the principles recognised in particular by the Charter of Fundamental Rights of the European Union.
>
> When certain rights and/or individual principles of the Charter are specifically involved, a second sentence may be added:
>
> 'In particular, this [act] seeks to ensure full respect for [right XX] and/or to promote the application of [principle YY]/[Article XX and/or Article YY of the Charter of Fundamental Rights of the European Union].'[119]

Carrying such a statement presupposes—in theory at least—that a fundamental rights scrutiny exercise has taken place. In order to comprehend how this does or should materialise, regard must be had to the Commission's drafting procedure.[120]

The initial stage, well before the preparation of a concrete draft, is that of the IA discussed above. It sets the agenda of the drafters, who—this is interesting to note—are not always lawyers, even though they do consult the legal affairs units in their departments, to the extent that those are in place. The identification of fundamental rights impacts is of

[119] Commission Decision, above n 22, 3; House of Lords, 16th Report, above n 23, 25.

[120] See Memorandum Prepared by Commission Services for the House of Lords, Select Committee on European Union, ibid p 49, www.publications.parliament.uk/pa/ld200506/ldselect/ldeucom/67/67.pdf.

particular importance for those initiatives whose implications are not obvious at first sight and that are undertaken in those Directorates General that are not accustomed to recognising conflicts in fundamental rights terms. This is the case for economic legislation (market regulatory instruments) and more generally for all legislation arising outside the area of justice, freedom and security.

After the IA, the desk officers in charge begin to elaborate a preliminary draft of the proposal. At this point, they may or may not have already included a recital confirming compatibility with the Charter. One factor that certainly influences whether a fundamental rights implication is identified at this level is the personal background of the drafters: whether they are legally trained or not and also in which legal culture such training has been received. Moreover, there is a difference in practice depending on the right at issue in a given context—it is clear that the main impact of the legislative scrutiny process will occur in relation to those rights that are extensively regulated at the EU level, such as data protection or free movement.[121] Simply put, more information about these rights will be directly available to the official(s) in charge.

Moreover, the use of 'secondary' sources for the assessment of the legislation will also depend on the legal culture of the officials involved. The Commission's 2009 Report states that even though the previous Communications as well as that Report 'deal with compliance with the Charter ... the Commission must ensure that its proposals comply not only with the Charter and the ECHR but also with United Nations human rights conventions which all the Member States have ratified'.[122] The primary source to consult is the Charter even though international treaties as well as national constitutions will also be taken into account. Undoubtedly, the most important international sources are those of the Council of Europe and, in particular, the ECHR. This also emerges from a survey of internal market legislation with an explicit reference to fundamental rights.[123] In order to ensure that the relevant desk officers possess the requisite knowledge, there is an official at Directorate General Justice in charge of compiling updates two to three times a week on the recent ECtHR and Court of Justice of the EU jurisprudence on fundamental rights. The same person will also provide a briefing in the event of important national constitutional developments (decisions of the German Constitutional Court that have EU implications are particularly well known). The extent to which regard will be had to national constitutions may, however, also be contingent on another factor, namely, the extent to which it is important to secure a particular Member State's vote for the adoption of the proposal. A similar picture appears at the Legal Service scrutiny stage (examined below).

As soon as the work on the preliminary draft commences, the lead Service has to engage in an 'interdepartmental coordination'/'pre-consultation'. At this stage, the preliminary draft is forwarded—on a somewhat informal basis—to other Directorates General for comments. The Fundamental Rights Unit of the Directorate General Justice can provide particularly expert input on fundamental rights questions; this kind of cooperation is supposed to occur frequently between the Directorate General Justice and the Directorate

[121] This is reflected in the Commission Annual Report on the Application of the Charter of Fundamental Rights (2011), http://ec.europa.eu/justice/fundamental-rights/files/charter-brochure-report_en.pdf.

[122] 2009 Commission Report, above n 30, 2, fn 2.

[123] For the period 2001–11.

General Home Affairs. A specific request for an opinion of the Directorate General Justice will in practice only occur by other Directorates General when obvious fundamental rights implications arise. The Legal Service will normally be involved in any such upstream interdepartmental coordination, but it will typically confine itself to making preliminary statements on major legal questions. Concurrently with the preliminary draft, the Explanatory Memorandum is prepared, which is designed to provide explanations of the fundamental rights implications of the proposal in a separate heading. It has to thereby 'demonstrate how respect for fundamental rights has been achieved'.[124]

The key element in the Commission's methodology is the *formal* 'Interservice Consultation' (CIS), which is launched by the lead department once a proposal is sufficiently advanced. This mechanism involves all the Directorates General and Services that have a legitimate interest being asked for their opinion and, by contrast with the 'pre-consultation' stage, consultation of the Legal Service is mandatory at this stage.[125] It thoroughly examines the entire draft in order to assess its legality in light of fundamental rights, based on the lead Service's draft which reflects the formal position of that Directorate General and the accompanying Explanatory Memorandum, as well as the draft IA report and the preparatory documents drawn up in the course of the IA. In cases where the Legal Service arrives at a negative opinion, only the College of Commissioners itself can overturn this conclusion. Given that the Director General of the Legal Service is directly placed under the authority of the President of the Commission (who takes part in all meetings of the College), in practice this happens very rarely. What is important to stress here is that it is this mechanism that provides for formal and decisive fundamental rights scrutiny of legislative proposals.

Six years after the 2001 Decision, criticisms and doubts relating to whether Charter compatibility recitals are (in)-accurately reflecting the motivations behind the legislator's choices,[126] whether the reasons for including the recitals are sufficiently made public, as well as compliance with the Charter *in fact* persisted.

A survey of internal market legislation containing fundamental rights references adopted in the decade following the 2001 Decision[127] reveals two deficiencies in the implementation of 'the methodology'. The same shortcomings were also acknowledged in the Commission's 2009 Assessment Report.

The first concerns the recitals. In general terms, there has mostly been a use of the generic formula affirming compatibility with the Charter instead of specifically identifying which rights are concerned and have been considered during the scrutiny process. It is clear that the generic recital could find its way into legislation in the complete absence of a fundamental rights examination. One reason why this could perhaps have happened is the fact that the standard Charter compatibility recital was included in the Commission's drafting template. The inclusion of 'empty' compatibility statements suggests that they are not the outcome of any fundamental rights scrutiny, given that targeted recitals would evidence the exercise of identifying which right(s) is/are affected by a given piece of legislation and

[124] 2009 Commission Report, above n 30, 7.

[125] Commission, Rules of Procedure of the Commission (C(2000) 3614) [2000] OJ L208/26, Art 21.

[126] Voggenhuber Report, above n 34; and 2009 Commission Report, above n 30.

[127] The legal bases that have been considered here are Arts 93, 94 and 95 EC (now Arts 113, 115 and 114 TFEU, respectively) and the free movement provisions. In this period, some 43 pieces of internal market legislation were identified which contain a Charter compatibility recital.

the fact that some thought has been given to possible implications for that/those right(s). Furthermore, recitals that identify the particular right(s) at issue and state 'how the solutions found in the proposal serve to respect fundamental rights obligations'[128] are certainly more useful as a tool for legislative interpretation when the judicial review process is engaged.

Perhaps accordingly, the Commission announced in its 2009 Assessment Report that it will be 'more selective in including recitals on the Charter in its legislative proposals' in the future,[129] namely, only where 'a proposal has serious fundamental rights implications'[130] and, one may hope, where a thorough examination has been undertaken. This seems to be a reaction to the rhetorical question posed in characteristically British fashion by the House of Lords report as to whether the practice has perhaps 'erred on the side of caution' by including these recitals too systematically.[131]

Since 2001, the decision whether or not to include a standard recital has been made on an ad hoc basis by the respective lead Directorate General, under the oversight of the Legal Service. The decision is often guided by an evaluation of whether the proposal had a 'sufficiently specific link' with fundamental rights. The Commission[132] does not regard it as either possible or desirable to provide proper guidelines for this process. Rather, it places any responsibility to avoid an over-extensive use of the Charter compatibility recital, which would render its role trivial and less credible, on the departments. At the same time, the departments have to ensure that all serious fundamental rights questions arising in the drafting of the legislation are dealt with.[133] The actor who can decisively influence the development of this practice is the Commission Legal Service, since it has the authority to request inclusion or removal of the recitals from the legal text.

Despite its announced reluctance, the 2005 Communication nonetheless introduced two broadly phrased guidelines. First, the rule that Charter recitals *have* to be included when:

— it is clear that, particularly in the light of information provided by the impact assessment, a legislative proposal includes a *limitation* of a fundamental right which must be justified under Article 52 of the Charter; or where there is a direct or indirect difference in treatment that must be justified in relation to the general principles of equality before the law and non-discrimination;
— a legislative proposal is aimed at *implementing* or *promoting* a particular fundamental right.[134]

Second, whenever a Charter compatibility recital is to be included in the proposal, the Explanatory Memorandum has to give the reasons for the conclusion that fundamental rights have been respected. The rationale behind this rule was to avoid criticism that the recitals constitute mere lip service to fundamental rights. Indeed, this requirement highlights the second deficiency in the implementation of 'the methodology'. Most pieces of legislation that contain a compatibility recital do not offer any or sufficient explanations in

[128] 2009 Commission Report, above n 30, 7.
[129] ibid.
[130] ibid.
[131] House of Lords, 16th Report, above n 23, Minutes of Evidence, 4.
[132] 2005 Commission Communication, above n 25, 5, paras 20–21.
[133] ibid para 21.
[134] 2005 Commission Communication, above n 25, para 22.

their Explanatory Memoranda as to the extent to which a fundamental rights assessment has taken place and why the stated result (Charter compatibility) was achieved. The public account of the explanations should prove that serious consideration and legal argument has preceded the assessment. In the absence of such an account, it is reasonable to wonder about the extent to which fundamental rights deliberations have actually preceded the adoption of the instruments.

The Commission's acknowledgment of this malfunctioning[135] was followed by the announcement that:

> [I]t will now become the norm that where the legislative proposal does, indeed, have an impact on fundamental rights, as witnessed by its recitals, the Explanatory Memorandum must include a section justifying succinctly how fundamental rights obligations have been respected.[136]

It is clear that at least up until the introduction of the 2010 Commission strategy for the effective implementation of the Charter, the legislative scrutiny mechanisms have not been very effective in identifying and responding to fundamental rights issues.

Awareness of this also seems to have led to a new Inter-Service Group on Fundamental Rights in the Commission. The need for a horizontal approach regarding experience-sharing on fundamental rights IA and stock-taking of the progress made regarding implementation of the Charter strategy make this group necessary, with a view to enhancing mutual learning in this area and the mainstreaming of the Charter in all policies. This is because bilateral interventions of the Directorate General Justice or the Legal Service are deemed to be insufficient. The mandate of this Inter-Service Group relates to:

— coherence on the implementation of the Charter strategy;
— consistent interpretation and implementation of EU data protection requirements;
— knowledge and experience sharing between Directorate Generals on how to ensure that Commission initiatives respect the Charter and on how to assess the impact of such initiatives on fundamental rights, including data protection;
— facilitating the preparation of the Annual Report on the application of the Charter;
— strengthening the culture of fundamental rights and data protection within the Commission through the development of training activities and possible new tools.

It is certainly no coincidence that the establishment of this Group comes at a time that the Commission has launched an ambitious and large-scale reform package of the EU data protection *acquis* and, indeed, that its mandate singles out this fundamental right. On the one hand, this might be in order to back the reform package that aims to provide for a 'stronger and more coherent data protection framework in the EU'.[137] On the other hand, data protection is one of the most extensively regulated fundamental rights at the EU level, for which the Commission may feel special responsibility, which means that all the necessary information for conducting *ex ante* checks of legislative proposals are 'house-made' and

[135] 2009 Commission Report, above n 30, 8, para 23 ('The treatment of fundamental rights compatibility as a separate heading within the Explanatory Memorandum has not, perhaps, been as consistent as had been envisaged by the 2005 Communication').

[136] ibid.

[137] See Commission Proposal for a 'General Data Protection Regulation' (25 January 2012), COM(2012) 11 final, 2012/0011 (COD).

accessible to all officials. Finally, it would not be credible for the EU legislature to require enhanced data protection in the Member States, while not being able to live up to its own standards. Thus, the EU legislature may want to avoid instances such as the *Schecke*[138] or the *Digital Rights*[139] case (discussed further below).

What the real impact of this Group on building a fundamental rights culture within the Commission will be remains to be seen and, as is the case with most of 'the methodology', its performance will have to be judged on the face of the resulting legislative documentation (IA, Charter compatibility assessments and Explanatory Memoranda, and how those relate to each other) through future monitoring of the EU's legislative output.

When having regard to the instances of *internal market* legislation containing a compatibility recital a year after the Commission's announcement in 2009 that this will be accompanied by proper explanation, it emerges that none justify in the respective Explanatory Memoranda how fundamental rights obligations have been respected. However, a review of a smaller but more recent sample of internal market legislation[140] may indicate some, even if modest, improvement when compared to the first findings of malfunctioning described above: first, the generic Charter compatibility recital, which does not even indicate the Charter articles at issue, is used less. This indicates a positive development, as some thought must have been given to the possible fundamental rights implications in order to identify which fundamental rights are affected. Second, as regards providing justification in the Explanatory Memorandum for how fundamental rights obligations have been respected, we find in about half of the instruments such justification, and in some of these it is even of a detailed nature. Of course, the question whether there has been a clear overall shift in institutional mentality can only be properly answered by analysing in detail all legislation adopted since the 2011 Commission Communication. Still, the above gives some indication that things seem to be changing currently.[141]

What can be investigated more deeply, however, are the reasons for the identified malfunctioning and what may trigger or is currently triggering the fundamental rights reflex.

One of the explanations for the lack of effectiveness could be the lack of an authority, eg, a 'minister', in charge of monitoring the process. Such authority now rests with the Commissioner for Better Regulation, Interinstitutional Relations, the Rule of Law and the Charter of Fundamental Rights, who is currently Frans Timmermans. However, the first to have fundamental rights expressly within her political mandate was the Commissioner for Fundamental Rights, Justice and Citizenship. Viviane Reding held this post from 2010

[138] Joined Cases C-92/09 and C-93/09 *Volker und Markus Schecke GbR and Hartmunt Eifert v Land Hessen* EUI:EU:C:2010:662.

[139] Joined Cases C-293/12 and C-594/12 *Digital Rights Ireland Ltd and Kärntner Landesregierund et al. v Ireland* ECLI:EU:C:2014:238.

[140] Only legislation based on Art 114 TFEU of the consolidated version of the TFEU for the period 2013–14 containing a Charter reference has been considered. Nineteen such instruments have been identified.

[141] To be sure, this is not to suggest that the methodology has already reached a satisfactory level. There are also enough examples to demonstrate missed opportunity on behalf of the legislature to adequately consider fundamental rights implications of legislation. For a discussion, see I Butler, 'A Fundamental Rights Strategy for the European Union', Open Society Institute Policy Brief (May 2014), www.opensocietyfoundations.org/sites/default/files/fundamental-rights-EU-20140530_0.pdf; and I Butler, 'Ensuring Compliance with the Charter of Fundamental Rights in Legislative Drafting: The Practice of the European Commission', (2012) 37 *European Law Review* 397.

to 2014 and it was under her office that the 2010 Communication was adopted. But it is not quite true that such a monitoring instance did not already exist earlier in time. Since 2004, the Group on Fundamental Rights, Anti-discrimination and Equal Opportunities[142] was entrusted with the task of monitoring the legislative scrutiny process (but having in practice the Legal Service keeping the Group informed of developments).[143] Furthermore, 'in very special cases where proposals require a careful balance between several opposing fundamental rights',[144] it could produce policy guidelines.

However, in spite the presence of the repeatedly declared political will, as well as the existence of this entity (albeit a loose one) in charge of this subject matter since 2004, for a long time the methodology did not perform well. So the problem certainly does not lie in the lack of an 'internal' (from inside the Commission) authority that monitors 'the methodology'.

Another argument is that the methodology's performance is contingent on the existence of a fundamental rights *culture* within this institution, and that cannot be established from one day to the next. Institutional attitudes, behaviour and practices require time, a period of 'learning', in order to develop in a politically dictated direction. This is a plausible explanation, especially considering the current new trends, but it is submitted that it is not the only explanation.

A comparison with national law practice may lead to further insights in this respect. The 'tool' of declaring that a proposal is fundamentally rights compliant is analogous to the practice in the UK under section 19 of the Human Rights Act 1998. Under this provision, Ministers and their departments have to consider the impact on ECHR rights for every new legislative bill they seek to introduce. They assume individual responsibility for such compliance.[145] Like the EU system, compatibility is first tested at a less formal policy approval stage, where the Ministers' attention is drawn to possible substantive ECHR implications (in the EU, the IA stage). Subsequently, and only once a bill has been drafted, the formal document of compatibility 'is prepared by departmental lawyers in consultation with Law Officers and the Foreign and Commonwealth Office. This document is then passed to the Cabinet Legislation Joint Committee and ultimately forms the basis of the section 19 statement in each house'[146] (in the EU, the inter-service consultation stage). The test that has to be passed in order for the legislation to bear a section 19 statement of compatibility[147] is interesting: 'A Minister must be clear that, at a minimum, the balance of argument supports the views that the provisions are compatible' and that 'the provisions of the bill will stand up to challenge on Convention grounds before the domestic

[142] ibid n 27.

[143] House of Lords 16th Report, above n 23, 31, para 99.

[144] 2005 Commission Communication, above n 25, para 25; House of Lords, 16th Report, above n 23, 31, para 100.

[145] A Lester, 'Parliamentary Scrutiny of Legislation under the Human Rights Act 1998' (2002) 4 *European Human Rights Law Review* 432, in particular discussion on section 19, 434–36.

[146] ibid 434.

[147] Note that under the Human Rights Act 1998, the responsible Minister can also state that no declaration of compatibility can be made, but that the government nonetheless wishes to proceed with the bill. See Human Rights Act, 1998, c 42 (UK), s 19(1)(b).

courts and the Strasbourg Court'.[148] What is noteworthy about this is that the ministerial scrutiny exercise is thus pressed into a form of court-like scrutiny (this is also happening with regard to the parliamentary scrutiny undertaken by the Joint Committee on Human Rights). The risk is that the legislator will be merely concerned about pre-empting courts in finding human rights violations. This may have two implications—singular or cumulative. First, it may mean that the legislator will be paying less attention to furthering rights (fundamental rights as a shield not as a sword). Second, if constantly preoccupied about what the judicial standard of protection may be, it would prevent the legislator from finding its own fundamental rights standard. This is important where the ECHR is at issue because this provides only for a *minimum* level of protection. It is also important for areas where the courts typically grant discretion to the legislator (or, in ECHR language, 'a wide margin of appreciation').

Unlike in the EU, where the practice of declaring fundamental rights compatibility remained for a long time a fig-leaf exercise, in the UK, it proved to be of significant practical importance.[149] However, it is clear that this success is the result of the effective monitoring and reporting of the Parliamentary Joint Committee on Human Rights.[150] The anticipation of an imminent assessment as to whether a declared rights compatibility can be upheld or not, as well as the Committee's practice of writing to government and inquiring into reasons and consequences of provisions,[151] forces those declaring compatibility to take this task more seriously. The message to be learned for the EU system is therefore that the effective functioning of a compliance declaration by the initiator of legislation requires an *external monitoring mechanism*, which puts (public) pressure on the initiator to take that assessment seriously and which can finally lead to the endorsement of a fundamental rights culture.

As to the state of affairs in the EU today, as already noted above, change seems to be currently underway. If this is indeed the case, the question arises why this would be occurring at precisely this point in time. One explanation could be that there are now *reinforced external mechanisms* in place (these will be discussed in more detailed in sections 3.2–3.4 below). Yet, even if this is true, the following question still remains—what has caused such reinforcement? Alternatively, or in addition, it could be argued that now, 14 years since the emergence of the methodology, the time has arrived where the first signs of a slowly built culture—mainly built through repeated political declarations and announced commitments—is emerging.

However, there is also another explanation, which is to this author's mind more convincing since it has arguably an influence on both of the previously offered explanations. The 'fundamental rights reflex' has finally begun to be triggered because of the existence of real incentives. These incentives do not result from the latest proclaimed (2010) strategy of the Commission on the implementation of the Charter, since, as already stated, it did not impart anything new to what was already in place.

[148] Human Rights Act 1998, Guidance for Departments issued by the British Cabinet Office (February 2000), para 36, in Lester, above n 145, 435.

[149] Lester, above n 145, 434.

[150] ibid s III.

[151] House of Lords, House of Commons, Joint Committee on Human Rights, The Work of the Committee in 2001–05 Session, 19th Report of Session 2004–05, 16, www.publications.parliament.uk/pa/jt200405/jtselect/jtrights/112/112.pdf (hereinafter the 'JCHR, 19th Report').

Nor are the incentives the result of the Court 'pushing' the methodology through procedural review, as suggested by one commentator:

> It would be easy for the Court to grant legal bite to such a procedural requirement. It necessitates less a direct involvement with the substance of the legislation but rather merely a requirement that legislators direct their attention to fundamental rights. Measures could therefore be struck down not merely where they violate a fundamental right but also where the EU institutions have failed to give due consideration to whether a measure potentially violates a fundamental right.[152]

Yet, the Court never set out to do so and there would be several difficulties that it would have to face if it embarked on following such an approach. The first concerns the fact that the proper explanation as to why and how fundamental rights are respected in a given instrument is supposed to be included in the Explanatory Memorandum, given that the general tendency is to keep Preamble recitals as concise as possible. However, only the Commission produces these Memoranda at the very initial stage of lawmaking when drafting a legislative proposal. Consider therefore the following scenario: assume the Commission fails to mention in the Explanatory Memorandum fundamental rights considerations, but the matter is extensively discussed at a later stage, say by the European Parliament, and this discussion is visible in the European Parliament documentation, but not on the face of the instrument and the Memorandum accompanying it. Would the Court be required here to undertake research of the legislative history of the instrument in order to assess whether 'the EU institutions have failed to give due consideration to whether a measure potentially violates a fundamental right'? Or would it have to come to the conclusion that no such consideration has been given, due to the fact that the Explanatory Memorandum is silent on the matter and despite the fact that the institutions have actually discussed it?

The second problem that would arise is that such an approach could in fact lead to the opposite result of what it intended to achieve. It could reinforce the lip-service nature of the methodology. The institutions could become more concerned with asserting that due consideration has been given to fundamental rights or with seeking to justify why a (politically wanted) instrument does not violate fundamental rights, rather than with a substantial and objective assessment of fundamental rights compliance (or furtherance).

The final problem relates to political reality. It seems unlikely that the Court would strike down a piece of legislation that, if it were to conduct a substantial assessment, it would find in compliance with the fundamental rights requirement on the ground that the institutions did not explain why they have come to the same assessment.

As illustrated above, at least so far, the incentive for triggering the 'fundamental rights reflex' did not originate in the threat of procedural fundamental rights review of the type described above. What is actually causing a different attitude among the lawmakers originates in the two well-known novelties introduced by the Lisbon Treaty: the legally binding status of the Charter; and the accession of the EU to the ECHR (irrespective of how close or distant the conclusion of that process may be).[153]

Drafters of legal instruments in the Commission may already feel the effects of future accession. The fear that the ECtHR may declare an EU legal instrument to be in violation of

[152] D Chalmers, G Davies and G Monti, *European Union Law* (Cambridge, Cambridge University Press, 2010) 252.

[153] CJEU, *Opinion 2/13 on the accession of the EU to the European Convention on Human Rights* EU:C:2014:2475.

the ECHR is real and puts on the legislator pressure to keep its fundamental rights record straight.

In fact, competition from the Strasbourg Court also seems to be changing the Court of Justice of the EU's approach to fundamental rights issues. The increasing reference and framing of issues in fundamental rights terms, and the changed reasoning structure which takes the Charter (not the ECHR) as a first point of reference, certainly have to do with the legally binding status of this document, but it can also be suggested that the Court of Justice of the EU is additionally under pressure to be the *first* instance that pronounces itself on fundamental rights that are protected within both legal orders. This could in consequence also lead to a stricter level of fundamental rights review of EU legislation.

The recent *Schecke*,[154] *Test-Achats*[155] and *Digital Rights*[156] cases seem to be indicative of such a changed approach. In the first two cases, the Court invalidated parts of legislation and in the latter it struck down the entire Directive on fundamental rights grounds. The cases are notable because in the past it was very rare that the Court would do so.[157]

In *Schecke*, the Court declared two provisions of a Council regulation, which required the publication of the recipients of agricultural subsidies to be contrary to Articles 7 (privacy) and 8 (data protection) of the Charter. The case is also noteworthy because the Court relied for the first time exclusively on the Charter in order to invalidate secondary legislation. In *Digital Rights*,[158] it found the Data Retention Directive,[159] which imposed an obligation on Member States to retain data under the conditions defined therein for the purposes of investigation, detection and prosecution of serious crime (as defined under national law) to be a disproportionate interference with, again, the right to privacy and data protection. *Test-Achats*, on the other hand, concerned equal treatment. The Court invalidated a provision of the Directive concerning access to and supply of goods and services,[160] which allowed Member States to permit insurers to take gender into account when calculating insurance premiums and benefits.

These cases might be seen as implying that the Court's level of legislative scrutiny has altered dramatically with the advent of the Lisbon Treaty. However, one should be cautious

[154] *Volker and Hartmut Eifert*, above n 138.

[155] Case C-236/09 *Association Belge des Consommateurs Test-Achats ASBL and others v Conseil des ministres* EU:C:2010:662.

[156] *Digital Rights*, above n 139.

[157] The trend was instead that the Court would impose on the Member States the obligation to protect (EU) fundamental rights of its citizens when implementing EU law. See on this point A von Bogdandy and J von Bernstoff, 'The EU Fundamental Rights Agency within the European and International Human Rights Architecture: The Legal Framework and Some Unsettled Issues in a New Field of Administrative Law' (2009) 46 *Common Market Law Review* 1035, 1066 with reference to J Bast, 'Legal Instrument and Judicial Protection' in A von Bogdandy and J Bast (eds), *Principles of European Constitutional Law* (Oxford, Hart Publishing, 2009) 345. However, this is not to say that the Court would always adopt a hands-off approach; it has been, for example, active in fundamental rights review also prior to the entry into force of the Lisbon Treaty in the field of EU Counter-Terrorism Measures. See, for example, the pre-Lisbon Cases C-402 and 415/05 *P Kadi and Al Barakaat International Foundation v Council and Commission (Kadi I)* [2008] ECR I-6351; Case T-288/02 *Organisation des Modjahedines du people d'Iran (OMPI) v Council* [2006] ECR II-4665.

[158] Discussed in detail in ch 4.

[159] Directive 2006/24/EC on the retention of data generated or processed in connection with the provision of publicly available electronic communications services or of public communications networks and amending Directive 2002/58/EC (Data Retention Directive) [2006] OJ L105/54.

[160] Directive 2004/113/EC implementing the principle of equal treatment between men and women in the access to and supply of goods and services [2002] OJ L373/27.

of already drawing at this stage firm conclusions based on these three cases. It may be true that the Court may tighten its fundamental rights judicial review post-Lisbon. This is so because it is arguable that the Court had an 'easy' case of finding fundamental rights incompatibility in these three judgments. However, the *Schecke* and *Test-Achats* cases are to be distinguished here from *Digital Rights*.

As Lenaerts has suggested,[161] *Schecke* and *Test-Achats* are more concerned with the *decision-making process* than the substantive choices of the EU legislature. In *Schecke*, the reason why the Court failed certain provisions of the Council Regulation and the Commission Regulation at issue is because the legislature did not satisfy the principle of proportionality since 'it [was] possible to envisage measures which affect less adversely that fundamental right of natural persons and which still contribute effectively to the objectives of the European Union rules in question'.[162] What seems to be crucial in this case, and what the Court in fact condemns, is the fact that 'There [was] *nothing to show that*, when adopting [the contested provisions] … *the Council and the Commission took into consideration* methods of publishing information on the beneficiaries concerned which would be consistent with the objective of such publication while at the same time causing less interference with those beneficiaries' right to respect for their private life in general and to protection of their personal data in particular' (emphasis added).[163] In other words, it is the legislature's complete disregard of the question of proportionate interference with data protection that the Court denounces. Had the legislative history demonstrated that methods of data publication were taken into account which are less restrictive of data protection, but came to the conclusion that those do not effectively contribute to the EU's objectives (guaranteeing transparency and ensuring best use of public funds), it would have been much more difficult for the Court to invalidate the contested provisions. To be sure, this is different from the suggestion discussed (and dismissed) above that the Court could strike down legislation merely on a finding that the legislature failed to duly consider whether a measure potentially violates a fundamental right. This is so because that scenario entails the possibility of invalidating legislation merely on procedural grounds, with a complete disregard to substance, whereas in *Schecke*, the Court did find (substantively) that it is possible to envisage other less restrictive measures than what the legislation at issue offered. Only because this is the case does the procedural point become relevant: the onus is then on the legislature to demonstrate that these alternatives were considered and dismissed, which was not the case here.

In *Test-Achats*, the invalidation of the contested provision was due to the inconsistency of the measure.[164] The inconsistency or incoherence is due to the fact that the Directive at issue (Directive 2004/113/EC)[165] provided in its Article 5(1) that the 'use of sex as a factor in the calculation of premiums and benefits for the purposes of insurance and related financial services shall not result in differences in individuals' premiums and benefits'. In

[161] K Lenaerts, 'The European Court of Justice and Process-Oriented Review', College of Europe, Department of European Legal Studies, Research Paper in Law 01/2012.

[162] *Volker and Hartmut Eifert*, above n 138, [86].

[163] ibid [81].

[164] Lenaerts, above n 161; and C Tobler, 'Case C-236/09 *Association belge des Consommateurs Test-Achats ASBL, Yann van Vugt, Charles Basselier v Conseil des ministres*, Judgment of the Court of Justice (Grand Chamber) of 1 March 2011' (2011) 48 *Common Market Law Review* 2041.

[165] Directive 2004/113/EC, above n 160.

doing so, the legislator endorsed the view that the situation between men and women in this context is comparable and that is why there shall be no difference in treatment. Yet the Directive allowed for a derogation from that principle without any temporal limitation in Article 5(2): Member States could 'permit proportionate differences in individuals' premiums and benefits where the use of sex is a determining factor in the assessment of risk based on relevant and accurate actuarial and statistical data'. As pointed out by Tobler: 'Essentially, [the Court] reproaches the legislator for having started from the premise of comparability, as expressed in Article 5(1) and the preamble of the Directive, but then, by establishing the derogation of Article 5(2), not having carried it through.'[166] The Court did not question the legislator's very premise.[167]

Digital Rights is different from the above-mentioned cases in the sense that the Court here was very much concerned with the substantive choices of the legislator. In this case, however, it is submitted that the Court would have had a hard time explaining that the Data Retention Directive was in compliance with fundamental rights because this instrument was blatantly disproportionate. The Directive was highly controversial from the very outset and long before the Court's judgment. This is evidenced by reactions of the Article 20 Working Party and the European Data Protection Supervisor, who characterised the Directive as 'the most privacy invasive instrument ever adopted by the EU in terms of scale and the number of people it affects',[168] whose necessity had not been demonstrated.[169] It would have been very difficult to avoid conducting substantive fundamental rights review here by emphasising fundamental rights-compliant implementation on behalf of Member States along the lines in the *Family Reunification* case.[170] In the latter case, the Family Reunification Directive was at issue, which imposes specific positive obligations on Member States for protecting the fundamental right to family reunification and allows Member States to derogate from that right under specific circumstances, thereby also granting them a certain degree of discretion. The Court held that the derogation clauses did not run counter to the fundamental right to respect for family life. At the same time, it emphasised that Member States have to act in compliance with fundamental rights standards when derogating. The situation is different for the Data Retention Directive. This instrument imposes an *obligation* on Member States to interfere[171] with a fundamental right. The Court in essence replied that the legislator cannot do so without providing for clear and precise rules governing the extent of the interference and sufficient safeguards.[172] This appears logical because it is the EU legislator that creates the risk for a violation to occur (ie, an unjustified restriction with a fundamental right). This is not the case with regard to the Family Reunification Directive.

[166] Tobler, above n 164, 2054.

[167] ibid.

[168] Commission, Press Release EDPS/10/17, 'The "Moment of Truth" for the Data Retention Directive: EDPS Demands Clear Evidence of Necessity' (3 December 2010), http://europa.eu/rapid/press-release_EDPS-10-17_en.htm?locale=en

[169] See the detailed discussion in ch 4, s IV.B.

[170] Case C-540/03 *European Parliament v Council* (*Re Family Reunification*) [2006] ECR I-05769, EU:C:2006:429.

[171] The interference is obvious because data retention amounts to a derogation from the data protection principles set out in Directives 94/46/EC and 2002/58/EC, respectively. In fact, the function of the Data Retention Directive was to harmonise the Member States' possibility of derogating from Directive 2002/58/EC. See the discussion in ch 4.

[172] See discussion in ch 4.

There is one further point on judicial review that is worth noting. In *Digital Rights*, when assessing the proportionality of the measure, the Court referred to ECHR standards[173] in order to determine the applicable level of judicial review. It noted that 'the extent of the EU legislature's discretion may prove to be limited, depending on a number of factors, including, in particular, the area concerned, the nature of the right at issue guaranteed by the Charter, the nature and seriousness of the interference and the object pursued by the interference'.[174] The Court eventually applied a strict level of judicial review when assessing the fundamental rights compatibility of the Directive. It did so 'in view of the important role played by the protection of personal data in the light of the fundamental right to respect for private life the extent and seriousness of the interference with that right caused by Directive 2006/24'.[175] The EU legislature's discretion was thereby reduced.

Does this then mean that the conceptualisation of internal market legislation as legislation impacting on fundamental rights affects the level of review adopted by the Court?

In order to answer this question, it is necessary to distinguish between the proportionality assessment under the Charter (Art 52(1) CFR) and that under Article 5(4) TEU.[176] It is well established that in the case of internal market legislation, which 'entails political, economic and social choices on the [legislator's] part, and in which [the legislator] is called upon to undertake complex assessments', the test applied is whether the measure is 'manifestly inappropriate', having regard to the objective pursued.[177] So, wide discretion is granted to the legislator in this area of lawmaking. When proportionality is tested in the assessment of fundamental rights compatibility of legislation (under Article 52(1) CFR), in accordance with the ECHR approach, there are further variables (in addition to the area concerned) that the Court needs to take into account in deciding the applicable level of review (the type of right, the seriousness of the interference etc). This may result in a strict review, as in *Digital Rights*, or in a review granting wide discretion, as in *Karner*.[178]

However, what is to be noted is that this fundamental rights assessment is also relevant for the Article 5(4) TFEU proportionality assessment. This is so because fundamental rights are not only a separate (from Art 5(4) TFEU proportionality) *ground* of review, but are also a *standard* of review within the Article 5(4) TFEU proportionality assessment. This is in fact nothing other than the mirror image of the *ERT*[179] doctrine in negative integration case law. The Court held in this case that the assessment as to whether Member States can derogate from the free movement provisions has to be made in light of fundamental rights. Thus, a restriction to a free movement provision, which pursues a legitimate public interest, will not pass the justification stage if it constitutes a disproportionate interference with an EU fundamental right. Conversely, in positive integration, the EU legislator cannot be

[173] *S and Marper v UK* [GC] App Nos 30562/04 and 30566/04 (ECtHR, 4 December 2008) [102].

[174] *Digital Rights*, above n 139, [47].

[175] ibid [48].

[176] The Advocate General, unlike the Court, drew this distinction. However, he did not follow through with the two separate assessments.

[177] Case 380/03 *Germany v Parliament and Council* [2006] ECR I-11573 (hereinafter '*Tobacco Advertising II*') [145].

[178] See ch 5.

[179] Case C-260/89 *Elliniki Radiophonia Tileorassi AE (ERT) v Dimotiki Etairia Pliroforissis and Sotirios Kouvelas* [1991] ECR I-2925 (hereinafter '*ERT*').

considered to have employed appropriate means to achieve the harmonisation goal when these means violate EU fundamental rights.

Concretely in substantive terms, the above means that a measure that violates fundamental rights will always also fall foul of Article 5(4) TFEU because it will have to be considered 'manifestly inappropriate' to the objective pursued. In procedural terms, this would even imply an *ex officio* obligation for the Court to review fundamental rights compatibility of a measure when it is only asked to review proportionality of the measure under Article 5(4) TEU.

Note, however, that the converse is not necessarily true. A measure may be compatible with fundamental rights (say, because there is no interference with a fundamental right) but still be problematic from the point of view of Article 5(4) TFEU if it is 'manifestly inappropriate' for achieving the objective it claims to pursue.

Nevertheless, in this light, it can, again, not be concluded that the strict level of review employed to assess the fundamental rights compatibility of the Data Retention Directive marks a shift from the normally wide discretion granted to the EU internal market legislator. The level of review employed was rather the result of the ground of review (fundamental rights) tested by the Court and consequently the variables (the right at issue and the serious interference) that were at stake.[180] The Court did not consider Article 5(4) TFEU separately, but that would also not be necessary after it found a fundamental rights violation.[181] This is so not only because the measure was at that point in any event already declared illegal, but also because that assessment would (or should) have let to the same outcome, as explained above.

Even if the three cases discussed may not be sufficient to speak of a clearly altered trend in the levels of judicial review employed by the Court, their significance should not be understated: they urge the legislator to first reason in a transparent manner about fundamental rights considerations in the preparation of legislation, second, to adopt legislation that is coherent and, finally and most obviously, substantively in line with fundamental rights standards, failing which it will be struck down by the Court. This is a strong message that has been sent to the legislator and it has certainly already reached the latter's ears.[182]

Should such modus operandi become prevalent in the future, it may be suggested that both 'external' judicial pressure from the ECtHR and 'internal' judicial pressure resulting inter alia from the competition of the two European Courts may result in a strengthened *ex ante* scrutiny system.

One caveat has to be made here. Compliance with the ECHR is of course not tantamount to compliance with the Charter. This is so because the EU catalogue of rights includes more rights than the ECHR, notably economic and social rights, and also because the ECHR is only a *minimum* standard of protection. On that basis, one may express a warning that

180 These two variables seem in any event to have outweighed the other two variables mentioned by the Court: the area and the objective pursued. However, the Court does not mention the area of regulation (the internal market) and the objective pursued (public security/fighting serious crime) and how precisely they weighed in the determination of the applicable standard of review.

181 The *ex officio* point does not arise here because the referring court also posed a question about the Charter compatibility of the Data Retention Directive.

182 See, eg, Council, Guidelines on Methodological Steps to be taken to check fundamental rights compatibility at the Council's preparatory bodies, 16957/14 (16 December 2014) (hereinafter the '2014 Council Guidelines').

ECHR accession will not influence fundamental rights-proofing of legislation so as to turn it into an 'ECHR-proofing' exercise.

However, two trends suggest that this is unlikely to occur. First, as discussed above, empirical evidence suggests that the first source of reference for the drafters is the Charter and not the ECHR. Second, there is the fact that ever since the entry into force of the Lisbon Treaty, the Court has been on a very frequent basis referring to the Charter in its case law, as already stated above. The effect that this may produce is important. That is, a 'thickened'[183] fundamental rights jurisprudence, whose resonance—if it materialises—will influence the drafting exercise. This 'thickening' may not only take place in case the Court changes its approach so as to adopt a stricter fundamental rights review of EU legislation, but also if it will provide for more elaborate accounts on the scope of the rights that it recognises as fundamental.

In any case, a changed attitude of the officials involved in legislative scrutiny and compatibility assessments is to be welcomed whatever the source of the incentive. Having said that, it still remains to be seen the extent to which this changed attitude will actually result in a better use of the available legislative scrutiny tools and consequently to enhanced fundamental rights protection in the legislation.

iii. Monitoring Compliance: Charter Compliance Throughout the Legislative Process

The Commission's natural self-perception is that its status as the guardian of the Treaties implies the role of being the 'guardian of fundamental rights'.[184] It is from this role that a broader monitoring function is derived, namely, that of 'monitoring the work of the two branches of the legislative authority [the Council of Ministers and the European Parliament]'.[185] This should mean in practice that 'the Commission would react whenever amendments were presented by the Council or Parliament which it could not accept because it believed they violated fundamental rights'.[186] In its 2010 Communication, the Commission offers assistance to the other institutions to 'find an effective way to take into account the effects of their amendments on the implementation of the Charter'.[187] At the same time, it threatens that 'it will not hesitate to use all the means at its disposal, which may include requesting that the act be adopted unanimously or, where applicable, withdrawing its proposal or bringing an action for annulment of the provisions in question'.[188] In order to prevent this, importance is placed on a 'transparent inter-institutional dialogue', whereby the Parliament and the Council take fundamental rights into account when assessing the

[183] The expression is borrowed from von Bogdandy and von Bernstoff, above n 157, 1061.

[184] 2005 Commission Communication, above n 25, para 27.

[185] ibid para 28.

[186] House of Lords, 16th Report, above n 23, 27, para 85, with reference to interview statements made by Dr Ladenburger, Commission Legal Service, European Commission. The European Council in its Stockholm Programme has also noted the fact that fundamental rights implications may arise in the course of the legislative process when amendments are made which are not systematically reviewed. See 2009 Commission Report, above n 30, 8.

[187] 2009 Commission Report, above n 30, 8.

[188] ibid.

impacts of their amendments, 'decisions on amendments are taken at the appropriate level' and 'the Legal Service of the three institutions are fully involved'.[189]

A note of caution should be sounded here. It is true that a dialogue among the institutions, as presented, may enhance fundamental rights awareness and promote a common approach as to how this issue will be tackled. At the same time, however, a dialogue may lead to undesirable coordination among the institutions in the sense that compromises and trade-offs may be reached, instead of raising the standard of fundamental rights protection through external control. An additional question that arises is what would be a practical way of ensuring continuous fundamental rights assessments all along the legislative process. One possibility for achieving this would be to provide for an obligation that Explanatory Memoranda are updated if changes have been made in the passage of legislation which impact on fundamental rights, and if the issues have been debated for example in the European Parliament. The responsibility could lay with the Commission to do so when compiling the final text for publication.

B. The European Parliament

Traditionally, the European Parliament has been the most active and most concerned institution regarding fundamental rights protection among the lawmakers.[190] Yet, as regards *systematic* fundamental rights-proofing of EU legislation, so far it has only assumed a secondary role.

Unlike the Commission—the main responsible for that task under the current state of affairs—its role is merely reactionary in the sense that compliance with fundamental rights will only be assessed when raised in the committees dealing with the proposal. There are two ways that can lead to such an assessment. The first one is when a majority in the committee responsible would disagree with the Commission's assessment on fundamental rights and would therefore request an opinion from the European Parliament Legal Service on the legality of the proposal or, alternatively, when the legislation is subjected to

[189] This point is not made in the current inter-institutional agreement 'Common Approach to Impact Assessment', Council document 14901/05 (24 November 2005). However, the Commission has announced that it will propose such provision in the forthcoming revision of this agreement. See 2009 Commission Report, above n 30, 9.

[190] On 10 February 1977, the European Parliament issued a declaration of political principle on the definition of fundamental rights, which was adopted by the Council and the Commission and signed by the respective presidents on 5 April 1977. See *Joint Declaration by the European Parliament, the Council and the Commission Concerning the Protection of Fundamental Rights and the European Convention for the Protection of Human Rights and Fundamental Freedoms* [1977] OJ C103/1 (5 April 1977). On 12 April 1989, this was expanded in a Declaration of fundamental rights, which includes a comprehensive list of rights. The European Parliament then declared its determination 'to achieve a basic Community instrument with a binding legal character guaranteeing fundamental rights'. See European Parliament Resolution adopting the Declaration of Fundamental Rights and Freedoms [1989] OJ C120/51, 52, G. Based on this Declaration, on 10 February 1994, the European Parliament's Committee on Institutional Affairs drew up a list of human rights guaranteed by the EU. In 1993, the Committee on Civil Liberties and Internal Affairs was set up under the Maastricht Treaty and produced its first annual report. More generally, the European Parliament has repeatedly adopted resolutions on respect for fundamental rights in the EU and human rights beyond the EU. It had frequently called for EU accession to the ECHR and it has also done so for EU accession to the Council of Europe's Social Charter. Finally, the European Parliament has also called for the Protocol and Agreement on Social Policy and the Charter of Fundamental Social Rights to be incorporated into the Treaty. See www.europarl.europa.eu/factsheets/2_1_1_en.htm.

amendments. Thus, unlike the Commission Legal Service, the European Parliament Legal Service does not undertake a fundamental rights compliance check of all legislation passing through this institution.

It is at this point important to note that not all committees consider fundamental rights systematically, but certainly those whose subject matter is concerned with them, notably the Committee on Civil Liberties, Justice and Home Affairs (LIBE), the Committee on Women's Rights and Gender Equality (FEMM) and the Constitutional Affairs Committee (AFCO). By implication, fundamental rights concerns emerging in legislative dossiers that are not allocated to these committees are more likely not to be subjected to Legal Service scrutiny.

As regards the substance of the Legal Service's assessment, the sources relied upon will be primarily case law of the Court of Justice of the EU on the matter, in the absence of which regard will be had to the jurisprudence of the ECtHR.

The second route leading to fundamental rights-proofing is again reactive in character. It was brought about with the 2009 Decision of the European Parliament on the adaptation of Parliament's Rules of Procedure to the Treaty of Lisbon[191] and can be found in the following paragraph:

> Where the committee responsible for the subject matter, a political group or at least 40 Members are of the opinion that a proposal for a legislative act or parts of it do not comply with rights enshrined in the Charter of Fundamental Rights of the European Union, the matter shall, at their request, be referred to the committee responsible for the interpretation of the Charter. The opinion of that committee shall be annexed to the report of the committee responsible for the subject-matter.[192]

The obligation to respect fundamental rights during the examination of legislative proposals already existed previously (certainly since the introduction of the TEU), as well as an explicit reference in the Parliament's Rules of Procedure that legislative acts have to be in conformity with the Charter.[193] However, the novelty of this amendment consists in the introduction of a *new procedure* for scrutinising fundamental rights compliance.[194]

The Rule does not stipulate which will be 'the committee responsible' that shall receive such requests, but the Voggenhuber Report,[195] where this amendment originates, reveals that the initial intention was to involve the LIBE Committee,[196] which speaks for the same interpretation of the current rule. This would be logical, given that this Committee is

[191] European Parliament decision of 25 November 2009 on the adaptation of Parliament's Rules of Procedure to the Treaty of Lisbon (2009/2062(REG)).

[192] European Parliament, Rules of Procedure, 7th parliamentary term (July 2010), rule 36, para 2, www.europarl.europa.eu/sides/getDoc.do?pubRef=-//EP//NONSGML+RULES-EP+20100705+0+DOC+PDF+V0//EN&language=EN.

[193] Before the 2009 amendment, rule 34 of the European Parliament Rules of Procedure.

[194] Draft Report on the adaptation of Parliament's Rules of Procedure to the Treaty of Lisbon, Committee on Constitutional Affairs (28 July 2009), 2009/2062(REG), Rapporteur: David Martin.

[195] Voggenhuber Report, above n 34, para 15. See also European Parliament Resolution of 15 March 2007 on compliance with the Charter of Fundamental Rights in the Commission's legislative proposals: methodology for systematic and rigorous monitoring, 2005/2169(INI), para 15 ('[the European Parliament] contemplates the possibility of amending to this end Rule 34 of its Rules of Procedure, so as to entrust the Committee on Civil Liberties with the task of monitoring the consequences of legislative proposals, measures and regulations relevant to fundamental rights').

[196] (Then) Rule 34 should be changed 'so as to entrust the Committee on Civil Liberties, Justice and Home Affairs with the task of monitoring the consequences of legislative proposals, measures and regulations relevant to fundamental rights'.

entrusted with, inter alia, 'the protection within the territory of the Union of citizens' rights, human rights and fundamental rights, including the protection of minorities, as laid down in the Treaties and in the Charter of Fundamental Rights of the European Union'.[197]

The fact that this political committee (and not say the Committee on Constitutional Affairs (JURI))[198] is entrusted with fundamental rights-proofing of legislation will certainly reflect upon the type of scrutiny conducted. LIBE is more likely to provide for an examination that is thoroughly legally informed if it is to request an opinion from the Legal Service or from the FRA as it were, and it is not obvious to what extent that would happen systematically. Members of the European Parliament appear to be conscious of the time delay associated with requesting a Legal Service opinion regarding the legislative dossiers that are regularly before them, even though one would assume (and hope) that such a referral from another committee would be taken seriously. Certainly, the same 'time factor' also plays a great role when the European Parliament is considering requesting an official Opinion from the FRA (this is discussed further below). The necessity to receive real-time responses turns out to be a key determinant in practice. A further matter to be noted is that since most of the legislation that involves (at least obvious) fundamental rights issues is in any case passing through LIBE and since most of the remaining committees do not routinely pay attention to fundamental rights issues, the added value provided by the new rule 36 could be questioned. On the other hand, given the fact that 40 members can initiate this procedure, the rule could be used by LIBE (comprising more than 40 members) in order to bring a legislative dossier allocated to another committee under its scrutiny.

A final more general point to be noted is the practice of 'trialogues', which poses a challenge to fundamental rights examinations and represents a risk for bypassing such concerns. 'Trialogues' constitute informal meetings involving key actors and are intended to achieve compromise solutions, which are then submitted to the respective official institutional settings. However, this practice, which has been promoted as it proved to be highly efficient, 'curtails the possibility for public deliberation about the content of legislation',[199] including fundamental rights.

In sum, the current practice is that the European Parliament relies for the *systematic* scrutiny of *all* legislation principally on the Commission, which is expected to get it right. Yet it is arguable that especially in the post-Lisbon era, there rests a responsibility on the European Parliament to assume a more systematic role in *ex ante* protection. Lisbon did not only bring about the stated changes with regard to fundamental rights, but also regarding the legislative role of the European Parliament. The procedure previously known as 'co-decision' and now as 'ordinary legislative procedure' has been extended to a considerable amount of new areas, including fundamental rights sensitive areas (ex-third pillar), 'now

[197] www.eppgroup.eu/LIBE.

[198] According to rule 36 of the European Parliamentary Rules of Procedure, the role of JURI includes 'the interpretation and application of Union law and compliance of Union acts with primary law, notably the choice of legal bases and respect for the principles of subsidiarity and proportionality'. Fundamental rights are not expressly mentioned, but the Charter clearly constituted primary law, so that the check of legislation for compliance with the Charter could have fallen within this Committee's responsibilities. See European Parliament, Rules of Procedure, above n 192, Annex XVI.

[199] B de Witte, A Trechsel, D Damjanović, E Hellquist, J Hien and P Ponzano, 'Legislating after Lisbon—New Opportunities for the European Parliament', EUDO study (2010), Florence, 27. www.eui.eu/Projects/EUDO/Documents/EUDO-LegislatingafterLisbon(SD).pdf.

applying to 90% of internal laws'.[200] This rise in power in the lawmaking process also brings with it a responsibility to ensure that mechanisms are in place that can guarantee a high level of fundamental rights protection in the transformed institutional output. This is not to say that the European Parliament has not already proven post-Lisbon that it can take its responsibilities seriously;[201] rather, it is to make the point that it should assume a more systematic role. A systematic cooperation with the FRA would be one way to do so, and indeed this seems to be increasingly occurring.[202]

The relatively modest role of parliamentary control at the EU level can be contrasted with two examples of national legal orders where Parliament plays a much more central role in *ex ante* fundamental rights review. These are the examples of Finland and the UK. These two countries have in common the fact that they adhere to the principle of parliamentary sovereignty, which accounts for the pivotal function assigned to these committees, as opposed to post hoc judicial rights review.

In Finland, the main form of constitutional—including fundamental rights—review takes the form of *ex ante* control. It is the parliamentary Constitutional Law Committee (CLC) that is mainly responsible for such review,[203] which is, however, not conducted for *all* legislative proposals. The importance of this committee becomes obvious when noting that its opinions are normally decisive as to the constitutionality of a bill subject to scrutiny. This is so because of the primary nature of *ex ante* control and conversely the fact that judicial review is a 'measure-of-last-resort' in this system.[204] This is of course very different from the EU, where the Court has been the initiator of fundamental rights review in the EU legal order, and given the institutional history and role of the European Parliament in the EU and the consequent absence of any doctrine similar to that of parliamentary sovereignty.

Interestingly, the procedure for reference to the CLC resembles the new European Parliament procedure for fundamental rights scrutiny discussed above (Rule 36 of the Rules of Procedure), to the extent that the plenary session or other committees may request the CLC (in the EU 'the committee responsible for the interpretation of the Charter') to review a bill. Indeed, a committee has a duty to do so if there are doubts regarding the proposal's constitutionality.[205]

There is one peculiarity in the Finnish system that the EU system could learn from. This concerns the interaction of the executive with this committee. Even though the normal procedure is that Parliament decides to request constitutional review from the CLC,[206] the

[200] ibid 26.

[201] See, eg, the European Parliament's refusal to consent to the EU–US Agreement on the transferring on financial messaging data (the 'SWIFT Agreement'). The Agreement was voted down in Plenary on 10 February 2010.

[202] See the European Parliament's request Opinions from the FRA, discussed further below in s III.D.

[203] See K Tuori, 'Combining Abstract *Ex Ante* and Concrete *Ex Post* Review: The Finnish Model' paper presented in the UNIDEM Seminar 'Definition and Implementation of Human Rights and Popular Sovereignty in Europe', Frankfurt am Main (15–16 May 2009), www.venice.coe.int/webforms/documents/CDL-UD (2010)011-e.aspx.

[204] ibid 5 (according to Art 106 of the Finnish Constitution, courts can only set aside in a case at hand a piece of legislation when there is an evident conflict with the Constitution. However, this can hardly be established when the CLC has expressly found in the *ex ante* review that the statute is in compliance with the Constitution).

[205] Article 38(2) of the Rules of Procedure of the Finnish Parliament. In the EU, such a duty exists if the committee responsible, a political group or at least 40 members consider the proposal or parts of it to be incompatible with the Charter. See rule 36 of the European Parliament Rules of Procedure, above n 192.

[206] See Art 32 of the Rules of Procedure of the Finnish Parliament.

main initiator of a constitutional review initiative is most of the time in fact the executive. The reason for this is that there is no centralised administrative constitutional review in place due to time and resource constraints.[207]

In the European model of *ex ante* review, the Commission believes to have the necessary time and resources so as to be the main responsible in this system. This is why this institution has initiated the 'methodology' and has put itself in its centre. Yet, even if this is accepted, a procedure foreseeing a referral by the Commission to the European Parliament could still be conducive to enhanced fundamental rights protection. For example, a procedure could be introduced whereby the Commission could in the event of particular sensitive or controversial proposals, where doubts still persist, request the European Parliament to scrutinise it for fundamental rights compliance, by involving the European Parliament Legal Service, LIBE or AFCO, before the proposal leaves the Commission. This might be especially useful in cases where the proposal would not be allocated to these Committees when reaching the European Parliament.

In our second example, the UK, the Joint Committee on Human Rights (JCHR) plays a key fundamental rights scrutiny role. Its set-up came hand in hand with the incorporation of the ECHR into the UK legal system through the Human Rights Act 1998 (HRA). Although the HRA does not explicitly foresee the creation of such parliamentary committee, already from the early stages of incorporation debates, there was political consensus for it. The reason for this was—in the JCHR's own appraisal—that it 'was seen as an important part of the constitutional compromise that was struck between parliamentary sovereignty and human rights in the terms of the Act'.[208] Since the HRA does not allow the courts to strike down legislation, but merely to make a declaration of incompatibility where it is deemed necessary, it is for the government and Parliament to decide on how to remedy the situation if such a declaration is made.[209] One of the JCHR's task is indeed to monitor such declarations of incompatibility as well as Strasbourg judgments (which may result in remedial orders that in any event have to be reported on), with a view to 'pressing the Government to take action and, in appropriate cases, recommending what action should be taken'.[210] Other tasks of the Committee include pre-legislative scrutiny, aimed at examining the human rights implications of policies before they are set out in a legislative text and with a view to minimising compatibility problems of primary legislation.[211] This type of scrutiny is reminiscent of the IA method discussed above, but it is interesting that Parliament is given a say even before a proposed text is adopted, without it being considered disruptive for the drafting process. To the contrary, this is considered to be constructive for the drafting process. The JCHR also engages in post-legislative scrutiny, assessing whether implementation of legislation has produced 'unwelcome human rights implications',[212] and legislative scrutiny when bills pass through Parliament. This is the part of the Committee's

207 In case of doubts about the constitutionality of a bill, the Chancellor of Justice will commonly request from government to include in it the need for a reference to the CLC.

208 JCHR 19th Report, above n 151, 12–13.

209 ibid 13.

210 House of Lords, House of Commons, Joint Committee on Human Rights, The Committee's Future Working Practices, 23rd Report of Session 2005–06 (JCHR 23rd Report 2005–06) 21.

211 ibid 19.

212 Ibid 20.

work that is given special weight. Two key principles already established in the first working session of the JCHR are notably absent in parliamentary fundamental rights scrutiny in the EU: 'the principle of comprehensive scrutiny of all Government bills, and the principle of seeking detailed evidence from the Government, when necessary, on the human rights compatibility of bills before arriving at final views on them'.[213]

As regards the former point, it is interesting to note a mechanism introduced by the JCHR in one of its reports in order to manage its workload. The Committee considered the principle that *all* legislative proposals be scrutinised,[214] and revised it by introducing a sifting process.[215] This means that the JCHR's Legal Adviser is responsible for reviewing all bills, within a week of their introduction, in order to establish according to agreed criteria whether they pass an established threshold, that is, whether a given bill raises 'sufficiently significant human rights issues'. If it does not, it is 'cleared from scrutiny'. Since, as noted above, one common argument for the Commission's predominant assumption of *ex ante* scrutiny is precisely its availability of resources, it could be proposed that other bodies with fewer resources could adopt this type of mechanism in order to still be involved in the process.

The principle of seeking detailed evidence from government is linked to the section 19 statements discussed above in which Ministers declare the deemed human rights compatibility of legislation. An interesting parallel with the EU is that the early declarations of compatibility constituted 'stark assertions of compatibility, with little if any explanation of the reasons for concluding that rights were not engaged or, if rights were engaged, little explanation why the proposed action should, nevertheless, be construed as a proportionate response to a compelling social problem'.[216] The incentive for changing this unsatisfactory state of affairs came from the JCHR, which established the said principle and pressured ministers to provide further explanations, eventually forcing the government to change its departmental guidance and requiring that specific explanatory notes be prepared for the bills carrying such statements.[217] Also noteworthy is the fact that there was initial resistance against more detailed explanations making recourse to an argument that will sound familiar (consider the discussion of the Commission Legal Service's role above), namely, that legal advice to government is confidential. However, the JCHR was not intimidated by this argument, continuing to pressure for more information, even after the introduction of the explanatory notes.

This leads to the second point: the reason why the JCHR could afford assuming such an uncompromising stance. The underlying philosophy of the HRA is to engage *all three* branches of government, and the Committee was able to make a strong case that Parliament was 'the missing player … unless Parliamentarians have the energy and skill to raise the questions ad hoc'[218]—a situation that had to be remedied.

[213] JCHR 19th Report, n 151, 16.

[214] In order to be able to focus on other tasks like 'pro-active policy oriented work' to 'shape the human rights agenda'; JCHR 23rd Report, above n 210, 5.

[215] What follows is taken from ibid 13 et seq.

[216] J Hiebert, 'Parliament and the Human Rights Act: Can the JCHR Help Facilitate a Culture of Rights?' (2006) 4 *International Journal of Constitutional Law* 1, 24, with reference to relevant documentation.

[217] ibid 25–26.

[218] Lord Lester, JCHR Minutes of Evidence (14 March 2001), House of Lords 66-I, HC 332-I, question 28.

The UK example illustrates that insistence on interaction between all branches of government during the *ex ante* scrutiny process can lead to an improved system of protection. As already noted above, the European Commission has acknowledged that more of a 'transparent inter-institutional dialogue'[219] is needed. However, the Commission's concern here lies with draft amendments undertaken by the other institutions once the proposal leaves the Commission, since its compliance statements only apply to the text as adopted at that stage. Our concern is different here. It is about questioning the Commission's assumptions of compatibility in the first place (for example, for legislation in respect to which no substantive amendments have been made) and involving other institutions than the Court in order to do so. A predominant reliance on one actor (in our case, the Commission) as well as a general assumption of correctness of its assessment, as seems currently to be the case in the EU, is undesirable.

C. The Council

Unlike the Commission and the European Parliament, the Council of Ministers was the institution that did not have 'standing procedures and a structural framework to guarantee that all fundamental rights are respected in all draft proposals'[220] when the Charter became legally binding. This the Council had acknowledged in the documentation of an informal meeting of the Justice and Home Affairs Ministers in 2011, which came as a response both to the Commission's Communication on a strategy for the effective implementation of the Charter, as well as to the European Parliament's Resolution on the situation of fundamental rights in the EU (2009–10). At the same time, it identified three measures already in place that could be used in order to fulfil its fundamental rights scrutiny duty: first, as the European Parliament does, considering the possibility of requesting an opinion from its Legal Service when the question of compatibility with fundamental rights arises; second (and this is peculiar to the Council), relying on Member States' expertise. Since 'Member States are the first check point where compliance with obligations resulting from the Charter as well as the constitutional traditions and international obligations common to the Member States is usually scrutinized',[221] each Member State should check a proposal against compatibility with the Charter before submitting it to a Council working group.[222] Third, the Council also invites reflection on 'a more visible, structured or even new fundamental rights scrutiny procedure',[223] which should, however, not be 'a burdensome, time-consuming process'.[224] Attention is drawn to two options: first, involving (already established) different Council formations in assessing fundamental rights impacts and compliance—this is similar to the process of referral to a specialised committee under the new rule 36 of the

[219] 2010 Commission Communication, above n 7, 8 et seq.

[220] Council discussion document, 'The Role of the Council in Ensuring the Effective Implementation of the Charter of Fundamental Rights in the Legislative Process', informal meeting of the Justice and Home Affairs Ministers (20–21 January 2011).

[221] ibid 2–3.

[222] ibid 2.

[223] ibid 3.

[224] ibid.

European Parliament's Rules of Procedure; and, second, making use of the FRA in developing policies and legislation.

As a follow-up to this announced reflection, later that year the Council adopted Guidelines for checking the fundamental rights compatibility at the Council's preparatory bodies.[225] Framed as 'non-binding advice', the aim is awareness-raising in the preparatory bodies[226] or, one could say, the introduction of a fundamental rights culture. The guidelines stipulate that they should be used at the beginning of the first reading of any proposal.[227] Envisaging their use from the very beginning may be an expression of the fact that no general assumption of fundamental rights compliance of a given proposal is accepted, but even if this is not the reason for such early use, in any event, it leaves the possibility open for taking a fundamental rights perspective even on proposals that do not blatantly raise these issues or which would not be subject to amendments by the Council (other than on the ground of fundamental rights compliance). The need for further checks on any compromise proposal is also recognised, but what is even more interesting to note is that such a need is also expressed with regard to those that result from a trialogue with the European Parliament.[228] As already noted above, this is the stage in the legislative process where the strategic interest of the institutions would be to avoid adding a further element liable to compromise adoption of a proposal after difficult negotiations in the conciliation procedure have been concluded. At the same time, it is the stage where fundamental rights are more susceptible to being compromised or to not being given adequate attention, precisely in view of the informal nature of the negotiations and the pressing objective of reaching agreement. It is therefore a surprising but all the more welcome development that this is conceded by the Council in this document.

Another interesting point to note relates to the sources that should be used in order to examine compatibility with the Charter. Next to the obvious reference to the Charter and the case law of the Court, the guidelines draw attention to thematic reports, publications etc produced by institutions, bodies, offices and agencies of the EU and of the Council of Europe, as well as the FRA, whose expertise should be used. The Council has expressly communicated its willingness to involve the FRA in the compatibility-check process.[229]

Regarding the guidance for assessing whether a proposal limits a fundamental right and whether this limitation is in compliance with the Charter, this document does not provide for great novelties when viewed against the various Commission Communications. Rather, it is a summarised version of the Commission's Fundamental Rights 'checklist'. What is specific to the Council Guidelines is that in case of doubt, they advise consulting the Council Legal Service, making use of the national experts' expertise in the Member State and consulting the Working Party on Fundamental Rights, Citizenship and Free Movement of Persons (hereinafter the 'FREMP Working Party') or another preparatory body specialising in a specific fundamental right.

[225] Guidelines on Methodological Steps to be taken to check fundamental rights compatibility at the Council's preparatory bodies, 10140/11 (18 May 2011). On a discussion of these Guidelines, see Morijn, above n 106.

[226] ibid 2.

[227] ibid 4.

[228] ibid.

[229] See also Council Conclusions on the Council's actions and initiatives for the implementation of the Charter of Fundamental Rights of the European Union, 3092nd General Affairs Council meeting (23 May 2011), paras 36–37.

Overall, it can be said that the essence of the guidance for assessing the Charter compatibility of legislation provided herein does not impart anything new in substance, but having such a written document in place may well turn out to be of practical importance in the sense that it can be invoked and relied upon during negotiations.

In December 2014, the Council adopted a new set of revised guidelines.[230] These include practical changes relating to enhancing awareness and changes to the wording of the fundamental rights checklist.

As regards the former, two small yet useful insertions are worth noting: first, the Council Secretariat is to include the revised guidelines in the general training of incoming Presidencies;[231] and, second, the FREMP Working Party should be kept informed of all Council Legal Services legal assessments and advice on fundamental rights matters through the insertion of its acronym in the relevant documentation.[232]

As regards the wording of the checklist, three changes have to be pointed out, which have been inspired by the test that the Court has adopted in fundamental rights review in the *Schecke* and *Digital Rights* cases discussed above and cited in the revised Guidelines.[233] First, when checking the content of fundamental rights at issue in order to assess the compatibility of the proposal with the Charter (step 1), ECHR law has been expressly included in the checklist as a source for understanding the Charter rather than being merely listed in the Annex. Second, when assessing whether there is a limitation to fundamental rights and, if so, whether it is in compliance with the Charter, an additional element has been included, which requires asking whether the essence of the right(s) is respected. Finally, Article 52(1) CFR concerning legitimate limitations of fundamental rights is expressly spelled out in the checklist with reference to the applicable case law.

The 2014 Guidelines do not include any groundbreaking changes from the first Guidelines adopted in 2011, but the revised version includes some improvements and the fact that they constitute a recurring item on the Council's Agenda is to be welcomed, even if it is certain that it is the Court's recent case law that has drawn attention to this matter. The fact that the Council is reacting by aiming to improve its framework for *ex ante* fundamental rights assessments is a positive development.

A final novelty in the practices of the Council to be noted is the Hungarian presidency's introduction of a new 'tradition',[234] namely, 'adopting an evaluation of the application of the Charter of Fundamental Rights at Council level', which will become 'a compulsory component of the EU's annual work'.[235] In view of its retrospective character, this practice does not contribute much to ensuring that concrete policies and legislation are fundamental rights-compliant. However, it can still provide for added value in terms of institutional learning, as it forces the Council to think about its actions in fundamental rights terms and as it also places a certain burden on it to actually take action in furtherance of the Charter rights in view of the upcoming evaluation.

[230] 2014 Council Guidelines, above n 182.

[231] ibid 2.

[232] ibid 11.

[233] ibid 4.

[234] Hungarian Presidency website, General Affairs Council, 'Protection of Fundamental Rights at Council's Agenda', www.eu2011.hu/news/protection-fundamental-rights-council's-agenda.

[235] See Council Conclusions, above n 229.

D. The FRA

With the advent of the FRA in 2007,[236] another layer of fundamental rights protection has been added at the EU level. In addition to the so far prevalent judicial and (less visible) legislative protection of fundamental rights, administrative rights protection has been added to the system.[237] The FRA was not erected out of a ground zero, but is the product of a transformation of the earlier European Monitoring Centre on Racism and Xenophobia (EMCRX).[238] In the same vain, another 'quasi-predecessor' also has to be mentioned, namely, the EU Network of Independent Experts in Fundamental Rights.[239] The designation 'quasi-' is employed because there is some overlap between the previous functions of the Network[240] and the EMCRX on the one hand and the current functions of the FRA on the other. Thus, even though some administrative-like elements of rights protection pre-existed, this the first time that an EU administrative body has been established that covers *all areas* of fundamental rights protection (as listed in the Charter) under EU law. Yet, two caveats have to be made here. The first is that the areas of activity of the FRA are set out in its Multiannual Framework (MAF).[241] Notably, the current MAF[242] does not provide for fundamental social rights, so that work in this field can only be pursued if it is possible to link it to any of the other 'areas of activity' (eg non-discrimination).[243] Second, the current Regulation, being adopted pre-Lisbon, defines the scope of the Agency's work as falling 'within the competences of the Community' as laid down in the EC Treaty. This means that currently the FRA cannot conduct work on its own initiative that falls within former third pillar matters (police and judicial cooperation).

The purpose of this section is not to provide a detailed account of the history, set-up and areas of activities of the FRA, which has already been done elsewhere.[244] Rather, its focus is

[236] FRA Founding Regulation, above n 6.

[237] On the notion of 'administrative rights protection' and advocating that EU administrative law scholarship should embrace this concept, see von Bogdandy and von Bernstoff, above n 157.

[238] Council Regulation (EC) No 1035/97 of 2 June 1997 establishing a European Monitoring Centre on Racism and Xenophobia [1997] OJ L151/1.

[239] Established by the Commission (formerly the Directorate General Justice and Home Affairs) in 2002 in response to the European Parliament Resolution of 5 July 2001 (Rapporteur: Thiery Cornillet) on the situation of fundamental rights in the European Union (2000/2231 (INI)), and was dissolved in 2006.

[240] M Scheinin, 'The Relationship between the Agency and the Network of Independent Experts' in Alston and de Schutter, above n 85, 85.

[241] FRA Founding Regulation, above n 6, Art 5.

[242] Council Decision No 252/2013/EU of 11 March 2013 establishing a Multiannual Framework for 2013–2017 for the European Agency for Fundamental Rights [2013] OJ L63/14 (hereinafter the 'MAF Decision 2013').

[243] The current 'areas of activity' of the FRA are: 1) access to justice; 2) victims of crime, including compensation to victims; 3) information society and, in particular, respect for private life and protection of personal data; 4) Roma integration; 5) judicial cooperation, except in criminal matters; 6) rights of the child; 7) discrimination based on sex, race, colour, ethnic or social origin, genetic features, language, religion or belief, political or any other opinion, membership of a national minority, property, birth, disability, age or sexual orientation; 8) immigration and integration of migrants, visa and border control and asylum; 9) racism, xenophobia and related intolerance. See MAF Decision 2013, above n 242, Art 2.

[244] Alston and de Schutter, above n 85; and GN Toggenburg, 'The EU Fundamental Rights Agency: Satellite or Guiding Star?' (2007) *SWP Comments* 5. See also references in GN Toggenburg, 'Fundamental Rights and the European Union: How Does and How Should the EU Agency for Fundamental Rights Relate to the EU Charter of Fundamental Rights?' EUI Working Paper LAW 2013/13, http://cadmus.eui.eu/bitstream/handle/1814/28658/LAW_2013_13_Toggenburg.pdf?sequence=1, 4

on the question what impact does, could or should the FRA have on the position of fundamental rights in EU legislation. In order to tackle this issue, it is necessary to consider first the role and the powers of this body.

The objective of the FRA is stipulated in the Founding Regulation. It shall:

> [P]rovide the relevant institutions, bodies, offices and agencies of the Community and its Member States when implementing Community law with assistance and expertise relating to fundamental rights in order to support them when they take measures or formulate courses of action within their respective spheres of competence to fully respect fundamental rights.[245]

Assistance, expertise and support are the key words here. They are directed to the EU institutions and bodies on the one hand, and the Member States when implementing EC law (now EU law) on the other. This is also reflected in the FRA's tasks. These include data collection and dissemination and development of standards to improve the comparability, objectivity and reliability of data at the EU level; the publishing of conclusions, opinions and reports on specific thematic topics, and in relation to proposals in the course of legislative procedures but only (!) when such is requested by one of the EU institutions; the publication of an annual report on the fundamental rights situation in the EU; and the development of a communication strategy to increase fundamental rights awareness in civil society.[246]

These tasks read together with the objectives reveal that the nature of the FRA is hybrid. One leg of its work is collecting and producing reliable high-quality data on fundamental rights issues across the EU. The other leg is to engage civil society through, inter alia, the Fundamental Rights Platform. The third leg is the least developed so far—it is the task of providing assistance and expertise in order to actually support the EU institutions in their actions or the Member States when implementing EU law. This state of affairs is to a considerable extent due to the FRA's own motion for development. Since it came to life in 2007, building up its research and data collection abilities has been the component that has been mostly focused upon in-house. This has also been the Commission's vision of the FRA: a function that is limited to data collection. However, the awareness that a purely research function of the FRA does not provide for added value at the EU level, and cannot justify its existence as a separate EU body has reached the Agency, certainly at the directorate level. The FRA is in the process of aligning its self-understanding according to its broader mandate, thus developing its advisory function in a more systematic manner, subject to constraints of mandate and resources.

What does *not* fall within the competence of the FRA is, first, individual rights protection[247] and, second, an *ex officio* (ie, not depending on a request by the institutions) legislative scrutiny role. In other words, the FRA was denied the two main tools capable of providing it with real teeth as an instrument that fosters an EU fundamental rights policy.

The absence of the latter is relevant for our purposes, as it could arguably have had a real impact on fundamental rights protection in EU legislation. A glimpse into the legislative history of the FRA reveals the controversy around this point and the fact that the

[245] FRA Founding Regulation, above n 6, Art 1.

[246] ibid Art 4.

[247] This contrasts with some other national human rights institutions which do have such competence, as noted by Toggenburg, 'The EU Fundamental Rights Agency', above n 244, 5.

Commission's opposition was mainly responsible for the current result.[248] The possibility of expressing a stance on the legality of Commission proposals was completely ruled out in the Commission's initial proposal.[249] It was later successfully amended by the European Parliament[250] so as to provide in the final Regulation establishing the FRA that it can formulate and publish opinions and reports on Commission proposals, but only if this is requested by one of the institutions[251]—clearly a compromise solution. So far, this has happened seven times.[252] Interestingly, the first request came from the French Council Presidency of the time. It did not come from the European Parliament (as all other Opinions did), which is the most reactive institution regarding fundamental rights concerns and certainly the only one supporting the idea for establishment of this body from the outset,[253] ie, when it was first raised by a *Comité des Sages* in 1998.[254]

Dissatisfaction with this development has been expressed in the literature and in a UK House of Lords Report compiled in 2005.[255] In particular, it has been argued that the denial of such an *ex officio* legislative scrutiny competence was regretful since it 'would not have represented the competence to establish non-compliance within the framework of infringement proceedings, but merely the possibility of examining relevant proposals and opinions at all stages of the legislative process from the perspective of a human rights expert'.[256] In reality however, and as will emerge in the discussion below, this possibility of *ex officio* legislative scrutiny was and remains very delicate.

[248] See on this point GN Toggenburg, 'The Role of the New EU Fundamental Rights Agency: Debating the "Sex of Angels" or Improving Europe's Human Rights Performance?' (2008) 3 *European Law Review* 384.

[249] Commission, Proposal for a Council Regulation establishing a European Union Agency for Fundamental Rights, Proposal for a Council Decision empowering the European Union Agency for Fundamental Rights to pursue its activities in areas referred to in Title VI of the Treaty on European Union (30 June 2005) COM(2005) 280 final.

[250] European Economic and Social Committee, Opinion on the Proposal for a Council Regulation establishing a European Union Agency for Fundamental Rights—Proposal for a Council Decision Empowering the European Union Agency for Fundamental Rights to pursue its activities in areas referred to in Title VI of the Treaty of the European Union, SOC/216 COM (2005) 280 final (14 February 2006); and LIBE Committee Report (1st reading/single reading), A6-0306/2006 (26 September 2006).

[251] FRA Founding Regulation, above n 6, Art 4(2).

[252] FRA Opinion on proposal for a Council Framework Decision on the use of Passenger Name Records (PNR) (28 October 2008) and follow-up FRA Opinion on the Proposal for a Directive on the use of Passenger Name Record (PNR) data for the prevention, detection and prosecution of terrorist offences and serious crime (14 June 2011); FRA Opinion on the draft Directive regarding the European Investigation Order (EIO) (23 February 2011); FRA Opinion on the proposed EU Regulation on property consequences of registered partnerships (11 June 2012); FRA Opinion on the proposed EU data protection reform package (9 October 2012); FRA Opinion on the confiscation of proceeds of crime (4 December 2012); and FRA Opinion on a proposal to establish a European Public Prosecutor's Office, (6 February 2014), www.fra.europa.eu/fraWebsite/research/opinions/op-pnr_en.htm.

[253] M Nowak, 'The Agency and National Institutions for the Promotion and Protection of Human Rights' in Alston and de Schutter, above n 85, 97, citing European Parliament Working Document of 25 March 2004 on the proposal for a Council Regulation on the European Monitoring Centre on Racism and Xenophobia (recast version), EU Doc PE 339.635, Rapporteur: Swiebel, 5.

[254] *Leading by Example: A Human Rights Agenda for the European Union for the Year 2000*, above n 4.

[255] House of Lords 16th Report (n 23) 32–33. In particular, the NGO Justice and the Law Society saw a legislative scrutiny role for the FRA. Interestingly, the expert witness for the Commission, Dr Clemens Ladenburger, expressed the view that 'the possibility of the Agency scrutinising proposals and draft legislation was something to be considered'.

[256] Toggenburg, 'The EU Fundamental Rights Agency', above n 244, 5.

At this point, it is appropriate to examine the impact of this development on fundamental rights protection in the legislative process. This examination will be undertaken by inquiring into the reasons/arguments for denying the FRA such a scrutiny role. Once exposed, they will be juxtaposed to the (relative) merits of granting the FRA such a mandate.

The formal explanation would be that the Commission is the guardian of the Treaties and therefore is also responsible for ensuring that fundamental rights are respected in the legislative process. On that ground, the proclaimed message is that since the Commission takes this role very seriously, it cannot outsource this task to another body, like the FRA. There is some merit to this argument, but only to the extent that it imposes on the Commission a fundamental rights scrutiny role. It does not follow from it that an *additional* instance of legislative scrutiny has to be ruled out, because it would not imply 'outsourcing', but added protection. Put differently, it is not obvious why the Commission's designated role as the guardian of the Treaties, or the guardian of fundamental rights, should exclude an institutional arrangement providing for a check on whether it performs that function well when conducting legislative scrutiny.

In addition to this 'no outsourcing justification', however, there are a series of more pragmatic explanations that seem to have played a decisive role. These are linked to the Commission's role and power in the legislative process as well as to the realities of its drafting business.

One justification that has been put forward for the Commission's denial to grant the FRA a more important role in that respect is the fear that it 'could be politically instrumentalised during the legislative process'.[257] This is certainly a legitimate concern and it is linked to the reason that probably carried the biggest weight for limiting the FRA's mandate, namely, the fact that the Commission may not want to compromise its room for manoeuvre within its monopoly of legislative initiative[258] and, coupled to that, its role as a legislative broker. In other words, the fear that may be involved here concerns the possible constraint of what is 'perhaps the Commission's most essential power',[259] because involvement of the FRA would mean that an initiative could be questioned even before it leaves the Commission.

However, there may be a need for doing so. Consider the following: even if the Legal Service (or some members of it) is of the opinion that a given proposal is problematic from a fundamental rights point of view, its adoption might nonetheless go ahead if there is enough political pressure (emanating from within the Commission or from other institutions) to do so. One could think of some examples where this might have been the case in the past, like the Returns Directive[260] or the Data Retention Directive.[261] It is precisely for

[257] ibid 6.

[258] Arguably one of the key components of the EU's institutional balance. See P Craig, 'Democracy and Rule-Making within the EC: An Empirical and Normative Assessment' (1997) 3 *European Law Journal* 105.

[259] Minutes of a lunchtime conference debate on governance with Professor Majone (14 May 2002), http://ec.europa.eu/governance/docs/dej140502_en.pdf.

[260] Directive 2008/115/EC of the European Parliament and of the Council of 16 December 2008 on common standards and procedures in Member States for returning illegally staying third-country nationals [2008] OJ L348/98.

[261] Directive 2006/24/EC on the retention of data generated or processed in connection with the provision of publicly available electronic communications services or of public communications networks and amending Directive 2002/58/EC [2006] OJ L105/45.

this reason that a body, which is not involved in the legislative brokering, would substantially improve the system of protection.[262]

Relatedly, one could counter-argue that such arrangement would be in breach of the *Meroni* doctrine.[263] *Meroni* established that it is not permissible to delegate wide discretionary powers because it 'brings about an actual transfer of responsibility' as it 'replaces the choices of the delegator by the choices of the delegate'.[264] In our cases, granting the FRA an *ex officio* legislative scrutiny mandate could be seen as the delegation of a power by the legislator to the FRA, which could interfere with the Commission's agenda-setting power and power of initiative. The argument would go as follows: due to the breath of the Charter, any Commission proposal could be seen as implicating a fundamental right. This would in turn allow the FRA to have a say on each and every Commission proposal. As a consequence, the FRA could turn into a policy-shaping organ.

However, it is submitted that this argument cannot stand when the *ex officio* legislative scrutiny role for the FRA is one that does not produce any legal effects, ie, one that cannot halt a proposal and thereby alter its course in the law-making process. It is true that the de facto effect of such an *ex officio* scrutiny mandate could be one of agenda shaping, and that effect would already be triggered by the fact that FRA Opinions are public, unlike a Legal Service advice. However, that is not sufficient to invoke the *Meroni* doctrine because there would in fact be no delegation of powers in the sense of this doctrine; the choices of the Commission (to adopt a given proposal or not) would not be replaced by those of the FRA (which may come to the conclusion that a given proposal is violating fundamental rights).

As a side note, it may be worth pointing out in this context that the Court has moved towards allowing Agencies to have wide powers in the post-Lisbon context. This is evident in the recent *ESMA* judgment.[265] In this case, ESMA's powers to intervene, under certain conditions, in the financial markets of the Member States through legally binding acts was challenged. The Court found these powers unproblematic because they were 'precisely delineated [through substantive and procedural guarantees] and amenable to judicial review in light of the objectives established by the delegating authority'.[266]

Of course, none of this would be at issue in our context. The point is a more general one, namely, that the Court has moved away from a strict interpretation of *Meroni*. It is therefore even more difficult to imagine a scenario where this doctrine could be stretched to cover our proposed situation of granting the FRA an *ex officio* legislative scrutiny mandate.

One separate question that arises in this context is whether *ex ante* scrutiny of legislation should be duplicated. An argument could be advanced that since the EDPS is conducting such scrutiny in relation to data protection, there is no need for the FRA to do the same in

[262] See Lord Lester, House of Lords 16th Report, above n 23, Minutes of Evidence, Examination of Dr Clemens Ladenburger, Legal Service, European Commission 11, question 18, p 14, making the point that the transparent (open to the public) dialogue of an independent body similar to the FRA (ie, the Human Rights Committee) with the administration has greatly improved the system in the UK.

[263] Case C-9/56 *Meroni & Co, Industrie Metallurgische SpA v High Authority* [1958] ECR 133, 152. For an overview discussion of this doctrine, see S Griller and A Orator, 'Everything under Control? The "Way Forward" for European Agencies in the Footsteps of the *Meroni* Doctrine' (2010) 35 *European Law Review* 3.

[264] *Meroni*, above n 263, 152.

[265] Case C-270/12 *United Kingdom of Great Britain and Northern Ireland v European Parliament and Council of the European Union* (*ESMA*) EU:C:2014:18.

[266] ibid [53].

this area. This could be discarded on the ground that the opinions of the two bodies may differ, especially in areas where data protection may be conflicting with other fundamental rights. The two specialist opinions could thereby inform each other.

However, the general point with respect to *all fundamental rights* remains: the 'weaker' the scrutiny inside the administration, the stronger the case for the involvement of the FRA becomes, and since, despite promising undertakings in a line of communications, the Commission's internal system of fundamental rights-proofing is yet to prove itself (see discussion above), the case remains strong.

The *second* reason for denying *ex officio* legislative scrutiny mandate for the FRA relates to the quality of fundamental rights-proofing if it was to be entrusted to the FRA and not exclusively to the drafters and legal service, as is currently the case. It is, however, not evident why this should be the case. When having, for example, regard to the FRA Opinion produced by the Agency on the Proposal for a Council Framework Decision on the Use of Passenger Name Record data for law-enforcement purposes,[267] one rather gets the opposite impression. It is a well-informed and subtle analysis of the kind that one would wish for the Commission's Explanatory Memoranda.

Third, the question of institutional appropriateness could be raised. The argument is here that if the FRA were to be involved in the drafting process, then other Agencies would also have to be included, albeit for different reasons. Again, it is not obvious why this should be the case. What is at stake here is making a choice about which institutional players should be entrusted with the constitutional task of fundamental rights-proofing of legislation in order to ensure the fundamental rights compliance of EU (legislative) action. This aim has to be pursued not only because of a political commitment that has been undertaken at the EU level, but also because it has been enshrined as an obligation in primary EU law. This is why the FRA differs from the other Agencies—its mandate relates to a subject matter in relation to which such commitments of constitutional relevance and importance have been undertaken.

The *fourth* reason relates to the necessity of speedy action and reaction during the drafting stage where details as well as insights into the entire drafting history matter. This, it could be argued, requires by implication that the fundamental rights check of the proposal is undertaken internally. But here again, this is an argument for the Commission to have an internal scrutiny mechanism; it is not an argument against putting in place an additional outside mechanism.

The *final* reason relates to the question of resources (as currently allocated to the FRA), which speaks against its systematic involvement. The legislative activity of the institutions is considerable,[268] so in order for the FRA to be systematically involved in checking all legislative proposals—and doing so without causing significant delay—it would have to be an institution of great size with a significant amount of resources, which would imply a budget much larger than that currently in place.[269] This is a point that has been recognised by the

[267] PNR Opinion, above n 252.

[268] For statistics for the period 1980–2009, see UK House of Commons Library, 'How Much Legislation Comes from Europe?', Research Paper 10/6213 (October 2010), www.parliament.uk/briefing-papers/RP10-62.pdf. For the year 2009, the total number of adopted Council Directives, Regulations and Decisions was 697.

[269] Under the current structure, the FRA budget for 2012 was €20 million.

UK government, which expressed caution regarding a legislative scrutiny role for the FRA precisely because of this point.[270] Here it has to be acknowledged that if resources are limited (and cannot be enlarged), the tasks that the FRA can undertake are restricted as well. However, it does not follow from this that the FRA's mandate should be limited as a matter of principle. Had the FRA been given a legislative scrutiny power that is not dependent on a request, it could have used it, within its logistical capabilities, for proposals that it considered problematic from a fundamental rights point of view and which came to its attention, or by making use of a sifting process as discussed above with respect to the JCHR. Such approach could also be used in an initial 'test phase', on the basis of which an assessment could be made as to whether the FRA's actual and potential output is of such value that it would warrant an expansion of resources.

The preceding analysis has thus revealed that the presented reasons for limiting the FRA's mandate regarding legislative fundamental rights scrutiny do not stand on firm ground as arguments justifying such a move. The basic conclusion resulting from the above is: the FRA would have resulted in enhanced protection by virtue of the fact that it constitutes 1) an additional fundamental rights check 2) originating outside the administration, which 3) is capable of delivering assessments of a high quality. It is accepted that this can only be so if the FRA is sufficiently resourced. However, the current absence of such resources does not justify a limitation of the FRA's mandate as a matter of principle.

The above analysis could be accused of being irrelevant, since it concerns a matter that has been settled in the way described in the Founding Regulation. It is still important, however, to reflect upon the desirability of this development. In the words of Lord Lester, 'if one is going to go to the expense and trouble of setting up such a body … [it] should meet the need for a timely, quick, expert input … [in the legislative scrutiny process] of a transparent kind so that the public knows what is going on'.[271] Since this need has not been met, one may indeed wonder about whether the expense and trouble was worth going into. Moreover, reflecting upon these considerations is not as mundane a task as it might appear at first sight. As noted above, the Founding Regulation is very likely to be opened up for re-negotiation in the future. When this occurs, it will be a good opportunity to revisit some of the compromises made in that instrument, which do not appear to be sensible.

A reflection on the current value of the FRA requires identifying the FRA's usefulness absent an *ex officio* legislative scrutiny mandate. From the point of view of the Commission, the FRA's task of providing data is of considerable importance in relation to: 1) IAs; 2) assessments whether EU law is applied in compliance with EU fundamental rights at the Member State level in order to decide whether infringement proceedings should be brought; and 3) the compilation of the Commission's Annual Report. Since the Commission has no other means of determining the situation 'on the ground', the FRA is an invaluable source of information.

This last point seems to be fair. However, it fades when bearing in mind the fact that the Network of Independent Experts did already perform this information-source role.[272]

[270] House of Lords 16th Report, above n 23, 33.

[271] Lord Lester of Herne Hill, House of Lords 16th Report, above n 23, examination of Expert Witness Dr Clemens Ladenburger for the European Commission, at 14.

[272] The Network's tasks were identified as follows: '[1] To draft an annual report of the state of fundamental rights in the European Union and its Member States, assessing the application of each of the rights set out in the

As a matter of fact—and this relates to assistance of data for bringing infringement proceedings—the Network was capable of adopting country-specific reports. It has been debated whether the FRA can do so, since it will prepare reports 'on specific thematic topics'.[273] Moreover, the Network's role went beyond data administration, as its main task was 'one of *normative assessment* of that data on the basis of the Charter' (emphasis added).[274] In this respect, the approach adopted for the FRA constitutes one step back.

The FRA was subject to an external independent evaluation of its performance in the first five years of its existence. Based on the results of this evaluation, the FRA's Management Board issued 13 recommendations to the Commission,[275] which, however, do involve amendment of the FRA Founding Regulation. These can be broadly divided into two categories: first, recommendations that concern managerial aspects and relate to the practical functioning of the FRA (eg, the term of office and the voting arrangement of its Management Board, ensuring continuity of the work of national liaison officers etc); and, second, recommendations that relate to the substantive expansion or amendment of the FRA's tasks and scope of activity.

The latter included two suggestions already discussed above, namely, amending the FRA Founding Regulation in order to bring former third pillar matters (police and judicial cooperation) within its mandate. Arguably, this is a very sensible recommendation to make. Following the entry into force of the Lisbon Treaty, which abolished the pillar structure, there is no good reason to exclude this area of EU activity. The second is to this author's mind the most crucial amendment, which has to materialise in order to increase the added value of the FRA and for which the case has been built above,[276] that is, allowing the FRA to deliver *ex officio* opinions on the compatibility of EU legislation.

Other recommendations relate to:

— the FRA's potential role in the external fundamental rights policy and in UN Convention on the Rights of Persons with Disability monitoring;
— the possibility of allowing (a group of) Member States to request assistance from the FRA (within the scope of its mandate);
— granting the FRA a possible role in the Article 7 TEU framework; and
— tasking the FRA with data collection and analysis regarding respect for Article 2 TEU values.

The last two recommendations are to be seen against the background of the EU's 'rule of law crisis' and featured more prominently in the public eye. Granting the FRA a role in the

EU Charter of Fundamental Rights. [2] To provide the Commission with specific information and opinions on fundamental rights issues, when requested. [3] To assist the Commission and the Parliament in developing European Union policy on fundamental rights.' Scheinin, above n 240, at 85.

273 Article 4(1)(d); Scheinin, above n 240, 85; O de Schutter, 'The Two Europes of Human Rights: The Emerging Division of Tasks between the Council of Europe and the European Union in Promoting Human Rights in Europe' (2008) 14 *Columbia Journal of European Law* 509, 524; von Bogdandy and von Bernstoff, above n 157, 1054, arguing that the formulation is 'too vague … in foreclosing this important area of activity'.

274 Scheinin, above n 240, 85.

275 The recommendations to the Commission were issued in accordance with Art 31(1) of the FRA Founding Regulation on 4 June 2013, https://fra.europa.eu/sites/default/files/fra-management-board-recommendations-external-evaluation_0.pdf.

276 It is also supported in other academic writings. See Toggenburg, 'Fundamental Rights and the European Union', above n 244.

Article 7 TEU framework was advocated by Commissioner Reding[277] a few months after the Council called on the Commission[278] 'to take forward the debate in line with the Treaties on the possible need for and shape of a collaborative and systematic method to tackle'[279] the issue relating to the rule of law, and after the European Parliament called for 'Member States [to] be regularly assessed on their continued compliance with the fundamental values of the Union and the requirement of democracy and the rule of law'.[280] Reding was, however, vague on the possibility of involving the FRA in Member State monitoring, her comments being limited to regretting that 'the FRA is barred from analysing national situations'.[281]

One should note here that the FRA can and has looked at country-specific situations in the past, even if not very frequently. For example, the report on irregular crossing of the Greek land border (reporting on what has become known as the 'Evros crisis') was a country-specific report on a particular fundamental rights problem, even if this was entitled 'thematic situation report'.[282] However, what it cannot do is to investigate national situations in light of EU fundamental rights or international human rights obligations in areas that fall outside the scope of EU law. However, such data collection and analysis would be necessary for assessing respect for Article 2 TEU values and would thus be useful for Article 7 TEU proceedings.

As already noted above, the EU Network of Independent Experts on Fundamental Rights already conducted such assessments[283] and it would be possible, in theory, to expand the FRA's mandate so as to bring this matter within its tasks. However, as pointed out by the Council, this should not result in a duplication of resources,[284] given that there are monitoring mechanisms available both at the international (UN) level and at the regional (Council of Europe) level for monitoring the compliance of Member States with international/regional human rights obligations. Thus, what may in fact be necessary in the first place is to seek methods for networking, coordination and cooperation of existing institutions and structures,[285] and consequently also sharing of data (something that is already happening

[277] V Reding, 'The EU and the Rule of Law—What Next?' speech held at the Centre for European Policy Studies (4 September 2013), Press Release, http://europa.eu/rapid/press-release_SPEECH-13-677_en.htm.

[278] Prior to that, four Member States (Denmark, Finland, Germany and the Netherlands) also addressed the Commission on the issue of the rule of law.

[279] Council Conclusions on fundamental rights and the rule of law and on the Commission 2012 Report on the Application of the Charter of Fundamental Rights of the European Union, Justice and Home Affairs Council meeting, Luxembourg (6 and 7 June 2013), www.consilium.europa.eu/uedocs/cms_Data/docs/pressdata/en/jha/137404.pdf (hereinafter the 'JHA Council Conclusions 2013').

[280] European Parliament resolutions setting out various recommendations to the EU institutions on how to strengthen the protection of Art 2 TEU (the Rui Tavares Report of 2013; the Louis Michel and the Kinga Göncz Reports of 2014, www.europarl.europa.eu/committees/en/libe/reports.html), as cited in Commission Communication, 'A New EU Framework to Strengthen the Rule of Law' (19 March 2014), COM(2014) 158 final/2 (hereinafter the '2014 Commission Communication on the Rule of Law'), 3.

[281] Reding, above n 277.

[282] See FRA Report, 'Coping with a Fundamental Rights Emergency—The Situation of Persons Crossing the Greek Land Border in an Irregular Manner' (2011), http://fra.europa.eu/sites/default/files/fra_uploads/1500-Greek-border-situation-report2011_EN.pdf. The explanation or justification given was the following (ibid 10): 'while the current report focuses on Greece, it addresses an issue of EU relevance and importance'.

[283] On this point, see I Butler, 'How to Monitor the Rule of law, Democracy and Fundamental Rights in the EU', Policy Brief Open Society European Policy Institute (August 2013), http://ec.europa.eu/justice/events/assises-justice-2013/files/contributions/43.1how_monitor_rule_law_democracy_and_fundamental_rights_eu_en.pdf.

[284] JHA Council Conclusions 2013, above n 279.

[285] ibid. See also G Toggenburg, 'Was soll die EU können dürfen, um die EU- Verfassungswerte und Rechtsstaatlichkeit der Mitgliedstaaten zu schützen? Ausblick auf eine neue Europäische Rechtsstaatshygiene' OEGfE Policy Brief (9 September 2013), www.oegfe.at/cms/uploads/media/OEGfE_Policy_Brief-2013.10.pdf.

to a certain extent for the work that is carried out within the FRA's mandate). At the same time, there should be one body, which should be responsible for compiling the results of such exercises for the purposes of an Article 7 TEU assessment. The FRA would be a logical choice in this respect.

The Commission eventually responded to the Council by proposing a 'new EU Framework to strengthen the Rule of Law'.[286] However, this does not offer any new institutional arrangements and, relevant for the present purposes, it does not provide for a monitoring arrangement. The Council adopted its conclusions on the rule of law in December 2014.[287] It foresaw the establishment of a dialogue among the Member States within the Council to promote and safeguard the rule of law. This dialogue is to be conducted once a year in the General Affairs Council and prepared by the Presidency. Thematic debates will also be launched where necessary. What is relevant for our purposes is that this practice will be developed 'in a way which is complementary with other EU institutions and International Organisations, avoiding duplication and taking into account existing instruments and expertise in this area'.[288] However, the FRA is not mentioned in these Guidelines. In any case, how this practice will develop in concrete terms remains to be seen. An evaluation of the proposed dialogue practice is to be made by the end of 2016.

Whatever the follow-up will be with respect to the FRA Management Board's recommendations, one important point remains: before the EU can legitimately criticise fundamental rights situations prevalent at the national level (be those within or outside EU competence), it first has to make sure that it keeps its 'own house' in order. That is why an own motion legislative scrutiny mandate is the most crucial and imminent amendment to make.

It is interesting to ask at this point the question of how the FRA's mandate compares to its national equivalents, ie, to national human rights institutions (NHRIs). Even though NHRIs cannot be considered as exactly comparable to the FRA, as they operate in a different setting of political structure and powers,[289] the comparison seems useful. Both the EU and at the national level (if endorsing the view that *ex ante* legislative scrutiny should take place) have to make a decision as to which method to adopt and as to which institution to allocate this task to.

In 2004, the EU Network of Independent Experts on Fundamental Rights published an Opinion regarding the role of national institutions for the protection of human rights in the Member States of the EU.[290] The main finding, which is relevant for our purposes, is that in those countries of the EU where NHRIs do exist,[291] the majority does not attribute

[286] 2014 Commission Communication on the Rule of Law, above n 280.

[287] Conclusions of the Council of the European Union and the member states meeting within the Council on ensuring respect for the rule of law, General Affairs Council meeting (16 December 2014), www.consilium.europa.eu/uedocs/cms_data/docs/pressdata/EN/genaff/146323.pdf.

[288] ibid 1, point 5.

[289] G de Búrca, 'New Modes of Governance and the Protection of Human Rights' in Alston and de Schutter, above n 85, 32, pointing out that NHRI 'were originally conceived at the UN level as a kind of mediator between the international and national levels to educate, inform and advice local and national bodies and actors about international human rights obligations in an effort to further their implementation'.

[290] EU Network of Independent Experts on Fundamental Rights, Opinion no 1-2004, http://cridho.uclouvain.be/en/eu_experts_network/report_details.php?year=2004; see also the later FRA Report, 'National Human Rights Institutions in the EU Member States—strengthening the fundamental rights architecture in the EU' (hereinafter the 'FRA NHRI Report 2010').

[291] A total of 14 states in 2004: the Czech Republic, Cyprus, Denmark, France, Germany, Greece, Ireland, Latvia, Luxembourg, Poland, Portugal, Sweden, Spain and the UK. In 2007, after Bulgarian and Romanian accession, that number increased to 16. See www.nhri.net/NationalData.asp?ID=80.

to it any formal role for human rights-proofing of legislation.[292] A 'remarkable exception'[293] is that of Greece.[294] Furthermore, the overall assessment is that:

> In order to ensure that the legislation or regulation [Member States] adopt will comply with the requirements of human rights, States rely preferably either on expertise within ministerial departments, or on the evaluation made in the course of the parliamentary procedure, quite frequently by specialist units or parliamentary committees. A number of States, moreover, ensure a systematic or quasi-systematic human rights proofing of draft legislation by an independent instance (such as Belgium or in the Netherlands, the Council of State, whose consultation in many cases is obligatory).[295]

The position taken at the EU level thus reflects the prevalent stance at the national level. Most Member States do not see a need for granting NHRIs legislative scrutiny powers. The question arises as to why this is so. De Schutter's proposed explanation is that in these Member States, human/fundamental rights-proofing of legislation is perceived as a technical issue that requires a legalistic approach,[296] as opposed to the input of an 'instance representative of a wide range of societal interests, and, especially, of different segments of the civil society'[297] that provides for 'grass-roots knowledge'.[298]

This may well be an accurate account of the national level, but the described perception is not prevalent regarding fundamental rights protection at the EU level. Even if the most important and decisive actor in the process at the moment—the Commission Legal Service—conducts a technical/legalistic analysis, the EU cannot be said to have embraced an exclusively legalistic approach to fundamental rights scrutiny of legislation.

The reasons for this are as follows. First, unlike it is the case in the national legal orders,[299] at EU level fundamental rights are increasingly gaining an important role in IAs, which is for the most part not a legal exercise and is not conducted by lawyers. Second, civil society is engaged as part of the Commission's 'upstream preparatory consultation' where relevant stakeholders can participate. As announced in the 2010 Commission Communication, 'when the Commission opens consultations (green papers, communications, working papers, etc.) with interested parties on issues which may lead to new sensitive proposals, it will highlight any potential fundamental rights aspects in order to encourage contributions

[292] O de Schutter, himself a member of the EU Network of Independent Experts at the time, drew on this Opinion and highlighted that finding in his Report. See O de Schutter, 4th Round Table of European National Institutions for the Promotion and Protection of Human Rights and the Council of Europe Commissioner for Human Rights, 'When can National Human Rights Institutions successfully intervene in the process of adopting legislation?', CommDH/NHRI(2006)2, 4 et seq (hereinafter the 'De Schutter Report').

[293] ibid 6. See also FRA NHRI Report 2010, above n 290.

[294] According to Law 2667/1998, the GNCHR (National Commission for Human Rights) shall: 'submit recommendations and proposals, carry out studies, submit reports and give an opinion on the taking of legislative, administrative and other measures which contribute to the improvement of the protection of human rights' (Art 1(6)(b)), as well as 'examine the adaptation of Greek legislation to the provisions of international law on the protection of human rights and deliver an opinion in this connection to the competent organs of the State' (Art 1(6)(j)). On the basis of this provision, the GNCHR has issued and continues to issue opinions on fundamental rights compliance of legislative drafts. It normally chooses itself which drafts to scrutinise. It does not have the power to block drafts, nor are the ministries obliged to await its opinion before they submit their proposals to Parliament.

[295] De Schutter Report, above n 292, 11.

[296] ibid.

[297] ibid.

[298] ibid.

[299] ibid.

that will feed into the impact assessment'.[300] Information from civil society is also to be taken into account in the Commission's Annual Fundamental Rights Report.[301] Third, the recent amendments in the European Parliament's rules of procedure, discussed above, illustrate that legislative scrutiny at that institution has to be triggered by a (political) committee entrusted with fundamental/human rights issues, not a technical legal committee responsible for legislative scrutiny. Finally, the FRA does have *some* scope for providing opinions on legislative proposals (even if this is limited) and can assist the institutions that are endowed with this task indirectly through the provision of information.[302]

Therefore, the EU seems to be adopting a mixed approach, endorsing in the first place a technical/legalistic one, but leaving at the same time room for political and 'new governance' methods. This results from 'the methodology', which imposes various proofing obligations on different institutional actors. It is indeed the case that the EU system accumulates all methods of fundamental rights-proofing as existent in different EU Member States except one (namely, a 'Council of State'-like instance).[303] It is also noteworthy that, unlike the EU, no Member State has more than one of these methods in place.

IV. CONCLUSION

The table concluding this chapter, which borrows from and builds on the one presented by de Schutter,[304] summarises the above key findings. It illustrates the EU-specific problems related to the different legislative scrutiny options and how they are remedied through the other alternatives (combination of methods), which can function as safeguards.

Overall, it emerges from the system's set-up that there is considerable potential for providing effective scrutiny—if properly used and if the identified shortcomings are remedied.

There is good reason to believe that more attention will be paid to this process and its ongoing problems in the future, due to the incentives created by the institutional changes that the Lisbon Treaty has brought about. It is hoped that this will finally lead to the advent of a real fundamental rights culture in the legislative branch of the EU.

[300] 2010 Commission Communication, above n 7, 6.

[301] ibid 13.

[302] The question whether an involvement of the FRA would actually mean that different segments of society would be involved that provide for grassroots knowledge remains open. It is true that the FRA's mandate includes the obligation to 'develop a communication strategy and promote dialogue with civil society, in order to raise public awareness of fundamental rights and actively disseminate information about its work' (FRA Founding Regulation, above n 6, Art 4(1)(h)) and it is equally true that the FRA has launched in 2008 the FRP in order to realise that obligation, as expressed in Art 10 of the FRA Founding Regulation. But under the current state of affairs, the extent to which 'grass-roots knowledge' resulting from that structure directly impacts on the substance of an opinion to a legislative proposal seems to be limited.

[303] See de Schutter Report, above n 292, 11 et seq.

[304] The first column ('FR proofing method at national level') and the third column ('Advantage') for the tables on (1), (2B) and and (3) are directly (verbatim) borrowed from the de Schutter Report, above n 292. The third column in these tables reproduces the findings of the de Schutter Report in a summarised form. The second column ('EU equivalent'), the third column ('EU-specific shortcoming of the method') and the fourth column ('Safeguard when method fails') in these tables have been added by this author. Table (2A) on Council oversight is in its entirety attributable to this author.

SUMMARY OF FUNDAMENTAL RIGHTS—PROOFING IN THE LEGISLATIVE PROCESS

(1) Commission proposal

FR proofing method existing at national level	*EU equivalent*	*Advantage*	*EU specific shortcoming of the method*	*Safeguard*[305] *when method fails (combination of methods)*
Ministerial department taking the initiative of the proposal	Lead Service at the Commission taking the initiative of the proposal	— Increases understanding of human rights implications in the public servants' proposals — Serves mainstreaming and building of a human rights culture	Not all drafters have legal training; susceptible to political compromises/ lobbying	Checked by Legal Service (systematically) and by DG Justice (less systematically)
Specialised unit within government examines and advises on the proposal	Commission Legal Service, DG Justice, and the Fundamental Rights Unit consider the proposal	— Ensures an expert approach to human rights issues and adequate use of existing international and European standards	Legal Service: so far it did not have a strong will/courage to oppose Commissioners DG Justice: no compulsory consultation	Checked by EP (LIBE Committee and/or EP Legal Service)

(2A) Council oversight

(2B) Parliament oversight

[305] If the fundamental rights compliance of a legislative proposal, which is achieved through one (or a combination) of the described methods, is altered and negated in amendments during the legislative process, the Commission could act as a safeguard by making use of the following tools: 1) withdrawing the proposal; 2) requiring the act to be adopted at unanimity; 3) bringing an annulment action (2009 COM report, 8–9).

(2A) Council oversight

FR proofing method existing at national level	***EU equivalent***	***Advantage***	***EU-specific shortcoming of the method***	***Safeguard when method fails (combination of methods)***
No effective equivalent	Council Legal Service, making use of national experts' expertise in the Member State, FREMP Working Party consultation	Ensures an expert approach to human rights issues, incorporating Member State input and adequate use of existing international and European standards	There might be divergent levels of rights protection at the national level; the Council Legal Service and Working Party only get involved on request/referral	The FRA could have played a role by being able to intervene (at this stage) without depending on a request by one of the institutions

(2B) Parliamentary oversight

FR proofing method existing at national level	***EU equivalent***	***Advantage***	***EU-specific shortcoming of the method***	***Safeguard when method fails (combination of methods)***
Parliamentary committee	European Parliament LIBE Committee	Ensures transparency in evaluation, facilitates public opinion and media control and societal debate Opens up possibility of consultation of external experts, including NHRIs	Not all legislation is scrutinised/no systematic scrutiny Mostly political as opposed to legal assessment	No safeguard; *FRA could have played a role by being able to intervene (at this stage) without depending on a request by one of the institutions*

(3) Expert independent bodies (optional)

FR proofing method existing at national level	*EU equivalent*	*Advantage*	*EU specific shortcoming of the method*	*Safeguard when method fails (combination of methods)*
Specialised, independent instance located outside both government and Parliament (eg Council of State)	No EU equivalent	— Guarantees independence in the evaluation and ensures that it will not be subordinated to the need to reach political compromises — Insulates the evaluation from the pressure of public opinion	N/A	N/A
NHRI or equivalent institution	The EU Fundamental Rights Agency	— Ensures that the impact of the proposed legislation on a wide range of interests and existing standards of international and European human rights law will be taken into account	Limitation of FRA's legislative scrutiny mandate; action only upon request	No safeguard

4

Data Protection

I. INTRODUCTION

DATA PRIVACY IS an area, which the EU legislature has regulated on the basis of the internal market in two different ways. First, legislation with an internal market legal basis has been put in place, which aims at protecting the right: the Data Protection Directive (DPD),[1] characterised as 'one of the most remarkable instruments that the European Community has adopted in the field of fundamental rights',[2] which 'enshrines two of the oldest and equally important ambitions of the European integration process: the protection of fundamental rights and freedoms of individuals … on the one hand and the achievement of the internal market … on the other';[3] and the e-Privacy Directive,[4] which applies the principles established in the DPD to the electronic communications sector. Second, legislation was adopted, again on the basis of the internal market, to regulate a (legitimate) restriction of the right, namely the Data Retention Directive (DRD).[5] This instrument was also labelled as a historical decision, 'aimed at introducing, for the first time, the Europe-wide obligation to retain, for investigational purposes, billions of data relating to the communications of any and all citizens'.[6] Recently, the CJEU struck down this instrument on the ground that it constituted a disproportionate interference with fundamental rights (Arts 7, 8 and 52(1) CFR).

It is therefore clear that the EU legislator has achieved not only groundbreaking data protection, but also, for some years, groundbreaking data privacy restriction—all in the name of the establishment and functioning of the internal market.

This chapter aims to scrutinise these apparently paradoxical dimensions of the way in which market making has impacted on the right to data protection. It will commence with

[1] Directive 95/46/EC on the protection of individuals with regard to the processing of personal data and on the free movement of such data (Data Protection Directive) [1995] OJ L281/31.

[2] EU Network of Independent Experts in Fundamental Rights, Report on the Situation of Fundamental Rights in the European Union and its Member States (2002), http://ec.europa.eu/justice/fundamental-rights/files/cfr_cdf_2002_report_en.pdf, 15.

[3] Commission Communication, 'A comprehensive approach on personal data protection in the European Union', COM(2010) 0609 final (hereinafter 'Commission Communication 2010').

[4] Directive 2002/58/EC of the European Parliament and of the Council of 12 July 2002 concerning the processing of personal data and the protection of privacy in the electronic communications sector [2002] OJ L201/37.

[5] Directive 2006/24/EC on the retention of data generated or processed in connection with the provision of publicly available electronic communications services or of public communications networks and amending Directive 2002/58/EC (Data Retention Directive) [2006] OJ L105/54.

[6] Article 29 Data Protection Working Party, Opinion 4 /2005 on the Proposal for a Directive of the European Parliament and of the Council on the Retention of Data Processed in Connection with the Provision of Public Electronic Communication Services and Amending Directive 2002/58/EC (COM(2005)438 final of 21 September 2005), 1868/05/EN, WP 113 (21 October 2005).

the definition of the right, juxtaposing the EU definition with the ECHR definition and posing the question whether such a right has gained an autonomous meaning at the EU level (section II). It will then turn to an analysis of the regulation of data protection (section III), examining first of all the legislative history and content of the two instruments that establish the EU data protection framework. It will become immediately obvious that these internal market instruments stand out (in comparison to the legislation discussed in the subsequent chapters) in the sense that they were explicitly conceived as (also) being fundamental rights instruments from the outset. Therefore, and given the fact that data protection is the most regulated fundamental right of the EU, the central theme of this chapter will be the question to what degree this fundamental right has gained an autonomous definition of its scope at the EU level.

Against this background, the specific situation of clashes between fundamental rights arising within the scope of the Directives will be examined. It will illustrate that this situation poses a challenge to an autonomous definition of the EU right to data privacy, as well as to a uniform EU data protection policy. This part of the chapter will therefore necessarily focus on the relevant case law of the Court of Justice of the EU (the Court). It is thereby not only concerned with the relationship between the Court and the EU legislature but also with the relationship between the Court and national courts in the context of the preliminary reference procedure when examining the question of autonomy.

Section IV is devoted to the recently annulled DRD. This discussion is important not only for the purposes of demonstrating how such an EU-wide regulation of a fundamental rights restriction can be brought about based on the internal market, but also for informing any potential future legislative action in the field. The section will first lay down the content of the instrument. It will then examine the (fundamental rights) challenges posed to the Directive prior to its invalidation as well as the case (*Digital Rights Ireland*)[7] in which it was actually struck down.

Finally, the Commission's proposal for a new data protection framework will be scrutinised by asking whether its new legal basis has moved it away from the internal market. The question of autonomy is also raised (when looking at the relationship between the EU legislature and the national legislatures) by asking whether the nature of the instrument (a regulation rather than a directive) will bring about a more autonomous definition of the right at the EU level.

II. DATA PROTECTION AS A FUNDAMENTAL RIGHT

A. The ECHR Approach vis-a-vis the EU Approach

The ECHR does not expressly list data protection in one of its articles. However, such a right has been recognised in the case law of the ECtHR in the Convention system. In *Amann v Switzerland*,[8] the ECtHR held that 'the storing of data relating to the "private life" of an

[7] Joined Cases C-293/12 and C-594/12 *Digital Rights Ireland Ltd and Kärntner Landesregierund et al v Ireland* ECLI:EU:C:2014:238.

[8] *Amann v Switzerland*, App No 27798/95 (ECtHR, 16 February 2000).

individual falls within the application of Article 8(1) ECHR [the right to respect for private life]',[9] while the subsequent use of the information has no bearing on that finding.

On the basis of a dynamic interpretation[10] of Article 8 ECHR, modern means of communication and storage of data are also covered under this article: telephone conversations[11] and the practice of tapping telephone calls by using a device that registers automatically numbers dialled on a telephone, including time and duration;[12] covert listening devices installed by the police;[13] electronic files,[14] including databases storing fingerprints, cell samples and DNA;[15] monitoring of emails at the workplace;[16] messaging systems;[17] video recordings filmed by a CCTV camera;[18] recording conversations in visiting rooms of prisons[19] and voice recording at police stations.[20]

The ECtHR reiterated in *Amann* that the concept of 'private life' is to be interpreted broadly. Such a notion includes the 'right to establish and develop relationships with other human beings'[21] and also encompasses 'activities of a professional or business nature'.[22] This approach, as the ECtHR states, corresponds to that of the Convention on the Automatic Processing of Personal Data (Convention 108),[23] which is aimed at 'secur[ing] in the territory of each Party for every individual … respect for his rights and fundamental freedoms, and in particular his right to privacy, with regard to automatic processing of personal data relating to him'.[24] Such data is defined as being 'any information relating to an identified or identifiable individual'.[25] Whether or not such interferences amount to a breach of Article 8 ECHR will depend on an assessment of whether the disclosure was 'in accordance with the law', 'necessary in a democratic society' for a legitimate aim and proportionate. 'The justifications for interference should outweigh the detrimental effect that the very existence of the legislative provisions in question could have on the subjects'.[26] The proportionality assessment is guided by the guarantees contained in Convention 108.[27] This is inter alia

[9] ibid [65] (with reference to *Leander v Sweden*, App No 9248/81 (ECtHR, 26 March 1987) [48]).

[10] Also known as the principle of 'evolutive interpretation' under the ECHR system.

[11] *Klass v Germany*, App No 5029/71 (ECtHR, 6 September 1978) [41]; *Amann v Switzerland*, above n 8, [44]; and *Halford v UK*, App No 20605/92 (ECtHR, 25 June 1997) [44].

[12] *Malone v UK*, App No 8691/79 (ECtHR, 2 August 1984).

[13] *PG and JH v UK*, App No 44787/98 (ECtHR, 25 September 2001).

[14] *Leander v Sweden* (n 9) [48]; *Amann v Switzerland*, above n 8, [65]; *Rotaru v Romania*, App No 28341/95 (ECtHR, 4 May 2000) [42]–[43]; *Bouchacourt v France*, App No 5335/06 (ECtHR, 17 December 2009); *Gardel v France and MB v France*, App No 16428/05 (ECtHR, 17 December 2009); *Dimitrov-Kazakov v Bulgaria*, App No 11379/03 (ECtHR, 10 February 2011); and *Khelili v Switzerland*, App No 16188/07 (ECtHR, 18 October 2011).

[15] *S and Marper v UK*, App No 30562/04 (ECtHR, 4 December 2008).

[16] *Copland v UK*, App No 62617/00 (ECtHR, 3 April 2007).

[17] *Taylor-Sabori v UK*, App No 47114/99 (ECtHR, 22 October 2002).

[18] *Peck v UK*, App No 44647/98 (ECtHR, 28 January 2003).

[19] *Wisse v France*, App No 71611/01 (ECtHR, 20 December 2005).

[20] *PG. and JH v UK*, above n 13.

[21] ibid.

[22] ibid [56] (with reference to *Niemietz v Germany*, App No 13710/88 (ECtHR, 16 December 1992)); and *Halford v UK*, App No 20605/92 (ECtHR, 25 June 1997) [44].

[23] Council of Europe Convention of 28 January 1981 for the Protection of Individuals with regard to Automatic Processing of Personal Data (1 October 1985) ETS No 108 (hereinafter 'Convention 108').

[24] ibid, Art 1.

[25] ibid, Art 2.

[26] Opinion of the European Data Protection Supervisor of 26 September 2005 [2005] OJ L298/1, para 9; and *Dudgeon v UK*, App No 7525 (ECtHR, 22 October 1981).

[27] F Bignami, 'Protecting Privacy against the Police in the European Union: The Data Retention Directive', Duke Law School Working Paper Series, Paper 76 (2007), http://lsr.nellco.org/duke/fs/papers/76.

evidenced by the fact that the adequacy of the safeguards in the overall regime is central to that assessment.[28]

In the EU, data protection is recognised in a separate provision in the EU Charter of Fundamental Rights (the Charter) (Art 8). However, despite the enshrinement of data protection as a *freestanding* right, its basis is clearly that of privacy. The EU data protection regime expressly acknowledges that it is especially inspired by the right to privacy[29] in addition to Convention 108,[30] and the Court interprets and applies provisions of the DPD on the basis of Article 8 ECHR.[31]

It should be noted, however, that grounding data protection rights in the right to privacy mirrors one specific legal tradition. This is the approach of the Council of Europe as well as that of Belgium and the Netherlands. France, for example, grounds data protection in the right to liberty, while in Germany it finds its basis in the right to human dignity, and in the US it is based on principles of public law, such as fair information practices.[32]

The different foundations of data protection (across Europe and beyond) account for the different types of regulatory interventions one sees. In the EU, given the wide scope and dynamic interpretations of Article 8 ECHR (corresponding to Article 7 CFR), as interpreted by the ECtHR and followed by the Court of Justice of the EU, one may wonder what the recognition of a separate data protection right in the EU Charter may add to the substantive level of protection.

Article 8 CFR reads:

1. Everyone has the right to the protection of personal data concerning him or her.
2. Such data must be processed fairly for specified purposes and on the basis of the consent of the person concerned or some other legitimate basis laid down by law. Everyone has the right of access to data which has been collected concerning him or her, and the right to have it rectified.
3. Compliance with these rules shall be subject to control by an independent authority.

This Charter provision is exceptionally detailed, including the basic data protection principles laid down in the Data Protection Directive 95/46/EC (discussed in detail below at section III.A), which in turn came from Convention 108. In fact, the added value of the separate provision can be explained by inquiring into why in the early 1970s the need was felt to adopt Convention 108 as a *parallel regime* to Article 8 ECHR. As explained by the European Data Protection Supervisor (EDPS),[33] the answer lies in the 'limitations in the light of new developments, particularly in the area of information technology: the uncertain scope

[28] See, eg, *Leander v Sweden*, above n 9, [67].

[29] DPD, above n 1, Art 1: 'Member States shall protect the fundamental rights and freedoms of natural persons, and in particular their right to privacy with respect to the processing of personal data.'

[30] ibid, recital 11: 'Whereas the principles of the protection of the rights and freedoms of individuals, notably the right to privacy, which are contained in this Directive, give substance to and amplify those contained in the Council of Europe Convention of 28 January 1981 for the Protection of Individuals with regard to Automatic Processing of Personal Data.'

[31] Joined Cases C-465/00 *Rechnungshof v Österreichischer Rundfunk and others* and C-138/01 *Christa Neukomm* and C-139/01 *Joseph Lauermann v. Österreichischer Rundfunk* [2003] ECR I-4989.

[32] P de Herth and S Gutwirth, 'Data Protection in the Case Law of Strasbourg and Luxembourg: Constitutionalisation in Action' in S Gutwirth, Y Poullet, P De Hert, J Nouwt and C de Terwange (eds), *Reinventing Data Protection?* (Berlin, Springer, 2009) 10.

[33] PJ Hustinx, 'Data Protection in the European Union' http://www.edps.europa.eu/EDPSWEB/webdav/shared/Documents/EDPS/Publications/Speeches/2005/05-04-21_Data_Protection_EN.pdf.

of 'private life', the emphasis on protection against interference by 'public authorities' and the insufficient response to the growing need for a positive and pro-active approach, also dealing 'with other relevant organisations and interests'.[34]

The EU regime takes these considerations on board. It provides for the principles of fair processing, consent and legitimacy, which 'are not at the core of privacy and cannot satisfactorily be met by the case law of the Strasbourg Court'.[35] Furthermore, the ECtHR does not grant in a general way a right to access one's data on the basis of Article 8 ECHR,[36] as the EU Charter does. Nor does it envisage the general right to have one's data rectified. The ECHR does not apply data protection rules in relations between private parties, nor is there a ground in the ECHR for a right to have compliance with these rules subject to control of independent data protection authorities.[37] Finally, unlike under the EU regime and Convention 108, not all aspects of processing of personal data are covered by the ECHR.[38]

One may wonder why it was considered necessary to include such a particularly detailed provision in the Charter and not leave it to secondary EU legislation. The answer applies to any kind of constitutional entrenchment: first, the right at issue is considered so important (or fundamental) in the specific legal order that it should be placed in a hierarchically higher position than other provisions, thus enjoying greater weight in the event of conflict; and, second, the right shall be entrenched for the future and be subject to more cumbersome procedures in order to be amended (in our case, that would entail Treaty amendment).

B. An Autonomous Definition of the Right to Data Privacy in the EU?

The Court has recognised that the right to data privacy is a fundamental right for the purposes of EU law. It has done so expressly in the *Promusicae* case,[39] which was subsequently confirmed in *Satamedia*.[40] Both decisions will be discussed in further detail below; however, two aspects of the *Promusicae* judgment are worth highlighting already at this point.

[34] ibid, 1.

[35] Y Poullet and S Gutwirth, 'Data Protection in the European Union—The Contribution of the Article 29 Working Party to the Construction of a Harmonised European Data Protection System: An Illustration of Reflexive Governance' in O De Schutter and VM Lax (eds), *Human Rights in the Web of Governance—Towards a Learning-Based Fundamental Rights Policy for the European Union* (Brussels, Editions Juridiques Bruylant, 2010) 271.

[36] See *Leander v Sweden*, above n 9.

[37] Poullet and Gutwirth, above n 35.

[38] See, eg, *Pierre Herbecq and the Association Ligue des droits de l'homme v Belgium*, App Nos 32200/96 and 32201/96 (joined) (ECtHR, 14 January 1998) [97]: photographic systems obtaining visual data which is not recorded does not interfere with the applicant's private life because 'it is difficult to see how the visual data obtained could be made available to the general public or used for purposes other than to keep a watch on places' and 'the data available to a person looking at monitors is identical to that which he or she could have obtained by being on the spot in person … Therefore all that can be observed is essentially, public behaviour. The applicant has also failed plausibly to demonstrate that private actions occurring in public could have been monitored in any way'.

[39] Case C-275/06 *Productores de Música de España (Promusicae) v Telefónica de España SAU* [2008] ECR I-271 [63]: 'the situation … involves … a further fundamental right, namely the right that guarantees protection of personal data and hence of private life' (hereinafter *Promusicae*).

[40] Case C-73/07 *Tietosuojavaltuutettu v Satakunnan Markinapörssi Oy, Satamedia Oy* [2007] ECR I-7075 [53]–[54] (hereinafter *Satamedia*). See also *Heinz Huber v Bundesrepublik Deutschland* EU:C:2008:724, Opinion of Advocate General Maduro [30] (where he considers that data protection cases concern the right to privacy as included in Art 7 CFR. Interestingly, even though he refers to the CFR, he does not mention the more specific provision going beyond the ECHR).

The first is that the Court established in this case the fundamental status of the right to protection of personal data almost exclusively on the basis of the Charter, prior to its entry into force. This is important to note, as it constituted the widest use that had been made of the Charter to that point. It was notably the reverse from that of the Court in *Viking*[41] and *Laval*,[42] where fundamental social rights were at stake. In those judgments, it will be recalled, the Court, in order to identify the right at issue, availed itself of the Charter only in the last instance, basing itself primarily on international treaties to derive a general principle of Community law. In *Promusicae*, the Court only referred to Article 8 ECHR so as to note that it is substantially reproduced in Article 7 CFR, and cited Article 8 CFR without any supporting reference to international treaties or constitutional traditions common to the Member States in order to affirm its fundamentality. In other words, this is the first case where the Court applied an altered reasoning structure, that is, one that refers in the first instance to the Charter and only subsequently, if at all, to the ECHR and other international human rights treaties. This has now become standard practice, but only after the Charter gained legally binding force.[43]

Second, the Court's first reference cited in support of its statement in *Promusicae* that personal data constitutes a fundamental right was recital 2 of the e-Privacy Directive.[44,45] The subtle, albeit important point to be made relates to the Court's methodology: it is in the context of *recognising* the fundamentality of the right for the purposes of EU law that the Court *first refers to an internal market instrument*. This in its turn refers to the Charter, and Article 8 ECHR is mentioned last (almost in passing) as being the provision that Article 7 CFR reproduces.

The diverging approaches in *Promusicae* on the one hand and *Viking* and *Laval* on the other can be linked to developments surrounding the fate of the Charter. In view of the UK and Polish opt-out from the Charter's Solidarity Chapter contained in the Lisbon Treaty, and the confusion resulting out of this regarding the question which rights of the Charter will be applicable to which Member States (see discussion in chapter six), it might have seemed to be the 'safest' option. This is because the right would in any case constitute a general principle of EU law, irrespective of what the Charter provides. This allowed the Court to circumvent any possible asymmetry of fundamental rights protection between the Member States. Moreover, the same approach is maintained post-Lisbon.[46]

These difficulties obviously do not exist with regard to data protection since Chapter II is not subject to any opt-out Protocol. Still, the question remains why such an unprecedented

[41] Case C-438/05 *The International Transport Workers' Federation and the Finnish Seamen's Union v Viking Line ABP and OU Viking Line Eestt* [2007] ECR I-1077 (hereinafter *Viking*).

[42] Case C-341/05 *Laval un Partneri Ltd v Svenska Byggnadsarbetareförbundet and others* [2007] ECR I-11767 (hereinafter *Laval*).

[43] This 'new approach' has been confirmed by President of the CJEU, V Skouris, in his presentation at the Council Presidency Seminar on 'The Practical Implementation of the Charter of Fundamental Rights', co-organised by the Danish Council Presidency and the EU Fundamental Rights Agency, Copenhagen, 15–16 March 2012.

[44] e-Privacy Directive, above n 4.

[45] *Promusicae*, above n 39, [64].

[46] See, eg, Case C-271/08 *Commission v Germany* [2010] ECR I-7091, where the Court affirms the fundamentality of the right to collective bargaining by referring first to the European Social Charter (Art 6 thereof), subsequently to the Community Charter of the Fundamental Social Rights of Workers (Art 12 thereof), and only at last instance to the CFR. Admittedly, the Court does not refer explicitly to 'general principles' here, but the construction applied allows such an inference.

extensive use was adopted in *Promusicae* and not in other cases dealing with rights outside the Solidarity Chapter.[47]

Arguably, an answer can be found when considering the second aspect of the *Promusicae* case, ie, the primary reference to an internal market instrument for the identification of the fundamental nature of the right in question. It is obvious that the difference in the two cases lies in the fact that the right to take collective action at issue in *Viking* and *Laval* has not been the object of legislative specification, unlike the right to data protection. Recalling the recognition of a specific right—in contrast to 'discovering' its fundamentality—by pointing out to the specific instrument in which the legislature has already done so appears to have two advantages: first, it means that there is political approval at the Member State level not only for such recognition, but also for its promotion through regulation; and, second, the right is not only recognised in an abstract form, but its scope is also, at least to a certain extent, defined, something that is usually absent when the Court acknowledges a specific fundamental right as being protected by the EU legal order.[48]

One reason for the Court's extensive use of the Charter might simply be the fact that it is an authoritative text for the EU—despite its lack of legal force at the time—which goes beyond that of the ECHR, since it includes the right to data privacy expressly. However, there might also be an argument that this practice constitutes evidence for a specific claim, namely, that this right had gained an *autonomous* definition by virtue of EU intervention—one that does not need to be derived from the general principles doctrine. Von Bogdandy, writing at a time when the Charter was newly proclaimed, observed that 'the human rights jurisprudence is the least "autonomous" part of the supranational legal order. In no other field does the [Court] rely so much on the national legal orders and international law'.[49]

An argument can be made that exactly that autonomy might have been established with regard to the right to data privacy through a twofold intervention at the supranational sphere. The first intervention is the inception of the right to data privacy in the Charter, formulated in such a way as to leave no doubt that this is a right that requires protection through concrete action as set out in Article 7. The second intervention is the fact that concrete action has actually been taken at the EU level along the lines of the formulation in the Charter.

Of course, it always has to be remembered in this context that whatever the degree of autonomy in defining the fundamental rights at the EU level that are also covered by the ECHR, it will never be possible to speak of complete autonomy due to the cross-reference to the ECHR contained in the Charter itself. Article 52(3) CFR provides that insofar as the

[47] After the ECJ's first reference to the CFR in Case C-540/03 *European Parliament v Council of the European Union (Family Reunification)* [2006] ECR I-5769, there has been a series of cases where the Court adopted a less extensive use: 1) In Joined Cases C-402 and 415/05P *Kadi & Al Barakaat International Foundation v Council and Commission* [2008] ECR I-6351 [335], the right to effective judicial protection was identified as a general principle by reference to the constitutional traditions common to the Member States and Art 6 and 13 ECHR—the CFR is mentioned last as reaffirming this. 2) In Case T-69/04 *Schunk and Schunk Kohlenstoff-Technik v Commission* [2008] ECR II-2567 [28], [29], [35], the principle of legality was recognised as a general principle on the basis of the Member States' constitutional traditions and the ECHR—the CFR is not mentioned at all. 3) In Case C-127/08 *Blaise Bahetan Metock and others v Minister for Justice, Equality and Law Reform* [2008] ECR I-6241 [56], the CJEU cited its own case law in support of its recognition of the right to family life, none of which makes reference to the CFR.

[48] A von Bogdandy, 'The European Union as a Human Rights Organization? Human Rights and the Core of the European Union' (2000) 37 *Common Market Law Review* 1307, 1330.

[49] ibid 1333.

Charter contains rights that correspond to those guaranteed by the ECHR, the meaning and scope of these rights shall be the same as those laid down by the Convention (although EU law is not prevented from providing a higher level of protection). To that extent, primary EU law has limited its ability to provide for a fully autonomous definition of (certain) EU fundamental rights.

III. REGULATING DATA PROTECTION: THE DATA PROTECTION DIRECTIVE AND THE E-PRIVACY DIRECTIVE

The subsequent section aims to examine the two instruments that have been put in place by the European legislature in order to realise this right: the DPD and the e-Privacy Directive. It will become clear that these two pieces of internal market legislation are an illustration that a strong fundamental rights policy can and is actually being pursued on the basis of the internal market—the data privacy policy. Both of these instruments are considered here as positive fundamental rights policy measures not only because they are positive legal instruments, but also because they constitute enabling (as opposed to 'negative' constraining) instruments.[50] This section will first set out the actions of the EU legislature (legislative history and substantive content of the instruments) against which the claim to an autonomous definition of the right to data privacy will then be examined (in section III.C).

A. The Data Protection Directive 95/46/EC

i. Legislative History

'In the European Union data privacy is one of the oldest of human rights policies',[51] the first foundation stone of which was laid when the DPD was adopted in the mid-1990s, although the need for an EU wide data protection regime had already been voiced much earlier[52] by the European Parliament in the mid- to late 1970s.[53] This came subsequent to developments at the national level commencing with the adoption of the Hessen Act in 1970 and the Federal German law in 1976; the following suit of a number of European states (France, Denmark, Ireland, Luxembourg, the Netherlands and the UK) throughout the 1970s and 1980s; and further important developments took place at the international scene, such as the OECD Guidelines on the Protection of Privacy and Transborder Data Flows of Personal

[50] See the discussion on positive versus negative (fundamental rights) policy-making in G de Búrca, 'Convergence and Divergence in European Public Law: The Case of Human Rights' in P Beaumont, C Lyons and N Walker (eds), *Convergence And Divergence In European Public Law* (Oxford, Hart Publishing, 2002).

[51] Bignami, above n 27, 1.

[52] On a detailed analysis of the legislative history of the DPD, on which the summarised account here is largely based, see S Simitis, 'Data Protection in the European Union—The Quest for Common Rules' in *Collected Courses of the Academy of European Law*, European Community Law, Vol VIII, Book 1 (The Hague, Boston/London, Kluwer Law International/Martinus Nijhoff Publishers/Academy of European Law, 1997).

[53] The European Parliament passed a series of resolutions on the protection of the rights of the individual in the face of technical developments in data processing including those of 13 March 1975 [1975] OJ C60/48; of 3 May 1976 [1976] OJ C100/27; of 8 May 1979 [1979] OJ C140/34; and of 9 March 1982 [1982] OJ C87/39.

Data and, importantly, the adoption of the Council of Europe Convention on Data Protection of 1981 (Convention 108).[54]

The European Commission, however, refused to respond to calls for harmonisation aimed at protecting fundamental rights of individuals—as the European Parliament's resolutions were termed—for nearly two decades. The reason can be traced to its specific understanding of the subject matter, which was not perceived as a fundamental rights issue; rather, data was seen as marketable goods that had to be subjected to the common market rules.[55] Moreover, the Commission's take is evidenced in the first Community document tackling data processing: in a 1973 Communication[56] the two key actions identified as central for such a policy were to develop the capacity for a European-based data processing industry and to promote the effective use of data processing.[57] In other words, the general project was to establish a European information market rather than to restrict data processing in line with fundamental rights obligations.

Nevertheless, the Commission was not immune from increased pressure emanating from the Member State level, the international sphere and the European Parliament, where the need for common rules became an ever-more strongly expressed concern.[58] Therefore, it did eventually take some action, which took the form of a proposal recommending Member States to ratify Convention 108.[59] Proposing a harmonisation instrument was not an envisaged option. This changed in the early 1990s and the question is what triggered the Commission at the time to adopt a Communication,[60] and eventually a proposal (and an amended version) for a Directive,[61] containing explicit fundamental rights references not only in the Preamble but also in its very first provision as one of its objectives. Nothing had changed in the arguments that were put forward by the European Parliament throughout the years and that were discarded by the Commission. Simitis argues that this move mirrors the EU's move 'from the market to a polis' after the Single European Act, on the road to Maastricht and the signing of the TEU to Amsterdam.[62] As the EU evolved into a political project with its own political values and increased references to fundamental rights not only in policy documents but also in the Treaty, the Commission arguably 'had no choice' in this area but 'to reconsider its policies in order to align them with the European Union's obligation to respect and implement fundamental rights'.[63] It has also been suggested that Simitis' own involvement in the drafting process as Chairman of the Commission's drafting group,

[54] Convention 108, above n 23.

[55] Simitis, above n 52, 101.

[56] Commission Communication to the Council, *Community Policy on Data Processing*, 21 November 1973, SEC(73) 4300 final.

[57] ibid 2.

[58] Simitis, above n 52, 102; and ACM Nutger, *Transborder Flow of Personal Data within the EC* (Deventer, Kluwer Law & Taxation Publishers, 1990) ch VII and p 225. See also European Parliament, 'Resolution on the Protection of the Rights of the Individual in the face of Technological Developments in Data Processing' [1982] OJ C87/39.

[59] Commission Recommendation Relating to the Council of Europe Convention for the Protection of Individuals with Regard to Automatic Processing of Personal Data 81/679/EEC [1981] OJ L246/31.

[60] Commission 'Communication on the protection of individuals in relation to the processing of personal data in the Community and information society' of 13 September 1990 [1990] OJ C277/3.

[61] Commission Proposal for a Directive on the protection of individuals with regards to the processing of personal data and on the free movement of such data of 24 September 1990, 1990/0287(COD).

[62] S Simitis, 'From the Market to the Polis: The EU Directive on the Protection of Personal Data' (1995) 80 *Iowa Law Review* 440, 447–48.

[63] Simitis, above n 52, 105.

while being also the Chair of the Council of Europe's Data Protection Experts Committee and the data protection Commissioner of Hessen, played an important role in successfully advancing this dimension of the instrument.[64]

The Directive is a piece of internal market legislation and therefore it also had to be justified along these terms. According to the preamble of the DPD, its purpose is to harmonise different data protection regimes across the Member States, whose divergence is detrimental to a well-functioning internal market. As set out in recital 7 of the Directive, different domestic standards of fundamental rights protection across the (then) Community were considered to constitute an obstacle to the free movement of personal data. This in its turn is liable to hinder several economic activities in the internal market, 'distort competition and impede a number of authorities in the discharge of their responsibilities under Community law'.[65] The stated objective of the legislation is therefore to secure the free flow of data whilst ensuring 'a high level of protection in the [then] Community'.[66] With respect to such 'free flow of data', it will be remembered from the discussion in chapter two on case *Österreichischer Rundfunk*[67] that ensuring this objective does not presuppose that the Directive is applicable only in situations where there is an actual link with free movement. Rather, according to the Court,[68] the Directive applies to any data processing because any such data can move between Member States. The result is an internal market instrument that applies data protection rules to purely internal situations to a considerable extent.

In addition to *ensuring* the free flow of personal data, the legislature was also concerned with the fact that an increase in such cross-border flow is actually expected by virtue of both deeper integration of the common market[69] as well as an increase in scientific and technical cooperation.[70] The concern here does not seem to lie with facilitating the free movement of data, but rather with the consequences that might result from it. The obvious one is 'possible abuses by market actors or by government agencies as service providers'.[71] This is tantamount to an acknowledgment that European market integration can lead to endangering the protection of fundamental rights in the absence of re-regulation of domestic standards at the European level.

Given the reciprocal (negative) impact that market making and data privacy can have on each other (diverging fundamental rights standards impeding the market on the one hand and deeper market integration endangering the protection of fundamental rights on the other), recourse to Article 114 TFEU, the more general market regulative power in the Treaty, is sound. To speak of a *fundamental rights policy*, firmly based on a legal basis in the Treaties, that has as its object 'the establishment and functioning of the internal market' might trigger some initial scepticism. However, it is easily refuted once it is realised that the Directive has a dual aim which on the face of the language used in the instrument seems

[64] D Heisenberg, *Negotiating Privacy: The European Union, the United States and Personal Data Protection* (Boulder, Lynne Rienner Publishers, 2005) 62.

[65] DPD, above n 1, recital 7.

[66] ibid, recital 10.

[67] *Österreichischer Rundfunk*, above n 31, [40]–[41].

[68] ibid [47].

[69] ibid, recital 5.

[70] ibid, recital 6.

[71] Bignami, above n 27, 2.

to be of *at least equal weight.* As Advocate General Maduro has pointed out 'in the context of Directive 95/46, data protection is not merely incidental to the economic activity that may be facilitated by data processing; it is on par with it. This is expressed in the title of the Directive ... in recitals 2, 10, 11, 12 and, of course, in its numerous provisions imposing specific obligations on data controllers'.[72] This statement finds reflection in Article 1 of the Directive, which on the one hand imposes on Member States the obligation to protect data privacy (para 1) and on the other hand bars them from restricting or prohibiting the free flow of personal data for reasons relating to data privacy, precisely because common rules for such protection are set out in the instrument. Furthermore, recital 3 seeks to justify the choice of legal basis in these terms: 'the establishment and functioning of the internal market ... *require not only* that personal data should be able to flow freely from one Member State to another, *but also that the fundamental rights of individuals should be safeguarded*' (emphasis added).[73] This statement is particularly interesting not only in view of the fact that the legislature appears to be given an explicit mandate to take action on the basis of Article 114 TFEU in order to legislate on fundamental rights,[74] but also because it expresses the acknowledgment of a *duty* to do so.

A final point to note is that the free flow of personal data in the DPD is the element used to advance the economic argument for justifying harmonisation. This is in contrast to Convention 108, where the same issue was viewed in terms of competing fundamental rights: privacy (as enshrined in Art 8 ECHR) and free flow of information regardless of frontiers (as enshrined in Art 10 ECHR). In this context, the rules set out in the Convention are viewed as a set of legitimate restrictions to Article 10 ECHR, which allows for 'the protection of other individual rights and freedoms, in particular the right to respect for individual privacy'.[75] The fact that no emphasis was placed on this conception of the free flow of data may be seen as unsurprising when bearing in mind that an economic argument—not another fundamental rights argument—was necessary for justifying recourse to what is now Art 114 TFEU. But of course, the fundamental rights dimension (freedom of information) could have been acknowledged as coinciding with the economic dimension.

ii. The Provisions

As emerges from the above, the first provision of the Directive reflects the concerns referred to in the Preamble in a very simple way: the Directive will stipulate not only the permissible, but also the obligatory level of data protection across the EU, so as to preclude Member States from restricting the free flow of such data in the name of privacy protection deviating

[72] *Heinz Huber*, above n 40.

[73] DPD, above n 1, recital 3.

[74] It is not a revolutionary statement that internal market legislation can pursue several aims and still be legitimately based on Art 114 TFEU, as long as it removes some obstacle to trade, as this is what legislative practice and ECJ jurisprudence confirm; see Case C-491/01 *The Queen v Secretary of State for Health ex parte British American Tobacco (Investments) Ltd and Imperial Tobacco Ltd (BAT)* [2002] ECR I-11453, Opinion of Advocate General Geelhoed, [100]–[101]. See also the discussion in ch 1.

[75] Explanatory Report to Convention 108, 11, margin 109, as cited in Nutger, above n 58, 226.

from that provided for by the harmonising instrument. So, its core is to frame the EU right to data protection. The Directive does so by providing for:

1. general rules on the lawfulness of the processing of personal data (Chapter II);
2. judicial remedies, liability and sanctions (Chapter III);
3. conditions under which the transfer of personal data to third countries is permitted (Chapter IV);
4. provisions on codes of conduct (Chapter V);
5. an obligation to have supervisory authorities in place at the Member State level and the setting up of an advisory Working Party (Article 29 Working Party) at the European level (Chapter VI).In adopting the data privacy regime, the EU legislature was unsurprisingly strongly influenced by the one European data protection regime that came first in time—Convention 108,[76] to which all EU Member States are party.[77] The control system of information processing established under the DPD adopts some central provisions of the Personal Data Convention (even though in a more detailed manner). Hence, the five requirements of Article 5 of the Personal Data Convention on data quality are substantially reproduced in Article 6 DPD. These requirements are fairness and lawfulness, specific purposes, necessity, accuracy and limitations on the purpose and time of retention. Furthermore, both these instruments provide for prohibitions on the processing of sensitive data[78] and for the imposition of security measures to protect personal data,[79] as well as for a right to access the data and to having it rectified.[80]

Beyond these common features of the two regimes, the DPD also includes provisions on criteria for making the data processing legitimate,[81] information to be given to the data subject,[82] the data subject's right to object,[83] public and private liability,[84] as well as limitations on third-country transmission of personal data.[85]

iii. Enforcement, Harmonisation and Policy Development Through (New) Bodies of Governance

The most distinguishing feature of the EU data protection system, and the one that gives teeth to the European data privacy policy, is the mechanisms established under the DPD, aimed at enforcement, harmonisation and policy development in a broader sense.

These mechanisms comprise, first, at the national level, the requirement to establish in each Member State an independent data protection authority (DPA) responsible for

[76] See also F Bignami, 'The Case for Tolerant Constitutional Patriotism: The Right to Privacy before the European Courts' (2008) 41 *Cornell International Law Journal* 211, 225 ff for a discussion of how EU data protection legislation draws on this Convention.

[77] Note also that the EU aims to become a party to the Convention. For this purpose, amendments to the Convention were adopted in June 1999. See LA Bygrave, 'International Agreements to Protect Personal Data' in JB Rule and G Greenleaf (eds), *Global Privacy Protection—The First Generation* (Cheltenham, Edward Elgar, 2008).

[78] DPD, above n 1, Art 8; and Convention 108, above n 23, Art 6.

[79] DPD, above n 1, Art 17; and Convention 108, above n 23, Art 7.

[80] DPD, above n 1, Art 12; and Convention 108, above n 23, Art 8.

[81] DPD, above n 1, Art 7.

[82] ibid, Arts 10 and 11.

[83] ibid, Arts 14 and 15.

[84] ibid, Arts 23 and 24.

[85] ibid, Arts 25 and 26.

monitoring the application of the provisions adopted by the Member States pursuant to the DPD.[86] Those authorities are to have investigative powers, effective powers of intervention (ordering the blocking, erasure or destruction of data, imposing a temporary or definitive ban etc) and the power to engage in legal proceedings where national provisions implementing the Directive are violated or to bring these violations to the attention of the judicial authorities.[87] At the moment, all EU Member States have one DPA in place tasked with monitoring and ensuring data protection legislation in their territories.[88]

In some Member States, issues have arisen regarding the question of whether the authorities meet the requirement of 'act[ing] with complete independence', as required under Article 28(1) DPD. It should be noted that this wording was introduced only later in the negotiating process of the DPD, the original Commission proposals speaking of 'an independent authority'. The change in wording was deliberate, as the latter normally implies 'institutional separation', while 'functional independence' could be deemed as sufficiently meeting the requirements of the former wording.[89] Given that the approach to this issue (appointment of officials of DPAs, institutional embedding etc) was and is divergent across the Member States,[90] the changed wording was introduced in the Council in order to accommodate different approaches to independence, including institutional and functional approaches.[91]

The Court has broadly construed the requirement of 'complete independence' in a Commission action against Germany.[92] The case concerned authorities responsible for the monitoring of data processing outside the public sector in the German *Länder*, which were subject to state scrutiny and therefore were not held to meet the requirement of the Directive. 'Independence' was, on the basis of its 'usual meaning'[93] held to mean 'a status which ensures that the body concerned can act completely freely, without taking any instructions or being put under any pressure',[94] while 'complete' 'implies a decision-making power independent of any direct or indirect external influence on the supervisory authority'.[95]

However, despite the positions advanced by the Commission the Court did not explicitly refer to types of independence that this should include (ie, not using terminology such as 'institutional', 'functional', 'operational' or 'financial'). This might be explained by the fact that the case was both difficult and easy at the same time. It was difficult because the Court was faced with the question of establishing an EU model of independence for national supervisory authorities, despite the fact that the legislature intended to allow for precisely that flexibility and therefore did not provide a strict definition. As an additional difficulty, it had to be borne in mind that whatever definition was handed down

[86] ibid, Art 28.

[87] ibid, Art 28(3).

[88] EU Agency for Fundamental Rights, Report on Data Protection in the European Union: The Role of National Data Protection Authorities—Strengthening the fundamental rights architecture in the EU II (2010) (hereinafter 'FRA Report 2010').

[89] Simitis, above n 62, 462.

[90] See FRA Report 2010, above n 88, 19 (in Denmark and Latvia, for instance, the data protection authorities are attached to the Ministry of Justice, whereas in Ireland and Luxembourg, data protection officers are directly appointed by the government).

[91] Simitis, above n 62, 462.

[92] Case C-518/07 *Commission v Germany* [2010] ECR I-1885.

[93] ibid [18].

[94] ibid.

[95] ibid.

here, it would have to be applicable to all pieces of EU legislation containing the phrase 'acting with complete independence' (eg, the FRA Founding Regulation). The case was, however, also easy in a way, because not even 'functional' independence was guaranteed with respect to the authorities at issue (those dealing with data processing conducted by private persons and enterprises), due to the fact that they were subject to state oversight, ie, they were subject to binding instructions by their superiors, who had the power to revoke measures taken or to oblige the subordinate authority to take measures. This state oversight operated regardless of the question whether it affected the authorities' independent function.

In *Commission v Austria*,[96] the Court eventually provided some further guidance. The case concerned Austria's data protection authority, which has close personal and organisational connections with the Federal Chancellor's Office. The Court invoked the general principles it had established in *Commission v Germany*, but also held that functional independence, which was here guaranteed, is by itself not sufficient to protect the authority from all external influence and thus be independent.[97] In *Commission v Hungary*,[98] the Court had to deal with the premature termination of the national Data Protection Supervisor's term of office by the Hungarian government. The Court held that this termination, which was in contravention of the rules and safeguards contained in the applicable legislation, led to his independence being compromised for the purposes of Article 28(1) DPD. The reasoning was based on the holding in *Commission v Germany* that 'the *mere risk* that the State scrutinising authorities could exercise a political influence over the decisions of the supervisory authorities is enough to hinder the latter in the independent performance of their tasks' (emphasis added).[99] This is so for two reasons: first, because there should be no 'prior compliance'; and, second, because the DPAs must remain 'above all suspicion of partiality'.[100] In a situation such as the one in this case, none of these requirements could be said to be ensured.

The second novel and unique mechanism established at the European level is the Article 29 Working Party (WP)—the independent EU Advisory Body on Data Protection and Privacy, which is composed of representatives of the different national supervisory DPAs (the European Data Protection Supervisor (EDPS) having observatory status), representatives of the authorities established for the EU institutions and bodies and a representative of the Commission. The nature of the body is 'advisory' and it will act independently.[101] This body was set up to achieve four main objectives:[102]

1. Providing expert opinion from the Member State level to the Commission on questions of data protection.
2. Promoting the uniform application of the principles underlying the Directive in all Member States through cooperation between the data supervisory authorities. This objective reveals actually the reason why there was a need to establish such a WP:

[96] Case C-614/10 *Commission v Austria* EU:C:2012:631.
[97] ibid [42].
[98] Case C-288/12 *Commission v Hungary* EU:C:2014:237.
[99] ibid [53].
[100] ibid.
[101] DPD, above n 1, Art 29(1).
[102] See http://ec.europa.eu/justice_home/fsj/privacy/docs/wpdocs/tasks-art-29_en.pdf.

the pre-existence of DPAs at the national level and the need to network them at the European level, thus repurposing '[o]ld national institutions ... with new pan-European goals'.[103]

3. Advising the Commission on any Community measures affecting the rights and freedoms of natural persons with regard to the processing of personal data and privacy.
4. Making recommendations to the public at large and in particular to Community institutions on matters relating to the protection of persons with regard to the processing of personal data and privacy in the EC.[104] The body produces Opinions, which, even though they are not legally binding, are still considered to be quite influential. Furthermore, the Commission has an obligation to respond to the opinions and recommendations of the WP.[105]

The degree of influence of the body can furthermore be illustrated by the quite remarkable fact that it was the WP which was responsible for the inclusion of a separate data protection right in the EU Charter.[106] As one commentator has observed, 'it could be said that Art 29 of the Data Protection Directive has officially installed a kind of "privacy lobby group" at the heart of the European institutions'.[107] But, as in part evidenced in its list of tasks and in part in its practice, the WP assumes a double role: on the one hand, it has an (institutionalised) lobbying and 'watchdog function',[108] while on the other hand, it is an administrative independent authority,[109] which also acts as a mediator operating by the principle of consensus. This mediation happens along two axes: the mediation among *national* data protection authorities and that from the national to the EU level.

A further body emerging from the Directive is the 'Article 31 Committee' established by Article 31 DPD to assist the Commission. It takes the form of a more traditional comitology committee, is composed of Member States' representatives and is chaired by a Commission representative. The task of the Article 31 Committee is to review implementing measures of the Commission. If the Commission's measures are not in compliance with the opinion of the committee, they are communicated to the Council, which can take a different decision, acting by qualified majority voting. The crucial difference in relation to the WP is that the latter acts not only in a reactive but also in a proactive manner by advising and pressuring the Commission on new developments in the field.[110]

A final body of the EU data protection system should be mentioned at this point, despite the fact that its set up is not envisioned in the DPD: the EDPS, who is tasked with monitoring the EU administration's processing of personal data, providing advice on policies and legislation that affect privacy, and cooperating with similar authorities to ensure coherent

[103] A Newman, 'Innovating European Data Privacy Regulation: Unintended Pathways to Experimentalist Governance' in CF Sabel and J Zeitlin (eds), *Experimentalist Governance in the European Union* (Oxford, Oxford University Press, 2010) 35.

[104] See DPD, above n 1, Art 30 for the details of the tasks.

[105] ibid, Art 30(5).

[106] Poullet and Gutwirth, above n 35, 270, pointing out (at note 54) that S Rodota, then Chairman of the Art 29 WP, 'played a great role in the adoption of this article by the drafters'.

[107] ibid 254.

[108] See, eg, DPD, above n 1, Art 30(2): 'If the Working Party finds that divergences likely to affect the equivalence of protection for persons with regard to the processing of personal data in the Community are arising between the laws or practices of Member States, it shall inform the Commission accordingly.'

[109] Poullet and Gutwirth, above n 35, 291.

[110] Newman, above n 103, 33.

data protection.[111] It is notable that both the EDPS and the WP can and do conduct *ex ante* fundamental rights scrutiny of legislation out of their own motion—something which the FRA is barred from doing (see the discussion in chapter three). The EU has therefore somehow singled out and strengthened *ex ante* control of this specific fundamental right, which is the function of several bodies (including the FRA).

The EDPS was established by a Regulation concerning data processing by (then) Community institutions.[112] This Regulation is based on (ex) Article 286 EC (introduced by the Treaty of Amsterdam)—a specific legal basis for data protection rules binding EU institutions, para 2 of which requires the establishment of an independent supervisory body. The relevant point to note for the present purposes is the trigger for the introduction of this separate legislation and body. Namely, this was the discrepancy arising after the coming into force of the DPD: the existence of specific obligations imposed from the EU to the Member State level, but no such obligations binding the EU institutions.

In other words, 'spill-over' was at work here. The introduction of a regime aimed at the 'establishment and functioning of the internal market' led to the adoption of an explicit and specific fundamental rights regime binding (then) Community institutions, and a new legal basis for doing so in the Treaties. Moreover, it is interesting to note that the 'actor' lamenting such discrepancy and pushing for the extension of data protection rules to EU institutions was a DPD body: the WP.

This latter point leads to an observation that is as valid for the WP as it is for the EDPS: both bodies seem to have created 'a life of their own' as guardians of personal data protection by interpreting their mandate broadly[113] and by allying with different and changing institutional actors (the best allies at any given time). With their creation initiated by the DPD, the EU has brought into existence bodies that are key players in the further evolution of EU data protection policy.

B. The e-Privacy Directive 2002/58/EC

i. Legislative History

The e-Privacy Directive was preceded by a Directive on data protection and privacy protection in the telecommunications sector (Directive 97/66/EC).[114] The Commission's proposal for this instrument was adopted at a point earlier in time than the proposal for the general DPD,[115] although it can safely be assumed that preparation of the instruments

[111] See www.edps.europa.eu/EDPSWEB/edps/cache/off/EDPS and Arts 41, 46 and 47 of Regulation (EC) No 45/2001 on the protection of individuals with regard to the processing of personal data by the Community institutions and bodies and on the free movement of such data [2001] OJ L8/1 for more details on the EDPS' mandate, duties and powers.

[112] Regulation (EC) No 45/2001, above n 111, Art 41.

[113] The WP, for instance, gets involved on issues relating to the internet, even though these are covered by the e-Privacy Directive. See also Poullet and Goutwirth, above n 35, 266; and Newman, above n 103, 39 (the EDPS arguing that its advisory role extended to the first as well as the third pillar matters).

[114] Directive 97/66/EC concerning the processing of personal data and the protection of privacy in the telecommunications sector [1998] OJ L24/1.

[115] Commission Proposal for a Council Directive concerning the protection of personal data and privacy in the context of public digital telecommunications networks, in particular the integrated services digital networks (ISDN) and public digital mobile network, COM/90/314/FINAL—SYN 288, [1990] OJ C277/12. The proposal was adopted on 27 July 1990.

did not happen in isolation from each other but rather informed each other.[116] The rapid introduction of this instrument was explained as being necessary for establishing a Community-wide market in telecommunications services and equipment, which was hampered by divergent legal, regulatory and technical provisions concerning data protection in this fast-growing sector.[117] Developments were indeed rapid. With the explosion of the Internet throughout the 1990s and the fast and continuous technological evolution to date, not only the introduction but also the need for constant adaptation of this legislative framework appears to be an inevitable consequence. So only three years after the entry into force of Directive 97/66/EC, the Commission already tabled a new legislative proposal in order to update and extend the provisions of that Directive to the electronic communications sector. However, it did not introduce major changes to the substance of the pre-existing Directive. At the end of the process stood the e-Privacy Directive, repealing the previous instrument. This was again to be amended, first by the DRD[118] (discussed below) in 2006 and subsequently as part of a broader review process of the 'telecom package' in 2009.[119]

ii. The Provisions

The e-Privacy Directive[120] applies the principle of data privacy established by the general DPD to the electronic communications sector. It lays down the obligation for Member States to ensure the confidentiality of communications—and the related traffic data—made over a public communications network.[121] In particular, the listening to, tapping and storage of communications and the related traffic data by persons other than the users will be prohibited.[122]

The Directive also addresses the issue of data retention and specifies that the principle of data privacy may be restricted to safeguard national security, defence, public security and to allow criminal investigations if the restriction is necessary, appropriate and proportionate within a democratic society.[123]

[116] ibid, recital 9 (referring to a Council Directive implementing the general principles of Convention 108 into (then) Community law, which was not yet adopted at the time).

[117] ibid, recital 12.

[118] DRD, above n 5.

[119] This process included a review of Directive 2002/21/EC on a common regulatory framework for electronic communications networks and services [2002] OJ L108/33; Directive 2002/19/EC on access to, and interconnection of, electronic communications networks and associated facilities (Access Directive) [2002] OJ L108/7; Directive 2002/20/EC on the authorisation of electronic communications networks and services (Authorisation Directive) [2002] OJ L108/21; Directive 2002/22/EC on universal service and users' rights relating to electronic communications networks and services (Universal Service Directive) [2002] OJ L108/51; and the e-Privacy Directive, as well as a review of Regulation (EC) No 2006/2004 on cooperation between national authorities responsible for the enforcement of consumer protection laws [2004] OJ L364/1. The e-Privacy Directive was amended by Directive 2009/140/EC of the European Parliament and of the Council of 25 November 2009 amending Directives 2002/21/EC on a common regulatory framework for electronic communications networks and services, 2002/19/EC on access to, and interconnection of, electronic communications networks and associated facilities, and 2002/20/EC on the authorisation of electronic communications networks and services [2009] OJ L337/37.

[120] e-Privacy Directive, above n 4.

[121] ibid, Art 5(1).

[122] ibid.

[123] ibid, Art 15(1).

The main provisions of the Directive deal with the following:

1. The unsolicited communications ('spamming') in relation to which an 'opt-in' approach is established, ie, it is only allowed in respect of subscribers who have given their prior consent.[124]
2. Location data other than traffic data (cookies): users must give and have the possibility to withdraw their consent for the processing of that data and must be provided with precise information on their purpose for that end.[125]
3. Public directories: Member States will have to ensure that subscribers give their prior consent before they are included in a directory.[126]

C. Limits to the Autonomous Definition of the Right to Data Protection: The Directives and Conflicting Fundamental Rights

The preceding exposition illustrates that the two named instruments—which find their sole legal basis in the internal market—lay down a detailed framework for data protection in the EU, which goes beyond that of the Council of Europe. At the same time, the incoherence of the overall system is striking, being characterised by a discrepancy between the former first pillar regulation (having a general framework in place) and the former second and third pillar regulation (having a scattered regime in place).[127] The Lisbon Treaty has introduced the necessary basis for remedying this situation, which the EU legislature is now in the process of acting upon (see discussion below in section V).

Yet even within the former first pillar, questions arise as to the degree to which the legislature actually laid down the framework for a uniform policy on data privacy when adopting these instruments, in the sense that the scope of protection, which is to be afforded to this right is satisfactorily defined, at the European level, for European law purposes.

The cases that will be discussed below will prove that this policy faces a challenge when it comes to dealing with the hardest of the hard tasks in fundamental rights law in general and in creating an autonomous definition for the EU's fundamental rights in particular: resolving conflicts of fundamental rights as they appear within the ambit of EU law.

[124] ibid, Art 13.

[125] ibid, Art 9, recitals 24–25.

[126] ibid, Art 12, recitals 38–39.

[127] See FRA Report 2010, above n 88, 16–18. For example, within the former third pillar, the different data protection rules included in the Convention implementing the Schengen Agreement and concerning the Schengen Information System (SIS) [2000] OJ L239/19; the Europol Convention and the rules governing transmission of data to third countries and bodies [1995] OJ C316/2; the Rules of Procedure on the processing and protection of personal data at Eurojust [2005] OJ C68/1; the data protection rules for the Customs Information System, under the Convention on the use of information technology for customs purposes [1995] OJ C316/34; and the data protection rules under the Convention on Mutual Assistance in Criminal Matters [2000] OJ C197/15. At the same time, the Council Framework Decision on the protection of personal data processed in the framework of police and judicial cooperation in criminal matters is a horizontal data protection instrument for the third pillar, but only covers transborder flows of data between national law enforcement authorities. See Council Framework Decision 2008/977/JHA of 27 November 2008 on the protection of personal data processed in the framework of police and judicial cooperation in criminal matters [2008] OJ L350/60.

i. Promusicae: *Clashing Fundamental Rights in Clashing Directives*

Promusicae[128] concerned two fundamental rights—the right to property and the right to data privacy—engaged in an intriguing way. The protection of both rights was the subject of separate directives, both of which are aimed at regulating the internal market.

Simple as the facts of the case may have been, the Court was presented with rather complicated legal circumstances. Promusicae, a non-profit-making organisation of producers and publishers of musical and audiovisual recordings applied for a preliminary court order against Telefónica, an internet service provider. The measure involved disclosure of personal data of users of its services who, through the peer-to-peer file exchange program KazaA, shared files on their personal computers and were providing access to material in which Promusicae held exploitation rights. The request was made in order to bring civil proceedings against the persons concerned for engaging in unfair competition and infringing intellectual property rights. After the preliminary measure was ordered, Telefónica appealed, arguing that under the relevant national law, this type of data could only be communicated for criminal investigations or for the purpose of safeguarding public security and national defence, but not for civil proceedings. Promusicae counter-argued that the relevant national law must be interpreted in light of three EC Directives which concern: 1) the free movement of information society services (Directive 2000/31/EC);[129] 2) the protection of copyright (Directive 2001/29/EC);[130] 3) the enforcement of intellectual property rights (Directive 2004/48/EC—the 'IP enforcement directive');[131] and 4) Articles 17(2) and 47 CFR.

In light of the above, the CJEU was asked whether (then) EC law, and in particular the listed Directives, read in light of the two Charter provisions, require Member States to lay down an obligation to communicate personal data in the context of civil proceedings, in order to ensure the effective protection of copyright.[132] The Court provided its answer in three steps.

a. Step 1

At the outset, the CFEU brought the e-Privacy Directive into play. It found no obligation to disclose personal data in the context of civil proceedings in order to protect copyrights. Article 5(1) of the Directive provides for a general confidentiality obligation, which can be restricted on the basis of Article 15(1) to safeguard national security, defence, public security and the prevention, investigation, detection and prosecution of crimes. Clearly, this list does not cover civil proceedings. However, as Article 15 makes reference to the fact that the grounds listed are those also referred to in Article 13(1) DPD, it chose to read into Article 15

[128] *Promusicae*, above n 39.

[129] Directive 2000/31/EC of the European Parliament and of the Council of 8 June 2000 on certain legal aspects of information society services, in particular electronic commerce, in the Internal Market [2000] OJ L178/1 (hereinafter the 'Directive on Electronic Commerce').

[130] Directive 2001/29/EC of the European Parliament and of the Council of 22 May 2001 on the harmonisation of certain aspects of copyright and related rights in the information society [2001] OJ L167/10.

[131] Directive 2004/48/EC of the European Parliament and of the Council of 29 April 2004 on the enforcement of intellectual property rights [2004] OJ L195/16 (the 'IP enforcement directive').

[132] *Promusicae*, above n 39, [41].

an 'Art 13 DPD ground of restriction'—'the protection of rights and freedoms of others',[133] which includes the right to property.[134] It should be noted (and will be discussed in further detail below) that this does not follow logically from a straightforward interpretation of the provision, but it did allow the Court to find that the e-Privacy Directive allows a restriction to the confidentiality obligation for the protection of the right to property. Hence, it concluded on this point that the Directive allows the Member States to lay down an obligation of disclosure, although the wording of Article 15 does not compel them to do so.[135]

b. Step 2

As the first question was answered in the negative, the Court continued by examining whether the three Directives relied on by Promusicae in the national proceedings required the Member States to lay down such an obligation of disclosure. It acknowledged that the purpose of the Directives is the effective protection of industrial property, but it also pointed out that each of the three instruments contains a provision providing explicitly 'that such protection cannot affect the requirements of the protection of personal data'.[136] Furthermore, none of the three instruments, or the TRIPS Agreement, requires the Member States to lay down an obligation to communicate personal data in the context of civil proceedings.[137]

At this stage, the Court concluded that the Directives cannot provide an answer to the problem because of their cross-reference: the data protection regime allows a restriction for the protection of the right to property; conversely, the regime for the protection and enforcement of intellectual property rights allows a restriction for the protection of data privacy. In view of this situation, the Court chose to proceed to its final step—an analysis of the situation in fundamental rights terms.

c. Step 3

The Court commenced by referring to the Charter provisions that were identified in the order for reference: Article 17 CFR—the protection of the right to property, including intellectual property, Article 17(2) and Article 47 CFR—the right to an effective remedy. It noted that both of these rights are general principles of Community law.[138] It went on to recognise that the other fundamental right involved is data protection.[139]

Having recognised that both rights at issue are fundamental, the Court reached the point where it had to face the crux of the matter, that is, the need to reconcile those conflicting rights. Yet, it managed to circumvent this difficult task. It did so by first pointing out that

[133] DPD, above n 1, Art 13(1)(g).

[134] *Promusicae,* above n 39, [53].

[135] ibid [54]–[55].

[136] ibid [57]. These provisions are: Art 1(5)(b) of Directive 2000/31/EC, above n 129; Art 9 of Directive 2001/29/EC, above n 130; and Art 8(3)(e) of Directive 2004/48/EC, above n 131.

[137] *Promusicae,* aboven 39, [57]–[60]. The specific provisions that were interpreted as not laying down such an obligation are: Art 8(1) of Directive 2004/48/EC, above n 131; Arts 15(2) and 18 of Directive 2000/31/EC, above n 129; Arts 8(1) and (2) of Directive 2001/29, above n 130; and Arts 41, 42 and 47 of the TRIPS Agreement.

[138] *Promusicae,* above n 39, [62].

[139] ibid [63].

the mechanisms for reconciling the conflicting rights are to be found on the one hand in the Directives themselves, which stipulate the limits to their scope of protection, and on the other hand in the national provisions which transpose those instruments.[140] Since the provisions of the Directives are, however, formulated in general terms, the Court acknowledged that the Member States have the necessary discretion to define the terms of their transposition measures. Taking this as its point of departure, it gave to the referring court the following 'guidance' on the issue: when transposing the Directives, as well as when the domestic courts and authorities are interpreting national law in their light, an interpretation has to be relied on which allows for a 'fair balance to be struck between the various fundamental rights protected by the Community legal order'.[141] Furthermore, they must 'make sure that they do not rely on an interpretation of them which would be in conflict with th[e] fundamental rights [protected by Community law] or with the other general principles of Community law'.[142]

The merits of this answer may be questioned. The gist of the Court's reply is that the conflicting rights have to be subject to a balancing exercise and that this balance must be fair, without giving any further guidance on what this means in the specific situation before it. Put simply, it refused to answer the question of reconciliation between two conflicting fundamental rights in a situation falling within the scope of (then) Community law. The implications of this approach are clear—in a situation where both the legislature and the Court (ie, both processes of market integration) fail to regulate the issue, disparate standards of fundamental rights protection will prevail across the Member States. Obviously, this state of affairs works in opposition to the twin rationales of the legal instruments in question: given that national courts are liable to balance the conflicting rights differently, varying domestic regimes of protection will arise, creating obstacles to trade and allowing for jurisdiction shopping.

There is a further issue to be raised, that is, the fact that the Court *chose* to address the problem posed in front of it in terms of conflicting fundamental rights that are given expression in the two 'conflicting' Directives.

It will be recalled that the referring court only sought an interpretation of the three Directives relating to e-commerce and intellectual property (IP) rights protection and enforcement. However, since 'that circumstance does not prevent the Court of Justice from providing the national court with all the elements of interpretation of Community law which may be of use for deciding the case before it whether or not that court has referred to them in the wording of its question',[143] the Court was of course free to take account of the right to data privacy and the relevant Directive.[144] However, on a straightforward construction of Article 15(1) of the e-Privacy Directive, secondary legislation does actually provide a concrete answer to the problem of this case. It emerges from the discussion of the Court's reasoning that the crucial step 3 (analysis of the situation in fundamental rights terms) was only reached because no answer could be found in the Directives given their

140 ibid [66].

141 ibid [68].

142 ibid.

143 ibid [42] (citing Case C-392/05 *Alevizos* [2007] ECR I-3505 [64]).

144 ibid [44] (the CJEU observes that the national law provision transposing Directive 2000/31 on e-commerce and not allowing the communication of personal data for the purpose of bringing civil proceedings is implementing the right to private life, which is also required under the DPD and the e-Privacy Directive).

cross-reference to each other's interests. However, this was artificially constructed because Article 15(1) does not contain a ground of restriction for the rights of others, as is provided for in Article 13(1)(g) DPD. The argument that this ground of restriction can be derived when reading Article 15(1) in conjunction with Article 13(1) DPD can only stand if the reference in the e-Privacy Directive to the latter named provision is viewed in isolation, that is, as Advocate General Kokott reasoned in her Opinion,[145] when disregarding the fact that Article 15(1) itself lists certain grounds of exceptions 'as referred to in Article 13(1)'. It would arguably follow that only those grounds that are expressly included in Article 15(1) of the e-Privacy Directive are applicable in the electronic communications sector—it being a deliberate choice of the legislature, as the Commission had argued,[146] not to replicate Article 13(1) DPD in the e-Privacy Directive. Consequently, and based on this interpretation, the outcome would be the 'rights and freedoms of others', here the protection of IP rights, cannot justify the communication of the personal traffic data.

Even if perhaps not very evident at first sight, this technical aspect of interpretative construction was the turning point of the case. It was subsequently followed in *LSG-Gesellschaft*,[147] and the pressing question is why the Court felt compelled to follow such a course of action. In other words, why did the Court focus on the underlying principles of the Directives—more than what the actual provision at issue stipulates—so as to refer the issue back to the national court. And a further question: should the Court overturn the choices made at the legislative level regarding the possible relationship of the conflicting rights?

These questions will have to be left open for the time being, but what is important to note at this stage is that the Court was not ready to accept that a reconciliation of the conflicting rights at issue was a matter that should be decided at the EU level.

ii. Satamedia: *Clashing Fundamental Rights within the DPD*

Satamedia[148] is another case where the Court was presented with conflicting fundamental rights in a situation where the DPD was applicable. This time, however, the conflicting fundamental rights at issue—the right to data privacy on the one hand and freedom of expression on the other—are protected by one and the same instrument: Directive 95/46/EC.

The facts were the following: Markinapörssi collects public data from the Finnish tax authorities and publishes extracts of those in a regional newspaper each year. The data consists of the names and surnames of a large number of natural persons with an income above a certain threshold, the approximate amount of earned and unearned income, as well as details relating to the wealth tax levied on them. The relevant newspaper, which contained a statement that the data disclosed may be removed on request without a charge, has as its main purpose the publication of personal tax information. Markinapörssi transferred the data published in the newspaper on CD-ROM to Satamedia so that these could be disseminated by a text-messaging system. In this context, both companies signed an agreement with a mobile telephone company, putting in place, on Satamedia's behalf, a text-messaging service by which mobile phone users are able to receive the information published in the

[145] *Promusicae*, above n 39, Opinion of Advocate General Kokott at [86].

[146] ibid [87].

[147] Case C-557/07 *LSG-Gesellschaft zur Wahrnehmung von Leistungsschutzrechten GmbH v Tele2 Telecommunication GmbH* [2009] ECR I-1227.

[148] *Satamedia*, above n 40.

newspaper on their mobile for a charge. However, the data can be removed from that system on request. Following complaints from individuals who claimed infringement of the right to privacy, the Finnish data protection authority brought proceedings to prohibit the data processing activities at issue.

The domestic court referred essentially four questions.[149] First, can the handling of the data described above be regarded as 'processing of personal data' within the meaning of Article 3(1) DPD? Second, are the activities involving the processing of personal data covered by Article 9 DPD so that they can be considered to be carried out solely for journalistic purposes? In that respect, is the fact that the principal aim of the activities is publication relevant for the determination of that issue? Third, does Article 17 DPD preclude the publication of data, which has been collected for journalistic purposes and subsequently transferred for commercial purposes? Fourth, do personal data files containing, solely and in unaltered form, material already published in the media fall outside the scope of the DPD altogether?

After answering the first question in the positive, with reference to the definitions provided for in *Österreichischer Rundfunk*[150] and Article 2(b) DPD,[151] the Court turned to the fourth question and examined whether Article 3(2) DPD, which limits the scope of the Directive in two situations, is applicable.[152] It answered this in the negative. The first alternative of that provision relates only to activities of the state and not to those of private companies like the ones in question. It was also clear that the second alternative did not apply because making collected data accessible to an unrestricted number of people cannot be considered a purely personal or household activity.[153] The CJEU further held that there are no other limitations to the scope of the Directive (Art 13 permits derogations only in certain cases, which do not extend to the provisions of Art 3) and that 'a general derogation from application of the directive in respect of published information would largely deprive the directive of its effect'.[154]

Having brought the situation within the scope of the Directive, the Court turned to the question of reconciling data protection with freedom of expression (examined under question 2).[155] It started with a teleological approach by pointing to the objective of the DPD: data protection and free movement of data. It also observed that this objective must be reconciled with the fundamental right to freedom of expression. This is reflected in recital 37 of the Directive, which suggests that it is the object of Article 9 DPD to reconcile the two specific fundamental rights—the resulting obligation to do so lies on the Member States.[156] The Court then reiterated the requirements that must be fulfilled for the derogations/limitations/exemptions in the Directive to apply (Art 9 DPD). First, processing must be solely for journalistic purposes or the purpose of artistic or literary expression, 'which fall within the scope of the fundamental right to freedom of expression'.[157] Second, they

[149] ibid [34].
[150] *Österreichischer Rundfunk*, above n 31, [64].
[151] *Satamedia*, above n 40, [35]–[37].
[152] ibid [38]–[49].
[153] ibid [44].
[154] ibid [48].
[155] ibid [50]–[62].
[156] ibid [54].
[157] ibid [55].

have to be provided for only insofar as they are necessary in order to reconcile the two fundamental rights.[158]

The Court then gave guidance on how the reconciliation mechanism encapsulated in Article 9 is to be applied. As regards the 'weight' that the two rights shall assume in the reconciliation exercise, it noted with reference to freedom of expression that notions that are related to that freedom, such as journalism, are to be interpreted broadly. Regarding privacy, it stated that the derogations/limitations relating to data protection as contained in the DPD must only apply insofar as strictly necessary.[159] Furthermore, the Court offered some clarification[160] on the meaning of 'solely for journalistic purposes', noting three points: first, Article 9 applies not only to media undertakings but also to every person engaged in journalism;[161] second, the fact that a publication is made for profit-making purposes does not mean that it is not made 'solely for journalistic purposes'; third, account must be taken of the evolution and proliferation of methods of communication, so that the medium that is used to transmit the data 'is not determinative' as to whether an activity is undertaken 'solely for journalistic purposes'.[162] From these considerations, it concluded that if the sole objective of the activities at issue is 'disclosure to the public of information, opinions or ideas', it would fall under that notion. Whether this is the case is for the national court to determine.[163]

In this case—once again—the Court seemed to be quite reluctant to engage in an assessment so as to offer a detailed account of how the clash of fundamental rights should be resolved. The lack of guidance is not manifested to the same degree as in the *Promusicae* case; this is not surprising, since in *Satamedia* a conflict between the specific rights at issue was predicted and specifically addressed in the Directive. In Article 9, the legislature laid down the obligation (and not only the possibility) to derogate from the provisions of this instrument if two conditions are met. The first one serves to define the scope of the right to freedom of expression, which falls under that provision, and is more limited than the scope of Article 10 ECHR. The second one is to stipulate that the concept/principle of 'necessity' needs to be satisfied for the derogation to apply.

In line with ECHR reasoning, the legislator clarified that the right to data privacy as contained in the DPD has to be restricted to the extent that a legitimate aim is pursued (here journalistic purposes or artistic/literary expression), but only if the restriction is necessary for pursuing that aim (the Court also reading into this clause the term 'strictly' necessary).

On the basis provided for by the legislature, the Court's interpretation was a rather modest intervention, leaving the substantive assessment of the question whether the situation fell within Article 9 DPD to the domestic court. The result is that the Court gave detailed guidance only in relation to the first of the two conditions, which have to be met for Article 9 DPD to be applicable, ie, it clarified the meaning of 'journalistic activities' and held that this concept is to be interpreted broadly. It did not take any stance on (and indeed did not even mention) the meaning of necessity in this context, which contains the obligation to balance the two conflicting rights by applying the concept of proportionality. This is to be

[158] ibid.
[159] ibid [56].
[160] ibid [58]–[61].
[161] ibid [58].
[162] ibid [60].
[163] ibid [62].

contrasted with the Court's ruling in *Huber*,[164] where it was held (in relation to Art 7(e) DPD—listing the situations in which data processing may be lawful)—that the concept of necessity contained therein has an independent meaning in Community law that cannot vary between the Member States. The explanation given for this approach was the need to ensure an equivalent level of protection in all Member States.

In the case at issue, however, one can observe again the Court's reluctance to provide for substantive answers when the reconciliation of the right to data privacy with another conflicting fundamental right is at stake. At this point an attempt will be made to explain the Court's approach.

iii. Making Sense of the Court's Abstaining Approach (or Not)

Advocate General Kokott's Opinion in *Satamedia* is particularly helpful when attempting to explain the Court's stance, as she urged the Court to afford the national court a wide margin of appreciation. She drew her conclusion by reviewing the CJEU's case law on conflicts between fundamental rights (and fundamental freedoms) and observed that the Court has sometimes been reluctant to spell out detailed guidance on how the reconciliation exercise between conflicting interests is to be resolved.[165] This is particularly so where data protection is concerned. However, in other instances, it has offered strict scrutiny ('intensive Prüfung').[166] According to the Advocate General, the Court adopts the latter approach in cases concerning predominantly transnational activities, and when active union citizens in transnational situations are concerned, the Court's interference will be particularly intensive. In deciding which approach should prevail in the situation before her, the Advocate General observed that with respect to the DPD, after *Österreichischer Rundfunk*, it is established that purely internal situations are also covered by the Directive.[167] From this she concluded that transnational activities are only exceptionally protected. Consequently, in view of 'the wide scope of the Directive, which (according to the Advocate General) almost goes beyond the establishment and functioning of the internal market', the Court—when balancing colliding fundamental rights in the context of the DPD—should afford a wide margin of appreciation to the Member States.

The Advocate General's position seems to follow logically. Nonetheless, it sits rather uncomfortably against the following contemplations. First, Directive 95/46—at its core is a harmonising measure '*intended … to ensure that the level of protection of the rights and freedoms of individuals with regard to the processing of personal data is equivalent in all Member States* [recital 8]' (emphasis added).[168] 'Thus, it has been held that the harmonisation of those national laws is not limited to minimum harmonisation but

[164] *Heinz Huber*, above n 40, [52].

[165] Reference is made to the following cases: *Promusicae*, above n 39; *Österreichischer Rundfunk*, above n 31; Case C-368/95 *Vereinigte Familiapress Zeitungverlag- und Vertriebs GmbH v Heinrich Bauer Verlag* [1997] ECR I-3689; Case C-36/02 *Omega Spielhallen- und Automatenaufstellung v Oberbürgermeisterin der Bundesstadt Bonn* [2004] ECR I-9609; Case C-244/06 *Dynamik Medien* [2008] ECR I-9609; and Case C-112/00 *Eugen Schmidberge Internationale Transporte und Planzüge v Republic of Austria* [2003] ECR I-5659.

[166] *Laval*, above n 42; *Viking*, above n 41; and Case C-265/95 *Commission v France* [1997] ECR I-6959 are cited.

[167] *Österreichischer Rundfunk*, above n 31, [42] ('the applicability of Directive 95/46 cannot depend on whether the specific situations at issue … have a sufficient link with the exercise of the fundamental freedoms guaranteed by the Treaty').

[168] *Heinz Huber*, above n 40, [50].

amounts to harmonisation which is generally complete.'[169] By shifting the resolution of conflicts between the right to data privacy and other fundamental rights to the Member State level, the objective of equivalent protection is liable to be frustrated by the different national solutions to the problem of reconciliation.

Second, the core element of the Advocate General's reasoning—transposing the rationale of the level of scrutiny that the Court applies in the free movement case law when conflicting fundamental rights are at stake to the level of scrutiny that should be applicable when it interprets the provisions of the relevant harmonisation measures—is problematic. It suggests that the Court may interpret the same provision differently in different contexts. This is dangerous in relation to a *harmonisation* measure, which will be applicable to all situations falling within its scope, irrespective of what position they will assume on the spectrum of transnationality.

Advocate General Kokott did not seem to be concerned with this because she considered that the greatest number of situations falling under the Directive will be purely internal in view of its wide scope (as noted above, applicability of the Directive does not depend on whether the situation at issue has a sufficient link with one of the fundamental freedoms).[170] The Advocate General appeared to be saying that a few situations, which, even though truly transnational still escaped the Court's (normally) strict scrutiny, can be traded off against the many situations where the Court should take a reserved stance. However, even if one was to agree with such a trade-off, a problem remains: how is an assessment to be made on the question whether a situation is or is not transnational (as that is a prerequisite for making the statement that transnational situations are only exceptionally covered by the Directive, as she does)? After all, the reason why the Court gave a wide definition to the scope of the Directive is precisely that difficulty. In its own words:

> A contrary interpretation [to the one that applicability of the DPD does not depend on an actual link with the exercise of fundamental freedoms] could make the limits of the field of application of the directive particularly unsure and uncertain, which would be contrary to its essential objective of approximati[on].[171]

The observations made thus far demonstrate that an explanation of the Court's reserved stance in solving fundamental rights clashes arising within the scope of EU harmonisation measures cannot be easily provided for by pointing out the Court's apparent logic for doing so in its fundamental freedoms case law.

Perhaps an answer is to be found by searching for more theoretical responses, which could be viewed as underpinning the Court's approach. One such attempt has been undertaken by Bignami.[172] For her, the question of how much discretion/margin of appreciation should be left to the Member States when clashing fundamental rights are concerned is a problem that can be formulated along the lines of intolerant constitutional patriotism versus constitutional pluralism/constitutional tolerance thinking. In essence,[173] the former

[169] ibid [51]; see also Case C-101/01 *Criminal Proceedings against Bodil Lindqvist* [2003] ECR I-12971 [96] (hereinafter *Lindqvist*).

[170] *Österreichischer Rundfunk*, above n 31, [42].

[171] ibid.

[172] Bignami, above n 76.

[173] Admittedly, the following account can be qualified as oversimplified. However, to provide a detailed exposition of the complex theory surrounding the two concepts would go beyond the scope of this chapter. Hence, the concepts are used as presented by the author discussed. For an overview of different ways in which constitutional

concept[174] embraces the idea that 'it is possible to root … European citizenship in a set of commonly held ideals [contained in a constitution and experienced as part of a constitutional culture] about the right and good mode of conducting life in a human community'.[175] The problem with this approach is, according to its critics, that it can trigger intolerance towards those that do not adhere to the particular common set of beliefs/values of the constitutional patriots.[176] This is seen as particularly problematic in the European context since intolerance towards diversity undermines the European constitutional system, which is firmly based on constitutional tolerance. That tolerance, as authors like Weiler[177] contend, is (inter alia) manifested in the European judicial dialogue. On the one hand, the Member States accept the pronouncements of the Court and hence subordinate themselves to the will of other political communities,[178] while on the other hand, the Court also defers to the views of the national courts.[179] The conclusion is that 'the European constitutional order is intrinsically pluralist, and any effort to impose a hegemonic belief system in the interest of constitutional patriotism would be antithetical to the character of Europe'.[180]

Our main concern lies with the position that deference to national courts assumes in this theory (at least for Bignami). In discussing the particular example of the right to privacy clashing with the right to freedom of expression at the European level, Bignami asserts that the deference doctrine is key to resolving the tension between constructing a supranational constitutional order on the one hand and respecting national constitutionalism on the other.[181] Since 'The European constitutional order is still too thin to settle many of the heated conflicts among rights-holders that emerge routinely at the national level',[182] the Court adopts the correct approach in affirming that the right to (data) privacy is a principle which is respected at the EU level, yet leaves the substantive task of balancing it with a conflicting right to the national court. The paradigm case, which is discussed in order to illustrate that the Court follows such a 'correct approach', is *Lindqvist*.[183]

It is worth taking a closer look at this judgment as it involved a challenge to the DPD itself on the basis that it infringes the right to freedom of expression. The case concerned information that was communicated through a personal website that Mrs Lindqvist set up for the benefit of her work as a catechist in her local parish in Sweden, as she wanted to allow parishioners preparing for their confirmation to be able to obtain information they might need.[184] The pages contained information about Mrs Lindqvist as well as her

pluralism can be conceived, see M Avblelij and J Komárek (eds), 'Four Visions of Constitutional Pluralism', EUI Working Papers Law 2008/21.

[174] Which could also be classified as a sub-form of civic nationalism; see J-W Müller, 'Three Objections to Constitutional Patriotism' (2007) 14 *Constellations* 197, 201, as cited in Bignami, above n 76.

[175] Bignami, above n 76 216.

[176] ibid.

[177] ibid 217.

[178] See JHH Weiler, 'In Defence of the Status Quo: Europe's Constitutional Sonderweg' in JHH Weiler and M Wind (eds), *European Constitutionalism Beyond The State* (Cambridge, Cambridge University Press, 2003) 7–23, as cited in Bignami, above n 76.

[179] F Bignami, 'Creating European Rights: National Values and Supranational Interests' (2005) 11 *Columbia Journal of European Law* 241, 272 and 279, as cited in Bignami, above n 76.

[180] Bignami, above n 76, 217–18.

[181] ibid 245.

[182] ibid 214.

[183] *Lindqvist*, above n 169.

[184] ibid [12].

colleagues in the parish, the content of which included jobs, hobbies, family circumstances and telephone numbers.[185] In one case she also stated that one colleague had injured her foot and was therefore on half-time leave,[186] which constitutes sensitive data under the DPD. Mrs Lindqvist had not informed her colleagues or acquired their consent, nor did she inform the Swedish data protection authority, but removed the pages promptly when her colleagues objected.[187] The public prosecutor brought an action against her for breach of the Swedish law on personal data (implementing the DPD). She was prosecuted and fined under that law. On appeal, the Swedish court referred several questions relating to the interpretation of the DPD.

In its sixth question it asked whether in a case such as that in front of it, the provisions of the DPD 'bring about a restriction which conflicts with the freedom of expression or other freedoms and rights, which are applicable within the [EU] and enshrined in inter alia Article 10 ECHR'.[188] The Court's reply to this provided for a precedent of deference, which was relied upon in the *Promusicae* judgment.

The Court first noted that the twin objectives of the Directive—free flow of data and safeguarding the fundamental rights of individuals—may be inconsistent with one another.[189] The mechanisms allowing those different rights and interests to be balanced are, first, contained in the directive itself and, second, result from the adoption of the national implementing provisions and their application by the national authorities.[190] This phrasing, it will be recalled, was subsequently followed in identical terms in *Promusicae*.

Next, the Court stated that the provisions are framed in general terms, but that even though 'the Member States have a margin for manoeuvre in implementing [the DPD] … there is nothing to suggest that the regime it provides for lacks predictability or that its provisions are, as such, contrary to the general principles of Community law and, in particular, to the fundamental rights protected by the Community legal order'.[191]

The conclusion is the same as in *Promusicae*. It is for the national authorities and courts to ensure a fair balance between the rights and interests in question and that 'they do not rely on an interpretation of it which would be in conflict with the fundamental rights protected by the Community legal order or with the other general principles of Community law, such as inter alia the principle of proportionatily'.[192] It is in view of this precedent that a commentator was led to infer that the ruling in *Promusicae* is 'unsurprising', that it 'makes perfect sense' and that it 'is not really new',[193] since it is based on the previous *Lindqvist* judgment.

For the advocates of constitutional pluralism, this deference to the national court is to be welcomed and is hailed as one that tolerates constitutional diversity. Arguably—and this is to reinforce the argument—it has also been applied in the fundamental freedoms case law, namely in *Omega*,[194] albeit in a different form, that is, not shifting the question of balancing

[185] ibid [13].
[186] ibid.
[187] ibid [14].
[188] ibid [72].
[189] ibid [79].
[190] ibid [82].
[191] ibid [85].
[192] ibid [87].
[193] X Groussot, 'Rock the KaZaA: Another Clash of Fundamental Rights' (2008) 45 *Common Market Law Review* 1745, at 1758.
[194] *Omega*, above n 165.

back to the domestic court, but accepting its views on the matter. In that way, the national standard providing for a specific outcome of the conflicting interests is transformed into the EU standard. In this case, the national (German) court was afforded a 'margin of discretion' in assessing whether a restriction to the free movement of services was justified in the public interest of protecting human dignity, a constitutionally protected right in Germany.[195] The Court of Justice noted that: 'It is not indispensable … for the restrictive measure issued by the authorities of a Member State to correspond to a conception shared by all Member States as regards the precise way in which the fundamental right or legitimate interest in question is to be protected.'[196] In adjudicating on the justification of the restriction (proportionality), it relied closely on the finding of the national court and held that the measure was justified.[197]

On the basis of this reasoning in *Omega*, it appears that: 'The Court found that it is *not* necessary that all Member States apply the same standard, even if it concerns a restriction of one of the fundamental economic freedoms.'[198] Hence, this variation (from Member State to Member State) of the EU standard of fundamental rights protection leads to the result that: 'To this extent, the autonomous EU standard is not autonomous at all.'[199]

Does the discussion thus far lead to the inevitable conclusion that the same must apply to the right to data privacy? As a matter of the Court's case law and therefore at a purely descriptive level, this is indeed the case. Based on the cases discussed above, there does not seem to be an autonomous EU standard of the right to data privacy to the extent that it clashes with other fundamental rights. However, the assertion that this *ought to* be the case based on a theory of constitutional pluralism, as presented above, is questionable.

This emerges from the following: the theory of constitutional pluralism, when used as a legitimisation for the Court's deferring stance, faces the same problem as already mentioned above with respect to Advocate General Kokott's explanations—that is, the rationale for harmonising the right to data privacy.

The reason why Article 114 TFEU (ex Art 95 EC) constitutes a legitimate legal basis for the EU's data protection regime is that it is aimed at harmonising *disparate* national standards of data protection, which are seen as liable to hinder the establishment and functioning of the internal market. Respecting constitutional diversity—which in itself is a laudable idea—must be limited when legislation aimed at complete harmonisation of the protection of a fundamental right is adopted under this specific legal basis. This is because that diversity is the very reason for EU intervention in the first place. The Court is not free to be tolerant of constitutional diversity to the same degree when it is called to interpret a harmonising legislative instrument as when it decides cases dealing with the free movement provisions. Consequently (here again), references to that latter type of case law in support of the pronouncement that 'on tough constitutional questions … the Court of Justice [rightly] gives precedence to national constitutionalism'[200] are not very helpful.[201]

195 ibid [31].

196 ibid [37].

197 ibid [39].

198 LB and JHR, 'The Relative Autonomy of the EU Human Rights Standard' (2008) 4 *European Constitutional Law Review* 199, 204.

199 ibid.

200 Bignami, above n 76, 237.

201 The validity of Bignami's statement is contestable when taking account of the *Viking*, above n 41 and *Laval*, above n 42, cases, where the Court did *not* adopt a deferential stance despite ruling on the 'tough constitutional question' of balancing the right to take collective action on the one hand and market rights on the other.

A contrary argument would go as follows: the EU legislature has reached quite an extensive level of harmonisation, *but at a general level only.* It has done so by guaranteeing the right to data privacy 'through prophylactic protection',[202] including the conferral on data subjects of specific rights in relation to their personal data, the imposition of specific obligations on data controllers, the obligation on Member States to establish a supervisory mechanism etc (see the discussion in section III.A). It therefore constitutes a 'centralized regulatory framework designed to achieve transparency, accountability and consistency in the application of the rules governing the collection, processing and distribution of data'.[203] If this is in fact achieved, the diversity arising in the limited context of a restriction of the right to data privacy by a conflicting fundamental right might not be sufficient to justify a claim that the entire regime is ineffective in contributing to the establishment and functioning of the internal market, whilst achieving a high level of data protection. In essence, the argument would be that the overall regime achieves enough harmonisation, so that some scope of diversity for constitutionally sensitive issues is affordable.

This proposition could, however, be dismissed because of the simple premise that the 'limited' context of clashing fundamental rights is not so limited after all. It is inherent in the very nature of data protection that it will conflict with freedom of expression and, as *Lindqvist* proves, the entire data protection regime can be challenged on that ground. This is also true with respect to the protection of IP rights where one of the biggest problems faced is the conflict with the right to data privacy.[204]

Therefore, if national laws relating to the protection of fundamental rights are aimed at being fully harmonised in view of the fact that their divergence is detrimental to the establishment and functioning of the internal market, it is difficult to maintain that an important source for this national divergence—different definitions/solutions for how fundamental rights relate to each other—can be tolerated.

In any case, by reserving to itself the last word on whether the national balances between fundamental rights that come within the scope of EU law are in compliance with EU fundamental rights, it seems that the Court has only postponed rather than truly deferred the issue.

iv. A New Direction in the Case Law Away from Abstention?

a. Clashing Fundamental Rights in Clashing Directives: Data Protection (and Freedom of Expression/Information as well as Freedom to Conduct a Business) versus Intellectual Property Rights

Perhaps aware of the difficulties examined above, the Court subsequently and for the first time gave some further—albeit once again cautious—guidance in a situation resembling the *Promusicae* scenario. In *Bonnier Audio AB*,[205] the applicants held exclusive rights in the

202 WJ Long and M Pang Quek, 'Personal Data Privacy Protection in an Age of Globalization: The US-EU Safe Harbor Compromise' (2002) 9 *Journal of European Public Policy* 325, p 331.

203 R Wong and J Savirimuthu, 'All or Nothing: This is the Question? The Application of Art 3(2) Data Protection Directive 95/46/EC to the Internet' (2008) 25 *John Marshall Journal of Computer & Information Law* 241, 243.

204 Germany, for instance, was reluctant to implement the IP enforcement directive because it considered it to conflict with German data protection rules.

205 Case C-461/10 *Bonnier Audio AB et al v Perfect Communication Sweden AB* EU:C:2012:219.

reproduction, publication and distribution of audiobooks and claimed that their rights had been infringed through file sharing on the Internet. They applied for an injunction against Perfect Communications Sweden AB ('e-Phone'), ordering the disclosure of data (more specifically, the name and address of persons using the Internet Protocol address from which it is assumed that the files in question were sent). The injunction was granted and e-Phone opposed this in the main proceedings. In this case, the Member State concerned had decided to lay down an obligation to communicate personal data for the purposes of civil proceedings, something that was legitimate under the interpretation of the e-Privacy Directive read in conjunction with the IP enforcement Directive, as provided for in *Promusicae* and *LSG-Gesellschaft*.

The Court held that the national legislation in question 'must be regarded as *likely, in principle, to ensure a fair balance* between the protection of intellectual property rights enjoyed by copyright holders and the protection of personal data enjoyed by internet subscribers or users' (emphasis added).[206] This was because a disclosure order required:[207]

1. '[T]hat there be clear evidence of an infringement of an intellectual property right';
2. '[T]hat the information can be regarded as facilitating the investigation into an infringement of copyright or impairment of such a rights';
3. '[T]hat the reasons for the measure outweigh the nuisance or other harm which the measure may entail for the person affected by it or for some other conflicting interest'.

Since the national law provided for these requirements, the Court could attribute to it the characteristic that seems to be decisive, namely, that the law enables the national court 'to weigh the conflicting interests involved, on the basis of the facts of each case and taking due account of the requirements of the principle of proportionality'.[208] So the substantive outcome of that balancing exercise is not touched upon here, only the fact that the national law allows for balancing. It is probably for this reason that the Court does not accept such law unconditionally as being in compliance with EU law, but introduced somehow awkwardly the caveated terms 'likely' and 'in principle'. What this means in practice, however, is, again, that the national court is left with little concrete guidance as to what such 'fair balance' should entail.

Having said that, two further recent cases are worth mentioning where the Court did not leave the substantive outcome of balancing to national courts, but held that the injunction at issue (again for the enforcement of intellectual property rights) would not strike a fair balance between the protection of intellectual property on the one hand and the opposing fundamental rights involved, including the freedom to conduct a business, data protection as well as the right to receive and impart information on the other.

Scarlet Extended[209] concerned an injunction requesting the defendant party to put a system in place for filtering all electronic communications passing through its services, particularly those using file-sharing software. The proposed system applied indiscriminately to all its customers, as a preventive measure, and operated exclusively at the defendant's own expense and for an unlimited period. The Court noted that such an injunction would

[206] ibid [60].
[207] ibid [58].
[208] ibid [59].
[209] Case C-70/10 *Scarlet Extended v SABAM* (*SABAM*) EU:C:2011:771 (hereinafter *Scarlet Extended*).

'require active observation of all electronic communications conducted on the network of the ISP [Internet Service Provider] concerned and, consequently, would encompass all information to be transmitted and all customers using that network'.[210] Hence, it concluded that this would amount to a general monitoring obligation, which is prohibited under the e-Commerce Directive.[211] This could have already been the end of the matter. One could argue that this was the legislature's solution between the conflicting interests when adopting the e-Commerce Directive, which, according to the explicit wording in its Preamble, is aimed at ensuring the free movement of information society services, which in turn 'can in many cases be a specific reflection in [then] Community law of a more general principle, namely freedom of expression as enshrined in Article 10(1) [ECHR]'.[212] The Court, however, deemed it necessary to continue and also assess the injunction in broader fundamental rights terms. In this context, it brought the freedom to conduct a business (Art 16 CFR) into play, which (unlike privacy and freedom of expression as protected under the ECHR) was not put forward in the referring question. The clash between this right and intellectual property was the key fundamental rights conflict identified by the Court between the parties to the proceedings. The balance was struck in favour of the defendant ISP, whose fundamental rights would have been 'seriously infringed'. This was because '[the injuction] would require that ISP to install a *complicated, costly*, permanent computer system *at its own expense*, which would also be contrary to the conditions laid down in Article 3(1) of Directive 2004/48, which requires that measures to ensure the respect of intellectual-property rights should not be unnecessarily complicated or costly' (emphasis added).[213]

In essence, the Court is saying that the enforcement of the interests of IP rights-holders, which are in essence financial, cannot impose a disproportionate financial and administrative burden on the intermediary (the ISP). In doing so, it seems to be merely applying the balance already encapsulated in Directive 2004/48. Therefore, the Court did no more than it would have done had it merely relied on the provisions of the instruments, without characterising this as a fundamental rights exercise. It then proceeded to deal with the fundamental rights clashes identified in the preliminary reference, namely, again on the one side, those of IP rights-holders and, on the other side, the data protection and freedom of expression rights of the ISP's customers—the alleged perpetrators of IP rights. Interestingly, no detailed assessment was undertaken. The Court only pointed out that the named rights *may* be infringed,[214] and yet its overall finding was that there was no fair balance struck between IP rights and the other two rights. Regarding data protection, the Court noted that the injunction 'would involve a systematic analysis of all content and the collection and identification of users' IP addresses from which unlawful content on the network is sent. These addresses are protected personal data because they allow those users to be precisely identified'.[215]

Moreover, the system might not be able to distinguish adequately between lawful and unlawful content, thereby also interfering with freedom of expression (or, more precisely,

[210] ibid [39].
[211] ibid [40].
[212] Directive 2000/31/EC, above n 129.
[213] *Scarlet* Extended, above n 209, [48].
[214] ibid [50]–[52].
[215] ibid [51].

'freedom of information').[216] The Court then acknowledged that what is 'lawful' content will of course vary from Member State to Member State. The same variation exists with regard to works that in some Member States are considered to fall within the public domain.[217] Therefore, it might not be surprising that no further concrete analysis was provided.

The main reasoning in *Scarlet Extended* has also been applied to *SABAM v Netlog*.[218] This case concerned an injunction sought against the owner of a social networking platform (Netlog) obliging him to introduce a system for filtering information stored on its platform in order to prevent files which infringe copyright being made available. The system was again costly, complicated, permanent and at Netlog's own expense. The Court's answer was thus predictable: repeating the findings in *Scarlet Extended* almost verbatim,[219] it held that such an injunction would not strike a fair balance between, on the one hand, the protection of IP rights enjoyed by the copyright holders and, on the other hand, the freedom to conduct a business, the protection of personal data and the right to receive or impart information.

The fact that the Court has given a concrete answer to these cases is to be welcomed. However, one should be cautious in concluding on this limited basis that it has already altered its deferential stance. These cases were in a sense easy not only because they concerned the imposition of *positive obligations* on intermediaries, which raises the bar for establishing proportionality, but also because with respect to the determining analysis of the clash between IP rights and the freedom to conduct a business, the criteria for conducting such assessment (ie, enforcement measures cannot be 'complicated' and 'costly') are stipulated in Directive 2004/48. It is certain that the Court will be faced with further preliminary questions in this line of case law. Any general conclusion will have to await these developments.

b. Clashing Fundamental Rights within the DPD: Data Protection ('the Right to be Forgotten') versus Freedom of Expression and the Freedom to Conduct a Business

One landmark decision indicating a new direction in the case law concerning conflicting fundamental rights within the DPD has been handed down most recently in *Google Spain*,[220] although it has to be stated from the outset, unlike in the previously discussed cases, that the Court did not *expressly* put the conflict in these terms.

In this case, the applicant, Mr Costeja González, complained, among other things, that he had the right to request from Google the removal of links that would appear upon typing his name into the search engine 'Google Search'. The links directed users to an online version of a newspaper article that would link his name to insolvency proceedings for the recovery of social security debts. Publication of the webpage was lawful and

[216] ibid [52].

[217] ibid.

[218] Case C-360/10 *Belgische Vereniging van Auteurs, Componisten en Uitgevers CVBA (SABAM) v Netlog NV* EU:C:2012:85.

[219] ibid [46]–[52].

[220] Case C-131/12 *Google Spain SL, Google Inc v Agencia Española de Protección de Datos (AEPD), Mario Costeja González* EU:C:2014:317.

the information contained therein was truthful. Mr González sought the removal of the link merely on the ground that he found the information prejudicial and wanted it 'to be forgotten'.

The Court agreed that such a right can exist under EU law. Even though it was left to the national court to apply the relevant EU test, the Court made clear that Mr González is very likely to fulfil the necessary requirements. In doing so, there seems to be a clear departure from the case law described above in sections III.C.i and III.C.ii. It will be recalled in that case law, the Court seemed to follow a pattern: it would (1) explicitly phrase the conflict at hand as a clash of fundamental rights; (2) those rights would need to be reconciled by 'striking a fair balance'; and (3) that would be a task left entirely to the national court. In this case, however, the Court seems to be doing the complete opposite.

This judgment has received much attention not only in data but also tech business circles, spawning the so-called 'right to be forgotten', as promoted by Commissioner Reding[221] and picked up by the mainstream media, and rendering it famous beyond the EU law scene. Yet it should be noted that the 'right to be forgotten' is not expressly mentioned in the Court's reasoning, although it is included in the referring question[222] and in the submissions to the Court.[223] The Advocate General, on the other hand, explicitly referred to this in his Opinion in order to conclude that the current DPD does not provide for such a right.[224]

Interestingly, the name of such a right is also not to be found in any currently binding law of the EU. It is contained in the Commission proposal for a new Data Protection Regulation (DPR) (as part of a broader new legislative data protection package, which is further discussed below),[225] but the wording has been abandoned at the first reading stage in the European Parliament. This was already the case at the moment the judgment was handed down. The relevant article used to read 'the right to be forgotten and to erasure' and now it only refers to 'the right to erasure'.[226]

The Explanatory Statement to the European Parliament legislative report[227] does not offer an explanation for the deletion of the 'right to be forgotten'; it merely states that this right should be read in light of the right to erasure and the right to rectification. A plausible

[221] See, eg, V Reding, 'The EU Data Protection Reform 2012: Making Europe the Standard Setter for Modern Data Protection Rules in the Digital Age', SPEECH/12/26, Press Release, http://europa.eu/rapid/press-release_SPEECH-12-26_en.htm; and European Parliament Debate on the Protection of individuals with regard to the processing of personal data—Processing of personal data for the purposes of crime prevention (11 March 2014) Procedure 2012/0011(COD), intervention by V Reding.

[222] *Google Spain*, above n 220, [20], question 3 and [89] (for an indirect reformulation by the Court of that question).

[223] ibid [90].

[224] ibid. See also Opinion of Advocate General Jääskinen at [22] and [109].

[225] Commission, Proposal for a Regulation of the European Parliament and of the Council on the Protection of Individuals with Regard to the Processing of Personal Data and on the Free Movement of Such Data (General Data Protection Regulation), (COM(2012) 11 final, 2012/0011 (COD)). Article 17 of this proposal reads 'right to be forgotten and right to erasure'.

[226] European Parliament Committee on Civil Liberties, Justice and Home Affairs, Report on the proposal for a regulation of the European Parliament and of the Council on the protection of individuals with regard to the processing of personal data and on the free movement of such data (COM(2012)0011–C-7-0025/2012–2012/011(COD)), A7-0402/2013 (22 November 2013). See especially Draft European Parliament Legislative Resolution Amendment 28, recital 54 and Amendment 122, Art 17.

[227] ibid.

reason for the deletion is the confusion as to what such a right actually entails or what it can realistically entail, as well as how it could be implemented and enforced.[228]

The Court ruled on the material and territorial scope of the Directive as well as on the responsibility of the operator and the data subjects' rights. As regards the first two, it suffices to say that Google Spain was qualified as a 'controller' 'processing personal data'[229] and fell within the territorial scope of the Directive.

The real interest of the present discussion concerns the latter two points (Questions 2c and 2d and 3 of the judgment). With respect to the extent of the responsibility of the operator, the Court commenced by setting out the legal framework. First, the right to erasure (Art 12(b) DPD), which the data subject may invoke against the controller (here Google),[230] applies not only when the data is inaccurate or incomplete, as listed in that Article. The Court held that this provision is non-exhaustive and that the right to erasure can also arise when other conditions of lawfulness of data processing, as spelled out in the DPD, are not observed.[231] These criteria for lawfulness are to be found in Article 6 DPD relating to the quality of data and in Article 7, which sets out the criteria for making data processing legitimate. Paragraph (f) of Article 7 is relevant in the present case. It provides that data may be processed only if it 'is necessary for the purposes of the legitimate interests pursued by the controller or by the third party or parties to whom the data are disclosed, except where such interests are overridden by the fundamental rights and freedoms of the data subject which require protection under Art 1(1)'. In other words, Article 7(f) allows the weighing of conflicting interests, although it should be noted that the provision does not expressly refer to the *fundamental rights* of the controller or third parties. A further relevant provision is Article 14(1)(a) DPD, which obliges Member States to grant the data subject the right to object to the processing of data relating to him at least in the cases referred to in Article 7(e) and (relevant for our case) (f).

Having set out the legal framework, the Court proceeded to its interpretation. First, it found *a serious interference* with the right to privacy and the protection of personal data in the given circumstances, given that the number of interconnected information received through a search via an engine based on one's name can lead to establishing 'a more or less detailed profile' of the data subject, something that would be very difficult to achieve in the absence of the search engine.[232] The effect of that interference is further heightened due to the importance of the Internet and search engines in modern society as well as its ability to render information ubiquitous.[233]

For the Court, the following results from this:

> [I]n light of the seriousness of the interference it is clear that it cannot be justified by merely the economic interest which the operator of such an engine has in that processing. However, in as

228 See also J Kühling, 'Rückkehr des Rechts: Verpflichtung von "Google und Co." zu Datenschutz' (2014) 14 *Europäische Zeitschrift für Wirtschaftsrecht* 527, 530 (pointing out that the term is more generally misleading); and ML Ambrose and J Ausloos, 'The Right to Be Forgotten across the Pond' (2013) *Journal of Information Policy* 1 (arguing that the Commission proposal seemed to be conflating two already known rights: the old *droit à l'oubli* (right to oblivion) and the right to erasure).

229 *Google Spain*, above n 220, [25]–[41].

230 The question as to whether Google was in fact a 'controller' was in itself a contentious question, but was answered in the affirmative by the Court (the Advocate General came to the opposite conclusion on that point).

231 *Google Spain*, above n 220, [70].

232 *Google Spain*, above n 220, [80].

233 ibid.

> much as the removal of links from the list of results could, depending on the information at issue, have effects upon the legitimate interest of internet users … a fair balance should be sought in particular between that interest and the data subject's fundamental rights under Articles 7 and 8 of the Charter. Whilst it is true that the data subject's rights protected by those articles also override, as a general rule, that interest of internet users, that balance may however depend, in specific cases, on the nature of the information in question and its sensitivity for the data subject's private life and on the interest of the public in having that information, an interest which may vary, in particular, according to the role played by the data subject in public life.[234]

This quoted passage is difficult to understand for three reasons. First, one would think that both the 'economic interest of the operator' and the 'legitimate interest of the Internet users' to receive information can be termed as fundamental rights, namely, the freedom to conduct a business (Art 16 CFR) and the right to receive information under freedom of expression (Art 11 CFR). Yet, unlike the case with data protection, the Court did not identify either of these as such, nor did it make a reference to the Charter as regards these two interests/rights.

Second, the language of the judgment suggests that the Court has attributed different weight to these two interests/rights. The economic interests of the operator are easily dismissed as not being sufficient to justify a serious interference with data protection and privacy rights. By contrast, the interests of Internet users shall be subjected to a 'fair balance'—the formula, it will be remembered, the Court of Justice of the EU—like the ECtHR– normally uses when conflicts of fundamental rights are at stake, in order to balance two equals.

Once one does term both of these 'interests' in question as 'fundamental rights', the obvious question arises: why should one fundamental right (freedom of expression) be subjected to a 'fair balance' test against data protection, but not the other one (freedom to conduct a business)? One answer could be that there is a normative hierarchy between fundamental rights and the freedom to conduct a business assumes a lower rank than freedom of expression in that hierarchy. That, however, would be difficult to sustain when read against *Sky Österreich*,[235] where the Court applied the 'fair balance' test precisely between these two fundamental rights, implying that they carry equal weight. Perhaps the reason for this differentiated treatment lies in the fact that the Court thought the scope of the freedom to conduct a business was not triggered at all, hence no reference to Article 16 CFR. But this should have been explained in the judgment. Moreover, the argument does not explain why there is no reference to Article 11 CFR, while at the same time the 'fair balance' formula is employed.

This leads to the third point. Even though reference is made to a 'fair balance' with regard to the 'legitimate interest of internet uses' it appears, at first sight at least, that the Court is not in fact applying this. This is because in a next step it articulates the presumption that the data subjects' rights *override as a general rule* that interest. This appears odd. The 'balance' does not seem to be fair at all, but rather strongly tilted towards the side of data protection/privacy rights of data subjects. The Court does not stop here, however. It establishes that the presumption can be rebutted. Determining conditions can be the nature of the information and its sensitivity for the data subject's private life, and the interest of the public in having that information, which may vary depending on the role of the data subject in public life.

[234] ibid [81].

[235] Case C-283/11 *Sky Österreich GmbH v Österreichischer Rundfunk* EU:C:2013:28.

These conditions are reminiscent of some of the criteria set out by the ECtHR for how to strike a 'fair balance' between the right to private life and freedom of expression, and, more specifically, press freedom in the two leading cases of *Von Hannover (No 2)* and *Axel Springer*,[236] even if in these cases the ECtHR—unlike the Court of Justice of the EU—expressly qualified the situation as one of two conflicting fundamental rights that deserve *equal* respect.

The ECtHR affords the Member States a wide margin of appreciation in balancing the conflicting rights. At the same time, it has identified six criteria that are relevant for the balancing exercise:[237]

a) the contribution to a debate of general interest;
b) how well known is the person concerned and what is the subject of the report?;
c) the prior conduct of the person concerned;
d) the method of obtaining the information and its veracity;
e) the content, form and consequences of the publication;
f) the severity of the sanction imposed (not listed in *Von Hannover*).

It is clear that the *Google Spain* criteria *are* contained in ECHR law, even though notably there is no reference whatsoever to the ECHR. However, it is also obvious that the list of the ECtHR is longer than what the Court pronounced here. In particular, it is difficult to see conditions (c), (d) and (f) being included in the Court's test. This may be explained by the factual difference of the ECtHR cases, which did not concern the online environment and in any case also did not concern the publisher itself.[238]

The Court did point out that it makes a crucial difference whether processing by a search engine or a web publisher is at issue. In the present situation, it noted that the express derogation from the data protection requirements can apply in the latter case 'when processing is carried out solely for journalistic purposes', as spelled out in Article 9 DPD, whereas it said that does not appear to be so in the former case.[239]

Article 9, it will be remembered, concerns the relationship between data protection and specific forms of freedom of expression, namely, journalistic expression as mentioned by the Court, but also (even though not mentioned) artistic and literary expression. For the Court, the journalistic expression derogation did not apply in the present case. Hence, receiving indexed links to webpages upon searching a name does not fall within the scope of the right to receive journalistic information here.

One could criticise this based on the fact that without a search engine, the right to receive journalistic (and in fact any kind of) information in an online environment becomes meaningless. Given the vast amounts of information on the Internet, the search engine becomes an indispensable portal for all users. However, the counter-argument would be that Google is not itself producing information/opinions/ideas, it is merely re-organising data. Moreover, typing the name in the search engine is only one means of accessing that data.

[236] *Von Hannover v Germany (No 2)*, App Nos 40660/08 and 60641/08 (ECtHR, 7 February 2012); and *Axel Springer AG v Germany*, App No 39954/08 (ECtHR, 7 February 2012).

[237] *Axel Springer*, above n 236, [90]–[95].

[238] In *Axel Springer*, the legality of an injunction against republication of an article about a celebrity was at stake, whereas in *Von Hannover (No 2)*, it was the legality of an injunction against any further publication of celebrity photographs that had already appeared in a German magazine.

[239] *Google Spain*, above n 220, [85].

The particular information itself would be available and could be retrieved not only when searching the newspaper's website but also when searching other terms in Google. Practically speaking, typing into a search engine terms like 'insolvency' and/or the name of the newspaper could lead to the same results as if one were to type the name of the applicant. At the same time, it would prevent an easy means to create a more or less complete profile of a person based on a search of his or her name.

The distinction between processing by a web publisher as opposed to a search engine is important in a further respect according to the Court: the grounds under Article 7 DPD, which make processing legitimate, may not coincide, but also, if they do so, the substantive balance under Articles 7(f) and 14(1)(a) DPD can vary. This is so because both the legitimate interests and the consequences of the processing for the data subject can be different.[240]

For the Court, the latter is indeed so in the present case. Since Google-searching a name makes it much easier to access the personal information and facilitates dissemination thereof, this is considered a more significant interference than publication of the information on the webpage. Thus, the conclusion is reached that in order to comply with the DPD:

> [A]nd in so far as the conditions laid down [by Articles 12(b) and 14(1)(a) DPD] are in fact satisfied, the operator of a search engine is obliged to remove from the list of results displayed following a search made on the basis of a person's name links to web pages, published by third parties and containing information relating to that person, also in a case where that name or information is not erased beforehand or simultaneously from those web pages, and even, as the case may be, when its publication in itself on those pages is lawful.[241]

The Court then turned to the final question, namely, whether the same provisions under the same circumstances enable the data subject to require the operator of a search engine to remove the links to webpages published lawfully by third parties and containing true information 'on the ground that that information may be prejudicial to him or that he wishes it to be "forgotten" after a certain time'.

The Court repeated its interpretation of Article 12(b) and recalled when reading it against Article 6(1)(c)–(e) DPD that 'even initially lawful processing of accurate data may, in the course of time, become incompatible with the directive where those data are no longer necessary in the light of the purposes for which they were collected or processed. That is so in particular where they appear to be inadequate, irrelevant or no longer relevant, or excessive in relation to those purposes and in the light of the time that has elapsed'.[242] Therefore, if data is incompatible with the Directive based on the above-described grounds, that information as well as the links appearing in a list of (here Google) search results would have to be erased.[243] The Court further noted that the processing of data must be authorised under Article 7 DPD for the entire period during which it is carried out.[244] Next, it stated that in order to have a right such as that invoked by Mr González, it is not necessary that the information included in the list of result causes prejudice to the data subject.[245]

240 ibid [86].
241 ibid [88].
242 ibid [93].
243 ibid [94].
244 ibid [95].
245 ibid [96].

In its next step, the Court repeated its general test, which sets out the balance that is to be struck between the conflicting rights and interests: the data subject's rights (contained in Articles 7 and 8 CFR) override, as a rule, the economic interest of the search engine operator and the interest of the public in finding that information through typing the name in the search engine, unless there is 'a preponderant interest of the general public in having, on account of inclusion in the list of results, access to the information in question'.[246] When applying the above test to the facts of the case, it concluded:

> [H]aving regard to the sensitivity for the data subject's private life of the information contained in those announcements and to the fact that its initial publication had taken place 16 years earlier, the data subject establishes a right that that information should no longer be linked to his name by means of such a list.

Therefore, and as there does not seem to be 'a preponderant interest of the public' in this case, which, however, is still left for the national court to establish, removal of the links from the list of search results can be required by the data subject.[247]

It is clear that the Court of Justice of the EU guided the national court very closely, in essence directing it to the conclusion that under the present circumstances, the applicant had the right to request erasure of the said links from Google. As already stated above, this marks a clear departure from the deferent approach identified in previous case law. In this instance, the balance was struck in favour of data protection.

Some commentators have criticised the judgment for getting the balance wrong or for not balancing at all.[248] However, at a closer look, it appears—at least as regards the interests of internet users/freedom of expression—the Court did balance according to ECHR criteria and was careful to formulate the outcome in very narrowly defined circumstances that are particular to the present case.

Two problematic aspects remain, however. The first concerns the pronounced presumption that data protection overrides, as a rule, the interests of Internet users. This is obviously problematic as soon as the situation falls within freedom of expression (the Charter does not suggest any hierarchy between the two). Moreover, it seems particularly unnecessary given that the Court has recourse to ECHR criteria in order to balance the two interests/fundamental rights at stake. Second, the fact that the interests conflicting with data protection are not qualified as fundamental rights is questionable. This is so even if—as suggested above—one views such balance as justifiable from a freedom of expression perspective and if there might be good reasons to not bring the situation within the freedom to conduct a business. As regards the latter, given the novelty of and scarcity of case law on this right combined with the fact that no guidance can be found in ECHR law (and indeed little of it in national constitutional law), more explanation would have been due.

Without wanting to take away from the positive development that the Court made a first clear move away from deference in this line of case law, one cannot help but wonder about the weaknesses in the judgment. One cannot help but think that the Court wanted

[246] ibid [97].
[247] ibid [98].
[248] See, eg, the blog posts of S Peers, 'Google Spain and the EU's Data Protection Directive', http://inforrm.wordpress.com/2014/05/16/google-spain-and-the-eus-data-protection-directive-steve-peers; and G Vassal-Adams, 'Case Comment', http://eutopialaw.com/2014/05/16/case-comment-google-spain-sl-google-inc-v-agencia-espanola-de-proteccion-de-datos-mario-costeja-gonzalez/#more-2455.

to demonstrate just how seriously it is taking data protection. In this context, it must have been influenced by the sensitive position that data protection has taken in the public eye in recent times and most prominently due to the 'Prism-Tempora-Snowden' affair. One commentator even observed that in times where the enforceability of data protection on the Internet is being called into question, in a double-strike (the other case being the *Data Retention* judgment discussed below) the Court restored the 'rule of data protection law'.[249] It might have been just this impression that the Court wanted to give to the outside world.

In the meantime, as a reaction to this judgment, Google has introduced special forms that allow data subjects to request erasure of links.[250] Less than two months after the judgment had been handed down, the press reported that some 50,000 removal requests had been filed with Google.[251] This appears to demonstrate a more than negligible public interest, even if the numbers might not be impressive when compared to the amount of copyright removal requests (driven by the economic interests of the media and recording industries)[252] that Google receives on a weeklybasis.[253]

To be sure, even if the judgment can be embraced as one that has brought the right to data protection closer to an autonomous definition at the EU level, one may question the extent to which it is de facto capable of bringing about an enhanced level of data protection, given the difficulties relating to the territorial application of the Directive. However, this only demonstrates the limits of attempting to regulate a global medium and its operators regionally.

IV. REGULATING RESTRICTIONS TO DATA PROTECTION: THE (INVALIDATED) DATA RETENTION DIRECTIVE 2006/24/EC

The European legislature has not only attempted to set an EU standard of data privacy, but it had also enacted an EU regime for harmonising a restriction to this right. Acting on an internal market legal basis, it had in quite some detail defined the extent to which the right should be encroached upon (Europe-wide) in order to pursue the investigation, detection and prosecution of serious crime, as defined by each Member State in its national law. An EU balance was thereby struck between the protection of the right and the named (EU) public interest.

The instrument setting up this regime was the DRD,[254] a controversial piece of legislation that was struck down in the *Digital Rights Ireland* judgment (discussed further below).[255]

[249] Kühling, above n 228, 527 ('Mit einem Doppelschlag hat der EuGH nicht weniger als die' Herrschaft des Datenschutzrechts 'wiederhergestellt').

[250] Google, 'Search Removal Request under Data Protection Law in Europe', https://support.google.com/legal/contact/lr_eudpa?product=websearch.

[251] L Sandoval, 'Google Deletes Search Result in Europe, Abides by "Right to Be Forgotten Rule"', Tech Times, www.techtimes.com/articles/9370/20140630/google-deletes-search-results-in-europe-abides-by-right-to-be-forgotten-rule.htm.

[252] For statistics on copyright owners and reporting organisations, see www.google.com/transparency report/removals/copyright/reporters/?r=last-month.

[253] Google receives 12,000,000 weekly requests to remove URLs due to alleged copyright infringements. For relevant statistics, see www.google.com/transparencyreport/removals/copyright.

[254] DRD, above n 5.

[255] *Digital Rights Ireland*, above n 7.

The Commission's Explanatory Memorandum[256] provided as grounds for proposing this instrument the following: due to changes in business models and service offerings (flat rates, free e-communications services etc) in the electronic communications sector (networks and services), operators no longer store traffic data. This in turn was considered as problematic from the point of view of combating organised crime and terrorism. The Memorandum[257] also explicitly states the background against which this proposal has to be seen, namely, the Madrid bombings in 2004 and the following call of the European Council on the Council to examine proposals for rules on data retention. This was confirmed in a subsequent European Council and Justice and Home Affairs Council meeting of July 2005 after the London bombings. The key motivation for adopting this proposal is thus clear, but, of course, the Commission also provided the internal market argument: a number of Member States had either already or were about to adopt legislation for data retention purposes. Under these circumstances, it is explained, it was 'urgent'[258] to adopt harmonising measures at the EU level on the matter.

The DRD's essential function was to harmonise possible Member State action under Article 15(1) of the e-Privacy Directive. This provision allows Member States to restrict the data confidentiality obligations laid down in the Directive for various purposes, including the one named above, if necessary, appropriate and proportionate within a democratic society (the conditions for justifying a restriction to Art 8 ECHR). With the advent of the DRD, this legal permissibility was transformed into an obligation to retain data, according to the rules specified therein. Thus, with the entry into force of the DRD, Article 15(1) of the e-Privacy Directive did not apply to data required by the former named Directive. That is obviously no longer the case after *Digital Rights Ireland*.

To the extent that the European legislature had removed from the Member States the margin of discretion for deciding whether and to what extent this right can be restricted for combating serious crime, it had made a step forward towards defining more clearly the scope of the EU right to data privacy and thereby towards its autonomous definition of this right. That definition could of course not break completely loose from what is requested under the ECHR and it is quite clear that the European legislature considered itself bound by that standard. Evidence for this is to be found in recital 9 of the DRD, which makes extensive reference to the ECHR in order to conclude 'The adoption of an instrument on data retention that complies with the requirements of Article 8 ECHR is therefore a necessary measure'. At this point, it is of course clear that the Directive certainly did not comply with the privacy and data protection standard of the Charter.

A. The Provisions

The key provision of the DRD was Article 3, which laid down the obligation to retain data by way of derogation from Articles 5, 6 and 9 of the e-Privacy Directive. The types of data

[256] Commission, Proposal for a Directive on the retention of data processed in connection with the provision of public electronic communication services and amending Directive 2002/58/EC (COM(2005) 438 final).

[257] ibid 2–3.

[258] ibid. Note that also the sense of 'urgency' seems to suggest that the measure's prime objective is to combat serious and organised crime. That of course does not exclude the internal market basis as being the correct one. See also discussion in ch 2; and Case C-301/06 *Ireland v European Parliament and Council of the European Union* [2009] ECR I -593.

that should be retained were listed in Article 5 DRD and did not include content data.[259] Two types of data were, however, covered by the Directive, despite the objections of the European Parliament,[260] which followed the Article 29 WP's recommendations:[261] unsuccessful call attempts[262] and location data lasting the entire call. The latter makes it possible to track the movement of the mobile communication equipment (or the person using it).[263] Another point of disagreement between the institutions[264] was the period of data retention. The outcome of a compromise was to set a minimum of six months and a maximum of two years.[265] Furthermore, the Directive provided the obligation to retain data in accordance with a number of data security principles[266] and storage requirements.[267] In relation to the former, it set up a monitoring mechanism requiring Member States to designate an authority responsible to supervise the application of the security principles.[268] The DRD also imposed a record-keeping obligation on the Member States, by requiring them to provide the Commission with statistics on the data retained on an annual basis.[269]

B. Challenges to the DRD

A controversy surrounding the question of the correct legal basis for the instrument in question initiated with the very first proposal of France, Ireland, Sweden and the UK for a third pillar Framework Decision on data retention,[270] and came formally to an end with the Court's judgment in *Ireland v Parliament*.[271] In this decision, the Court rejected Ireland's action for annulment and confirmed that what was then Article 95 EC—the legal basis, which the Commission proposed,[272] and on the basis of which the Directive was finally adopted—constituted the correct choice.

In deciding the case, the Court had to deal with technical legal questions relating to the division of competences between the three pillars of the EU and relating to the conditions that need to be fulfilled in order to justify recourse to the provision in question; however, expressed in substantive terms, the Court was ruling on *whether it is possible to restrict on the basis of a market-regulative power a fundamental right for the exclusive aim of fighting serious crime.*

[259] DRD, above n 5, Art 5(2).

[260] European Parliament Committee on Civil Liberties, Justice and Home Affairs, Report on the proposal for a directive of the European Parliament and of the Council on the retention of data processed in connection with the provision of public electronic communication services and amending Directive 2005/58/EC (COM(2005)0438–C6-0293/2005–2005/0182(COD)), A6-0365/2005 (28 November 2005) 33–35.

[261] Article 29 Data Protection Working Party, above n 6.

[262] DRD, above n 5, Art 3(2).

[263] ibid, Art 5(f)(2).

[264] See Bignami, above n 27, 14–15 for a discussion about the way the disagreement evolved.

[265] DRD, above n 5, Art 6.

[266] ibid, Art 7.

[267] ibid, Art 8.

[268] ibid, Art 9.

[269] ibid, Art 10.

[270] Draft Framework Decision, Council Doc 8958/04 (28 April 2004). The legal basis proposed was Arts 31(1)(c) and 34(2)(b) TEU.

[271] *Ireland v European Parliament*, above n 258.

[272] European Data Protection Supervisor, Proposal for a Directive of the European Parliament and of the Council on the retention of data processed in connection with the provision of public electronic communication services and amending Directive 2002/58/EC, COM(2005) 438 final (21 September 2005).

The technicalities of the Court's assessment of the competence question across the former first pillar and the third pillar will not concern us further here. However, what is noteworthy in this case is the concern of the EDPS that the legislature has to ensure respect for fundamental rights when adopting an instrument on data retention. This was not subject to examination in *Ireland v Parliament*. The Court declined to undertake a fundamental rights scrutiny with a laconic one-line observation: 'the action brought by Ireland relates solely to the choice of the legal basis and not to any possible infringement of fundamental rights'.[273]

The Court's decision to uphold the DRD contributed to a more autonomous definition of data privacy for the purposes of EU law, as its restriction in the interest of 'investigation, detection and prosecution of serious crime' was harmonised at the EU level. This was the case up until the decision in *Digital Rights Ireland*, where the referring court expressly posed the question of fundamental rights compliance.[274] The Court handed down a short judgment with a strong message: the Directive violates Articles 7, 8 and 52(1) CFR and is therefore invalid.

As a prelude to this case, it should be noted, the EU definition received challenges from two fronts: first, from national judiciaries (national constitutional courts); and, second, from the EU data protection authority (the EDPS).

As regards the former, three constitutional courts—of Germany,[275] Romania[276] and the Czech Republic[277]—struck down the national implementing law. The difference between the German and the Romanian decision is noteworthy:[278] the former followed the Court of Justice of the EU in *Ireland v Parliament* and was careful to make a distinction between data retention (which the Directive is supposed to harmonise) and access to data for law enforcement purposes (which is governed by national law).[279] This approach allowed it to conclude that there is no need to make a preliminary reference to the Court of Justice of the EU: since the German Constitution does not include an outright prohibition of data retention, it is possible to transpose the Directive in line with the German Constitution and therefore the question of a potential conflict between EU law and German Basic Law does not arise. The Romanian Constitutional Court on the other hand attacked data retention and therefore implicitly the DRD. Taking ECHR case law[280] as its basis, it held that 'the obligation to retain the data, established by Law 298/2008, as an exception or derogation from the principle of personal data protection and their confidentiality, empties, through

[273] *Ireland v European Parliament*, above n 258, [57].

[274] *Digital Rights Ireland*, above n 7.

[275] *Vorratsdatenspeicherung*, BverfG (2 March 2010) 1 BvR 256/08.

[276] Romanian Constitutional Court, Decision No 1258 (8 October 2009), Romanian Official Monitor No 789 (23 November 2009). For an unofficial English translation, see: www.legi-internet.ro/fileadmin/editor_folder/pdf/decision-constitutional-court-romania-data-retention.pdf.

[277] Czech Constitutional Court, Judgment on the provisions of section 97, paragraph 3 and 4 of Act No 127/2005 Collection on electronic communications and amending certain related acts as amended, and Decree No 485/2005 Collection on the data retention and transmission to competent authorities (22 March 2011), Official Gazette of 1 April 2011, www.mpo.cz/dokument147108.html.

[278] As pointed out by K de Vries et al, 'The German Constitutional Court Judgment on Data Retention: Proportionality Overrides Unlimited Surveillance (Doesn't it?)' in S Gutwirth, Y Poullet, P De Hert and R Leenes (eds), *Computers, Privacy and Data Protection: An Element of Choice* (Dordrecht, Springer, 2011) 3.

[279] The CJEU makes that distinction for assessing competences across the former pillars, retention being a first pillar matter and access a third pillar matter.

[280] *Rotaru v Romania*, App No 28341/95 (ECtHR, 4 May 2000); *Sunday Times v UK*, App No 6538/74 (ECtHR, 26 April 1979); and *Prince Hans-Adam of Liechtenstein v Romania*, App No 42527/98 (ECtHR, 12 July 2007).

its nature, length, and application domain, the content of this principle'.[281] Similarly, in an obiter dictum, the Czech Constitutional Court doubted that data retention is necessary, efficient and appropriate when viewed in relation to new modes of criminality (eg, the use of anonymous sim cards).[282] It should be noted that 'constitutional' problems in relation to transposing laws have also occurred in Bulgaria,[283] Cyprus[284] and Hungary.

In the meantime, the Commission had adopted its evaluation report[285] as foreseen in Article 14 of the DRD. The report's purpose is to assess Member States' application of the Directive and its impact on economic operators and consumers in light of new technological developments and with a view to establishing whether amendments are necessary. Two aspects of the report are particularly noteworthy. First was the overall finding that the Directive 'has not fully harmonised the approach to data retention and has not created a level-playing field for operators'.[286] Data retention differed to a considerable extent across the Member States[287] beyond the leeway provided for by the Directive, thus missing the objective of creating a level playing field for service providers and consumers. The second is that the report addressed the fundamental rights dimension—the applicable standards and the criticisms voiced in this regard—despite the fact that this is not strictly required under the Article 14 evaluation.[288] The need to create better conditions for the industry and to strengthen data protection was to be tackled in the Commission legislative proposal, which was to be tabled in 2012. The Commission also commissioned an external study in order to examine 'whether and how an EU approach to data preservation[289] might complement data retention', which found that the two are indeed complementary.[290] Finally, the Commission also set up the 'Data Retention Expert Group' to advise on best practice in the implementation of the DRD. This Group no longer exists following the invalidation of the DRD.

[281] As cited in de Vries et al, above n 278.

[282] Commission Evaluation Report on the Data Retention Directive (2006/24/EC), COM(2011) 225 final (hereinafter 'Evaluation Report 2011') 20.

[283] The Bulgarian Supreme Administrative Court (judgment of 11 December 2008) declared a provision of a law partly transposing the DRD as unconstitutional. The provision in question allowed 'security services and other law enforcement bodies' to have access 'to all retained data by Internet and mobile communication providers' without permission of a court, cited by de Vries et al, above n 278, 15.

[284] Evaluation Report 2011, above n 282, 20–21. In Cyprus, 'court orders issued under the transposing law were held to be unconstitutional'; see Supreme Court of Cyprus Appeal Case Nos 65/2009, 78/2009, 82/2009 and 15/2010-22/2010 (1 February 2011).

[285] Evaluation Report 2011, above n 282.

[286] ibid, point 8.3.

[287] For example, in relation to limitations to the use of data, data storage and reimbursement of costs for complying with data retention rules.

[288] See Evaluation Report 2011, above n 282; and Opinion of the EDPS on the Evaluation Report from the Commission to the Council and the European Parliament on the Data Retention Directive (Directive 2006/24/EC) (31 May 2011) 2, para 2, https://secure.edps.europa.eu/EDPSWEB/webdav/shared/Documents/Consultation/Opinions/2011/11-05-30_Evaluation_Report_DRD_EN.pdf.

[289] Also known as 'quick freeze'. Under this concept, a person or organisation 'is required by a state authority to preserve specified data from loss or modification for a specified period of time'. Unlike the case with 'data retention' usually (and under the DRD certainly), 'data preservation' covers not only non-content data but also content data. See Center for Strategy and Evaluation Services (CSES), 'Evidence of Potential Impacts of Options for Revising the Data Retention Directive: Current Approaches to Data Preservation in the EU and in Third Countries' (November 2012) 4, http://ec.europa.eu/dgs/home-affairs/what-we-do/policies/police-cooperation/data-retention/docs/drd_task_2_report_final_en.pdf (hereinafter the 'Data Preservation Study 2012').

[290] ibid.

After the Commission evaluation report had been issued, the EDPS provided an Opinion[291] on this report challenging the legality of the DRD. He conducted that analysis and found that data retention as provided for in the Directive is not necessary,[292] that it could have been regulated by less restrictive means and that it lacked foreseeability, referring to the fact that access to data is not regulated by the Directive, ie the question of 'who' can access the data and 'for what purpose', since it is for Member States to define what is a 'serious crime' and who qualifies as a 'competent authority'.[293]

Against this background, a declaration that the DRD violates fundamental rights—important as it is both for data protection law and as a warning signal for the EU legislature to respect fundamental rights more generally—may not seem very surprising. The judgment in *Digital Rights Ireland* was therefore arguably to be expected.

The Court followed the derogations rule contained in Article 52(1) CFR in its legality review. At the outset, it had no difficulty finding an interference with Articles 7 and 8 of the Charter.[294] Interestingly enough, the Court specifically noted that the retention of data on a widespread scale may 'have an effect on the use, by subscribers or registered users, of the means of communication'[295] and is '*likely to generate in the minds of the person concerned the feeling that their private lives are the subject of constant surveillance*' (emphasis added).[296] In other words, it may be said that the mere existence of this kind of widespread data retention may be an interference per se with the relevant rights. It also swiftly dismissed the possibility that the essence of the fundamental rights at issue was affected (the Directive did not apply to the content of e-communications and it did provide for certain principles of data protection and security).[297] On the question of legitimate aim, the Court was again easily satisfied that the Directive genuinely met an objective of general interest, namely, the fight against serious crime and therefore public security.[298]

The case turned on the question of proportionality. The Court failed the Directive under this test on four counts, which essentially related to the absence of 'clear and precise rules governing the extent of the interference' in the Directive[299] and of sufficient safeguards:

1. its mass-surveillance character with a general absence of limits;
2. its failure to regulate access to data (this point is interesting when laid alongside the Court's finding in *Ireland v Parliament* that the DRD was based on the correct legal basis, precisely *because* it was *not* regulating access to data. Post-Lisbon, this is not problematic as a single instrument regulating both retention and access can be adopted under the specific data protection legal basis (Article 16 TFEU), which underscores its importance);

[291] ibid.

[292] Evaluation Report 2011, above n 282; and Opinion of the EDPS, above n 288, 11–12. 1) It involves 'the use of retained data for far too wide a range of purposes and by far too many authorities'. 2) 'The maximum retention period of two years appears to go beyond what is necessary'. 3) The security measures are not sufficiently harmonised. 4) Uncertainty as to whether all categories of retained data are necessary.

[293] Opinion of the EDPS, above n 288, 12–14.

[294] It also noted, although without entering any deeper analysis, that the Directive might also be problematic from the point of view of freedom of expression (Art 11 CFR).

[295] *Digital Rights Ireland*, above n 7, [28].

[296] ibid [37].

[297] ibid [39]–[40].

[298] ibid [41].

[299] ibid [65].

3. data retention periods were not regulated in a way limited to what is strictly necessary; and
4. the absence of sufficient safeguards relating to data security.

The Court's approach is broadly in line with the views of the EDPS mentioned above on the question of necessity of the measure. However, there is one point not addressed in the Court's reasoning, which has direct consequences for future lawmaking on the subject. This is worth pointing out, as it is not clear whether the subject of data retention will disappear from the EU regulatory scene.

The EDPS took issue with data retention as a tool for combating serious crime, noting that alternative and less restrictive means might be available for achieving the same aim, such as data preservation.[300] Importantly, the EDPS called on the Commission to consider this tool as an *alternative* to data retention in its planned IA (for proposing amendments to the Directive based on its Evaluation Report).[301] The Court, on the other hand, did not enter this debate on alternatives at all. It merely noted, rather swiftly, at the stage of assessing the appropriateness of the measure that data retention is 'a valuable tool for criminal investigations'[302] and later focused on ensuring more *definitional* specificity for the identification of situations justifying retention obligations.[303] The implication for a potential future proposal in this area is that there will be no need to prove empirically the need to impose data retention obligations on Member States. Therefore, a future impact assessment is most likely only going to be concerned with empirics seeking to justify the particular limits and safeguards to data retention that will be chosen.

At the moment, there is no official documentation suggesting that a new proposal on data retention *will* be adopted.[304] Should that materialise, it will be interesting to see what the narrative will be for justifying the need for such action, particularly in times when concerns for control over one's data feature prominently in public debates so that they cannot be easily dismissed by the objective or rhetoric of fighting serious crime and terrorism, which, it will be remembered, provided the key impetus for the DRD.

In the meantime, the more imminent question concerns that of national implementing laws.[305] Some national implementing laws were annulled in judgments handed down by the respective constitutional courts shortly after the Court of Justice of the EU judgment[306]

[300] Evaluation Report 2011, above n 282, 10, para 45; and Opinion of the EDPS, above n 288, (data preservation is explained as 'temporarily securing or "freezing" of certain telecommunications traffic and location data relating only to specific suspects of criminal activity, which may subsequently be made available to law enforcement authorities with a judicial authorisation').

[301] Evaluation Report 2011, above n 282, para 56.

[302] *Digital Rights Ireland*, above n 7, [49].

[303] See ibid [60] for more details on the Court's approach to the use of the term '*serious* crime'.

[304] In the European Parliament Debate of 16 April 2014 (eight days after the judgment had been handed down), Commissioner Malström left both possibilities (re-adoption or no adoption of a new Data Retention Directive) explicitly open. See www.europarl.europa.eu/ep-live/en/plenary/video?debate=1397667684985.

[305] For the questions posed by Dutch MEP Sophie In't Veld to Commissioner Malström, as well as for the questions concerning implementing laws, see http://www.statewatch.org/news/2014/may/eu-letter-malmstrom-judgment-data-retention-directive.pdf.

[306] F Böhm and D Cole, Study on Data Retention after the Judgment of the Court of Justice of the European Union (30 June 2014), www.janalbrecht.eu/fileadmin/material/Dokumente/Boehm_Cole_-_Data_Retention_Study_-_June_2014.pdf, 55–56.

(eg, Austria,[307] Slovenia[308] and for the second time Romania),[309] while other Member States are eager to maintain data retention rules equivalent or similar to those implementing the Directive (eg, the UK).[310] This is problematic as it is clear that national laws seeking data retention would fall under Article 15(1) DRD and that action would have to be in compliance with the requirements spelled out in that Article and EU fundamental rights as also interpreted in *Digital Rights Ireland*.[311]

Be that as it may, it can be concluded that with the invalidation of the DRD, the EU moved again one step away from the road to creating an autonomous definition of data protection/restriction. However, this move was both necessary and desirable in order to stay true to the objective of ensuring a high level of data protection within the EU.

V. PROPOSAL FOR A COHERENT DATA PROTECTION FRAMEWORK FOR THE TWENTY-FIRST CENTURY: MOVING AWAY FROM THE INTERNAL MARKET, MOVING CLOSER TO AUTONOMY?

The need to revise the data protection regime was voiced by the European Council in 2010 in the framework of the Stockholm Programme.[312] Against the backdrop of rapid technological developments and globalisation, it called on the EU to address the necessity for increased exchange of data while ensuring respect for privacy[313] and urged that a 'comprehensive strategy' should be adopted for protecting data privacy within and outside the EU.[314] In this context, it invited the Commission to (among other things) 'evaluate the functioning of the various instruments on data protection and present, where necessary, further legislative and non-legislative initiatives to maintain effective application of the above[315] principles'.[316] The Commission had in fact already engaged with this matter a year before the adoption of the Stockholm Programme. In May 2009, it had kicked off the review of the present regime with a high-level conference and a number of studies as well

[307] Austrian Constitutional Court (VfGh), Decision G 47/2012 et al regarding data retention (27 June 2014). For an English extract, see www.vfgh.gv.at/cms/vfgh-site/attachments/1/5/8/CH0006/CMS1409900579500/erwaegungeneng28082014.pdf.

[308] Constitutional Court of the Republic of Slovenia, Judgment U-I-65/13-19 (3 July 2014). Decision available only in Slovenian: www.ip-rs.si/index.php?id=272&tx_ttnews[tt_news]=1256&cHash=2885f4a56e6ff9d8abc6f94da098f461.

[309] Romanian Constitutional Court, Decision No 440 (8 July 2014), Official Press Release only in Romanian: http://privacy.apti.ro/decizia-curtii-constitutionale-date-trafic.

[310] Data Retention and Investigatory Powers Act 2014.

[311] On a discussion of the effect of *Digital Rights Ireland* on Member States' law, see the leaked Legal Opinion of the European Pariament, 'Re: LIBE—Questions Relating to the Judgment of the Court of 8 April 2014 in Joined Cases C-293/12 and C-594/12 *Digital Rights Ireland and Seitlinger and others*—Directive 2006/24/EC on Data Retention—Consequences of the Judgment', 15 et seq, https://s3.amazonaws.com/access.3cdn.net/27bd1765fade54d896_l2m6i61fe.pdf.

[312] The Stockholm Programme—An open and secure Europe serving and protecting citizens [2010] OJ C115/1.

[313] ibid, point 2.5.

[314] ibid.

[315] ibid: purpose limitation, proportionality, legitimacy of processing, limits on storage time, security and confidentiality, respect for the rights of the individual, control by national independent supervisory authorities and access to effective judicial redress.

[316] ibid.

as a public consultation.[317] The fact that revision of the old regime was due seems to have been all too apparent.

That revision should be based on a new legal basis introduced by the Lisbon Treaty under Title II on 'provisions having general application'. Such separate legal basis on data protection was already envisaged during negotiations and included in the drafting of the (failed) Constitutional Treaty.

It is another example of a specific fundamental rights legal basis being contained in primary EU law. As it happened in the area of social policy, we can once again witness a development whereby EU legislative activity was pursued through the internal market before it had gained its own distinct place in the Treaties. Henceforth, one single legal basis applies to data processing by both EU institutions and Member States (including both public and private data processing). Excluded from regulation under this legal basis are rules on data processing by Member States when they fall within the area of Common Foreign and Security Policy.[318]

The Article in question, albeit new, constitutes a combination of already existing provisions that gradually entered the EU law landscape in the form of primary and secondary EU law. Thus, Article 16(1) TFEU[319] is a restatement of Article 8(1) CFR and Article 16(2) TFEU is essentially based on the DPD and (ex) Article 286 EC.[320] Article 16(2) TFEU reads:

> The European Parliament and the Council, acting in accordance with the ordinary legislative procedure, shall lay down the rules relating to the protection of individuals with regard to the processing of personal data by Union institutions, bodies, offices and agencies, and by the Member States when carrying out activities which fall within the scope of Union law, and the rules relating to the free movement of such data. Compliance with these rules shall be subject to the control of independent authorities.

The question arising is whether the new legal basis has actually extended the regulative powers of the EU in relation to data protection. The UK's House of Lords EU Select Committee, while commenting on the equivalent provision[321] contained in the Constitutional Treaty, cautioned that it should be made clear that what is now contained in the first sentence of Article 16(2) TFEU 'does not confer any general power on the Union to legislate on data protection'. But except for data processing related to CFSP and the limited fields falling 'outside the scope of Union law', such as national security and personal household activities,[322] it is difficult to imagine an area of activity that could not be covered by this provision. This is so after the Court's decision in *Lindqvist* and *Österreichischer Rundfunk* (not

[317] Commission Communication 2010, above n 3, 3. For the responses to the Commission's public consultation, see http://ec.europa.eu/justice/news/consulting_public/nes_consulting_0003_en.htm.

[318] Article 16(2) TFEU, last para. In this case, rules must be laid down by a Council Decision based on Art 39 TFEU.

[319] 'Everyone has the right to the protection of personal data concerning them.'

[320] The same was noted with regard to the equivalent provision in the Constitutional Treaty by the HL Select Committee on the European Union, Session 2002–03, 22nd Report, www.publications.parliament.uk/pa/ld200203/ldselect/ldeucom/106/106.pdf.

[321] Though not exactly identical provision: Art 36a of the Constitutional Treaty, which is commented upon by the HL Select Committee (ibid) lacks the reference contained in Art 16 TFEU that the rules be subject to the control of independent authorities, and to the specific rules for the Common Foreign and Security Policy. The analogy can be drawn nonetheless with the remainder.

[322] Also exempted from the material scope of Art 2 of the proposed Commission Proposal for a Regulation on the protection of individuals with regard to the processing of personal data and on the free movement of such data, COM(2012) 11 final (hereinafter 'the General Data Protection Regulation').

delivered at the time the House of Lords made its comments), which made clear that the DPD covers not only data processing in cross-border and economic situations—and hence under 'rules relating to the free movement of data'—but also in domestic non-economic situations. Therefore, what the House of Lord Select Committee was worried about seems to have been already established law before the introduction of Article 16 TFEU. One substantial difference in the new legal basis is that rules on data processing in the area of police and judicial cooperation can take the form of a regulation or directive (with the ordinary legislative procedure applying, the Court of Justice of the EU having full jurisdiction in reviewing the measure, and the instrument being capable of direct effect),[323] but this is of course a consequence that comes with the abolition of the pillar structure and is true for many former third pillar matters. The real distinctiveness of the new legal basis is rather that *one legal instrument* could be adopted regulating data protection in the internal market as well as in the area of police and judicial cooperation, and in theory also data processing by EU institutions.

Overall, it can be said that the 'three carefully put together elements'[324] that once 'fell apart'[325] in the early 1990s seem for the most part to be coming together again two decades later with the introduction of Article 16 TFEU. The advantage is that one of the key problematic aspects of the old regime—the problem of fragmentation—is now capable of being tackled.

This also seems to be the direction that the Commission is set on taking. Following the entry into force of the Lisbon Treaty, it responded to the call in the Stockholm Programme by adopting a Communication on 'A comprehensive approach on personal data protection in the European Union' in 2010.[326] Basing itself on the findings of the public consultation and the studies conducted, it came to the conclusion that the core principles of the DPD as well as its technologically neutral character should be maintained. On the other hand, five challenges were identified:[327]

1. the need to clarify and specify the application of data protection principles to new technologies beyond the e-Privacy Directive;
2. enhancing the internal market dimension through increased harmonisation in order to increase legal certainty, lessen the administrative burden and ensure a level playing field for economic operators and other data controllers;
3. improving international data transfers in a globalised world, permeated by uncertainties and problems as to applicable law and allocation of responsibility;
4. ensuring effective enforcement through, inter alia, the strengthening of DPAs; and

[323] In other words, what was called 'the Community method' will be henceforth applicable in a former third pillar area.

[324] Simitis, above n 52, 116.

[325] ibid. The three elements Simitis referred to are those contained in the Commission's proposals from 1990: 1) 'A Directive was to regulate processing that fell within the scope of Community law.' 2) 'A Declaration of the Representatives of the Governments of the Member States meeting within the Council was to extend the Directive's principles to all other processing in the public sector.' Thus, this also includes processing in the area of policy and judicial cooperation 3) 'A Commission Resolution, to be joined by the other institutions of the Communities was to ensure the Directive's demands would also be respected within every institution and body of the European Communities' (COM(90) 314 final—SYN 288).

[326] The Stockholm Programme, (above n 312.

[327] ibid 3–4.

5. improving coherence of the data protection legal framework through an 'overarching instrument applying to data processing operations in all sectors and policies of the Union, ensuring an integrated approach as well as seamless, consistent and effective protection'.

While attempting to tackle these challenges, the Commission noted that: '[It] will give the highest priority to ensuring respect for the fundamental right to data protection … while at the same time enhancing the internal market dimension and facilitating the free flow of personal data.'[328] The wording used in the Communication demonstrates that the Commission has maintained exactly the same kind of 'dual aim', at least as far as the weight that these two purposes shall assume, as contained in the DPD. The Commission thus identified six 'key objectives'. In the first two places stood the strengthening of individuals' rights[329] and enhancement of the internal market dimension.[330] Third came the need to revise the data protection rules in the area of police and judicial cooperation in criminal matters as part of a 'comprehensive approach to data protection'. Fourth was the desire to improve the rules on the global dimension of data protection (international data transfers). Last of all, strengthening the institutional arrangements for better enforcement of data protection rules, in particular the strengthening of DPAs and the Article 29 WP's role in coordinating the positions of DPAs.

As announced in the Communication, which received overall support from the European Parliament and the Council, the Commission tabled a legislative reform package on data protection in January 2012. It should be noted that revision of the EU data protection regime goes in parallel with similar processes running at the international level, namely the OECD[331] and the Council of Europe, that is currently assessing revision of Convention 108[332] with the broad dual objective of dealing with 'challenges for privacy resulting from the use of new ICTs [and] to strengthen the Convention's follow up mechanism'.[333] While the EU, acting as an observer, will pay attention to ensure the coherence of EU law with the Convention as has been the case so far, the Council of Europe proposal also states as one of its objectives to ensure coherence and compatibility with the legal framework of the EU. Interestingly, the EU legislature, once influenced by this instrument, is now acting as a forerunner with its proposal for a comprehensive data protection framework.

However high the Commission's ambitions for an 'overarching instrument' may have been, the final choice in the reform package[334] is one of two legal instruments: a General

[328] Commission Communication 2010, above n 3, 4.

[329] ibid 5–9.

[330] Ibid 10.

[331] See OECD report, Working Party on Information Security and Privacy, 'The Evolving Privacy Landscape: 30 Years after the OECD Privacy Guidelines' (6 April 2011), www.oecd.org/dataoecd/22/25/47683378.pdf.

[332] Proposals for the Modernisation of Convention 108, T-PD-BUR(2012)01EN, www.coe.int/t/dghl/standard-setting/dataprotection/TPD_documents/T-PD-BUR_2012_01_EN.pdf. The EU's stance in these negotiations is obviously dependent on the current EU internal negotiation of the data protection package. See, eg, Commission note on provisions of the draft text that the Commission 'intends to leave open or maintain a reservation until a compromise is reached between the EU legislators', Document 15765/13 (6 November 2013), www.statewatch.org/news/2013/nov/eu-com-coe-convention-108-multicolumn-15765-13.pdf.

[333] Proposal for the Modernisation of Convention 108 (ibid) 1.

[334] Also including a Commission Communication on 'Safeguarding Privacy in a Connected World: A European Data Protection Framework for the 21st Century', COM(2012) 9 final (hereinafter the 'Commission Communication 2012').

Data Protection Regulation[335] and a Directive[336] applicable to former third pillar matters. Both instruments have passed (at the time of writing) through the first reading at the European Parliament, receiving broad endorsement from this institution.[337] It appears that the Member States clearly considered it necessary to allow for sufficient flexibility on their side, granted by the fact that, unlike with the Regulation, they enjoy discretion in the implementation of the instrument. The EDPS has criticised exactly this choice of splitting the areas of regulation and having a directive in former third pillar matters, which he considers as providing 'for an inadequate level of protection, by far inferior to the proposed Regulation',[338] as not contributing to comprehensiveness and as being a missed opportunity in tackling the problem of fragmentation.

A detailed analysis of the reform package, which is not based on the internal market, would go beyond the scope of this chapter. Nonetheless, the following aspects of the draft General Data Protection Regulation are worth noting. First, the internal market dimension of data protection continues to form a central motivation behind the instrument. This is despite the fact that the Regulation is formally no longer based on the internal market provisions. For one thing, this is evidenced by the way in which the Commission explains the need for effective data protection rules to be drawn from fundamental rights considerations as well as economic considerations: 'a high level of data protection is also crucial to enhance trust in online services and to fulfil the potential of the digital economy, thereby encouraging economic growth and the competitiveness of EU industries'.[339] Furthermore, as noted above, the reform package expressly acknowledges it as a key objective: enhancing the internal market dimension is considered as 'essential if the Single Market is to function and to stimulate economic growth, create new jobs and foster innovation',[340] an objective that is linked to the aim of establishing a Digital Single Market by the date of 2016. The approach is unsurprising given that data have been characterised as 'the oil of the 21st century'. What is noteworthy, however, is that these key objectives are carried over to the new system under the specific legal basis on data protection. The need for achieving such enhanced harmonisation determined the nature of the legal instrument chosen: the DPD is to be replaced by a regulation in the interest of uniformity and effectiveness.

This brings us to the second point and back to the discussion undertaken above, namely, the question of the extent to which the EU has achieved an autonomous definition of data protection at the EU level. Putting a Regulation in place, which will be interpreted and applied in exactly the same manner across 28 EU Member States suggests, at least at first sight, a definite move towards such autonomy. However, when taking a closer look at the provisions of the Regulation, it emerges that it again leaves considerable room for variation

[335] General Data Protection Regulation, above n 322; note that this proposal is also to amend Directive 2002/58/EC.

[336] Commission Proposal for a Directive on the protection of individuals with regard to the processing of personal data by competent authorities for the purposes of prevention, investigation, detection or prosecution of criminal offences or the execution of criminal penalties, and the free movement of such data, COM(2012) 10 final.

[337] For a summary of the voting, see 'Progress on EU Data Protection Reform now irreversible following European Parliament vote', Press Release (12 March 2014), http://europa.eu/rapid/press-release_MEMO-14-186_en.htm.

[338] Opinion of the European Data Protection Supervisor on the data protection reform package (7 March 2012) 4, para 20 (hereinafter the 'EDPS Opinion 2012').

[339] Commission Communication 2012, above n 334, 2.

[340] ibid.

across the Member States. As the EDPS has pointed out,[341] there are four categories of rules contained in the proposed Regulation that allow for coexistence between national law and EU law:

1. provisions that build on national law;[342]
2. national law that builds on the Regulation;[343]
3. provisions allowing national rules in relation to specific data processing situations,[344] covering freedom of expression, health, the employment context, professional secrecy or other equivalent obligations of secrecy and churches and religious associations. It is important to note especially with regard to freedom of expression[345] that the ground for reconciling freedom of expression with the right to the protection of personal data (which Member States have to provide) is as narrowly defined as it used to be in the DPD, ie, in relation to 'processing of personal data carried out solely for journalistic purposes or the purpose of artistic or literary expression'—a definition that appears somehow limited in the age of the Internet (blogging etc);
4. section 5 of the draft Regulation explicitly allows Member States (and also EU law) to restrict the scope of a series of provisions of the Regulation when such is a necessary and proportionate measure in a democratic society to safeguard a list of interests, including again as in Article 13 DPD 'the rights and freedoms of others'.

Admittedly, using the legislative tool of a Regulation may make some practical difference: to the extent that the General Data Protection Regulation mandates national legislation to strike a balance between conflicting rights, 'these will now have to take the form of special laws rather than elements of general data protection laws, which would have to be abrogated within the scope of the proposed regulation'.[346]

Still, the general point remains: the choice of a Regulation over a Directive will not alter the fact that potential conflicts between this and other fundamental rights will continue to persist as the main theme and most important challenge not only to an autonomous EU definition of data privacy but also in building the Digital Single Market.

VI. CONCLUSIONS

The EU data protection regime constitutes a unique instance of EU fundamental rights harmonisation driven by a concrete policy whose general framework is set out by internal market instruments that have been explicitly conceived in fundamental rights terms. The

[341] EDPS Opinion 2012, above n 338, 9–10, paras 50–55.

[342] For example, Art 6 stating in relation to some grounds for lawful processing listed in the Regulation that they have to be provided for either in EU law or the law of the Member State to which the controller is subject (Art 6(3)(b)).

[343] For example, the proposed Regulation providing for a right to a judicial remedy against a supervisory authority or against a controller or processor (Arts 74 and 75). See General Data Protection Regulation, above n 322.

[344] ibid, ch IX.

[345] Article 80 of the General Data Protection Regulation, above n 322.

[346] C Ladenburger, 'FIDE 2012—Session on "Protection of Fundamental Rights Post-Lisbon—The Interaction between the Charter of Fundamental Rights, the European Convention of Human Rights and National Constitutions"—Institutional Report', 41, www.fide2012.eu/index.php?doc_id=88.

first instrument (the DPD) came to life at a time when the EU was progressing (in Simitis' words) 'from the market to the *polis*', while in competence terms, the entire regime has made the same shift with the introduction of a specific legal basis in the Lisbon Treaty, even if market considerations continue to be key for advancing the general framework. These developments have made the EU move from a position of lagging behind and being forced to follow national and international developments in data protection to that of a forerunner today.

The legislative implementation of the right has not only set out data protection principles, but it has also created new bodies of governance, most notably the WP, contributing to the necessary continuous reassessment of the regime at the micro-level (amendments to directives) and at the macro-level (eg, achieving insertion of a separate article on data protection in the Charter).

With this implementation, data protection has become one of the most regulated fundamental rights at the EU level and therefore one that has achieved a degree of an autonomous EU definition (of its scope) far higher than most other rights. Such scope was further delineated through the DRD, which harmonised (legitimate) restrictions to the right. It was the only internal market instrument having such an explicit purpose up until its annulment by the Court in the *Digital Rights Ireland* case.

However, the autonomous drawing of the scope of data protection faces two important challenges. One challenge has been implicitly expressed by national constitutional courts and explicitly by the EDPS and the CJEU: the disagreement as to how the legislature had delineated the restrictions to data protection in the DRD (*Digital Rights Ireland*). The other one originates in the fact that it is in the inherent nature of data protection to conflict with other fundamental rights, such as notably freedom of expression (expressly recognised in the DPD), and in the e-communication sector intellectual property.[347] In this context, the CJEU has initially taken a deferential stance, leaving the substantive balancing of fundamental rights to national courts (*Promusicae* and *Satamedia*). However, recent case law suggests a more proactive approach of less deference—in some cases a cautious one (*Bonnier Audio AB*, *Scarlet Extended* and *SABAM v Netlog*), but in one recent instance a definite one endorsing a high level of data protection (*Google Spain*).

Deference means that the seemingly autonomous EU definition of data protection is not so autonomous after all. It is also liable to undermine the entire harmonisation regime, since an important source for diverging standards is that of providing different solutions as to how different fundamental rights relate to each other.

The new proposal for the general framework on data protection (the Draft General Data Protection Regulation), despite taking the form of a Regulation, allows a considerable degree of coexistence between national and EU law, and, most notably, it allows Member States and the EU to restrict the scope of a number of provisions 'for rights and freedoms of others'. This suggests not only that conflicting fundamental rights will continue to be the most important question in relation to the data protection regime, but also that the onus will be on the Court to decide the level of harmonisation and therefore also the level of autonomy of the EU right to data protection.

[347] See, eg, the provision on measures based on profiling (Art 20 of the proposed General Data Protection Regulation) capable of conflicting with most of the rights contained in the CFR.

5

Freedom of Expression

I. INTRODUCTION

THIS CHAPTER WILL discuss three different forms of the right to freedom of expression that have been regulated—or attempted to be subject to harmonisation—in the internal market. The different areas raise different points of concern and it should be clear from the outset that the chapter does not attempt to link them in any (artificial) way. Rather, it serves to expose the different forms of actual and potential interference by the European legislator with this right through internal market legislation.

The different forms of freedom of expression discussed in the three subsequent sections concern media pluralism, the right to receive and impart information and the right to commercial expression.

The first section will discuss an instance of failed regulation—the Media Ownership Directive. It will thereby illustrate the importance of political obstacles that need to be overcome in order to achieve (sensitive) fundamental rights regulation on the basis of the internal market. It is apparent that if the political will is absent, the instrument is more susceptible to be criticised on legal grounds, *in casu*, the lack of competence.

The second section will discuss the Audiovisual Media Services Directive. It will demonstrate that the right to receive and impart information has been actively promoted on the basis of the internal market. It has been done so, however, on the basis that this right coincides with the internal market freedom to provide services. This is reflected in the regulatory approach.

The third, and final, section will review advertising regulation with the aim of assessing the level of protection granted to commercial expression through internal market legislation. It will emerge that formally a fundamental rights status is granted to this right in the EU legal order. However, closer analysis of the wording and legislative history of the instruments as well as jurisprudence of the CJEU (the Court) reveals that the fundamental rights discourse in this area may serve as mere rhetoric.

II. MEDIA PLURALISM—HOW THE REGULATORY PROCESS CAN FAIL

Even if the legal requirements, which render the regulation of fundamental rights on the basis of the internal market legitimate, are met (see chapter two), it does not mean that successful regulation is guaranteed. There is one obstacle that shapes the evolution of the EU's system of competences in general[1] and one which is liable to constitute a determining

[1] AV Bausili, 'Rethinking the Methods of Dividing and Exercising, Powers in the EU: Reforming Subsidiarity and National Parliaments', Jean Monnet Working Paper No 9/02.

factor on a question as sensitive as that of whether a particular fundamental right shall be subjected to supranational regulation in particular: the presence or absence of a political will. This factor has already played a significant role in blocking adoption of an instrument regulating a value that is linked to the fundamental right to freedom of expression, namely, media pluralism. The protection of this value requires (different forms of) positive intervention. Such intervention was attempted at the EU level with a view to regulating media ownership.

The circumstances leading to this failure will be discussed in due course. Before doing so, however, it is useful to lay out the said link between media pluralism, freedom of expression and the internal market.[2]

The first point to note is that media pluralism has been recognised and protected under the ECHR system.[3] This does not result from the wording of the Convention, but rather from the dicta of the ECtHR[4] as well as Council of Europe statements.[5] It is true with respect to internal media pluralism (plurality of voices in the media), as well as external media pluralism (diversity of media ownership and 'plurality of independent and autonomous media outlets and providers').[6,7] The EU Charter of Fundamental Rights (the Charter) goes a step further than the ECHR in expressly stipulating that 'the freedom and pluralism of the media shall be respected';[8] the Court has also recognised the link between media pluralism and freedom of expression, and that already at a time pre-dating the Charter.[9] At the same time, it has accepted in its jurisprudence that media pluralism constitutes an overriding requirement relating to the general interest, which can justify a restriction to free movement.[10]

[2] On a discussion of this entanglement, see F Barzanti, 'Governing the European Audiovisual Space: What Modes of Governance Can Facilitate a European Approach to Media Pluralism?', EUI Working Papers, RSCAS 2012/49, available at: http://cadmus.eui.eu/bitstream/handle/1814/23914/RSCAS_2012_49.pdf?sequence=1.

[3] On a discussion of media pluralism under the ECHR system, see E Komorek, 'Is Media Pluralism a Human Right? The European Court of Human Rights, the Council of Europe and the Issue of Media Pluralism' (2009) 3 *European Human Rights Law Review* 395.

[4] See, eg, *Handyside v UK*, App No 5493/72 (ECtHR, 7 December 1976); *Lingens v Austria*, App No 9815/82 (ECtHR, 8 July 1986); *Jersild v Denmark*, App No 15890/89 (ECtHR, 23 September 1994).

[5] See, eg, Recommendation CM/Rec(2007)2 of the Committee of Ministers to Member States on media pluralism and diversity of media content (adopted by the Committee of Ministers on 31 January 2007 at the 985th meeting of the Ministers' Deputies).

[6] B Klimkiewicz, 'Is the Clash of Rationales Leading Nowhere? Media Pluralism in European Regulatory Policies' in A Czepek, M Hellwig and E Nowak (eds), *Press Freedom and Pluralism in Europe: Concepts and Conditions* (Bristol, Intellect, 2009) 47.

[7] *Informationsverein Lentia v Austria*, App No 37093/97 (ECtHR, 28 November 2011) [38]: '[Imparting] information and ideas of general interest ... cannot be successfully accomplished unless it is grounded in the principle of pluralism.'

[8] Article 11(2) CFR.

[9] Case C-260/89 *ERT* [1991] ECR I-2925 [4]; Case C-288/89 *Stichting Collectieve Antennevoorziening Gouda* [1991] ECR I-4007 [23]; Case C-353/89 *Commission v The Netherlands* [1991] ECR I-4069 [30]: 'The protection of the pluralism which that Dutch policy seeks to safeguard is *connected with* freedom of expression, as protected by Article 10 of the [ECHR], which is one of the fundamental rights guaranteed by the Community legal order' (emphasis added). Admittedly, the relationship between media pluralism and freedom of expression is ambiguous; see S Craufurd, *Broadcasting Law and Fundamental Rights* (Oxford, Clarendon Press, 1997) 196. However the quoted passage as well as statements of the EU Institutions suggest that in the EU legal order, the two are viewed as inextricably linked rather than the former being a restriction to the latter. In support of this, see Commission Decision 97/606/EC (26 June 1997) pursuant to Art 90(3) of the EC Treaty on the exclusive right to broadcast television advertising in Flanders, recital 13: 'The Commission accepts that a cultural policy and the *preservation of pluralism, which is an aspect of the freedom of expression*' (emphasis added).

[10] See, eg, *Gouda*, above n 9; and *Commission v The Netherlands*, above n 9.

This is noteworthy as two implications follow from this. First, it appears that the link between the concept of media pluralism and the fundamental right to freedom of expression has at least so far, not impacted on the way it is balanced with market freedoms in the negative integration process. It is treated like any other overriding requirement in the public interest. This would also mean then that it is not possible to rely on this ground in order to justify overtly discriminatory national measures.

Second, despite the acknowledged connection to freedom of expression, and the assurance that the latter is a fundamental right guaranteed by the Community legal order, the maintenance of pluralism is understood as a cultural policy, not a *fundamental rights* policy. Thus, the derogatory ground is subordinated to the market freedoms. In light of this, it is not very surprising that the Court has frequently found measures aimed at maintaining pluralism unjustified[11] and that it will not take a deferring stance when subjecting the measure or review under the market freedoms—something that is normally the case when fundamental rights considerations are involved.[12]

However, later case law on universal services[13] may suggest that the Court is taking a deferring stance.[14] In these cases, national 'must carry' obligations[15] imposed under national law on undertakings providing electronic communications networks where challenged on the ground that they infringe EU law and sought to be justified on the ground that they aim to guarantee pluralism as connected to freedom of expression. In these cases, the Court did not hold the measures to be unjustified and allowed some discretion to the national court to assess proportionality. Nevertheless, it was careful to provide for detailed guidance. In particular, in *United Pan-Europe Communications*,[16] after the Court repeated its by-now standard formula connecting media pluralism as a cultural policy to freedom of expression, it afforded to the Member States a wide margin of discretion, relying on (inter alia) *Schmidberger*,[17] precisely because this fundamental right was at issue.[18] However, the Court was at the same time also quick to point out that the 'legislation cannot render legitimate discretionary conduct on the part of the national authorities which is liable to negate

[11] See Barzanti, above n 2, 13 and Craufurd, above n 9, 186: this is signalling that the audiovisual sector is circumscribed by the Treaty.

[12] Case C-438/05 *The International Transport Workers' Federation and the Finnish Seamen's Union v Viking Lince ABP and OU Viking Line Eestt* [2007] ECR I-10779 (hereinafter *Viking*); and Case C-341/05 *Laval un Partneri Ltd v Svenska Byggnadsarbetareförbundet and others* [2007] ECR I-11767 (hereinafter *Laval*) seem to constitute an exception. However, there the same pattern can be identified (see discussion in ch 2): the fundamental right is not balanced directly against free movement provisions, but subsumed into the public interest ground of the protection of workers and therefore subordinated to the free movement provisions.

[13] Case C-336/07 *Kabel Deutschland Vertrieb und Service GmbH & Co KG v Niedersächsische Landesmedienanstalt für privaten Rundfunk* [2008] ECR I-10889; and Case C-250/06 *United Pan-Europe Communications Belgium and others* [2007] ECR I-11135.

[14] D Doukas, 'The EU Media Market and the Interplay between the Legislature and the Judiciary' in P Syrpis (ed), *The Judiciary, the Legislature and the EU Internal Market* (Cambridge, Cambridge University Press, 2012) 170.

[15] In *Kabel Deutschland*, above n 13, the national law required analogue cable network operators to provide access to their cable network to all television programmes allowed to be broadcast terrestrially. The question was whether Art 31(1) of the Universal Services Directive 2002/22/EC precludes such a law; in *United Pan-Europe Communications*, above n 13, national legislation required cable operators to broadcast programmes transmitted by certain private broadcasters; in this case, the law was examined on the basis of Art 49 EC.

[16] *United Pan-Europe Communications*, above n 13.

[17] Case C-112/00 *Eugen Schmidberger Internationale Transporte und Planzüge v Republic of Austria* [2003] ECR I-5659.

[18] *United Pan-Europe Communications*, above n 13, [44].

the effectiveness of provisions of Community law relating to a fundamental freedom'.[19] This amounts, as a matter of fact, to curbing considerably the scope of discretion previously granted on the ground that a fundamental right is involved.

Yet, the fact that this national policy objective has been subjected to the rules of the internal market and has therefore led to a loss of autonomy on the part of the Member States to protect this interest means that this interference could be addressed within the positive integration process if the divergent national regulatory regimes put the establishment and functioning of the internal market at risk (see discussion in chapter two). Moreover, the legislator would have the opportunity to grant more weight to media pluralism than what it currently enjoys under the status of an overriding requirement in the public interest.

Such intervention for regulating one aspect of media pluralism, more specifically media concentration, has been attempted at the EU level with the proposed Media Ownership Directive. However, it failed at an early stage of the lawmaking process. The reasons for such a failure will concern us in what shall follow.

It has been argued that the absence of a clear competence contributed significantly to the failure of this instrument.[20] It is true that such an absence gave the players involved in the pre-legislative/legislative process room to pull into opposing directions (market making versus safeguarding pluralism), which ultimately did not lead to a compromise. It is, however, submitted that the internal market legal basis could have been correctly used for adoption of such a directive. The remainder of this section will, first, set out that argument and, second, illustrate the true reasons that lead to failure in the legislative process.

The well-known history of the named instrument dates back to the early 1990s with calls from the European Parliament inviting the Commission to take legislative action for combating media concentration.[21] The Commission responded in 1992 with the publication of a Green Paper on 'Pluralism and Media Concentration in the Internal Market: An Assessment of the Need for a Communitarian Action',[22] which, after a long elaboration process, led to a proposal for a directive on 'Concentration and Pluralism in the Internal Market' four years later. However, this, as well as a renamed follow-up proposal,[23] was eventually abandoned. The renaming from 'media pluralism' to 'media ownership' was arguably deliberate in order 'to deflect the focus away from pluralism … towards the aim of removing obstacles to the Internal Market'.[24]

In terms of substance, a maximum share of audience reach (calculated differently for 'monomedia ownership' and 'cross-media ownership') was set,[25] and certain thresholds

[19] ibid [45].

[20] Barzanti, above n 2, 18.

[21] European Parliament Resolution of 15 February 1990 on Media Takeovers and Mergers [1990] OJ C68/137; and European Parliament Resolution of 16 September 1992 on Media Concentration and Diversity of Opinions [1992] OJ C284/44.

[22] European Commission, Green Paper on 'Pluralism and Media Concentration in the Internal Market: An Assessment of the Need for a Communitarian Action, COM(92) 480 final (hereinafter '1992 Green Paper').

[23] European Commission, Explanatory Memorandum On Media Ownership in the Internal Market, DG XV, February 1997.

[24] G Doyle, 'From "Pluralism" to 'Ownership': Europe's Emergent Policy on Media Concentrations Navigates the Doldrums' (1997) *Journal of Information, Law and Technology* 1, 9, www2.warwick.ac.uk/fac/soc/law/elj/jilt/1997_3/doyle.

[25] For a more detailed discussion, see A van Loon, 'EU Involvement in National Television Ownership and Control Policies and Practices' in European Audiovisual Observatory (ed), *IRIS Special, Television and Media Concentration—Regulatory Models on the National and the European Level* (Council of Europe, 2001) 64.

on media ownership were envisaged, even though never proposed, during the preparatory process. The second proposal of 1997 also included a flexibility clause, which allowed the exclusion of certain broadcasters from the upper limits for media ownership, provided these were not infringed in more than on Member State at the same time.[26]

The proposed directive found its legal basis in the internal market. This choice appears to be justified, at least in principle. As Craufurd Smith has argued:

> Perhaps the strongest justification for Community involvement is that media ownership rules restrict the freedom to provide services under Art 49 EC and that the complexity created by different national rules discourages companies from entering new markets. These impediments may be removed under the combined force of Arts 49, 55, and 57(2) EC, or the rules approximated under Art 95 EC. To be legitimate, a genuine objective of any such measure must be to complete the internal market, but there remains considerable scope during the drafting of such legislation to take into account various policy objectives, among them media pluralism. Moreover, all EC legislation must comply with fundamental rights and also, by virtue of Art 151(4) EC, take cultural aspects into account 'in particular in order to respect and promote the diversity of its cultures.[27]

The cited passage assumes the same conditions that have been set out in chapter two as prerequisites for regulatory action: there must be divergent national regulatory regimes which restrict free movement and are putting the unity of the internal market at risk, irrespective of what other interest the legislator may pursue.

This was indeed the case with respect to media ownership rules, according to Commissioner Mario Monti, who put this explanation forward when announcing his intention to submit a draft proposal for coordinating national media ownership rules. In particular, he pointed out that 'different Member States had launched projects to modernize their national rules on media ownership and media activities'[28] and that 'this might result in a refragementation of the internal market'.[29]

More concretely, arguments are still made in academic literature that there is considerable divergence among national rules, which calls for action in the interest of the internal market. The freedom of establishment is impeded due to the fact that there are significantly different national rules in place with respect to prohibitions on being active in the media depending on the market share.[30] The freedom to provide services is liable to be hampered by national concentration rules that hinder the transmission of broadcasts, with the result that undertakings may move to another country in order to transmit from there. As a response, Member States could restrict the free movement of broadcasts.[31] In addition,

[26] For a more detailed discussion on the content of the two (1996 and 1997) proposals, see Doyle, above n 24.

[27] S Craufurd, 'Rethinking European Union Competence in the Field of Media Ownership: The Internal Market, Fundamental Rights and European Citizenship', (2004) 29 *European Law Review* 652, 663.

[28] Van Loon, above n 25.

[29] ibid. See also C Palzer and C Hilger, 'Rechtliche Rundschau der europäischen audiovisuellen Informationsstelle' (2001) 8 *IRIS Plus* 1; Commission on Concentration in the Media (KEK), First Report on Media Concentration, 'Securing Diversity of Opinion against Media Concentration' (Konzentrationsbericht)', both cited in G Gounalakis and G Zagouras, 'Publizistische Vielfaltsicherung—Eine Aufgabe für Europa?' (2008) 13 *Juristische Zeitung* 652, 658.

[30] Contrast, for example, the German attempt at the ordinary legislative level to secure a plurality of voices in TV (see Gounalakis and Zagouras, above n 29, fn 44) with the Greek constitutional rule, which prohibits simultaneous activity in the media sector (if a main shareholder of a media undertaking) and the public works sector. This rule was eventually held by the CJEU to be contrary to EC Public Procurement law in Case C-213/07 *Michaniki AE v Ethniko Simvoulio Radiotileorasis, Ipourgos Epikratias* [2008] ECR I-999.

[31] Gounalakis and Zagouras, above n 29 (my translation).

the current state of affairs could be seen to be distorting competition, as there are two parameters which determine competition in the media that vary across the EU: cross-media activity is not only assessed on the basis of different scales of measurement but also on the degree to which it is allowed or restricted varies.[32] Moreover, recent policy analysis suggests that a possible legal framework on media ownership should focus on broadcasting and print media, since in these sectors there is national legislation in place providing for different limits (while pointing out that such instruments would contain many exceptions for reasons such as different market sizes).[33] It also draws attention to the fact that 'concentration is a tendency that can be observed also in the new media markets and thus it could be worth introducing ownership thresholds', while not limiting global competition and hampering investment.[34]

Notwithstanding the above (if empirically justified), one argument that could be made against supranational regulation is based on the principle of subsidiarity. However, it appears that it can equally be refuted.[35] This is so in view of the fact that the problem of media concentration has long ceased to be a national one, ever since media undertakings have expanded across national borders.[36] As one author has noted, 'national regulators have been often confronted with over-spills of broadcasting across borders and are finding it difficult to maintain pluralism in their domestic markets, especially when they deal with international media conglomerates whose national affiliations are weak'.[37] The problem is highlighted by the fact that most national regulatory regimes—due to their domestic focus—are not taking the audience reach of media undertakings outside the national borders into account.[38] In addition, it is clear that digital pay-television, the film, the music industry, advertising and the Internet are dominated by regional and international players,[39] and programme rights are often sold on a European scale and not for individual national markets.[40] 'On top of this, concentrations between already powerful players are increasingly tolerated and perceived by the Commission as inevitable.'[41] As the problem has become transnational, it is clear that national authorities will not be able to address it on their own account; rather, a joint effort by all Member States is needed.[42]

The above suggests that a significant part of the answer to the failure of this instrument may lie somewhere else. It appears that the serious impediment to supranational regulation

[32] ibid. See also Commission, above, n 22.

[33] The Centre for Media Pluralism and Media Freedom (CMPF), 'European Union Competencies in Respect of Media Pluralism and Media Freedom', RSCAS Policy Papers 2013/01, 73, http://cmpf.eui.eu/Documents/CMPFPolicyReport2013.pdf (hereinafter 'CMPF Report 2013').

[34] ibid.

[35] See Gounalakis and Zagouras, above n 29, 660.

[36] See A Harcourt, 'Engineering Europeanization: The Role of the European Institutions in Shaping National Broadcasting Regulation', (2002) 9(4) *Journal of European Public Policy* 736; see also B Klimkiewicz, 'Media Pluralism: European Regulatory Policies and the Case of Central Europe', RSCAS, EUI Working Paper No 2005/19, 5, www.eui.eu/RSCAS/WP-Texts/05_19.pdf.

[37] M Ariño, 'Competition law and Pluralism in European Digital Broadcasting: Addressing the Gaps' (2004) 54 *Communications & Strategies* 97, 124, with reference to M Feintuck, 'Regulating the Media Revolution: In Search of the Public Interest' (1997) *Journal of Information, Law and Technology* 3, www2.warwick.ac.uk/fac/soc/law/elj/jilt/1997_3/feintuck.

[38] Gounalakis and Zagouras, above n 29, 655.

[39] Ariño, above n 37, 124.

[40] ibid.

[41] ibid.

[42] ibid.

was/is one of political difficulties[43] rather than legal obstacles. However, it is acknowledged that these would not have reached these dimensions had there existed an explicit competence to regulate media pluralism supranationally. Yet this is not a complete answer to what had occurred, especially when paying attention to the fact that other sensitive areas have been regulated on the basis of the internal market in the absence of a self-standing competence.

With respect to the failed media ownership directive, Harcourt and Radaelli have described the failed process in the following terms: 'what to the Commission appeared a perfectly straightforward single market issue twisted itself out of control as the ensuing policy process became increasingly politicized'.[44]

The first internal market Green Paper was indeed formulated along the lines on which the argument for a competence has been built above, namely, in market making terms. The Commission acknowledged at the outset that 'the protection of pluralism as such is primarily a matter for the Member State'.[45] However, at the same time, it pointed out that there existed disparities between national rules that have as their purpose the safeguarding of media pluralism, which actually or potentially may impact on the functioning of the internal market. The following concerns were listed:

— a Member State could possibly restrict the free movement of broadcasts in the event of genuine circumvention of one of these laws;
— the establishment of media companies in another Member State could be limited;
— restrictions and distortions of competition are introduced;
— uncertainty in the law, harmful to the competitiveness of companies, could result from diverging views on what constitutes circumvention;
— such laws limit access to the activities and to the ownership of the media, when access should be facilitated so as to permit the establishment of the single market and secure the competitiveness of media companies which pluralism requires.[46]

At this stage, the Commission had not specified what form of action it envisaged. In fact, it even contemplated not taking action at all (the other two options were: 1) action relating to transparency; and 2) harmonisation of national laws). What it did, however, in this Green Paper is to call for a deliberately wide consultation of various stakeholders[47] in order to gain support for the initiative, but thereby also placing the issue very much in the political arena. The outcome was to propose a second Green Paper on 'Pluralism and Media Concentration in the Internal Market',[48] which kept the internal market rationale, but this time focused on the information society.

[43] Gounalakis and Zagouras have arrived at the same conclusion. See Gounalakis and Zagouras, above n 29 661.

[44] AJ Harcourt and CM Radaelli, 'Limits to EU Technocratic Regulation?' (1999) 35 *European Journal of Political Research* 110.

[45] Commission, above n 22, 7.

[46] ibid 8.

[47] The stakeholders involved were the European Parliament (in favour of harmonisation), the Economic and Social Committee (in favour of harmonisation), Member States, national interest groups, national government departments and European federations. Harcourt and Radaelli, above n 44, 112 list those and discuss this. In total, over 70 organisations had sent written reports to the Commission; see P Iosifidis, 'Pluralism and Media Policy in the European Union' (1997) 1 *The Public* 85, 95.

[48] Follow-up to the Consultation Process relating to the Green Paper on 'Pluralism and Media Concentration in the Internal Market—An Assessment of the Need for Community Action', COM(94) 353 final.

However, the political tension started emerging when the European Parliament called for tough measures to safeguard pluralism—this is where it saw the focus—and to restrict media ownership.[49] As the tension accelerated, the Commission had to convince the Parliament, especially the *Committee on Culture, Youth, Education and the Media* that maintaining the internal market logic was the only possible way to proceed with harmonisation.[50] A deal was eventually struck and the Parliament agreed to support the internal market argument. In return, it asked the Commission for a public commitment for the safeguarding of pluralism.[51] The Commission thereby managed to win the European Parliament over to its side, following which Commissioner Monti submitted a proposal for a Directive to the College of Commissioners.

At this point, although the draft was widely agreed upon, opposition emerged, most unexpectedly, from within the Commission: one of the Commissioners objected to the proposal on the grounds of media pluralism.[52] This triggered renewed criticism from the European Parliament, in particular, as regards the proposal's failure to take content pluralism in audience share into account.[53]

In addition to the tensions among and within the involved institutions, there was a further hindrance to the process, namely, powerful industry actors that were lobbying against the proposal.[54] Furthermore, it resulted from the consultation process following the publication of the Green Paper that the industry did want to see the national rules on media ownership changed in order to meet the new reality of globalisation and technological development.[55] However, they opposed harmonisation; what they envisaged was that if new rules on media ownership were to be adopted, those should de-regulate rather than provide for further regulation.[56] As one author has commented, those industry actors were also supported by the German as well as the UK government and they 'eroded the efforts of the Commission'.[57]

In conclusion, the foregoing example is a good illustration of the various political difficulties that may lead to failure of the regulation of a sensitive issue even if the legal requirements are met. In fact, with respect to the measure under discussion—to put it bluntly—everything that could have gone wrong went wrong: there was strong opposition between, within and outside the lawmaking institutions. However, it is obvious from the discussion above that the absence of an explicit competence did not mean an impossibility of adopting the measure. Still, this competence was to remain with the

[49] European Parliament, Report of the Committee on Culture, Youth, Education and the Media on the Commission Green Paper 'Pluralism and Media Concentration in the Internal Market' (5 January 1993), Document EN/RR242/242609, PE 204.759 final (Rapperteurs Fayot/Schinzel).

[50] Harcourt and Radaelli, above n 44, 113.

[51] Harcourt and Radaelli, (ibid) interviewed MEPs and received confirmation for that statement.

[52] The Commissioner is Commissioner Oreja (DG X). See ibid, fn 19: 'In an interview with Harcourt in 1996, a Commission official stated "Oreja was a surprise, we didn't expect Oreja".' However, the 'battle' within the Commission involved also other Commissioners: Bangemann (DG X), Brittan (DG I), Papoutsis and Santer—Commission President at the time. CMPF Report 2013, above n 33, 47.

[53] C Tongue, Report on 'The Future of Public Service Television in a Multi-Channel Digital Age', European Parliament Committee of Culture, Youth, Education, Sports and the Media (19 September 1996).

[54] M Christensen, 'Contentious Terrain in EU Information Society Policies: Media Pluralism and Freedom of Expression' (2008) 45 *Mediekultur* 80, 84.

[55] Iosifides, above n 47, 95.

[56] ibid 96.

[57] Klimkiewicz, above n 36, 5.

Member States, which have been 'equally reluctant to limit mergers of dominant national players'.[58]

The ultimate consequence of these political obstacles is that the supranational regulation of external media pluralism (comprising media ownership) is to a great extent left to EU competition law and to the free movement rules as applied by the Court. In both instances, it seems that the market interest will—more often than not—prevail. This is so with regard to competition law because of the limited extent to which non-economic considerations can be taken into account.[59] With regard to the Court's free movement jurisprudence, it is due to the conception of media pluralism as a cultural policy exception that functions as a narrow exception to the free movement rule.

At the same time, it is important to appreciate that regulating media ownership/concentration is only one means for promoting media pluralism. Examples for protecting internal media pluralism through European harmonisation, based on the internal market, do already exist, albeit in limited form; they are to be found in the Audiovisual Media Services Directive (discussed in detail below) and, more specifically, in the rules establishing European quotas, as well as the right to short news reporting.[60] They are also present in the EU's Information Society framework, that is, in electronic communications[61] and in the regulatory framework for radio spectrum policy.[62] Implicit regulation on media pluralism is in this respect found in, for example, provisions regarding frequency allocations and universal access.[63] Media pluralism is also sought to be promoted by allowing, under certain conditions, state aids for public service broadcasting. As Protocol No 29 to the Lisbon Treaty stipulates, 'the system of public broadcasting in the Member States is directly related to the democratic, social and cultural needs of each society and to the need to preserve

[58] Klimkiewicz, above n 6, 52.

[59] Ariño, above n 37, 113; Craufurd, above n 27. But note also the European Parliament's observation that 'EU competition law is somewhat limited in its ability to address media concentration issues because the activities creating concentration of media ownership at vertical and horizontal level in the new Member States have not reached the financial threshold at which EU competition law would apply'. See European Parliament Resolution of 25 September 2008 on concentration and pluralism in the media in the European Union, P6_TA(2008)0459.

[60] Directive 2010/13/EU of the European Parliament and of the Council of 10 March 2010 on the Coordination of Certain Provisions laid down by law, regulation or administrative action in Member States concerning the provision of audiovisual media services ('Audiovisual Media Services Directive') [2010] OJ L95/1 (hereinafter 'AVMSD'), Art 16 and Art 14. See Barzanti, above n 2, 18.

[61] Directive 2002/21/EC laying down a common regulatory framework for electronic communications network and services [2002] OJ L108/33 (hereinafter 'Framework Directive'); Directive 2002/20/EC on the authorisation of electronic communications networks and services [2002] OJ L108/21 (hereinafter 'Authorisation Directive'); Directive 2000/29/EC on access to, and interconnection of electronic communications networks and associated facilities [2000] OJ L169/1 (hereinafter 'Access Directive'); Directive 2002/22/EC on universal service and users' rights relating to electronic communications networks and services [2002] OJ L108/51 (hereinafter 'Universal Service Directive'). The first three named directives have been amended by Directive 2009/140/EC on Better Law-making [2009] OJ L337/37 and the latter by Directive 2009/136/EC on Citizens' Rights [2009] OJ L337/11.

[62] European Parliament and Council Decision No 676/2002/EC on a regulatory framework for radio spectrum policy in the European Union [2002] OJ L108/1, recital 3: 'Radio spectrum policy in the Community should contribute to freedom of expression, including freedom of opinion and freedom to receive and disseminate information and ideas, irrespective of borders, as well as freedom and plurality of the media.'

[63] See Christensen, above n 54, 85. See also, for example, Art 31(1) of the Universal Services Directive 2002/22/EC, which allows Member States to impose 'must carry' obligations on undertakings providing e-communications networks, if, inter alia, they are necessary to meet general interest objectives like media pluralism. See Universal Services Directive, above n 61.

media pluralism'.[64, 65] Finally, there are also other 'soft modes' that have been explored, such as the initiative on ERASMUS for journalists.[66] However, the European Parliament continues to be dissatisfied with the state of affairs and to pressure on the issue.[67]

The Commission had to react to the pressures emanating from both this institution and from civil society. In 2007, Commissioners Reding and Wallström presented a three-step approach to fellow Commissioners, comprising:

1. a Commission Staff Working Document on Media Pluralism;[68]
2. an independent study on media pluralism in EU Member States aimed at the development of indicators[69] and leading to a tool for assessing risks and identifying threads to media pluralism (the Media Pluralism Monitor);
3. a Commission Communication on the indicators for media pluralism in the EU Member States followed by a public consultation.[70]

The Media Pluralism Monitor—the output of the second step—is currently being tested in a pilot implementation,[71] whereas the third step seems to have been abandoned.

A series of other initiatives on media pluralism followed as of 2011. The timing suggests that the 'Hungarian crisis'[72] served as a catalyst in this respect, although other Member States like Italy (especially on the issue of media concentration) have also been for a long time the subject of focus.[73] All of the initiatives relate to the establishment of groups of experts to study, explore and form opinions and issue recommendations on media pluralism: the establishment of the High Level Group on Media Freedom and Pluralism in 2011 tasked with 'draw[ing] up a report for the Commission with recommendations for the respect, protection, support and promotion of pluralism and freedom of the media in Europe';[74] the establishment of the Centre for Media Pluralism and Media Freedom in 2012,[75] which is to reflect and advise on these issues, and finally the EU Media Futures

64 Protocol (No 29) on Services of General Interest [2010] OJ C83/312.

65 See also Commission Decision 2005/842/EC on the application of Article 86(2) of the EC Treaty to State aid in the form of public service compensation granted to certain undertakings entrusted with the operation of services of general economic interest [2005] OJ L312/67.

66 Feasibility study for the preparatory action 'Erasmus for Journalists' (March 2011) submitted to the Commission by Economisti Associati, The Evaluation Partnership, European Journalism Center, http://ec.europa.eu/information_society/media_taskforce/doc/mobility/erjo_part2_report.pdf.

67 See, eg, the 2008 European Parliament Resolution, above n 59; and European Parliament Resolution of 21 May 2013 on the EU Charter standard settings for media freedom across the EU (2011/2246(INI)), P7_TA-PROV(2013)0303, A7-0117/2013.

68 Commission Staff Working Document, 'Media Pluralism in the Member States of the European Union' (16 January 2007), SEC(2007)32.

69 The final output is available here: http://ec.europa.eu/information_society/media_taskforce/pluralism/study/index_en.htm.

70 Commission, 'Media Pluralism: Commission Stresses the Need for Transparency, Freedom and Diversity in Europe's Media Landscape' (16 January 2007), IP/07/52, http://europa.eu/rapid/press-release_IP-07-52_en.htm.

71 The pilot implementation is led by the CMPF of the European University Institute: http://www.eui.eu/news/2013/12-11-thecmpfselectstheninecountriestoconductthepilot.aspx.

72 See the European Parliament Resolution of 10 March 2011 on media law in Hungary, P7_TA(2011)0094.

73 See, eg, European Parliament Resolution of 22 April 2004 on the risks of violation, in the EU and especially in Italy, of freedom of expression and information (Art 11(2) of the Charter of Fundamental Rights), P5_TA(2004)0373; Motion for a Resolution on freedom of information and media pluralism in Italy and the European Union (14 October 2009), PE428.701v01-00.

74 High-Level Group on Media Freedom and Pluralism, http://ec.europa.eu/information_society/media_taskforce/pluralism/hlg/index_en.htm.

75 CMPF, above n 71.

Forum set up in 2011 'to debate how to improve the policy framework for European media industries'[76] and 'issue recommendations on how best to incentivize quality content and journalism while seizing the benefits of the digital revolution'.[77]

It is evident that the Commission sought 'formalised' support in deliberating on any possible future action, while the European Parliament has been very clear and articulate on what is needed. In its own words:

> 4. [The European Parliament] [r]eaffirms that the EU legislative framework for media pluralism and media concentration still remains inadequate and that it is therefore *urgent* for the Commission to finally take action using existing Community powers in the fields of the internal market, audiovisual policy, competition, telecommunications, State aid, public service obligations and the fundamental rights of citizens, in order to define the minimum essential conditions that all Member States are obliged to respect to ensure, guarantee and promote freedom of information and an adequate level of media pluralism;
> 5. In this respect, deplores the lack of political will of Member States and the inaction of the Commission as the political engine of the Union and urges the Commission to finally issue without delay a proposal for a directive on media pluralism and concentration, as requested several times by the European Parliament and as announced by the Commission itself; (emphasis added).[78]

Along the same lines, calls for a legislative initiative were expressed again in 2011.[79]

However, a subsequent LIBE Committee Working Document[80] revealed that for the European Parliament, several points for future actions were also in need of clarification. Its position in this document seemed far less 'absolute' than previously. First, the question of competence should be revisited by asking the European Parliament Legal Service for its opinion on whether it is possible to adopt a legislative measure in the field, an example that other institutions could follow and on which the Centre of Media Pluralism and Media Freedom should (continue) its work.[81] Second, even if there is such competence, the extent to which a legislative measure could be 'the solution' to all relevant problems of media freedom/pluralism was posed as an open question, and other means such as self-regulation and back-up interventions should be considered, while ensuring that no further power of media control is handed over to the government.[82] The Working Document also sought a wide and open debate with stakeholders and other organisations, and the identification and consolidation of international standards such as those of the Council of Europe. The European Parliament was thereby no longer hinting at quick and 'urgent' action, but at a slower process of deliberation and pooling of expertise.

[76] EU Media Futures Forum, http://ec.europa.eu/information_society/media_taskforce/pluralism/forum/index_en.htm.

[77] ibid.

[78] 2008 European Parliament Resolution, above n 59.

[79] 2011 European Parliament Resolution, above n 72, para 6.

[80] European Parliament, LIBE Committee Working Document 2 on EU Charter: Standard Settings for Media Freedom across the EU (11 June 2012), PE491.183v02-00 (Rapporteur: R Weber).

[81] ibid, point (d).

[82] ibid, point (e).

The Working Document also repeated a point that the European Parliament has already expressed in the past, namely, entrusting the FRA with the task of monitoring media pluralism in the Member States. The problem here, however, is that the FRA's mandate precludes any monitoring function. Given the European Parliament's insistence on the issue, it will be interesting to see whether a potential re-negotiation of the FRA Founding Regulation[83] may bring it to the negotiation table.

A further interesting point is the possibility of reviewing the Audiovisual Media Services Directive (AVMSD) in order to harmonise and network national regulatory authorities at the EU level, which is reminiscent of the Article 29 Data Protection Working Party[84] and may prove in fact more effective in monitoring the situation Europe-wide. Attention is also paid to a series of specific issues, such as the fact that the independence of journalists has to be guaranteed, that public service broadcasters should not be subject to political interference and that the challenges of new media should be taken on.

The resulting European Parliament Resolution of 2013[85] echoes this more cautious phrasing of key points in part. On competence, the European Parliament is careful to point out that the EU has such to promote, inter alia, media pluralism in specific media-related fields[86] and at least as much as it has competence over other general interests which are pursued in the AVMSD.[87] Yet, it does call once again on the Commission 'to propose concrete measures to safeguard media pluralism, including a legislative framework for media ownership rules introducing minimum standards for Member States'.[88]

The European Parliament made sure to point to other non-legislative media pluralism initiatives, which shall be pursued, 'such as monitoring, self-regulation and codes of conduct as well as activation of Article 7 TEU when appropriate'.[89] In this vein, it also emphasised, for example, the importance of establishing self-regulatory bodies of the media and 'bottom-up efforts initiated by European journalists'.[90] Monitoring is one such non-legislative means on which the report placed great emphasis. This will be conducted and reported in all Member States on an annual basis. This resolution is more ambiguous than the LIBE Working Document on who should be entrusted with this task, mentioning 'the Commission, the Fundamental Rights Agency and/or the EUI Centre for Media Pluralism and Media Freedom'.[91] This may be due to the above-described limitation of the FRA and the absence of a self-standing competence on media pluralism, which makes the point contentious.

The resolution also repeated its calls on the Commission to evaluate and revise the AVMSD. This will be done not only in order to network national regulatory authorities at the EU level, eg, through the establishment of a 'European Regulator's Association for

[83] See discussion in ch 3, s III.D.
[84] See discussion in ch 4, s III.A.iii.
[85] European Parliament Resolution of 21 May 2013 on the EU Charter: Standard Settings for Media Freedom Across the EU (2011/2246(INI)).
[86] ibid, point (s).
[87] ibid, para 33.
[88] ibid, para 19.
[89] ibid, para 33.
[90] ibid, para 26.
[91] ibid, para 32.

audiovisual media services';[92] but also in order to put in place 'an appropriate legislative and administrative framework to guarantee effective pluralism'.[93] Therefore, the AVMSD shall be revised to include rules ensuring that national regulatory authorities enjoy independence and have sanctioning powers. Moreover, rules relating to transparency, media ownership, media concentration and conflicts of interest should be included.[94]

In conclusion, the LIBE Committee did in fact acknowledge both in its Working Document and Resulting European Parliament Resolution how multifaceted the problem of media pluralism is and that it is unlikely to be fully solved with the adoption of one directive on media ownership. However, it also sought institutional back-up on the question of competence, but in doing so revealing implicitly that pursuing such an instrument will continue to rank high on its agenda. This is confirmed by the European Parliament Resolution, which again calls also for legislative action.

As regards the AVMSD, the Commission had already presented a Green Paper[95] before the adoption of this European Parliament resolution. The document points out that its purpose is not to reflect a pre-determined outcome; it will not necessarily lead to a legislative proposal. Rather, it will 'open a broad, public discussion on the implications of the on-going transformation of the audiovisual media landscape'.[96] It also picks up on national regulatory authorities in the context of the media pluralism discussion, although the concern is not the independence of the national regulatory authorities, but rather their potential role in imposing obligations on operators to provide access to electronic programme guides.

The subsequent Council conclusions on media freedom and pluralism[97] clearly de-emphasised the legislative dimension. For example, both the matter of preventing excessive concentration of media ownership and that of ensuring independence of regulatory audiovisual authorities are issues that should be dealt with by Member States according to the Council.

In conclusion, we have seen that the supranational regulation of media concentration through a directive has not been seen favourably by Member States and the powerful media industry, which has led to a hands-off approach on behalf of the legislator, but given that media pluralism has been said to be 'without doubt the biggest failure of the EP',[98] continuous efforts for achieving (at least partial) supranational regulation are to be expected, and with it also the instrumentalisation of the competence argument.

[92] ibid, paras 35–36.

[93] ibid, para 34.

[94] ibid, para 35.

[95] European Commission, Green Paper 'Preparing for a Fully Converged Audiovisual World: Growth, Creation and Values' (24 April 2013), COM(2013) 231 final (hereinafter '2013 Green Paper').

[96] ibid 14.

[97] Council Conclusions and of the Representatives of the Governments of the Member States, meeting within the Council on media freedom and pluralism in the digital environment, Education, Youth, Culture and Sport Council meeting (26 November 2013), www.consilium.europa.eu/uedocs/cms_data/docs/pressdata/en/educ/139725.pdf.

[98] In the sense of being a very significant point on its agenda, but it has failed to successfully push for EU legislation on the matter. K Sarikakis, *Powers in Media Policy: The Challenge of the European Parliament* (Bern, Peter Lang, 2004) 132, in Klimkiewicz, above n 6, 60.

III. THE AUDIOVISUAL MEDIA SERVICES DIRECTIVE—PROMOTING FREEDOM OF EXPRESSION/TO PROVIDE SERVICES

The AVMSD[99] is the most obvious example of an internal market instrument that regulates freedom of expression, or rather a specific form of it: the right to receive and impart information.[100]

In the words of the Preamble to the AVMSD: 'This Directive enhances compliance with fundamental rights and is fully in line with the principles recognised by the Charter of Fundamental Rights of the European Union, in particular Article 11 thereof.'[101]

The history of this instrument commences with the adoption of the Television without Frontiers Directive (TVWFD). This was adopted in 1989[102] on the basis of then Article 47(2) and 55 EC and was amended in 1997[103] in order to respond to technological developments. The Directive established the core principle that Member States shall ensure freedom of reception and shall not restrict retransmission on their territory of television broadcasts from other Member States.[104] A number of minimum rules were laid down with respect to a number of coordinated areas, in relation to which Member States are obliged to respect this obligation and follow the country of origin principle (ie, all broadcasts comply with the law of the Member State from which they emanate—Article 2). The basic rules as contained in the new AVMSD are the following:

1. Provisions applicable to all audiovisual media services (Chapter III):

   Member States shall ensure that audiovisual media service providers make a number of information relating to it available to recipients (Article 5). Member States shall also ensure that audiovisual media services do not contain incitement to hatred (Article 6), and encourage that services are gradually made available to people with a visual or hearing disability (Article 7). They shall also ensure that audiovisual commercial communications comply with a list of requirements, aimed at promoting health, minors, the environment and importantly also certain fundamental rights: human dignity and equal treatment (Article 9(1)(c) (i) and (ii)).

2. Provisions only applicable to on-demand audiovisual media services (Chapter IV):

   On-demand services harmful for minors shall only be made available in a way to ensure that they cannot normally be heard or seen by them (Article 12). Member States shall also ensure that on-demand services promote the production of and the access to European works (Article 13).

[99] AVMSD, above n 60.

[100] Article 11(1) CFR and Art 10(1) ECHR.

[101] AVMSD, above n 60, recital 16.

[102] Council Directive 89/552/EEC of 3 October 1989 on the Coordination of Certain Provisions laid down by law, regulation or administrative action in Member States concerning the Pursuit of Television Broadcasting Activities [1989] OJ L298/23 (hereinafter 'TVWFD 1989').

[103] Directive 97/36/EC of the European Parliament and of the Council of 30 June 1997 amending Council Directive 89/552/EEC on the Coordination of Certain Provisions laid down by law, regulation or administrative action in Member States concerning the Pursuit of Television Broadcasting Activities [1997] OJ L202/60 (hereinafter 'TVWFD 1997').

[104] TVWFD 1989, above n 102, Art 2; AVMSD, above n 60, Art 2.

3. Exclusive rights and short news reports in TV broadcasting (Chapter V):

   Member States may take measures to ensure that broadcasters do not broadcast on an exclusive basis events of major interest to society so that a large part of the public is excluded from following them (Article 14). Equal, fair and reasonable access for broadcasters to events of high interest to the public, which are transmitted on an exclusive basis by a broadcaster shall be guaranteed (Article 15).

4. Promotion of distribution and production of TV programmes (Chapter VI):

   Member States shall ensure that broadcasters reserve for European works a majority proportion of their transmission time (Article 16) and that they reserve at least 10 per cent of their transmission time, or 10 per cent of their programming budget, for European works created by producers who are independent of broadcasters (Article 17).

5. Advertising, TV sponsoring (Chapter IV):

   The Directive provides a 20 per cent maximum proportion of hourly transmission time allowed for advertising (Article 23) and sets procedures for interrupting programmes (Article 20). Furthermore, it provides that the advertisements must conform to certain ethical considerations, in particular the protection of minors and that the advertisements must comply with certain criteria concerning advertisements for alcoholic beverages (Article 22).

6. Protection of minors (Chapter V):

   Member States shall take measures to ensure that television broadcasts by broadcasters under their jurisdiction do not include programmes, which might seriously impair the physical, mental or moral development of minors, in particular those that involve pornography or gratuitous violence. Other programmes that may have the same effect should be transmitted in an appropriate time and preceded by acoustic warnings or visual signals (Article 27).

7. Right of reply in TV broadcasting (Chapter VI):

   Any natural or legal person, whose legitimate interests have been damaged, shall have a right of reply or equivalent remedy (Article 28).

The successor to the TVWFD, the AVMSD, was proposed in 2005. The reason for such an initiative was the perceived need to respond to changes in the media environment and to extend the scope of the Directive. The main innovations that the AVMSD brought about are, first, to extend its scope so as to cover all content services, regardless of the technology delivering them. That means to include 'pull'/'on demand'/'non-linear services', but to apply differentiated rules to them. Second, new more relaxed rules on advertising and product placement were introduced.

The reasons for taking action in this area have been attributed, in the first place, to 'exogenous factors, which were epitomized by the development of satellite broadcasting, the proliferation of TV broadcasters and the rapidly increasing deficit with the US in audiovisual trade'.[105] The motives for the adoption of the TVWFD can be distilled from

[105] M Burri-Nenova, 'Cultural Diversity and the EC Audiovisual Media Services Directive: Beyond the Handsome Rhetoric', NCCR Trade Working Paper No 2009/9, April 2009, 3.

Commission statements. They are basically twofold, namely, economic and cultural, and include the following aims: 1) making the European film and television programme industry more competitive and 'more open to the world market'; 2) ensuring 'its share of the overall growth of the audiovisual sector'; 3) placing it 'in a position to realise its potential in terms of employment'; and 4) promoting European cultures 'without causing any individual country to lose its identity'.[106]

In addition to that, however, the Commission has also identified the importance of ensuring freedom of expression and media pluralism as 'requirements of a democratic society'[107] that constitute reasons for establishing the European audiovisual space. In the Commission's early Green Paper on the Establishment of the Common Market for Broadcasting,[108] which came in response to a resolution from the European Parliament,[109] this dimension finds striking emphasis. The Paper has a threefold purpose, the very first of which is 'to demonstrate the importance of broadcasting (radio and television) for European integration and, in particular, for the free democratic structure of the European Communities'.[110] It also reveals that its drafters perceived an inextricable link between 'Community-wide television broadcasting' and 'fundamental rights of freedom of information and opinion which are binding on the Community'.[111] The assumption is that, on the one hand, the former is already guaranteed by virtue of the latter (international human rights instruments like the ECHR, the Universal Declaration of Human Rights and the International Covenant on Civil and Political Rights (ICCPR) are cited in support) and that Western democracies have taken a 'fundamental … decision … to promote free transmission of information as an expression of political freedom'.[112] On the other hand, the Green Paper also stated that the transmission of radio or TV signals is captured by the (then EEC) Treaty and, more specifically, the rules on the internal market, respect for which has to be ensured.[113] The initiative was built on the basis of this latter 'economic approach' and was subsequently endorsed in the Commission's White Paper on the Internal Market.[114]

That the free transmission of broadcasting services has an indisputably strong internal market link is clear since the 1970s, where the Court established in *Sacchi* that 'a television signal must by reason of its nature be regarded as provision of services'.[115] The Court's move

[106] Commission Green Paper, 'Strategy Options to Strengthen the European Programme Industry in the Context of the Audiovisual Policy of the European Union' (6 April 1994), COM(94) 96 final, 1.

[107] Communication from the Commission to the Council and Parliament on Audiovisual Policy (21 February 1990), COM(90) 78 final, 21.

[108] Commission Green Paper, 'Television without Frontiers—Green Paper on the Establishment of the Common Market for Broadcasting, especially by Satellite and Cable' (14 June 1984), COM(84) 300 final.

[109] European Parliament Resolution on Broadcasting and Television in the European Community [1982] OJ C87/110.

[110] ibid 15.

[111] ibid 38.

[112] ibid.

[113] ibid 23.

[114] Commission White Paper to the European Council, 'Completing the Internal Market' (14 June 1985), COM(85) 310 final.

[115] Case 155/73 *Giuseppe Sacchi* [1974] ECR 409 [6]; Case 52/79 *Procureur du Roi v Marc JVC Debauve and others* [1980] ECR 833; Case 62/79 *Coditel v Ciné-Vog Films* (*Coditel I*) [1980] ECR 881; and Case 262/81 *Coditel v Ciné-Vog Films* (*Coditel II*) [1982] ECR 3381.

in this case meant that broadcasting regulation per se came within the scope of the Treaty (the free movement of services). Therefore, adoption of the TVWFD meant to provide for a concretisation (albeit only partial) of the freedom to provide services in this sector.[116] The internal market requirement necessary for adopting the directive was also fulfilled as 'it is … clear from the eighth, ninth and tenth recitals in the preamble to the Directive that the obstacles which the Community legislature intended to abolish are those which result from disparities existing between the provisions of the Member States concerning the pursuit of broadcasting activities and of distribution of television programmes'.[117] These obstacles were thought to obstruct the internal market in television services. Hence, the ultimate endeavour to construct an audiovisual space along market building terms comes as no surprise.

This does not, however, mean that it was uncontroversial at the time. The Commission's approach was seen critically by many actors (although it was welcomed by the European Parliament), which considered audiovisual broadcasting to be a cultural rather than an economic activity, on which there is no EU competence).[118]

In any event, what is clear is that there was no lamentation that the Directive was a fundamental rights instrument for which the EU lacked competence. This is probably so because the rights dimensions was seen as one that 'simply' coincided with the internal market dimension.

In the words of the legislator in the first TVWFD: 'this right [the free movement of services] as applied to the broadcasting and distribution of television services is also a specific manifestation in Community law of a more general principle, namely the freedom of expression as enshrined in Art 10(1) [ECHR]'.[119] This statement imparts in effect that the freedom to provide the specific service, other than a fundamental market freedom, is at the same time a fundamental right, linked to Article 10(1) ECHR and as such is protected in EU law.

What has to be emphasised, however, is that this 'coincidence' is imperfect in the following sense: even though the free transmission of broadcasting signals can assume both classifications, the *overall* regulatory framework through which it is to be guaranteed will vary based on the conceptualisation that will be driving the process.

The difference can be illustrated when comparing the EU instrument with the Council of Europe's Convention on Transfrontier Television (ECTT),[120] and this despite the fact that the former was adopted shortly after the latter, following its basic structure and

[116] See Case C-412/93 *Société d'Importation Edouard Leclerc-Siplec v TF1 Publicité SA and M6 Publicité SA* [1995] ECR I-179.

[117] Joined Cases C-34, 35 and 36/95, *Konsumentombudsmannen (KO) v De Agostini (Svenska) Förlag AB and TV-Shop I Sverige AB* [1997] ECR I-3843 [25].

[118] P Goerrens, 'Interplay between Relevant European Instruments—ECTT and TVWF Directive: Competition or Complementarity?' in *IRIS* Special, *Audiovisual Media Services without Frontiers, Implementing the Rules*, European Audiovisual Observatory (2006), 2.

[119] TVWFD 1989, above n 102, Preamble, 8th 'whereas clause'.

[120] Council of Europe, European Convention on Transfrontier Television (5 May 1989), ETS No 132 (hereinafter 'ECTT').

provisions.[121] The existing degree of convergence is a result of a carefully coordinated negotiations and drafting process, paralleled by many formal and informal interactions.[122]

Parallel developments on the issue in the two legal orders were ongoing (the impetus coming from the EU side this time)[123] as the ECTT was undergoing its second revision process in light of the adoption of the AVMSD, with the aim of aligning, as far as possible, the two instruments.[124] However, in 2011, the process of revising the ECTT was discontinued. This was due to the EU's position, namely, the fact that it has exclusive external competence over most of the issues covered by the ECTT and did not intend to become party to it.[125] This being the case, and given that many provisions of the ECTT 'might not necessarily be in line with the EU *acquis*',[126] Member States cannot become separately and individually party to the Convention. Given that this position still holds true today, the Committee rejected[127] on the same grounds recent calls by the Parliamentary Assembly[128] to resume work on the ECTT in 2014.

Despite the described link of the AVMSD's predecessor to the Council of Europe Convention and several references in the Preamble to fundamental rights, one could hold that the two instruments are in their basis different: the underlying rationale of the ECTT is freedom of expression, while that of the TVWFD/AVMSD is the single market.[129]

The Explanatory Report to the ECTT states that the objective, which was pursued by the Member States to the Convention, was '*to strengthen the free exchange of information and ideas* by encouraging the transfrontier circulation of television programme services on the basis of a number of commonly agreed basic standards' (emphasis added).[130] This is

[121] As the Commission has also stated: 'The objectives and principles and the field of application of the Convention and the Directive are nearly the same.' See European Commission website on Audiovisual and Media Policies, http://ec.europa.eu/avpolicy/info_centre/a_z/index_en.htm#e9. The Convention lays down minimum rules in fields such as advertising (Ch III) and sponsorhip (Ch IV), and aims to protect individual rights, like human dignity and the protection of minors. The parties to the Convention undertake to comply with those rules and guarantee in return the transfrontier transmission and retransmission of television broadcasting services. Note that one important difference concerns the enforcement mechanisms: for the AVMSD, it is the Commission and the CJEU; for the ECTT, it is the Convention's Standing Committee, which, however, has only an advisory role. See ECTT, above n 120, Arts 20–22.

[122] Goerrens, above n 118.

[123] Draft Second Protocol Amending the European Convention on Transfrontier Television and its Explanatory Report (24 September 2009), T-TT(2009)007FIN_en (hereinafter 'Draft 2nd Protocol Amending the ECTT') 27: 'One of the major relevant political developments was the second revision of the Television without Frontiers Directive within the framework of the European Community, since the Convention, at the time of its preparation, had been negotiated in parallel with the drafting of this directive.'

[124] See the preliminary UK Consultation Report of September 2008 'Council of Europe Transfrontier Television Convention (TTV)', para 20, www.culture.gov.uk/images/consultations/TTV_prelimconsultationsept08.rtf.

[125] Standing Committee on Transfrontier Television (T-TT), http://www.coe.int/t/dghl/standardsetting/media/t-tt/default_EN.asp.

[126] Council of Europe, Committee of Ministers, 'Revision of the European Convention on Transfrontier Television' (23 September 2014), Reply to REC 2036 (2014), Doc 13605.

[127] ibid.

[128] Council of Europe, Parliamentary Assembly, Recommendation 2036(2014) on 'Revision of the European Convention on Transfrontier Television' (31 January 2014).

[129] Burri-Nenova, above n 105, 6. Note also the concern expressed during the revision process of the ECTT that even though the concerns reflected in the AVMSD which correspond to Council of Europe concerns are to be retained, those which are market-driven should not 'unwittingly [be] introduced into the Council of Europe's ambit'. See Council of Europe Doc 1177518 December 2008, 'The regulation of audiovisual media services', Report, Committee on Culture, Science and Education, Explanatory Memorandum by Mr McIntosh, para 11, http://assembly.coe.int/ASP/Doc/XrefViewHTML.asp?FileID=12289&Language=en.

[130] See the revised (1st revision) ECTT and its Explanatory Report, T-TT(2000)008, para 28, at 28.

fundamentally different from the objective underlying the TVWFD and the AVMSD. The Preamble of the former (1997 amended version) provided that 'the primary objective of this Directive … is to create the legal framework for the free movement of services',[131] while the latter states that the cross-border provision of audiovisual media services is one of the ways of pursuing the objectives of the EU and that therefore: 'Certain measures are necessary to permit and ensure the transition from national markets to a common programme production and distribution market, and to guarantee conditions of fair competition without prejudice to the public interest role to be discharged by the audiovisual media services.'

What is hinted at in political declarations finds confirmation in the provisions of the respective instruments. The first difference is the fact that the main obligation to ensure free transmission and retransmission is linked in the ECTT to Article 10 ECHR. Indeed, the obligation imposed on the Member States to the ECTT in the first place is to ensure freedom of expression in accordance with Article 10 ECHR.[132] No such obligation is imposed in the AVMSD.

The second distinctive feature is the explicit media pluralism provision in the ECTT, which is absent in the AVMSD. Media pluralism is there instead inserted in various recitals of the Preamble, but it is also implicit in the provisions of the instrument, for example, in the European quota rule or in the rules on short news reporting.[133]

The explicit references to media pluralism in the AVMSD Preamble are of varying character: first, we find affirmations/proclamations that the audiovisual policy should safeguard media pluralism and respect Article 11 of the Charter;[134] second, the objective of ensuring media pluralism serves as a justification for adopted rules.[135] Lastly, Member States are reminded that 'it is essential [for them to] ensure the prevention of any acts … which may promote the creation of dominant positions which would lead to restrictions on pluralism'.[136]

However strong and frequent the rhetoric in the Preamble, this choice ultimately proves once more how difficult it is to agree on media pluralism issues at the EU legislative level. By contrast, the ECTT requires—in a substantive provision—its Contracting Parties to 'endeavour to avoid that programme services transmitted or retransmitted by a broadcaster or any other legal or natural persons within their jurisdiction … endanger media pluralism'.[137] The draft second protocol revising the ECTT goes even further in that it also asks its Contracting Parties 'to promote full transparency of ownership of media service

[131] TVWFD 1997, above n 103, recital 7. See also Case C-6/98 *Arbeitsgemeinschaft Deutscher Rundfunkanstalten (ARD) v Pro Sieben Media AG* [1999] ECR I-7599 [42] (the Court held that 'the attainment of the objective of Directive 89/552 … is to ensure freedom to provide television broadcasting services').

[132] See ECTT, above n 120, Art 4; and Draft 2nd Protocol, above n 123, Art 6 renumbering Art 4 of ECTT to Art 3 of ECTT.

[133] See AVMSD, above n 60, recital 48 which acknowledges that broadcasting rights for events of high interest to the public may be acquired but also emphasises that 'it is essential to promote pluralism through the diversity of news production and programming across the Union…'. See also recital 55 stressing that short news reporting rights should be granted to broadcasters in order 'to safeguard the fundamental freedom to receive information and to ensure that the interests of viewers in the Union are fully and properly protected'.

[134] AVMSD, above n 60, recitals 12; 34 last sub-sentence 'pluralism of information should be a fundamental principle of the Union'; and 48.

[135] AVMSD, above n 60, recitals 5 and 48.

[136] AVMSD, above n 60, recital 8.

[137] ECTT, above n 120, Art 10*bis*.

providers'[138] and to 'encourage broadcasters with a public service mission to play an active role in promoting social cohesion and integrating all communities, social groups and generations ... while respecting their different identities and needs'.[139]

On the other hand, and as regards the substantive provisions of the Directive aimed at promoting media pluralism, their importance for the latter should be noted even if the legislator did not expressly frame the matter as such. This becomes evident in the *Sky Österreich* case, where the Court held that Article 15 AVMSD seeks 'to safeguard the fundamental freedom to receive information, guaranteed under Article 11(1) of the Charter, and to promote pluralism of the media in the production and programming of information in the European Union, protected under Article 11(2) of the Charter'.[140] As already stated above, Article 15 AVMSD grants to broadcasters for the purposes of short news reports the right to have access on a fair, reasonable and non-discriminatory basis to events of high interest to the public that are transmitted by other broadcasters on an exclusive basis. This provision (more specifically Article 15(6) AVMSD) was challenged in *Sky Österreich* on the ground that it violated Article 17 (right to property) and Article 16 (freedom to conduct a business) of the Charter. The Court rejected both claims.[141] As regards the former, it held that there was no interference with Article 17(1) CFR.[142] As regards the latter, it found that the limitations that Article 15(6) imposes on the freedom to conduct a business are proportionate and ensure a fair balance between the rights and freedoms at issue. The Court imposed a detailed proportionality analysis, finding that the limitations to the freedom to conduct a business where 'confined within precise limits'[143] and that the legislature 'was entitled ... to give priority, in the necessary balancing of the rights and interests at issue, to public access to information over contractual freedom'.[144]

Finally, it should be noted that the Green Paper on 'Preparing for a Fully Converged Audiovisual World'[145] dedicates a section explicitly on media pluralism[146] and sees not only the above-named provisions as relevant for that, but also the cornerstone principle of the directive, ie, the free circulation of audiovisual media services based on the country of origin principle.

Still, the ECTT and the AVMSD are of a different character. This comes to the fore—albeit more indirectly—when considering the restrictions/derogatory measures to the principle of free transmission in the respective instruments. The draft revised Convention,[147] in almost identical terms as the AVMSD,[148] allows Member States to 'take measures' in respect to on-demand services, if those are necessary on the ground of a list of legitimate reasons (public policy, public health, public security and consumer protection) and proportionate

[138] Draft 2nd Protocol Amending the ECTT, above n 123, Art 15 renumbering Art 10(a) ECTT to Art 12; and Art 12(1).

[139] ibid; see Art 12(2) and (3).

[140] Case C-283/11 *Sky Österreich GmbH v Österreichischer Rundfunk* EU:C:2013:28 [51] (hereinafter *Österreich*).

[141] For a detailed discussion, see W Hins, 'The Freedom to Conduct a Business and the Right to Receive Information for Free: *Sky Österreich GmbH* v *Österreichischer Rundfunk*' (2014) 51 *Common Market Law Review* 665.

[142] *Sky Österreich*, above n 140, [40].

[143] ibid [61].

[144] ibid [66].

[145] 2013 Green Paper, above n 95.

[146] ibid, s 3.2, at 13.

[147] See Draft 2nd Protocol Amending the ECTT, above n 123, Art 39 introducing a new Art 29.

[148] AVMSD, above n 60, Art 3(1)(4).

to those objectives. Even though the obligation is the same, it is questionable whether the balancing exercise will be the same. In the AVMSD, the restrictions will be balanced, in the classic internal market logic, against the free movement provisions, whereas within the ECTT framework, the derogation will be one against a human right. One could argue that if the balancing is undertaken in the fundamental rights logic rather than in that of the market freedoms, the threshold to pass the proportionality test in order to justify the restriction may be higher, and consequently so may the level of protection. However, if one takes the position that fundamental rights and internal market freedoms have the same hierarchical position in the Treaty and are thus of equal value, then it should not make a difference how one classifies the freedom to broadcast. Nevertheless, it seems that there would certainly remain one difference: the legitimate grounds on the basis of which Article 10 ECHR can be restricted constitute a considerably shorter list than what can qualify as an overriding requirement in the public interest under the Court's free movement case law.

The AVMSD also contains provisions that can be qualified as harmonised 'restrictions', to be found in the articles laying down content requirements. It should be noted in that respect that the classification of these requirements as 'restrictions' is dependent on the conceptualisation chosen for the Directive. If one focuses on the freedom of expression dimension, content requirements will certainly always qualify as 'restrictions' (which may be subject to justification). However, if one focuses on free movement of services, this will not be the case, given that the Directive's provisions apply irrespective of whether the service moves.

In the remainder, we shall focus on the fundamental rights dimension, whereby the Directive could be viewed as restricting freedom of expression. The following content requirements deserve attention: 1) the European quota rules (Chapter VI); 2) the provision on the protection of minors (Chapter VIII); and 3) the obligation imposed on Member States to ensure that the media services provided under their jurisdiction 'do not contain any incitement to hatred based on race, sex, religion or nationality'.[149]

European quota rules were already included in the predecessor to the AVMSD (the TVWFD) and have been criticised for restricting freedom of expression already at that time.[150] These rules impose on Member States the obligation to reserve a majority proportion of the transmission time of television broadcasts for European works.[151] Furthermore, Member States are required to ensure that the broadcasters reserve 10 per cent of their transmission time and at least 10 per cent of their programming budget for European works created by independent producers.[152] With regard to non-linear services, Member States shall ensure that the service providers promote, 'where practicable and by appropriate means, the production of and access to European works'.[153]

The critical argument is that certain 'voices' and information are prevented from being expressed and heard due to the simple reason that they are not European. Under ECHR

[149] ibid Art 6.

[150] A von Bogdandy, 'Europäischer Protektionismus im Medienbereich' (1992) 9 *Europäische Zeitschrift für Wirtschaftsrecht* 15, discussed by B de Witte, 'The European Content Requirement in the EC Television Directive—Five Years After' (1995) *The Yearbook of Media and Entertainment Law* 101, 116.

[151] AVMSD, above n 60, Art 16. Art 10 ECTT contains an equivalent provision; see ECTT, above n 123.

[152] ibid Art 17.

[153] ibid Art 13(1); Member States have to report every four years on the implementation of this provision to the Commission.

law, TV broadcasters enjoy a right to compose their programmes independently,[154] and this is certainly encroached upon in view of the fact that the quota regulation influences the content of the programme.[155]

Such restriction should be capable of justification, one would assume, on the basis of two arguments. The first one is that in the context of an international/European market where there is 'a tendency to homogenise programming in the broadcasting sector',[156] this rule promotes diversity of expression and therefore promotes pluralism. At this point, a restriction of one aspect of freedom of expression is justified by the promotion of another such aspect. The second argument can be made on the basis that it aims to protect cultural rights by seeking to ensure the European cultural identity. The problem that has been put forward is that neither of these grounds is listed in Article 10(2) ECHR, the provision under which restrictions can be justified, although it seems that those provisions could be justified on the ground of 'rights of others' mentioned in Article 10(2),[157] as both grounds (pluralism and cultural identity) can be presented as fundamental rights concerns. The question is thus whether a fair balance has been struck between the two interests, which in view of the above considerations could be answered in the positive.

A similar kind of balancing exercise can be attributed to Chapter VIII. The provisions therein impose on Member States the obligation to take appropriate measures not to include 'programmes, which might seriously impair the physical, mental or moral development of minors, in particular programmes that involve pornography or gratuitous violence' (Art 27(1)) and other programmes which might so impair children's physical mental or moral development, except when it is ensured that minors will not see or hear such programmes (eg, through the choice of time) (Art 27(2)). The protection of minors translates here into a fundamental rights obligation: the protection of children's rights. Thus, the question is again one of conflicting rights. Freedom of expression is balanced against the rights of children.[158] This balance seems to be in line with international standards, although it has to be acknowledged that there is 'little legal elaboration of these issues by international courts'.[159]

However, the third content requirement relating to hate speech, which at its core aims to ensure respect for human dignity, cannot be viewed in these (balancing of rights) terms. This is so given that, under ECHR jurisprudence, hate speech is not protected by freedom of expression (Art 11 ECHR).[160] So here the legislature cannot be accused of restricting

[154] *Groppera Radio AG and others v Switzerland*, App No 10890/84 (ECtHR, 28 March 1990).

[155] O Castendyk, E Dommering and A Scheuer (eds), *European Media Law* (Dordrecht, Kluwer Law International, 2008) 443.

[156] K Bhattacharjee and T Mendel, 'Local Content Rules in Broadcasting' (March 2001), www.article19.org/pdfs/publications/local-content-rules.pdf.

[157] De Witte, above n 150, 117.

[158] Article 17(e) of the UN Convention on the Rights of the Child provides that Contracting States shall: 'Encourage the development of appropriate guidelines for the protection of the child from information and material injurious to his or her well-being, bearing in mind the provisions of articles 13 and 18.' Article 13 provides that children shall have the right to receive and impart information, while Art 18 grants parents the primary responsibility for the upbringing and development of the child.

[159] Center for Law and Democracy, 'Freedom of Expression and the Regulation of Television to Protect Children: Comparative Study of Brazil and Other Countries' (March 2012), www.law-democracy.org/wp-content/uploads/2010/07/Report.Brazil-and-Watersheds.pdf.

[160] *Erbakan v Turkey*, App No 59405/00 (ECtHR, 6 July 2006).

freedom of expression. What it did instead is to take positive steps to protect human dignity by mainstreaming it into the regulation of audiovisual media services.

In sum, on an overall assessment, it can be concluded that the AVMSD is indeed in the first place a market liberalisation measure. It is an instrument that is primarily concerned with the liberalisation of transfrontier broadcasts of on-demand services and one that provides considerable loosening of advertising requirements (in comparison to the TVWFD), like the abolishment of the daily advertising limit, the allowing of more advertising breaks in certain programmes and the liberalisation of new forms of advertising.[161] The described differences between this instrument and the ECTT then only serve to highlight the point.

At the same time, and as we have seen, the AVMSD does mainstream other non-market interests into the regulation. This mainstreaming involves both fundamental rights interests, as well as other non-market interests, especially in the regulation of commercial communications. The extent to which such regulation of commercial communication (more broadly in the EU, but also with respect to this instrument) is also conceived by the legislature in fundamental rights terms will be discussed in the following section.

IV. REGULATING COMMERCIAL EXPRESSION IN THE INTERNAL MARKET

A. Commercial Expression—What is the Status in EU Law?

At the outset, and before analysing the relevant internal market legislation, an explanation of the introduced term 'commercial expression' has to be provided, especially since it is not commonly used in EU terminology.

In historical terms, one can trace the constitutional protection of this form of expression to the US Supreme Court.[162] This development has happened at a time much earlier than in the European courts (the ECtHR and the Court of Justice of the EU) and, notably, after initial reluctance on the part of the US Supreme Court to afford First Amendment Protection to such speech. On the other side of the Atlantic and, more specifically, in the jurisprudence of the ECtHR, the issue arose first in *Barthold v Germany*,[163] but it was not until the *Markt Intern*[164] decision that the question whether (purely) commercial expression is covered by Article 10 ECHR was expressly answered in the affirmative.

A difficult, widely debated and still unsettled question in the US context concerns the definition of 'commercial speech'. Whether the examined speech falls into that category or

[161] See discussion by A Harcourt, 'Introduction' in G Terzis (ed), *European Media Governance—The Brussels Dimension* (Bristol, Intellect Books, 2008) 20.

[162] For an institutional historic and comparative account between the US, Canada and Europe, see RA Shiner, *Freedom of Commercial Expression* (Oxford, Oxford University Press, 2003) chs 2–5.

[163] *Case of Barthold v Germany*, App No 8734/79 (ECtHR, 25 March 1985) [58] ('A criterion as strict as this in approaching the matter of advertising and publicity in the liberal professions is not consonant with freedom of expression. Its application risks discouraging members of the liberal professions from contributing to public debate on topics affecting the life of the community if ever there is the slightest likelihood of their utterances being treated as entailing, to some degree, an advertising effect. By the same token, application of a criterion such as this is liable to hamper the press in the performance of its task of purveyor of information and public watchdog'). See also the dissenting opinion of Judge Pettiti: 'freedom of expression in its true dimension is the right to receive and to impart information and ideas. Commercial speech is directly connected with that freedom'.

[164] *Markt Intern Verlag v Germany*, App No 10572/83 (ECtHR, 20 November 1989).

not is important, as it not only determines whether it is within the realm of constitutional protection, but also which level of scrutiny will be applicable (commercial speech is normally afforded a lower level of protection than other speech). The definitional question is also relevant for the purposes of our subsequent analysis, since only the legislation regulating this form of expression will qualify for examination.

The definitional effort undertaken by the US Supreme Court reads as follows:

> The [US] Supreme Court has identified three characteristics of commercial speech, while being careful to note that none is necessary or sufficient for speech to be classified as commercial. According to the Court, speech that is concededly an advertisement, refers to a specific product, and is motivated by economic interest may properly be characterized as commercial speech.[165]

One should add to this also a further phrase, which has been used by the US Supreme Court, namely, speech that does 'no more than propose a commercial transaction'.[166] It is evident from the citation that the attempt to give a positive meaning to this concept has not delivered precision. In looking for answers on what can qualify as commercial speech, it has been commented that 'the attempts to construe a positive definition by stating what commercial speech is, are definitely overshadowed by statements as to what commercial speech is not'.[167]

By contrast, the ECtHR has never provided a definition of what commercial expression entails, but neither the inclusion of commercial expression within the Convention's realm of protection nor the definitional absence of it are very surprising when considering the fact that the wording of Article 10 ECHR is very wide and has been interpreted as not 'distinguish[ing] between the various forms of expression'.[168] It is therefore clear that under the ECHR, whether protection will be granted—to whatever form of expression—or not will turn on the question of justification under Article 10(2) ECHR. What type of expression is at stake will, however, play a role within that assessment. Under ECHR jurisprudence, three different levels of scrutiny have been applied depending on the type of expression. Those are, first, purely commercial, second, mixed commercial and public, and, third, purely public. The widest margin of appreciation is afforded to the first-mentioned category,[169] the strictest scrutiny is applied in the last-mentioned and when mixed speech is concerned, the ECtHR will weigh which of the two types is predominant.

As regards the EU legal order, it has to be remarked that commercial expression is not expressly included in the Charter. Article 11 CFR, however, reproduces the first generic sentence of Article 10 ECHR,[170] so that the same approach could be held to be applicable in the EU context.

[165] *Securities and Exchange Commission v Wall Street Publishing Institute Inc d/b/a Stock Market Magazine* 851 F 2d 365 (USCA DC Cir 1988) 372, as cited by Shiner, above n 162, 7.

[166] *Pittsburgh Press Company v Pittsburgh Commission on Human Relations et al* 413 US 376 (1973) 385, as cited by Shiner (ibid).

[167] J Krzemińska, 'Freedom of Commercial Speech in Europe', Zentrum für Europäische Rechtspolitik Universität Bremen, http://aei.pitt.edu/3043/02/JKrzeminska_EUSA_paper.doc.

[168] *Müller v Switzerland*, App No 10737/84 (ECtHR, 24 May 1988) [27]. See also DJ Harris, M O'Boyle and C Warbick, *Law of the European Convention on Human Rights* (Oxford, Oxford University Press, 1995) 373, as referred to in Shiner, above n 162, 96: 'there appears to be no expression which is not protected at all by paragraph 1 of Article 10 because of its content'.

[169] *Markt Intern Verlag*, above n 164.

[170] Article 11(1) CFR and Art 10(1) ECHR 'Everyone has the right to freedom of expression. This right shall include freedom to hold opinions and to receive and impart information and ideas without interference by public authority and regardless of frontiers.'

The Court of Justice of the EU does as a matter of fact follow the ECHR's jurisprudence when reviewing measures restricting *advertising*.[171] The first case in which the above approach was applied in the EU order is *RTL*,[172] where the Court not only affirmed that advertising restrictions may amount to 'a restriction on the freedom of expression as enshrined in Art 10(1) of the ECHR',[173] but also cited ECtHR jurisprudence in order to assess the applicable level of review, noting that 'national authorities have a discretion in deciding whether there is a pressing social need capable of justifying a restriction on freedom of expression … such a discretion is particularly essential in commercial matters and especially in a field as complex and fluctuating as advertising'.[174]

Therefore, like the ECtHR, the Court of Justice of the EU affords a wide margin of appreciation to the national authorities when reviewing Member State measures restricting advertising for their compatibility with freedom of expression, more specifically Article 10 ECHR.

The above thus leads to one—for our purposes relevant—finding: Even though the Court of Justice of the EU, like the ECHR, has not provided for a definition of what constitutes commercial expression,[175] it is clear that advertising[176]—the quintessential type of commercial speech[177]—is protected under the fundamental right to freedom of expression, both under the ECHR and under EU law. Hence, any legislation regulating advertising falls within the scope of our analysis.

These observations also provoke a question, that is, whether the fundamental rights dimension thus accepted by the Court is also mirrored in the legislative instruments. The relevant inquiry is twofold: first, does the legislator demonstrate consciousness that what is regulated constitutes interference with freedom of expression (legitimate or not)?; and, second, how does the Court assess those legislative choices?

B. Advertising Regulation: An Assessment Through the Fundamental Rights Lens

In the examination that is to follow, the EU advertising rules as contained in internal market legislation which function as restrictions to commercial expression, will be divided

[171] The ECtHR held unanimously that professional advertising fell within the scope of Art 10 ECHR. See *Groppera Radio AG v Switzerland*, above n 154.

[172] Case C-245/01 *RTL Television GmbH v Niedersächsische Landesmedienanstalt für privaten Rundfunk* [2003] ECR I-0000 [73]. See subsequently Case C-71/02 *Herbert Karner Industrie-Auktionen GmbH v Troostwijk GmbH* [2004] ECR I-3025 [50]; Case 380/03 *Germany v Parliament and Council* ECR I-11573 (hereinafter '*Tobacco Advertising II*') [154], [155]; Case C-479/04 *Laserdisken ApS v Kulturministeriet* [2006] ECR I-8089 [63], [64]; and Case C-421/07 *Frede Damgaard* [2009] ECR I-2629 [26], [27].

[173] *RTL*, above n 172, [68].

[174] ibid [73], with reference to *Verein gegen Tierfabriken v Switzerland*, App No 24699/94 (ECtHR, 28 June 2001) [66]–[70] (hereinafter '*VGT*').

[175] Note though that two of its Advocates General have provided for the following options: Advocate General Fenelly in his Opinion in Case C-376/98, *Germany v Parliament and Council* [2000] ECR I-8419 (hereinafter '*Tobacco Advertising I*') [153]: 'the provision of information, expression of ideas or communication of images as part of the promotion of a commercial activity and the concomitant right to receive such communication'; similarly, see Advocate General Alber in his Opinion in *Karner*, above n 172, [75]: 'the dissemination of information, the expression of ideas or the dissemination of images in the course of the promotion of an economic activity and the corresponding right to receive such information'.

[176] Advertising is understood as commercial advertising in this section.

[177] E Barendt, *Freedom of Speech* (Oxford, Oxford University Press, 2005) ch XI.

into two groups: content-based rules (section IV.B.i) and content-neutral rules (section IV.B.ii).[178] Within the former category, the analysis will be organised around four thematic units: (a) misleading commercial speech; (b) disclosure requirements; (c) prohibited speech for unlawful products; and (d) prohibited speech for lawful products. The content-neutral rules category is subdivided into the following: (a) rules on the manner of distributing advertising content; (b) and time, frequency and placement rules.

i. Content-Based Rules

a. Misleading and Comparative Advertising

Horizontal Legislation:

The Misleading and Comparative Advertising Directive[179] (MCAD) and the Unfair Commercial Practices Directive[180] (UCPD)

Unlike in the US context, where misleading commercial speech falls outside the scope of the First Amendment altogether,[181] the ECtHR has held that 'freedom of expression may sometimes be restricted, especially to prevent unfair competition and untruthful or misleading advertising'.[182] Thus, both the MCAD and the UCPD have to be viewed as regulated restrictions (lawful or not) to the freedom of expression.

The MCAD has as its aim the protection of traders[183] against misleading and comparative advertising and lays down the conditions under which comparative advertising is permitted.[184] The Directive's underlying rationale is clearly market functioning, as is evidenced by the fact that the emphasis is placed on the trader who should be able to make best use of the internal market, on avoiding distortions of competition and on enabling the execution of advertising campaigns beyond national boundaries.

This instrument does not contain any reference to fundamental rights; the legality of the measure has never been contested on the ground that it violates freedom of (commercial) expression, nor does it include a standard recital affirming compatibility with the Charter. This latter observation is interesting for two reasons. First, it suggests that the legislator

[178] Note that this distinction is employed in US jurisprudence on the First Amendment. Under that jurisprudence, restrictions on content-based rules are in general perceived as worse than content-neutral restrictions and trigger a stricter level of judicial scrutiny. For a critical discussion, see RG Wright, 'Content-Based and Content-Neutral Regulation of Speech: The Limitations of a Common Distinction', University of Miami Law Review, 2006. Available at SSRN: http://ssrn.com/abstract=1158603.

[179] Directive 2006/114/EC [2006] OJ L376/21 concerning misleading and comparative advertising (codified version) repealing Directive 84/450/EC and Directive 97/55/EC [1997] OJ L290/18 (hereinafter 'MCAD').

[180] Directive 2005/29/EC of the European Parliament and of the Council of 11 May 2005 concerning unfair business-to-consumer commercial practices in the internal market and amending Council Directive 84/450/EEC and Directives 97/7/EC, 98/27/EC and 2002/65/EC of the European Parliament and of the Council and Regulation (EC) No 2006/2004 of the European Parliament and of the Council ('Unfair Commercial Practices Directive') [2005] OJ L49/22 (hereinafter 'UCPD').

[181] *Central Hudson Gas Electric Corp v Public Service Commission of New York* 447 US 557, 100 S Ct 2343, 65 L Ed 2d 341 (1980) 566: 'For commercial speech to come within that provision, it at least must concern lawful activity and not be misleading.'

[182] *Stambuk v Germany*, App No 37928/97 (ECtHR, 17 October 2002) [39].

[183] Despite the fact that the consumer is also mentioned in the preamble (recital 4), unfairness against consumers is not covered by the Directive.

[184] MCAD, above n 179, Art 1.

was not concerned or aware of any fundamental rights implications that the instrument may have. The second reason, relates to its sister directive, the UCPD on unfair business-to-consumers commercial practices. This Directive harmonises national laws on unfair commercial practices, in that it defines what such practices entail and in providing for a prohibition of those. It also incorporates the provisions of the MCAD on business-to-consumer relations, ie, those that deal with advertising that reaches or is directed at consumers, and limits the latter's scope to comparative advertising in business-to-business relations.[185] Interestingly, this instrument does contain the standard general formula affirming that the Directive 'respects the fundamental rights and observes the principles recognised in particular by the Charter of Fundamental Rights'.[186] The question arises why the latter instrument contains such an acknowledgment while the former does not. The recital can be read as pronouncing that this Directive respects the fundamental right *of freedom of expression* and observes the principle *of consumer protection* as pronounced in the Charter. It is not clear, however, what *specific* fundamental rights issues the drafters saw this instrument to trigger, especially since the Commission's Explanatory Memorandum,[187] as well as the rest of the legislative-procedural documentation,[188] is completely silent on the matter.

One way in which freedom of expression may become relevant[189] is in relation to marketing communications, which formally appear as media content.[190] These are covered under the UCPD,[191] but not under the MCAD. Since it is difficult to assess when media content will have to qualify as a marketing communication, if the latter concept is too generously applied to media content, the Directive, or its application, could be challenged on the ground that it unduly restricts the freedom of the press. It is important to note that the concern here is the restriction of freedom of non-commercial expression if this is illegitimately classified as commercial expression—it is not the claim that commercial expression is restricted in order to promote a public interest unrelated to speech (such as consumer protection).

A claim along these lines has, however, been dealt with by the Court in *Karner*.[192] This case concerned the repealed Directive 84/450/EEC[193] on Misleading and Comparative Advertising in a context where a national law prohibiting the advertisement of goods as

[185] UCPD, above n 180, Art 14.

[186] ibid, recital 25.

[187] Commission Proposal for a Directive concerning unfair business-to-consumer commercial practices in the Internal Market and amending Directives 84/450/EEC, 97/7/EC and 98/27/EC ('Unfair Commercial Practices Directive') (18 June 2003) COM(2003) 356 final 2003/0134 (COD).

[188] See, eg, the European Parliament Committee Recommendation tabled for plenary (2nd reading), Draft European Parliament Legislative Resolution, A6-0027/2005, pointing out that the Directive 'will mark, for both consumers and professionals in the EU, a step forward in terms of a more secure legal framework and the fuller protection of the rights enshrined in the Charter of Fundamental Rights of the Union'. Again, there is no mentioning of which rights are at stake.

[189] This argument has been made by G Howells, HW Micklitz and T Wilhelmson, *European Fair Trading Law—The Unfair Commercial Practices Directive* (Burlington, VT, Ashgate, 2006) 55.

[190] Examples of where the line between media content and advertising is easily blurred are as follows: website sponsorship, affiliation, remunerated search tools, use of meta-data and links, referrals and reviews. See Green Paper, 'European Consumer Protection' COM(2001) 531 final 8, cited in Howells, Micklitz and Wilhelmson (ibid).

[191] See also UCPD, above n 180, Art 11 and Annex 1 on advertorials.

[192] *Karner*, above n 172.

[193] Council Directive 84/450/EEC of 10 September 1984 relating to the approximation of the laws, regulations and administrative provisions of the Member States concerning misleading advertising [1984] OJ L250/17.

being from an insolvent estate was challenged, inter alia, on the ground that it violated Article 10 ECHR.

The case's contribution in the discussed area is the following. First, the Court has accepted the argument for the purposes of EU law that a restriction on advertising characterised as 'unfair' qualifies as a restriction to freedom of expression as guaranteed in EU law. Second, it proves that in this area—commercial expression—the Court follows closely ECHR case law, something that is not necessarily true for other areas of fundamental rights.

Third, it demonstrates the Court's great willingness to accept the restriction as justified. Since it affords wide discretion to the national legislators, the contested measure will pass the reasonableness and proportionality test if the objective pursued is legitimate.

Specific Legislation:

The Cosmetics Regulation[194] Amending Directive 88/667/EC and Directive 76/768/EEC; the Foodstuffs Directive[195] Consolidating and Repealing Directive 79/112/EEC; the Package Travel Directive;[196] the Trademark Directive;[197] the Community Trademark Regulation,[198] the Directive Relating to Foodstuffs Intended for Particular Nutritional Uses;[199] the Regulation on Nutrition and Health Claims Made on Food;[200] and the First[201] and Second[202] Tobacco Products Directive (TPD1 and TPD2)

All of the above listed internal market directives contain provisions that are tantamount to prohibiting misleading advertising with respect to those products.[203] There is no reference to freedom of expression in the listed legislation and, up until the TPD2, the same was true

194 Regulation (EC) No 1223/2009 of the European Parliament and of the Council on Cosmetic Products (recast) [2009] OJ L342/59 (hereinafter 'Cosmetics Regulation').

195 Directive 2000/13/EC [2000] OJ L109/29. See also the more specific Food Supplements Directive 2002/46/EC [2002] OJ L183/51, Arts 6(2) and 7.

196 Council Directive 90/314/EEC of 13 June 1990 on package travel, package holidays and package tours [1990] OJ L158/59 (hereinafter 'Package Travel Directive'). Article 3 requires that brochures made available for a consumer indicate the price and a list of 'adequate information'.

197 Directive 2008/95/EC of the European Parliament and of the Council of 22 October 2008 to approximate the laws of the Member States relating to trademarks [2008] OJ L299/25 (hereinafter 'Trademarks Directive').

198 Council Regulation (EC) No 207/2009 of 26 February 2009 on the Community Trademark [2009] OJ L78/1.

199 Council Directive 89/398/EEC of 3 May 1989 on the approximation of the laws of the Member States relating to foodstuffs intended for particular nutritional uses [1989] OJ L186/27, as amended by Directive 96/84/EC of the European Parliament and of the Council of 19 December 1996 amending Directive 89/398/EEC on the approximation of the laws of the Member States relating to foodstuffs intended for particular nutritional uses [1997] OJ L48/20; Directive 1999/41/EC of the European Parliament and of the Council of 7 June 1999 relating to foodstuffs intended for particular nutritional uses [1999] OJ L172/38; and Regulation EC (No) 1882/2003 of the European Parliament and of the Council of 29 September 2003 adapting to Council Decisions 1999/468/EC the provisions relating to committees which assist the Commission in the exercise of its implementing powers laid down in the instruments subject to the procedure referred to in Article 251 of the EC Treaty [2003] OJ L284/1.

200 Regulation (EC) No 1924/2006 of the European Parliament and of the Council of 20 December 2006 on nutrition and health claims made on foods [2006] OJ L404/9.

201 Directive 2001/37/EC of the European Parliament and of the Council on the approximation of laws, regulations and administrative provisions of Member States concerning the manufacture, presentation and sale of tobacco products (hereinafter 'TPD1').

202 Directive 2014/40/EU of the European Parliament and of the Council of 3 April 2014 on the approximation of the laws, regulations and administrative provisions of the Members States concerning the manufacture, presentation and sale of tobacco and related products and repealing Directive 2001/37/EC (hereinafter 'TPD2').

203 Cosmetics Regulation, above n 194, Art 6(3); Foodstuffs Directive, above n 195, Art 2(3); Package Travel Directive, above n 196, Art 3; Trademark Directive, above n 197, Art 5(3)(d); Directive relating to foodstuffs

for the procedural documentation of all instruments. Furthermore, so far, these instruments have not been challenged on the ground that they violate freedom of commercial expression in front of the Court.[204]

The Regulation on nutrition and health claims on food and, more specifically, its provision that alcoholic beverages (above 1.2 per cent by volume of alcohol) shall not bear health claims was challenged on fundamental rights grounds in *Deutsches Weintor*.[205] In this case, Deutsches Weintor was prevented from marketing its wine as 'easily digestible', indicating reduced acidity levels. However, interestingly, the fundamental right it invoked was not commercial expression, but the freedom to choose an occupation (Art 51(1)) and the freedom to conduct a business (Art 16 CFR). The Court held that a claim such as the one at issue was 'ambiguous or even misleading'[206] and it eventually found that the absolute prohibition in the Regulation of a claim such as that at issue was necessary in order to protect the fundamental right to health and was also proportionate.

The final TPD2 does not contain a reference to freedom of expression, but it is to be found in the documentation of its legislative history.[207] Interestingly for the present purposes, at the first reading stage of the proposal[208] the Legal Affairs Committee (JURI) of the European Parliament found the labelling measures problematic. It noted that the prohibition of 'any labelling that suggests that a particular products is less harmful than others' is problematic because: 'Manufacturers must be able to communicate that [information] if this is scientifically proven and if it is not misleading.'[209] Similarly, it proposed the deletion of what is now Article 13(c) TPD (prohibition of references to taste, smell, flavourings or other additives or the absence thereof)[210] because 'customers should not be deprived of information about the product as long as it is not misleading'.[211] The Committee did not expressly mention Article 11 CFR; however, when reading the opening sentence of the opinion that makes express reference to freedom of expression, it can be concluded that this right is meant here.

The question is then whether it could be held that the type of labelling prohibited under the Directive could be perceived as misleading per se. In light of *Deutsches Weintor*, this is not to be ruled out. Moreover, it is notable that JURI's opinion was not followed in the final instrument, which preserved the originally proposed position. In the meantime, the TPD2 (more precisely the implementing law) has been challenged in front of an English court, also on fundamental rights grounds, and the judge has made an order for a preliminary

intended for particular nutritional uses, above n 199, Art 2(2); Regulation on nutrition and health claims made on food, above n 200, Arts 1(2), 10(2) and 14(2); TPD1, above n 201, Art 7; and TPD2, above n 202, Art 13.

[204] See, however, the Opinion of Advocate General Maduro in Joined Cases C–236/08, C–237/08 and C–238/08 *Google France Google Inc v Louis Vuitton and others* [2010] ECR I-2417. In the context of keyword based advertising (display of advertising through the entering of (trademarked) terms into search engines on the Internet), he juxtaposes trademark protection with freedom of expression and commercial activity.

[205] Case C-544/10 *Deutsches Weintor* EU:C:2012:526.

[206] ibid [52].

[207] See discussion in ch 7, s III.

[208] European Parliament Report on the proposal for a directive concerning the manufacture, presentation and sale of tobacco and related products, A7-0276/2013 (COM(2012)0788—C7-0420/2012—2012/0366(COD)), Opinion of the Committee on Legal Affairs for the Committee on the Environment, Public Health and Food Safety (25 June 2013).

[209] ibid.

[210] ibid, Amendment 45 proposing the deletion of Art 12(c) of the Commission TPD proposal.

[211] ibid.

reference to the Court of Justice of the EU.[212] However, at the time of writing, it is not yet clear what fundamental rights arguments the claimants will plead in front of the Court.

The above demonstrates the general absence of references to commercial expression in the legislation and pre-legislative history of instruments regulating misleading and comparative advertising. The TPD2 is one recent example where freedom of expression was debated during the lawmaking process. However, in that case, the European Parliament Legal Service in fact seemed to be implying that prohibiting misleading speech (which allegedly was not at issue, which is why the provisions prohibiting certain forms of claims were contested) in advertising is not problematic from a freedom of expression point of view, in the sense that it would be easily justifiable for legitimate interests. This finds further support in *Deutsches Weintor*, even if the right tested is not commercial expression. Especially given the wide discretion that the Court normally grants to the legislature in advertising, it does not seem likely that it would have arrived at a different conclusion had the commercial expression argument been invoked; perhaps the litigants were even aware of the difficulty to succeed on a commercial expression claim in front of the Court and this is why Articles 15 and 16 CFR have been invoked instead. However, this remains pure speculation.

If it is true that the prohibition of misleading advertising is easily justifiable from a freedom of expression point of view, may this then explain the general overall absence of references to commercial expression in the legislation discussed? This conclusion would assume that the legislator was mindful of this dimension. Admittedly, it is difficult to arrive at this general conclusion from one example, especially given that there is no indication of such debate in the making of the other instruments.

There are other arguments that could explain the lacking debate on commercial expression. One explanation might be that most of these instruments have been first adopted before adoption of the Charter and at a time when fundamental rights scrutiny of EU legislation during the drafting process was not yet systematically applied.[213] This is, however, not a fully satisfactory explanation given that there are instruments, which have been adopted before adoption of the Charter, that do include statements of compatibility with fundamental rights as guaranteed by the ECHR and/or as general principles of Community law.[214] An argument from chapter three might provide further explanation here: the Commission Directorate General, European Parliament Committees and Council formations as well as stakeholders involved in the regulation of advertising would not typically conceive of the matter in fundamental rights terms.

[212] *R (on the application of Philip Morris and others v Secretary of State for Health* (2014) EWHC 3669 (Admin). Note that another reference has been made by an English court to the CJEU in other proceedings challenging the compatibility of Art 20 TPD2 with EU law, namely, *R (on the application of Pillbox 38 (UK)) v Secretary of State for Health*, CO/3234. Note also that Poland has brought a direct action against the EU institutions, although not invoking fundamental rights grounds: Case C-358/14 *Republic of Poland v European Parliament and Council of the European Union* (action brought on 22 July 2014).

[213] This practice emerged after proclamation of the Charter and Commission Decision of 13 March 2001 on the Application of the Charter of Fundamental Rights of the European Union SEC (2001) 380/03. See the discussion in ch 3.

[214] Examples of internal market legislation include the TVWFD 1997, above n 103, recital 15; Directive 95/46/EC on the protection of individuals with regard to the processing of personal data and on the free movement of such data [1995] OJ L281/31, recital 10; and Directive 98/44/EC on the legal protection of biotechnological inventions, [1998] OJ L213/13, recital 43.

This is not to say that the relevant actors are always oblivious to fundamental rights implications more generally. A recent example demonstrates the legislator's general attention to fundamental rights, but no conceptualisation of the regulation of misleading advertising in freedom of expression terms, that is, the Commission Proposal for a new Package Travel Directive.[215] Its Explanatory Memorandum provides that fundamental rights have been respected; the rights identified are the freedom to conduct a business (Art 16 CFR) and consumer protection (Art 38 CFR), not freedom of expression. According to the explanations, Article 16 CFR is respected while Article 38 CFR is ensured, and the same is stated in the Preamble of the Proposal,[216] but there is no indication in the Explanatory Memorandum that commercial expression was at any point considered, nor is there any such reference to be found in the current legislative process.[217] Notably, the lead Directorate General of this proposal was the Directorate General Justice—the Commission Directorate General responsible for fundamental rights.

Whatever the definite reasons for a lacking fundamental rights conceptualisation, what is clear is that if it does lack from the outset, a re-conceptualisation in subsequent targeted amendments and recast versions will be more difficult, but that will not necessarily be the case when an instrument is completely re-negotiated (as the TPD2). In any case, we know from *Karner* that despite absence of such acknowledgment, implications on the right to commercial expression can arise nonetheless and will be recognised as such by the Court.

b. Disclosure Requirements

The Consumer Credit Directive[218] *Amending Directive 87/102/EEC; the Package Travel Directive;*[219] *the Pharmaceuticals Directive 2001/83/EC*[220] *Laying Down a Community Code Relating to Medicinal Products for Human Use as Amended by Directive 2004/27/EC;*[221] *Directive 2014/40/EU*[222] *on Manufacture, Presentation and Sale of Tobacco Products (the Second Tobacco Products Directive—TPD2) and its Predecessor, Directive 2011/37/EC (the First Tobacco Products Directive—TPD 1)*[223]

The Consumer Credit Directive harmonises certain aspects of the laws, regulations and administrative provisions of the Member States concerning agreements covering credit for consumers.[224] It requires standard information to be included in advertising concerning

[215] Commission Proposal on package travel and assisted travel arrangements, amending Regulation (EC) No 2006/2004, Directive 2011/83/EU and repealing Council Directive 90/314/EEC, COM(2013) 512 final (9 July 2013).

[216] ibid, recital 42.

[217] At the time of writing, the proposal is awaiting the Council first reading position.

[218] Directive 2008/48/EC of the European Parliament and of the Council of 23 April 2008 on credit agreements for consumers and repealing Council Directive 87/102/EEC [2008] OJ L133/66 (hereinafter 'Consumer Credit Directive').

[219] See Package Travel Directive, above n 196.

[220] Directive 2001/83/EC of the European Parliament and of the Council of 6 November 2001 on the Community code relating to medicinal products for human use [2001] OJ L311/67 (hereinafter 'Pharmaceuticals Directive').

[221] Directive 2004/27/EC of the European Parliament and of the Council of 31 March 2004 amending Directive 2001/83 on the Community code relating to medicinal products for human use [2004] OJ L136/34.

[222] TPD2, above n 202.

[223] TPD1, above n 201.

[224] Consumer Credit Directive, above n 218, Art 1.

credit agreements, which indicates an interest rate or any figures relating to the cost of the credit to the consumer.[225] It also imposes on credit intermediaries an obligation to indicate in advertising (and documentation) intended for consumers the extent of his or her powers, in particular whether he or she works exclusively with one or more creditors or as an independent broker.[226] The advertising regulation at issue here takes the form of disclosure requirements.

The Directive contains a fundamental rights recital, including not only the generic statement affirming compatibility with the Charter, but also specifying which rights the legislator perceived to be specifically affected. Data protection, the right to property, non-discrimination, protection of family and professional life, and consumer protection are included. Despite this acknowledgment, the procedural history does not reveal any further attention to fundamental rights considerations, a pattern that is of course not unusual especially pre-Lisbon.[227] More importantly, however, freedom of expression is not mentioned. The reason may be found in the fact that from a freedom of expression point of view, disclosure requirements are uncontroversial.

As Barendt has noted, 'negative freedom of speech covers a right not to be forced to subscribe to opinions one does not hold, not a right to withhold information'.[228] This consideration is based on the idea that the best argument for granting fundamental rights protection to commercial speech is based on the consumers' rights to receive information in order to make informed economic choices. Viewed from that perspective, since the speakers' rights derive from the recipients' interests, 'there is no good reason for holding that advertisers have any right not to provide information'.[229]

If it is true that no fundamental rights concerns arise with respect to disclosure requirements, this may explain the fact that no fundamental rights references can be found in other instruments containing them. This is so for the Package Travel Directive, which requires that brochures made available to a consumer indicate the price and a list of 'adequate information'.[230] It is also true for directives outside the 'services' field, namely, the Pharmaceuticals Directive,[231] and the first Directive on manufacture, presentation and sale of tobacco products (TPD1). Again, the legislative history of all of these instruments reveals no consideration of advertising as commercial expression within the fundamental rights domain.

The TPD1 contained the best-known disclosure requirement. It imposed the obligation on tobacco manufacturers to indicate on the cigarette packets the ingredients in a way that a certain percentage of the surface is covered, as well as to include warning signs indicating the risks that come with smoking.[232] This Directive was challenged on several grounds, including that the provision containing the described disclosure requirements violates fundamental rights.[233] However, the fundamental right pleaded was not freedom of expression;

[225] ibid Art 4.

[226] ibid Art 21(a).

[227] See the discussion in ch 3.

[228] Barendt, above n 177, 412.

[229] ibid.

[230] Package Travel Directive, above n 196, Art 3. This Article also requires that no misleading information is included.

[231] Pharmaceuticals Directive, above n 220, Art 89.

[232] TPD1, above n 201, Art 5.

[233] Case C-491/01 *R v Secretary of State for Health ex parte British American Tobacco (Investments) Ltd and Imperial Tobacco Ltd* [2002] ECR I-11453 (hereinafter '*BAT*').

rather, the applicants argued that the provisions violated the right to property because the required large warning signs seriously infringed intellectual property rights.[234] Yet this line of argumentation may come as no surprise when considering the fact that in the Directive's Preamble, the obligation of transparency of product information is opposed to the 'commercial and intellectual property rights of the tobacco manufacturers'[235] and not to their right to freedom of expression. This fact in turn is consistent with the finding above that disclosure requirements are a non-issue in fundamental rights terms.

In the second Tobacco Products Directive, the disclosure of ingredients (tar, nicotine and monoxide levels) on the sides of packs was replaced with health warnings, so this is the relevant disclosure requirement maintained in the directive. The freedom of expression argument was raised in the legislative history of this document. However, it is not an argument that the mandatory disclosure (of the health risks) is per se problematic from a freedom of expression point of view, but that the specific regulation proposed in the directive (the original proposals included plain packaging and 75 per cent coverage of the surface of packs with warning signs, see discussion in Chapter 7) interferes with promotional speech in a disproportionate manner or prohibits it de facto altogether. It will therefore be discussed below at section IV.B.i.d.

c. Prohibited Speech for Unlawful Products

The Pharmaceuticals Directive 2001/83/EC;[236] the AVMSD[237]

The Pharmaceuticals Directive lays down, among other things, a comprehensive regime regulating advertising of medicinal products for human use.[238] It provides for a definition of 'advertising of medicinal products' and prohibits the marketing of products in respect of which no marketing authorisation has been granted.[239] Furthermore, it prohibits the advertising of medicinal products to the general public (different rules apply to qualified professionals), which are available on medical prescription only, contain psychotic or narcotic substances and are not intended for use without the intervention of a medical practitioner.[240] Direct distribution of medicinal products for promotional purposes is also prohibited.[241] The AVMSD applies this regulation to the audiovisual media services sector.[242]

234 ibid [143].
235 TPD1, above n 201, recital 26.
236 Pharmaceuticals Directive, above n 220.
237 AVMSD, above n 60.
238 Pharmaceuticals Directive, above n 220, Title VIII and VIII(a).
239 ibid, Art 87.
240 ibid, Art 88.
241 ibid, Art 88(6).
242 Article 21 prohibits teleshopping for medicinal products which are subject to a market authorisation within the meaning of the Pharmaceuticals Directive; Art 9(f) prohibits audiovisual commercial communication for products available only on prescription; Art 10(3) provides that the sponsorship of audiovisual media services shall not promote specific medicinal products or medical treatment available only on prescription in the Member State within whose jurisdiction the media service provider falls; Art 4(b) prohibits product placement of medical products or medical treatment available only on prescription in the Member State under whose jurisdiction the media service provider falls. See Pharmaceuticals Directive, above n 220.

This Pharmaceuticals Directive does not contain a reference to fundamental rights, nor does it include a Charter compatibility statement. Still, a case has arisen within the scope of this Directive where a violation of freedom of expression was argued. This concerns a restriction of commercial expression in relation to banned products (for which no market authorisation has been granted).

The case is *Damgaard*[243] and the facts were these: Mr Damgaard, a journalist, stated on his website that a medicinal product (Hyben Total) contained an ingredient relieving a certain type of pain and that it is available for sale in two other countries. This statement was made after a marketing authorisation for Hyben Total was refused. Mr Damgaard was not linked to or paid by the manufacturer. The national agency for medicinal products commenced criminal proceedings, alleging that the website post constituted advertising within the meaning of the Pharmaceuticals Directive and therefore had to be prohibited since the marketing of the product in question is prohibited in Denmark.

The first question to be answered was whether Mr Damgaard's actions constituted advertising within the meaning of the Pharmaceuticals Directive. The definition stipulated in the Directive reads: 'any form of door-to-door information, canvassing activity or inducement designed to promote the prescription, supply, sale or consumption of medicinal products'.[244] The Court held that it was for the national court to determine whether Mr Damgaard's actions constituted advertising within the meaning of that provision.[245] However, it did give some guidance on the issue. First, it noted that the definition focuses 'on the purpose of the message, and does not state anything with regard to the people disseminating the information'.[246] Second, it maintained that even where the dissemination of information is 'carried out by an independent third party [de jure and de facto] outside any commercial or industrial activity',[247] it can constitute 'advertising' for the purposes of the Directive. The reason is that it can even in that context 'harm public health, the safeguarding of which is the essential aim of [the Directive]'.[248] Interestingly, the Advocate General came to a very different conclusion, namely, that 'a lack of connection between the author of the information and the sellers or manufacturers of the medicinal products and the non-commercial or non-industrial nature of the activity of that independent third party may … be a strong indication that a message does not have promotional content'[249] and consequently does not constitute advertising within the meaning of the Pharmaceuticals Directive.

The Court, however, gave a wider interpretation to the meaning of 'advertising', holding that this concept does not require any commercial or industrial activity to be involved. This is important in light of the Court's next step, where it tackled Mr Damgaard's claim that his criminal conviction resulted in a violation of his right to freedom of expression. Crucially, it cited *Karner*[250] in order to hold that the level of judicial review should be that of reasonableness and proportionality, the applicable standard for the commercial use of

243 *Damgaard*, above n 172.
244 Pharmaceuticals Directive, above n 220, Art 86(1).
245 *Damgaard*, above n 172, [23].
246 ibid [20].
247 ibid [22].
248 ibid.
249 Opinion of Advocate General Colomer in ibid, point 82.
250 Note also that the Court no longer refers here to the jurisprudence of the ECHR.

freedom of expression.[251] However, this is contradictory in view of the Court's previous claim that non-commercial advertising is also covered by the Directive. The argument can be made that the Court's interpretation of the relevant provision is so wide-reaching as to be capable of affecting journalistic/editorial freedom of expression (consider, for example, editorials on pharmaceuticals in health and lifestyle magazines) and that therefore a different, less deferring standard of judicial review should be applicable. The Court in this case, as in *Karner*, even though referring to reasonableness and proportionality, did not undertake any analysis in this regard; it merely proclaimed that if Mr Damgaard's activity were to be found to constitute advertising for the purposes of the Directive, 'his conviction could be considered reasonable and proportionate, in the light of the legitimate aim pursued, namely the protection of public health'.[252]

Thus, according to the Court, a criminal conviction for non-commercial advertising of an unauthorised medicinal product is in line with the Pharmaceuticals Directive and does not violate freedom of expression. As in *Karner*, the non-commercial public interest objective of the Directive seems to weigh so heavily in the Court's assessment that it does not see it as necessary to undertake a proportionality analysis, but can arrive straight at the conclusion. However, this case appears controversial in view of the fact that this almost absolute deferential approach is applied in a case involving speech that is not commercial. One factor in support of the Court's quick disposal of the fundamental rights argument is the fact that a banned product was at issue. Yet, even the Advocate General, who was careful to take this factor into account, observed that the Court has accepted that 'freedom of expression [enables] expression to be given to opinions which differ from those held at an official level'.[253]

d. Prohibited Speech for Lawful Products

The First[254] and Second[255] Tobacco Products Directive (TPD1 and TPD2); the Tobacco Advertising Directive 2003/33/EC[256] and its Predecessor, the Annulled Tobacco Advertising Directive 98/43/EC;[257] and the AVMSD[258]

As already stated above, the EU regime on a tobacco products regulation contains provisions that can be seen as restricting or prohibiting promotional speech. Most of the controversy arising in the context of the TPD2 concerned the proposal on 'plain packaging', which precludes the use of all branding (including colours, images, trademarks etc).[259] This was eventually rejected, as it was considered problematic from the perspective of intellectual

[251] *Damgaard*, above n 172, [27].

[252] ibid [28].

[253] Opinion of Advocate General Colomer in ibid [72], citing Case C-340/00 *P Commission v Cwik* [2001] ECR I-10269 [22].

[254] TPD1, above n 201.

[255] TPD2, above n 202.

[256] Directive 2003/33/EC of the European Parliament and of the Council of 26 May 2003 on the approximation of laws, regulations and administrative provisions of the Member States relating to the advertising and sponsorship of tobacco products [2003] OJ L152 (hereinafter 'Tobacco Advertising Directive II').

[257] Directive 98/43/EC of the European Parliament and of the Council of 6 July 1998 on the approximation of laws, regulations and administrative provisions of the Member States relating to the advertising and sponsorship of tobacco products [1998] OJ L213 (hereinafter 'Tobacco Advertising Directive I').

[258] AVMSD, above n 60.

[259] See the detailed discussion in ch 7.

property and trademarks. Commercial expression was, however, also invoked by stakeholders (NGOs) to oppose plain packaging, but it did not find ambitious treatment in the IA and further legislative history (merely a general reference that freedom of expression was affected (see the discussion in chapter seven) and the comments of JURI discussed above).

The trademarks argument was also used for debating the size of health warnings, which the TPD1 included and the TPD2 maintained, although by increasing the size. This argument was made in fundamental rights terms, but what is more interesting for the present purposes is the link to commercial expression. When the TPD2 proposal was passing through the first reading stage, JURI (in discussing the difficulties arising with respect to Art 17 CFR) put forward that 'trade marks could also not properly fulfil their … advertising function'.[260] The Committee did expressly refer to freedom of expression at this stage and it is certainly possible to argue that the increased size of warnings also restricts *commercial* expression. It is interesting to note in this respect that Sweden made a statement in the Council noting that 'the proposed increase of size of … [health] warnings may pose great difficulties in terms of compatibility with the Swedish constitution'.[261] It added that 'it is not certain if or how Sweden can implement the Directive'[262] and that 'Swedish constitutional rules concerning freedom of the press and freedom of expression are being examined regarding text warnings, contents declarations and similar product information'.[263] The Council therefore must have been aware of this dimension, given the possible clash with national constitutional law. It is in this light even more interesting to see what fundamental rights arguments will be invoked in the preliminary reference challenging the TPD2 and how the Court may react.[264]

Directive 2003/33/EC (the first Tobacco Advertising Directive), which was adopted after the successful challenge to Directive 98/43/EC (the second Tobacco Advertising Directive), imposes an almost outright EU ban on tobacco advertising. The AVMSD extends this ban to audiovisual media services[265] and the TPD2 prohibits advertising of e-cigarettes.[266]

The tobacco advertising field is marked by stark controversy, not only because of the question of competences,[267] but also because the regulation amounts to an almost outright ban on the advertising of tobacco products in print, radio broadcasting, information society services and sponsorship. Only a few exceptions are allowed for publications intended for professionals in the tobacco trade and those originating in third countries and not principally intended for the Community market. Thus, a particularly grave and very evident restriction is imposed on commercial expression in order to pursue a public interest—the

260 TPD2, above n 202.

261 Council of the European Union, Proposal for a Directive concerning the manufacture, presentation and sale of tobacco and related products (first reading), Interinstitutional File 2012/0366 (COD), 7346/14 ADD1 (10 March 2014) 3.

262 ibid.

263 ibid.

264 In the cases mentioned above in n 212.

265 In particular: Art 9(1)(d) prohibits commercial communication for cigarettes and other tobacco products; Art 10(2) provides that audiovisual media services or programmes shall not be sponsored by undertakings whose principle activity is the manufacture or sale of tobacco products; and Art 11(4) stipulates that programmes shall not contain product placement of tobacco programmes or product placement from tobacco manufacturers/undertakings. See AVMSD, above n 60.

266 TPD2, above n 202, Art 20(5).

267 See the relevant discussion in ch 2.

protection of health. Both the annulled Tobacco Advertising Directive and its successor contain fundamental rights references. This may not be very surprising, however, in light of the absolute nature of the measure.

The second Tobacco Advertising Directive stipulates that it respects and observes the Charter, and, in particular, it 'seeks to ensure respect for the fundamental right to freedom of expression'.[268] The annulled Directive on the other hand is phrased in more negative terms; it states that all forms of advertising (direct or indirect) should be regulated 'without prejudice to the fundamental principle of freedom of expression'.[269] However, both recitals in the Preamble declare by implication that the respective ban on tobacco advertising does not violate freedom of expression or, in other words, is a legitimate restriction to this right. In the famous *Tobacco Advertising I* case,[270] this claim, which was contained in the Preamble was challenged by Germany.[271] The applicants made reference to Article 10 of the ECHR and the fact that commercial speech is included in the scope of this right, as it is also recognised by EU law. The applicants also urged the Court not to afford a wide margin of appreciation to the legislature when balancing this right with other interests, like the completion of the internal market or public health, and referred to the fact that the Directive provided for an almost total prohibition on advertising. The Court did not enter this discussion at all as the case was decided on the question of the choice of legal basis and the measure was held invalid on that ground.[272] By contrast, Advocate General Fenelly dealt in his Opinion with this issue extensively and adopted a 'Strasbourg-like' approach in his assessment.[273] The following aspects of his opinion are noteworthy.

First, the Advocate General discussed explicitly why commercial expression should be protected under (then) EC law. As noted above, the Court has not dealt with this so far. The Court has accepted the inclusion of this doctrine by referring to Article 10 ECHR and ECtHR case law, but it has not discussed the justification of this approach. Advocate General Fenelly's explanation is the following: he acknowledges that commercial expression is different from political, journalistic, literary and artistic expression, but in his opinion it warrants protection nonetheless because:

> [P]ersonal rights are recognised as being fundamental in character, not merely because of their instrumental, social functions, but also because they are necessary for the *autonomy, dignity and personal development of individuals.* Thus, individuals' freedom to promote commercial activities derives not only from their right to engage in economic activities and the general commitment, in the Community context, to a market economy based upon free competition, but also from their inherent entitlement as human beings freely to express *and receive views* on *any* topic, including the merits of the goods or services which they market or purchase.' (emphasis added)[274]

[268] Tobacco Advertising Directive II, above n 256, recital 7.

[269] Tobacco Advertising Directive I, above n 257, recital 9.

[270] *Tobacco Advertising I*, above n 175.

[271] Opinion of Advocate General Fenelly in ibid [54].

[272] There appears to be a pattern in the Court's judicial review case law, that is, when the legality of the directive is tested on multiple grounds—and, in particular, choice of incorrect legal basis and violation of fundamental rights—the Court will give priority to the question of competences and, if infringed, the case will be concluded on that point; the fundamental rights question will be avoided.

[273] On this, see L Woods, 'Freedom of Expression in the European Union (2006) 12(3) *European Public Law* 371, 382.

[274] Opinion of Advocate General Fenelly in *Tobacco Advertising I*, above n 175, [154].

The Advocate General thus seems to be relying on two arguments in order to justify the protection of commercial expression. It should be noted that these are not new arguments, but have appeared in earlier jurisprudence of the US Supreme Court (the first argument)[275] and the Supreme Court of Canada (the second argument).[276] The first one is more evident but also less convincing than the second one. Advocate General Fenelly uses 'the standard grounds within liberal political morality for the high value given to freedom of expression'[277]—autonomy, dignity and personal development of individuals. This argument is difficult to sustain for commercial expression and especially commercial advertising since the right is mostly ascribed to corporations, as in the instant case to the tobacco manufacturing companies. It simply does not make sense to hold that the right to advertise fosters the autonomy, dignity and self-fulfilment of these corporations.[278] The second argument may be that consumers[279] have a right to receive information in order to make informed economic choices for their lives, which is important for the development of their autonomy and self-fulfilment. There is certainly more strength to this argument. Even so, it can also be criticised on the ground that 'the making of informed or better economic choices [is] neither necessary nor sufficient to individual self-fulfilment'.[280] This is so because some people may feel self-fulfilled without being at all concerned about their economic choices, while guaranteeing utmost care in this area does not necessarily lead those who are concerned about it to self-fulfilment.[281]

The Advocate General's basis for recognising commercial expression for the purposes of EU law thus seems to be resting on weak theoretical ground. It is indeed difficult to apply the classic justifications for protecting freedom of expression to commercial advertising. In light of this, it may not be surprising that the discussion has so far been avoided by both the ECtHR and the Court of Justice of the EU.

The second aspect of the Opinion relates to the applicable level of judicial review. Advocate General Fenelly opined that the standard of review when assessing the proportionality of legislative choice should be different when reviewing fundamental rights.[282] The normal standard of review when assessing legislative choices in complex fields is to ask the question 'whether the exercise of such discretion is vitiated by a manifest error or a misuse of powers or whether [the institutions] did not clearly exceed the bounds of [their] discretion'.[283] However, according to the Advocate General, that should not be the approach here, where fundamental personal rights are at issue. The level of review should rather be the one adopted by the ECtHR when commercial expression is at stake: the restriction is acceptable 'where the competent authorities *on reasonable grounds*, had considered the restrictions to be *necessary*' (emphasis added).[284]

[275] US Supreme Court, *Virginia State Pharmacy Board v Virginia Citizens Consumer Council* 425 US 748 (1976).

[276] *Ford v A-G of Quebec*, Supreme Court of Canada (1988) 2 SCR 712, 767.

[277] Shiner, above n 162, 104.

[278] ibid 400.

[279] The Advocate General refers not expressly to consumers but human beings, who have the right to receive information 'on any topic, including the merits of the goods or services which they market or purchase'; see Opinion of Advocate General Fenelly in *Tobacco Advertising I*, above n 175.

[280] Barendt, above n 177, 402.

[281] ibid.

[282] Opinion of Advocate General Fenelly in *Tobacco Advertising I*, above n 175, [157].

[283] Case C-180/96 *UK v Commission* [1998] ECR I-2265 (hereinafter '*BSE*').

[284] Opinion of Advocate General Fenelly in *Tobacco Advertising I*, above n 175, [158].

The standard of review that the Advocate General advocated here—the ECtHR standard—is the one that the Court later followed in *Karner*. However, the Opinion differs from that case, to the extent that the Advocate General, like Advocate General Alber in *Karner*, did undertake a proper assessment and gave a more concrete meaning to the test set out above. In the Advocate General's Opinion, the legislature has to fulfil three requirements in order to satisfy the stipulated test:

1. The legislator has to 'supply coherent evidence that the measure will be effective in achieving the public interest objective'[285] (here the protection of public health through the reduction in tobacco consumption).
2. It has to be proven that 'less restrictive measures would not have been equally effective'.[286]
3. The restriction must be proportionate, 'having regard to the public interest envisaged, no matter how efficiently pursued'.[287]

The Advocate General proceeded to considering the applicable evidentiary requirements and the actual evidence that was presented during the proceedings in order to conclude that the legislator had reasonable grounds to believe that a comprehensive prohibition on tobacco advertising would achieve the public interest objective.[288] He also accepted that 'a nearly total ban on advertising an economic activity is a particularly grave intrusion on the exercise of the right of free expression',[289] which placed a greater onus on the legislator to prove that a more limited restriction would not be effective; this the legislator had done in the Advocate General's view. Finally, he also deemed the measure proportionate in view of the reduction in consumption levels that it would lead to. However, the same conclusion was not reached with regard to diversification products because it was not evident that the advertising of those products would have an effect on the consumption levels of tobacco products, and no evidence was adduced in that respect. Hence, the Advocate General reached the same conclusion as the Court, which examined the issue under the separate question of competences.

After annulment of this first Tobacco Advertising Directive, the legislator adopted the second instrument, which again laid down an almost outright ban on tobacco advertising, but did not cover the controversial diversification products, and furthermore contained a free movement provision. The two key problems on the basis of which the first Directive failed were thus rectified. However, this instrument was also challenged by Germany in *Tobacco Advertising II*[290] on several grounds, including on the basis that the Directive violated the freedom of expression. This time, the Court had no choice but to deal with that claim, as all other grounds were rejected (note that this issue was dealt with as a last point). Yet the applicant's argument was made along a different line in the instant case (probably because the Advocate General's message in the first case had been heard).

[285] ibid [159].
[286] ibid.
[287] ibid [165].
[288] ibid [163].
[289] ibid [164].
[290] *Tobacco Advertising II*, above n 172.

The applicant argued in essence that the prohibitions to advertise in the press, other printed publications and radio advertising, with a few allowed exceptions, 'would have the effect of denying the press significant advertising income, or even contribute to the closure of certain undertakings, and would, ultimately, prejudice the freedom of expression guaranteed by Article 10 of the ECHR'.[291] In other words, the argument was that a restriction to commercial expression violates the freedom of the press.

The Court's reply was rather short. First, it held on the basis of the '*Market Intern*-formula' (as in *Karner*) that the applicable level of review should be that of reasonableness and proportionality. That is already peculiar, since it merely noted the following: even if the measures at issue 'have the effect of weakening freedom of expression indirectly, journalistic freedom of expression, as such, remains unimpaired and the editorial contributions of journalists are therefore not affected'.[292] Once again, the Court did not undertake any thorough analysis of the fundamental rights argument. A finding that editorial and journalistic freedom remained unaffected was enough to conclude that freedom of expression/press freedom was not violated. It is difficult to understand the Court's syllogism, as it does not seem to be answering the question properly. The Court did not address the issue of whether freedom of expression can be successfully invoked if the regulation of commercial expression (the advertising ban) endangers the viability of press undertakings, which depend on the advertising revenues. Moreover, if the measure is scrutinised on the ground that it restricts the freedom of the press, why is the less strict level of review applied that normally pertains to cases where a violation of commercial expression is alleged?

In trying to comprehend the Court's reasoning, one should have regard to one commentator's observation that the Court's approach is similar to that taken by the ECtHR in *Murphy*.[293,294] This case concerned a prohibition on broadcasting religious advertisements. One of that Court's decisive contemplations was to distinguish between coverage of religious matters in advertisements on the one hand and in broadcasted programmes (documentaries, debates, films etc) on the other.[295] A total prohibition of such speech with respect to the former was legitimate since (among other reasons) the latter remained unaffected. The reasoning was that prohibiting the promotion of religious speech through a commercial means (buying advertising time) does not impinge, on an overall assessment, on that speech since there are other means of exercising it. It is, however, difficult to see how this line of argumentation can be transposed to the claim put forward in *Tobacco Advertising II*. The advertising ban in that case meant that there are no other ways of exercising the speech involved. The only way to transpose the ECtHR reasoning to the present case would be if one were to read the *Murphy* ruling as a broader statement that advertising bans would only be held to infringe press freedom if they have an impact on editorial freedom (note that the Court did not examine that question properly, but only stated that it does not) and that any other consideration will not be accepted. It is doubtful that this is what the ECtHR said in *Murphy*, but this is the only statement that seems to follow from the Court's reasoning.

[291] ibid [153].
[292] ibid [156].
[293] *Murphy v Ireland*, App No 44179/98 (ECtHR, 10 July 2003).
[294] E Dommering, 'Part 1 Primary European Law' in Castendyk, Dommering and Scheuer, aboven 155, 75.
[295] *Murphy*, above n 293, [74].

To summarise on tobacco advertising, the two Directives are examples of commercial expression implications of internal market instruments being acknowledged by a fundamental rights reference in the Preamble. The legislative process leading to the first Tobacco Advertising Directive does not reveal any further elaboration on fundamental rights by the legislature, whereas the link between advertising and fundamental rights has been further acknowledged during the lawmaking process[296] of the second Tobacco Advertising Directive. Mindfulness to that dimension was, however, inevitable after the Opinion of Advocate General Fenelly in *Tobacco Advertising I*,[297] even if the Court remained silent on the matter in that case. Yet this was to change in *Tobacco Advertising II*, where the Court confirmed its generous stance towards advertising restrictions.

ii. Content-Neutral Rules

a. Rules on the Manner of Distributing Advertising Content

***The e-Commerce Directive*[298] *and the e-Privacy Directive*[299]**

The listed Directives lay down rules on unsolicited commercial communications (spamming). The e-Commerce Directive imposes on those Member States that permit unsolicited commercial communications to ensure that it is clearly and unambiguously identifiable as such when reaching the recipient.[300] It also imposes an obligation that service providers undertaking such communications regularly consult and respect the opt-out registers.

The instrument contains two references to freedom of expression, the first one of which had been inserted by the European Parliament in its amendments at first reading: recital 9. It reads as follows: 'the free movement of information society services can in many cases be a specific reflection in Community law of a more general principle, namely freedom of expression as enshrined in Article 10(1) of the Convention for the Protection of Human Rights and Fundamental Freedoms, which has been ratified by all the Member States; for this reason, directives covering the supply of information society services must ensure that

[296] See Commission Proposal for a Directive of the European Parliament and of the Council on the approximation of the laws, regulations and administrative provisions of the Member States relating to the advertising and sponsorship of tobacco products, COM(2001)0283 [2001] OJ C270E. The proposal states: 'Advertising is an important economic activity which stems from the *most fundamental rights*. However, legislators in *Member States have felt the necessity to restrict the exercise of those rights in order to protect public interest and especially to protect health*. These restrictions, which often reach a total ban, concern in particular advertising for certain products, no matter whether their sale is legal or not. Such restrictions exist in Member States for drugs, guns, pharmaceuticals, alcohol, toys, etc' (emphasis added).

[297] Confirmed in European Parliament Committee Report tabled for plenary (first reading/single reading), A5-0344/2002. The report acknowledged the point in the 'Appraisal': 'As a footnote, your rapporteur would further state that, after amendment, the new proposal seems to cater for the other grounds of annulment endorsed by Advocate General Fennelly in his opinion, but not considered by the Court (proportionality, fundamental rights to property and to pursue a professional activity, *freedom of expression*, inadequate statement of reasons)' (emphasis added).

[298] Directive 2000/31/EC of the European Parliament and of the Council of 8 June 2000 on certain legal aspects of information society services, in particular electronic commerce, in the Internal Market ('Directive on Electronic Commerce') [2000] OJ L178/1 (hereinafter 'e-Commerce Directive').

[299] Directive 2002/58/EC of the European Parliament and of the Council of 12 July 2002 concerning the processing of personal data and the protection of privacy in the electronic communications sector ('Directive on privacy and electronic communications') [2002] OJ L201/37 (hereinafter 'e-Privacy Directive').

[300] e-Commerce Directive, above n 298, Art 7(1).

this activity may be engaged in freely in the light of that Article, subject only to the restrictions laid down in paragraph 2 of that Article and in Article 46(1) of the Treaty'.[301] Interestingly, the recital further provides that the Directive 'is not intended to affect national fundamental rules and principles relating to freedom of expression'. This suggests a willingness to grant discretion to national laws on freedom of expression as long as the minimum guarantees in the ECHR are respected. The other recital concerns the removal or access to information in relation to illegal activities, which should be undertaken in compliance with the principle of freedom of expression.[302] It is also interesting to note that at the first reading stage in the European Parliament the Committee on Youth, Culture and Education proposed in its Opinion to also insert this more general opening recital—'freedom of expression in the new information services must be upheld in accordance with the European Convention on Human Rights, with particular reference to Article 10 thereof'—but which was not to be included in the final version.

This last attempted insertion is interesting for the fact that commercial expression could certainly be held to be covered by it. With regard to recital 9, one could assume that when reference is made to information society services, it also includes the commercial communications at issue, which are regulated (and to a certain extent restricted) in order to ensure a legitimate objective, namely, consumer protection. However, this has to be refuted when taking into account the meaning of the term 'information society services'. Article 2(a) of the e-Commerce Directive refers for a definition to Directive 98/48/EC,[303] which describes it as 'any service normally provided for remuneration, at a distance, by electronic means and at the individual request of a recipient of services'.[304] As it is the case that unsolicited commercial communications are normally not provided for remuneration (and if no consent has been given to receive such, certainly not individually requested), they hardly qualify as an information society service. If this is correct, then the quoted recital cannot be taken to refer to what qualifies in our analysis as commercial expression. This is not to say that it does not constitute commercial expression as a matter of principle as accepted by the Court, but only that there is no such explicit acknowledgment in the instrument and during the law-making process.

The e-Privacy Directive provides for stricter regulation[305] than the e-Commerce Directive in this field. It lays down the general rule that unsolicited commercial communications are not allowed without the consent of the subscribers or in respect of subscribers who do not wish to receive those. If electronic details of customers have been collected in the context of a sale or a service, those details can be used for direct marketing purposes by the same natural or legal person, provided the customers are given the opportunity to object. Furthermore, the practice of sending these communications with a disguised sender, or without a valid address to which a request can be send that such communication cease, is prohibited.

[301] ibid, recital 9.
[302] ibid, recital 46.
[303] Directive 98/48/EC laying down a procedure for the provision of information in the field of technical standards and regulations [1998] OJ L217/18.
[304] ibid, Art 1(2)(a).
[305] e-Privacy Directive, above n 299, Art 13.

This Directive includes several references to fundamental rights[306] not only in its Preamble but also in the main text. This is unsurprising in view of the fact that it seeks to harmonise national laws aimed at the protection of a specific fundamental right, namely, data privacy (discussed in chapter four) and, in fact, all these references relate only to that right. Obviously, the regulation of unsolicited commercial communications in this instrument is aimed at precisely this objective. The main idea, to put it in simple terms, is that an email address (where these communications are received) forms part of the private sphere and therefore warrants special protection. As such, the rules at issue impose a restriction on commercial expression in order to protect another fundamental right. However, the conception thus described is not mirrored in the language of the Directive, nor is it so in the rest of the legislative documentation. Furthermore, it appears unlikely that a claim alleging an unjustified restriction of freedom of expression would be successful before the Court. This is so in light of the Data Protection Directive 95/46/EC, which the e-Privacy Directive merely complements and the basic rules of which it applies to the electronic communications sector. This instrument contains a provision proposing a balance between freedom of expression and data protection. However, it states expressly that the sole type of expression that can be invoked—and only if necessary—in order to derogate from the data privacy rules is journalistic, literary and artistic expression,[307] not commercial expression.

Therefore, the following results from the above: the potential impact on commercial expression caused by regulation on unsolicited commercial communications is not expressly acknowledged in either of the instruments and no case has arisen so far which would challenge that impact. In the e-Commerce Directive, regulation takes a very light form and is pursued for a public interest, namely, consumer protection. In the e-Privacy Directive, regulation is stricter and the freedom to commercial expression is restricted in order to protect the fundamental right to data privacy. The balance struck by the legislator between the two rights is in this instance clearly in favour of the latter.

b. Time, Frequency and Placement Rules

The AVMSD

The AVMSD provides for substantive regulation on the distribution of advertising content. At the same time, it must be acknowledged that in comparison to its predecessor (the TVWFD), the content-neutral advertising rules in the current instrument have been considerably relaxed. This issue indeed played a central role in the amendment process and, as one commentator has observed: 'Ultimately, the directive may prove to be more important for its de-regulation of broadcast advertising than for its extension of Community content regulation into the Internet and mobile domains.'[308] The new AVMSD has thus led to a regulatory regime in this sector that is less restrictive of commercial expression compared to what was in place under the TVWFD.

[306] ibid, recitals 2, 7, 10, 11 and 12, and Art 1.

[307] Data Protection Directive, above n 214, Art 9.

[308] S Craufurd, 'Media Convergence and the Regulation of Audiovisual Content: Is the European Community's Audiovisual Media Services Directive Fit for Purpose?' (2007) *Current Legal Problems* 238, 242.

However, the changed approach was not triggered by concerns that the previous regime of advertising regulation was problematic from the fundamental rights perspective due to its far-reaching restriction of commercial expression. The true reason is rather to be found in market changes, which were also influenced by technological developments. The new reality in the media landscape is one of increasing market participants, mainly private broadcasters, whose main and often only revenue source is advertising revenues.[309] In light of restrictive advertising rules, competition in the European audiovisual industry appeared to be hampered. As the Commission has stated, 'free-to-air channels can better flourish in a media landscape where there is increasing competition for advertising revenues'.[310] Decreasing competitiveness due to advertising restrictions was and is also a problem because technological developments have allowed the market 'to move fundamentally on both sides of the Atlantic',[311] which means that the players will position themselves where the best opportunities are given and hence under the old regime, not in Europe.

The de-regulatory approach affording less protection to the viewer[312] was seen as justified in view of technological developments that brought about greater viewer choice (and with it the possibility of 'zapping' away from channels showing advertisements) and the possibility of avoiding advertising altogether (when recording transmissions). The perception was therefore that the 'transmission-consumer' can avoid excessive exposure to advertisements and consequently has not only more choice but also more responsibility. Thus, there appeared to be less need for a paternalistic regulatory approach and the balance had to be re-struck, according to the Preamble of the AVMSD, in order to 'remain proportionate with the general interest'.[313]

This re-balancing resulted in the following list of advertising rules as contained now in the new Directive:

— Where TV advertising or teleshopping is inserted during programmes, Member States have to ensure that the integrity of the programmes as well as the rights of the right-holders are not prejudiced (Art 20(1)).
— The transmission of films made for TV, cinematographic works and news programmes may be interrupted once for each 30-minute period; the same applies for children programmes, provided the programme is longer than 30 minutes (Art 20(2)).
— The proportion of TV advertising spots and teleshopping spots within a clock hour shall not exceed 20 per cent (Art 23(1)).
— Teleshopping windows shall be of a minimum uninterrupted duration of 15 minutes.

On the question whether the Directive's wording reveals awareness of fundamental rights implications, it can be observed that the Preamble contains three references to fundamental

309 See speech of H Ungerer at the Annual General Meeting European MultiMedia Forum (19 November 1996), http://ec.europa.eu/competition/speeches/text/sp1996_056_en.html. Ungerer noted these developments at a time when the TVWF was already undergoing its first amendment.

310 Commission, COM Press Release, 'Presenting the New Audiovisual Media Services without Frontiers Directive', Memo/07/206, http://europa.eu/rapid/pressReleasesAction.do?reference=MEMO/07/206

311 Ungerer speech, above n 309.

312 Woods' assessment of the balance struck in this instrument between the commercial interests of broadcasters and the advertiser is that it clearly favours the former; see L Woods, 'The Consumer and Advertising Regulation in the Television without Frontiers and Audiovisual Media Services Directive' (2008) 31 *Journal for Consumer Policy* 63.

313 AVMSD, above n 60.

rights.[314] The only one that could be read as acknowledging respect for commercial expression in the context of content-neutral rules is the Charter compatibility statement, identifying Article 11 CFR as being specifically affected.[315] This recital also stipulates that the Directive 'should not in any way prevent Member States from applying their constitutional rules relating to freedom of the press and freedom of expression in the media'.[316] However, it is obvious that this assertion is of limited value since the Member States will not be able to rely on it in order to argue exclusive jurisdiction on the matter, as only provisions of the main text and not of the Preamble are legally binding. The legislator's (political) message is that any interpretation of the Directive should show deference to the named national constitutional rules, as is the case with the e-Commerce Directive. Yet, in the event of a (unavoidable) clash, the provisions of the Directive would have to prevail. The motivations for inclusion of this recital are not obvious since the Explanatory Memorandum[317] does not impart anything in this respect, but it is noteworthy that no such references are to be found in the TVWFD of 1989, nor in the version of 1997.[318]

In any event, it is clear (at least since *RTL*)[319] that even content-neutral advertising rules can be characterised as restrictions to the freedom of expression under EU law and that the Court will assess this matter according to the EU standard of protection for freedom of expression. In *RTL*, the Court was faced with the question whether the advertising frequency rule under the TVWFD of 1989 infringes freedom of expression. RTL challenged that rule which provided that in the case of films, interruptions for advertising can only take place once for each period of 45 minutes, instead of the normal 20-minute rule (Art 11(3) TVWFD).

The basis of its argument was that the relevant provision was primarily aimed at protecting the integrity and artistic value of audiovisual works and editorial freedom, and that consumer protection was a secondary objective. Therefore, the first-mentioned protection cannot extend to films produced specifically for TV and designed to have advertising breaks, as that would constitute an unjustified interference. The interference would relate to the right to communicate and broadcast, which includes advertisements, as well as to the artistic freedom of the producer to make television programmes, including advertisements.

The Court replied that RTL's construction of Article 11(3) TVWFD was misconceived. The real aim of the frequency rules is to provide for a balanced protection between, on the one hand, the financial interests of television broadcasters and advertisers, and, on the other

[314] ibid, recitals 16, 48, 60.

[315] ibid, recital 16. Recital 48 appears to be aimed at the concern of media pluralism and recital 60 at the balance between human dignity and the protection of minors on the one hand and freedom of expression on the other.

[316] ibid.

[317] European Commission, Proposal for a Directive of the European Parliament and of the Council amending Council Directive 89/552/EEC on the coordination of certain provisions laid down by law, regulation or administrative action in Member States concerning the pursuit of television broadcasting activities, COM(2005) 646 final.

[318] Several other instruments include such statements with respect to freedom of expression in their Preambles, for example: e-Commerce Directive, above n 298, recital 9; Directive 98/48/EC, above n 303, recital 5; Directive 98/48/EC of the European Parliament and of the Council of 20 July 1998 amending Directive 98/34/EC laying down a procedure for the provision of information in the field of technical standards and regulations [1998] OJ L217/18; Directive 2003/6/EC of 28 January 2003 on insider dealing and market manipulation (market abuse) [2003] OJ L96/16, recital 44; Commission Directive 2003/125/EC of 22 December 2003 implementing Directive 2003/6/EC as regards the fair presentation of investment recommendations and the disclosure of conflicts of interest [2003] OJ L96/16, recital 11.

[319] *RTL*, above n 172.

hand, the interest of right-holders. These are not only writers and producers but also consumers as television viewers.[320] Indeed, the Court characterised the protection of consumers as viewers from excessive advertising as an *essential* objective of the provision.[321] Thus, even if it is accepted that the objective of protecting writers and producers is irrelevant here, RTL had clearly disregarded the other objective pursued by the named provision.

In subjecting the rule to a fundamental rights examination, the Court, based on what it concluded above, changed RTL's constellation of the argument. It did not examine whether the frequency rule constituted a restriction on the editorial freedom in broadcasting and on the artistic freedom of the producer, but rather undertook the following assessment. Initially, it acknowledged that advertising regulation may amount to a restriction of the freedom of expression, as referred to in the eighth recital in the TVWFD. It stated that the regulation may constitute a restriction to the freedom to broadcast. This restriction pursues a legitimate aim in accordance with Article 10(2), namely, consumer protection, and may be justified if proportionate. Note that the Court did not refer explicitly to commercial expression here, but it is clear that this is what was balanced (RTL's commercial speech as transmitted in broadcasting) against the objective of consumer protection. This can be concluded from the fact that the Court applied in its proportionality assessment the ECHR level of review applicable in 'commercial matters'.[322]

It is also interesting to note that the Court answered the question of proportionality promptly in the affirmative not only because of the wide margin of appreciation applicable in commercial matters, but also because of two other reasons: first, the restriction did not relate to advertising content; and, second, it did not constitute a prohibition, but a limit to frequency. This may suggest that the Court of Justice of the EU, like the US Supreme Court, considers the content-based advertising restrictions to constitute a graver interference with commercial expression and probably also to afford a stricter level of review.

However, when bearing in mind the discussion of the case law on content-based rules and especially *Tobacco Advertising II*, where an almost total advertising ban was at issue, it cannot be concluded that the Court applied a stricter level of review there.

C. Conclusion

The evaluation undertaken above leads to the following results. With regard to legislative practice, it is clear that *commercial* expression as a fundamental right has not been explicitly acknowledged in any of the final versions of the 19 discussed instruments that regulate advertising in the internal market (in fact, most of them do not contain a reference to fundamental rights at all), and only four of them refer to freedom of expression (the first and second Tobacco Advertising Directives, the AVMSD and the e-Commerce Directive). As the analysis has illustrated, out of these four directives, only with respect to one is it possible to say that the formal reference to freedom of expression is accompanied by (evidenced) mindfulness of the legislator regarding the Directive's implications for the freedom of *commercial* expression—the second Tobacco Advertising Directive. The impetus for this came

[320] ibid [62].
[321] ibid [64].
[322] ibid [73], citing *VGT*, above n 174.

from the Court's case on the first Tobacco Advertising Directive. We do, however, also find references to freedom of expression in the legislative process of one instrument, and even to commercial expression in the pre-legislative process, even though the final version does not include such an explicit reference (the TPD2).

This admittedly somewhat numerical approach to the posed question makes it possible to pronounce the conclusion that overall there is no substantive acknowledgment in the legislation that advertising regulation interferes prima facie with the right to commercial expression. This is at least what results from a survey of the language used in the adopted instruments and in the legislative documentation.

With regard to the contrasting Court's appraisal of advertising regulation, the analysis leads to four broader findings. The first finding is that ECtHR law has been consistently relied on in cases concerning commercial expression. Second, the Court has accepted in all the discussed cases that the various advertising rules which were allegedly restricting freedom of expression fall within the scope of protection of that right for the purposes of EU law. These were rules on misleading advertising (*Karner*), on the advertising of pharmaceutical products (*Damgaard*), on tobacco advertising (*Tobacco Advertising I* and *II*) and on the frequency of broadcasted advertisements (*RTL*). Third, the Court, unlike its Advocate Generals, has not undertaken in any of the cases a substantive review of the measures at issue. In view of the discretion granted to the national legislator (and it seems also to the European legislator—see in particular *RTL*), if the measure pursues a legitimate objective (*in casu* consumer protection and public health),[323] it will be held to be a justified restriction to the freedom of expression. This finding can lead to a further observation, namely, that the Court ranks those public interest objectives in such a context hierarchically higher than commercial expression as they will, so it seems thus far, automatically trump commercial expression. This is so despite the rhetoric used that they constitute a 'restriction that has to be justified'. Fourth, the Court's approach is always the same, irrespective of what kind of legitimate interest is at stake and irrespective of whether it examines a content-based or a content-neutral advertising rule.

In light of these findings, it can be concluded that even though commercial expression has been formally granted protection as a fundamental right in the EU legal order, there is not much substantive acknowledgment of it in the internal market legislation discussed or in the Court's methodology when dealing with such claims. However, this outcome may not be a stark surprise. It could be explained by the argument that despite the lengthy examination of advertising regulation through the fundamental rights lens undertaken herein, adopting necessarily a fundamental rights discourse in this area is at least as a matter of theory, not obvious at all.

Jurisprudentially, Shiner has provided for a strong account, arguing that commercial expression is philosophically unjustified. In his view, 'freedom of commercial expression

[323] On an explanation as to why the wide discretion is granted to public health when freedom of commercial expression is at stake, see Opinion of Advocate General Jääskinen in Case C-249/09 *Novo Nordisk AS v Ravimiamet* [2011] ECR I-3155 [49]–[50]: 'Public health must be safeguarded in order to guarantee the fundamental rights, human dignity, the right to life and the right to physical and mental integrity referred to in Articles 1 to 3 of the Charter. In the system of fundamental rights, the right to life is the foremost and must take precedence over the fundamental rights of freedom of action. Freedom of commercial expression is not at the heart of that fundamental right. Therefore, the Union legislature has a wide discretion with regard to the level of protection granted to public health and it is therefore not required to restrict itself to the minimum necessary to protect freedom of expression.'

does not promote the ends which make freedom of expression valuable'.[324] The author challenges the US approach of protecting commercial expression by asking the following 'tough questions', which, so he argues, the US Supreme Court had left unanswered in its seminal case *Virginia Board*[325]—the case in which the doctrine of commercial expression has its roots, also for the European Courts:

1. Why do business corporations enjoy a right to free speech that belongs primarily to natural persons?
2. How come the free flow of commercial information is touted as an unequivocal good, when economists acknowledge the importance of regulation of information in maintaining efficient markets? or
3. When most of what is protected is not in fact carrying information at all?
4. What is it about commercial speech, as opposed to political speech, which means it has to weigh so heavily in the balance against other social needs like public health?

These questions have not been dealt with by the Court of Justice of the EU or by the ECtHR, and it is not clear how mindful the Courts are to this debate, but it results from the above examination that in the EU context, the following replies can be given. There is in fact plenty of legislation regulating commercial expression in the EU, which when challenged on fundamental rights grounds has not been so far and is unlikely to be struck down in the future according to the Court's current approach on the issue (question 2). This is so because commercial speech does not actually weigh heavily in the balance against other social needs. The opposite is in fact the case (question 4). Therefore, business corporations have so far not de facto been able to rely on a right to freedom of expression under EU law in order to challenge regulation that is in place (question 1),[326] whether the expression at issue actually did or did not concern information (question 3).

Once Shiner's view is endorsed that commercial expression does not warrant acknowledgment in fundamental rights terms, the legislator's, for the most part, lack of such becomes entirely justified, and even more so when it comes to content-neutral rules, even though it is not clear whether this is also the reason for the approach taken. One pragmatic explanation might be found when considering the Court's case law. If the legislator knows that the legislation will in any case pass a fundamental rights test, it will be less concerned with explaining and attempting to justify any interference with it.

Equally, if commercial expression is dismissed as a fundamental right, the Court's deferring stance becomes justified. Moreover, it could even be argued that the Court could discontinue its practice of conceptualising commercial expression in fundamental rights terms and thereby could perhaps also attempt to influence the ECtHR to change its approach or at least to rethink the rationale upon which such protection is based. Given that the Court is at any rate deferential, reference or not to the *fundamental* freedom of commercial expression would not make any substantive difference in terms of outcome (if the current approach is to be maintained).

[324] Shiner, above n 162, 18.

[325] What follows is taken from ibid 69.

[326] Under ECHR law, the freedom of commercial expression has been successfully relied upon in order to challenge comparative advertising restrictions through a court injunction in *Krone Verlag GmbH & Co v Austria (No 3)*, App No 39069/97 (ECtHR, 11 December 2003).

6

Fundamental Labour Rights

I. INTRODUCTION

THIS CHAPTER WILL deal with two fundamental labour rights that the internal market legislator has and is in the process of regulating: the right to fair and just working conditions (section II) and the right to take collective action, including the right to strike (section III). Legislative intervention in these areas has been triggered by the case law of the Court, with the Commission package on the enforcement of the Posted Workers Directive and the exercise of the right to strike in the internal market coming as a response to the (in)famous case law quartet: *Viking*, *Laval*, *Rüffert* and *Commission v Luxembourg*.

The chapter will debate the interplay between negative and positive integration, and how the balance between the fundamental rights at stake and the market interest has been struck during both processes. It will become obvious that the apparent advantages of positive integration—responding to and/or pre-empting conflicts between fundamental rights and economic freedoms while not being constrained by the structural asymmetry between market values and non-market values in the internal market, as set out in the Treaties (and as construed by the Court with respect to the right to take collective action) do not materialise in the instant case.

II. THE RIGHT TO FAIR AND JUST WORKING CONDITIONS IN THE POSTED WORKERS DIRECTIVE 96/71/EC

This part of the chapter will deal with a piece of legislation that constitutes a 'focal point where the social and economic factors meet':[1] the Posted Workers Directive (PWD).[2] The concern will lie with the 'meeting' of the two competing values in the Directive as shaped by the interaction of the responsible institutions (the Court and the legislator). Bearing in mind that the Court has been the main initiator of regulation in this area, both with regard to the adoption of the PWD and with respect to recent legislative follow-up action, we will critically analyse how the legislator has responded both times in striking a balance between the competing interests. An analysis of this balance is important for assessing the fundamental rights dimension in the instrument.

[1] J Hellsten, 'From Internal Market Regulation to European Labour Law' (DPhil thesis, Hanken School of Economics, Helsinki, 2007), also published as an article: J Hellsten, 'On the Social Dimension in Posting of Workers, Reasoning on Posted Workers Directive, Wage Liability, Minimum Wages and Right to Industrial Action' (2006) 301 *Publication of Labour Administration* 34.

[2] Directive 96/71/EC of 16 December 1996 concerning the posting of workers in the framework of the provision of services [1997] OJ L18/1 (hereinafter 'PWD').

In order to do so, section II.A will commence with the legislative history and the content of the Directive. It will subsequently inquire whether the 'social factor' has been conceptualised by the legislator in fundamental rights terms or rather as an objective linked to social policy.

This point (choice of concept—policy discourse versus fundamental rights discourse) is relevant for the further question of the impact that a fundamental rights conceptualisation may have on the balance struck between the competing interests, which will be discussed in section II.B.

Sections II.C and II.D will deal with the interplay between the Court and the legislature. It will be illustrated that judicial interpretation has interfered and apparently altered the way in which the legislator attempted to allocate the weights. Subsequently, the political response to this and to the policy decisions leading ultimately to the Posted Workers Enforcement Directive 2014/67/EU (PWED)[3] will be discussed. The actual and potential role of fundamental rights considerations in these processes will be kept in focus throughout the analysis.

A. Legislative History of the PWD

i. Background

The origins of the PWD can be traced back to the Court's ruling in *Rush Portuguesa*, where it was held that:

> Community law does not preclude Member States from extending their legislation or collective labour agreements entered into by both sides of industry, to any person who is employed, even temporarily, within their territory, no matter in which country the employer is established.[4]

Although the question of extending domestic labour law to temporary workers was not really at issue in the case before the Court, it is interesting to see why it probably felt obliged to make such a statement.

At issue were certain provisions of French law which stipulated that employment of foreign workers without a work permit and the recruitment and bringing into France of foreign workers in breach of the monopoly held by the state *Office des migrations internationals* constituted offences. Rush Portuguesa had been fined for committing both of these offences. The question thus posed was whether this was a breach of (then) Article 49 EC. The Court's answer was in the affirmative, effectively holding that the specific rules of the

[3] Directive 2014/67/EU of 15 May 2014 on the enforcement of Directive 96/71/EC concerning the posting of workers in the framework of the provision of services and amending Regulation (EU) No 1024/2012 on administrative cooperation through the Internal Market Information System ('the IMI Regulation') [2014] OJ L159/11 (hereinafter 'PWED').

[4] Case C-113/89 *Rush Portuguesa v Official National d'Immigration* [1990] ECR I-1417 [18]. This dictum was also repeated in Case C-43/93 *Vander Elst (Raymond) v Office des Migrations Internationales* [1994] ECR I-3803 [23] and Case C-272/95 *Guiot & Climatec* [1996] ECR I-1905, although in the latter two cases, this was confined to legislation and collective agreements relating to minimum wages. Note that this phrase is reproduced verbatim in recital 12 of the PWD.

host country's labour system were violating a free movement provision: the freedom to provide service. This ruling seemed to have the potential for opening up the floodgates to future challenges to many different features of the host countries' labour law environment[5] and it appears that the Court (not providing for further explanation) was aware of this possibility, which in all likelihood led it to making the statement quoted above.

By bringing the matter within the free movement of services rather than the free movement of workers, the Court also in effect 'destroyed' the intended effects of the Acts of Accession of Greece, Spain and Portugal, which deferred application of the free movement of workers provisions when workers move to the 'old' Member States, for a transition period of up to seven years.[6] This derogation was adopted because old Member States greatly feared that cheap labour from less mature economies (new Member States) could flood the markets of old Member States, especially in the building sector.[7] The countries, which at the time were especially affected by the posting of workers, were France and Germany after reunification.[8]

Unsurprisingly, following this ruling, different Member States adopted diverse legislation extending their national labour laws to posted workers[9] and thereby 're-nationalising'[10] the matter. This in turn led the supranational legislator to take action in order to provide for common rules. The end result was the enactment of the PWD.[11]

The underlying principle of this instrument can be summarised in the following terms: whenever a worker employed by an employer established in one Member State is posted to another Member State in order to perform temporary work there, the latter ('host State') has the *obligation*[12] to apply to that employment relationship certain basic standards of its own labour laws (Art 3(1) PWD), while more favourable terms and conditions of employment than those set out in Article 3(1) PWD could still be applied (Art 3(7) PWD), the most controversial ones being those related to minimum wages, working times and equal

[5] P Davies, 'Market Integration and Social Policy in the Court of Justice' (1995) 24(1) *Industrial Law Journal* 74.

[6] M Schlachter, 'The Posting of Workers Directive—German Reactions and Perceptions', Formula Working Paper No 20, 2010, www.jus.uio.no/ifp/english/research/projects/freemov/publications/papers/2010/september/WP20-Schlachter-2010.pdf, 5.

[7] Because 'labour costs amount to a specifically high proportion of overall-costs of doing business there, as they usually constitute up to 50% of such costs': ibid 5.

[8] W Eichhorst, 'European Social Policy between National and Supranational Regulation: Posted Workers in the Framework of Liberalised Services Provision', Max-Planck-Institut für Gesellshaftsforschung, Discussion Paper 98/6, http://econstor.eu/bitstream/10419/43182/1/248171305.pdf, 13. Currently, the available data (for the years 2008 and 2009) suggest that Poland, France, Germany, Luxembourg, Belgium and Portugal are the main sending countries. Germany, France, Belgium, the Netherlands, Spain and Italy are the main receivers. See Commission Staff Working Document, Impact Assessment of 21 March 2012, 'Revision of the legislative framework on the posting of workers in the context of the provision of services', SWD(2012) 63 final (hereinafter 'IA posted workers 2012') 19.

[9] See B de Witte, 'Non-market Values in Internal Market Legislation' in NN Shuibhne (ed), *Regulating the Internal Market* (Cheltenham, Edward Elgar, 2006) 81, fn 69 and reference therein to Eichhorst, above n 8, 20–26.

[10] Eichhorst, above n 8, 27.

[11] Bercusson has commented that this was probably done so in order 'to try and head off an equivalent to the post-*Torfaen* confusion': B Bercusson, *European Labour Law* (Cambridge, Cambridge University Press, 1996) 401.

[12] This aspect indicates that the Directive goes further than the *Rush* principle, which merely provides that the Member States are *not precluded* from applying their labour standards. See ibid 402.

pay.[13] Furthermore, the 'host State' also has the *option* to apply certain other basic standards (Art 3(10) PWD).

It is worth remarking that when this principle operates, the labour standards applicable to the contractual relationship between employer and employee do not result out of an agreement between the two, and they would not be applicable under the system which governs their contractual relationship, ie, they would not be applicable in the 'home State'.[14]

ii. The PWD—Has the Instrument been Conceived in Fundamental Rights Terms? Can it be so Conceived?

The legislative-procedural documentation of the PWD suggests, for the most part, that this instrument was not conceived in fundamental rights terms,[15] but with two exceptions. One is to be found in the Commission's Explanatory Memorandum of its first proposal on a PWD,[16] which contained references to the Community Charter of Fundamental Social Rights of Workers (CCFSRW) and to the Action Programme (AP) for its implementation.[17] Given that the AP listed under its envisaged 'new initiatives' a 'Proposal for a Community instrument on working conditions applicable to workers from another State performing work in the host country in the framework of the freedom to provide services, especially on behalf of a subcontracting undertaking', this reference comes as no surprise.

Similarly, the second reference to be found is an amendment tabled by the European Parliament at first reading to include an opening recital that would identify this instrument as one that comes in response to the AP and therefore at the same time as one that implements fundamental social rights of workers.[18]

However, the European Parliament's amendment did not survive the final version of the PWD, which does not contain any fundamental rights reference or any hint that it has been shaped by fundamental rights considerations. It may be speculated that the abandonment of the European Parliament's amendment is linked to the fact that not all Member States had signed up to the CCFSRW at the time (the UK only signed in May 1997, a few months after the Directive had been adopted).

[13] Note also that these are the three subjects that would, in contrast to the rest of the subjects listed in Art 3, not be applicable anyway under international labour law, according to the Convention Applicable to the Law of Contractual Obligations [1980] OJ L266/1 (hereinafter 'Rome Convention'). W Däubler, 'Posted Workers and Freedom to Supply Services' (1998) 27 *Industrial Law Journal* 264.

[14] See generally P Davies, 'Posted Workers: Single Market or Protection of National Labour Law Systems?' (1997) 34 *Common Market Law Review* 571, 571–72.

[15] Commission, Proposal for a Directive concerning the posting of workers in the framework of the provision of services, COM(1991) 230 final, SYN-346 (hereinafter 'Commission Proposal 1991'); European Parliament Committee on Social Affairs, Employment and the Environment, Decision T3-0277/1992 and T3-0083/1993; Commission modified legislative proposal COM(1993) 225 final-SYN 346; Council Common Position (3 June 1996) COD 1991/0346.

[16] Commission Proposal 1991 (ibid).

[17] Commission, Communication Concerning its Action Programme relating to the Implementation of the Community Charter of Basic Social Rights for Workers, COM(1989) 568 final 22.

[18] Minutes of Proceedings of the Sitting of 10 February 1993 [1993] OJ C 72/78. The amendment reads: 'Whereas the action programme relating to the Community Charter of Fundamental Social Rights for Workers provides for the submission of a Community instrument to remove both the disadvantages faced by workers posted to work temporarily in a Member State and distortions of competition between undertakings.'

The next question arising then is whether the instrument can still be conceived in fundamental rights terms. A good starting point is the European Parliament's reference to the Commission AP. The heading under which the initiative is listed in the AP is that of 'free movement'. This is relevant because—as the AP notes—its chapters are grouped so as to correspond to the various sections of the CCFSRW. At first sight, the PWD seems to be implementing point two of the CCFSRW's free movement section, which provides:

> 2. The right to freedom of movement shall enable any worker to engage in any occupation or profession in the Community in accordance with the principles of equal treatment as regards access to employment, working conditions and social protection in the host country.

But this would not quite fit the final version of the PWD, for two reasons. The first is because there is no equal treatment with regard to *all* employment conditions: as noted above, only a core of host country labour standards is applied to the employment relationship of posted workers, who receive different treatment not only vis-à-vis workers who are nationals of the host state, but also vis-à-vis migrant workers. Second, social security standards expressly provided for in Article 2 CCFSRW are not covered by the relevant provision (Art 3) of the PWD. It results from this that the Directive is improperly implementing point 2 of the CCFSRW.

Furthermore, one can conceive of the PWD as legislation implementing the CCFSRW by focusing on provisions other than the articles on free movement, namely, point 5 on employment and fair remuneration and points 7–9 on improvement of living and working conditions. The focus shifts here from the rule that a posted worker be subjected to certain rules of the host country's labour law system, which is not a fundamental right according to the EU Charter of Fundamental Rights (the Charter) and the European Social Charter (ESC), to the mandatory protective legislation, which can be so conceived, by the ESC and the Charter. As regards the ESC, this is not only so in relation to the 'controversial standards' listed above,[19] but also with regard to all other standards (except one).[20]

The Charter, on the other hand, contains a more general clause relating to fair and just working conditions (Art 31 CFR), which the Explanations to the Charter acknowledge as based on provisions of the ESC, the CCFSRW and other Community instruments,[21] and to equality between men and women in employment, work and pay (Art 23, para 1 CFR). In a recent Impact Assessment (IA), the Commission has also drawn the link between Article 31 CFR and the working conditions applicable to posted workers within the framework of the PWD.[22] The conclusion can therefore be drawn that this instrument can be conceived in fundamental rights terms.

Against this background, the question arising is what impact such conceptualisation may have on the balance struck in the instrument. The simple and concrete question to be asked

[19] Minimum wage is protected in Art 4(1) ESC ('the Parties undertake to … recognise the right of workers to a remuneration such as will give them and their families a decent standard of living'), working time in Art 2(1) and 2(5) (rev)ESC, and equal pay in Clause E ESC.

[20] That is, with respect to the conditions for hiring out workers. See Art 3(1)(d) PWD.

[21] Article 31(1) is based on Art 3 (rev)ESC and point 19 of the ECCFSRW as regards the rights of workers; Art 26 (rev)ESC as regards dignity at work; but also Directive 89/391/EEC as regards health and safety at work. Article 31(2) is based on Art 2 ESC and point 8 ECCFSRW, and Directive 93/104/EC as regards certain aspects of the organisation of working time.

[22] See, eg, IA posted workers 2012, above n 8, 57.

is whether conceiving the non-market value at stake in fundamental rights terms leads de facto to a higher level of worker protection.

We shall investigate this potential correlation by scrutinising the actual balance struck in the final version of the PWD and will compare the deviation from the early amendments of the European Parliament. Admittedly, no generally valid conclusions as to causality can be drawn here on the basis of a single instance. Still, it is interesting for the present purposes to see whether such a correlation did in fact exist in the concrete case under examination.

B. The Legislator's Balancing Exercise in the PWD

The Preamble of the PWD reveals the three broad interests that are claimed to be addressed in this instrument. First, the *free movement of services* will be facilitated in situations involving the posting of employees temporarily abroad in order to perform work in a Member State other than that in which they are habitually employed.[23] While promoting this transnational provision of services, two further aims will be ensured: a *fair climate of competition*[24] and respect for the *rights of workers*.[25] It results from this that the Directive has multiple aims, but it is also clear that pursuing simultaneously the promotion of the economic freedom on the one hand and respect for workers' rights and fair competition[26] on the other means that a balancing exercise has to be undertaken which might result in placing more weight on one aim than the other. The subsequent analysis will be concerned with the question of how the balance has been struck. It will suggest that this instrument is aimed at a social policy consideration: to prevent social dumping. Its underlying principle (extending a set of mandatory rules for minimum labour protection to posted workers) operates so as to further that objective and provides for enhanced worker protection as regards labour rights.

That underlying principle could be appreciated as being per se restrictive of trade. Such a view is supported by the Court's early case law. This could be interpreted as meaning that the balance struck by the legislator on the basis of the legal bases relating to free movement of services is in favour of the non-market value/the fundamental social right. However, such a result, even if true, cannot call the internal market nature of the instrument in question (as illustrated in chapter two).

The analysis will also reveal that the level of worker protection was in fact fixed at a significantly lower level than what the European Parliament at first reading was aiming for, while having an understanding of the instrument as one implementing fundamental social rights. To be sure, the claim here is not that abandonment of the fundamental rights conceptualisation has led to a fundamental rights violation, but that implementation of the fundamental rights at issue (Arts 31 and 23 CFR) has occurred at a lower level. This does not alter the overall conclusion that on the face of the instrument, social considerations still

[23] ibid, recitals 1–4.
[24] ibid, recital 5.
[25] ibid.
[26] The perception is that cost-competition, ie, 'social dumping', is 'unfair competition and shall be avoided' (discussed below).

appear to be key, but it does tentatively suggest that there might be a correlation between the conceptualisation of the instrument in fundamental rights terms and the degree of worker protection pursued.

In demonstrating these points, it will be useful to try and disentangle (as far as possible) the three interests pursued in the PWD. This will be helpful in disclosing the degree to which each of them is attained.

i. How is 'Fair Competition' Achieved or 'Unfair Competition' Avoided?

In the first place, it is necessary to consider what kind of competition is perceived as desirable within the EU. It is clear that free competition between firms is, in principle, desirable in view of the fact that 'the opening-up of national markets into the internal-market results in productivity and welfare gains',[27] which is to have the effect of 'improv[ing] the social level of protection in the States'.[28] However, it is also true that through the exploitation of competition advantages in different Member States, competition between the social systems can arise; this can lead to the consequence of 'build[ing] up pressure to reduce the level of social protection',[29] thereby resulting in a 'race to the bottom'.[30] This kind of result is obviously also feared in the posting workers context, the competitive advantage in this situation being the labour cost. The Commission thus expressed the view that in the situation where a firm established in the 'host country' that has to comply with the host country's regulations with regard to pay is exposed to competition within the same territory with a firm based elsewhere, and the latter is not subject to the same obligations, 'legitimate competition between firms is ... overlaid by potentially distortive effects between national requirements'.[31] Even more to the point, the Commission described a situation where the posted workers receive lower wages and are subject to different working conditions than those that are applicable in the 'host State' as one that '*affect[s] fair competition* between undertakings and equality of treatment between foreign and national undertakings; it would from the social point of view be completely unacceptable' (emphasis added).[32]

In short, the above considerations make clear that when reference is made in the Directive with the aim of ensuring 'fair competition', what is meant is the prevention of cost-competition or 'social dumping', the direct answer to which is eliminating or reducing the main competitive advantage (cheaper labour) of the service provider established in another Member State. This is achieved by the 'pro "host-State"' regulative stance of the Directive. Hence, pursuance of this aim appears to be central to the Directive.

[27] R Giesen, 'Posting: Social Protection of Workers vs Fundamental Freedoms?' (2003) 40 *Common Market Law Review* 143, 144.

[28] ibid.

[29] ibid.

[30] On the meaning and role of this concept in European Community social policy, see generally C Barnard, 'Social Dumping and the Race to the Bottom: Some Lessons for the European Union from Delaware' (2000) 25 *European Law Review* 57.

[31] Explanatory Memorandum for a Council Directive concerning the posting of workers in the framework of the provision of services, para 12 in the Commission Proposal 1991, above n 15.

[32] ibid.

ii. How is Respect for the Rights of Workers Achieved?

The next question is whether and to what extent the Directive, with its underlying principle of protecting to a certain extent the host country's labour law system, contributes towards protecting workers' rights. Article 3(1) stipulates the central core of mandatory protective legislation applicable in the territory where the work is carried out which shall be guaranteed to posted workers. The following conditions of work and employment are covered: maximum work periods and minimum rest periods; minimum paid annual holidays; minimum rates of pay, including overtime rates; the conditions of hiring-out of workers, in particular the supply of workers by temporary employment undertakings; health, safety and hygiene at work; protective measures with regard to the terms and conditions of employment of pregnant women or women who have recently given birth, and of children and of young people; and equality of treatment between men and women and other provisions on non-discrimination.[33]

What is important to appreciate is that the Directive, whilst ensuring access to local protection, 'does not prevent the application of terms and conditions of employment which are more favourable to workers' (Art 3(7) PWD). This means that the posted workers benefit from the presumably higher minimum standards in the host State, but at the same time in case of higher home[34] standards, those higher standards remain applicable. In addition, discrimination between seconded workers and 'host State' workers regarding the core of protective legislation listed above is eliminated. These facts suggest that the Directive takes a highly protective stance for posted workers.

Finally, it is worth noting that the protection of workers is realised *through the measures taken to prevent unfair competition*, so the two issues are inextricably linked. One could even hold that the former interest is a functional result of pursuing the latter.

It is with respect to this objective that the European Parliament's amendments at first reading[35] made a considerable difference towards higher worker protection, for example, by including new matters in the list of mandatory terms and conditions of employment to be extended to posted workers: freedom of association, minimum working hours and equal pay for part-time work and social security insofar as not covered by Regulation EEC (No) 1408/71.[36] It also altered the existing one. The most interesting one for the subsequent discussion concerns rates of pay. According to this amendment, 'rates of pay as laid down in collective agreements' should be applicable, and only in the absence thereof should 'minimum rates of pay' be applicable.[37] The European Parliament also included a new provision stipulating that in case the home standards were providing for more favourable terms and conditions of employment, the Member States had to ensure that these home standards remained applicable.[38]

[33] Note that but for the provision regarding the conditions concerning the hiring-out of workers (Art 3(1)(d) of the Directive), all other matters listed are also covered by the ESC.

[34] Although, after *Laval*, it is settled that host standards above the minimum obligations set out in Art 3(7) PWD can only apply if the service provider voluntarily signs a collective agreement.

[35] Ibid, n 17.

[36] ibid, amendments no 21–23 respectively.

[37] ibid, amendment no 18.

[38] ibid, amendment no 32.

None of these amendments, which were clearly aiming at a higher level of worker protection than the original proposal, survived the final version of the PWD. However, they did come with—and perhaps as a result of—the European Parliament's view that this Directive was mainly concerned with the fundamental social rights of workers. Beyond the reference to the CCFSRW mentioned above, this is evidenced in further amendments, for example, when requesting mandatory rights language[39] or when stating that the need for coordinating national measures in this area arises 'until such time as these differences in social rights have converged'.[40]

iii. How (if at all) is the Free Movement of Services Promoted/Ensured? Is the PWD Legitimately Based on (ex) Article 47(2) and 55 EC?

This question of how the free movement of services is furthered concerns the most controversial part of the PWD and it links necessarily into a discussion of the choice of its legal bases,[41] which are directed at exactly that aim.

Considerable critique had been raised calling into question the Directive's 'internal market nature'.[42] The criticism is not merely directed at the consideration that free movement of services might not be the *main* aim of the Directive; it is rather the contemplation that the Directive is actually restrictive of the free movement of services. This is so not only in view of the CJEU's case law,[43] but it can also be derived from two further arguments. First is the fact that: 'The out-of-state provider of services has to meet the regulatory requirements of two [different] sets of labour laws, the home and the host State's, whereas the domestic provider needs to meet only the regulatory requirements of its own labour law'[44] (an obligation which, as seen above, is aimed at the protection of workers).

The counter-argument to this is that concrete obstacles to the free movement of services are removed through the provision of legal certainty. The PWD does so by 'allow[ing] the clear identification of the working conditions applicable to [posted] workers',[45] thereby removing the uncertainty that may arise out of the different criteria inspiring the conflict of law rules in the different Member States.

Second is the argument that by eliminating the main competitive advantage[46] (cheaper labour) of the employers of the posted workers, the former are less likely to obtain the contracts for carrying out this work; the result is therefore less provision of cross-border services and a hampering of the functioning of the internal market—the opposite from

[39] See eg, ibid, amendment no 2. The Commission proposal's recital 5 referred to 'measures ensuring respect for the rights of workers', whereas the European Parliament sought to change this so as to read 'measures *guaranteeing* the rights of workers'.

[40] ibid, amendment no 3.

[41] Articles 47(2) and 55 EC.

[42] See Davies, above n 14.

[43] Note that in Case C-165/98 *Mazzoleni* [2001] ECR I-2189 [24], the Court has readily accepted that the application of host state rules 'is liable to prohibit, impede or render less attractive the provision of services to the extent that it involves expenses and additional administrative and economic burdens'.

[44] Davies, above n 14, 585.

[45] ibid 592 and recital 6 of the Preamble of the PWD, above n 2.

[46] Although note that the possible competitive advantage in social security costs remains untouched by the Directive. See Hellsten, above n 1, 32.

what is claimed to be its goal. This will be examined in more detail by taking the most controversial requirement leading to cheaper labour cost, ie, the provision on minimum wages, as a concrete example.

The Directive aims to prevent unfair competition and, simultaneously, to protect posted workers *to the extent that their remuneration should not fall below that of the minimum wages in the host State*. It has to be noted, however, that the competitive advantage is *not completely* eliminated. The obligation relates to *minimum* pay. Therefore, since in most countries the wages that are paid are actually higher than the minimum and sometimes—mainly in collective agreements—'even widely exceed the compulsory provisions',[47] the competitive advantage, even though reduced, is still existent.[48] Recent estimations have shown significant wage differences between local workers and posted workers comprising around 50 per cent in France (2006 French Senate estimate), 25–28 per cent in Denmark between Eastern European and Danish building workers, and similar numbers in the German construction sector.[49]

It results from this that a considerable degree of competition based on cheaper labour is still possible, which also means that the Directive still 'allows essential pressure to lower actual wages [in the host State]'.[50] Of course, this pressure would be eliminated if the 'host State' were allowed to go beyond the minimum and apply its domestic labour standards on an equal basis to posted workers (ie, if the Directive was interpreted as a 'minimum' Directive). For a long time, it was unclear whether this is possible under Article 3(7) PWD,[51] until the Court took a stance in *Laval* (discussed below).

What should be noted is that not only a 'minimum' but also a 'maximum' Directive could be legitimately adopted on the basis of the internal market: as the discussion in chapter two has illustrated, an internal market provision can serve as a legitimate legal basis even if it has the effect of restricting trade or abolishing a certain market altogether.

Be that as it may, the following section will deal with the judicial intervention. It will illustrate how it took the Court only three instances of jurisprudence in order to turn the original balance between the competing interests on its head—it is now decided in favour of the market interest.[52]

C. The Judicial Intervention: *Laval, Rüffert* and *Commission v Luxembourg*[53]

Laval, Rüffert[54] and *Commission v Luxembourg* invited the Court to take a stance on, inter alia, the issue raised above as regards the delicate provisions of the Directive: Article 3(1)(c)

[47] ibid, with reference to C Barnard, *EC Employment Law* (Oxford, Oxford University Press, 2000) 170–80, especially 'Conclusions' at 179.

[48] Hellsten, above n 1, 32.

[49] IA posted workers 2012, above n 8, 20.

[50] ibid.

[51] PWD, above n 2.

[52] For an express confirmation of this view, see Case C-515/08, *Criminal Proceedings against Vítor Manuel dos Santos Palhota and others* [2010] ECR I-9133, Opinion of Advocate General Cruz Villalon at [44].

[53] For an overview discussion, see C Kilpatrick, 'The ECJ and Labour Law: A 2008 Perspective' (2009) 38 *Industrial Law Journal* 180.

[54] Case C-346/06 *Dirk Rüffert, in His Capacity as Liquidator of the Assets of Objekt und Bauregie GmbH & Co KG v Land Niedersachsen* [2008] ECR I-1989.

(minimum wages), Article 3(7) (is the PWD a minimum or a maximum Directive?) and Article 3(10) PWD (application of additional host State standards). All three instances deal in essence with the question to what extent and under what conditions the more protective host country standards (regarding matters listed in the PWD mandatory list (Art 3(7)) and matters not included in the PWD mandatory list (Art 3(10)) can be applied to the employment relationship in order to achieve a high level of worker protection.

i. The Court's Assessment in Laval

The Court had to interpret the PWD in light of (ex) Article 49 EC against the following factual background. In Sweden, the terms and conditions of employment, which have to be guaranteed to posted workers under the Directive, are those contained in legislative provisions. Most importantly, this does not apply to minimum rates of pay, since Sweden does not have legislation on minimum pay. Trade unions took action aimed at forcing the service provider established in another Member State to enter into negotiations with it on the rates of pay for posted workers and to sign a collective agreement containing more favourable conditions than those resulting from the relevant legislative provisions, while other terms related to matters not referred to in the relevant provision of the PWD. The question posed was whether (ex) Articles 12 EC (now Art 18 TFEU) and 49 EC (now Art 56 TFEU) and the PWD preclude a trade union from taking industrial action. The Court replied by interpreting the provisions of the Directive in light of Article 49 EC.

First, it held that a Member State in which the minimum rates of pay are not determined in accordance with one of the means provided for by the Directive is not entitled to impose on undertakings established in other Member States negotiation at the place of work, on a case-by-case basis,[55] especially since the wages that are sought to be imposed by the trade union are not minimum rates of pay.

In holding that Article 3(1) of the Directive relates *only to minimum rates of pay*,[56] the Court has set a clear limit as to how far the restriction to the freedom to provide services can go. For the Court, the Directive does not aim at fighting social dumping at every (market) cost.

The fear that allowing trade unions to bargain wages on a case-by-case basis, which makes the final wage obligation unpredictable, could potentially lead to 'protectionist bargains'[57] seemed to be all too imminent. In deciding the matter along these lines, the Directive is interpreted in a way that clearly puts more weight on the market consideration for the free movement of services than on the aim of combating social dumping; it also challenges labour law systems that are based on autonomy and collective bargaining, such as that of Sweden.

In its second point of examination, the Court analysed the matters that may be covered by the terms and conditions of work applicable to posted workers. It denied the host Member State the possibility of imposing on the service provider the more favourable conditions

[55] Case C-341/05 *Laval un Partneri Ltd v Svenska Byggnadsarbetareförbundet and others* [2007] ECR I-11767 [71].

[56] ibid [70].

[57] B Mestre, 'The Ruling Laval un Partneri: Clarification and Innovation' (2008) 1 *European Law Reporter* 2, 6.

contained in the collective agreement (which was not declared universally applicable and thus could not have similar effects to legislation) than the minimum protection provided for by law. The Court also held that the trade unions could not force upon the foreign service provider other conditions of work contained in collective agreements beyond those provided for by the PWD. According to the PWD (Art 3(10)), only authorities governed by public law could enlarge the scope of protection granted to posted workers, which was not done in this case.[58]

Here too, as in relation to the previous issue, the term 'minimum' played a crucial role, in the sense that the minimum standard of protection for posted workers stipulated in the PWD provides the maximum degree of an acceptable restriction to the freedom to provide services. In effect, this ruling suggests that the PWD—contrary to how Sweden interpreted it—is a maximum directive. This is supported by how Article 3(7) PWD is interpreted. The Court made it clear that this provision cannot be interpreted as meaning that the protection given can go 'beyond the [host State's] mandatory rules of minimum protection'[59] (unless the workers are given higher protection in their home country).

ii. The Court's Assessment in Rüffert:[60] *Posted Workers and Public Procurement*

Rüffert provides a possibility for observing the influence that the interpretation given to the Directive in *Laval* had in another area where market and social concerns meet, namely, public procurement. The facts in this case were as follows. Following a public invitation to tender, the Land of Lower Saxony awarded a contract to a German contractor to build a prison. According to the law of Lower Saxony on the award of public contracts, 'public contracting authorities may award contracts for building works … only to undertakings which pay the wage laid down in the collective agreements at the place where the service is provided'.[61] In order to obtain the contract, the building service provider need to undertake in writing to pay its employees those wages, to also impose that obligation to subcontractors and to monitor their compliance with it. Non-compliance with this obligation is sanctioned with a fine. The German company that undertook to comply with these obligations employed a Polish subcontractor whose workers were paid about half the rate fixed in the German collective agreement. Subsequently, the German company was fined and appealed the fine in the German court. The latter referred the following question to the Court: in a situation such as this, does Article 49 EC (now Art 56 TFEU) preclude a statutory obligation which requires the contractor in a public works contract to undertake to pay its employees at least the wages laid down by the applicable collective agreement.

The Court found that in the particular circumstances, involving the transnational provision of services, the law of Lower Saxony was incompatible with the PWD interpreted in the light of Article 49 EC. It started off its reasoning by taking into account the Directive and examining whether the rates of pay were laid down in accordance with one of the procedures provided for in Articles 3(1) and 3(8) PWD. The Court opined first that the law

[58] *Laval*, aboven 55, [84].

[59] ibid [80].

[60] See Kilpatrick, above n 53, annotated by P Davies, 'Case Note on Rüffert' (2008) 37 *Industrial Law Journal* 384.

[61] *Rüffert*, above n 54, [5].

of Lower Saxony cannot be considered to be a 'law' within the meaning of Article 3(1) PWD because it does not fix any minimum rates of pay.[62] Second, the collective agreement in question was not one that had been declared universally applicable pursuant to the German law transposing the PWD.[63] [64] Third, the collective agreement could not be treated as universally applicable on the basis of Article 3(1), 1st subpara, 2nd indent PWD in conjunction with the first subparagraph of Article 3(8) PWD because those provisions apply only where there is no system for declaring collective agreement universally applicable, which was not the case in Germany.[65] Fourth, the collective agreement could not fall under the second subparagraph of Article 3(8), because it is not 'generally applicable to all similar undertakings in the geographical area and in the profession or industry concerned'.[66] Therefore, since the answer was that the rates of pay were not laid down in accordance with the Directive's relevant procedures, such a rate could not be considered to constitute a minimum rate of pay within the meaning of the Directive (Art 3(1)(c)). At this point, the Court made reference to *Laval* and recalled its interpretation of Article 3(7) therein and the dictum that the provision of services cannot be made 'conditional on the observance of terms and conditions of employment which go beyond the mandatory rules for minimum protection'.[67] [68]

The interpretation continued, in line with *Laval*, that the level of protection which must be guaranteed to posted workers cannot go beyond the minimum protection provided for in the relevant provisions of the Directive (Art 3(1)(a)–(g)) because that would deprive it of its effectiveness.[69] It is important to note that the Court stressed expressly in this ruling what was already quite apparent in *Laval*. Its interpretation of the Directive is that it 'seeks in particular to bring about the freedom to provide services'.[70] In the view of the Court, this seems to be the Directive's main aim.

The Court continued by examining the law of the Land of Lower Saxony as to its compatibility with (ex) Article 49 EC. It held that the law constituted a restriction to the freedom to provide services and could not be justified by the objective of ensuring the protection of workers[71] because it applied only to a part of the construction sector (ie, only to public contracts and was therefore discriminatory) and it was not clear why the protection provided for by the national law was only necessary for a worker when working in the context of a public works contract.[72] The arguments invoking, first, the protection for independence in

[62] ibid [24].

[63] ibid [25].

[64] This point—that terms of collective agreements cannot be imposed on posted workers if the former are not universally applicable—was also confirmed in the later Case C-319/06 *Commission v Luxembourg* [2008] ECR I-4323.

[65] *Rüffert*, above n 54, [27].

[66] ibid [28].

[67] ibid [33].

[68] Similarly, in *Commission v Luxembourg*, above n 64, the Court held: 'the Community legislature intended, … to limit the possibility of the Member States intervening as regards pay to matters relating to minimum rates of pay. It follows that … adjustment of rates of pay other than the minimum wage to the cost of living does not fall within the matters referred to in the first subparagraph of Article 3(1) of Directive 96/71'.

[69] *Rüffert*, above n 54, [33]–[34].

[70] ibid [36]. The Opinion of Advocate General in the later *Santos Palhota* case, above n 52, 44, also states this in utterly clear words.

[71] *Rüffert*, above n 54, [38].

[72] ibid [40].

the organisation of working life by trade unions and, second, ensuring the financial balance of the social security systems were both dismissed.[73]

After *Laval*, it was fairly predictable that the Court would not follow the Opinion of Advocate General Bot[74] (delivered before the judgment in *Laval* was handed down), who came to the opposite conclusion. He found that the Directive does not preclude a measure such as the German law at issue. The key difference in the reasoning lies in the interpretation of Article 3(7). Advocate General Bot interpreted the provision as allowing enhanced protection going beyond the nucleus of mandatory rules stipulated in the Directive. Obviously, the interpretation is dependent on how one places the weights among the different objectives of the Directive, something that is not immediately obvious from the wording of the legislation—the Court, unlike the Advocate General, yielding more towards the market interest.

However, the Court's assessment on the question of whether the restriction to trade was justified under (ex) Article 49 EC can be challenged on the following ground. Instead of asking why the type of protection provided for by national law should be seen as necessary for the protection of workers engaged under public procurement contracts, but not for workers engaged under private contracts, the Court should have examined a different question—that is, in situations of public procurement, is it permissible to aim for higher standards of protection so that a restriction to the free movement of services can be justified on that ground?

At this point, another piece of internal market legislation that takes non-market values into account—ie, environmental and social considerations, the latter of which with implications for fundamental (social) rights[75]—becomes relevant: the Public Procurement Directive 2014/24/EU[76] and its predecessor Directive 2004/18/EC.[77] These instruments are good examples of how fundamental (social) rights can be 'mainstreamed'[78] (systematically integrated) into the EU's policies and actions.

Directive 2004/18/EC was enacted with the aim of simplifying and clarifying the pre-existing EU public procurement regime. It shed light on the previously unclear question whether it was possible to integrate social requirements into public procurement contracts.

[73] ibid [41]–[42].

[74] Opinion of Advocate General Bot in *Rüffert*, above n 54.

[75] Commission, Interpretative Communication of the Commission on the Community law applicable to public procurement and the possibilities for integrating social consideration into public procurement (COM (2001))—0566 final OJC 333 (28 November 2001) 0027—004. This communication provides guidance on the meaning of 'social considerations', which is broad and can mean to include 'measures to ensure compliance with fundamental rights, with the principle of equality of treatment and non-discrimination ... with national legislation on social affairs ... with Community directives applicable in the social field ... [and] concepts of preferential clauses (for example, for the reintegration of disadvantaged persons or of unemployed persons, and positive actions or positive discrimination in particular with a view to combating unemployment and social exclusion'. See especially Interpretative Communication, 'Introduction', para 11.

[76] Directive 2014/24/EU of 26 February 2014 on public procurement and repealing Directive 2004/18/EC [2014] OJ L94/65.

[77] Directive 2004/18 of 31 March 2004 on the co-ordination of procedures for the award of public work contracts, public supply contracts and public service contracts [2004] OJ L134/114. Note that Advocate General Bot took it into account (in *Rüffert*, above n 54, points 132–35), whereas the Court ignored it.

[78] On a detailed discussion of this concept, see O De Schutter, 'Mainstreaming Human Rights in the Europea Union' in P Alston and O De Schutter (eds), *Monitoring Fundamental Rights in the EU* (Oxford, Hart Publishing, 2005) 37ff.

While the former Directives did not provide explicitly for such a possibility, the Court had already accepted such.[79]

Directive 2004/28/EC gave recognition to that in Article 26 on contract performance: 'Contracting authorities may lay down special conditions relating to the performance of a contract, provided that these are compatible with *Community law* ... The conditions governing the performance of a contract may, in particular, concern *social* ... considerations' (emphasis added).

Directive 2014/40/EU aimed to strengthen the social considerations. It was enacted with a twofold objective: first, revision and modernisation of the previous public procurement rules 'in order to increase the efficiency of public spending';[80] and, second, 'better use of public procurement in support of common societal goals',[81] including, among others, employment and social inclusion. The second point is especially interesting for the present purposes, and it found translation in the substantive provisions of the Directive. In particular, the new article on contract performance (Art 70) now reads as follows:

> Contracting authorities may lay down special conditions relating to the performance of a contract, provided that they are linked to the subject-matter of the contract ... These conditions may include ... *social or employment-related* considerations. (Emphasis added)

The EU does indeed aim at *actively promoting* social considerations (including fundamental social rights) in the area of public procurement. However, the Court did not take this consideration into account when ruling on whether the Law of Lower Saxony was justified in the situation at issue.

A similar line was adopted in the more recent *Bundesdruckerei* case.[82] In this case, a Law of North Rhine-Westphalia was challenged, which provided the following: public service contracts (other than those concerning posted workers or in the field of public road and rail transportation) may be awarded only to undertakings which, at the time of the submission of the tender, have agreed to pay their staff a certain minimum hourly wage. The dispute arose between Bundesdruckerei and the Stadt Dortmund. The latter issued a call for tenders for a public contract. The former made it clear that if it were awarded the contract, a subcontractor established in another Member State would perform the services under the contract in that Member State. Bundesdruckerei also asserted that it could not comply with the minimum wage obligation stipulated in the Law of North-Rhine Westphalia, and applicable to the subcontractor according to the tendering specification, for two reasons: 'such a minimum wage was not provided for by collective agreements or by the law of the [other] Member States and payment of such a minimum wage was also not usual in that State in the light of the general standard of living there'.[83] Bundesdruckerei therefore sought exemption from the minimum wage obligation under the circumstances, which was rejected by the Stadt Dortmund.

[79] Case C-31/87 *Gebroeders Beentjes BV v State of the Netherlands* [1988] ECR 4635; Case C-255/98 *Commission v France* [2000] ECR I-7445.

[80] Directive 2014/24/EU, above n 76, recital 2.

[81] See also Commission Proposal on public procurement, COM(2011) 896 final (20 December 2011) 2.

[82] Case C-549/13 *Bundesdruckerei GmbH v Stadt Dortmund* ECLI:EU:C:2014:2235.

[83] ibid [10].

The question referred by the national court was in essence whether Article 56 TFEU and Article 3(1) PWD precluded the imposition of minimum wage obligations on the subcontractor in a situation such as that in the main proceedings. The Court's ruling on the scope of the question referred is particularly interesting for the present purposes. It rightly observed that, unlike in *Rüffert*, the PWD was not applicable in this situation.[84] It also acknowledged expressly that 'the public contract at issue in the main proceedings appears, in the light of its objective and the amount of the contract, to come within the scope of application of Directive 2004/18/EC'.[85] However, at the same time, it noted that according to Article 26 of the same Directive, 'such requirements [as laid down in the law of North Rhine-Westphalia] may be imposed only to the extent to which they are compatible with Community law'.[86]

The Court therefore immediately proceeded to test the national law with Article 56 TFEU. It found that it constituted a restriction, which may be justified by the objective of protecting employees and avoiding "social dumping" and the penalisation of competing undertakings which grant a reasonable wage to their employees'.[87] However, by referring to *Rüffert*, it found the measure inappropriate 'in so far as it applies solely to public contracts'.[88] It also held that the national law appears 'in any event disproportionate', because the fixed minimum wage 'bears no relation to the cost of living in the Member State in which the services relating to the public contract at issue are performed' and therefore 'prevents subcontractors established in that Member State from deriving a competitive advantage from the differences between the respective rates of pay'.[89]

We will not enter the debate on whether the Court's latter point on proportionality is convincing (consider, for example, the extent to which 'competitive advantages' in Member States where the contract is performed may have a social dumping effect on wages in the long run in the Member State where the contract is procured). It is the first-mentioned point on appropriateness of the measure that concerns us. Here again, the Court did not give weight to the fact that in public work contracts, higher standards of 'social protection' may be applicable than in private works contracts, as the codification in the Public Procurement Directives may suggest. The question is why that is.

The legal jigsaw looks like this: as noted above, Article 26 of the Public Procurement Directive accepts the inclusion of special conditions in the contract that relate to social considerations, but *only if they are compatible with EU law*. Here, the Court ruled that those conditions were *incompatible* with Article 56 TFEU, *in disregard of the special nature of public procurement*, which aims to meet not only the administrative need for work but also other public interest requirements such as social objectives.[90]

Clearly, at this point, the argument becomes circular: to argue that the restriction is justifiable *because* public procurement is at stake is not of much use when the Public

[84] ibid [24]–[27].
[85] ibid [28].
[86] ibid.
[87] ibid [31].
[88] ibid [32].
[89] ibid [34].
[90] Opinion of Advocate General Bot in *Rüffert*, above n 54, [113] with reference to V Martinez, 'Les péripéties du critère social dans l'attribution des marchés publics' in *Contracts publics, Mélanges en l'honneur du professeur Michel Guibal*, vol II (Montpellier, Presses de la facultés de droit de Montpellier, 2006) 251–52.

Procurement Directive stipulates that social objectives can only be furthered to the extent that those are compatible with EU law, *in casu* Article 56 TFEU.

The answer as to how this circle can be broken is predictable: someone has to take a stance on the issue and in the context of Directive 2004/18/EC, it was certainly not the legislator. The legislator recognised respect for the social interest, but at the same time it shifted the resolution of a potential conflict to the Court.

The Court did then take a stance in *Rüffert*, and the key finding was repeated in *Bundesdruckerei*. Implicitly, it weighed the internal market freedom above the interest to further social objectives through public procurement.

However, with adoption of the new Public Procurement Directive 2014/40/EU, the legislator seems to have taken a stronger stance in support of furthering social objectives in public procurement. As already stated above, one of the two explicit objectives in the revision of the public procurement regime was indeed to improve the framework's ability to achieve common societal goals.

When recalling the wording of Article 70 of the 2014 Directive and comparing it to the wording of Article 26 of the repealed 2004 Directive, two differences immediately become obvious. The first is the deletion (already at the Commission Proposal stage) of the reference to 'Community law', while the second is the inclusion of a reference to 'employment-related considerations'. The latter serves to add a more concrete ground next to the broad category of 'social considerations' and the former does away with the above criticism that the legislator shifts the responsibility for how to balance social considerations back to the Court.

It has been commented that this change is meaningless given that compliance with EU law is in any case required irrespective of whether it is written in a directive or not.[91] This may be true. And yet it is a very different signal that the legislator sends to the Court, when the reference to EU law is missing, as to how much weight to afford to the respective conflicting interests at stake. It is one thing for the Court to balance social considerations against internal market freedoms in the framework of a directive that expressly seeks and has as its objective to further social considerations in public procurement, but it is quite another matter to do so without that framework of reference.[92]

Directive 2014/40/EU was not applicable to the facts of either of the cases discussed *rationae materiae*. It remains to be seen how the Court will react in the context of the new legislation.

iii. The Court's Assessment in Commission v Luxembourg[93]

In this case, the Commission brought action against Luxembourg, arguing that the latter failed to fulfil its obligations in relation to Article 3(1) and (10) PWD and Articles 49

[91] Blogpost of AS Graells, 'CJEU Continues Reducing the Scope of Minimum Wage Laws When Public Contracts are Subcontracted (C-549/13)', http://howtocrackanut.blogspot.nl/2014/09/cjeu-continues-reducing-scope-of.html.

[92] See by analogy the discussion below on 'saving clauses' in s III.C.

[93] *Commission v Luxembourg*, above n 64. See also C Barnard, 'The UK and Posted Workers: The Effect of *Commission v Luxembourg* on the Territorial Application of British Labour Law' (2009) 38 *Industrial Law Journal* 122.

and 50 EC. Of particular interest are the holdings in relation to Article 3(10) PWD as they serve to restrict the social dimension of the Directive even further. The first sentence of Article 3(10) PWD allows Member States to apply terms and conditions of employment on matters other than those listed in Article 3(1), in the case of public policy provisions, provided that this happens on the basis of equal treatment and 'in compliance with the Treaty'. The latter conditions mean that the measures falling under this provision will nonetheless be assessed for compatibility with Article 56 TFEU (ex Art 49 EC). This is yet another instance of the legislature shifting an element of substantive resolution to the Court; the Court responded by taking and further reinforcing the line it had taken in the preceding judgments.

In the case under discussion, Luxembourg classified a set of measures as mandatory provisions falling under 'public policy' in its national legislation implementing the PWD. The Court handed down its interpretation of what 'public policy' entails in the context of the PWD in its 'preliminary observations'. It did so by providing a restrictive interpretation based on earlier case law:

> [The public policy classification] applies to national provisions compliance with which has been deemed to be so crucial for the protection of the political, social or economic order in the Member State concerned as to require compliance therewith by all persons present on the national territory of that Member State and all legal relationships within that State.[94]

Interestingly, the Court drew on Declaration No 10 to Article 3(10) PWD, as recorded in the minutes of the Council of the European Union, in order to support its construction of public policy, where it was noted that according to the Council and the Commission:

> [T]he expression 'public policy provisions' should be construed as covering those mandatory rules from which there can be no derogation and which, by their nature and objective, meet the imperative requirements of the public interest. These may include, in particular, the prohibition of forced labour or the involvement of public authorities in monitoring compliance with legislation on working conditions.[95]

It may be argued that the Court's solution merely reflects mindfulness to legislative statements. However, such a conclusion should not be reached too swiftly, given that the Declaration is not representative of all legislative actors. It reflects the views of the Council and the Commission only. In fact, the European Parliament has protested against such 'interpretative use' of a Declaration that it—as co-legislator—had not adopted.[96] Second, as Barnard has pointed out, the Court 'tightened up the criteria for public policy even further'[97] by holding 'that public policy may be relied on only if there is a genuine and sufficiently serious threat to a fundamental interest of society'.[98] One can only agree with Barnard that it is difficult to imagine any labour law (except laws against slavery) that could satisfy such a

[94] *Commission v Luxembourg*, above n 64, [29] with reference to Joined Cases C-369/96 and 376/96 *Arblade and others* [1999] ECR I-8453 [30].

[95] *Commission v Luxembourg*, above n 64, [32].

[96] European Parliament Resolution on Challenges to Collective Agreements in the EU, 2008/2085(INI) [2010] OJ C15E/50, para AA.

[97] Barnard, above n 93, 129.

[98] *Commission v Luxembourg*, above n 64, [50], with reference to Case C-54/99 *Église de scientologie* [2000] ECR I-1335 [17].

test,[99] with the consequence that this provision 'is interpreted … almost out of existence'.[100] Such an interpretation constitutes one more step towards 'closing' the list of Article 3(1) PWD and reinforcing the market interest in the Directive.

One important aspect to note with regard to the Court's approach is that neither of the cases conceptualises the social interest as one of fundamental social rights, that is, as an instrument that seeks to promote free movement of services, while ensuring that fundamental labour rights of posted workers are protected and provided for at a high level.

Arguably, such a conceptualisation would have made it harder for the Court to alter the balance in the Directive in the way just described. When the Court acknowledges that a directive embodies two fundamental rights,[101] it holds that 'a fair balance' has to be struck between the competing interests in the interpretation and application of the instrument.[102] In this light, it is more than questionable whether interpreting the PWD as a minimum directive strikes such 'fair balance'.

D. The Political Response

The subsequent analysis will reveal that the initial political responses can be divided into two camps. One challenges the Court's interpretation of the Directive; it is represented by the European Parliament. The other is that of the Council and the Commission, which responds to the controversies by not seeking to alter the judicial outcome. The focus there is rather on the issue of implementation and enforcement of the PWD that emerged prior to and separately from the case law quartet. Arguably, this position was already established in the Monti Report, which might be the explanation for a seemingly skewed analysis in the Commission's IA report.

i. Deviating from the Judicial Interpretation: The Position of the European Parliament

The first formal institutional statement expressly tackling the Court's judgments came from the European Parliament in the form of a Resolution in 2008.[103] It constitutes a frontal attack to the Court and puts fundamental rights at the heart of the matter.

The essential message conveyed with regard to the PWD is that the interpretations provided for by the Court do not provide for a fair balance between freedom to provide services and the protection of workers' rights, and, consequently, they do not reflect the intention of the legislator. However, it also acknowledged that the PWD has 'loopholes and

[99] A test which, as Barnard points out, is taken from the free movement of persons provisions applied to deported migrants: Barnard, above n 93, 129.

[100] ibid.

[101] As will be seen below (in s II.D), the market interest in this case can and has been identified by the legislator in fundamental rights terms. This is not to say that the internal market freedom *ought to be conceived* as a fundamental right, but only that it can be thus construed on the basis of the Charter. Furthermore, even if it is not thus construed, it is in any case afforded formally (at least) the same hierarchical rank in the Treaties as fundamental rights.

[102] See relevant discussion on *Promusicae* case in ch 4, s III.C.

[103] European Parliament Resolution on Challenges to Collective Agreements in the EU, above n 96.

inconsistencies and therefore may have lent itself to interpretations of the PWD'[104] contrary to those intended by the legislator.

The European Parliament called on the Commission to adopt legislative proposals in order to prevent conflicting interpretations in the future.[105] The opening paragraph (A) sets the tone of the Resolution, which is based on and permeated by fundamental rights considerations. The central message concerns the hierarchical relationship of the two competing interests, which necessarily affects their balancing in the legislation, and in turn in the judicial interpretation of such legislation. At a time before the entry into force of the Lisbon Treaty (but after its signature), the European Parliament stated in repeated and unequivocal terms that fundamental social rights are not inferior to the internal market freedoms; that this is so because they are constitutional rights in several Member States and enshrined in the Charter (paras 3 and 5); that it has to be made clear and ensured that economic freedoms should not be interpreted as infringing fundamental social rights (para 5); and that their proper balance should be reasserted in primary law 'in order to help avoid a race to lower social standards' (para 35). Crucially, the European Parliament also emphasised in this Resolution that *fundamental* social rights are at stake and that the weights have to be placed accordingly.

It is true that the Resolution does not refer explicitly to the right to fair and just working conditions as enshrined in the Charter. However, it does take a stance on the level of protection that the PWD is supposed to set out:

> [I]t must be made absolutely clear that the PWD and other directives do not prohibit Member States and social partners from demanding more favourable conditions, aimed at equal treatment of workers, and that there are assurances that Community legislation can be implemented on the basis of all the existing labour market models.[106]

Admittedly, the European Parliament was not unequivocal on whether the Directive *should* be revised,[107] even if that is implicit in the demands made.

This contrasts with the position of the Commission and the Council discussed below, so the question arises as to why the European Parliament had such a different stance. Part of the answer might be found when bearing in mind the internal institutional driver of the Resolution, namely, the Committee on Employment and Social Affairs (EMPL), which quite naturally would seek a re-balance in favour of the social interest. Furthermore, the emphasis of the fundamental rights dimension even before the entry into force of the Lisbon Treaty is one that also seems to be in line with the traditional role of the European Parliament as the institution that most forcefully pushes the fundamental rights agenda in the EU political landscape. Having said that, it is also clear that the issue most explicitly addressed as one of fundamental rights is the one that the Court already framed in such terms (the right to strike and its relationship with the economic freedoms). Still, the tone of the Resolution and the emphasis on fundamental social rights more generally certainly helped the European Parliament to phrase the demands more forcefully.

[104] ibid, para 26.
[105] ibid.
[106] ibid, para 32
[107] ibid, para 30.

ii. Endorsing the Judicial Interpretation: The Commission and the Council

Shortly after adoption of the European Parliament Resolution, in December 2008, the EPSCO Council meeting[108] took place. During this meeting, the Member States did acknowledge the need for an appropriate balance between the rights of posted workers and economic freedoms, but they did not see the need for opening up the PWD for amendment or review. The focus was instead placed on effective implementation. The reason may be that those Member States that were affected by the rulings had already changed their legislation.[109] Equally, the Commission agreed with the sufficiency and appropriateness of the current framework within which it deemed it possible to address all the issues raised, while involving social partners in the re-assessment of the situation.

The focus on effective implementation of the PWD and enhanced administrative cooperation in the field is an area in which the Commission had already taken action before and independently from the discussed cases.[110] It is against this background that the 'Expert Committee on Posting of Workers' (ECPW) emerged in December 2008,[111] following an invitation in the Council conclusions of 9 June 2008 (after *Laval* but before *Rüffert*) to institutionalise a pre-existing informal group on the posting of workers. This Committee is tasked with elaborating on and clarifying the implementation of the PWD, including the examination of problems linked to Article 3(10) PWD.[112] It is noteworthy that even though the discussions around the Court's case law and the centrality of fundamental rights arguments had at this point already moved centre stage, they are notably absent in this context.

In 2009, the Commission initiated four *ex post* evaluation studies on legal aspects, social and economic effects of posting of workers in the framework of the provision of services.[113] In the same year, Commission President Barroso announced his political priorities in front of the European Parliament plenary, and his position on the matter was remarkably different from the Commission's stance described above. From the initial position that there was no need for a legislative proposal, the President now announced that there was a need to adopt a separate Regulation in order to resolve problems linked to interpretation and

[108] Employment, Social Policy, Health and Consumer Affairs Council (EPSCO), Meeting of 17 December 2008, www.epha.org/a/3084.

[109] These Member States are: Denmark, Sweden, Luxembourg, and several 'Länder' of Germany. Note that only Luxembourg demanded the re-opening of the Directive in 2008. See IA posted workers 2012, above n 8, 15.

[110] Commission, Report from the Commission Services on the implementation of Directive 96/71/EC of the European Parliament and of the Council of 16 December 1996 concerning the posting of workers in the framework of the provision of services (2003) and implementation of Report Directive 96/71/EC concerning posting of workers in the framework of the provision of services (2006), www.ec.europa.eu/social/posted-workers; Commission Communication, Guidance on the posting of workers in the framework of the provision of services, COM(2006) 159 final; Staff Working Document SEC(2006) 439 for assisting Member States to achieve the results sought be the Directive and comply with the Community *acquis* as interpreted by the Court, regarding administrative requirements and control measures; Commission Communication, Posting of workers in the framework of the provision of services: maximising its benefits and potentials while guaranteeing the protection of workers, COM(2007) 304 final (finding insufficient quality of administrative cooperation and access to information); and Commission Recommendation of 31 March 2008 on enhanced administrative cooperation in the context of the posting of workers in the framework of the provision of services [2008] OJ C85/1.

[111] Commission Decision of 19 December 2008 setting up the Committee of Experts on Posting of Workers [2009] OJ L8/26.

[112] For a detailed task description, see ibid, Art 2.

[113] Listed in IA posted workers 2012, above n 8, 11–12.

implementation of the PWD. Moreover, opening up the PWD for re-negotiation was expressly acknowledged as a possibility. This was because the Commission President considered that 'the interpretation and the implementation of the Posted Workers Directive falls short of [respect for fundamental social rights and the principle of free movement of workers]'.[114] However, this changed positioning may not be surprising given the political context: the European Parliament's vote on the Commission President's second term the day after this speech and, in particular, the need to obtain the support of the socialist group.

The Monti Report followed shortly after. Apart from identifying the need for addressing the normative question concerning the status of the right to strike vis-a-vis economic freedoms, it also identified the need to respond to the practical question whether the PWD provides an apt framework in today's situation of increased posting of workers while protecting their rights.

It is important to appreciate that this report—together with the significant amount of preparatory studies and consultations—already manifestly framed the direction that was to be taken in the resulting Commission legislative package.

Monti's key recommendation for tackling the problems linked to the PWD was to:

> Clarify the implementation of the Posting of Workers Directive and strengthen dissemination of information on the rights and obligations of workers and companies, administrative cooperation and sanctions in the framework of free movement of persons and cross-border provision of services.[115]

In similar terms, the Single Market Act identified as a key action for social cohesion:

> Legislation aimed at improving and reinforcing the transposition, implementation and enforcement in practice of the Posting of Workers Directive, which will include measures to prevent and sanction any abuse and circumvention of the applicable rules.[116]

The agenda was set in a way that did not involve modification of the core controversial provisions of the PWD. No change of substance was envisaged. The focus lay on transposition, implementation and enforcement, including preventing abuse *of what is already there*, with a focus on enhancing the provision of information as well as administrative cooperation.

The pre-legislative process concerning the possible revision of the legislative framework on the posting of workers, which ultimately led to the PWED, commenced in 2011. That year the Commission contracted out an *ex ante* evaluation study to prepare the IA.[117] It is submitted that the outcome of the IA report, the resulting PWED proposal[118] and consequently also the final instrument were substantially pre-empted by the Monti Report and

[114] Commission, Press Release, Speech/09/391 (15 September 2009), http://europa.eu/rapid/pressReleasesAction.do?reference=SPEECH/09/391.

[115] M Monti, 'A New Strategy for the Single Market—At the Service of Europe's Economy and Society', Report to the President of the Commission, José Manuel Barroso (9 May 2010) (hereinafter 'Monti Report') 72.

[116] Commission Communication, Single Market Act—twelve levers to boost growth and strengthen confidence—Working together to create new growth, COM(2011) 206 final. This key action goes 'together with legislation aimed at clarifying the exercise of freedom of establishment and the freedom to provide services alongside fundamental social rights'.

[117] Multiple Framework Contract VT 2008/87, Preparatory study for an Impact Assessment concerning the possible revision of the legislative framework on the posting of workers in the context of services (VT/2010/126).

[118] Commission, Proposal for a Directive on the enforcement of Directive 96/71 concerning the posting of workers in the framework of the provision of services, COM(2012) 131 final (hereinafter 'COM Proposal PWED').

the Single Market Act, even though such analysis is supposed to start from neutral ground. The remainder will illustrate this point by having a closer look at the Commission IA.

iii. The Commission's IA Report

As Chapter 3 has demonstrated, IAs can serve as a tool for systematically integrating fundamental rights standard into policy proposals, both in the sense of preparing the ground for compatibility assessments with existing fundamental rights standards and in the sense of aiming for 'further realisation' of a given right. However, in demonstrating that the IA study was pre-empted by the Monti Report/Single Market Act context, it will also emerge in the discussion below that with respect to enhancing the regulation of fair and just working conditions in the posted workers context, fundamental rights considerations did not play any significant role in this report.

The IA of the PWED proposal identifies three (policy) problems that are directly linked to the PWD.[119] The first two are concerned with Article 4 PWD (cooperation on information) and Article 5 PWD (enforcement of obligations as well as prevention of abuse). The third problem tackles the issue that was of main significance in the case law and the one we shall focus on here: the controversy or unclear interpretation of terms and conditions of employment in Article 3 PWD—the provision that goes 'to the heart of the political compromise struck at the time of adoption of the Directive'.[120] The IA subdivides the issue into two categories.

The first category relates to the scope and level of terms and conditions of employment. According to the IA, following *Laval*, *Rüffert* and *Commission v Luxembourg*, the problem is not one of legal certainty regarding the core provisions at stake (Arts 3(7), 3(8) and 3(10) PWD); rather, it is one of implementing the rules set out due to the diverging industrial relations systems across the EU. Two problem-drivers are identified. One concerns the consequences for those countries that on the Court's interpretation fall outside the scope of the PWD, ie, those that do not set minimum wages by law or universally applicable collective agreements and those that do not provide for minimum wages etc.[121] The second problem-driver concerns the above-discussed controversies and disagreements (especially of the stakeholders) on the Court's rulings.

The second category identifies the unclear level of protection regarding the notion 'minimum rates of pay'. Again, two problem-drivers are listed: first, given that the definition of the concept is left to the host Member State, the constituent elements of 'minimum pay' are not clear, despite the fact that some indications have been given by the Court;[122] second: 'The Directive does not specify the method of comparison between the minimum rate of pay in the sending and the host Member State.'[123]

Following this problem definition, a baseline scenario of no policy change and four packages including varied combinations of regulatory and non-regulatory options are examined

[119] IA posted workers 2012, above n 8, 27ff.

[120] ibid 45.

[121] It is however curious that this situation is framed as 'a problem of implementation' since, in fact, it does not concern application of the PWD, but of primary Treaty law.

[122] See Case C-341/02 *Commission v Germany* [2005] ECR I-2733.

[123] IA posted workers 2012, above n 8, 39.

as to their appropriateness for tackling the identified problems. The analysis is made against three specific objectives: 1) better worker protection; 2) facilitating cross-border provision of services/ensuring fair competition; and 3) reducing tensions between national industrial relations systems and freedom to provide services/freedom of establishment.[124]

The policy option identified as the most suitable one involves regulatory intervention for remedying the first and second problem, while the third problem concerning Article 3 PWD is left to non-regulatory intervention. The IA rejects, among other things, legislative changes to Article 3(1), 3(7), 3(8) and 3(10) PWD that would enhance terms and conditions of employment of posted workers. Instead, it offers mainly interpretative guidelines regarding the Court's interpretation of Article 3 PWD. Among other things, it is acknowledged that this option does not address difficulties linked to the fact that some national industrial relations systems do not provide for minimum wages, even though it was one of the most controversial points arising from the case law.

The interesting question is how this overall result has been arrived at, and the answer seems to lie in the method used for comparing the different options available. Two points play an important role in this regard. The first one concerns the way in which the impacts are allocated. This is best explained on the basis of the concrete case. Take the 'optimal package' (regulatory intervention for problems 1 and 2, and non-regulatory intervention for problem 3 (Art 3 PWD))[125] and compare it with the 'rejected package' foreseeing regulatory intervention for all three problems.[126] The IA attributes the same 'positive' impact to both packages as regards the objective 'better protecting the rights of posted workers'. This is a curious result. On the one hand, we have maintenance of the status quo of Article 3 PWD as interpreted by the Court and, on the other hand, a substantive re-interpretation of it, which among others turns the PWD into a minimum Directive. How can both of them—all other things being equal—have the same degree of positive impact on protecting the (fundamental) rights of posted workers? One would assume that the package foreseeing regulatory intervention should be attributed a higher positive impact (or the 'preferred package' a more negative impact).

It could have been argued that the answer can be found in the indication that the 'rejected package' involves 'very uncertain results to the extent that the economic disincentive created for legal posting may seriously reduce the flow of posting, job opportunities or encourage undeclared work'.[127] However, this is not convincing for the following reasons. First, a reduced flow of posting per se has a negative impact on free movement of services and not on *workers' rights*. Similarly, a reduction of job opportunities does not have a negative impact on the *rights* of workers; it is an alleged consequence resulting from restricting the free movement of services. This consequence will not impact negatively on *posted* workers, but on *potential* posted workers in the home Member State. Finally, that increased worker's rights protection will encourage undeclared work is an odd argument to make when measuring the impact on workers' rights. It seems to suggest that if posted workers' rights are

[124] See Overview table in ibid 73. However, this objective is more relevant for assessing Problem 4—linked to the proposed Regulation.

[125] IA posted workers 2012, above n 8, Package B.

[126] ibid Package D.

[127] ibid Summary Table 73.

kept at a sufficiently low level, there will be no incentive for undeclared work, but surely the problem with undeclared work is one of enforcement, not of pushing workers' standards down to such a minimum level that the risk of not declaring the work is not worth running into.

In conclusion, it is not clear why the two packages are attributed the same degree of positive impact. And yet this attribution determined the choices made: by granting the same degree of positive impact on the objective of workers' rights protection to both packages; by attributing a negative impact on the objective of 'facilitating cross-border provision of services/improving climate of fair competition' on the 'rejected package' and a positive/very positive impact on the 'optimal package'; and by granting a neutral impact on 'reducing tension between national industrial relations systems and the freedom to provide services/freedom of establishment' on the 'optimal package', while granting on this point only a neutral/positive impact on the 'rejected package'.

The second point is of a more general nature and concerns the way in which the options are compared. The IA starts from the assumption that all three objectives are to be given the same weight. This, in itself, is not problematic, as long as it is remembered that the legislator is not constrained by such an approach. As we have seen in chapter two, the legislator is free to strike its own balance between market value and non-market value when re-regulating at the supranational level, also explicitly favouring the non-market value, even to the extent of prohibiting certain markets (eg, of tobacco advertising/of trade in certain food supplements).

However, there is a condition imposed on the legislator when fundamental rights are at stake, namely, balancing then becomes subject to the obligation that fundamental rights standards are respected and, in the case of positive rights, that a high level of protection is ensured in their implementation.

This then begs the question of the extent to which fundamental rights considerations actually played a role in this IA report. It is immediately obvious that they are certainly mentioned throughout the IA, which contrasts starkly with the pre-legislative stage of the PWD where such considerations are almost entirely absent (with the exception of the European Parliament report at first reading, as discussed above).

The IA identifies fundamental rights as one leg of the legal framework of posted workers.[128] It also lists a series of those that have to be taken into account in the preparation of the legislation: protection of personal data (Art 8), the freedom to choose an occupation and right to engage in work (Art 15), the freedom to conduct a business (Art 16 CFR), non-discrimination (Art 21 CFR), workers' right to information and consultation within the undertaking (Art 27 CFR), the right of collective bargaining and action (Art 28 CFR), protection in the event of unjustified dismissal (Art 30), fair and just working conditions (Art 31), family and professional life (Art 33 CFR), and the right to an effective remedy and to a fair trial (Art 47 CFR).

[128] This stands next to free movement (Art 56 TFEU), the provisions on furthering dialogue between social partners at the EU level and respect for the diversity of industrial relations system (Arts 151 and 152 TFEU) as well as the provision on the social market economy (Art 3(3) TEU).

The impact on fundamental rights is assessed throughout the IA for all examined options under the heading 'social impact', but the question is to what extent they *actually* influenced the outcome of the study—the regulatory option proposed.

The IA characterises fundamental rights both as a standard to comply with (concerning a series of fundamental rights that are not the core subject matter of regulation in the instrument, such as data protection) and as an objective to be achieved.[129]

The way to understand this is by appreciating that the listed objectives are to a certain extent coinciding with fundamental rights. For instance, the objective 'better protecting the rights of posted workers' can be matched with Article 31 CFR (fair and just working conditions) and the objective 'facilitating cross-border provision of services and improving a climate of fair competition' with Article 15 CFR (freedom to choose an occupation and right to engage in work) and Article 16 CFR (freedom to conduct a business). It is in this capacity that fundamental rights feature more strongly in the IA. This is so because their subsumption into these objectives means that they are also implicitly weighed against each other,[130] something that does not happen with those Charter rights that do not relate to the objectives.

However, precisely because of this coinciding, it has to be concluded that the fundamental rights conceptualisation did not make a substantive difference in this IA study. These interests would have been weighed anyway, even in the absence of the identification of that dimension. Furthermore, balancing these objectives that coincide with fundamental rights is not conducted against the background of established fundamental rights standards, for example, by taking relevant fundamental/human rights jurisprudence into account, but by applying a cost-benefit analysis.

iv. The Resulting PWED: Leaving the Substance of the PWD Intact

The actual proposal[131] resulting from this IA report, which set the tone for the legislative process, reflects its findings and does not seek to re-open the substance of the PWD. Consequently, the final instrument agreed in April 2014 also has as its subject matter the 'establish[ment of] a common framework of a set of appropriate provisions, measures and control mechanisms necessary for better and more uniform implementation, application and enforcement in practice of [the PWD]'.[132] It is basically aimed at improving information exchange, administrative cooperation, better definitions of key terms so as to avoid circumvention and abuse, as well as improving workers' rights of enforcement.

In accordance with the IA, some fundamental rights language did enter this instrument: a Charter compatibility recital is included in the Directive's Preamble,[133] listing rights that this Directive is said to respect and according to which it shall be implemented: Articles 8, 5, 16, 28, 31, 47, 48 and 50 CFR. The first six were already included in the initial Commission proposal, while Article 48 (the presumption of innocence and right of defence)

[129] IA posted workers 2012, above n 8, 45.

[130] The different options of intervention are compared as to the identified 'objectives', and fundamental rights do not feature explicitly and separately as such 'objectives'.

[131] COM Proposal PWED, above n 118.

[132] PWED, above n 3, Art 1(1).

[133] ibid, recital 48.

and Article 50 (*ne bis in idem*) have been added. This is not surprising in light of the substantive provisions of the PWED and, in particular, the provision on rights of defence.[134] It is with respect to these latter named rights (and access to justice more generally—see recital 34) that this instrument, on the face of its text, seems overtly concerned with *fundamental* rights.

On the other hand, the Explanatory Memorandum of the Commission proposal indicated a broader fundamental rights perspective. It referred to the Strategy for the effective implementation of the Charter[135] and provided that: 'people must be able to effectively enjoy their rights enshrined in the Charter when they are in a situation governed by Union law'.[136] This broad formulation is in line with the framing in the IA that fundamental rights are both an objective to achieve and a standard to comply with: the 'rights' referred to in the quotation can be seen to encompass not only workers' rights and the freedom to provide services understood in fundamental rights terms (Arts 31, 28, 16 CFR), the reconciliation of which is the objective of the PWD and by implication also that of the PWED, but also other fundamental rights that need to be ensured while regulating enforcement of the rules of posted workers (eg, rights of defence, as stated above).

Another fundamental rights dimension of this instrument should also be noted: the PWED contains a clause providing that it shall not affect fundamental rights as recognised in Member States and at the EU level (Art 1(2)), including the right to strike. Clearly, this comes in response to the Court's case law and will be discussed in detail below (section III.A.ii).

Irrespective of the question of the extent to which this Directive may 'improve' fundamental rights in the posted workers context, the important point remains that it leaves the substance of the PWD, which was at the heart of the *Laval* conflict, untouched.

However, the European Parliament's cooperation on an instrument that does not alter that substance is understandable,[137] given that the issues addressed in the PWED were a matter of real concern prior to and irrespective of the Court's judgment, as already stated above.

Some voices (from the Committee of Legal Affairs) were still raised in the European Parliament debate leading up to the voting of this instrument, calling for opening up and examining the substance of the PWD in the next legislative period.[138]

[134] Article 11 PWED on defence of rights, facilitation of complaints and back-payments in the enforcement context; Art 17(c) on grounds for refusal (for a requested authority to execute a request for recovery or notification of an administrative penalty and/or fine); and recital 45.

[135] Commission Communication, Strategy for the effective implementation of the Charter of Fundamental Rights by the European Union (19 October 2010), COM(2010) 573/4. See also discussion in ch 3.

[136] COM Proposal PWED, above n 118 11.

[137] This is not to say that negotiations were easy—quite the contrary. The proposal went through a difficult negotiation process with over 12 trialogues being held within a short time span and two rapporteurs (Emily Turunnen of the Committee on the Internal Market and Consumer Protection and Evelyn Regner of the Committee on Legal Affairs) asking for their names to be withdrawn from the reports. See the speech by L Andor, Member of the Commission, and the speech by E Regner, European Parliament parliamentary debate of 15 April 2014, Procedure 2012/0061(COD).

[138] Regner, European Parliament parliamentary debate (ibid).

E. Conclusion

Before judicial intervention, the PWD was an internal market instrument with a strong social dimension, essentially aimed at worker protection.

The legislative history reveals that this social dimension had not been conceived in fundamental rights terms, with two exceptions during the early phase of the proposal. This occurred during a period that was relatively proximate to the adoption of the CCFSRW and the Commission's AP for its implementation, which may explain the reference to fundamental social rights.

None of these references survived the final version of the Directive, and the PWD lacks a fundamental rights conceptualisation more generally. Interestingly, it emerged in the instant case that a correlation existed between the use of rights language and a higher level of social protection.

The analysis went on to illustrate how the Court reversed the balance as the legislator had intended it in the '*Laval* quartet' to strike it now in favour of the market interest. Heated debates in the EU institutions among stakeholders, in national governments and academia followed and made a political response to the problem inevitable.

So far, this response has led to the adoption of the PWED, which leaves the PWD—as the Court had interpreted it—intact. Both the Council in an early EPSCO meeting and the Commission in the Monti Report took a clear stance against re-opening the negotiations of the PWD, which implies tacit agreement with the Court's interpretation. The Council's position was facilitated by the fact that many Member States affected already sought adjustment of their national labour law systems in order to accommodate the requirements of the PWD. This may be either due to agreement with the Court's approach or due to the perception at the national level that attempting to reverse this position through positive integration might be in vain because of the majority's agreement with it. The position of the Commission does not come as a surprise, given its roots in the Monti Report seeking options for re-launching the single market and perceiving the bridging of economic and social objectives as necessary for boosting economic (!) integration.

It is arguable that this stance pre-empted the analysis conducted in the IA and might be the reason for some unclear steps in the methodology determining the recommendations of this report. It also emerged that the study was permeated by fundamental rights language, but that this was not determinative as to the final outcome of the study.

An earlier resolution of the European Parliament seems to take the opposite position of what the Commission presented in here, namely, one that sought re-negotiation of the PWD. However, this did not find its way back in the final PWED. Whether the matter will be revisited in the near or distant future remains an open question.

III. THE RIGHT TO TAKE COLLECTIVE ACTION AND ITS RECONCILIATION WITH ECONOMIC FREEDOMS

This section will analyse how the legislator has and is currently in the process of responding to the de-regulatory impact of *Viking* and *Laval* concerning the right to take collective action, including the right to strike, as guaranteed in the national legal orders. The two cases controversially brought the matter within the scope of EU law and called for a political response at the EU level that should reconcile fundamental labour rights with the internal market freedoms. This came with the Commission's package on the enforcement of the PWD and the exercise of the right to strike in the internal market context that will be analysed together with earlier legislative reconciliation attempts of the same interests. It will emerge that the legislative response is an ambiguous one, failing to take legal developments sufficiently into account that have occurred since the Court's pronouncement in these cases.

A. The Right to Take Collective Action in EU and International Case Law

The aim of this section is to scrutinise how the process of negative integration impacted on the right to take collective action. It will examine how the Court 'interfered' with fundamental social rights protection in *Viking* and *Laval*, how other judicial fora have interpreted the right and the consequences for the EU legislator resulting from this.

Given that these cases have been discussed exhaustively in academic literature in the aftermath of the Court's judgment,[139] the subsequent analysis will only focus on the main findings that have possible repercussions on positive integration.

i. The Right to Take Collective Action in EU Law: Viking *and* Laval

The circumstances of *Viking* and *Laval* should be briefly recalled here.

Viking concerned a Finnish passenger ferry operator that sought to reflag its vessel from Finland to Estonia in order to replace the Finnish crew with an Estonian crew and to enter into a collective bargaining agreement with an Estonian trade union. The Finnish Seamen's Union (FSU)—with the support of the International Transport Workers' Federation (ITF)—effectively prevented Viking to deal directly with an Estonian union and threatened strike action. Following Estonia's accession to the EU, Viking brought proceedings in the English courts to stop the ITF and the FSU from taking any action to prevent reflagging. The Court of Appeal referred preliminary questions to the CJEU, which essentially related to three issues: first, whether, collective action falls outside the freedom of establishment (ex Art 43 EC, now Art 49 TFEU); second, the question of horizontal direct effect, since the case is concerned with two private parties; third, whether collective action, such as that at issue, constitutes a restriction within the meaning of ex Article 43 EC and, if so, to what extent it may be justified.

Laval involved a Latvian company that hired out building workers to a Swedish company named Baltic. Laval, Baltic and the Swedish building workers' union began negotiations

[139] See, eg, B Bercusson, 'The Trade Union Movement and the European Union: Judgment Day' (2007) 13 *European Law Journal* 279; T Blanke, 'Die Entscheidungen des EuGH in den Fällen Viking, Laval und Rueffert—Domestizierung des Streikrechts und europaweite Nivellierung der industriellen Bezieungen', Oldeburger Studien zur Europäisierung und zur transnationalen Regulierung N 18/2008; ACL Davies, 'One Step Forwards, Two Steps Back? The *Viking* and *Laval* Cases in the ECJ' (2008) 37 *Industrial Law Journal* 126; N Reich, 'Free Movement v Social Rights in an Enlarged Union—The *Laval* and *Viking* Cases before the ECJ' (2008) 2 *German Law Journal* 125; C Joerges and F Roedl, 'Informal Politics, Formalised Law and "the Social Deficit" of European Integration: Reflections after the Judgments of the ECJ *Viking* and *Laval*' (2005) 15 *European Law Journal* 1.

with a view to concluding a collective agreement for the work on the Swedish building sites, but no such agreement was reached. Meanwhile, Laval had concluded a collective agreement with the Latvian building workers' trade union to which most of the workers were affiliated. As a response to this, the Swedish union began collective action, resulting to a blockading of all of Laval's sites in Sweden. Laval brought proceedings in the Swedish courts claiming the unlawfulness of the action and seeking compensation and an interim injunction. The national court stayed proceedings and asked the CJEU whether the PWD[140] and ex Article 49 EC (now Art 56 TFEU) precluded trade unions from taking collective action in the circumstances of the present case.

The three legal issues raised in *Viking* are also pertinent for resolving *Laval* and the subsequent (attempted) legislative response on how to reconcile the right to strike with the economic freedoms of the internal market.

a. The Question of Competence

In *Viking*, the Court answered the question of competence in the affirmative in dismissing three arguments put forward. First, the fact that there is no EU competence on the right to strike (ex Art 137(5) EC, now Art 153(5) TFEU) is irrelevant because Member States must in any event comply with EU law when exercising competences resting on them, according to previous case law.[141] Second, the fact that the right to strike is a fundamental right, as the Court expressly recognised here, is also irrelevant because fundamental rights must be reconciled with the requirements of the Treaty and in accordance with the principle of proportionality according to *Schmidberger*[142] and *Omega*.[143] Third, an analogy with the *Albany*[144] case was dismissed. According to the Court, the fact that an agreement or an activity is excluded from the competition provisions does not mean that the same holds true for the free movement provisions.[145]

The answer of the Court is of great significance when viewed in the light of the link between negative and positive harmonisation. It leads to the result that the right in question, the subject matter of which falls within the exclusive competence of the Member State, can feature as a legitimate ground for derogating from one of the common market freedoms. The direct consequence is that the European legislator gains some competence to legislate over it (though admittedly still not a direct competence), which would be absent was the right held to fall outside the scope of the provision in question.

140 PWD, above n 2.

141 Case C-438/05 *The International Transport Workers' Federation and the Finnish Seamen's Union v Viking Line ABP and OU Viking Line Eesett* [2007] ECR I-0779 [40].

142 'The protection of fundamental rights is a legitimate interest which, in principle, justifies a restriction of the obligations imposed by Community law, even under a fundamental freedom guaranteed by the Treaty': Case C-112/00 *Eugen Schmidberger, Internationale Transporte und Planzüge v Republik Österreich* [2003] ECR I-5659 [74].

143 Case C-36/02 *Omega Spielhallen* [2004] ECR I-9609.

144 Case C-67/96 *Albany International BV v Stichting Bedrijfspensioenfonds Textielindustrie* [1999] ECR I-5751 [60]: 'Under an interpretation of the Treaty as a whole which is both effective and consistent … agreements concluded in the context of collective negotiation between management and labour in pursuit of such [social policy] objectives must, by virtue of their nature and purpose, be regarded as falling outside the scope of Article 81.'

145 *Viking*, above n 141, [52]–[53].

b. The Question of Horizontal Direct Effect

The Court answered also this question in the affirmative,[146] because the collective action taken by FSU and ITF—which are not public law entities, but exercise their legal autonomy conferred under national law—is aimed at the conclusion of an agreement which is meant to regulate the work of Viking's employees collectively. For the Court, it was immaterial whether the entities are quasi-public and whether they have quasi-legislative powers.[147] This is arguably the most innovative[148] part of the CJEU's reasoning, which is said to have amounted to a 'revolution in the interpretation of the fundamental freedoms'.[149] The remarkable fact that Article 49 TFEU was held to be applicable here without any real explanation as to why that should be the case is relevant for the same reasons as the previous issue: an area that is normally according to Article 153 TFEU excluded from harmonisation is thereby subjected to negative integration, which opens up the door to positive integration.

c. The Fundamental Right to Strike as a Restriction to Economic Freedoms and How the Two should be Reconciled

The Court had no difficulty in finding a restriction as the collective action pursued by FSU had the effect of making Viking's exercise of its freedom of establishment less attractive or even pointless, inasmuch as it enjoyed unequal treatment vis-a-vis economic operators established in that state.[150] However, the Court's methodology on the question of justification warrants special consideration. In particular, the issue of how fundamental rights were 'categorised', ie, whether fundamental rights were included into the already-existing ground of justification or whether they constitute an independent ground of justification to be judged according to different parameters,[151] as the earlier *Schmidberger* case may (although admittedly not unequivocally) suggest.

When examining the Court's reasoning in *Viking*, it becomes obvious that in this case the emphasis was not placed on the fact that collective action is a fundamental right that clashes directly with a free movement provision, but rather at the *aim* to which the exercise of this right is directed. True, the Court recalled the *Schmidberger* formula, but it proceeded by concentrating on the fact that the exercise of that right is aimed at the protection of workers[152] and recalled in the same sentence that '*the protection of workers* is one of the *overriding reasons of public interest* recognised by the Court' (emphasis added).[153] In light of this approach, it is almost no surprise that, when referring to the objectives that need to

146 ibid [60]–[61] and [66].

147 ibid [64]–[65].

148 Mestre, 'The Ruling Laval Laval un Partneri', above n 57.

149 ibid.

150 *Viking*, above n 141, [72].

151 This position can be advocated on the following ground: if it is accepted that the aim of lawful derogations is to provide the Member Sates with the necessary regulatory autonomy, the protection of fundamental rights demands a higher degree of regulatory autonomy on the part of the Member States because they 'present … the core of social value choices about the balance between the individual's freedom and collective interest'. M Avbelij, 'European Court of Justice and the Question of Value Choices, Fundamental Human Rights as an Exception to the Freedom of Movement of Goods', Jean Monnet Working Paper 06/04, 57.

152 *Viking*, above n 141, [77].

153 ibid.

be balanced against each other, the Court refers to the market freedoms on the one hand and to social *policy objectives*[154] on the other. Hence, the *fundamentality* of the right at issue is lost out of sight and the balancing is essentially undertaken between the free movement provision and an 'overriding reason of public interest'—a narrow exception to the free movement rule which thus has to be interpreted strictly. Notably, the same methodology was adopted in *Laval*.[155]

This approach stands in striking contrast to the one adopted in *Schmidberger*, where the Court did not subject environmental protection (which was the aim of the demonstration that constituted a restriction to the free movement of goods) to the balancing exercise, but rather took into account the fact that the national authorities need to *respect fundamental rights* as guaranteed by both the ECHR and the Constitution of the Member State concerned in deciding to allow a restriction to be imposed on one of the fundamental freedoms enshrined in the Treaty.[156] Note that the point made here does not concern the fact that the fundamental right was qualified as a restriction to the free movement provision first. This is logical from the point of view of EU law. If the answer to the question of the existence of a restriction on a fundamental freedom would be in the negative (which is also a possibility), the situation would not be within the scope of EU law and the Court would not be able to pronounce itself on the issue—that would be the end of the matter.[157] Rather, the relevant question is that of how the balancing act is conducted (ie, what methodology is adopted for balancing) *once* the situation is brought within the scope of EU law. It is not only for those who endorse the view that fundamental rights should rank above the internal market freedoms that the Court's methodology in *Viking* and *Laval* does not make sense; it should be equally so for those[158] who endorse the view that fundamental rights and fundamental freedoms are of the same hierarchical rank.

In *Viking and Laval*, it is not very clear whether the Court merely sought a way to evade the question of the direct clash between fundamental rights and market freedoms or whether it subsumed fundamental rights in the category of 'overriding reasons in the public interest'. Lenaerts and Gutiérrez-Fons attempt to explain the different approach in *Viking* and *Laval* (by 'different', they mean 'stricter scrutiny' by the Court, but they do not acknowledge the methodological difference) by pointing out that the 'trade unions sought *protectionist* measures by struggling to keep jobs at home'(emphasis added).[159] The authors acknowledge that it is in principle legitimate for trade unions to seek to protect workers from social dumping, but Member States will not be denied a wide margin of appreciation in that respect when such action leads to protectionism,[160] the prohibition of which is, so the authors say, 'a fundamental EU value'.[161] The statement raises the following problems.

[154] ibid [79].

[155] *Laval*, above n 55, [101]–[107].

[156] See *Schmidberger*, above n 142, [76].

[157] V Skouris, 'Fundamental Rights and Fundamental Freedoms: The Challenge of Striking a Delicate Balance' (2006) 17 *European Business Law Review* 225, 236.

[158] See, eg, Judge Skouris, ibid.

[159] K Lenaerts and JA Gutiérrez-Fons, 'The Constitutional Allocation of Powers and General Principles of EU Law', (2010) 47 *Common Market Law Review* 1629, 1666.

[160] The exact wording used is 'equally trade unions are not entitled to shield local labour markets from competition coming from Member States with low average wages': ibid.

[161] ibid 1667.

First, note that the vice that 'protectionism' is in this context aimed at is a restriction of the free movement of services. In this conception, trade unions are not allowed to try to keep jobs at home and thereby hamper the posting of workers (which in EU law falls under the services provisions, not workers as noted above).[162] This is not necessarily self-evident, since the very purpose of the PWD was to recognise the capacity of Member States to protect their own employment markets against social dumping whilst also offering free movement. The authors do make a distinction between protection against social dumping (which is allowed) and protectionism (which is not allowed). However, the problem here is that protecting national workers from 'social dumping' will always lead to some degree of protectionism: the more host labour standards are maintained for posted workers, the less of a competitive advantage the foreign undertaking will have, the less likely it is that posting will take place and the result is that more jobs 'are kept at home' (see discussion on the PWD above). Consequently, the moment that the social dumping argument is raised, protectionism could be ascribed to it.

Second, the economic freedom also seems to rank above the fundamental right in this analysis, as the methodology for balancing, which was criticised above, is maintained. The authors refer to the fact that it may be legitimate for trade unions to seek to *protect workers* (recall the discussion on subsuming the right to take collective action into the 'overriding requirement in the public interest category'). However, why is it not stated that trade unions have a fundamental right to take collective action? Why is there a need to justify the exercise of a fundamental right in the first place, while there is no such need to exercise the free movement of services?

There is a further point made by the authors. They seem to be not only concerned with protectionist effects but also with *motive*. The relevant passage is worth citing in full:

> [H]ad the Scandinavian trade unions in *Laval* and *Viking* reacted to cheaper labour coming from the Baltic States *with a transnational mindset*, perhaps seeking to raise standards throughout the EU rather than seeking to exclude workers from other Member States, the ECJ might have been more sympathetic to their claims. For example, fears of social protectionism might have been alleviated had the Scandinavian trade unions joined forces with their Baltic counterparts to provide a 'European solution' to intra-Union relocation or to the remuneration of posted workers. (emphasis added)[163]

However, where the objective is necessarily justifiable since it corresponds to the exercise of a fundamental right, then it might be said that motive is irrelevant. By analogy, in its

[162] The authors give a social dimension to this argument: 'Otherwise, the ECJ might have tilted the balance in favour of a "social Europe" that arguably *excludes a large part of its* new *citizens*.' ibid, emphasis added, with reference to A Rosas, 'Finis Europae socialis?' in JC Piris et al (eds), *Chemins d'Europe, Mélanges en l'honneur de Jean-Paul Jacqué* (Paris, Dalloz, 2010) 606–07. Similarly, Advocate General Kokott explains the CJEU's approach in *Viking* and *Laval* by the fact that there were 'adverse effects on Union citizens engaged in cross-border activities' in Case C-73/07 *Tietosuojavaltuutettu v Satakunnan Markinapörsi Oy, Satamedia Oy (Satamedia)* [2008] ECR I-9831, Opinion of Advocate General Kokott, point 50. The posted workers cannot be said to be 'included' in this 'social Europe', as a matter of principle, insofar as they do not enjoy equal pay for equal work. Rather, the citizens who directly (and certainly in the short term) profit from this 'inclusion' are the companies that post (the posted workers would only profit if it were the case that they would not have a job if it was not for the posting, which is an empirical question). Indeed, the very point of the purported exercise of the right to strike here was to argue that the posted workers would not be benefiting from having jobs without proper social rights and protections.

[163] Lenaerts and Gutiérrez-Fons, above n 159, 1666–67.

free movement case law where the 'objective' being pursued is a fundamental freedom, the CJEU has consistently concentrated on effect and not on, say, the motivation of the worker (*Carpenter*)[164] doing the moving.

To conclude, it is open to question whether the different approach in *Viking* and *Laval* is related to the fact that fundamental *social rights* were at issue. It is certainly remarkable. Indeed, it may be said that the very criticisms or rationalisations of the judicial balancing act which have been offered to justify the divergences point to the need for comprehensive and calibrated internal market legislation, which seeks to strike an appropriate balance between the interests at stake. However, as will be seen below, this has failed to materialise.

What is clear is that the issue of categorisation raises immensely important questions as to the normative value of the economic freedoms and fundamental rights, respectively, and as to what hierarchical relationship they stand to each other. The Court's subsumption of fundamental rights into the category of overriding reasons of public interest implies that they assume a lower position.

In the meantime, the Charter has gained legally binding force, which means that both its own text and the sources that are cross-referred therein have to be taken as a starting point for the recognition of the right, as well as for determining the scope of protection when clashing with economic freedoms. The Charter—at least on the face of its text—also suggests that economic freedoms and fundamental rights are at least of equal rank. It will emerge below that the currently legally binding regime has the potential to significantly challenge the Court's approach in *Viking* and *Laval*.

ii. The Fundamental Right to Take Collective Action, Including the Right to Strike and its Reconciliation with the Economic Freedoms Post-Lisbon

a. The Charter

The right to take collective action is enshrined in Article 28 CFR along the following terms:

> Workers and employers, or their respective organisations, have, in accordance with Union law and national laws and practices, the right to negotiate and conclude collective agreements at the appropriate levels and, in cases of conflicts of interest, to take collective action to defend their interests, including strike action.

In setting out the right as protected under EU law, the ESC, the CCFSRW and Article 11 ECHR have to be taken into account.[165]

b. The ECHR

Until recently, the right to collective bargaining and the right to enter into collective agreements were *not* considered an inherent element of Article 11 ECHR.[166] The ECtHR has,

[164] Case C-60/00 *Mary Carpenter v Secretary of State for the Home Department* [2002] ECR I-6279.

[165] The Explanations to the Charter provide that this Article is based on Art 6 ESC, on points 12–14 CCFSRW and Art 11 ECHR. Explanations Relating to the Charter of Fundamental Rights [2007] OJ C303/1 26.

[166] *Swedish Engine Drivers' Union v Sweden*, App No 5614/72(ECtHR, 6 February 1976) [39]; *Schmidt and Dahlström v Sweden*, App No 5589/72 (ECtHR, 6 February 1976) [34].

however, departed from its previous longstanding position in its decision in *Demir and Bakayra*[167] to hold the opposite—that 'the right to bargain collectively with the employer has, in principle, become one of the essential elements of the "right to form and to join trade unions for the protection of [one's] interests" set forth in Article 11 of the Convention'.[168] The ECtHR based its 'complete u-turn'[169] on its previous case law on developments in labour law at the international and the national level, and the practice of Contracting States. The international sources drawn upon are ILO Convention No 98 (on the Right to Organise and Bargain Collectively) and No 151 (on labour relations in the public service); Article 6 ESC; and, finally and very interestingly, Article 28 CFR. Reference to these sources is of crucial importance in this context not only because they led the ECtHR to recognise the right under the Convention, but also because they are relied upon in the substantive assessment of whether a restriction to this right is 'necessary in a democratic society'/'proportionate'.[170] Following and relying on *Demir and Baykara*, the ECtHR handed down its judgment in *Enerji Yapi-Yol Sen v Turkey*[171] explicitly recognising the right to strike as an essential element of collective bargaining under Article 11 ECHR. In doing so, it made reference to ILO Convention No 87.

The question thus arising is what impact does all of the above have on the content of the right to take collective action/right to strike under EU law? Since the ECHR now covers the right to take collective action, Article 28 CFR has to be interpreted as providing as a minimum the same level of protection. This has two implications. First, the level of protection provided for in the ECtHR has to be followed by the CJEU by virtue of Article 52(3) CFR. Second, since the ECtHR itself relies on universal (the ILO Conventions) and on regional instruments (the ESC) for determining the content of the right,[172] the conclusion could be drawn (as was done by Ewing and Hendy)[173] that the same must be relied on in order to determine the scope of the EU right.[174] This is important, given that both the ILO position and the ESC pose a direct challenge to CJEU jurisprudence, as will be illustrated in what follows.

c. The ILO

The Report of the ILO Committee of Experts on the Application of Conventions and Recommendations on the *BALPA* case is particularly relevant in this respect.[175] BALPA was a trade union that threatened strike action against British Airways (BA) when the latter

[167] *Demir and Baykara v Turkey*, App No 34503/97 (ECtHR, 21 November 2006) [14]. See also KD Ewing and J Hendy QC, 'The Dramatic Implications of *Demir and Baykara*' (2010) 39 *Industrial Law Journal* 2.

[168] *Demir and Baykara*, above n 167 [38].

[169] Ewing and Hendy, above n 167, 7.

[170] *Demir and Baykara*, above n 167, [162]–[170].

[171] *Enerji Yapi-Yol Sen v Turkey*, App No 68959/01(ECtHR, 21 April 2009). See also *Danilenkov and others v Russia*, App No 67336/01(ECtHR, 30 July 2009).

[172] *Demir and Baykara*, above n 167, [147]–[148] and [149]–[150] (with reference to universal and regional instruments, respectively).

[173] Ewing and Hendy, above n 167, 40ff.

[174] The reference to the Charter under the 'regional instruments' obviously does not add anything to the point made here.

[175] ILO, Report of the Committee of Experts on the Application of Conventions and Recommendations (2010), www.ilo.org/public/libdoc/ilo/P/09661/09661%282010-99-1A%29.pdf.

decided to set up a wholly owned subsidiary airline in France. BA responded that it would apply for an interim injunction based on the argument that according to *Viking* and *Laval*, the strike action was unlawful, and that it would claim damages of such a significant amount if strike action were to take place nonetheless as to deter BALPA from pursuing this course of action.

The ILO Committee of Experts examined whether the impact of the CJEU's decisions at the national level was such as to deny workers' freedom of association rights under Convention No 87. It found that this was indeed the case—in three steps:

1. In elaborating the permissible restrictions that may be placed on the right to strike, the Committee 'has never included the need to assess the proportionality of interests bearing in mind a notion of freedom of establishment or freedom to provide services' and it 'finds no basis to reverse its position here'.
2. The Committee noted with 'serious concern the practical limitations on the effective exercise of the right to strike in the BALPA scenario'. This is so because the 'omnipresent threat of an action for damages that could bankrupt the union possible now in the light of the *Viking* and *Laval* judgements creates a situation where the rights under the Convention cannot be exercised'.
3. The Committee rejected the argument that the judgments are only of limited impact since they are only limited to free movement of services and freedom of establishment. It reasoned that 'in the current context of globalization, such cases are likely to be ever more common, particularly with respect to certain sectors of employment'. The conclusion thus reached was 'the doctrine that is being articulated in these ECJ judgements is likely to have a significant restrictive effect on the exercise of the right to strike in practice in a manner contrary to the Convention'.[176]

Point 1 calls the balancing exercise conducted in *Viking* and *Laval* into question. As already seen above, in *Viking* and *Laval*, in a classic free movement law manner, the right to strike has to be a justified and proportionate restriction to an economic freedom. However, the CJEU could only ask for an examination of other less restrictive means than strike action because it relied on pre-*Demir* ECtHR case law on the question of suitability, stating that collective action is only one way to protect interests of trade union members. Following *Enerji*, this is no longer tenable. Any interference with the right to strike is a prima facie violation of Article 11(1) ECHR, which can only be justified on the basis of Article 11(2) ECHR. It is true that freedom of establishment or freedom to provide services could be read into the Article 11(2) ECHR list of 'rights and freedoms of others', but it would still be necessary to demonstrate the pursuance of a 'pressing social need' in order to demonstrate that the restriction is 'necessary in a democratic society'. If the ECtHR is to follow ILO Convention No 87 in determining this point, the restriction is going to fail the test; if it decides to deviate, it would still make a substantive difference to the CJEU's approach not only because it changes the burden of proof but also because that is a high burden to overcome.

d. The ESC

Another important challenge to the CJEU's case law has come from the European Committee of Social Rights (ECSR) handing down a decision under the collective complaints

[176] ibid 209.

procedure in *LO and TCO v Sweden*.[177] In this case, the Swedish trade unions (LO and TCO) challenged Swedish legislation that was amended following the *Laval* judgment in order to bring it into line with CJEU jurisprudence (the so-called *Lex Laval*). The amended law provided in essence that industrial action could only be taken against a foreign service provider posting workers if the conditions demanded relate to minimum rates of pay and/or correspond to the conditions contained in a collective bargaining agreement concluded at a central level that are generally applied throughout Sweden to corresponding workers within the sector in question.

The ECSR obviously ruled on the compliance of Swedish law with the ESC, but in doing so, it indirectly challenged EU law. The ECSR's remarks on the relationship between EU law and the ESC are in any event highly interesting beyond the purposes of the *Laval* discussion. The ECSR commenced by noting that the fact that national provisions are based on EU law does not remove them from the ambit of the Charter, and the same goes for national provisions based on preliminary rulings (the *Laval* judgment). The ECSR then expressly dismissed the idea that any type of presumption of compatibility of EU law with the ESC can apply, as is the case with ECHR law.[178] This is so because:

> [N]either the current status of social rights in the EU legal order nor the substance of EU legislation and the process by which it is generated would justify a general presumption of conformity of legal acts and rules of the EU with the European Social Charter. Furthermore the Committee notes that the EU has not taken steps to accede to the European Social Charter at the same time as the European Convention on Human Rights.[179]

This is remarkable not only because it highlights the different position of fundamental social rights in EU law,[180] but also because a *specialised external* body questions both the substance of EU legislation (adopted or failed to be adopted when such is required in order to realise a fundamental social right) and, very interestingly for the purposes of this book, the manner in which it is adopted.

Turning to the substance of the case, the important points that the Committee noted were the following: first, under Article 6(2) ESC, Contracting States have the obligation to actively *promote* the conclusion of collective agreements and States 'should not interfere in the freedom of trade unions to decide themselves which industrial relationships they wish to regulate in collective agreements and which legitimate methods should be used in their effort to promote and defend the interest of the workers concerned'.[181] The Swedish law, however, 'impose[d] "substantial limitations" on the ability of Swedish trade

[177] *Swedish Trade Union Confederation (LO) and Swedish Confederation of Professional Employees (TCO) v Sweden*, Complaint No 85/2012 (ECSR Decision, 20 November 2014).

[178] *Bosphorus v Ireland*, App No 45036/98 (ECtHR, 30 June 2005).

[179] *LO and TCO v Sweden*, above n 177, [74].

[180] For a discussion of this in the pre-Lisbon context, see B de Witte, 'The Trajectory of Fundamental Social Rights in the EU' in G de Búrca and B de Witte, *Social Rights in Europe* (Oxford, Oxford University Press, 2005). Central arguments made therein are still valid today, eg, the fact that general principles of EU law single out the ECHR, but not the ESC (see Art 6(3) TEU); the rights versus principles dichotomy in the Charter, which the CJEU has been confronted with recently (see, eg, Case C–176/12 *Association de médiation sociale v Union locale des syndicats CGT and others (AMS)* ECLI:EU:C:2014:2 and especially the Opinion of Advocate General P Cruz Villalón); and in Case C-282/10 *Maribel Dominguez v Centre Informatique du centre Ouest Atlantique* EU:C:2012:33, Opinion of Advocate General Trstenjak; in addition, as the ECSR noted in the quoted passage, the fact that the EU shall accede to the ECHR (Art 6(2) TEU), but not to the ESC.

[181] *LO and TCO v Sweden*, above n 177, [111].

unions to make use of collective action in establishing binding collective agreements on other matters and/or to reach agreements at a higher level'.[182] It was therefore in violation of Article 6(2) ESC.

Second, a restriction of the right to take collective action as provided for in Article 6(4) ESC is only lawful if prescribed by law, pursued for a legitimate aim and necessary in a democratic society (Art G ESC). However, 'national legislation which prevents a priori the exercise of the right to collective action, or permits the exercise of this right only in so far as it is necessary to obtain given minimum working standards would not be in conformity with Article 6§4 of the Charter … [i]f the *substance* of this right is to be respected, trade unions must be allowed to strive for the improvement of existing living and working' (emphasis added).[183] The reference to the 'substance of this right' is reminiscent of Article 52(1) CFR, which refers to the 'essence' of rights.[184] It becomes interesting when considering Barnard's suggestion for a revised proportionality test for balancing economic freedoms with fundamental rights.[185] The suggestion is to add a further limb to the proportionality test in order to examine whether the essence of a right is affected. It appears then that for the ECSR, the Swedish legislation would indeed fail under this limb. Indeed, it might be said that this approach would be a mirror effect of the sort of reasoning that Lenaerts and Gutiérrez-Fons rely upon in relation to the fundamental freedoms and the threat of protectionism.

The ECSR also pointed out that the free movement of services 'cannot be treated, from the point of view of the system of values, principles and fundamental rights embodied in the Charter, as having a greater a priori value than core labour rights'.[186] When looking at the provisions of the Swedish law, the Committee found the restriction disproportionate and in violation of Article 6(4) ESC.

Finally, the ECSR found the measure to be in violation of Article 19(4)(a) and (b) ESC providing that (lawful) migrant workers have the right to enjoy treatment no less favourable than national workers as regards: a) remuneration and other employment and working conditions; and b) trade union membership and collective bargaining. A crucial step for arriving at that conclusion was the qualification of posted workers as *migrant workers*. This of course challenges the entire EU posted workers regime, which has been regulated under the 'free movement of services' rather than workers provisions,[187] and is remarkable in that regard, although understandable from the perspective of the ESC, which obviously does not contain any consideration for the free movement of services.

It emerges from the above discussion that both the ILO and the ECSR have entered into a direct collision with the current EU approach on the right to strike. The extent to which the ECtHR will take these into account should the occasion arise can then also have real implications for the EU legal order, especially in view of the EU accession to the ECHR.

[182] ibid [112].

[183] ibid [120].

[184] See also the following blog post: http://marcorocca.wordpress.com/2013/11/22/a-european-clash-of-legal-orders-the-european-committee-of-social-rights-on-the-swedish-lex-laval.

[185] C Barnard, 'A Proportionate Response to Proportionality in the Field of Collective Action' (2012) 37 *European Law Review* 117, 133ff.

[186] ibid [122].

[187] See also blog post above n 184.

All we know to date is that within the 'new legal context' post-Lisbon (but before the *LO and TCO v Sweden* decision), the EU legislature responded to the Court's case law and the relationship between the two conflicting interests at stake with two legislative proposals. It did so by using, inter alia, a tool already employed in legislation before the case law under discussion.

iii. The Legislative Approach: 'Saving' the Right to Take Collective Action from the Economic Freedoms?—Monti I, Monti II, Services and Posted Workers

The case law discussed in the previous section triggered the legislator's need to provide for a political response to the controversy surrounding the judicial solution of the matter. This response culminated in the Commission proposals for the PWED[188] and for a Regulation on the exercise of the right to take collective action within the context of the freedom of establishment and the freedom to provide services:[189] the so-called draft 'Monti II' Regulation. Meanwhile, this draft Regulation was withdrawn by the Commission after it was challenged by national parliaments under the new subsidiarity control mechanism introduced in the Lisbon Treaty, while the PWED has been enacted (see discussion above).

Both instruments were closely modelled on the suggestions put forward in the 2010 report of Mario Monti.[190] The draft regulation carries the 'Monti' epithet because it contains contrivances (such as an 'early warning mechanism') already inserted in a Regulation inspired by the same person, the 'Monti' Regulation ('Monti I'),[191] which is applicable to the free movement of goods.

Both the PWED and draft 'Monti II' make use of 'saving clauses' for addressing the relationship between the internal market legislation at issue and the right to take collective action. 'Saving clauses' exclude the fact that internal market legislation could have an effect on the exercise of the right to take collective action.[192] [193] Such tools were, however, already employed in two instances of legislation adopted prior to the *Viking* and *Laval* case law, namely, the 'Monti I' Regulation as well as the Services Directive (SD).

In what follows, initially, the effectiveness of 'saving clauses' will be examined as introduced in its originator ('Monti I') and then in a somewhat altered form in the SD and finally as included in the Commission's most recent legislative action (the PWED and the (failed) draft 'Monti II'). A discussion of the latter instrument remains important despite its withdrawal for demonstrating that the alleged benefits of a legislative response do not always materialise, especially when it comes to politically sensitive issues, which a direct clash between economic freedoms and fundamental (social) rights almost inevitably involves.

188 COM Proposal PWED, above n 118.

189 Commission, Proposal for a Council Regulation on the exercise of the right to take collective action within the context of the freedom of establishment and the freedom to provide services COM(2012) 130 final (hereinafter 'Draft "Monti II" Regulation').

190 Monti Report, above n 115.

191 Council Regulation (EC) No 2679/98 of 7 Dec 1998 on the functioning of the internal market in relation to the free movement of goods among the Member States [1998] OJ L337/8, Art 2 (hereinafter '"Monti I" Regulation').

192 Directive 2006/123/EC on Services in the Internal Market [2006] OJ L376/36 (hereinafter 'Services Directive (SD)').

193 See also T Novitz, 'Labour Rights as Human Rights: Implications for Employers Free Movement in an Enlarged European Union' (2006–07) 9 *Cambridge Yearbook of European Legal Studies* 358.

a. The 'Monti I' Regulation

The 'Monti I' Regulation[194] sets up an early warning system whereby Member States with relevant information in relation to any obstacle or threat to the free movement of goods that is leading to serious disruption, causing serious loss to the individuals affected and requires immediate action[195] shall communicate this to the Commission.

The Commission will then transmit it to the Member States.[196] When an obstacle occurs, the Member States have the obligation to take all necessary and proportionate measures so that the free movement of goods is assured. They must communicate this to the Commission.[197] The Regulation is thus mainly concerned with procedure rather than with a substantive balancing exercise between economic freedoms and fundamental rights. Crucially, however, it also provides for the following provision in Article 2:

> The Regulation may not be interpreted as affecting in any way the exercise of fundamental rights as recognised in Member States, including the right or freedom to strike. These rights may also include the right or freedom to take other actions covered by the specific industrial relations systems in Member States.[198]

b. The SD

It is well known that the controversial SD has had a long pre-legislative and legislative history.[199] Building and complementing the existing *acquis* in this area,[200] it is an instrument aimed at reducing barriers to the free movement of services and the right to establishment. It takes a horizontal approach in the sense that all services are covered by it unless expressly excluded. The most controversial part of the initial Commission proposal was the application of the 'country of origin principle',[201] which determined that the applicable law for the service provider was that of the country of establishment and not that of the 'host State' to which the services may be provided on a temporary basis. When the proposal reached the European Parliament, this principle was abandoned. The scope of the SD had also been altered through the inclusion of a saving clause in the spirit of the 'Monti I' Regulation. This provides that the 'Directive shall fully respect the right to negotiate, conclude, extend or enforce collective agreements, and the right to strike and to take industrial action according to the rules governing industrial relations in the Member State'.[202] Furthermore,

[194] See D Chalmers, C Hadjiemmanuil, G Monti and A Tomkins, *European Union Law* (Cambridge, Cambridge University Press, 2006) 502–03.

[195] 'Monti I' Regulation, above n 191, Art 1(1)(a)–(c).

[196] ibid, Art 3.

[197] ibid, Art 4.

[198] ibid, Art 2.

[199] See generally B de Witte, 'Setting the Scene: How Did Services Get to Bolkestein and Why?', EUI Working Paper LAW No 2007/20.

[200] Although the SD also provides for confusion as to the grounds of legitimate derogations from the freedom to provide services. Article 16(3) of the Directive provides a considerably shorter list of legitimate derogations than the Court's list of mandatory requirements, whereas recital 40 defines the concept of 'overriding reasons relating to the public interest' in making reference to the full list of mandatory requirements as recognised by the Court. See ibid 10–11.

[201] Commission Proposal for a Directive on services in the internal market COM(2004) 0002, Art 16.

[202] European Parliament Resolution on the application of Directive 96/71/EC on the posting of workers(2006/2038(INI)), P6_TA-PROV(2006) 0061, A6-0308/2006 (16 February 2006), Amendment 9, recital 6(d) (new).

it will not affect the exercise of fundamental rights, including the right to take industrial action. However, what should be noted is that the saving clause did not survive the final version of the Directive in this form, but was amended in the following way:

> This Directive does not affect *the exercise of fundamental rights as recognised* in the Member States and *by Community law*. Nor does it affect the right to negotiate, conclude and enforce collective agreements and to take industrial action *in accordance with* national law and *practices which respect Community law*. (emphasis added)[203]

It becomes immediately obvious that the wording of the clauses in the two instruments is not identical. The 'Monti I' Regulation appears to place great importance on respect for fundamental rights generally, and the right to take collective action specifically, by seeking to pre-empt any possible interference of this instrument with such rights. It does so by giving clear guidance to all authorities responsible for its application and interpretation, when stating that this instrument shall not be interpreted *in any way* in a manner that may affect fundamental rights. It could therefore be assumed that the effect of this 'saving clause' is to exclude from its scope of application *any situation* where the Regulation with its objective of ensuring the free movement of goods might adversely affect the exercise of fundamental rights.

However, the 'saving clause' contained in the final version of the SD has a narrower formulation than the 'Monti I' Regulation. First, it does not refer to the 'right' to strike (although recital 14 does, and it seems that it is actually included).[204] Second, it states that the rights that shall not be affected have to be in conformity with '*practices, which respect Community law*'.[205] This phrasing indicates that the right to take collective action, which is intended to be 'saved' and which falls according to Article 153(5) TFEU outside the competences of the EU, can only be so 'saved' to the extent that it is exercised in accordance with EU law. Two issues need to be analysed in this regard.

First of all, the question is what does the expression 'saving' with respect to Article 1(7) SD mean? Does it imply a total exclusion from the reach of the SD, identical to Article 2 of 'Monti I', which expressly excludes certain sectors from its scope of application?[206] Barnard argues for exactly that position by referring to statements of various politicians made before the European Parliament and the House of Lords EU Select Committee.[207] At the same time, she also points out, against the background of *Viking*[208] and *Laval*,[209] that it is 'clear [that] barriers created by national employment laws—even if exempted from the Directive—may nevertheless be caught by [ex] Article 43 and 49 of the EC Treaty unless those rules can be justified and the steps taken are proportionate'.[210] Therefore, even though the right in question is 'saved' for the purposes of the Directive, it is not 'saved' for the

[203] Services Directive, above n 192, Art 1(7).

[204] C Barnard, 'Employment Rights, Free Movement under the EC Treaty and the Services Directive', Mitchell Working Paper Series, 5/2008, www.law.ed.ac.uk/file_download/series/44_employmentrightsfreemovementundertheectreatyandtheservicesdirective.pdf, 21.

[205] See ibid 22; and Novitz, above n 193.

[206] Barnard, above n 204, 22.

[207] ibid.

[208] *Viking*, above n 141.

[209] *Laval*, above n 55.

[210] Barnard, above n 204, 23.

purposes of the Treaty.[211] Orlandini expresses a similar view by rejecting that Article 1(7) SD, Article 2 of the 'Monti I' Regulation and recital 22 of the PWD[212] could be read to mean 'absolute immunity that … result[s] in the mere acknowledgment of the compatibility with Community law of whatever a Member State lays down on the subject'.[213] This can be concluded on the basis of the consideration that any right—even those over which the EU institutions do not have competence—has to be reconciled with the 'Community integration process' and thus become relevant from the moment of a clash with EU law.[214]

This latter consideration leads to the second matter that needs to be examined. This is the argument that by making reference to 'Community law' (now 'Union law'), the legislator does not really provide an answer to the question of the extent to which the right at issue can restrict the freedom to provide services without infringing EU law. This state of affairs has been criticised as constituting 'abdication of political responsibility to the Court in difficult circumstances',[215] since the burden of deciding on this issue is left to the CJEU. However, when taking the statement made above into account that no right, even if apparently excluded from the scope of secondary legislation, enjoys absolute immunity, but has to be reconciled with EU law, it appears that inclusion (or not) of the formula requiring respect for 'Community law' does not make any difference to the degree to which the right to take collective action can be 'saved' from interference of EU law with it.

On the other hand, it could be maintained that there does remain a pertinent difference between a regulatory instrument that refers to such a formula and one that does not. In the latter case, which would be that of the 'Monti I' Regulation, the right to take collective action seems to fall, on the basis of its wording, completely outside the scope of the legislation, as long as it is exercised in a way that is recognised in the Member State concerned, whereas, as regards the SD, collective action that has been assessed to be incompatible with the Treaty falls within its scope of application. However, one substantial argument that could make this assertion redundant is that the CJEU in any case enjoys jurisdiction to rule on secondary legislation, both in order to interpret the meaning of its provisions and in order to decide on the compatibility of the legislation with EU law. In both of these situations, the Court will rule on the matter in light of primary EU law. Hence, whatever the 'saving clause' provides for, it has to be in any case compatible with the Treaty and the Court will be the final instance ruling on the matter.

[211] This can be contrasted with 'saving clauses' in US federal legislation in relation to which it has been commented that 'straightforward rules of statutory construction dictate that the state laws related to the subject matter of the clause should not be displaced'. Furthermore, 'savings clause(s) should be seen as evidencing the intent *not* to occupy the field' and they should 'weigh against a finding that state law poses an obstacle to the accomplishment of federal purposes': SB Zellmer, University of Nebraska at Lincoln—College of Law, 'Saving Saving Clauses from Judicial Preemption' (29 August 2007), http://ssrn.com/abstract=1010625, 43.

[212] PWD, above n 2, recital 22: 'this Directive is without prejudice to the law of the Member States concerning collective action to defend the interests of trades and professions'.

[213] G Orlandini, 'Right to Strike, Transnational Collective Action and European Law: Time to Move On?', Jean Monnet Working Paper 8/07, www.jeanmonnetprogram.org/papers/07/070801.pdf, 30.

[214] ibid. See also on this point JHH Weiler, 'Fundamental Rights and Fundamental Boundaries: On Standards and Values in the Protection of Human Rights' in NA Neuwahl and A Rosas, *The European Union and Human Rights* (The Hague, Martinus Nijhoff Publishers, 1995) 65–66.

[215] Novitz, above n 193, 375.

Having said that, it may be wondered what is the use of these clauses in internal market legislation in a situation where the rights aimed to be 'saved' are to be subjected to a reconciliation exercise *in any case*? One possible answer could be that the legislator is sending a message to the Court that stresses the need to place great weight on the protection of fundamental rights in the internal market context; it does so by creating a presumption that the legal instrument aimed at promoting a common market freedom shall not interfere with fundamental rights. If this is true, then there still remains the question whether the legislature, when including two differently phrased clauses of the type cited above, is sending two different messages. Syrpis and Novitz perceive the clause in the Monti Regulation—in view of its broader phrasing—as 'perhaps the clearest statement in favour of the autonomy of national systems'[216] and argue that if such a clause was used for the SD (as initially proposed, but which did not survive the final draft), it would have 'provided a clear indication to the Court of the weight to be afforded to the various interests at stake'. This indication would therefore make it more likely for the Court either to decide in cases like *Viking* and *Laval* that the trade unions' actions are not captured by the free movement provisions of the Treaty or to consider the actions as justified and proportionate.[217] On the basis of these assertions, the message of the 'Monti-type' saving clause seems to be an attempt to persuade the Court, when faced with a conflict between free movement rights and collective labour rights, to resolve it by following the legislature's footprints and giving preference to the latter, whereas a clause of the type in the SD does not seem to take any stance as to the relationship between the conflicting interests and conveys nothing more than what is already known, namely, that it is for the Court to strike a balance between the two. The Court did then strike a balance in *Viking* and *Laval* by turning the presumption contained in the 'Monti-type' saving clause on its head, ie, by being concerned with the right to take collective action not to interfere with one of the internal market freedoms.

Although it is not at all clear how far the legislator's message would have reached the ears of the Court had the saving clause in its initial form remained in place, it is still important to inquire into the extent to which it is feasible for the legislature to influence the Court on how to place the weights when fundamental freedoms and fundamental rights clash. There is a case to be made that there is no (and should not be) room for legislative interference in this kind of situation. In the words of Edward:

> [I]f the EU is an organization exercising conferred (as opposed to sovereign) powers—powers conferred *by* the Treaties—does the democratic mandate stop where the Treaties stop? Even more specifically, do the Four Freedoms, as interpreted by the Court, have a 'constitutional' validity with which the political institutions are not entitled to interfere *au gré*?[218]

The quotation makes the point that the very nature of the EU—a treaty-based international organisation enjoying conferred powers only—mandates the exclusion of any legislative, say, on how the contours of the Treaty provisions should be drawn. It is for the Court to assess the contours of the Treaty provisions and it is for the legislator to act within those

[216] P Syrpis and T Novitz, 'Economic and Social Rights in Conflict: Political and Judicial Approaches to Their Reconciliation' (2008) 33 *European Law Review* 411, 417.

[217] ibid 417–18.

[218] D Edward, 'Guest Editorial: Will There Be Honey Still for Tea?' (2006) 43 *Common Market Law Review* 623.

boundaries when legislating. If the political actors were to disagree, they are always free to amend the Treaties.

Such a position is, however, not tenable with regard to EU law. It fails to take into account the inextricably entangled relationship between the Court and the institutions in the market building process, and the fact that both are needed in this process. As the SD states, 'a genuine internal market for services cannot be achieved by relying [solely] on direct application of [ex] Arts 43 and 45 of the Treaty'.[219]

If both processes (negative integration and positive integration) work towards a common end set out in the Treaties, the following question arises: why should only the former inform the latter and not also the other way round? This is especially so in a situation where the Treaty does not provide for clear guidance on how to balance the interests at issue, which is indeed true for the case of direct collision between the market freedoms and fundamental rights.

Furthermore, the position expressed in the quotation above does not sit well with the Court's case law. In *Ratti*,[220] the Court held that national derogations from free movement provisions are not permissible once the area has been harmonised by EU legislation. This means that the Court itself not only recognises but also gives priority to the way in which the legislator shapes the contours of the Treaty in reconciling (national) derogations, which include fundamental rights, with the economic freedoms of the internal market. The Court will certainly always be the last instance assessing whether the legislative choices are in line with the Treaty, but it is at the same time clear that so far it has granted the legislator a wide margin of discretion, especially when economic legislation is at stake. The matter is of course more difficult when the legislator seeks to directly overturn a judicial decision, but it is more difficult politically and practically speaking (because the Court will always have the last word as to the compliance of secondary law with the Treaties) rather than as a matter of principle.

The assessment so far suggests that at the time of *Viking* and *Laval* and in the area of services—unlike in the area of free movement of goods—the legislator had missed the opportunity to contribute to the question of how the interests should be placed in case of conflict between fundamental rights and economic freedoms. Such a contribution can indeed be valuable. This is so in view of the following: in not being as constrained by the seemingly paramount primacy granted to the economic freedoms in the internal market's system of rules as the Court, the legislator could provide impetus for a higher degree of fundamental rights protection within the internal market than has been witnessed in the cases *Viking* and *Laval*.

We shall therefore turn at this point to the two instruments that appear (at least at first sight) to respond to exactly that missed opportunity: the draft 'Monti II' Regulation and the PWED. The purpose will be to investigate what kind of impetus they have provided.

Both instruments originate in the Monti Report.[221] Professor Monti's report came in response to a formal invitation by Commission President Barroso, who wished to receive options and recommendations for re-launching the Single Market—a key strategic objective

[219] Services Directive, above n 192, recital 6.
[220] Case C-148/78 *Minister Pubblico v Ratti* [1979] ECR 1629.
[221] Monti Report, above n 115.

for the Commission.[222] In his letter, President Barroso also pointed out that the economic crisis has enhanced concerns about the social dimension of market(s). In this respect, he emphasised a principle of the Lisbon Treaty (but already contained in the Treaty of Rome) that 'the Union … shall work … for a highly competitive social market economy'.

In the chapter entitled 'Building Consensus on a Stronger Single Market', the Monti Report deals with the situation of economic freedoms and workers' rights after the case law quartet (*Viking*, *Laval*, *Rüffert* and *Commission v Luxembourg*).[223] The Court's decisions on the direct collision between the right to strike and the economic freedoms and the application of the PWD are so important as to warrant special treatment in this grand Single Market strategy because, per Monti, they:

> [R]evived an old split that had never been healed: the divide between advocates of greater market integration and those who feel that the call for economic freedoms and for breaking up regulatory barriers is code for dismantling social rights protected at national level.
>
> The revival of this divide has the potential to alienate from the Single Market and the EU a segment of public opinion, workers' movements and trade unions, which has been over time a key supporter of economic integration.[224]

Overcoming the split is presented as necessary for moving on with economic integration. This point is noteworthy, as it presents economic integration as the end goal, not social cohesion or both.

An important statement made concerns the question of which actor—the judiciary or the legislator—does or should resolve the matter. The Monti Report provides a clear answer:

> There is a broad awareness among policy makers that a clarification on these issues should not be left to future occasional litigation before the ECJ or national courts. Political forces have to engage in a search for a solution, in line with the Treaty objective of a 'social market economy'.[225]

We shall be concerned with this legislative response in the remainder.

The PWED contains the following 'saving clause':

> Art 1(2) PWED:
>
> This Directive shall not affect in any way *the exercise of fundamental rights as recognised* in Member States *and at Union level*, including the right or freedom to strike or to take other action covered by the specific industrial relations systems in Member States, in accordance with national law and/or practice. Nor does it affect the right to negotiate, conclude and enforce collective agreements and to take collective action in accordance with national law and/or practice. (emphasis added)[226]

The draft 'Monti II' Regulation laid down the general principles and rules applicable at the EU level with respect to the exercise of the fundamental right to take collective action within the context of the freedom of establishment and the freedom to provide services.[227] It contains a 'saving clause' like Article 2 of 'Monti I', 'a mechanism for the informal solution

[222] Mission letter from the President of the European Commission, Brussels (20 October 2009), Pres(2009) D/2250.

[223] Monti Report, above n 115, ch 3, 68ff.

[224] ibid 68.

[225] ibid 69.

[226] COM Proposal PWED, above n 118.

[227] Draft 'Monti II' Regulation, above n 189, Art 1(1).

of labour disputes', and—being modelled along the lines of 'Monti I'—it also provides for an early warning or 'alert mechanism'.[228]

The draft 'Monti II' Regulation states in its Article 1(2):

> This Regulation shall not affect in any way *the exercise of fundamental rights as recognised in the Member States*, including the right or freedom to strike or to take other action covered by the specific industrial relations systems in Member States in accordance with national law and practices. Nor does it affect the right to negotiate, conclude and enforce collective agreements and to take collective action in accordance with national law and practices.

As the emphasis shows, the PWED saving clause contains in the first sentence a reference to the 'Union level' that is absent in 'Monti II'. At first sight, it could be suggested that the same issue (of not taking a stance on how to balance the conflicting interests) arising with respect to the SD is also applicable here, if one were to understand 'at Union level' as corresponding to the phrase 'by Union law', which was the original wording used in the Commission proposal. However, one would think that the change of words was deliberate in order to connote something else, that is, only the fact that the rights to be 'saved' are also respected at the EU level, but in fact not meaning the EU fundamental rights (whose scope and level of protection may be different from the fundamental rights of Member States). That understanding would in any event make more sense when considering the second sentence, which does not make any reference to 'Union law' or the 'Union level'. It would be illogical to subject the right to strike to two standards (the EU standard and national law and practices) while the right to negotiate, conclude and enforce collective agreements and the right to take collective action were held only to one standard (national law and practices). On the other hand, if the proposed reading was intended, why not replicate the sentence of 'Monti I'?

The saving clause of 'Monti II' is in its first sentence in essence a reproduction of 'Monti I' with its exclusive reference to national law, while the second sentence adds a further specification of a right especially targeted by this Regulation. Does the above then lead to the conclusion that, within the context of the PWED, the legislator is not taking any specific stance as to 'the right to strike or to take other action covered by the specific industrial relations systems', whereas the 'Monti II' Regulation gives an indication to the Court in favour of the fundamental right?

This impression may indeed be gained if one views the saving clause in isolation. However, the draft Regulation also provides for another crucial provision, which gives an altered image. It suggests that the two interests shall be afforded exactly the same weight:

> The exercise of the freedom of establishment and the freedom to provide services enshrined in the Treaty shall respect the fundamental right to take collective action, including the right or freedom to strike, and conversely, the exercise of the fundamental right to take collective action, including the right or freedom to strike, shall respect these economic freedoms[229] (Art 2 of the Draft 'Monti II' Regulation)

[228] ibid, Art 4.

[229] Draft 'Monti II' Regulation, above n 189, Art 2.

The Explanatory Memorandum further clarifies what the legislator means. The basic assumption is 'that there is no inherent conflict between the exercise of the fundamental right to take collective action and the freedom of establishment and the freedom to provide services enshrined in and protected by the Treaty, with no primacy of one over the other'.[230] Furthermore, Article 2 recognises that in situations of conflict, the interests will have to be reconciled in accordance with the principle of proportionality, but according to the Explanatory Memorandum, such must be '*in line with standard practice by courts and EU case law*' (emphasis added).[231]

This latter phrase then suggests that all the Regulation aims to do is to confirm and codify the case law, at least as regards the holding that the proportionality test is to be applied in situations of a clash between the interests at stake. This is further evidenced by the remarks in the Explanatory Memorandum on restrictions to economic freedoms. It explains that the *protection of workers* can constitute *overriding requirements in the public interest.*[232] This is true of course, but it seems to replicate the Court's methodology on reconciling economic freedoms with the right to take collective action. In the present context, one would expect the identification of the fundamental right to be capable of restricting the internal market freedoms and not to be an overriding requirement that constitutes a narrow exception to the free movement rule, as already discussed. In any case, the Explanatory Memorandum also does not seem to suggest that a re-balancing between economic freedoms and fundamental rights is in order post-Lisbon. The section on the Lisbon Treaty[233] makes three key points. First, it indicates that the internal market shall work towards a highly competitive social market economy (Art 3(3) TEU). Second, it stipulates that according to CJEU case law, the internal market freedoms have to be implemented in accordance with the social policy objectives as included in Article 151 TFEU. Third, it points out that according to Article 152 TFEU, the EU aims to recognise, promote and further strengthen the role of social partners at the EU level, facilitate dialogue and respect their autonomy while taking account of the diversity of national systems.

However, it is not clear how this 'Lisbon context' should translate into a concrete balancing test, and there is furthermore no indication that this should lead to an altered approach of that taken by the Court in *Viking* and *Laval.* On the contrary, the potential of the saving clause contained in Article 1(2) to indicate another direction to the Court is fading in light of the points discussed above. What is more, two provisions (Art 1(2) and Art 2) in fact seem contradictory, and that would have been already good reason for rejecting the Commission's proposal as it stood. If the Regulation provides that the right to take collective action, including the right to strike, has to be reconciled in a proportionate manner with the free movement provisions, how can it be possible that the Regulation does 'not affect' that right as recognised in the Member States? It does so by definition, and the question is which of the two provisions was intended to prevail. If the latter was intended, one cannot but agree with Ewing's criticism that the draft 'Monti II' Regulation '[1] writes into a legislative

230 Draft 'Monti II' Regulation, above n 189, Explanatory Memorandum 12.

231 ibid.

232 ibid 5.

233 ibid 3.

form and preserves in aspic a judicial formulation [2] that was out of date within a year of its expression'.[234]

Confirmation for the first point may also be found in the fact that the stakeholder, BusinessEurope, did not seem to see much added value in this draft Regulation.[235] The European Trade Union Confederation (ETUC) on the other hand welcomed 'the idea of a so-called Monti II regulation … as a positive step in the right direction'.[236] However, once the draft text was available, the European Trade Union Institute (ETUI) published a critical policy brief on the matter taking issue, inter alia, with Article 2 of the draft on the attempted reconciliation of the right to strike with economic freedoms along the lines of Ewing's argumentation presented above.[237]

The ETUC's initial optimistic approached can also be explained by the fact that it envisaged the draft Regulation to come *in addition* to a Social Progress Protocol—a demand it had expressed during the consultation phase.[238] The purpose of the Social Progress Protocol should have been 'to give priority to fundamental social rights over economic freedoms'.[239] It is not entirely clear, however, what the terms of such prioritisation would be. The Monti Report refers to a differently phrased demand of the trade unions, one that is unequivocal in its terms. In other words, a 'social progress clause' should be introduced which 'immunises' the right to strike from the impact of the free movement rules[240]—a demand that has also been expressed by the European Economic and Social Committee.[241] This would of course mean that the masters of the Treaties disagree with the Court's move of bringing the right to strike within the scope of EU (internal market) law, and it would alter the status quo by way of Treaty amendment. Monti dismissed this option in his report as not being 'realistic … in the short term'.[242]

Realistic or not in the short term, the real question is to what extent such move might be necessary in the long term. This is where Ewing's second point comes to play. It alludes to the fact already discussed above that the ILO does not recognise in the form of a permissible restriction the need to balance the right to strike with the freedom of establishment and the freedom to provide services by applying the principle of proportionality. Here, if the ECtHR is eventually going to follow ILO jurisprudence closely, a serious need for such a Social Progress Protocol could in fact arise, unless of course the CJEU is going to deviate

[234] K Ewing, 'The Draft Monti II Regulation—An Inadequate Response to Viking and Laval', www.ier.org.uk/resources/draft-monti-ii-regulation-inadequate-response-viking-and-laval.

[235] Draft 'Monti II' Regulation, above n 189, Explanatory Memorandum 7.

[236] ibid.

[237] Note, however, that the draft could be seen to have provided for added value to the following extent: first, it presents the colliding interests at stake as being on the same level ('no primacy of one over the other') and not as the right to strike being a narrow exception to the free movement rule, like the pronouncement of the Court in *Viking* and *Laval* suggested. One could therefore hold that it deviates to a certain extent from the Court's case law (but note that this does not match with the ECHR, which clearly places the right to strike higher than any 'legitimate interest' which may justify an interference with the right). However, again here, the reference to this case law is contradictory.

[238] Draft 'Monti II' Regulation, above n 189, Explanatory Memorandum 5.

[239] ibid.

[240] Monti Report, above n 115, 70.

[241] European Economic and Social Committee Opinion on the 'Social Dimension of the Single Market', 2011/C 44/15 (11/02/2011).

[242] Monti Report, above n 115, 70.

from previous case law and hold that the right to strike falls outside the scope of the free movement provisions (as the argument was made by the pleading parties and was rejected by the Court in the two cases).

The draft instrument was, however, also problematic from another point of view, namely, incorrect choice of legal basis. The draft Regulation was in fact not proposed as an internal market measure, but it found its legal basis in Article 352 TFEU (ex Art 308 EC). This is the so-called flexibility clause that gives the EU the power to act where it should prove necessary within the framework of the policies defined in the Treaties to attain one of the objectives set out in the Treaties, where these do not provide the necessary powers. In the present context, founding the instrument on this legal basis is problematic since the Treaties expressly preclude the legislative regulation of the right to strike at the EU level (Art 153(5) TFEU).[243] Such preclusion cannot be evaded by having recourse to this provision, as Article 352(3) TFEU confirms.[244]

It is arguable that the internal market competence should have been used for adopting this instrument—indeed, this would have been the only possible route for harmonsiation. This is so because the Court brought the right to take collective action, including the right to strike, within the scope of the free movement rules, thus subjecting it to de-regulation. As a corollary, the EU legislator should be free to adopt legislation in order to re-regulate the matter (provided the necessary conditions are met; see the discussion in chapter two). This cannot be called into question by the exclusionary rule in Article 153(5) TFEU. As the Court has stated in *Tobacco Advertising I*,[245] the fact that the Treaty precludes harmonisation of a certain matter (in that case public health) 'does not mean that harmonisation measures adopted on the basis of other provisions of the Treaty cannot have any impact on the protection of human health [in our case, the right to strike]'.[246] The Court also noted that 'other articles of the Treaty may not, however, be used as a legal basis in order to circumvent the express exclusion of harmonisation laid down in Article 129(4) [in our case read Article 153(5) TFEU] of the Treaty'.[247] But *Tobacco Advertising II*[248] confirms that this will not be the case 'provided that the conditions for recourse to Article 95 EC as a legal basis are fulfilled'. This means that in the instant case, the legislator would have to prove that there are divergences in national laws on the right to strike (or future obstacles that are likely to occur) to such a degree that they are liable to put the establishment and functioning of the internal market at risk or distort competition, and it would be for the legislator to substantiate that assertion (see the discussion in chapter two).

Provided that this (empirical) requirement is satisfied, the obvious choice for a legal basis would seem to be Article 114 TFEU; however, here we also find a hurdle. Article 114(2)

[243] As the Danish Parliament (European Affairs Committee) also noted in its reasoned opinion of 3 May 2012 (on the Draft 'Monti II' Regulation) under the subsidiarity control mechanism.

[244] This is a point that the Dutch House of Representatives also put forward in its reasoned opinion of 22 May 2012, and the Luxembourg Chamber of Deputies in its reasoned opinion of 15 May 2012. The Portuguese Parliament in its reasoned opinion of 30 April 2012 also makes the point that Art 352 TFEU cannot be used to circumvent the exclusionary rule in Art 153(5) TFEU, but without making reference to Art 352(3) TFEU.

[245] Case C-376/98 *Germany v Parliament and Council (Tobacco Advertising I)* [2000] ECR I-8419.

[246] ibid [78].

[247] ibid [79].

[248] Case C-380/03 *Federal Republic of Germany v European Parliament and Council of the European Union (Tobacco Advertising II)* [2006] ECR I-11573.

TFEU precludes the adoption of measures of approximation that relate to the rights and interests of employed persons, which the right to strike does relate to. Therefore, the only remaining appropriate legal basis left is Article 115 TFEU. The Explanatory Memorandum unfortunately does not discuss these obvious difficulties, but merely states that Article 352 TFEU is the appropriate legal basis.

Meanwhile, the proposal has already been successfully challenged on another ground, namely, the principle of subsidiarity. The principle concerns the question whether the regulatory intervention at issue is better pursued at the EU level than at the Member State level. This point is taken seriously in the legal basis of the draft Regulation. Article 352 TFEU stipulates that the Commission shall draw the attention of national parliaments to proposals based on this Article. It shall do so by using the procedure for monitoring subsidiarity under Article 5(3) TEU. The Protocol on the Application of the Principle of Proportionality and Subsidiarity gives national parliaments the opportunity to scrutinise draft legislative acts as to their respect for the principle of subsidiarity and to send reasoned opinions to the Presidents of the European Parliament, the Council and the Commission when their finding is in the negative.[249] When reasoned opinions represent one-third of all votes allocated to the national parliaments, the 'yellow card' is raised, which means that the draft must be reviewed.[250] The draft Monti II Regulation reached that threshold stage, with 12 reasoned opinions being submitted to the Commission. This is the first time that this has occurred since the entry into force of the Lisbon Treaty. At the end of the review process, the Commission has the choice of deciding to maintain, amend or withdraw the draft. Given the lack of support for the instrument, including, it seems, the lack of enthusiasm for the instrument from the Commission itself, the last-named scenario materialised (rather quickly) in the instance case.

B. Conclusion

The above discussion leads us to the following findings. The legislator has responded to the Court's case law, pre- and post-*Viking* and *Laval* dealing with a direct collision between the right to take collective action, including the right to strike and economic freedoms. It did so by introducing 'saving clauses' in two enacted instruments and in two draft instruments, one of which has been withdrawn before it could leave the Commission stage on subsidiarity grounds.

In the context of these (draft) instruments, 'saving' means the exclusion from the scope of application of the instruments in question in situations in which it may affect the right. However, that does not imply absolute immunity for this right, as it is only 'saved' for the purposes of the instrument, not for the purposes of the Treaty.

The function of 'saving clauses' may then legitimately be seen as questionable in light of this consideration. However, it is submitted that their role can be seen as one of sending a

[249] Protocol No 2 on the application of the principles of subsidiarity and proportionality, annexed to the Treaty on the European Union and the Treaty on the Functioning of the European Union by the Treaty of Lisbon of 13 December 2007 [2010] OJ C83/206, Art 6.

[250] ibid, Art 7(2).

message to the Court as to the respective weight that the fundamental rights in question should assume. This should inform the Court's reconciliation exercise.

This role of the legislator should not be dismissed on the ground that the principle of conferred powers precludes the legislator to interfere with the validity and scope of the internal market freedoms. This is especially so given that the Court will be inevitably the final instance ruling on the matter.

On the question of the concrete impetus provided by the legislator, we have seen that pre-*Viking* and *Laval*, there was one instance of unequivocal favouring of national autonomy ('Monti I') and one instance of leaving the matter entirely to the Court (the SD). After *Viking* and *Laval*, the Commission produced one equivocal saving clause (the draft PWED) and one that is seemingly unequivocal, but is contradicted by another provision in the same draft instrument (the draft 'Monti II').

The message sent by the saving clauses in the Commission's recent package aiming to respond to the case law is therefore an ambiguous one, obviously driven and caught between two conflicting aims: one the one hand, calming down the concerns of various stakeholders (most notably trade unions) that fundamental social rights will not be compromised by the economic freedoms and, on the other hand, affirming the Court's case law, whose substance has meanwhile received a challenge from the international level—a fact that was not sufficiently reflected in the 'Monti II' proposal, even if the Explanatory Memorandum acknowledged the developments in the relevant fora.

IV. FINAL CONCLUSION

In respect to both rights discussed in this chapter—the right to fair and just working conditions and the right to take collective action—we have seen that legislative intervention has been triggered by initial judicial de-regulation (*Rush Portuguesa* in the former case and *Viking* and *Laval* in the latter). The classic and often described scenario of positive integration following negative integration seems to be materialising here, although legislative action in the posted workers context goes one step further in that positive integration was called into question by a new round of Court-steered negative integration.

Distinct controversial points arise in the two areas, but what they have in common is that the current political response is a concealed endorsement of the judicial stance. It is not presented as a codification exercise seeking to set out in clearer terms what the Court has laid down, nor is it one that introduces new elements of harmonisation in order to push integration in this field. The impression is rather that legislative action serves to grant political legitimacy to the core findings in the controversial case law of the Court.

7

Health

I. INTRODUCTION

A. Health in the Internal Market

THE PROTECTION OF human health ranks high among the non-market values that have been pursued through internal market regulation. This is so despite the fact that an explicit legal basis (Art 168 TFEU) is available in a separate Treaty title devoted to health protection, ever since the entry into force of the Maastricht Treaty.

An explanation for *why the protection of public health* is given such prominent status in the internal market can be discerned from the content of the Treaty legal basis for health. Article 168 TFEU (ex Art 129 EC) provides that attaining a high level of human health protection should be ensured in the definition and implementation of all EU policies and activities. The Treaty of Lisbon added a repetition of this obligation in a general mainstreaming clause (Art 9 TFEU), where the protection of health is listed as one of a series of other social objectives.[1] In substance, Article 9 TFEU does not add much to the already existing mainstreaming obligation in Article 168 TFEU, but it does reinforce the status of health as a general EU policy, and so achieving a high level of health protection while pursuing other policies, such as the realisation of the internal market, is not only legitimate but also mandatory under the Treaty rules.

Importantly, the same mainstreaming obligation is also included in the internal market legal basis (Art 114(3) TFEU). The existence of legislation that on its face aims to achieve a high level of health protection while regulating the market could therefore be taken as proof that the legislator is taking this obligation seriously. This is not surprising when bearing in mind the EU's longstanding commitment to pursue a health policy, evidenced by the fact that coordinative action has been taken long before the introduction of the specific health legal basis and the mainstreaming clause.[2] Still, the question remains as to *why the internal market* has served as fertile ground for pursuing action in this field.

Again, the content of Article 168 TFEU is a useful starting point. It accounts for a characteristic of public health that has remained unaltered since Maastricht: the fact that it constitutes a 'flanking policy'. This means that harmonisation of national laws and regulations is

[1] Other objectives listed: employment, adequate social protection and the fight against social exclusion.

[2] T Hervey and J McHale, *Health Law and the European Union* (Cambridge, Cambridge University Press, 2004) 173, with reference to the 'Europe Against Cancer' programme, Decision 88/351/EEC [1988] OJ L160/52 and the 'Europe Against AIDS' programme [1991] OJ L175/26. These actions were based on the 'gap-filling' legal basis contained in Art 235 EEC (now Art 352 TFEU) and Art 2 EEC, which stated as one of the Community objectives the 'raising of the standard of living'.

excluded from EU competence, and EU activity is limited to coordinative action. Recourse to an internal market legal basis like Article 114 TFEU seems an obvious choice[3] in these circumstances, where a political will for approximation is present and provided that a convincing link to the establishment and functioning of the internal market can be established. The need to meet this latter requirement should not be underestimated, as the famous *Tobacco Advertising I*[4] case has taught us. And yet, on the condition that this requirement is met, pursuing health objectives can be the primary or sole motivation of the legislator (see discussion in chapter two).

Ultimately, the reason why we find such a great bulk of 'internal market health legislation' is that it has not been very difficult to meet this 'market requirement' in the health domain. That in turn is due to the fact that the EU institutions, including the Court of Justice of the EU (the Court), have viewed and construed health matters on a market making or market enabling rationale rather than a social policy rationale. This approach was pursued because of the original and to a large part persisting focus of the EU's mandate on creating an internal market, and the resulting operation of the free movement rules as interpreted by the Court, but also precisely because of the limited supranational competence. It is also facilitated by the fact that healthcare 'traditionally … has more "market traces" (pharmaceuticals, remedies, medical equipment, private suppliers etc.) than other social policy fields'.[5]

More concretely, construing health matters on such a market making rationale, and bringing them consequently within internal market competence, has meant that health has been perceived as a factor of production, medical goods and services have been perceived as a trading commodity and national health measures have been qualified as obstacles to cross-border trade. This requires further elaboration. First, health has been perceived as a factor of production in the sense that a uniformly high level of health and safety at work will lead to better productivity and will ensure the free movement of workers. The other side of the coin is that the absence of (high) uniform standards in workplace health and safety may lead in a common or internal market to 'social and ecological dumping where business would be able to take advantage of differences in standards, and hence costs, between Member States'.[6] Both motivations have led to the adoption of directives on health and safety at work, and it will be remembered that before the entry into force of the Single European Act, harmonisation in the field of occupational health and safety was not possible under Article 118 of the Treaty of Rome. In the absence of an explicit competence, the first directives in this area were based on the internal market.[7]

[3] Other choices that have been made include: common agricultural policy, transport, environmental policy, consumer protection, competition policy, research and technological development, development cooperation and social policy. See Hervey and McHale, above n 2, 85. The extent to which the EU can adopt regulatory action of course differs in these fields.

[4] Case C-376/98 *Germany v European Parliament and Council of the European Union* ECLI:EU:C:2000:544 (hereinafter *Tobacco Advertising I*)

[5] W Lamping, 'European Integration and Health Policy—A Peculiar Relationship' in M Steffen (ed), *Health Governance in Europe* (London, Routledge, 2005) 28.

[6] E Mossialos and M McKee, *EU Law and the Social Character of Health Care* (Cambridge, Cambridge University Press, 2002) 46.

[7] For a discussion, see G Majone, 'The European Community as a Regulatory State', *Collected Courses of the Academy of European Law*, European Community Law, Vol V, Book 1 (The Hague, Boston/London, Kluwer Law International/Martinus Nijhoff Publishers/Academy of European Law, 1994).

Second, national health measures fall squarely within internal market rules, because the Court has de facto construed their subject of regulation as a trading commodity. Thus, medical goods and services[8] are not afforded any special status due to their (public interest) nature, and their free movement has to be guaranteed subject to the same conditions as any other good or service. As a result, EU regulation of medical devices, pharmaceuticals and food safety has been based on the free movement of goods rationale; the regulation of (medical) professional qualifications aims to guarantee the free movement of persons (medical personnel); and the latest Directive on the Application of Patients' Rights in Cross-border Healthcare shall ensure the freedom to provide services. This construction by the Court is a logical consequence of its previous case law, but it is not the one that is prevalent at the national level. For example and with respect to the last-mentioned Directive, out-patient care has been construed as a pure economic service at the EU level, even though at the national level, 'social services in general are usually part of public services which are regulated by social law'.[9]

Third, in addition, national measures not regulating medical goods, services and health professionals, but which are adopted with the aim of pursuing public health may have adverse effects on cross-border trade and thus may justify EU regulatory intervention replacing national standards of health protection in this field—the regulation of tobacco advertising, clinical trials and biotechnology are examples for this.

B. Questions of Inquiry and Areas of Examination

In view of extensive EU activity in the field of health protection based on the internal market, the following questions will be investigated in this chapter: first, whether the institutions have conceptualised the instruments in fundamental rights terms and the extent to which they can be so conceived; and, second, the question of the concrete impact that adoption of the rights discourse has had or could have had on the substance of the legislation.

This task will be approached by analysing three examples of EU legislation in more detail. The choice of the instruments has been made based on the consideration that the instruments assume a particular position on a spectrum that mirrors the 'market-health relationship' of the instrument. At one end (the beginning), we find the legislation constituting market intervention with the purpose of pursuing health protection—market-correction policies. At the other end (the end) is the legislation that has been adopted for market building purposes and that incidentally has the effect of protecting health—market-building policies. In this chapter, we will examine legislative intervention in three areas. Two of them will mirror the two ends of the market-health relationship spectrum: orphan medicinal products regulation (the beginning) and patient mobility (the end). A third area (among many that could have been chosen) represents the 'middle ground': tobacco control policies.

[8] Privately remunerated (Joined Cases C-286/82 and 26/83 *Luisi and Carbone v Ministero del Tesoro* [1984] ECR I-377) or reimbursed under a national social security system (Case C-158/96 *Kohll v Union des caisses de maladie* ECR I-1931)

[9] Lamping, above n 5, 30.

Conceiving of legislation in the way just proposed instead of subjecting it to two distinct categories is deliberate. On the face of the text of the instruments, it is for the most part difficult to discern the goal pursued, which would determine the straightforward allocation into one category rather than another. Take as an example (and there are countless of those) investments in biotechnological research. It is almost impossible to assess whether the primary goal is to create and improve health opportunities or to strengthen the competitive position of the pharmaceuticals industry on the global markets.[10] It is also true that the distinction between market-making and market-correcting policies is not clear-cut *in principle*, and not only with respect to the market–health relationship. This is not only so because of the identified difficulty in discerning the primary motive for intervention when reviewing the text of the legal instruments, but also based on the 'means' criteria used for such categorisation, ie, what tools the legislation uses in order to 'build the market'.

Legislation for market-making policies is said to be directed at:[11]

— the removal of trade and competition barriers;
— the abolishment of tariffs and other quantitative restrictions;
— the establishment of common product standards;
— the establishment of a level playing field for all market players.

Market-correcting interventions on the other hand are supposed to constitute interventions that have a restrictive impact on competition.[12] The aim here is to 'avoid market effects that are considered deviant or anomalous, such as ethical reasons, considerations related to social welfare and public health'.[13]

The dividing line between the two blurs most obviously when considering the scenario of a prohibition of certain economic activities as opposed to placing restrictions on the exercise of such. Prohibiting an economic activity has the most restrictive impact on competition in the sense that it bans it completely. At the same time, it establishes a level playing field for the market actors (a market-making characteristic)—every actor has to follow the same rule of not pursuing that activity when competing on the market. The point to note is that the correct categorisation is not a straightforward exercise since many instruments 'combine aspects of both'.[14]

To be sure, the fact that an instrument is of a market-correcting nature does not mean that it cannot at the same time be lawfully based on an internal market provision. This is so despite the fact that the Treaty bases are formally articulated in market-making terms.

In light of the above difficulties of categorisation, support for the line-up of the instruments proposed herein will be taken from inquiring into the legislative history of the instruments and asking what triggered mobilisation of the political process *in fact*, leading finally to adoption of the instruments.

Finally, it should be noted that there might also be policies with primary goals other than the market or health, which also promote health substantively, such as education.[15]

[10] Steffen, above n 5, 9.

[11] S Boessen and H Maarse, 'The Impact of the Treaty Basis on Health Policy Legislation in the European Union: A Case Study on the Tobacco Advertising Directive' (2008) 8 *BMC Health Services Research* 1, 3.

[12] ibid.

[13] ibid.

[14] ibid.

[15] Steffen, above n 5, 9.

However, these fall outside the scope of the overall study to the extent that they do not find their legal basis in the internal market.

A crucial issue has to be addressed before analysing the harmonisation practice. An understanding of the concepts of 'public health' and the fundamental 'right to health' has to be provided, with a view to assessing the differences between the two notions, and the strengths and weaknesses they carry with them when pursuing their respective goals. This is a necessary task for answering the question of the impact that rights language may have on the law-making process and its output. This is so given that the language employed in the EU Charter of Fundamental Rights (the Charter) regarding health resembles that of the public policy notion.

II. PUBLIC HEALTH VERSUS HEALTH AS A FUNDAMENTAL HUMAN RIGHT

A. The Definitional Exercise

i. Public Health Policy

The one definition of the policy framework that has been characterised as one 'that has perhaps best stood the test of time'[16] is the following:

> Public health is the science and art of preventing disease, prolonging life and promoting physical health and efficacy through organized *community* efforts for the sanitation of the environment, the control of communicable infections, the education of the individual in personal hygiene, the organization of medical and nursing services for the early diagnosis and preventive treatment of disease, and the development of social machinery which will ensure *every individual in the community* a standard of living adequate for the maintenance of health; so organizing these benefits in such a fashion as to enable every citizen to realize his birthright and longevity. (emphasis added)[17]

This definition consists of the following constitutive elements:

— First, it provides for three general aims: 1) ill-health prevention (preventing diseases); 2) promotion of good health (prolonging life and promoting physical health and efficacy); and 3) enabling every citizen to realise his birthright and longevity.

— Second, the aim of promoting good health shall be achieved by five means: 1) the sanitation of the environment; 2) the control of communicable infections; 3) the education of the individual in personal hygiene; 4) the organisation of medical and nursing services for the early diagnosis and preventive treatment of disease; 5) the development of a social machinery ensuring an adequate standard of living for maintaining health.

— Third, public health relates to achieving health protection in a specific community and for individuals within that community (see emphasis in quotation above).

[16] JP Koplan et al, 'Towards a Common Definition of Global Health' (2009) 373 *The Lancet* 1993, http://qs1939.pair.com/cfhisf/web/fckeditor/uploaded/File/publications/intro%20page%20links/Toward%20a%20Definition%20of%20GH%20June%202009PracticalGlobal%20PublicHealth.pdf.

[17] C Winslow, 'The Untilled Field of Public Health' (1920) 2 *Modern Medicine* 183–91, as cited in ibid.

ii. The Fundamental Human Right to Health

The ESC provides for a 'right to protection of health' in its Article 11 (Rev):

> With a view to ensuring the effective exercise of the right to protection of health, the Contracting Parties undertake, either directly or in co-operation with public or private organizations, to take appropriate measures designed to inter alia:
>
> 1) Remove as far as possible the causes of ill-health;
> 2) Provide advisory and educational facilities for the promotion of health and the encouragement of individual responsibility in matters of health;
> 3) Prevent as far as possible epidemic, endemic and other diseases, as well as accidents.

It is obvious that this is a broad provision, covering health protection/promotion, prevention, as well as healthcare.[18] The latter, even though not expressly referred to in this Article, falls within its scope according to the Conclusions of the European Committee of Social Rights (ECSR).[19] The ECSR has enumerated six elements of the right to health.[20] Of particular relevance among these for the subsequent analysis (section II.B) are the following: first, the obligation resting on the Contracting Parties (all EU Member States constitute such) to have a healthcare system in place that is accessible to the entire population and that includes 'public health arrangements making generally available medical and para-medical practitioners and adequate equipment consistent with meeting its main health problems ensuring a proper medical care for the whole population';[21] second, the requirement that collective bodies are required to bear all, or at least part, of the cost of health services;[22] and, third, environmental health, including the promotion of good health through the control of tobacco (as well as alcoholism and drugs).

Two more general aspects of Article 11 (rev)ESC should be noted. The first is that in relation to obligations involving positive action, ie, public expenditure, states may not rely on lack of resources in order to justify a failure to fulfil these obligations.[23] Second, the obligations resulting from this provision have been identified to be of a general nature. As a

[18] The three pillars of health policy under Hatzopoulos' analysis. See V Hatzopoulos, 'Health Law and Policy: The Impact of the EU' in G de Búrca (ed), *EU Law and the Welfare State* (Oxford, Oxford University Press, 2005) 112.

[19] Council of Europe, *Case Law on the European Social Charter* (Strasbourg, Council of Europe, 1982) 104; European Social Charter, Committee of Independent Experts, Conclusions I 59.

[20] 'Conclusions', ibid. Also discussed by T Hervey, 'We Don't See a Connection: The "Right to Health" in the EU Charter and European Social Charter' in G de Búrca and B de Witte (eds), *Social Rights in Europe* (Oxford, Oxford University Press, 2005) 311, with reference to B Toebes, *The Right to Health as a Human Right in International Law* (Antwerp, Intersentia, 1999). The other three include: 1) providing special measures that are ensuring the protection of health of members of vulnerable groups as well as their access to healthcare; 2) providing health education; and 3) providing measures such as vaccination, disinfection and the control of epidemics in order to combat/prevent epidemic and endemic diseases.

[21] European Social Charter, Conclusions, above n 19, as cited in Hervey, above n 20.

[22] ibid.

[23] Hervey, above n 20, 312, with reference to DJ Harris and J Darcy, *The European Social Charter* (Prague, Hotei Publishing, 2001), citing the German reunification case: European Social Charter, Committee of Independent Experts, Conclusions XII-2 74.

result, states are allowed a wide margin of discretion,[24] and therefore are rarely found to be in non-compliance with the obligations of Article 11 (rev)ESC.[25]

The ESC also includes the right to social and medical assistance in its Article 13 (rev)ESC. According to this provision, parties undertake:

1) to ensure that any person who is without adequate resources and who is unable to secure such resources either by his own efforts or from other sources, in particular by benefits under a social security scheme, be granted adequate assistance, and, in case of sickness, the care necessitated by his condition;
2) to ensure that persons receiving such assistance shall not, for that reason, suffer from a diminution of their political or social rights;
3) to provide that everyone may receive by appropriate public or private services such advice and personal help as may be required to prevent, to remove, or to alleviate personal or family want;
4) to apply the provisions referred to in paragraphs 1, 2 and 3 of this article on an equal footing with their nationals to nationals of other Parties lawfully within their territories, in accordance with their obligations under the European Convention on Social and Medical Assistance.

Unlike the case with Article 11 (rev)ESC, not all Member States have accepted Article 13.[26]

In the EU, the right to health is included in Article 35 CFR. More specifically, the provision is entitled 'health care' and therefore gives the impression of being of a more confined nature. The Convention on the Future of Europe did however base this article on that of Articles 11 and 13 (rev)ESC as well as Article 168 TFEU (ex Art 152 EC). This may suggest that Article 35 can be read as including a wider scope than its strict wording would suggest, so as to cover in particular the content of Article 11 (rev)ESC.

Article 35 CFR reads: 'Everyone has the right of access to preventive health care and the right to benefit from medical treatment under the conditions established by national laws and practices. A high level of human health protection shall be ensured in the definition and implementation of all Union policies and activities.'

This Article consists of two elements.[27] The first sentence pertaining to 'health care' is phrased as an individual entitlement, whereas the second sentence imposes on the EU a mainstreaming obligation to ensure in all its policies and activities a high level of health protection (and not just healthcare).

To be more precise, the first sentence of this provision contains two distinct entitlements: first, it guarantees in conjunction with Articles 20 and 21 CFR equal access to preventive healthcare;[28] and, second, it provides for an individual right to medical treatment.[29] However, the question is whether it results from this that every person has a justiciable right to invoke these entitlements. It has been suggested that the answer should be in the negative.

[24] European Social Charter, Conclusions I, above n 19.
[25] Hervey, above n 20, 314.
[26] On this point and on the Council of Europe treaties dealing with health/healthcare more generally, see T Hervey and J McHale, 'Article 35—The Right to Health Care' in S Peers, T Hervey, J Kenner and A Ward (eds), *The EU Charter of Fundamental Rights* (Oxford, Hart Publishing, 2014) 954–56.
[27] Hervey, above n 20, 315.
[28] J Meyer, *Kommentar zur Charta der Grundrechte der Europäischen Union* (Baden-Baden, Nomos, 2006) 398.
[29] ibid.

This is so, first, because of the practice relating to ex Article 152 EC, which forms the basis of Article 35 CFR, and, second, because this intention was repeatedly stressed in the Convention on the Future of Europe.[30]

German legal literature[31] understands Article 35 CFR to provide for the following guarantees: first, protection of the individual against the state's interference with the individual's health; second, protection of the individual against discriminatory state measures for access to healthcare; and, third, an active duty rests on the state (or EU institutions) to protect individuals against interference of third parties with the right to healthcare and medical treatment. This duty concerns the monitoring and directing of private behaviour through the adoption of prohibitions and commandments.

Given that there is scarce case law on this provision, it is difficult to provide for an accurate account of what exact guarantees it entails in terms of its substantive scope and potential justiciability. Thus far, Article 35 CFR has featured in the case law in two ways. First, the Court has referred to it in its free movement case law relating to national legislation regulating pharmacies.[32] There, the second sentence of Article 35 CFR has been used to merely underline the importance of the public health objective as an exception to the free movement rules. It did certainly not apply any changed balancing test (of the *Schmidberger* type, for example) by invoking Article 35 CFR, which seems not to have made any substantive difference to the outcome. Second, the Court referred to Article 35 CFR in judicial review proceedings concerning a challenge to the Regulation on nutrition and health claims made on food.[33] More specifically, the total prohibition of the 'health claim' 'easily digestible' in the marketing of wine was challenged based on Articles 15 and 16 CFR (freedom to choose and occupation and freedom to conduct a business). The Court juxtaposed the right to health to the Article 15 and Article 16 challenges, asserting that a 'fair balance' must be struck between the competing rights. This, the Court found, was the case here because 'the prohibition at issue does not in any way affect the actual substance of the freedom to choose an occupation or of the freedom to conduct a business'.[34] Article 35 CFR functioned here as an 'equal weight' counter-claim to the action brought.

It is in any event clear that the Court did not conceptualise Article 35 as an individual guarantee in either of these cases.[35] It is to be expected that most adjudicative use of the individual guarantees the right entails will be made of this provision when combined with other 'justiciable' rights, such as non-discrimination.

It is also important to note the qualification provided for in the first sentence 'under the conditions established by national laws and practices'. For the EU's harmonisation practice, it means that whenever the EU acts within the already limited competences provided for by

[30] ibid 399.

[31] Meyer, above n 28.

[32] Joined Cases C-159/12–C-161/12 *Alessandra Venturini v ASL Varese et al* EU:C:2013:791; Case C-84/11 *Marja-Liisa Susisalo, Olli Tuomaala and Merja Ritala* EU:C:2012:374; Joined Cases C-570 and 571/07 *José Manuel Blanco Pérez and María del Pilar Chao Gómez v Consejería de Salud y Servicios Sanitarios* [2010] ECR I-4629.

[33] Challenge to Regulation (EC) No 1924/2006 of the European Parliament and of the Council of 20 December 2006 on nutrition and health claims made on foods [2006] OJ L404/9, as cited in case Case C-544/10 *Deutsches Weintor eG v Land Rheinland-Pfalz* EU:C:2012:526.

[34] *Deutsches Weintor*, above n 33, [58].

[35] Hervey and McHale, above n 26, 960.

the Treaty, it is ensured that the responsibility for the organisation of the national healthcare system and medical treatment rests firmly with the Member States.

As regards the mainstreaming obligation contained in the second sentence, the Charter is not adding anything beyond what was already included in Article 168 TFEU (ex Art 152(1) EC) and Article 9 TFEU. This is so despite the fact that it has been described as a 'super-mainstreaming' obligation,[36] since it is not obvious how a mainstreaming obligation included in the Charter could be different from one that is 'merely' listed in the Treaty, given that the Charter and the Treaty have the same legal value.[37]

B. Differences, Similarities and the Preferred Approach

The question of differences between the two notions has already been addressed in debates concerned with the best approach for achieving good health at the global level. These debates concentrate on the one hand on the different movements directed at that aim, like the health equity movement, the 'social determinants movement', 'primary healthcare', 'traditional public health', 'new public health' or 'global health', and on the other hand on the (international) fundamental human right to health. The features that have been said to make the rights framework stand out from the rest can be summarised as follows:

1) The addressees: the right to health has been said to focus on individuals as opposed to (defined) communities.
2) The aim: the rights framework is concerned with conduct and processes (eg, transparency, participation, non-discrimination, equal treatment and accountability) as opposed to outcomes, since there is no right to a certain level of health.[38]
3) The methodology: the rights framework applies a role-obligation analysis in identifying rights-holders and duty-bearers.
4) The mandatory nature: the rights framework is not optional. It is the only approach that is 'underpinned by universally recognised moral values and reinforced by legal obligations'.[39]

The last two characteristics serve to make the case for the imperative application of the rights-based approach, while the first two are commonly referred to in order to point to its shortcomings. It will be shown that these have been overtaken in view of the development of the interpretation of the right to health.[40]

[36] Hervey, above n 20 315, with reference to J Kenner, *EU Employment Law: From Rome to Amsterdam and Beyond* (Oxford, Hart Publishing, 2002) 544.

[37] Article 6(1) TEU.

[38] Note though that traditional health policy analysis has also been criticised for focusing more on means to achieving health, such as organisation and financing of healthcare, than on health itself; see J Prah Ruger, 'Toward a Theory of a Right to Health: Capability and Incompletely Theorized Agreements' (2006) *Yale Journal of Law & Humanities* 273, 276.

[39] P Hunt and G Backman, 'Health Systems and the Right to the Highest Attainable Standard of Health' (2008) 20 *Health and Human Rights* 81, 90.

[40] K Rasanathan, J Norenhag and N Valentine, 'Realizing Human Rights-Based Approaches for Action on the Social Determinants of Health' (2010) 12 *Health and Human Rights: An International Journal* 1, 4–5.

As regards the addressees of the different frameworks, the definitions provided above show that the public health framework is indeed focused on the community. It makes explicit and strong reference to communities and rights, and when reference is made to the individual, it is an understanding of realising the individual's birthright and longevity through community efforts and community well-being.

Yet it is also evident that the fundamental rights framework covers both the individual and the community. The definition and interpretation of Article 11 (rev)ESC, covering 'the three pillars of health policy',[41] namely, health protection/promotion, prevention and healthcare, makes this clear. Furthermore, the wording of the first sentence of Article 35 CFR, which is seemingly concerned with the individual ('everyone has the right…'), might be held to be inadequately reflecting the scope of this provision were it to be interpreted in line with the requirements under the ESC.

As regards health outcomes, the criticism that a human rights approach is not concerned with such can be dismissed when having regard at the international level to the recent WHO report on a human rights-based approach to health. It aims at *capacity development* in order to ensure that duty-bearers meet their obligations and rights-holders claim their rights.[42] Outcomes certainly do matter in the ESC context. This is more generally implied in the statement of the ECSR that: 'The aim and purpose of the Charter being a human rights protection instrument, is to protect rights not merely theoretically, but also in fact.'[43] More specifically, it is evidenced by the Committee's approach to prevention policies. It takes account of actual statistics and evidence in order to assess the effectiveness of the policies in question. For example, the Committee measures the effectiveness of tobacco control policies by looking into the numbers (increase or decrease) of tobacco consumption. Another illustration is the case where the Committee has taken into account the actual status of health of Roma (which was 'inferior to that of the general population')[44] in order to arrive at the finding that a State has failed to fulfil its positive obligations of ensuring that Roma 'have adequate access to healthcare, in particular by failing to take reasonable steps to address the specific problems faced by Roma communities stemming from their often unhealthy living conditions and difficult access to health services'.[45]

This example also illustrates the way in which 'results' are given attention in a human rights framework through the accountability requirement, which stands next to that of establishing duties and obligations. It includes monitoring conduct and assessing performance and outcomes. In Hunt and Backman's view, 'accountability is one of the most important features of human rights—and also one of the least understood'.[46] As a result of the latter, it comes as no surprise that this aspect is often overlooked, but that does not mean that the rights framework, if applied in this way, would be oblivious to the question of actual outcomes.

[41] Hatzopoulos, above n 18.

[42] WHO, 'A Human Rights-Based Approach to Health', www.who.int/hhr/news/hrba_to_health2.pdf.

[43] European Committee of Social Rights, *International Commission of Jurists v Portugal* 1/1998 (Decision on the merits of 9 September 1999), para 4.

[44] European Committee of Social Rights, *European Roma Rights Center (ERRC) v Bulgaria* 48/2008 (Decision on the merits of 18/02/2009), para 49.

[45] ibid.

[46] Hunt and Backmann, above n 39, 87.

The question whether better outcomes are actually achieved due to the right to health being protected is of course thereby not directly answered. Research at the international level has shown that there is no correlation between ratification of human rights treaties and health or social outcomes.[47] For our purposes, it is equally important to consider whether recognition and constitutional entrenchment of the right to health leads to better health outcomes in EU Member States. The intuitive answer here seems to be also in the negative.[48]

On this account, the first two features supposedly distinguishing the public health framework from the fundamental rights framework are in fact illustrating further convergence. Furthermore, this convergence seems to be speaking in favour of applying a rights-based approach to achieving good health. This is so because it covers the advantages of the public health framework (paying due attention to collectivity and outcomes ((1) and (2)), but at the same time, it adds to it the distinctive features of its methodology and legally binding nature ((3) and (4)). The rights framework has been praised precisely because of these latter two features as providing a 'powerfully normative set of criteria'[49] in defining obligations and establishing accountability—normally resting on the state—'for meeting basic human needs'.[50]

However, and perhaps unsurprisingly, as we are concerned with a right from the 'socio-economic' category that requires progressive realisation, these characteristics are not only considered as the strength of this framework, but also, and at the same time, its weakness.[51] In this regard, it has been asserted that three features of the right 'conspire to displace the legal relevance of the right to health'.[52]

First, economic and social rights, such as the right to health, are conceived as positive and thus non-justiciable rights. It follows that they are unsuitable for litigation and are better left to contestation in the democratic processes. Second, legal rights are thought of in terms of remedies. This is in fact the reason why the methodology is one of establishing rights-holders and duty-bearers. It is done in order to assess the direction in which relief will flow. But the problem is that '[a] successful enforcement of a right is measured by the form of relief to the claimant. Where multiple—or possibly countless—duty-holders exist [as it is the case with the right to health], an appropriate remedy remains elusive'.[53] Third, its complex outlook renders its conception as a 'right' impossible: health can be conceived both as

[47] A Palmer et al, 'Does Ratification of Human-Rights Treaties Have Effects on Population Health?' (2009) 373 *The Lancet* 1987, cited in Rasanathan et al, above n 40, 4.

[48] Undertaking a study on this matter falls outside the scope of this chapter, but some indication for this can be found when having regard to the data provided by the OECD on the 'two most widely used health indicators'—life expectancy and healthcare spending as a percentage of GDP (although note that this method for measuring progress in health and healthcare has been criticised). See MC Wolfson and D Lievesley, 'Making Progress in Health and Healthcare', OECD conference in Istanbul (June 2007); see also, OECD health data for 2011, http://stats.oecd.org/index.aspx?DataSetCode=HEALTH_STAT.

[49] L London, 'What is a Human Rights-Based Approach to Health and Does it Matter?' (2008) 10 *Health and Human Rights* 65, 68.

[50] ibid.

[51] ibid.

[52] KG Young, 'Securing Health through Rights' in T Pogge, M Rimmer and K Rubenstein (eds), *Incentives for Public Health: Patent Law and Access to Essential Medicines* (Cambridge, Cambridge University Press, 2010) 6. What follows is a summarised version of Young's three features.

[53] ibid 7, with reference to LL Fuller, 'The Forms and Limits of Adjudication' (1978) 92 *Harvard Law Review* 353, 394–98.

a private good (eg, individual 'consumption' of healthcare based on market mechanisms) and as a public good (eg, collective 'consumption' of healthcare that is protected by environmental, occupational and public health laws), and depends in its practical realisation on 'the countless (and often merely risk-allocative) choices made by institutions, among them clinics and hospitals … pharmaceutical companies, insurance companies, international financial institutions, bureaucracies, legislatures, agencies, schools, families, as well as by individuals'.[54]

These are all valid criticisms and, at the same time, Young's contention has to be accepted that they can only be seen as a weakness of the *right* to health when the aim one targets is 'institutional certainty' (the right is either realised or not), 'jurisdictional certainty' (realisation happens at the local, national, regional or international level as opposed to in some or all of them combined) and 'court-led reforms'.[55] If institutional and jurisdictional uncertainty is accepted and if reform is sought simultaneously through multiple sites of action, 'judicial, legislative [the focus of this chapter] and popular',[56] the rights conception becomes an important tool.

Against this background, two specific strengths of the rights framework come to the fore.[57] First, if the indivisibility between socio-economic rights and civil and political rights is accepted, the rights framework forces policy-makers 'to spend as much time considering and developing health policies in terms of obligations to fulfil the right to health, as they do in developing elaborate and potentially impressive commitments to eradicating discrimination or violation of dignity'.[58] It may be added here, that this 'fulfilment' could in any case not fall below the standards set by the legal texts providing for the right, and courts or court-like bodies interpreting it. Second, rights language helps to foster social movements and mobilise civil society, whose involvement is in turn crucial for the realisation of rights in general and this right in particular. One of the best examples here is the response to the HIV/AIDS pandemic by civil society around the world, where many successful movements have increasingly grounded their advocacy arguments in a human rights framework.[59] In sum, the rights framework instigates proactive rights policy work through legislative and popular action,[60] which stands next to the capacity of redress of violations through adjudicatory and accountability mechanisms. This is important precisely because of the limitations that adjudicatory and accountability mechanisms face, especially, but not exclusively, within the socio-economic sphere.

The observations made so far suggest that application of a rights framework is not merely a paper obligation to be found in constitutional and international texts which neither does nor can substantively contribute to promoting health in real life terms. On the contrary, it is portrayed as a concept that brings additional benefits to the framework(s) of other disciplines concerned with health and of which the various actors can make functional use.

[54] Young, above n 52, 8.
[55] ibid 9–10.
[56] ibid 10.
[57] The following attributes are identified by London, above n 49, 67–68.
[58] ibid 67.
[59] WHO, The World Health Report, 'Changing History' (2004), 45–47, www.who.int/whr/2004/en/report04_en.pdf.
[60] See, eg, Young, above n 52, 9–10.

However, it is important to point out that the application of a rights-based approach is not the one and only unequivocal solution for realising a high level of health among populations and for achieving health equity. When standing in isolation, its limits emerge very quickly. Consider that so far, it has offered scarce, if any solutions, to the following core problem for achieving good health: it fails to tackle the issue of resource allocation and the question of how to prioritise when conflicting health needs are at issue. Important as this point may be, we shall not go into further detail as it is of little concern to EU health legislation (which never regulates budgeting and priority setting in health systems).

Suffice it to say that in view of the complexity of the subject matter of health, any attempt to *fully* conceptualise, institutionalise and theorise the right of it is bound to hit hard ground, in view not only of the many intertwined disciplines and approaches that are necessarily involved, but also because each and every discipline and perspective faces its own limits. So, for example, a policy, ethical or economic approach equally struggles to give neat answers to the question of prioritisation.[61] Unresolved disagreement about the right to health (in terms of content and scope) has also made the task of its theorisation difficult.[62] From the 'rights in legislation angle', we also have to accept that: 'At best, legal instruments offer a partial solution to health inequities.'[63] Finally, 'even if the violation of individual rights contributes to health inequities, not all health inequities can be explained by rights violations'.[64]

Based on all of the above, the following conclusions can be drawn:

1) Public health policy and the right to health (as defined above) differ in the sense that the latter adds to the former a distinct methodology, namely, a role-obligation analysis (1) that enables legal enforceability (2).
2) Even if (1) and (2) are limited in the field of socio-economic rights like health,[65] the framework provides for two further characteristics that speak for its application: policy-makers and legislators are compelled to realise not only the individual, but also the collective dimension of the right, in accordance with fundamental human rights standards to which they are committed (3); and the mobilisation of civil society leading to upstream change and influencing such policy and legislative processes is facilitated (4).
3) It has to be acknowledged that the application of a rights framework in health matters *alone* will not lead to a solution of all core challenges to good health (which includes better health outcomes and health equity); rather, a collaboration of all relevant disciplines is essential.

[61] Hunt and Backman, above n 39, 86.

[62] Prah Ruger, above n 38. For an attempt to tackle the theorisation task from a sociological angel, see K Milburn, 'The Importance of Lay Theorising for Health Promotion Research and Practice' (1996) 11 *Health Promotion International* 41, http://heapro.oxfordjournals.org/content/11/1/41.full.pdf. For a recent account from legal theory, see P Eleftheriadis, 'A Right to Health Care' (2012) 40 *Journal of Law, Medicine & Ethics* 286.

[63] Rasanathan et al, above n 40, 6.

[64] ibid.

[65] Since the judicial forum is not the ideal place for making complex resource allocation decisions, something that has also been generally and implicitly acknowledged by courts when granting a wide margin of discretion to states in this fields.

4) Even though a rights-based approach is not a panacea, its application is still necessary because in the absence of a *rights* conceptualisation, utilitarian bureaucratic imperatives easily take over,[66] which may inter alia disadvantage and marginalise vulnerable groups.

III. MARKET–HEALTH HARMONISATION PRACTICE AND THE ROLE OF FUNDAMENTAL RIGHTS

Based on the above, the scheme of inquiry for the three regulatory areas under examination will take the following form: first, the motives for market intervention will be examined. Second, the fundamental rights dimension of the instruments will be analysed. As regards the latter the specific questions that will be asked are the following: can the legislation be conceived in fundamental rights terms, and if so has it been so conceived; and what is the potential significance of adopting a fundamental rights conception as regards the legislation at issue.

A. Orphan Medicinal Products: Regulation (EC) No 141/2000[67]

i. The Motives for Market Intervention

Certain medicinal products are called 'orphan' because they aim to diagnose, prevent or treat medical conditions that are so rare that the cost of developing and marketing them would under normal conditions not be recovered by their sales. As a consequence, the pharmaceutical industry would not be willing to develop them under normal market conditions. This is a problem that several patients' associations had pointed out and requested EU action for years. In 1998, after a lengthy preparatory phase, the Commission responded to this[68] and to the Community framework for action in public health,[69] which indeed identified rare diseases as a priority area for Community action within that framework.[70] It put forward a proposal with the aim of creating market conditions and providing incentives for the pharmaceutical industry to research, develop and place these medicinal products on the market. In doing so, the EU was following the footprints of the US,[71] which was the first country to enact such forms of regulation in the 1980s, with considerable success.[72]

[66] C O'Cinneide, 'The Right to Health: Perspective from Judges and Advocates', UCL lecture, www.youtube.com/watch?v=QUAih7KRA-o.

[67] Regulation (EC) No 141/2000 of the European Parliament and of the Council of 16 December 1999 on orphan medicinal products [2000] OJ L18/1 (hereinafter 'Orphan Medicinal Products Regulation').

[68] Commission, Proposal for a European Parliament and Council Regulation (EC) on orphan medicinal products (98/C 276/05) COM(1998) 450 final–98/0240(COD).

[69] Commission, Communication on the Framework for Action in the Field of Health COM (1993) 559 final. See also Commission, Proposal for a Decision adopting a Programme of Community Action 1999-2003 on Rare Diseases in the Context of the Framework for Action in the Field of Public Health COM (1997) 225 final.

[70] Commission, Communication on the Framework for Action in the Field of Public Health, COM(1997) 225 final, recital 5.

[71] US Orphan Drug Act of 1983.

[72] See, among many, JL Valverde, Editorial (2001) 3 *Pharmaceuticals Policy and Law* 1–5; see also contributions in this volume.

Under the EU system, the incentive is essentially realised by creating a central marketing authorisation system[73] for designated orphan medicinal products and by providing, as a general rule, market exclusivity throughout the EU for a 10-year period.[74] The single market authorisation is granted by the Commission decision on the basis of a scientific evaluation undertaken by the European Medicines Agency (EMA).

It is clear that market intervention has occurred in this case with, if not the exclusive then certainly the main aim of pursuing the protection of health by correcting market failure resulting from the profit principle. This can be discerned not only from the circumstances of the proposal's genesis but also from statements of the institutions during the law-making process.[75] The justification contained in the instrument itself as to why action is best taken *at the EU level* (or why the principle of subsidiarity has been met) provides further insights. The explanation, according to the Preamble, is 'in order to take advantage of the widest possible market and to avoid the dispersion of limited resources'.[76] So the justificatory rationale is not that for having a more efficiently functioning market, but for tackling more efficiently the problem of a lack of orphan medicinal products (this is so because the smaller the scale of the market, the bigger the problem of low capacity for return becomes). However, the Regulation does offer a reason for justifying the internal market legal basis by stating that 'action at Community level is preferable to uncoordinated measures by the Member States which may result in distortion of competition and barriers to intra-Community trade'.[77] It is certainly not the case that there did exist uncoordinated action among the Member States at the time of the adoption of the proposal. This was explicitly made clear in the Preamble,[78] but the market requirement could still be satisfied if the aim of the measure was to prevent 'the emergence of such obstacles to trade resulting from the divergent development of national laws. However, the emergence of such obstacles must be likely and the measure in question must be designed to prevent them'.[79] There is some evidence that France (but only

[73] The central market authorisation procedure has become compulsory since November 2005. See Regulation (EC) No 726/2004 of the European Parliament and of the Council of 31 March 2004 laying down Community procedures for the authorisation and supervision of medicinal products for human and veterinary use establishing a European Medicines Agency [2004] OJ L136/1.

[74] Orphan Medicinal Products Regulation, above n 67, Art 8. Further EU incentives include a reduction of fees payable to the EMA, research support through the multi-annual Framework Programmes for Research and Technological Development and Protocol assistance. See Commission Staff Working Document on the experience acquired as a result of the application of Regulation (EC) No 141/2000, SEC(2006) 832 (20 June 2006).

[75] See Opinion of the European and Economic Social Committee (EESC) on the Proposal for a European Parliament and Council Regulation (EC) on Orphan Medicinal Products (COM(1998) 450 final—98/0240 (COD)) of 27 January 1999, SOC/007, point 2.1: 'The primary aim of the Commission proposal, which is based on Art 100a of the EC Treaty and takes the legal form of a Regulation, is then to create conditions likely to encourage the pharmaceutical industry and its research centres to tackle the issue of rare diseases adequately, as already happens in the USA and Japan' (hereinafter 'Opinion of the EESC on Orphan Medicinal Products'). See also European Parliament Committee on the Environment, Public Health and Consumer Protection Report of 24 February 1999, A4-0078/99, Explanatory Statement: 'The purpose of this proposal is to ensure that the pharmaceutical industry can concentrate on the research, development and marketing of medicinal products which would not otherwise be marketed because they would not be commercially viable, or because they concern rare diseases affecting only a few people or in certain very specific cases the diseases concerned are those where considerable numbers are affected but they are unable to pay for these drugs.'

[76] Orphan Medicinal Products Regulation, above n 67, recital 3.

[77] ibid.

[78] ibid.

[79] Case C-58/08 *R on the Application of Vodafone and others v Secretary of State for Business, Enterprise and Regulatory Reform* [2010] ECR I-4999 [33] and the case law cited therein (hereinafter *Vodafone*).

France) was ready to take action,[80] and so it is unsurprising that this country provided the main impetus for this measure; whether that is enough to fulfil the market requirement is, however, doubtful. An alternative 'economic' reason that has been provided, even though it is not contained in the legislation itself, is that 'in the absence of an adapted legislative framework in Europe, some large laboratories, in particular the British multinationals established on American soil, registered orphan medicines in Washington'.[81]

In the legislative reports (of all institutions involved) leading to adoption of the proposal, no particular effort was made to give further explanation as to whether the conditions justifying the internal market legal basis were in actual fact satisfied, and the impression gained is that no particular attention was paid to that requirement. There are two possible scenarios that could have occurred. The first one is that the requirement was met, but the institutions simply failed to properly explain this. Considering the fact that the text was adopted before the Court delivered its judgment in *Tobacco Advertising I*, this would not seem unsurprising. The other possibility is that the requirement was not met, but given the consensus among the institutions and the Member States, the measure was simply never challenged.

ii. The Fundamental Rights Dimension

a. Can the Legislation be Conceived in Fundamental Rights Terms? Has it been so Conceived?

Undoubtedly, the Regulation can be conceived in fundamental rights terms. If translated into the language of the ESC, one would say that it aims to make generally *available* of medical equipment (Art 11(3)); in addition, it aims to achieve equal treatment for patients suffering from rare conditions who 'should be entitled to the same quality of treatment as other patients'.[82] It is important that this is one of the opening statements in the Preamble of the Regulation. It is also emphasised in the Opinion of the European Economic and Social Committee (EESC), which characterises the regulation as 'represent[ing] an important move in the direction of solidarity with patients who are left at the margins of medical advances, because they suffer from rare diseases'.[83] Even more interestingly, the EESC provides for a rare example of explicit EU institutional reference being made to the fundamental right to health per se by stating that the proposal aims 'to counter what is now the unacceptable marginalization experienced by such patients, who are denied equality in terms of a *fundamental right of all citizens: the right to health*' (emphasis added).[84] The reference is even more remarkable in view of the fact that the Charter was not even proclaimed at the time of this statement. The reason may be that the strongest dimension of the right to health was at issue here, namely, its combination with the principle of equality, which is also a well-established general principle of EU law. At the same time, such reference should

[80] F Grossetête, 'Research and Development of Orphan Drugs: At Last a European Regulation' (2001) 3 *Pharmaceuticals Policy and Law* 7: 'France is the only Member State to have created, in the same year [in 1995 during the French Presidency of the Council] a ministerial task force on orphan medicines.'

[81] ibid.

[82] Orphan Medicinal Products Regulation, above n 67, recital 2.

[83] Opinion of the EESC on Orphan Medicinal Products, above n 75, 6 et seq.

[84] ibid.

not be overstated, as it did not find its way into the final text adopted. The final instrument has not been conceived in fundamental rights terms.

b. The Potential Significance of a Fundamental Rights Conception

Realisation of the Right to Health, But Scope for Improvement

From a fundamental human rights point of view, this instrument certainly seems laudable as it aims to pursue realisation of the right to health. However, there are two ways in which the Regulation could be improved from the same point of view. Both relate to achieving equal access to medicines. While the first obligation is specific to international human rights law, the second one could be based on regional and national constitutional traditions.

The first suggested improvement can be based on observations of the UN special rapporteur on the right to the highest attainable standard of health and makes clear how applying explicitly a (international) human rights framework of the right to health can make a substantive difference to the content of the legislation. The special Rapporteur found that 'States not only have a duty to ensure that existing medicines are available within their borders, they also have a responsibility to take reasonable measures to ensure the much-needed new medicines are developed and thereby become available',[85] *especially* to developing and poor countries.

What is crucial here is the fact that the responsibility resting on states relates to health protection beyond their own territory. This contrasts with the notion of 'public health', which comes with a specific understanding of the geographical reach. It is concerned with 'issues that affect the health of its population of a particular *community or country*' (emphasis added).[86] On this understanding, the obligation of public health protection resting on the EU institutions would be confined to the territory of the EU. This has also been the express understanding of the Commission. It stated with respect to the instrument under discussion that the 'orphan regulations [did] strive to deliver on the fundamental objective of improving public health *in the EU*' (emphasis added).[87]

However, it has to be acknowledged that it is possible to arrive at the same understanding of an extended geographical reach without applying a fundamental human rights framework. Instead, one could employ notions like 'global health' or 'international health'. This is certainly so with regard to the mainstreaming obligation expressed in Article 9 TFEU (the general clause) and Article 114 TFEU, as these provisions refer to the notions of 'human health' and 'health', respectively, as opposed to public health.[88] They could therefore be

[85] UN General Assembly Report, 'The Right of Everyone to the Enjoyment of the Highest Attainable Standard of Physical and Mental Health', A/61/338 (2006) 13, paras 47–48.

[86] Koplan et al, above n 16. Note that when reference is made to 'public health' as a legitimate ground of derogation from the free movement provisions, the protection of public health is limited to the territory of the Member State invoking the derogation.

[87] See Commission Staff Working Document on the experience acquired as a result of the application of Regulation (EC) No 141/2000 on Orphan Medicinal Products and account of the public health benefits obtained (Document on the basis of Article 10 of Regulation (EC) No 141/2000); http://ec.europa.eu/health/files/orphanmp/doc/orphan_en_06-2006_en.pdf..

[88] Note that the same would not seem to be possible with regard to the health legal basis, Art 168 TFEU, which stipulates that EU action complementing national policies 'shall be directed towards improving *public* health' (emphasis added).

interpreted in light of the alternative notions offered that have a wider geographical reach. The first alternative (global health) has been understood in this respect to 'Focus … on issues that directly or indirectly affect health but that can transcend national boundaries',[89] whereas the second one (international health) 'Focuses on health issues of countries other than one's own, especially those of low-income and middle-income'.[90]

The EESC was somehow in line with this latter approach when stating that progress in the sector of rare diseases 'could make a decisive contribution to improving living conditions in the developing countries, where investment in research is almost completely lacking. Such a move would place Europe at the centre of solidarity with the developing countries, and should constitute Europe's preferred approach in the future'.[91]

But even more interestingly, at first reading at the European Parliament, the committee in charge (on environment, public health and consumer protection) proposed two amendments in the Preamble whereby a call was made on the Commission to put forward a proposal that would tackle the problem of orphan medicinal products in relation to diseases prevailing in developing countries.[92] Attention was drawn to the fact that additional incentives may be necessary for researching and developing medicinal products that occur predominantly in the (poor) tropical regions and not in the EU. However, these proposed amendments did not survive and were only included in the Rapporteur's explanatory statement. The reason for this was, as he explained, that the introduction of a policy to research and develop these kinds of diseases was not really the purpose of the proposed regulation at issue. The rhetorical use of rights language could have been employed here in a strategic way, although it is clear that such use would only be effective if employed systematically and beyond a single reference in the Preamble of one instrument.

In any case, the matter was thus left for the future, but has not been tackled to date. It is this inaction, however, which is subject to a different judgment, depending on whether one views it from a human rights perspective or not. The difference is the following: unlike a public health approach, a rights framework *imposes a duty* on states that reasonable measures are taken to develop and make available much-needed medicines to poor and developing countries. Absence of such action would constitute a human rights violation. The human rights methodology of identifying duty-bearers therefore comes into play here.

The second way in which the instrument could be improved from a fundamental rights perspective relates to its nature as a measure that pursues equal treatment between patients suffering from rare medical conditions and those that suffer from common ones. In this respect, it has been pointed out (on behalf of the medical technology industry)[93] that the Orphan Medicinal Products Regulation does not address the unequal situation faced by patients who suffer from rare diseases and are in need of medical devices[94] as opposed to

[89] Koplan et al, above n 16, 1994.

[90] ibid.

[91] Opinion of the EESC on Orphan Medicinal Products, above n 75, point 3.1.6.

[92] European Parliament, Report on the Proposal for a European Parliament and Council Regulation on Orphan Medicinal Products, Draft Legislative Resolution, A4-0078/99, amendments 1 and 2, recital 2a (new).

[93] EUCOMED discussion paper, 'Rare Diseases and Medical Devices in the European Union', www.eucomed.org/uploads/Modules/Publications/Rare%20diseases%20and%20medical%20technology.pdf.

[94] Examples offered: patients suffering from Parkinson's disease in need of deep brain stimulation treatment, which involves the use of an active implantable device; patients suffering from Multiple Sclerosis with severe spasticity in need of a programmable, implantable drug delivery pump. See ibid.

those in need of drug-based treatment. This is so because medical devices are excluded from the scope of the Regulation.[95] As such, this is a situation where rights language would draw the legislator's attention to precisely these kinds of problems, which otherwise are more easily overlooked.

Restricting Other Fundamental Rights

As a last issue, it should be noted that a fundamental rights discourse can be applied to the Regulation not only in order to portray it as a rights-promoting instrument (making medicines generally available), but also as a rights-restricting instrument. This argument was put forward by the applicant in the *Behring* case.[96] Behring applied to receive orphan status for one of its medicinal products, which the EMA dismissed for a number of reasons, in particular because the applicant already held a marketing authorisation for this product. The applicant, in contesting the Commission's decision, alleged that the provision of the legislation laying down the procedure for designation (of a medicinal product being 'orphan') and removal from the register[97] was unlawful. The claim was made on the ground that it violated the right to property and the freedom to pursue a profession, as well as the equal treatment principle. The Court dismissed all three of these claims, but the way it did so is interesting. With respect to the first two grounds of allegation, it held:

> [A]lthough the right to property and freedom to pursue a trade or profession are general principles of European Union law, they are not absolute, but must be viewed in relation to their function in society. Consequently, the exercise of those rights may be restricted, provided that those restrictions in fact correspond to objectives of public interest pursued by the European Union and do not constitute, in relation to the aim pursued, a disproportionate and intolerable interference, impairing the very substance of the rights so guaranteed. The importance of the objectives pursued may justify restrictions which bring about even substantial negative consequences for certain economic operators.[98]
>
> In the present case, the fact that it may become impossible for the applicant to make use of its right to use the procedure for mutual recognition in a situation where a competing undertaking obtains market exclusivity for an improved medicinal product is a possible consequence of the implementation of Regulation No 141/2000. Nevertheless, such a consequence can in no way be regarded as impairing the very substance of the property right or of the freedom to pursue a trade or profession. The restriction on the economic exploitation of human fibrinogen developed more than 40 years ago by the applicant does not represent a disproportionate or intolerable sacrifice when compared with the objectives of public interest pursued by the European Union legislature.[99]

Two points are worth noting. First, the Court did not frame the matter in fundamental rights terms. Despite the fact that the applicants argued on the basis of a violation of '*fundamental*

[95] Orphan Medicinal Products Regulation, above n 67, Art 2. See also Directive 65/65/EEC relating to medicinal products [1965] OJ L22/369, as amended by Directive 2001/38/EC [2001] OJ L 311/67 (Art 1 of Directive 65/65/EEC defines 'medicinal product' as 'any substance of combination of substances presented for treating or preventing disease in human beings or animals' also 'with a view to making a medical diagnosis or to restoring, correcting or modifying physiological functions in human beings or in animals is likewise considered a medicinal product').

[96] Case T-264/07 *CSL Behring GmbH v European Commission and the EMA* [2010] ECR II-4469.

[97] Orphan Medicinal Products Regulation, above n 67, Art 5(1) (and Art 2(4) of the implementing Regulation).

[98] *Behring*, above n 96, [99].

[99] ibid [100].

principles of the same rank as the primary legislation of the European Union and, accordingly, the Treaty' (emphasis added),[100] the Court considered the *general* principles, without stating that those at stake were fundamental human rights.[101] Having said that, it has to be acknowledged that the approach adopted is in fact reminiscent of fundamental rights adjudication. Second and equally, what is posed on the other side of the scale is, again, not a fundamental right, but a public interest objective. Thus, formally not only the political institutions, but also the Court construes the Orphan Medicinal Products Regulation in public health/health policy terms.

B. Tobacco Control Regulation

The EU has been an important player in tobacco control policy, passing some of the most progressive laws for the purpose of public health protection in the fields of tobacco advertising,[102] tobacco product regulation[103] and tobacco taxation.[104] Even though the discussion herein is limited to the instruments rooted in internal market legal bases, it should be

[100] ibid [67].

[101] An interesting side point to note is the submission that the principles at issue are of the same rank as the Treaty. Unfortunately, however, the Court did not enter any discussion as to the hierarchical relationship between fundamental rights as general principles and other primary Treaty law.

[102] See, eg, Directive 98/43/EC on the approximation of the laws, regulations and administrative provisions of the Member States relating to the advertising and sponsorship of tobacco products [1998] OJ L213/9 (annulled); Directive 2003/33/EC on the approximation of the laws, regulations and administrative provisions of the Member States relating to the advertising and sponsorship of tobacco products (replacing Directive 98/43/EC) [2003] OJ L152/16; Directive 89/552/EEC of the Council of 3 October 1989 on the coordination of certain provisions laid down by law, regulation or administrative action in Member States concerning the pursuit of television broadcasting activities [1989] OJ L298/23 (hereinafter 'TVWF Directive—TV Advertising Ban'), as amended by Directive 97/36/EC of the European Parliament and of the Council of 30 June 1997 amending Council Directive 89/552/EEC on the coordination of certain provisions laid down by law, regulation or administrative action in Member States concerning the pursuit of television broadcasting activities [1997] OJ L202/60 (hereinafter 'TVWF'), later amended by Directive 98/43/EC of the European Parliament and of the Council of 6 July 1998 on the approximation of the laws, regulations and administrative provisions of the Member States relating to the advertising and sponsorship of tobacco products [1998] OJ L213/9 (hereinafter 'AVMSD').

[103] Directive 89/622/EEC of the Council of 13 November 1989 on the approximation of the laws, regulations and administrative provisions of the Member States concerning the labelling of tobacco products [1989] OJ L359/1, amended by Directive 92/41/EEC of the Council of 15 May 1992 amending Directive 89/662/EEC on the approximation of the laws, regulations and administrative provisions of the Member States concerning the labelling of tobacco products [1992] OJ L158/30. With regards to tar yield, see Directive 90/239/EEC of the Council of 17 May 1990 on the approximation of the laws, regulations and administrative provisions of the Member States concerning the maximum tar yield of cigarettes [1990] OJ L137/36, recast by Directive 2001/37/EC of the European Parliament and of the Council of 5 June 2001 on the approximation of the laws, regulations and administrative provisions of the Member States concerning the manufacture, presentation and sale of tobacco products [2001] OJ L194/26. The recast Directive has now been repealed by Directive 2014/40/EU of the European Parliament and of the Council of 3 April 2014 on the approximation of the laws, regulations and administrative provisions of the Member States concerning the manufacture, presentation and sale of tobacco products and repealing Directive 2001/37/EC [2014] OJ L127/1 (hereinafter 'Tobacco Products Directive').

[104] Directive 92/79/EEC of the Council of 19 October 1992 on the approximation of taxes on cigarettes [1992] OJ L316/8; Directive 92/80/EEC of the Council of 19 October 1992 on the approximation of taxes on manufactured tobacco other than cigarettes [1992] OJ L316/10 and Directive 95/59/EC of the Council of 27 November 1995 on taxes other than turnover taxes which affect the consumption of manufactured tobacco [1995] OJ L291/40, as amended by Directive 2002/10/EC, of the Council of 12 February 2002 as regards the structure and the rates of excise duties applied on manufactured tobacco [2002] OJ L46/26; Directive 2003/117/EC of the Council of 5 December 2003 amending Directives 92/79/EEC and 92/80/EEC, in order to authorise the French Republic to

borne in mind that the EU has also pursued tobacco control through other venues. Internal market regulation is only one pillar, albeit the biggest 'pillar', of the overall policy. The other venues through which it is pursued is Health and Safety at Work,[105] and a number of Council Resolutions/Recommendations, which are, however, not binding.[106]

i. The Motives for Market Intervention

a. General

When inquiring into the legislative history, it is obvious that the trigger for political mobilisation was health considerations. The above-listed instruments were adopted following the launch of the Europe Against Cancer (EAC) programme of 1987.[107] The EAC 'always included a substantial commitment to the anti-smoking campaign',[108] which is already visible from its very first action plan,[109] Chapter I of which is concerned with the 'Fight Against Tobacco'.[110] This included among its proposed actions: 'Upwards alignment of taxation on tobacco manufactured in the European Community' (action 1); 'Harmonization of cigarette labelling in the European Community' (action 4); 'Prohibition of cigarettes with a high tar content' (action 5); 'Harmonization of the standards for the components of tobacco smoke' (action 6); and 'Prohibition of tax-free sales of tobacco in the European Community' (action 7). These goals had to be pursued through concrete legislative action. In the EU context, this meant that the institutions were in need of a legal basis. Ex Article 95 EC (now Art 114 TFEU) served as such for all of the above-listed actions, except the tax directives, which are based on Article 93 EC (now Art 113 TFEU) in the absence of a more specific 'health'-legal basis, and in view of the practical impossibility of using the 'general legal basis' (ex Art 308 EC, now Art 352 TFEU) due to the unanimity requirement. This explanation of the motives holds true for all of the above-listed instruments. Finally, it should be noted that these proposed actions that were implemented by the EU in the form of internal market measures are also existing obligations in the WHO Framework Convention on Tobacco Control (FCTC), to which the EU and all its Member States are party.[111]

prolong the application of lower rates of excise duty to tobacco products released for consumption in Corsica [2003] OJ L333/49; and Directive 2010/12/EC of the Council of 16 February 2010 amending Directives 92/79/EEC, 92/80/EEC and 95/59 on the structure and excise duty applied on manufactured tobacco; and Directive 2008/118/EC [2010] OJ L50/1, repealed by Directive 2011/64/EU of the Council of 21 June 2011 on the structure and rates of excise duty applied to manufactured tobacco [2011] OJ L176/24.

[105] For a list of measures, see THE ASPECT Consortium, 'Tobacco or Health in the European Union— Past, Present and Future', http://ec.europa.eu/health/ph_determinants/life_style/Tobacco/Documents/tobacco_fr_en.pdf.

[106] Listed in ibid.

[107] Resolution of the Council and the Representatives of the Governments of the Member States on a 'Programme of Action of the European Communities Against Cancer' (meeting within the Council of 7 July 1986), [1986] OJ C184/19, 20; and Commission, 'Europe Against Cancer Programme'—Proposal for a plan of action, 1987 to 1989 [1987] OJ C50/1.

[108] L Trubek, M Nance and T Hervey, 'The Construction of Healthier Europe: Lessons from the Fight against Cancer' (2008) 26 *Wisconsin International Law Journal* 804, n 25, with reference to Hervey and McHale, above n 2, 368–84.

[109] There were three action plans in total with one extension: 1987–89; 1990–94; 1996–2000 and extension 2001–02.

[110] See Europa Press Release 'Europe Against Cancer'—Action Plan 1987–1989, MEMO/86/159, 10/12/1986.

[111] Council Decision of 2 June 2004 concerning the conclusion of the WHO Framework Convention on Tobacco Control [2004] OJ L213/8.

The legal basis for this action was what was then Article 95 EC (now Art 114 TFEU, internal market), Article 152 EC (now Art 168 TFEU, health) and Article 133 EC (now Art 207 TFEU, common commercial policy).

b. Tobacco Advertising Directive 98/43/EC Annulled and Replaced by Directive 2003/33/EC

The first Tobacco Advertising Directive has its roots in the EAC programme and, more specifically, the European Experts Cancer Committee established by the EAC.[112] Out of all the tobacco control measures, politically, this was the most difficult one—'the most intensively lobbied dossier in the history of EU health policy-making'.[113] It was adopted following 10 years of difficult negotiations only in order to be annulled by the Court shortly after on the ground of inappropriate choice of legal basis.[114] The original proposal and the final legislative act make it clear that the Commission framed the instrument in market-making terms. The very first recital of Directive 98/43/EC explains that differences in the Member States' laws relating to advertising and sponsorship of tobacco products are likely to hinder the movement of the products carrying advertisement (newspapers, magazines etc), impede the freedom to provide services and distort competition. Approximation was therefore seen as necessary, leading in the final instance to a total EU ban on tobacco advertising. Note, however, that the initial 1989 Commission proposal did not foresee such a total ban.[115] This idea was only later introduced by the European Parliament after the Committee on the Environment, Public Health and Consumer Protection (ENVI) advised the plenary for such an amendment. The plenary adopted it[116] because of its improved public health rationale; it did not enter into any serious discussion about the market-making nature of the instrument.[117] The Commission did not endorse this in its following amended proposal,[118] as it considered it premature in light of existing laws at the national level (only two states, Italy and Portugal, had total bans in place), but it did eventually do so in its subsequent proposal after a qualified majority could not be reached in the Council and in light of increasingly stringent measures being adopted in the Member States. It was, however, this absolute prohibition that led the Court (in *Tobacco Advertising I*) to arrive at the conclusion that the internal market did not constitute an appropriate legal basis for this first Directive.[119] The Court

[112] Boessen and Maarse, above n 11, 3; and Trubek et al, above n 108, 824.

[113] S Adamini et al, 'European Policymaking on the Tobacco Advertising Ban: The Importance of Escape Routes' (2011) 6 *Health Economic, Policy and Law* 65, 66.

[114] There has been a vast amount of literature describing the legislative path leading to the adoption of the Directive and the *Tobacco Advertising I* judgment annulling it. See, eg, T Hervey 'Up in Smoke? Community (Anti) Tobacco Law and Policy' (2001) 26 *European Law Review* 26.

[115] Commission Proposal for a Council Directive on the advertising of tobacco products in the press and by means of bills and posters COM(89) 163 final/2—SYN 194.

[116] European Parliament, Minutes of the Proceedings of the Sitting of Wednsday 14 March 1990 (first reading) [1990] OJ C96/42.

[117] Boesse and Maarse, above n 11.

[118] Commission, Amended Proposal for a Council Directive on the authorized advertising of tobacco products in the press and by means of bills and posters (19 April 1990), COM(90) 147 final—SYN 194.

[119] *Tobacco Advertising I*, above n 4.

accepted that prohibiting the advertising of tobacco products in periodicals, magazines and newspapers could be based on ex Article 100a EC (now Art 114 TFEU). However, the Directive also covered (in Art 3(1)) types of advertising of tobacco products that could not be 'justified by the need to eliminate obstacles to the free movement of advertising media or the freedom to provide services in the field of advertising'.[120] Furthermore, it did not ensure free movement of products that were in compliance with its provisions (in Art 5). The total ban therefore did not serve the interests of the internal market (see on these points the discussion in chapter two).[121]

The second Tobacco Advertising Directive was adopted in order to replace the annulled first version. The reason for intervention and the presented rationale for justifying action does not differ in substance from the first instrument. However, and of course unsurprisingly, the legislature has closely followed the dicta of the Court.[122] This Directive was again challenged before the Court on the ground that the internal market legal basis constituted an inappropriate choice. Since the Court had accepted in principle that tobacco advertising regulation could legitimately have such a legal basis, in the absence of the problematic provisions that could not be linked to the establishment and functioning of the internal market mentioned above,[123] it is no surprise that it upheld the later instrument.

c. Tobacco Products Regulation: Directive 2014/40/EU

The Tobacco Products Directive is the result of a very hotly debated legislative dossier and it seems to have overtaken the Tobacco Advertising Directive as the most lobbied dossier in the history of EU health policy-making.[124]

The proposal followed two Commission reports on the application of Directive 2001/37/EC (in 2005 and 2007), two pieces of scientific advice by the Scientific Committee on Emerging and Newly Identified Health Risks (SCENIHR) (in 2008 and 2009)[125] and a public consultation.

The public consultation generated an unprecedented amount of responses, with more than 85,000 contributions. The Commission was careful to point out that the volume of responses, positive as it may seem at first sight, appears to be largely the result of several

[120] ibid, para 99.

[121] A parallel can be drawn here with the US, where difficulties of reconciliation emerged between, on the one hand, the Cigarette Smoking Act of 1969 and the Cigarette Labelling Act of 1969 and, on the other hand, the Interstate Commerce Act. See also the attempts by the Food and Drug Administration to introduce an extensive advertising rule and prohibition of trade in certain products in 1996, which was struck down by the Supreme Court. See TE Novotny and HM Mamudu, 'Progression of Tobacco Control Policies: Lessons from the United States and Implications for Global Action', HNP, World Bank, Discussion Paper (May 2008) 9.

[122] Acknowledged in the Commission Explanatory Memorandum, COM(2001) 0283.

[123] *Tobacco Advertising I*, above n 4, [98].

[124] Neil Corlett, Spokesperson of the European Parliament ALDE Group even suggested that this is 'one of the most lobbied dossiers in the history of the EU institutions.' Audiovisual interview available at: www.vieuws.eu/eu-institutions/parliament-agenda-alde-priorities-for-the-week-of-23-sept-2013.

[125] Tobacco Products Directive, above n 104, recital 2.

citizen mobilisation campaigns that took place in some Member States.[126] This is also evidenced by the type of contributions and the origin of the contributors.[127,128]

Attempts of non-legislative actors to influence this piece of legislation were remarkable. The associated lobbying scandals overshadowed the legislative process: most prominently the so-called 'DalliGate' affair,[129] but also the leak to the media of internal tobacco industry documents suggesting that the tobacco lobby employed several delaying tactics.[130] The scandals did delay the process, but the final instrument was still adopted and entered into force two years after the Commission tabled its first proposal—this is relatively quick compared to the first Tobacco Advertising Directive.

The Tobacco Products Directive 2014/40/EU (TPD) repeals its predecessor, Directive 2001/37/EC. The latter was a recast version, which in turn repealed previous directives. These:

1) introduced regulation on the labelling of tobacco products, making warnings and the indication of tar and nicotine yield, and other product information on unit packets of tobacco products obligatory;
2) provided for a prohibition of the marketing of certain types of tobacco for oral use; and
3) set maximum tar yields.

The recast Directive maintained all of the above actions, but it also went further through the introduction of a reduced EU ceiling for tar yield levels (based on new scientific evidence) and that of maximum permissible nicotine and carbon monoxide levels. This was maintained in the TPD.

The TPD brought about further changes and new features. Among the most important ones are the following:

1) New rules on labelling and packaging: mandatory picture and text health warnings shall cover 65 per cent of the surface, while the previous printing of tar, nicotine and carbon monoxide levels on packages will be replaced with health warnings. Unit packets of cigarettes will need to have a standard shape and contain a minimum of 20 cigarettes. No slim 'lipstick-style' packs or 'pocket money' packs will be allowed

[126] One such campaign was organised by a group representing over 75 per cent of Italian tobacconists. See Commission, Report on the public consultation on the possible revision of the Tobacco Products Directive 2001/37/EC (July 2011), Health and Consumers Directorate D 4, http://ec.europa.eu/health/tobacco/docs/consultation_report_en.pdf.

[127] A total of 57 per cent of all citizens' responses (which accounted for 96 per cent of the survey response) were duplicate responses and almost two-thirds of the responses came from only two Member States: Italy and Poland. See ibid 6–9.

[128] In this regard, tobaccotactis.org (an online academic resource launched by the Tobacco Control Research Group of the University of Bath, UK) suggests that this was a tactic by the tobacco lobby in order to 'flood' the consultation and delay the process. See www.tobaccotactics.org/index.php/TPD:_Delaying_the_Process_of_Consultation.

[129] John Dalli, former health Commissioner, was forced to resign in October 2012 after an anti-fraud investigation linked him to an attempt to influence the legislative process in return for compensation. Meanwhile Dalli has brought an action in front of the General Court seeking annulment of the decision of termination of his office and compensation for moral and material prejudice (Application T-562/12 *Dalli v Commission*).

[130] 'Tobacco Giant Philip Morris Spent Millions in Bid to Delay EU Legislation' (*The Guardian*, 7 September 2013), www.theguardian.com/business/2013/sep/07/tobacco-philip-morris-millions-delay-eu-legislation.

(Art 10 TPD). As regard product presentation, promotional and misleading features will not be allowed on packs (Art 13 TPD).

2) Regulation of ingredients, including the banning of certain types/quantities of 'flavourings' (Art 7 TPD).
3) Mandatory reporting of ingredients and emissions for manufacturers and importers of tobacco products (Art 5 TPD).
4) New rules for e-cigarettes introducing safety and quality requirements, reporting obligations and extending the rules on tobacco advertising to e-cigarettes (Art 20 TPD).
5) New rules to combat the illicit trade of tobacco products through an EU-wide tracking and tracing system (Art 15 TPD).

The TPD maintains the ban on snus (oral tobacco) and it does not introduce the much-debated 'plain packaging' requirement (further discussed below), although it allows Member States to introduce further measures in this regard (Art 24(2) TPD). It also does not ban cross-border distance sales, but allows Member States to do so.

The reason for initiating the legislative process leading to the TPD was to 'update and complete'[131] the regime laid down by its predecessor, Directive 2001/37/EC.[132] Revision was explicitly foreseen in the latter-named Directive (Art 11) and was called for by both co-legislators.[133] The reasons put forward for this action concerned the need to reflect three kinds of developments, namely, in science (eg, on tobacco flavourings and the effectiveness of health warnings), the market (an increasingly diversified tobacco products market, with the emergence of new products like e-cigarettes and new patterns of use of traditional products)[134] and international law (the FCTC entered into force in 2005).[135]

The presented 'overall objective'[136] and argument justifying the legal basis is the same as for the predecessor Directive 2001/37/EC[137] and as for regulating tobacco advertising: disparities (still) exist between the national regulatory regimes, which are 'liable to constitute a barrier to trade and to impede the smooth functioning of the internal market in tobacco products, and should, therefore, be eliminated'.[138] So, as with the previous instruments, the functioning of the internal market shall be improved while taking as a base a high level of health protection, and in this case especially for young people.[139] It is indeed notable that two out of the three mentioned developments driving the need for revision relate to the health rationale. So, the scientific developments concern inter alia new findings on the effectiveness of health warnings to inform consumers about the health consequences of

[131] Commission, Proposal for a Directive on the approximation of the laws, regulations and administrative provisions of the Member States concerning the manufacture, presentation and sale of tobacco and related products, COM(2012) 788 final, Explanatory Memorandum 2 (hereinafter 'Commission Proposal Tobacco Products Directive').

[132] Directive 2001/37/EC, above n 103.

[133] Commission Proposal Tobacco Products Directive, above n 131, 2.

[134] Commission, Second Report on the Application of the Tobacco Products Directive, COM(2007) 754 final (27 November 2007) 11 et seq.

[135] Tobacco Products Directive, above n 103, recital 1; and Commission, Memo 'New Rules for Tobacco Products', http://europa.eu/rapid/press-release_MEMO-14-134_en.htm.

[136] Commission Proposal Tobacco Products Directive, above n 132, Explanatory Memorandum, 2.

[137] Directive 2001/37/EC, n 103, recital 2.

[138] Directive 2014/40/EU, above n 103, recitals 22 and 23.

[139] Tobacco Products Directive, above n 103, recitals 19 and 21.

tobacco use and change their attitude and behaviour.[140] The international development concerns the entry into force of the FCTC—a Convention whose objective is 'to give priority to the right to protect public health'.[141]

Still, the economic argument is here in principle stronger than with regard to tobacco advertising, as we are concerned with the regulation of an economic activity as opposed to the prohibition of one. Having said that, it is interesting to note the remarks made by the Committee on Legal Affairs at the European Parliament first reading stage,[142] which noted that 'it is difficult to see how the proposed (de facto) ban on menthol and on slim cigarettes could improve the functioning of the internal market', given that 'not a single Member State has banned slim cigarettes or menthol or is even considering it. Thus, the ban will neither remove nor prevent the emergence of obstacles to fundamental freedoms'.

Eventually, the ban of slim cigarettes did not find its way into the final instrument, whereas that of menthol (a 'characterising flavour' under the Directive)[143,144] will be applicable after a transitional period.[145] The Explanatory Memorandum merely states that 'some Member States have … adopted legislation or concluded agreements with industry allowing or prohibiting certain ingredients'.[146] The same is repeated in the final Directive.[147] It is not mentioned that the ingredients alluded to are the problematic 'characterising flavours', nor is it stated how many/which Member States have adopted legislation. The IA Report provides for some indication, stating that 'at least one Member State [Denmark] has declared that it will discuss a national ban on "candy cigarettes" if no action is taken at EU level' and that 'Member States will seek inspiration from other [non-EU] jurisdictions'.[148] This seems to be a rather thin basis for meeting the legal basis threshold, but the same assertions are in essence repeated in the Preamble of the TPD.[149] Here again, the explanation might be found in the fact that there was Member State support.[150]

A similar point arose with respect to the introduction of an EU ceiling for carbon monoxide levels in the predecessor Directive 2001/37/EC. The market argument was not obvious here. At the time of the proposal of this instrument, certainly no Member State had such a ceiling in place,[151] and it is doubtful whether the fact that some third countries had

[140] Sambroek Research International, Report prepared for the Commission, 'A Review of the Science Base to Support the Development of Health Warnings for Tobacco Packages', http://ec.europa.eu/health/tobacco/docs/warnings_report_en.pdf.

[141] WHO, Framework Convention on Tobacco Control (FCTC), Preamble, first sentence. For the full text of the Convention, see: http://whqlibdoc.who.int/publications/2003/9241591013.pdf.

[142] Opinion of the Committee on Legal Affairs for the Committee on the Environment, Public Health and Food Safety (25 June 2013), A7-0276/2013, Procedure 2012/0366(COD).

[143] This falls under the definition of a 'characterising flavour' under the Directive.

[144] For cigarettes and roll-your-own tobacco.

[145] As will all tobacco products with characterising flavours, whose EU-wide sales volumes represent three per cent. See Tobacco Products Directive, above n 103, Art 7(14).

[146] Commission Proposal Tobacco Products Directive, above n 132, Explanatory Memorandum, 5.

[147] Tobacco Products Directive, above n 103, recital 15.

[148] Commission Staff Working Document, Impact Assessment accompanying the Proposal for a Directive concerning the manufacture, presentation and sale of tobacco and related products (19 December 2012), SWD(2012) 452 final 41 (hereinafter 'TPD IA').

[149] Tobacco Products Directive, above n 103, recital 15.

[150] According to the IA Report, 'a majority of Member States also supports some kind of regulation in the context of the public consultation': TPD IA, above n 148, 41.

[151] ibid, point 5.

introduced such and that some Member States have reporting requirements in place would justify intervention on the basis of the internal market. Of course, here also, it could be argued that future regulatory activity in this field is likely to arise, leading to future obstacles to the internal market, but no evidence was put forward supporting such an argument. In fact, the ground on which the Commission considered the introduction of this provision to be justified is 'scientific evidence' which basically links carbon monoxide in cigarettes to cardiovascular diseases in smokers.

The Explanatory Memorandum of Directive 2001/37/EC also makes it clear that it was introduced pursuant to the recommendations of the Commission's High Level Cancer Experts Committee in Helsinki in October 1996 to take such a course of action. The necessity for action is openly stated. It stems from the aim to ensure a high level of public health protection. The same motive is by implication carried over to the successor TPD, which is only meant to 'update and complete' its predecessor.

d. Tobacco Control Through Taxation: Directive 2011/64/EU

Similar to Article 114 TFEU, harmonisation of indirect taxation under Article 113 TFEU also requires that these harmonising measures are 'necessary for the establishment and functioning of the internal market'. Also in this area, the main motive for intervention has been the protection of health.

The first harmonising measures were taken in the early 1990s. Yet, discussions on the topic had already been conducted in the framework of the White Paper on Completing the Internal Market in 1985, where the Commission had proposed full harmonisation of excise duties on tobacco products. The Council rejected this approach, however, on the ground that it was not perceived as a necessary step for the establishment and functioning of the internal market. The regulatory history unfolded instead in the following piecemeal fashion. First, two types of minimum excise duty levels were set in Directive 92/79/EC approximating taxes on cigarettes and providing for a system combining both, *ad valorem* ('fixed percentage of the product's retail price') and specific rates ('excises levied at a fixed amount per quantity').[152] Second, Directive 92/80/EC approximated taxes on tobacco products other than cigarettes and gave Member States the choice between an *ad valorem* duty or a specific duty or a mixture of the two, and providing for minimum rates of these duties. Third, a Directive was adopted which sets out the general principles and definitional categories for different types of manufactured tobacco: Directive 95/59/EC on taxes other than turnover taxes which affect the consumption of manufactured tobacco.

This basic regime was further amended (as a result of the duty resting on the Commission to examine every four years 'the smooth operation of the single market, the real value

[152] S Cnossen, 'Tobacco Taxation in the European Union', CESIFO Working Paper No 1718 (May 2006) 7, www.econstor.eu/bitsream/10419/25763/1/51698196X.PDF. Cnossen discusses the two concepts and makes the point that 'the choice between specific and *ad valorem* taxation depends on whether the primary aim of the policy is to discourage consumption or to raise revenue and on whether improvements in product quality are deemed desirable or not'.

of excise-duty rates and the wider objectives of the Treaty'),[153,154] most recently by Directive 2010/12/EU. This instrument 'foresees a gradual increase in the EU minimum taxation levels on cigarettes and fine cut tobacco up to 2014 and 2018 respectively. The Directive also aims to contribute to reducing tobacco consumption by 10% within the next 5 years'.[155] All amendments have been assembled and codified in a single act: Directive 2011/64/EU.[156]

Directive 2010/12/EU is an interesting example of health considerations being mainstreamed during the IA stage of the proposal and substantively affecting the shaping of the regulatory regime. In assessing potential measures for modernising or adding more transparency to the structure of excise duties on tobacco products and ensuring a level playing field for the operators, the IA evaluated three options. The first—no policy change option—was dismissed on the ground that several persistent problems, including fiscal instability and distortions of competitions, would be left untackled. The second option consisted of changing only the structure of excise duties on cigarettes. This option 'would create a tax floor for all cigarettes in the EU'[157] and: 'It would also reduce the tax and price gap between Member States more than the other options and, to an appreciable extent, integrate public health concerns.'[158] However, and most interestingly, the second option was dismissed on the ground that this approach would 'not sufficiently take account of health considerations'.[159] That is why the third option was finally endorsed, namely, that of changing minimum rates of excise duties on cigarettes as well as the structure.[160] The language of the Preamble of course presents the Directive as an instrument whose adoption has been motivated equally by the aim of achieving the establishment and functioning of the internal market and pursuing public health protection. But the Explanatory Memorandum reveals that public health protection had a pivotal role to play in this revision of the instrument, particularly in view of the EU becoming party to the WHO FCTC, and the Member States demanding higher levels of human health protection 'and consequently higher European minima for excise duties on tobacco'.[161] The Council seems to have expressed the most 'honest' stance by explaining the purpose of the Directive in the following terms: 'The directive is *intended to ensure a higher level of public health protection* by raising minimum excise duties on cigarettes, whilst bringing the minimum rates for fine-cut tobacco gradually into line with those for cigarettes' (emphasis added).[162]

[153] This duty is laid down in Art 4 of Directive 92/79/EEC and Art 4 of Directive 92/80/EEC, and extends to the relevant provisions of Directive 95/59/EC. See n 104 above.

[154] Directive 2002/10/EC and Directive 2003/117/EC; see n 104 above.

[155] Commission, Taxation and Customs Union, Legislation, http://ec.europa.eu/taxation_customs/taxation/excise_duties/tobacco_products/legislation/index_en.htm.

[156] Directive 2011/64/EU, above n 104.

[157] Commission, Proposal for a Council Directive amending Directives 92/79/EEC, 92/80/EEC and 95/59/EC on the structure and rates of excise duty applied on manufactured tobacco, Explanatory Memorandum (16 July 2008), COM(2008)0459.

[158] ibid.

[159] ibid.

[160] And abolishing the 'Most Popular Price Category' (MPPC) concept.

[161] See Explanatory Memorandum COM(2008)0459, above n 157, 3.

[162] Council Press Release 15767/09 (Presse 324) (10 November 2009), www.consilium.europa.eu/uedocs/cms_data/docs/pressdata/en/ecofin/111018.pdf.

ii. The Fundamental Rights Dimension

a. Can the Legislation be Conceived in Fundamental Rights Terms? Has it been so Conceived?

Can the Legislation be Conceived in Fundamental Rights Terms?

It is certainly possible to construct all of the above instruments in terms of the fundamental right to health, even if the legislature has for the most part and for a long time refrained from doing so.

More specifically, it is possible to understand the instruments as aimed at fulfilling and protecting the fundamental right to health, also in combination with other fundamental rights like the right to life (Art 2 CFR and Art 2 ECHR), children's rights (Convention on the Rights of the Child, GC14, para 23), prohibition of inhuman and degrading treatment (Art 3 ECHR and Art 7 ICCPR) and access to information (Art 11 CFR, Art 10 ECHR and Art 14 ICESCR). All of these have been used as a basis for advocating an 'emerging human right to tobacco control' at the international level.

In terms of the ESC, the legislation could be seen as fulfilling the obligation to remove as far as possible the causes of ill-health as provided for by Article 11(1) (rev)ESC. The consumption of tobacco has been characterised as an epidemic by the WHO and in the FCTC as it 'is the leading cause of preventable death and is estimated to kill more than 5 million people each year worldwide'.[163] Furthermore, the ECSR has specified what is required under Article 11(3) ESC with respect to tobacco control measures:

> The Committee recalls that to be effective, any prevention policy must restrict the supply of tobacco through controls on production, distribution, advertising and pricing. In particular, the sale of tobacco to young persons must be banned as must smoking in public places, including transport, and advertising on posters and in the press should also be prohibited. The Committee assesses the effectiveness of such policies on the basis of statistics on tobacco consumption.[164]

Has the Legislation been Conceived in Fundamental Rights Terms?

Up until the latest Tobacco Products Directive, none of the instruments listed above had been conceptualised in terms of the fundamental right to health, nor had any such reference been made during the legislative process of any of these Directives.

In fact, the only reference to fundamental rights was found in the Preamble to the second Tobacco Advertising Directive (2003/33/EC), which affirms its compatibility with the Charter and, in particular, with the right to freedom of expression,[165] not the right to health. The Commission Proposal to this Directive included that recital already,[166] and the Explanatory Memorandum provided: 'Advertising is an important economic activity which stems from

[163] WHO, Report on the 'Global Tobacco Epidemic 2009'—Executive Summary 1, http://whqlibdoc.who.int/hq/2009/WHO_NMH_TFI_09.1_eng.pdf.

[164] European Committee of Social Rights (ECSR), 240th Session (7–11 December 2009), Conclusions: Georgia, Art 11.

[165] Tobacco Advertising Directive, above n 103, recital 18.

[166] Commission, Proposal on the approximation of the laws, regulations and administrative provisions of the Member States relating to the advertising and sponsorship of tobacco products, COM(2001)0283, recital 17.

the most fundamental rights.'[167] There is no specification here as to which fundamental rights are meant, but it is clear that 'advertising' cannot be seen as stemming from the right to health; rather, the reference to 'the most fundamental rights' would suggest that freedom of expression was alluded to here.[168] If one were to put the emphasis on the reference to 'economic activity', one could also think of the right to property and freedom to pursue a commercial activity. This suggestion would also seems to be in line with the Explanatory Note of the European Parliament Committee Report at first reading, providing: 'after amendment, the new proposal seems to cater for the other grounds of annulment endorsed by Advocate General Fennelly in his opinion, but not considered by the Court (proportionality, fundamental rights to property and to pursue a professional activity, freedom of expression, inadequate statement of reasons)'.[169]

In the new Tobacco Products Directive, fundamental rights language was already very prominently used at the pre-legislative stage and informed the entire legislative process. Health conceived as a fundamental right may have not been the only or the most prominent argument in these debates, but the fact that it featured as such and that it was advanced as a counter-argument to allegations of (other) fundamental rights violations is significant. The way in which it did feature in the legislative history of this proposal will be described in what follows.

The Commission's IA Report[170] states that 'particular attention was given to the Fundamental Rights Charter'[171] as required under the Commission Operational Guidance on Taking Account of Fundamental Rights in Impact Assessments.[172] More interestingly, in asserting the overall fundamental rights compliance of the IA Report's contents, it points out that it affects Articles 11, 16 and 17 CFR, but that the obligations imposed are necessary to improve the functioning of the internal market while ensuring a high level of health protection. Health is here not conceived as a fundamental right. This also becomes evident from the section of the report setting the overall context where health is presented as the mainstreaming obligation in Article 114(3) TFEU.[173] Similarly, the Report addresses early on the role of *public health* considerations: 'While all options identified seek to improve the functioning of the internal market, the protection of public health has played a key role in designing/shaping the policy options.'[174] In line with this, it uses 'health impacts' as one of the assessment categories, which is equally not conceived in fundamental rights terms.

Out of the fundamental rights listed as being affected, freedom of expression, does not receive any further reference and the right to health only one, while the freedom to conduct

[167] Explanatory Memorandum, ibid, s 7.1.

[168] The ECtHR has held that freedom of expression is 'one of the basic conditions for the progress of democratic societies and for the development of each individual'. See *Handyside v UK*, App No 5493/72 (ECtHR, 7 December 1976) [49].

[169] European Parliament, Report on the proposal for a Directive of the European Parliament and of the Council on the approximation of the laws, regulations and administrative provisions of the Member States relating to the advertising and sponsorship of tobacco products, A5-0344/2002 (COM(2001) 283—C5-0274/2001—2001/0119(COD)), Explanatory Note, Appraisal.

[170] TPD IA, above n 148.

[171] ibid 2.

[172] Commission Staff Working Paper, Operational Guidance on taking account of Fundamental Rights in Commission Impact Assessments (6 May 2011), SEC(2011)567 final.

[173] TPD IA, above n 148, 1.

[174] See, eg, TPD IA, above n 148, 48.

a business and even more the right to property seem to have received the most attention. An example for this can be found in the proposed policy options for regulating smokeless tobacco (STP), which are considered a proportionate limitation to the freedom to conduct a business, justified in order to protect public health.[175] Notably, the legitimate aim is not phrased as a fundamental right. By contrast, when evaluating the option of prohibiting cross-border distance sales of tobacco products, the report juxtaposes Article 16 CFR with Article 35 CFR, even if not very prominently.[176] Apparently this is the only real reference to health as a fundamental right in the IA Report.

The right to property and, more specifically, intellectual property and trademarks becomes relevant for regulating packaging and labelling under the TPD. This has already been clear since the *BAT* case.[177] In the specific context, this fundamental right is relevant for the plain packaging debate. Plain packaging is 'standardised colour, font, size and position of brand name and brand variant on packages'[178] and is recommended under the FCTC.[179] Plain packaging or 'standardised packaging' was envisaged as a possible policy option in the IA. The IA Report addresses the possible intellectual property implications; however, it is not featured in any of the IA categories, but curiously in a separate section entitled 'The view of stakeholders', although also here without a Charter reference.[180] The tobacco interest groups raised the fundamental right to property and intellectual property very forcefully in their responses to the public consultation—unsurprisingly so, as the same argument has already taken a central position in the debates and challenges (in national constitutional law and international trade law) surrounding the introduction of the first law on plain packaging in Australia.[181] Plain packaging was eventually rejected as a policy option in the IA Report. However, the reasons offered at the IA stage of 'comparing the options' are not

[175] ibid 76.

[176] The juxtaposition is explicit with reference to the relevant Charter articles only in a footnote (fn 106), whereas the actual text speaks of 'the principles of health protection'. See TPD IA, above n 148, 106.

[177] Case C-491/01 *R v Secretary of State for Health ex parte British American Tobacco (Investments) Ltd and Imperial Tobacco Ltd* [2001] ECR I-11453 (hereinafter *BAT*).

[178] TPD IA, above n 148, 92.

[179] Guidelines for implementation of Article 11 of the WHO Framework Convention on Tobacco Control (Packaging and labelling of tobacco products), www.who.int/fctc/guidelines/article_11.pdf.

[180] TPD IA, above n 148, 95. Incidentally, this supports the point made in ch 3 for a separate fundamental rights IA category, as not all fundamental rights will easily fit the 'social impacts' category.

[181] The law (the Tobacco Plain Packaging Act 2011) was unsuccessfully challenged in front of the High Court of Australia (*JT Int'l l SA v Commonwealth* [2012] HCA 43 (Austl)) on the grounds of acquisition of property on unjust terms under the Australian Constitution. The case turned on the meaning of the term 'acquisition' and the claim failed essentially because the Act did not amount to acquisition of a proprietary benefit on behalf of the government. For a discussion, see MS Kennedy, 'Australia's Tobacco Plain Packaging Act: Convergence of Public Health and Global Trade' (2013) 39(2) *North Carolina Journal of International Law & Commercial Regulation* 591, 611 et seq. At the international level, Ukraine, the Dominican Republic and Honduras filed complaints with the WTO for alleged violations of TRIPS, TBT and GATT. For a discussion of plain packaging and international trade law, see, eg, S Frankel and D Gervais, 'Plain Packaging and the Interpretation of the TRIPS Agreement' (2013) 46(5) *Vanderbilt Journal of Transnational Law* 1149; M Davison, 'Plain Packaging and the TRIPS Agreement: A Response to Professor Gervais' (2013) 23 *Australian Intellectual Property Journal* 160; A Alemanno and E Bonadio, 'Do You Mind My Smoking? Plain Packaging of Cigarettes under the TRIPS Agreement' (2011) 10 *John Marshall Review of Intellectual Property Law* 450.

expressly linked to fundamental rights considerations.[182] The chosen option was preferred because: 'It addresses in particular the concerns of the tobacco industry as it leaves a certain space on the package for manufacturers to display their trademark.'[183] Interestingly, shortly after the TPD's entry into force, Ireland notified the Council[184] and the Commission[185] of plans to introduce standardised plain packaging of tobacco products. At the time of writing, the Bill has been halted in the legislative process (second stage) due to the standstill period relating to the notification procedure. The UK[186] and France[187] have followed suit.

Indeed, stakeholders seem to have played a key role in this legislative process. As already stated above, the stakeholder consultation[188] had an unprecedented turnout, and its evaluation must have constituted a challenge.[189] According to the Commission's report, the topic of consumer information/tobacco labelling and hence plain packaging was the most controversial one, generating the most responses.[190]

The Member States were in general in favour of improving consumer information, but plain packaging was contentious. Half of the Member States supported its introduction, alongside other changes, while a minority wanted the maintenance of existing regulation and was strongly against plain packaging.[191] Predictably, the NGOs were divided on the issue according to affiliation. The public health organisations supported the proposed changes on consumer information/labelling and endorsed plain packaging, while smokers' rights groups opposed it.[192] As regards the industry representatives,[193] again predictably, the tobacco and cigar industry was opposed to almost the entire spectrum of proposed changes. Other industry representatives pointed to the danger of increasing illicit tobacco trafficking and the pharmaceutical industry advocated better consumer information.[194] Notably, the citizens responding to this consultation were 'largely in favour of maintaining the status quo'.[195]

[182] The report instead points out that plain packaging 'would reduce the possibilities for brand differentiation, in particular affecting high margin/premium brands and impact more negatively on revenues/profits due to the drop in consumption'. See TPD IA, above n 148, 95.

[183] TPD IA, above n 148, 96.

[184] Notification in accordance with Directive 98/34/EC of the European Parliament and of the Council of 22 June 1998 laying down a procedure for the provision of information in the field of technical standards and regulations [1998] OJ L204/37; and Council Document, 'Employment, Social Policy, Health and Consumer Affairs' (12 June 2014), ST 10876/14.

[185] Commission, Notification Details, 'Public Health (Standardised Packaging of Tobacco) Bill 2014' (UK), http://ec.europa.eu/enterprise/tris/en/search/?trisaction=search.detail&year=2014&num=277.

[186] Commission, Notification Details, 'The Standardised Packaging of Tobacco Product Regulations' (Ireland), http://ec.europa.eu/enterprise/tris/en/search/?trisaction=search.detail&year=2014&num=427.

[187] Ministère des Affaires Sociales de la Santé et des Droits des Femmes, Programme National de Réduction du Tabagisme (25 September 2014), www.sante.gouv.fr/IMG/pdf/250914_-_Dossier_de_Presse_-_PNRT_2_.pdf.

[188] Commission, Public consultation on the possible revision of the Tobacco Products Directive 2001/37/EC, http://ec.europa.eu/health/tobacco/consultations/tobacco_cons_01_en.htm.

[189] Commission, Report on the public consultation on the possible revision of Tobacco Products Directive 2001/37/EC (July 2011), http://ec.europa.eu/health/tobacco/docs/consultation_report_en.pdf, 22 ('The experience gained with the management of the large volume of response will help shape how future consultations of this nature can be effectively and efficiently carried out') (hereinafter 'Commission Report Public Consultation TPD 2011').

[190] ibid 13.

[191] ibid 13.

[192] ibid 14.

[193] ibid 15.

[194] ibid.

[195] ibid.

When conducting a simple key term search of the submitted responses of NGOs and industry within the materials that could be searched,[196] it becomes evident that those opposing stricter regulation of the manufacture, presentation and sale of tobacco products, and especially plain packaging, used the right to property, intellectual property and trademarks as well as the right to engage freely in an economic activity as strong arguments, while also linking these (even if not always) to the fundamental rights discourse (generically termed as fundamental property rights and less often linked to the ECHR). Another fundamental rights argument used against stricter regulation was that of commercial free speech, but it does not feature as prominently as the above-mentioned rights.

Obviously, those advocating tobacco control used the protection of health as a strong counter-argument, but they generally conceptualised it as *public health*. They also linked it to the WHO FCTC (discussed further below). At least within the (admittedly limited) materials searched, health was only exceptionally linked to fundamental rights.

Given this pre-legislative background and especially the IA Report, it may be unsurprising that the Commission's proposal included a fundamental rights recital, which echoes its preparatory work (the public consultation and the IA Report):

> The proposal affects several fundamental rights as laid down in the Charter of Fundamental Rights of the European Union, notably the protection of personal data (Art 8), the freedom of expression and information (Art 11), freedom of economic operators to conduct business (Art 16), and the right to property (Art 17). The obligations imposed on manufacturers, importers and distributors of tobacco products are *necessary to improve the functioning of the internal market while ensuring a high level of health and consumer protection* as set out in Articles 35 and 38 of the Charter of Fundamental Rights of the European Union. The application of this Directive should respect the EU law and relevant international obligations. (emphasis added)[197]

Interestingly, the final piece of legislation includes a fundamental rights recital, which takes a different form:

> The obligation to respect the fundamental rights and legal principles enshrined in the Charter of Fundamental Rights of the European Union is not changed by this Directive. Several fundamental rights are affected by this Directive. It is therefore necessary to ensure that the obligations imposed on manufacturers, importers and distributors of tobacco and related products *not only guarantee a high level of health and consumer protection, but also protect all other fundamental rights* and are proportionate with respect to the smooth functioning of the internal market. The application of this Directive should respect Union law and relevant international obligations. (emphasis added)[198]

At first glance, the two formulations seem very similar, but a closer look suggests that a different emphasis is placed on the right to health, with health assuming a more prominent role in the final version. The recital of the Commission proposal starts off by identifying Articles 8, 11, 16 and 17 as fundamental rights that this proposal 'affects'; these fundamental

[196] It should be noted that this type of search is only partially indicative as not all submissions were in English. The submission of respondents who identified themselves as affiliated to government authorities (note that this self-identification was not verified by Directorate General Health and Consumers) could not be searched for key terms as they were submitted in the original country of origin language and no translation was available at the time of writing.

[197] Commission, Proposal for a Tobacco Products Directive, above n 131, recital 45.

[198] Tobacco Products Directive, above n 103, recital 59.

rights constitute the starting point; it then continues by explaining that the obligations the proposal imposes (ie, the interference) are necessary in order to improve the functioning of the internal market while also ensuring a high level of health and consumer protection. Reference is here made to Articles 35 and 38 CFR, but is understood as standing next to the internal market as legitimate interests justifying restrictions to the other listed fundamental rights.

The language of recital 59 TPD, on the other hand, does not suggest that a specific fundamental right is taken as a starting point. Moreover, health and consumer protection are the only fundamental rights singled out specifically. Recital 59 states that several fundamental rights are affected and therefore it draws attention to the necessity that a high level of health and consumer protection are guaranteed *next to all other fundamental rights.*

The final wording of recital 59 was agreed at the fifth trialogue meeting.[199] However, change happened incrementally. The European Parliament amendment changed the logic of the penultimate sentence construing health as a mainstreaming obligation along the lines of Article 114(3) TFEU.[200] The Council introduced the more general first sentence that the Directive does not change the obligation to ensure respect for EU fundamental rights[201] and the deletion of Articles 8, 11, 16 and 17 CFR as fundamental rights affected by the legislation occurred at the trialogue stage.

The fact that the European Parliament was concerned with giving a more prominent role to health in the Preamble can also be discerned from another of its proposed amendments. In its draft legislative resolution, it proposed a separate recital pointing to the obligation that Member States should respect Articles 7(b) and 12 ICESCR on the rights for safe and healthy working conditions and the right of everyone to the enjoyment of the highest attainable standard of physical and mental health.[202] Interestingly, reference was made to Article 37 CFR on environmental protection and not to Article 35 CFR. This is curious given that the provisions of the ICESCR cited are expressly concerned with health—the link to environmental health is obviously there, but it is not clear why Article 37 CFR was preferred as a reference over Article 35 CFR.

The Opinion of the Committee on the Internal Market and Consumer Protection (IMCO) had its own perspective on the same issue. Like ENVI, it proposed inclusion of

[199] Council, Proposal for a Directive concerning the manufacture, presentation and sale of tobacco and related products—Analysis of the final compromise text with a view to an agreement (17 December 2013) (first reading), ST 17727/2013 INIT, Interinstitutional file: 2013/0366(COD), Legislative deliberation.

[200] European Parliament, Report on the proposal for a directive of the European Parliament and of the Council on the approximation of the laws, regulations and administrative provisions of the Member States concerning the manufacture, presentation and sale of tobacco and related products, A7-0276/2013, COM(2012)0788—C7-0420/2012—2012/0366(COD)), amendments adopted by the European Parliament on 8 October 2013, amendment 43, proposal for recital 45.

[201] Council of the European Union, ST 11483/2013 INIT and ST 11483/2013 COR 1 (24 June 2013), Interinstitutional File 2012/0366(COD), Proposal for a Directive concerning the manufacture, presentation and sale of tobacco and related products (first reading)—General Approach; and Council of the European Union (13 December 2013), ST 17506/13, Interinstitutional File 2012/0366(COD), Proposal for a Directive concerning the manufacture, presentation and sale of tobacco and related products (first reading)—Preparation for the informal trialogue, Legislative deliberation.

[202] European Parliament Report A7-0276/2013, above n 201, Draft Legislative Resolution, amendment 44, inclusion of new recital 45(a).

Articles 7(b) and ICESCR in the Commission fundamental rights recital,[203] but it also added next to Article 38 CFR a reference to Article 35 CFR on consumer protection. However, this may not be surprising, given the nature of the Committee, whose mandate also specifically includes consumer protection. In this case, these considerations were again sifted out of the legislative text.

The Committee on Legal Affairs (JURI) is of course the one Committee that would naturally be expected to adopt a fundamental rights perspective, and so it did in this context. But it was not concerned with the fundamental right to health; rather, it was concerned that 'some provisions in the Commission's proposal also raise serious doubts as to their conformity with fundamental rights, such as the right to property, the right to freedom of expression and information and the freedom to conduct business'.[204]

JURI contended that the proposal contains several measures that are problematic from an intellectual property rights perspective, but it especially took issue with the Commission's proposal to increase the size of health warnings to 75 per cent.[205] It asserted that this was a disproportionate restriction to Article 17 CFR and was problematic in light of national constitutional law as well as international treaties such as TRIPS, for two reasons: first, trademarks would be deprived of one of their main functions because there would not be enough space available for information that would distinguish products of different producers; second, trademarks could also not fulfil other functions such as advertising. JURI therefore suggested setting the size of health warnings at 50 per cent, which would still be in line with the FCTC. The final TPD eventually set the size at 65 per cent.[206]

The Committee also found the labelling measures problematic, and linked the issue to Article 11 CFR and the right to receive and impart information. It noted that: 'Manufacturers must be able to communicate that a certain product is less harmful than others if this is scientifically proven and if it is not misleading.'[207] In a similar fashion, it proposed the deletion of what is now Article 13(c) TPD (prohibition of references to taste, smell, flavourings or other additives or the absence thereof)[208] because 'customers should not be deprived of information about the product as long as it is not misleading'.[209] Notably, JURI's opinion was not followed in the final instrument, which preserved the originally proposed position.

A final objection of JURI concerned a provision prohibiting nicotine-containing products (like e-cigarettes) if they are not authorised by the Medicinal Products Directive.[210] The problem was that it is not clear whether these products fell within the Medicinal Products Directive at all and the implications for the products that do not was a ban. JURI noted that this was not in line with *public health* objectives of the proposal because it involved banning

[203] ibid, Opinion of the Committee on the Internal Market and Consumer Protection for the Committee on the Environment, Public Health and Food Safety (20 June 2013), amendment 22, recital 45.

[204] ibid, Opinion of the Committee on Legal Affairs for the Committee on the Environment, Public Health and Food Safety (25 June 2013).

[205] Commission Proposal for a Tobacco Products Directive, above n 131, Art 9(1)(c).

[206] See Tobacco Products Directive, above n 103, Art 10(1)(c).

[207] Opinion of the Committee on Legal Affairs for the Committee on the Environment, Public Health and Food Safety (25 June 2013), above n 204.

[208] European Parliament Report A7-0276/2013, above n 200, Opinion of the Committee on Legal Affairs, Amendment 45, proposed deletion of Art 12(c) Commission Proposal TPD.

[209] ibid.

[210] Directive relating to Medicinal Products, above n 95.

products that are less harmful than tobacco products and that could also be conducive to quitting smoking. The entire draft provision was deleted at the draft legislative report stage[211] and the TPD makes clear that e-cigarettes are regulated by that Directive unless they are subject to the Medicinal Products Directive.[212] However, the important point is that, here again, health was not linked to fundamental rights.

The above discussion has demonstrated that health as a fundamental right featured in the legislative history of this instrument from the very outset—even if it did not receive the most ambitious treatment. Yet the bigger point still remains that in the context of EU tobacco control legislation, this seems to be the first time that the obligations imposed by the legislation are linked to health as a fundamental right, and therefore could be said to mark a shift.

In searching for the reasons explaining the general absence of linking health and fundamental rights in the EU's tobacco control measures and its first appearance in the latest TPD, it may be useful to look at the FCTC and (the reasons for) its conceptualisation.

The FCTC provides for obligations relating to the regulation of fields with respect to which the EU had adopted measures before the Convention was even adopted (among others and for our purposes relevant: advertising, labelling and information, contents of tobacco products and taxation policies). It is noteworthy that this text also does not phrase the obligations provided for therein in fundamental human rights terms, although the link to the right to health, to women's rights and to children's rights is expressly acknowledged in the Preamble.[213] Melissa Crow has investigated the reasons for this omission, interestingly noting that the use of human rights references was actually discussed at different points of treaty negotiation.[214] Specifically, the possibility was debated to include a paragraph on the right to health in the Preamble or in the main text of the Convention and noting that: 'Due account should be taken of human rights issues.'[215] Even more interestingly, she found the following reasons for such omission (but not excluding that there may have been also others):

> [1] the absence of lack of involvement of organizations with experience in rights-based approaches in the negotiations, [2] the public health community's relative unfamiliarity with international human rights law, [3] the controversial status of the right to health under international law, and [4] the competing concerns of many governments involved in the negotiations about retaining certain sovereign rights.[216]

[211] European Parliament Report A7-0276/2013, above n 200.

[212] Tobacco Products Directive, above n 103, recital 36 and Art 20(1).

[213] Recalling the preamble to the Constitution of the WHO 'which states that the enjoyment of the highest attainable standard of health is one of the fundamental rights of every human being without distinction of race, religion, political belief, economic or social condition', and referring to the Convention on the Elimination of all forms of Discrimination against Women (CEDAW) Convention, and to the Convention on the Rights of the Child (CRC). Also noted by C Dresler and S Marks, 'The Emerging Human Right to Tobacco Control' (2006) 28 *Human Rights Quarterly* 599, 646, and ME Crow, 'Smokescreens and State Responsibility: Using Human Rights Strategies to Promote Global Tobacco Control' (2004) 29 *Yale Journal of International Law* 209, 222.

[214] Crow, ibid, 222, fn 78.

[215] Crow, ibid, referring to the 'Proposed Draft Elements for a WHO Framework Convention on Tobacco Control: Provisional Texts with Comments of the Working Group', Intergovernmental Negotiating Body and the WHO Framework Convention on Tobacco Control, 1sts Sess, Provisional Agenda Item 8, 5 and 16, WHO Doc A/FCTC/INB1/2 (2000).

[216] Crow, ibid, with reference to a telephone interview conducted with Allyn Taylor, Adjunct Professor, University of Maryland Law School, Former Senior Legal Advisor to WHO Tobacco Free initiative.

These three reasons could indeed also be of some explanatory value for the way in which the EU has approached tobacco control regulation.

First, as regards the participants and the question who was/is typically involved in the law-making process and what their experience is in adopting rights-based approaches we can observe the following: at the Commission level, the Directorate General responsible for putting forward the proposals was the Directorate General Health and Consumers, with the exception of Directive 2010/12/EU, the responsible Directorate General for which was the Directorate General Taxation and Customs Union. The Commission has traditionally not viewed economic legislation from the fundamental rights lens, and the same appears to be true for health legislation (which has an internal market legal basis). At the European Parliament, the committees responsible for the legislation were: for the Tobacco Advertising Directive (No 2), the Committee on Legal Affairs (JURI) and the Internal Market and Consumer Protection (IMCO) with the associated Committee on the Environment, Public Health and Food Safety (ENVI); for the latest Tobacco Product Directive, the ENVI Committee; and for the Tobacco Taxation Directive, the Committee on Economic and Monetary Affairs (ECON). None of these Committees would typically frame these issues in fundamental rights terms, so that the lack of such conceptualisation may not be very surprising. In the case of the TPD, the fact that both the responsible Committee (ENVI) and IMCO linked health to fundamental rights may be evidence for an emerging shift towards adopting a fundamental rights culture (compare discussion in chapter three) outside the obvious institutional fora (here the Committee on Civil Liberties, Justice and Home Affairs (LIBE)).

Second, when having regard to the stakeholders participating in public consultations, a similar picture emerges as regards the link between type of actors and the type of contributions. This emerges from both the Public Consultation preceding the TPD (hereinafter the 'TPD Consultation') discussed above and the Public Consultation on smoke-free environments (hereinafter the 'SFE Consultation').[217] The latter was launched as a result of the Green Paper, 'Towards a Europe Free from Tobacco Smoke: Policy Options at EU Level',[218] which was aimed at assessing 'the best way to tackle smoking in the EU'.[219] Even though this consultation is not linked to the instruments discussed, it is still useful in helping to identify general trends regarding the types and perceptions of stakeholders involved in tobacco control policies. This is especially so given the difficulty of evaluating and discerning real trends from the TPD Consultation.[220]

[217] Contributions to the consultation by 306 stakeholers, http://ec.europa.eu/health/tobacco/law/free_environments/free_environments_consultation/index_en.htm.

[218] Commission, Green Paper 'Towards a Europe Free from Tobacco Smoke: Policy Options at EU Level', COM(2007) 0027.

[219] ibid, 3.

[220] This is so due to the sheer amount of responses and the attempt by some stakeholders to 'flood' the consultation (see nn 126 and 127 above). See also Commission Report Public Consultation TPD 2011, above n 190 Executive Summary, 2: ('It is difficult to draw firm conclusions from the outcome of the public consultation procedure. In general, opinions varied significantly between and also within categories of respondents. Arguments provided by respondents in the 'free text' sections of the consultation present a variety of different justifications for policy action.')

The first observation to be made concerns the types of participants: no human rights NGO participated in the TPD Consultation or the SFE Consultation. This is in line with the general observation of the special rapporteur for the right to health (Hunt) finding that human rights NGOs do not have the right to health high on their advocacy agenda—if at all.[221]

The second observation concerns the substantive contributions of the participants. As regards the SFE Consultation, only a very minor number of health-related organisations showed their awareness of fundamental rights implications. Next to the specific questions as to which concrete policy option the stakeholders preferred,[222] the consultation questionnaire also inquired into whether there are 'any further quantitative or qualitative data on the health, social or economic impact of smoke-free policies which should be taken into account'.[223] In asking for qualitative and/or quantitative data, the question aims in essence at relevant sources of information. It is interesting to see that out of 80 health-related organisations,[224] only four (all of which based in Finland)[225] answered to this the following: the human right to the highest possible standards of health and the right to a healthy environment, as stated in the Constitution of the World Health Organization, the Convention on the Rights of the Child, the Convention on the Elimination of all Forms of Discrimination Against Women and the Covenant on Economic, Social and Cultural Rights, should be taken into account. It is also noteworthy that none of them made reference to EU sources or national constitutional law on the right to health. Similarly, in the TPD Consultation we find only two health-related NGOs that point to the right of all people to the highest attainable standard of health and these are Finland-based.

With respect to the contributions of national, regional and local authorities and national parliaments in the SFE Consultation, the picture becomes even more homogeneous. Most contributions came from national health ministries, and none of them linked tobacco control policies to fundamental rights. None of them made statements to the effect that health policies are a specific form of a fundamental rights policy or that it is a policy with fundamental rights implications. Similarly, in the TPD Consultation we find most responses under the 'heading' Governments and Ministries of EU Member States to be originating from national health ministries, and none of them linked health to fundamental rights. This may not be surprising. As again Hunt has put it, the reason is that 'Health professionals run the key international health organisations, as well as ministries of health across the globe … [however] … most health professionals whom the Special Rapporteur meets have not even heard of the right to health. If they have heard of it, they usually have no idea what it means, either conceptually or operationally'.[226]

[221] P Hunt, 'The Health and Human Rights Movement: Progress and Obstacles' (2008) 15 *Journal of Law and Medicine* 714, 720. See also Report of the Special Rapporteur on the right of everyone to the enjoyment of the highest attainable standard of physical and mental health, Implementation of General Assembly Resolution 60/251 of 15 March 2006 entitled 'Human Rights Council', A/HRC/4/28 (17 January 2007), www.unfpa.org/derechos/documents/PaulHunt07_en_000.pdf.

[222] Should there be a total or partial ban on smoking in all enclosed public spaces and working places; should there be legally binding or non-binding measures.

[223] This question can be found in the returned contributions of the Stakeholders to the SFE Consultation, above n 216.

[224] Health NGOs, scientific institutions, professional organisations, pharmaceutical industry.

[225] ASH Finland, Cancer Society of Finland, Finnish Heart Association, Pulmonary Association Heli.

[226] Hunt, above n 221, 722.

Third, the controversial status of the right to health under international law holds true as a possible explanation for lack of reference to it also for our purposes, and its ambiguous status under EU law should be added to that. With respect to international law, it has been observed that the difficulties relate to its unclear scope and normative meaning, the problems of implementation and justiciability.[227] In EU law, similar problems arise when trying to define the content of the right to health for reasons that have been already pointed out above: the reference back to national law in the first sentence of Article 35 CFR; the non-justiciable mainstreaming obligation in the second sentence, which we find replicated in Article 168 TFEU and Article 9 TFEU and specifically for the internal market also in Article 114(3) TFEU; finally, scarce judicial reference to and pronouncements on the scope and content of this right.[228] However, the cautious approach of the Court also constitutes an opportunity for the institutions to proactively embrace the rights concept and fill in the void—an opportunity which barely has been made use of.[229] The TPD seems to signal a first new approach.

Of course—and this links to the fourth point—the fact that the Charter refers to national law and practices has to do with the fact that health is an area that Member States are keen to keep within their own sphere of competence, at least to the extent that legislative harmonisation interferes with resource-allocative decision-making.

b. The Potential Significance of a Fundamental Rights Conception

Regulation in Line with International and Regional Fundamental Human Rights Standards

When having regard to the ESC observations cited above, it immediately becomes clear that the EU measures are in line with the type of 'prevention policy' foreseen by the ESC.[230] The same is true for the international right to health in General Comment No 14, whereby 'the failure to discourage production, marketing and consumption of tobacco' is considered a violation of that right.[231] Even though not framed as a fundamental rights policy, the standard dictated by fundamental rights is—intentionally or not—observed by the EU regulatory regime to the extent that there is a legal competence to take action.

[227] See among many, A Hendriks, 'The Right to Health in National and International Jurisprudence' (1998) 5 *European Journal of Health Law* 389.

[228] The Court has already referred to Art 35 CFR, but with respect to the mainstreaming obligation (2nd sentence). See Joined Cases C-570/07 and 571/07 *José Manuel Blanco Pérez and Chao Gómez* [2010] ECR I-9047, para 65, and the Advocate General Opinion in Case C-137/09, *Marc Michel Josemans v Burgemeester van Maastricht* [2010] ECR I-13019, point 26; see also Advocate General Opinion in Case C-249/04 *Novo Nordisk AS v Ravimiamet*, [2011] ECR I-3155, point 49 deriving a mandatory obligation to protect public health in order to 'guarantee the fundamental rights, human dignity, the right to life and the right to physical and mental integrity referred to in Articles 1 to 3 of the Charter', but citing also Art 35 CFR as one of the 'relevant' fundamental rights.

[229] One exception: Commission, Communication on 'Solidarity in Health: Reducing Health Inequalities in the EU' (20 October 2009), COM(2009) 567 final, SEC(2009) 1396, SEC(2009) 1397.

[230] ECSR Conclusions 2009, above n 164. It should be added that the policies are in line with the ESC to the extent that the EU has competence to adopt such measures. For example, the prohibition of advertising on posters as foreseen by the ECSR, even though attempted by the first Tobacco Advertising Directive, exceeded EU competence. See UN Committee on Economic, Social and Cultural Rights, General Comment No 14 (2000), 'The Right to the Highest Attainable Standard of Health', UN Doc E/C.12/2000/4 (2000).

[231] UN Committee on ESCR, Comment No 14 (ibid).

Added Value in Linking Tobacco Control to Fundamental Human Rights: Social and Political Mobilisation

It has been established above that the application of fundamental rights language could be conducive to social mobilisation influencing or bringing about regulatory change, although it has to be said from the outset that legislative intervention is only one among several other methods (eg, school-based education, media campaigns and clinical interventions)[232] for tackling the tobacco problem.

In speaking about added value here, one question is whether fundamental rights language served to *initiate* that process. However, the answer is in the negative. At the EU level, high-ranking health professionals (cancer experts and doctors) provided the real trigger for initiating and developing action. As already noted above, the tobacco legislative regime is a direct result of the EAC programme. This came about, after the Chernobyl catastrophe, because of 'political pressure from influential cancer experts on at least two Heads of State of the larger Member States',[233] as well as 'the recommendations of an expert committee'.[234] And doctors continued to play the pivotal role in developing the EAC's strategies (this group carried all the tactical use of funding, the gathering of data and the dissemination of new knowledge).[235]

Another question is whether fundamental rights language did actually lead to different outcomes in the substance of the legal regime. It is clear that up until the TPD, the fundamental right to health had not played any role *during* the legislative process. It is also clear that the right to health featured the legislative process of the TPD, but it seems that intellectual property rights framed as fundamental rights played a far more important role in shaping the substance than health conceived as a fundamental right. Of course, the concept of *public health* was crucial in advancing the instrument as its legislative history demonstrates.

In the US context (and interestingly by the (anti-)tobacco movement itself), it has been noted that human rights arguments should be used alongside other means 'to achieve desired social change'[236] more generally and with regard to tobacco control specifically, and that *sole* reliance on fundamental rights language may even be detrimental to a given movement.

This leads to the further argument that needs to be made: the fact that the importation of fundamental rights language may not only serve to make a political difference for those furthering the cause of protecting health through tobacco control, but also for those on the other side: the tobacco companies. The language of fundamental rights can thus be 'co-opted'[237] or, to put it in more neutral and generally valid terms, little is to be gained

[232] Novotny and Mamudu, above n 121.

[233] Trubek et al, above n 108, 814, with reference to A Gilmore and M McKee, 'Tobacco Control Policy in the European Union' in E-A Feldman and R Bayer (eds), *Unfiltered: Conflicts over Tobacco Policy and Public Health* (Cambridge, MA, Harvard University Press, 2004), 224. The names listed are: Professor M Tubiana persuading President F Mitterand and Professor U Varonese influencing Prime Minister B Craxi.

[234] Trubek et al, above n 108.

[235] ibid 814–17.

[236] PD Jacobson and A Banerjee, 'Social Movements and Human Rights Rhetoric in Tobacco Control' (2005) 14 *Tobacco Control* ii45, ii48.

[237] PD Jacobson and S Soliman, 'Co-opting the Health and Human Rights Movement' (2002) 30 *Journal of Law, Medicine & Ethics* 705.

(politically) through the use of fundamental rights language if both sides to a debate can have recourse to it.

The US experience demonstrates how successful the tobacco industry has been in doing so, especially in a setting where individual civil rights (as opposed to collective rights) are afforded stronger protection or are placed in a superior position, such as the American case.[238] The advancement of arguments about rights of individual freedom, property rights and equal treatment for those pursuing personal social behavioural choices like smoking has successfully changed the terms of the tobacco control debate in some US states, 'allow[ing] the industry to enact legislation favourable to its own interest'[239] and, as a result: 'Public health advocates had a hard time reframing the issue in terms of protecting the community.'[240]

In the EU no such infiltration influencing the legislative process in this way occurred until the TPD. However, a fundamental rights argument *was* advanced during litigation by the party *opposing* tobacco control legislation. The argument was not made by the tobacco industry, but by Germany, which sought judicial review and annulment of the first[241] and also the second Tobacco Advertising Directive 2003/33/EC.[242,243] In *Tobacco Advertising II* (discussed in chapters two and five), at least at first sight, rights language seems to have made a legal difference in putting the legislator in a defensive position. Germany argued that two provisions of the Directive[244] infringed freedom of expression, which, it was argued, 'is ensured [in EU law and under the ECHR] in particular, from the point of view of the financing of press products, by advertising revenue and unimpeded commercial communication'.[245] The structure of this conflict under the ECHR, which is followed by the Court of Justice of the EU, is the following: 'freedom of expression, including commercial expression [see discussion in chapter five] enjoys protection as a fundamental right, but may also be subject to certain limitations justified by objectives in the public interest'.[246] The 'protection of health' is an expressly acknowledged ground of derogation/legitimate aim in Article 10(2) ECHR, but it is clear that this is an asymmetrical relationship, putting

[238] ibid.

[239] ibid 708, with reference to PD Jacobson, J Wasserman, and KR Raube, 'The Politics of Anti-smoking Legislation: Lessons from Six States' (1993) 18 *Journal of Health Politics, Policy and Law* 787.

[240] Jacobson and Soliman, above n 237.

[241] TVWF Directive, above n 102.

[242] Directive 2003/33/EC, above n 102.

[243] Case C-380/03 *Germany v Parliament and Council* [2006] ECR I–11573 [129] et seq [hereinafter *Tobacco Advertising II*].

[244] Directive 2003/33/EC, above n 102, Art 3 (prohibiting advertising in printed media and information society services, except for those intended exclusively for professionals in the tobacco trade and those which are printed and published in third countries, where those publications are not principally intended for the Community market) and Art 4 (prohibiting all forms of radio advertising for tobacco products and sponsorship).

[245] *Tobacco Advertising II*, above n 243 [131].

[246] In line with Art 10(2) ECHR, these have to be in accordance with the law, motivated by one or more legitimate aims in the provision and necessary in a democratic society. See ibid [154]. See also previous case law of the Court of Justice of the EU: Case C-368/95 *Vereinigte Familiapress Zeitungverlag- und Vertriebs GmbH v Heinrich Bauer Verlag* [1997] ECR I–3689 [26]; Case C-60/00 *Mary Carpenter v Secretary of State for the Home Department* [2002] ECR I–6279 [42]; Case C-112/00 *Eugen Schmidberger Internationale Transporte und Planzüge v Republic of Austria* [2003] ECR I–5659 [79]; and Case C-71/02 *Herbert Karner Industrie-Auktionen GmbH v Troostwijk GmbH* [2004] ECR I-3025 [50].

the onus of proof on the legislature to establish a proportionate intervention in order to protect health, which is not framed as a fundamental right.[247]

In this case, the Court had no difficulty to uphold the legislative intervention aimed to protect health, for three reasons: first, the wide discretion granted to the EU legislature when complex assessments in relation to political, economic and social choices are to be made;[248] second, the obligation resting on the EU legislature to ensure a high level of human health protection;[249] finally, the fact that under the ECHR and followed by the Court of Justice of the EU,[250] states are granted a wide margin of appreciation when commercial expression is at issue. Thus, the seemingly 'defensive position' of the legislature for the judicial review proceedings is outweighed by two important moves of the Court: deference to the legislative process and taking seriously the health mainstreaming obligation, whose use is here not only one of shaping legislation but also of impacting on the standard of review.

In the TPD context, we certainly find the tobacco-friendly NGOs and the tobacco industry using individual freedom, the right to property, freedom of expression as well as the freedom to conduct a business as strong fundamental rights arguments opposing strict regulation. Moreover, the Commission and the European Parliament Legal Service advanced the same arguments, which demonstrate their salient role in this legislative process. Recourse to fundamental rights language did not come here (either on the side of the stakeholders or the institutions) in response to health advocates building the health and fundamental rights nexus. As discussed above, this was certainly still very much under-represented as a tool used by health advocates at the pre-legislative stage of the proposal. One could speculate that the reverse might be true, namely, that the health and fundamental rights link entered the debates as a response to the fundamental rights arguments opposing regulation.

C. Patient Mobility: Directive 2011/24/EU on the Application of Patients' Rights in Cross-Border Healthcare[251]

i. The Motives for Market Intervention

Directive 2011/24/EU is one of the most strongly debated pieces of legislation to emerge in recent years in the EU internal market regulatory landscape. The stated aim of the Directive is to facilitate access to safe and high-quality cross-border healthcare and to promote cooperation on healthcare between Member States.[252] In addition, it aims to clarify its relationship with the existing regulatory framework on the coordination of social security systems as regards the application of patients' rights.[253]

[247] An ECHR example where freedom of expression was unsuccessfully pleaded by an anti-smoking association which was prohibited to use certain words and a picture in an anti-smoking publicity: *Österreichische Schutzgemeinschaft für Nichtraucher and Robert Rockenbauer v Austria*, App No 17200/91 (European Commission of Human Rights, 1991).

[248] *Tobacco Advertising II*, above n 243 [145].

[249] ibid [147].

[250] ibid [155]; *Karner*, above n 246 [51].

[251] Directive 2011/24/EU of the European Parliament and of the Council of 9 March 2011 on the application of patients' rights in cross-border healthcare [2011] OJ L88/45 [hereinafter 'Patient Mobility Directive'].

[252] ibid, para 1.

[253] ibid.

When investigating into the motives for market intervention, 'clarification' appears to be the key word. The language of the Commission's proposal,[254] as well as its IA,[255] makes this obvious. The reason why clarity was needed is explained by the original genesis of the proposal. It was triggered by a very active Court in the application of the free movement provisions relating to (health) services, evolving in parallel to the regulative regime on the coordination of social security systems under Regulation 883/2004.[256] The Patient Mobility Directive is in fact a prime example of legislative harmonisation being directly triggered by the process of negative market integration. The landmark cases in the area were *Kohll*[257] and *Decker*,[258] followed by *Smits and Peerbooms*,[259] *Müller-Fauré/Van Riet*,[260] *Watts*[261] and *Commission v France*.[262]

Even though the Commission made a point of stressing that 'The Court's ruling on the individual cases ... are clear in themselves and no pre-condition may be required for the exercise of the rights of patients recognised by the Court',[263] it still acknowledged that it was concerned with improving legal certainty and clarity regarding cross-border care.[264] This was to be achieved in order to ensure 'a more general and effective application of the freedoms to receive and provide health services'.[265]

It is a fact that the internal market in health services was not working. The Commission came to this finding in a 2003 report[266] on the basis of information provided by the Member States.[267] The general appraisal was that Member States do not have a common understanding of the Court's case law on the matter and consequently also draw different conclusions regarding reimbursement of treatment undergone in another Member State. The report further found that the Court's case law is to a large part incompletely or incorrectly implemented.

[254] Commission, Proposal for a Directive on the application of patient's rights in cross-border health care (2 July 2008), COM(2008) 414 final 2 [hereinafter 'Commission Proposal Patient Mobility Directive'].

[255] Commission staff working document—Accompanying document to the proposal for a Directive of the European Parliament and of the Council on the application of patients' rights in cross-border healthcare—Impact assessment (COM(2008) 414 final), SEC(2008) 2164.

[256] Regulation EC (No) 883/2004 on the coordination of social security systems [2004] OJ L200/1.

[257] Case C-158/96 *Raymond Kohll v Union des caisses de maladie* [1998] ECR I-1931.

[258] Case C-120/95 *Nicolas Decker v Caisse de maladie des employés privés* [1998] ECR I-1831.

[259] Case C-157/99 *BSM Geraets-Smits v Stichting Ziekenfonds VGZ and HTM Peerbooms v Stichting CZ Groep Zorgverzekeringen* [2001] ECR I-5473.

[260] Case C-385/99 *VG Müller-Fauré v Onderlinge Waarborgmaatschappij OZ Zorgverzekeringen UA and EEM van Riet v Onderlinge Waarborgmaatschappij ZAO Zorgverzekeringen* [2003] ECR I-4509.

[261] Case C-372/04 *R (on the Application of Yvonne Watts) v Bedford Primary Care Trust and Secretary of State for Health* [2006] ECR I-4325.

[262] Case C-512/08 *Commission v France* [2010] ECR I-8833.

[263] Commission Proposal, Patient Mobility Directive, above n 254, 6.

[264] ibid, 1.

[265] ibid.

[266] Commission Staff Working Paper, Report on the Application of Internal Market Rules to Health Services: Implementation by the Member States of the Court's Jurisprudence (28 July 2003), SEC (2003) 900, discussed by W Sauter, 'The Proposed Patient Mobility Directive and the Reform of Cross-Border Healthcare in the EU', TILEC Discussion Paper No 2008-034 (September 2008), 31 et seq.

[267] Provided during the consultation process on the follow-up by the Member States to the Court's jurisprudence relating to reimbursement of medical expenses incurred in another Member State.

The matter was initially to be addressed in the abandoned 'Bolkenstein Directive proposal', but was later taken out of the horizontal Services Directive.[268] Following this, the Council and the European Parliament specifically requested a sectoral proposal from the Commission. After a lengthy consultation and preparation period, the Commission adopted its proposal in 2008. The draft had to go through two readings at the European Parliament and heated debates before it was finally adopted in 2011—more than a decade after discussions on the topic had commenced. The matter has been so delicate because 'one of the traditional functions of the welfare State, the organization of care policy, finds itself under the influence of EU [internal market] law'.[269]

In summary, the Directive provides for basic rules aimed at achieving three main goals:[270]

— First, it sets out to clarify the rights of mobile patients by setting out rules on the reimbursement of costs of cross-border healthcare in order to facilitate access to it: 1) the Member State of affiliation will be responsible for reimbursement up to the level of costs that would have been assumed by the Member State of affiliation had the healthcare been provided in its territory without exceeding the actual costs of healthcare received. This is so unless Regulation 883/2004 is applicable as set out in the Directive;[271] 2) the Member State of affiliation will determine the healthcare for which an insured person is entitled and the level of assumption of those costs;[272] 3) the Member State shall not make the reimbursement of costs of cross-border healthcare subject to prior authorisation except in cases set out in the Directive;[273] In general, rules on reimbursement may be limited based on overriding requirements in the public interest (as set out in the Directive).
— Second, it aims at ensuring access to high-quality and safe cross-border healthcare.[274] This is the point at which the Directive provides for some added value to the case law.[275] It requires Member States to ensure the common principles of EU health systems[276] and, to that end, includes obligations relating to the provision of information to patients, transparent complaints procedures, systems of professional liability, data protection etc.
— Third, the Directive aims at furthering European cooperation between healthcare systems.

[268] Directive 2006/123/EC of the European Parliament and of the Council of 12 December 2006 on services in the internal market [2006] OJ L376/36 [hereinafter 'Services Directive'].

[269] S de la Rosa, 'The Directive on Cross-border Healthcare or the Art of Codifying Complex Case Law' (2012) 49 *Common Market Law Review* 15, 17.

[270] See Services Directive, above n 269 Art 1 on subject matter and scope. See also A Vassiliou, 'Patients' Rights in Cross-border Healthcare' in B Rangoni Machiavelli and F Velo (eds), Healthcare Policy and Fundamental Rights in Europe—Conference Proceedings (2008), 7–17. For a detailed analysis of the Directive, see de la Rosa, above n 269.

[271] Patient Mobility Directive, above n 251, Art 7(4).

[272] ibid, Art 7(3).

[273] ibid, Art 7(8).

[274] See in particular ibid, Art 4.

[275] See W Palm and R Baeten, 'The Quality and Safety Paradox in the Patients' Rights Directive' (2011) 21 *European Journal of Public Health* 272.

[276] As set out in the Council, Conclusions on Common Values and Principles in European Union Health Systems OJ [2006] C 146/1. These principles are at the basis: universality, access to good quality care, equity and solidarity.

There is a separate point worth noting with regard to the motives for regulative intervention. It concerns the following contradiction already pointed out by some commentators. One the one hand, a case had to be made for the *need* of legislation regulating access to cross-border healthcare. It had to be established that either a significant number of patients are already moving across borders to access healthcare or that they will do so in the future. The IA rejects the former case, but supports the latter: 'the extent of crossborder healthcare is growing, and is likely to continue to grow in the future'.[277] On the other hand, if there are in fact major flows of moving patients, they will also have major impacts on national healthcare systems, which means that derogations from the rule of no prior authorisation requirement (or, from the perspective of the Member State of treatment, the rule of equal treatment of patients) will increasingly have to be justified, thus frustrating the entire regime.[278]

The question that thus arises is 'why bother' with regulation?[279] Part of the answer has already been provided: because the Court's case law had to be clarified and made visible to EU patients in order to build the internal market in healthcare services. The other part of the answer relates to opportunism. As Sauter has pointed out, part of the intention might be to go 'the first step on the road toward creating further incentives for greater efficiency in healthcare, setting in motion a process that will be difficult to stop'.[280] A kind of 'indirect harmonisation' might be achieved in this respect if it is true that certain healthcare systems will be more able to support the new regime than others.

ii. The Fundamental Rights Dimension

a. Can the Legislation be Conceived in Fundamental Rights Terms? Has it been so Conceived?

Viewed from a fundamental rights perspective, the Directive on the Application of Patients' Rights in Cross-border Healthcare regulates access to healthcare (Art 11(1) (rev)ESC), but only in cross-border situations. The same obligation of allowing everyone access to healthcare is enshrined in Article 35 CFR, although 'under the conditions established by *national* laws and practices'. How does this relate to the content of the Directive? Evidently, the instrument interferes with the national conditions for accessing healthcare in cross-border situations, most obviously by establishing the general rule of prohibiting prior authorisation (albeit with exceptions). The reason why the EU can interfere in this field is a situation discussed already in chapter five with regard to the Audiovisual Media Services Directive The fundamental rights coincides with the internal market freedom. Here specifically, the fundamental right to access healthcare coincides in a cross-border situation with the

[277] Commission Staff Working Document—Accompanying document to the Proposal for a Directive on the application of patients' rights in cross-border healthcare, Summary of the Impact Assessment, SEC(2008)2164, 2. Although, considering the very low numbers to begin with (780,000 extra patients receive treatment), it is still questionable whether a strong case for intervention has been established.

[278] This point has been noted by Sauter, above n 266, 37, with reference to C Barnard, 'Between a Rock and a Soft Place: Internal Market v Open Coordination in EU Social Welfare Law' in M Dougan and E Spaventa (eds), *Social Welfare and EU Law* (Oxford, Hart Publishing, 2005).

[279] Barnard, ibid.

[280] Sauter, above n 266, 38.

freedom to receive a service. Internal market rules thus bring the matter within the competence of the EU, something that is permissible under the Charter.[281] Therefore, the first sentence of Article 35 is relevant in conceptualising the substantive aim of the Directive of allowing patients to access cross-border healthcare[282] in fundamental rights terms, but not in seeking an answer as to who should be regulating the matter (the EU or Member States) within the limited field of cross-border healthcare.

The final version of the instrument does not contain any reference to Article 35 CFR, nor is there any indication that it has been conceptualised in terms of the fundamental right to health, but is built on the free movement on services rationale.

However, the Directive does acknowledge respect for other fundamental rights in its Preamble like data protection[283] and equal treatment.[284] The documentation of the legislative process reveals that the initial Commission proposal[285] also included next to the general Charter compatibility statement the sentence that: 'The right of access to healthcare and the right to benefit from medical treatment under conditions established by national law and practices are recognised by Article 35 of the Charter of Fundamental Rights of the European Union.' It is not obvious what the motives were for removing this recital. Yet, given the above observations, it could be suggested that the reference to 'national laws and practices' contained in that Article might have been considered as unnecessarily misleading in this context.

By contrast, the mainstreaming obligation contained in the second sentence of Article 35 CFR forms the opening recital of the Directive—only that not the Charter, but the identical wording of Article 168(1) TFEU is referred to. However, given that mainstreaming is not a fundamental right, but a method for realising fundamental rights and other legitimate interests by taking them as objectives in policies into account (see the discussion in chapter three), a reference to it via the Charter would not have made a substantial contribution to conceptualising the instrument in fundamental rights terms.

Interestingly enough, this mainstreaming obligation was falsely used in the early Opinion of the Committee for Economic and Monetary Affairs, which stated:

> Pursuant to Article 35 of the Charter of Fundamental Rights of the European Union and Article 152(1) of the EC Treaty, *Member States* must ensure a high level of health protection. At present the health services on offer vary substantially between Member States. This situation should be further developed and preserved with high standards of quality. (emphasis added)[286]

Neither Article 168 (1) TFEU (ex Art 152(1) EC) nor Article 35 CFR requires Member States to ensure 'a high level of health protection'; rather, *the EU* shall ensure this aim in the implementation and definition of its policies. The focus was perhaps on Member States at that stage of the proposal given that it imposed on them a particular obligation to 'define

[281] See Art 51(2) CFR: 'the Charter does not modify powers and tasks as defined in the treaties'.

[282] See Vassiliou, above n 270, 10: 'The overall aim of the proposal is to provide patients with better opportunities and access to healthcare, regardless of their place of residence while, at the same time, fully respecting national responsibilities for healthcare.

[283] Patient Mobility Directive, above n 251, recital 25.

[284] ibid, recital 13.

[285] Commission Proposal Patient Mobility Directive, above n 254.

[286] European Parliament, Opinion of the Committee for Economic and Monetary Affairs (10 March 2009), A6-0233/2009, Rapporteur: Harald Etti.

clear quality and safety standards for healthcare provided on their territory' and to have monitoring as well as sanctioning mechanisms in place for achieving these standards.[287] At the same time it was acknowledged that: 'The Member States of treatment shall be responsible for the organisation and the delivery of healthcare.'[288] However, this obligation did not survive the final text of the Directive[289] in view of strong objections from the Member States on competence grounds.[290]

b. The Potential Significance of a Fundamental Rights Conception

The Directive's Compliance with Regional Fundamental Human Rights Standards

As we have seen above, the ESC requires from its contracting parties to have a healthcare system in place that is accessible *to the entire population*. In assessing this obligation, the ECSR also takes into account Council of Europe Parliamentary Assembly Recommendation 1626 (2003) on 'reform of health care systems in Europe: reconciling equity, quality and efficiency', which places emphasis on 'effective access to healthcare for all, without discrimination'.[291]

In considering the Directive's compliance with this standard, the division of tasks between the EU and the Member States has to be kept in mind. As noted, the EU level does not interfere with Member States' responsibility to have and to organise a functioning healthcare system that would endorse the principles of equity, quality and efficiency. It does however contribute to broadening the element of non-discrimination. Whereas that would only be applicable within the jurisdiction of a particular Member State under the ESC, EU internal market law makes this obligation applicable for the moving patient when he or she is moving between Member States. It is important to note here that the moving patient does not have to be an EU citizen. The definition of 'patient' under the Directive instead applies to 'any natural person who seeks to receive or receives healthcare in a Member State'.[292] This is in line with the fundamental rights requirement that the right of people to access healthcare 'must be determined on the basis of their humanity, not their status'.[293] However, the equal treatment obligation in the Directive does not require that everybody accessing or seeking to access healthcare *within* a Member State receive equal treatment (for example, irregular migrants in many cases do not receive the same treatment as citizens and regular

[287] Commission Proposal Patient Mobility Directive, above n 254, Art 5(1).

[288] ibid.

[289] All that is provided on quality and safety is, according to Art 4(1) of the Patient Mobility Directive, that: 'cross-border healthcare shall be provided in accordance with … (a) the legislation of the Member State (b) standards and guidelines on quality and safety laid down by the Member State of treatment (c) Union legislation on safety standards'.

[290] Palm and Baeten, above n 275, 273.

[291] European Committee of Social Rights, Conclusions 2005, Statement of Interpretation on Article 11, para 5, 10.

[292] Patient Mobility Directive, above n 251, Art 3(h) and 3(b) ('insured persons are defined under the Directive as "persons, including members of their families and their survivors, who are covered by Art 2 of Regulation (EC) No 883/2004 and who are insured persons within the meaning of Art 1(c) of that Regulation' and 'nationals of a third country who are covered by Regulation (EC) No 859/2003 or Regulation (EU) No 1231/2010, or who satisfy the conditions of the legislation of the Member State of affiliation for entitlement to benefits').

[293] T Hervey, 'The "Right to Health" in EU Law' in T Hervey and J Kenner (eds), *Economic and Social Rights under the EU Charter of Fundamental Rights* (Oxford, Hart Publishing, 2003) 197.

migrants),[294] which rests within the Member State's competence, but it requires the principle to be applied to patients coming from other Member States[295] and with regard to the rules applicable to the reimbursement of costs for the Member State of affiliation.

The Directive can also be seen as enhancing patients' *accessing rights* because of the broadening of the geographical scope within which healthcare can be accessed. In doing so, it enables individuals to access rights they would be deprived of were they confined to the geographical reach of their own Member State. Take as a concrete example the situation of waiting times and waiting lists in the UK. The ESC has stated that 'the organisation of healthcare in the United Kingdom is manifestly not adapted to ensure the right to health for everyone'.[296] An individual who is prevented from accessing healthcare because he or she is put on such a waiting list in one county nonetheless has accessing rights in another country (and cannot be subject to prior authorisation if certain conditions are met).[297] This of course does not mean that the Member State's (here the UK's) obligations under the ESC, and perhaps also under the first sentence of Article 35 CFR[298] are discharged. The European Parliament Committee on Economic and Monetary Affairs at first reading of the Directive seemed to be alert about this point.[299] However, it does mean that the individual's rights can be fulfilled nonetheless.

Added Value of Adopting a Fundamental Rights Conceptualisation: Emphasising the Collective Dimension of the Right to Health?

The elaborations above have demonstrated that the Directive on patients' rights to cross-border healthcare can be seen as an instrument that enhances the fundamental right to health. However, what becomes also immediately obvious is that it enhances only a particular dimension of that right, namely, the individual as opposed to the collective one. This is unsurprising given that the Directive is in essence a market-making instrument that aims to establish the same level-playing field for all service receivers (patients) and service providers (doctors, hospitals etc) in cross-border healthcare.

The collective dimension of the right to access healthcare would correspond to what is construed in the Directive as a 'public health' exception to the free movement rule. The focus shifts here from the individual, who should have 'clear and effective rights', be 'empower[ed] and [have] access [to healthcare]', as well as 'choice[s] and opportunities',[300] to the community. For our purposes, 'community' has two meanings in this context: the 'Member

[294] See FRA Report, 'Migrants in an Irregular Situation: Access to Healthcare in 10 European Union Member States' (2011), http://fra.europa.eu/fraWebsite/attachments/FRA-2011-fundamental-rights for irregular-migrants-healthcare_EN.pdf.

[295] Patient Mobility Directive, above n 251, Art 4(3).

[296] ECSR Conclusions XV-2, United Kingdom, 599. Note that the ECSR did not pronounce here a violation of Art 11(1) ESC yet, but sought further information on the way waiting lists are managed.

[297] As set out in Art 8(5) of the Patient Mobility Directive, codifying the Court's pronouncements in *Watts*, above n 261, [68].

[298] See Hervey, above n 293, 208. Hervey argues that this would be the case *if* the findings of the ECSR can be extended to the substantive content of Art 35 CFR.

[299] European Parliament, Opinion Committee for Economic and Monetary Affairs, above n 286: 'The possibility of cross-border health care must not encourage individual Member States to cease to develop their health institutions, nor should it provide an incentive for them to promote treatment abroad.'

[300] Vassiliou, above n 270.

State level community' and the 'EU level community'. The community at the Member State level has a right to have a functioning healthcare system in place (with a view to improving health in that community). The Directive affords consideration to this through the provisions allowing Member States to derogate from the no-prior-authorisation rule (directed to the Member State of affiliation) and the equal treatment rule (directed to the Member State of treatment), for reasons related to ensuring sufficient and permanent access to healthcare within the Member State.[301] However, competence constraints prevent the EU from going further and regulating that collective dimension. As we have already seen, the matter is so sensitive that Member States already rejected the mere obligation to define clear quality and safety standards for the delivery of healthcare on that ground. Promoting the collective dimension of the right to health for the 'EU level community' (for example, by aiming to reduce health inequalities within the EU) would fail on the same ground. Because of the competence structure and the political status quo, it seems that there would have been no meaningful role, at least under the current circumstances, for a fundamental rights conceptualisation of the Directive in terms of creating both legal obligations and political incentives for giving more emphasis on the collective dimension of the right to health.

IV. CONCLUSION

The starting point of this chapter has been that the protection of health is a non-market value enjoying a very high rank among those pursued through internal market legislation—something that is also reflected in the number of existing instruments in this area.

These instruments can be differentiated based on their market-making or market-correcting nature. The EU legislature has intervened both in order to avoid market effects that would undermine the protection of health (market-correcting policies) and in order to build a market, thereby incidentally protecting health (market-making policies).

The three examples of harmonisation practice discussed represent each of the two categories (market-making or market-correcting) and one that has overlapping features. The inquiry focused on the actual and potential conceptualisation of 'health' in these instruments, distinguishing between the notions of 'public health' and 'the fundamental human right to health'. It also tested the identified advantages (section II.B) of a fundamental rights approach to the right to health.

The inquiry led to the following findings:

1) Up until the latest Tobacco Products Directive, none of the discussed instruments had been conceived in fundamental rights terms. This was so irrespective of their market-making or market-correcting nature; it was also more generally true beyond the examples discussed. In the TPD, the link to health as a fundamental right was made, even if modestly, in the context of a debate where other fundamental rights (intellectual property, freedom to conduct a business and freedom of expression) were forcefully argued against strict tobacco control measures.

[301] Patient Mobility Directive, above n 251, Arts 4(3) and 7(9).

2) All of the discussed instruments can be conceptualised in fundamental rights terms. When doing so, it emerges that the market-correcting instrument (the Orphan Medicinal Products Regulation) is concerned with furthering the collective dimension of the right to health, whereas the market-making instrument (the Patient Mobility Directive) with the individual dimension of this right.
3) Those instruments that have not been conceptualised in fundamental rights terms were not in violation of regional human rights standards and, more specifically, those of the ESC, due to the absence of such conceptualisation—quite to the contrary in fact. However, with respect to the Orphan Medicinal Products Regulation, it has been demonstrated that the instrument could be further improved from an international as well as regional/national human rights perspective for achieving equal access to medicines. A fundamental or human rights approach to this instrument could have made a difference in this respect.
4) Despite the generally valid statement that a fundamental rights approach brings with it two concrete advantages (section II.B), in the instant cases their impact was or would have been limited.

As regards the potential of rights language for triggering social and political mobilisation, the example of EU tobacco control measures demonstrates that it was neither rights language nor human/fundamental rights advocates, but the targeted and organised efforts of cancer experts and health professionals that brought about regulatory change. However, the example of the TPD has shown that the (collective dimension of the) fundamental right to health can be advanced against individual fundamental rights arguments opposing regulation.

With respect to its potential for compelling policy-makers and legislators to realise the collective dimension of the right to health, the example of patient mobility has shown that such could not and cannot materialise in the instant case because of the EU's *limited competence* in the field of healthcare.

Finally, the strongest dimension of the right to health, its combination with non-discrimination, is to a large extent already guaranteed by virtue of the internal market freedoms, which are firmly based on that principle.

In conclusion, within the specific EU (internal market) context, so far there seems to have been little added value in linking health to fundamental rights. This might change if an environment is created where a proliferated use is made of fundamental rights arguments opposing health regulation.

8

Conclusions

I. HARMONISING FUNDAMENTAL RIGHTS PROTECTION THROUGH THE INTERNAL MARKET

THIS BOOK HAS placed the debate on the relationship between fundamental rights and economic freedoms in the positive integration process. At the beginning of the study stood the question of why it is important to pursue a fundamental rights policy that is specific to the internal market, and under what circumstances the institutions can do so.

We have established that the EU legislator not only has a competence to pursue fundamental rights protection through the internal market (chapter two), but also arguably a duty to do so[1] (chapter three). This can be seen as an opportunity not only to respond to but also to pre-empt clashes between the two interests arising in the negative integration process.

Once this is recognised, our focus can shift to an examination of the existing fundamental rights harmonisation practice based on the internal market. This book sought to tackle precisely that analysis. It examined internal market legislation in the area of four fundamental rights: data protection, freedom of expression, fundamental labour rights (fair and just working conditions and the right to take collective action) and the right to health.

II. EXISTING HARMONISATION PRACTICE

A review of internal market legislation through the lens of the said four rights or sets of rights leads to the following core findings: fundamental rights regulation pursued through the internal market exists, and it does so for a long time, but it is to a great extent not explicit or visible. This triggers the question of what factors drive not only the adoption of such regulation but also the kind of conceptualisation chosen by the legislator. Five determinants of the role of fundamental rights in internal market legislation emerge within the remits of this study. Finally, possible consequences flowing from employment (or not) of a fundamental rights conceptualisation are revealed. This is important for assessing the extent to which such choice matters for fundamental rights protection in and through internal market legislation.

[1] Such duty can be based on the mainstreaming obligation contained in the Charter: Art 51(1) provides that the EU institutions 'shall promote the application' of the rights contained in the Charter 'in accordance with their respective powers'.

A. Fundamental Rights Regulation: Existent but to a Great Extent not Explicit/Visible

The study has revealed the existence of a considerable amount of internal market legislation not merely incidentally impacting on fundamental rights but also having at its core the regulation/harmonisation of fundamental rights protection. This portfolio of laws did not—as might have been expected—emerge as a response to the millennium-era calls for a fundamental rights policy, but can be traced back to initiatives as early as the 1980s.[2] For the most part, such legislation is not expressly phrased in fundamental rights language. Only four exceptions to this general finding were identified.

First and most remarkable is the area of data protection, which met fundamental rights issues head on and expressly adopted fundamental rights language. The current regime is soon to be replaced by new legislation that will be based on a new and explicit legal basis for data protection introduced by the Lisbon Treaty[3] and placing the EU regulation on this issue beyond the internal market.[4] However, this is not a novel phenomenon: a similar evolution took place for social policy, which was initially pursued through the internal market (eg, the Collective Redundancies Directive[5] and the Acquired Rights Directive)[6] before it gained a distinct place in the Treaties with the entry into force of the Maastricht Treaty. It should be noted that this new legal basis for data protection carries over the influence of the internal market element in that it is also to be used for legislating on the rules relating to the free movement of data.

The second example of an instrument overtly concerned with a value linked to the fundamental right of freedom of expression would have been the (failed) Media Ownership Directive.[7] It emerged from our discussion (chapter five) that fundamental rights language in the title of the instrument was intentionally abandoned (the change from 'media pluralism' to 'media ownership regulation'), along with a shift in the nature of the regulation, moving away from the media pluralism objective. In that sense, the two draft versions reflect the two opposing camps in the negotiation process, which could not overcome their differences—leading to the initiative's abandonment altogether.

A further instrument expressly concerned with a fundamental right arose as a direct response to the controversial case law in *Viking*[8] and *Laval*[9]—the draft Monti II Regulation.[10]

[2] See, eg, Commission Green Paper, 'Television without Frontiers—Green Paper on the Establishment of the Common Market for Broadcasting, especially by Satellite and Cable', COM(84) 300 final (14 June 1984).

[3] Article 16 TFEU.

[4] See discussion of the proposed data protection package in ch 4.

[5] Council Directive 75/129/EEC of 17 February 1975 on the approximation of the laws of the Member States relating to collective redundancies [1975] OJ L48/29.

[6] Council Directive 77/187/EEC of 14 February 1977 on the approximation of the laws of the Member States relating to the safeguarding of employees' rights in the event of transfers of undertakings, business or parts of businesses [1977] OJ L61/26.

[7] Commission Proposal on 'Concentration and Pluralism in the Internal Market' as a follow-up to the Commission Green Paper on 'Pluralism and Media Concentration in the Internal Market: An Assessment of the Need for Communitarian Action', COM(92) 480 final (23 December 1992).

[8] Case C-438/05 *International Transport Workers' Federation and the Finnish Seamen's Union v Viking Line ABP and OU Viking Line Eesett* [2007] ECR I-0779.

[9] Case C-341/05 *Laval un Partneri Ltd v Svenska Byggnadsarbetareförbundet and others* [2007] ECR I-11767.

[10] Commission Proposal for a Council Regulation on the right to take collective action within the context of the freedom of establishment and the freedom to provide services, COM(2012) 130 final.

This initiative also fell at the Commission proposal stage. Once again, the opposition to the draft Regulation came from the national level, although this time from national parliaments, under the subsidiarity control mechanism. It is the first example of an instrument that received such a challenge (being 'yellow carded') and was withdrawn on that ground. This draft instrument is worth mentioning here despite the fact that it had Article 352 TFEU as a legal basis (and not an internal market provision), for the following reasons: 1) the internal market was arguably the only possible route for harmonisation in this area (chapter six); 2) the example demonstrates how difficult it might be for a response to or mitigation of court rulings via the legislative process to materialise. This is evidenced in the poor legislative drafting, which contained conflicting messages as to how the fundamental right at stake and the internal market freedoms were to be reconciled (chapter six). This is a reflection of the difficult negotiation process, leading to an inclusion of a variety of contradictory statements in the Preamble; 3) the instrument is also noteworthy as an example of fundamental social rights regulation (even though it deals with a 'negative' right from that category).

In contrast, certain current legislation, which directly impacts fundamental rights, is nevertheless not conceptualised as such. One example is the Audiovisual Media Services Directive (AVMSD), although its Preamble does acknowledge that the Directive 'enhances compliance with fundamental rights and is fully in line with … Article 11 [CFR]'.[11] Despite the fact that the internal market dimension is emphasised in the main body of the instrument, it is still interesting for this investigation because of its origins. The early Commission vision in the 1980s of this initiative[12] was that it would be an indispensable means for fostering the integration project and, in particular, the free democratic structure of the (then) European Communities. In reality, history has shown that the current Directive is more of a market liberalisation tool than anything else.

B. Determinants of the Role of Fundamental Rights in Internal Market Legislation

Whether or not fundamental rights protection will be pursued through the internal market and whether it will be done so explicitly depends on a series of determinants. In other (political science) words, it depends on the kind of 'agenda-setting' mechanisms operating in the field. 'Agenda-setting is about having an issue considered by policy-makers'[13] and is contingent on the strategies adopted by the policy actors involved at a given political moment in time. Evidently, it is also contingent on the institutional and constitutional context in which these actors operate. For our purposes, within these latter variables, we shall single out the interaction between the judiciary and the legislator given its relevance for this study. Finally, the subject matter at issue, meaning which right(s) is/are affected and not which policy is at issue, will also be considered as a separate feature.

[11] Directive 2010/13/EU of the European Parliament and of the Council of 10 May 2010 on the coordination of certain provisions laid down by law, regulation or administrative action in Member States concerning the provision of audiovisual media services (Audiovisual Media Services Directive) [2010] OJ L95/91, recital 16.

[12] See Commission Green Paper, above n 2.

[13] S Princen, 'Agenda-Setting Strategies in EU Policy Processes' (2011) 18 *Journal of European Public Policy* 927.

Thus, the determinants of the role of fundamental rights in internal market legislation will be divided into five categories: first, the political context; second, the constitutional context, namely, one of limited competence and that endorses a formally equal hierarchical relationship between market freedoms and fundamental rights; third, the incentives provided (and not provided) by court rulings in the negative integration process; fourth, the extent to which the institutional apparatus at the pre-legislative and legislative stage supports fundamental rights mainstreaming and fundamental rights conceptualisation of internal market legislation; and, finally, the type of right affected may have an influence on this process.

i. Political Context

The political context is an obvious (non-legal) determinant. It is well known that decision-making at the EU level involves the complex interaction of a large variety of actors from the national and European levels. This is no different for internal market legislation harmonising fundamental rights protection.

The question whether a certain matter will be included in the EU policy agenda and, if so, how depends on elements that apply in understanding EU policy-making. A list of driving motives, which occurred in the field of the present study, were as follows.

First, 'spillover(s) from other EU policies demanding a European solution'.[14] This book has postulated a simple starting point for the necessary analysis: the internal market's potential to impact on national fundamental rights standards may trigger the need for harmonisation of fundamental rights protection at the EU level.

Second, there may be a 'functional logic' for solving problems collectively.[15] This is especially relevant for the area of data protection, where the advent of new technologies, and especially the Internet, along with deeper market integration has transposed problems to the transnational level, overcoming national physical boundaries and thereby demanded a correlative response, as soon as the matter became a politically important issue at the national level (especially for the 'big' Member States). Given the obvious reciprocal relationship between data protection regulation and the market, and in the absence of a more specific legal basis until the Lisbon Treaty, the internal market route was an obvious choice (chapter four).

Third, domestic interest group pressures for regulation at the EU level have been a telling influence.[16] Here one should also add pressures on EU institutions exercised by pan-European networks and interest groups. This was the case for the Orphan Drugs Regulation[17] and for the EU tobacco control policies. The nature of stakeholders playing a key role in the placement of an item on the EU policy agenda will also be key in shaping the framing of these issues. Thus, in the area of health regulation, it emerged from this study that the

[14] ibid.

[15] I Bache and S George, *Politics in the European Union* (Oxford, Oxford University Press, 2006) ch 24, 'Policies and Policy-Making in the European Union', 355.

[16] ibid.

[17] Regulation (EC) No 141/2000 of the European Parliament and of the Council of 16 December 1999 on orphan medicinal products [2000] OJ L18/1.

advocacy groups involved were health specialists/health associations that do not typically frame issues in fundamental rights terms. This is predictably mirrored in most of the legislation, which does not link health to fundamental rights (chapter seven). In the recent Tobacco Product Directive (TPD2),[18] such a link was made modestly and, interestingly in a context where the opponents of regulation made strong use of fundamental rights arguments (eg, intellectual property, the freedom to conduct a business and freedom of expression), in order to challenge both the proposed and the eventually adopted legislation.[19]

A further factor is the receptiveness of the governments of Member States to 'European approaches to problems because it allows them to escape political unpopularity for the measures that are necessary'.[20] Such opportunism was not easily exercised by Member States governments within the field of this study. The instruments discussed replaced or sought to replace divergent national fundamental rights standards. However, such divergence may imply disagreement about the most fundamental national value judgments, which render the negotiation and adoption of a harmonisation measure at the EU level very difficult. One could predict that the draft Monti II Regulation would have encountered precisely that difficulty (had it passed the subsidiarity challenge posed by national parliaments), as some of the reasoned opinions by national parliaments indicate.[21] This difficulty is of course mitigated when there is already some common ground, which has been agreed through international cooperation outside the EU framework. The example of data protection, where the pre-existing Council of Europe Convention was closely followed by EU legislation, is a case in point.

Legislation may also be initiated at the EU level because one of the institutions advocates it. It is interesting to note that the two examples of failed internal market-fundamental rights legislation were exactly of such type, and fell through mainly because of Member State opposition. The draft Media Pluralism/Ownership Directive was adopted in response to repeated calls for action by the European Parliament. The initiative could not survive fierce disagreement among and within the institutions, but also importantly the opposition of Member States, which were, in turn, subject to powerful lobby groups. The draft Monti II Regulation, on the other hand, appeared to be the result of political campaigning on behalf of Commission President Barroso during his second pre-election period. The Commission was in fact not very insistent on this proposal, as was made clear by its decision to immediately withdraw the initiative when the 'yellow card' was raised by the national parliaments instead of attempting to re-draft it. In reality, this sort of practice would dramatically

[18] Directive 2014/40/EU of the European Parliament and of the Council of 3 April 2014 on the approximation of laws, regulations and administrative provisions on the manufacture, presentation and sale of tobacco and related products and repealing Directive 2001/37/EC [2014] OJ L127/1 (hereinafter 'TPD2').

[19] See discussion in ch 7, s III.B and ch 5, s IV.B.

[20] Bache and George, above n 15.

[21] Compare, for example, the UK reasoned opinion with that of Portugal. The former challenges supranational harmonisation on the ground of lacking evidence substantiating such necessity in a situation where the Court's judgment is arguably clear (as regards reconciliation of the right to strike with internal market freedoms)—a position that indicates endorsement of that judgment, whereas the latter provides that 'it is not uncommon for Portuguese constitutional law to accord greater legal value to social rights compared with economic rights' (at 5). The reasoned opinions are available on the Platform for Parliamentary Exchange IPEX: www.ipex.eu/IPEXL-WEB/result/simple.do?text=reasoned+opinion&start=.

reduce the difference between a 'yellow card' and a 'red card', since opposition at the first hurdle could be seen to kill Commission initiatives.

It is difficult to identify a fixed or exhaustive list of political variables. So, for example, the adoption of the Data Retention Directive[22] seems to have been the result of a 'particular political appropriation'[23] of events, together with a functional logic for collective problem-solving. This was perhaps combined with a sense that it might be more difficult to pursue a particular initiative at the national level. The challenges by national constitutional courts may evidence this.[24] Of course, the verdict of the Court of Justice of the EU (the Court) that the Directive was unlawful proves that the EU route was not easier as a matter of EU law, but rather as a matter of EU (and national) politics.

Having set out the policy drivers, it is important to point to factors that help us to understand why an item will or will not eventually make it on the agenda. In simplified terms, agenda-setting theory identifies three central processes: the problem definition or problem recognition stage; the stage where proposals for addressing the problem are put forward; and politics, including obvious factors like the political climate, changes in relevant offices etc. When all of these factors (or at least two out of three) coalesce during a critical and favourable moment, the item will be adopted. This moment is called a 'policy window' or a 'window of opportunity'.

Within this broad framework, policy actors can adopt strategies to push an item on or to take it off the agenda. Critical factors are the type of 'venues' (which policy-maker(s) and therefore which Commission Directorate General, European Parliament Committee, Council formation could be/is adopting a proposal) and the type of 'frames' (what language/conceptualisation/terms) chosen. These arguably stand in a correlative relationship: framing influences the venue, but the reverse is also true.

Seen in this light, the general finding above that most internal market legislation is not expressly conceptualised in fundamental rights terms may not be surprising. As an example, the Directorate General Internal Market is less likely to frame an issue in rights terms and, conversely, if a stakeholder chooses the Directorate General Internal Market as a 'venue', he, she or it will only succeed when the issue is properly framed in economic/market terms.

Framing legislation in market terms is of course also necessary for demonstrating that the legal basis requirements are satisfied.[25] Yet, it is important to point out that framing legislation in a way as to prove that its adoption is necessary for the establishment and functioning of the internal market does not preclude that the fundamental rights dimension is

[22] Data Retention Directive 2006/24/EC of the European Parliament and of the Council of 15 March 2006 on the retention of data generated or processed in connection with the provision of publicly available electronic communications services of public communications networks and amending Directive 2002/58/EC [2006] OJ L105/54.

[23] M De Goede, 'The Politics of Preemption and the War on Terror in Europe' (2008) 14 *European Journal of International Relations* 161, 171.

[24] Note that the only two Member States that voted against the measure in the Council were Ireland and Slovakia.

[25] Weatherill even argues that any type of legislation will pass the Court's legal basis test provided it is framed in a prescribed way, including key terms and phrases of tests laid down in the Court's legal basis case law. S Weatherill, 'The Limits of Legislative Harmonization Ten Years after *Tobacco Advertising*: How the Court's Case Law has Become a "Drafting Guide"' (2011) 12 *German Law Journal* 827. See also the discussion in ch 2.

also recognised. However, in purely policy strategy terms, that fundamental rights framing will not be so relevant in order to 'sell' it to the policy-makers. On the contrary, as we have seen above, such emphasis may even work to hinder adoption of the instrument, as, once again, the failed attempt to regulate media ownership demonstrates.

ii. The Sensitivity of Constitutional Context

A vital precondition for the pursuit of a fundamental rights policy will be satisfaction of the legal requirements for having recourse to the internal market legal basis. Even if the legislator enjoys wide discretion in making use of this legal basis, the 'market' threshold requirement will always have to be passed as prescribed by the Court's legal basis case law (chapter one). The example of media pluralism illustrates how such an argument can be instrumentalised in order to oppose harmonisation (chapter five), and the analysis of 'health as a fundamental right' (as opposed to health as a 'public policy') in the EU context has revealed that limited competence may help to explain the limited added-value of a fundamental rights approach in this area.

Once the legal basis requirements are satisfied, divergent national regulation can be harmonised in a manner that ensures a high level of fundamental rights protection.

In some instances however, such as the draft Monti II Regulation, harmonisation can also involve the difficult task of reconciling two values that appear to enjoy (at least formally) the same hierarchical rank in the Treaties. This is not only the case because both constitute primary EU law, but also because the internal market freedoms can be expressed in fundamental terms based on the provisions of the EU Charter of Fundamental Rights (the Charter).[26]

Formulating a legislative initiative as one involving the meeting of these two values or as one involving a 'clash of titans'[27] may slant the legislative process towards a difficult path of negotiation, as both interests will be claimed as equal 'heavyweights' by the opposing sides. Under such a conceptualisation, a 'quiet' technocratic approach to regulation seems almost impossible (see the example of media pluralism in chapter five). Moreover, in these circumstances, the adoption of clauses such as Article 2 of the draft Monti II Regulation, which aim to reconcile the conflicting interests and state nothing more (each value/right can be subject to a proportionate restriction in the interest of the other) might not be very surprising. At the same time, such outcomes are deeply unsatisfactory, as they severely limit the added value of legislative intervention.

[26] The free movement of workers, services and freedom of establishment are protected under Article 15 CFR, which reads: '1. Everyone has the right to engage in work and to pursue a freely chosen or accepted occupation. 2. Every citizen of the Union has the freedom to seek employment, to work, to exercise the right of establishment and to provide services in any Member State.' And free movement of goods could be read into Art 16 CFR on the freedom to conduct a business.

[27] The formulation was used by SA de Vries in 'The Protection of Fundamental Rights within Europe's Internal Market after Lisbon—An Endeavour for More Harmony' in SA De Vries et al, *The Protection of Fundamental Rights in the EU After Lisbon* (Oxford, Hart Publishing, 2013) 59.

iii. The Institutional Apparatus (Mainstreaming Fundamental Rights Through IAs and ex ante *Fundamental Rights Compatibility Assessments of Legislation)*

Once a political will is present and a legal basis is identified, policy strategists and legislative drafters will be called to the drafting board. It is evident that harmonisation practice is at first instance influenced by the operation of *ex ante* fundamental rights protection mechanisms during this policy definition and legislative drafting stage (chapter two). The first such mechanisms for systematic scrutiny—IAs and Charter compatibility assessments—were initiated by the Commission in 2001.[28] This study has shown that a robust and comprehensive fundamental rights culture inside the institutions had not been achieved up until Lisbon, although it has to be acknowledged that shifts in institutional cultures need time to materialise and are certainly dependent on incentives which make such shifts pressing. The incentives provided by the Lisbon Treaty (the legally binding Charter and the envisaged EU accession to the ECHR), the Commission's revived emphasis on this fundamental rights culture building process[29] and the recent expansion (through the introduction of new procedures)[30] of *ex ante* scrutiny to all institutions involved in lawmaking appear promising. At the same time, it is regrettable that the role of the Fundamental Rights Agency (FRA) in fundamental rights-proofing of legislation continues to be dependent on a request by one of the institutions. Arguably, when it comes to EU internal incentives, this is the one non-judicial mechanism which could have real teeth in ensuring fundamental rights protection and conceptualisation where necessary, as well as forcing a shift in mentality amongst law-makers, given its location outside the lawmaking institutions.

Until the fundamental culture fully materialises, its absence is arguably more likely to impact on legislation that is not obviously concerned with fundamental rights, such as internal market legislation.[31] This is the case because for the institutional actors involved (the relevant Directorate General, the European Parliament Committee and the Council Working Group), the fundamental rights implications in the formulation, negotiation and drafting of these instruments are more easily overlooked or disregarded. The type of actors involved account to a considerable extent for the broad absence of fundamental rights language in internal market legislation thus far. This can of course be mitigated through building systematic synergies with those actors that do already have the necessary 'fundamental rights-reflex' (Directorate General Justice, the Legal Services of the respective institutions, the FRA etc). A serious attempt is currently being made to enhance these synergies (eg, through inter-departmental cooperation but also increased involvement of the FRA)—it will be interesting to see how this will translate de facto in the legislative output.

[28] Decision on the Application of the Charter of Fundamental Rights of the European Union, SEC (2001) 380/3 as replaced by the Commission Communication, 'Compliance with the Charter of Fundamental Rights in Commission Legislative Proposals: Methodology for Systematic and Rigorous Monitoring', COM(2005)0172.

[29] Commission Communication, 'Strategy for the effective implementation of the Charter of Fundamental Rights by the European Union', COM(2010) 573/4 (19 October 2010).

[30] European Parliament, Rules of Procedure, 7th Parliamentary term (July 2010), Rule 36.

[31] As opposed to legislation from the Area of Freedom Security and Justice.

iv. The Incentives Provided by the Court

The presence or absence of negative integration in a given field can provide specific incentives for the legislator to act—to clarify and codify negative integration. The prime example for this is the Directive on the Application of Patients' Rights in Cross-border Healthcare.[32] When legislation is adopted as a direct response to negative integration, the legislator may often follow the Court's conceptualisation of a given non-market value, so it is not surprising that in this example the approach is one of 'public health', as employed by the Court as a legitimate ground of derogation from the free movement provisions. However, the early legislative history of the Posted Workers Directive demonstrates that this does not necessarily have to be so.[33] Despite the fact that the initiating case law[34] did not contain any fundamental rights language, the European Parliament attempted to conceive of the instrument as one implementing the Community Charter of Fundamental Social Rights of Workers. This conceptualisation did not survive until the final enacted version and it could be argued that its abandonment would have been more difficult had the Court conceived of the matter in fundamental rights terms.

In certain areas, the legislator may want to pre-empt Court-led integration or it may seek to mitigate certain rulings, such as the controversial *Viking-Laval* line of case law. However, chapter six has revealed that subsequent legislative attempts in the area reflect a concealed endorsement of the judicial decisions and do not suggest that the legislator has seized the opportunity to inform the integration debate.

However, there are also occasions where the legislator does take the lead in the *absence* of negative integration. Within the present study, data protection (chapter four), tobacco control measures (chapter seven) and commercial expression regulation (chapter five) fall within this category. The initiators of legislation (Member States, national and pan-European lobbying groups), as already mentioned above, are then the ones that will provide the framing of the instrument.

v. The Type of Right Affected

Three core findings emerge with respect to the relevance of the right in question.

First, as already noted, in areas where the fundamental right at stake coincides with a market freedom, the market freedom will be emphasised in the legislation, such as is the case for the AVMSD and the Patient Mobility Directive.

In other areas, where the right in question has not received an ambitious treatment in the case law, the approach of the legislators may also be one that ignores a possible fundamental rights dimension of the instrument. For instance, in the field of advertising (covering both rules that regulate content and content-neutral rules), internal market legislation is not

[32] Directive 2011/24 of the European Parliament and of the Council of 9 March 2011 on the application of patients' rights in cross-border healthcare [2011] OJ L88/45.

[33] See Commission Proposal for a Directive concerning the posting of workers in the framework of the provision of services, COM(91) 230 final—SYN 346 (1 August 1991).

[34] Case C-113/89 *Rush Portuguesa v Official National d'Immigration* [1990] ECR I-1417, ECLI:EU:C:1990:142.

phrased in terms of the fundamental freedom to *commercial* expression,[35] and the legislative history reveals that such a conceptualisation was largely absent[36] during the lawmaking process (chapter five). This may partly be explained by the institutional actors involved in drafting consumer legislation. However, a separate and specific reason linked to the type of right at issue may be the fact that both the ECtHR and the Court of Justice of the EU have (arguably justifiably) adopted a very deferential approach to State regulation of commercial expression. In the EU context specifically, the lack of substantive review of legislation and the seemingly automatic prevalence of the public interest (consumer protection and public health) over commercial expression begs the question of the criteria, which the legislator would have to take into account to ensure fundamental rights compliance in this field. Similarly, if the current approach is maintained, it is extremely difficult to contemplate circumstances where such legislation could be struck down for violating fundamental rights standards. Nevertheless, the relative lack of leadership from the legislator in fundamental rights conceptualisation suggests that (at least currently) this is largely a judge-led phenomenon.

Finally, the 'generation' of the right (civil and political as opposed to economic and social) may affect the process. Chapters six and seven revealed that legislation dealing with social rights is not conceptualised in fundamental rights terms (see, eg, the Posted Workers Directive, the draft Posted Workers Enforcement Directive[37] and health legislation). The one clear exception to this was the draft Monti II Regulation, which concerned the right to strike—a right that, according to the classic typology of negative rights or civil and political rights (those that require governments to abstain from interfering with them) and positive rights or economic and social rights (those that require positive action, progressive realisation and wealth re-distribution), would fall into the former category

However, there is obviously no difficulty in framing rights from the first (civil and political rights) category that require positive intervention in fundamental rights terms. This is the case for data protection legislation, which requires that independent data protection authorities are put in place.

C. Consequences of Adopting a Fundamental Rights Approach

The survey conducted above raises a number of important consequences for the legislative process and for substantive fundamental rights protection. To the extent that overarching conclusions can be drawn from areas that differ in terms of both interests involved and context, it is important to foresee the practical result of the adoption of the various models identified above. These will be considered below by focusing on the substantive content of legislation as well as on the potential impact on judicial review by the Court.

[35] Although the Tobacco Advertising Directive 2003/33/EC does refer to freedom of expression in its Preamble. See Directive 2003/33/EC of the European Parliament and of the Council of 26 May 2003 on the approximation of the laws, regulations and administrative provisions of the Member States relating to the advertising and sponsorship of tobacco products [2003] OJ L152/16.

[36] See TPD2, above n 18. TPD2 is one exception, although also here *commercial* expression is not expressly referred to, but it can be inferred from the wording used.

[37] Commission Proposal for a Directive on the Enforcement of Directive 96/71/EC concerning the posting of workers in framework of the provision of services, COM(2012) 131 final (21 March 2012).

i. The Absence of a Fundamental Rights Conceptualisation does not Necessarily Lead to a Violation of Fundamental Rights Standards in the Legislation

A perhaps counter-intuitive finding in the era of fundamental rights 'mainstreaming' is that the absence of a rights conceptualisation of given legislation as raising rights issues does not appear to correlate to violation of fundamental rights standards. This is reflected in the examples of advertising and health legislation and is true both for instruments that are of a positive (enabling) nature for fundamental rights policy-making as well as for those that are of a negative (constraining) nature.

Advertising regulation is in the latter category. As discussed above, compliance with fundamental rights standards is easily achieved in this area whether or not this dimension is taken into account, given the judicial 'hands-off' approach when it comes to restrictions of commercial expression.

Health legislation prohibiting tobacco advertising (Directive 2003/33/EC)[38] also falls within this category. The legislation can be framed both as restricting commercial expression and at the same time as protecting the right to health. Despite the instrument not being termed in the latter terms, it is still in compliance with both rights.[39]

The Patient Mobility Directive is yet another example of an instrument regulating fundamental rights that is not termed in fundamental rights terms. Here, a fundamental rights conceptualisation would add nothing, given that the relevant principle of non-discrimination—which plays a pivotal part in the Directive—is a cornerstone of the internal market in any event.

Compliance with fundamental rights standards also materialises for those health instruments that are positive in nature. The term 'positive' is here not used for characterising instruments with resource-allocative implications, but for those that nonetheless require positive intervention by the legislator. This category includes the Orphan Drugs Regulation (establishing market exclusivity for orphan drugs for a determined period and putting in place a central marketing authorisation system) as well as for most of the tobacco product regulations (those instruments regulating labeling, tar yield levels as well as the manufacture, presentation and sale of tobacco products). The potential of fundamental rights here would be to force Member States to adopt certain strategies rather than finding out what the best strategies are to control/eliminate tobacco consumption.

ii. A Fundamental Rights Conceptualisation may not Always Provide Added Value

Especially with regard to tobacco control measures, it is interesting to see that the legislator has pursued all the actions required in light of the ESC standard without having explicit regard to a human rights-based approach. The reason might be that this same standard is derived from tested public health strategies and scientific arguments, and not from fundamental rights considerations. In practice, therefore, fundamental rights may have little added substantive value.

[38] Tobacco Advertising Directive, above n 35.

[39] See ch 7, s III.B.

As concerns legislation regulating commercial expression, the legislator's decision to take the 'safe'[40] route of not adopting a fundamental rights approach has been explained above (section II.B.v). However, it can also be justified in light of the fact that commercial expression seems to stand on weak theoretical underpinnings,[41] and the justificatory rationale for protecting this form of speech through the fundamental rights angle has not been satisfactorily provided by the Court of Justice of the EU or the ECtHR.

One added value of fundamental rights language in the sphere of socio-economic rights is that it facilitates the mobilisation of civil society, thereby leading to upstream change and influencing policy and legislative processes. However, when taking the field of EU tobacco advertising regulation as a frame of reference, it emerges that it was the scientific argument rather than the fundamental rights argument that was driving the initiation of the policy process in the EU. The developments surrounding the TPD2[42] illustrate that fundamental rights arguments (relating to intellectual property, freedom to conduct a business and freedom of expression) can also be raised in order to oppose the same regulation that could be initiated by having recourse to another fundamental rights argument (the right to health).[43]

iii. The Correlation Between a Fundamental Rights Conceptualisation and a Higher Standard of Fundamental Rights Protection

Despite the difficulties in establishing general rules of causality based on specific examples taken in this study, this point is worth mentioning. It emerged, for instance, when investigating the legislative history of the Posted Workers Directive,[44] where the European Parliament amendments at first reading provided for an understanding of the instrument as one implementing the Community Charter of the Fundamental Social Rights of Workers (CCFSRW), which was eventually abandoned. This amendment came alongside other substantive amendments tabled by the European Parliament striving for a higher level of worker protection in the instrument than what was achieved in the final version.

iv. Is there any Impact on the Balancing of the Conflicting Interests?

The classic method for balancing competing interests in EU legislation is the proportionality test. One question that may be raised after this study is whether the presence or absence of a fundamental rights approach affects the balancing of the (fundamental) non-market value and the economic value in the legislation. It is clear that in the process of negative integration, there is a structural asymmetry between the two. The non-market value is always construed as a narrow exception to the free movement rule. This asymmetry seems

[40] *If* the current approach is to be maintained.

[41] See ch 5, ss III et seq.

[42] TPD2, above n 18.

[43] See ch 7, s III.B.

[44] Commission Proposal for a Directive concerning the posting of workers in the framework of the provision of services, COM(91) 230 final—SYN 346 (1 August 1991).

to be—to a certain extent—remedied by the *Schmidberger* formula,[45] although this was not applied in that manner in *Viking* and *Laval.*

The same is not true for positive integration. When the legislator pursues harmonisation based on the internal market, it has the freedom to choose the regulatory option to adopt. The instrument can be either of a market-making or of a market-correcting nature (chapter one). This is the case even if the internal market legal bases seem to be formulated in market-making terms. This is indeed where the value lies in achieving market integration via the legislative as opposed to the judicial route.

Whether or not legislation is expressly termed as one harmonising fundamental rights protection, the balance struck between the competing values in the instrument (and, more generally, the level of fundamental rights protection adopted) will also always have to be in compliance with fundamental rights standards, as that is a condition for the legality of EU acts. However, one advantage that explicit adoption of a rights approach may bring about is that the legislator's attention is drawn to such standards and to the relevant case law. It also increases transparency for and the awareness of the subjects affected by the legislation.

This brings us to the next point, which concerns judicial review of legislation. It is established case law that in the case of economic legislation, the legislator enjoys a wide discretion as to the means of approximation (the 'harmonisation technique') chosen for achieving the desired results.[46] Furthermore, as the Court has observed in *Vodafone*,[47] when reviewing the respect of the principle of proportionality[48]—codified in Article 5(4) TEU—when exercising its conferred powers, the EU legislature 'must be allowed a broad discretion in areas in which its action involves political, economic and social choices and in which it is called upon to undertake complex assessments and evaluations'.[49] At the same time, the legislator 'must base its choice on objective criteria'.[50] The applicable standard of review in these situations is that of whether 'the measure is *manifestly inappropriate* having regard to the objective which the competent institution is seeking to pursue' (emphasis added).[51]

This means that the standard of judicial review applied is not a strict one. However, if economic legislation is also conceptualised as fundamental rights legislation or as legislation impacting on fundamental rights, will that affect the standard of review employed by the Court?

[45] Case C-112/00 *Eugen Schmidberger Internationale Transporte und Planzüge v Republic of Austria* [2003] ECR I-5659 [74] ('the protection of those rights is a legitimate interest which, in principle, justifies a restriction of the obligations imposed by Community law, even under a fundamental freedom guaranteed by the Treaty such as the free movement of goods').

[46] Case C-217/04 *UK v Parliament and Council* [2006] ECR I-3771 [43]; Case C-66/04 *UK v Parliament and Council* [2005] ECR I-0000 [45].

[47] Case C-58/08 *R (on the Application of Vodafone Ltd and others) v Secretary of State for Business, Enterprise and Regulatory Reform* [2010] ECR I-4999 (with reference to previous case law).

[48] Requiring that 'measures implemented through Community [now EU] law provisions be appropriate for attaining the legitimate objectives pursued by the legislation at issue and must not go beyond what is necessary to achieve them'. See ibid [51].

[49] ibid [52]; Case C-380/03 *Germany v Parliament and Council (Tobacco Advertising II)* [2006] ECR I-11573 [145].

[50] ibid.

[51] ibid.

The discussion in chapter three[52] has shown that the Article 5(4) TFEU proportionality assessment also has to take into account fundamental rights compliance of legislation. This is because legislation that violates fundamental rights will also have to be considered 'manifestly inappropriate' to the objective pursued. The fundamental rights assessment should therefore be the starting point when applying the 'manifestly inappropriate test' to internal market legislation. How strict the proportionality test will be within the fundamental rights assessment will then depend on a number of variables, such as 'the area concerned, the nature of the right at issue guaranteed by the Charter, the nature and seriousness of the interference and the object pursued by the interference'.[53] In that respect, in *Digital Rights*, the Court has followed the ECtHR's approach.[54]

A different test is applied when the measure is perceived as one involving two conflicting fundamental rights. This is the situation when, on the one hand, limits on economic activity laid down by the legislation are construed as limits to a fundamental right, such as the freedom to conduct a business and, on the other hand, when the public policy aim driving such restriction is also construed in fundamental rights terms. In such situations, the Court will employ the 'striking a fair balance' test. This test will be remembered from the discussion on *Promusicae* (chapter four) on the interpretation of conflicting rights in legislation, but it is also employed in judicial review cases.[55]

An interesting question in this context is whether conceptualising the interest pursued by the legislation as one of public policy as opposed to a fundamental right makes any difference in terms of the level of review applied. Formally, the answer appears to be positive, as the test is re-framed as one of 'striking a fair balance' so that the public policy is elevated to the same level as the fundamental right invoked. However, it seems that at least for all those instances where the fundamentality of the right is not substantially different from the policy understanding of it by the Court and the legislator (or where the latter feeds into the understanding of the former), there will be no substantive impact on the level of judicial review applied.

III. FINAL CONCLUSION: DON'T JUDGE A BOOK BY ITS COVER

The conclusion of this study inexorably leads us to the observation that the obvious assumptions flowing not only from initial key observations but also from first findings of this research are in stark contrast to the position resulting from further investigation and a bird-eye's view on the collection of individual findings. Three points emerge in this regard.

First, the finding that a fundamental rights conceptualisation is largely absent in internal market legislation may have triggered a general assumption or suspicion that there is a 'fundamental rights deficit' in this legislative action. This deficit is to be understood as implying violations of fundamental rights standards in the legislation, that there is a lack

[52] In more detail, s III.A.ii.

[53] Joined Cases C-293/12 and C-594/12 *Digital Rights Ireland Ltd and Kärntner Landesregierund et al v Ireland* ECLI:EU:C:2014:238 [47].

[54] ibid.

[55] See, eg, Case C-544/10 *Deutsches Weintor eG v Land Rheinland Pfalz*, Judgment of 6 September 2012 (not yet reported).

of furtherance of those standards and that the adoption of a strong value-oriented internal market policy is not being incentivised.

The present study (within its remits) has painted a much more varied picture. It is, for example, striking to see that the instrument that was most clearly problematic from a fundamental rights perspective—the Data Retention Directive—was within the one area where fundamental rights find the most explicit recognition. One perhaps trite but important observation to be made in this respect is that political incentives can constitute a main challenge in this area, which cannot be counterbalanced by the attention drawn to fundamental rights standards through the use of fundamental rights language. Furthermore, the large absence of fundamental rights language in the health area might have prompted the adoption of low levels of health protection, but in fact the opposite is true. On the other hand, abandonment of a fundamental rights discourse has also proved to lead to lower levels of protection. As already stated above, this becomes obvious when juxtaposing the proposal for a Media Pluralism Directive to the draft Media Ownership Directive and also when comparing the Posted Workers draft at the European Parliament first reading stage with the final text, while in other areas, the added value and indeed the justification for adopting such an approach may be questionable (see the discussion on commercial expression in chapter five).

Second, at first sight, one might assume that the emergence of a variety of policy structures (a separate fundamental rights portfolio within the Commission with a Commissioner at its apex and the establishment of the FRA) would have contributed to dramatic changes in fundamental rights protection in the EU more generally and within the internal market specifically. This book did not focus on the general picture of the EU's fundamental rights policy. Nevertheless, based on the research conducted, some general observations can be made which have repercussions for fundamental rights-internal market policy and which rebut the above-mentioned assumption. For instance, both institutions could be seen as not meeting the initial expectations, when considering, for example, the hesitant moves of the Commission during the Roma crisis or the fact that the FRA is a much weaker body than was initially anticipated.[56] Furthermore, it is true that the *ex ante* fundamental rights scrutiny processes have received a revival and stronger emphasis. At the same time, it should be noted that the Commission's new 'methodology'[57] does not introduce any groundbreaking changes compared to the pre-existing scrutiny tools,[58] while the introduction of new procedures in the other institutions is notable. The advent of a true fundamental rights culture across the institutions still remains to be proven. Finally, despite all the emphasis on policy tools, it should not be overlooked that currently the most important incentives for bringing about *change* in the institutional culture seem to come on the one hand from the legally binding Charter and on the other hand from the envisaged EU accession to the ECHR.

As to future developments, it can be anticipated that more fundamental rights language will enter legislative instruments, and certainly that more legislation will be the object of

[56] Given that it has neither a monitoring role nor an unconstrained legislative scrutiny mandate.

[57] Commission Communication, above n 29.

[58] Although there are procedural novelties in the European Parliament and the Council of Ministers.

litigation on fundamental rights grounds[59] (be that on points of interpretation or validity challenges). The prognosis should therefore be that there is a substantially higher level of fundamental rights protection in and through (internal market) legislation still to come.

Notes of caution against over-enthusiasm are to be sounded on both points. The increased use of fundamental rights language in litigation could also serve to increasingly frame the conflicting interests at stake as conflicts between fundamental rights (the 'fundamental' market interest versus the 'fundamental' non-market interest), both for judicial review purposes and for the interpretation of legislation. Viewed against the critique of judicialisation[60] and (over-)employment of balancing exercises,[61] the de facto results achieved in such a process may not always be the most optimal. This is so when viewed from the perspective of achieving a proper law–politics balance[62] in fundamental rights protection, but also from the perspective of legal certainty and the harmonisation objective.[63] In addition, employing such a methodology may not always provide for added value, as we have seen above.

With respect to the increased use of fundamental rights references in the legislation, even though recent developments appear promising, it still remains to be seen whether that will go beyond a strengthened 'lip service' exercise.[64] As this research has demonstrated, fundamental rights language in pre-legislative and legislative documentation is not always indicative of the degree to which such considerations were actually taken seriously into account during the lawmaking process. In fact, it has emerged that more often than not, the 'Charter compatibility recitals' constituted such lip service, at least until the entry into force of the Lisbon Treaty. We have also seen that fundamental rights language in the legislation does not always provide for better protection in practice in the application of the laws.

These last considerations should not, however, lead to neglecting this topic. On the contrary, in the post-Lisbon era, where, perhaps more than ever, fundamental rights stand in the spotlight, a momentum has been created for a conscious approach to dealing with and enhancing fundamental rights protection in and through internal market legislation—a moment that should be seized by the EU institutions.

IV. EPILOGUE

As we have seen, the internal market can constitute an 'entrance point' through which not only fundamental rights but also a variety of other non-economic objectives can and

[59] The increasing amount of fundamental rights litigation is already starkly evident; see Commission, 2011 Report on the Application of the EU Charter of Fundamental Rights, COM(2012) 169 final (16 April 2012); and Joined Report of the Danish Council Presidency and the EU Fundamental Rights Agency, 'Bringing the Charter to life—opportunities and challenges of putting the EU Charter of Fundamental Rights into practice' (15–16 March 2012), http://fra.europa.eu/sites/default/files/copenhagen-seminar-report.pdf.

[60] R Dehousse, *The European Court of Justice: The Politics of Judicial Integration* (Basingstoke, Macmillan, 1998).

[61] D Kennedy, 'The Critique of Rights in Critical Legal Studies', http://duncankennedy.net/documents/The%20Critique%20of%20Rights%20in%20cls.pdf, 197.

[62] M Dawson, 'The Political Face of Judicial Activism: Europe's Law-Politics Imbalance', Maastricht Faculty of Law, Working Papers (2012-1).

[63] See discussion in ch 4 on Case C-275/06 *Productores de Música de España (Promusicae) v Telefónica de España SAU* [2008] ECR I-271 in s III.C.i.

[64] See I Butler, 'Ensuring Compliance with the Charter of Fundamental Rights in Legislative Drafting: The Practice of the Euroepan Commission' (2012) 37 *European Law Review* 397.

are typically regulated. Internal market legislation is never only concerned with market objectives.[65] Among the possible non-market objectives that can be pursued, this book has singled out fundamental rights as deserving special attention for the following reasons: fundamental rights are one of the EU's foundations; they are central to its ethos; they constitute a measure for the legality of all EU action; they go to the core of the EU integration project; and they are capable of posing the most challenging conflict when colliding with internal market freedoms—the 'clash of titans' scenario, as already stated above.

At the same time, fundamental rights also go to the core of the constitutional structures of the Member States who may have diverging views both on the question of what count as fundamental rights and, more often, on the question of their scope. In the case of maximum harmonisation (as in the case of data protection), the EU standard set out in the instrument will entirely replace and therefore also eliminate any national diversity on the matter. It will also prevail over national constitutional law,[66] even if the Treaty imposes the obligation on the EU to respect the identity of Member States inherent in their constitutional structures.[67] One question that might be posed in this context is therefore whether it is justifiable that elimination of such diversity will be dependent on the operation of the market mechanisms as unfolding on the European scene. As will be recalled, only if a sufficient connection to the 'establishment and functioning of the internal market' can be established will there be a competence to harmonise. In other words, the operation of market mechanisms will decide either which national fundamental rights standards should be harmonised or the regulatory area within which common fundamental rights standards should be mainstreamed. And this 'selection mechanism' could be criticised for being dependent on the market.

This brings us back to the starting point of this book, namely, to the point of advocating a move away from negative to positive integration. Once it is established that fundamental rights as protected in national law are caught by the free movement rules, Member States have already potentially lost a certain degree of autonomy for dictating the permissible degree of protection of the rights at issue. The 'selection mechanism' already starts operating at this point and comes to full manifestation once a measure is subjected to the Court's balancing exercise. Given that excluding fundamental rights from the scope of the free movement rules is unrealistic, the real question is *which process* is better placed to address the matter under these circumstances. In this book, the case has been made for positive integration for three reasons: 1) the legislator is not constrained by the structural asymmetry between market and non-market values which affects balancing of the conflicting interests in the negative integration process and, connected to that, may take full advantage of the potential for market correction during positive integration; 2) the balancing of conflicting interests can be addressed in a conscious generally valid manner by the legislator as opposed to in ad hoc solutions by the Court; and 3) in finding the appropriate 'EU fundamental rights standard', there will be democratic participation (through the European

[65] B de Witte, 'A Competence to Protect: The Pursuit of Non-market Aims through Internal Market Legislation' in P Syrpis (ed), *The Judiciary, the Legislature and the EU Internal Market* (Cambridge, Cambridge University Press, 2011).

[66] Case C-213/07 *Michaniki AE v Ethniko Simvoulio Radiotileorasis, Ipourgos Epikratias* [2008] ECR I-999; Case C-399/11 *Stefano Melloni v Ministero Fiscal* [2008] ECR I-999.

[67] Article 4(2) TEU.

Parliament), while at the same time Member State participation can feed into the EU definition of the most appropriate standards to be applied, thus compensating for their loss of autonomy during negative integration.

This is not to say that harmonisation will always be the most appropriate solution. In certain instances, the definition and implementation of fundamental rights (as operating within the scope of EU law) at the national level may be desirable, as that 'may favour experimentation in each Member State of original solutions, most suitable to the local context'.[68] But there are two points to be made in response here. One is that, in the absence of harmonisation, this will only be possible so long as the Court does not strike down the national standard as constituting an unjustifiable barrier to trade, such as was the case in *Viking* and *Laval*, and so long as the national standard is not threatened by externalities resulting from the operation of the internal market (eg, regulatory competition). The other is that harmonisation does not preclude respect for the local standard (as long as it does not fall below the level of protection provided for in the EU) in the case of minimum harmonisation. Outside the internal market, it is even possible to find an instance of legislation that refers back to national constitutional standards in its substantive provisions.[69] It would be possible for internal market legislation to do the same.

In this light, it is even more mandatory that the legislator adopts a conscious and explicit fundamental rights policy in the internal market. This means not only that the choices as to minimum or maximum harmonisation, deference to national constitutional law or a lack thereof, the appropriate levels of protection and the rights chosen for mainstreaming result from awareness of the fundamental rights dimension at stake in given circumstances. It also means that the legislator keeps a close eye on the developments in negative integration and takes a serious and courageous role as an equal partner in the construction of an internal market that is firmly based on respect for fundamental rights, also to the extent of seeking to influence and alter situations detrimental to fundamental rights that are brought about by Court rulings. This, after all, is its duty under the Charter.

[68] O de Schutter, 'A New Direction for the Fundamental Rights Policy of the EU', Working Paper Series: REFGOV-FR-33 (2010), 13.

[69] Council Framework Decision 2008/913/JHA on combating certain forms of and expressions of racism and xenophobia by means of criminal law [2008] OJ L328/55, Art 7.

Bibliography

LITERATURE

Adamini, S et al, 'European Policymaking on the Tobacco Advertising Ban: The Importance of Escape Routes' (2011) 6 *Health Economic, Policy and Law* 65.

Agerbeeck, FR, 'Freedom of Expression and Free Movement in the Brenner Corridor: The Schmidberger Case' (2004) 29(2) *European Law Review* 255.

Alemanno, A, 'Fundamental Common Market Freedoms v Fundamental Individual Rights in the EU; What Role for the ECJ after Omega?' (2005) *EU Focus* 2.

—— 'A Meeting of Monds on Impact Assessment—When Ex Ante Evaluation Meets Ex Post Judicial Control' (2011) 17 *European Public Law* 3 485.

Alemanno, A and Bonadio, E, 'Do You Mind My Smoking? Plain Packaging of Cigarettes under the TRIPS Agreement' (2011) 10 *John Marshall Review of Intellectual Property Law* 450.

Alston, P and de Schutter, O (eds), *Monitoring Fundamental Rights in the EU—The Contribution of the Fundamental Rights Agency* (Oxford, Hart Publishing, 2005).

Alston, P and Weiler, JHH, 'An Ever Closer Union in Need of a Human Rights Policy' (1998) 9 *European Journal of International Law* 658.

—— 'The European Union and Human Rights: Final Project Report on an Agenda for the Year 2000' in *Leading by Example: A Human Rights Agenda for the European Union for the Year 2000: Agenda of the Comité des Sages and Final Project Report* (Florence, Academy of European Law, EUI, 1998).

Ambrose, ML and Ausloos, J, 'The Right to be Forgotten across the Pond' (2013) *Journal of Information Policy* 1.

Ariño, M, 'Competition law and Pluralism in European Digital Broadcasting: Addressing the Gaps' (2004) 54(2) *Communications & Strategies* 97.

Avbelij, M, 'European Court of Justice and the Question of Value Choices, Fundamental Human Rights as an Exception to the Freedom of Movement of Goods', Jean Monnet Working Paper 06/04.

Avblelij, M and Komárek, J (eds), 'Four Visions of Constitutional Pluralism', EUI Working Papers Law 2008/21.

Bache, I and George, S, *Politics in the European Union* (Oxford, Oxford University Press, 2006).

Bailleux, A, *Les interactions entre libre circulation et droits fondamentaux dans la jurisprudence communautaire. Essai sur la figure du juge traducteur* (Brussels, Bruylant, 2009).

Barendt, E, *Freedom of Speech* (Oxford, Oxford University Press, 2007).

Barnard, C, 'Social Dumping and the Race to the Bottom: Some Lessons for the European Union from Delaware' (2000) 25(1) *European Law Review* 57.

—— 'Employment Rights, Free Movement under the EC Treaty and the Services Directive', Edinburgh, Europa Institute, Mitchell Working Paper Series, 5/2008.

Barnard, C, 'The UK and Posted Workers: *The Effect of Commission v Luxembourg* on the Territorial Application of British Labour Law' (2009) 38(1) *Industrial Law Journal* 122.

Barzanti, F, 'Governing the European Audiovisual Space: What Modes of Governance Can Facilitate a European Approach to Media Pluralism?', EUI Working Papers, RSCAS 2012/49.

Bast, J, 'Legal Instruments and Judicial Protection' in A Von Bogdandy and J Bast (eds), *Principles of European Constitutional Law* (Oxford, Hart Publishing, 2009), 345–98.

Bausili, AV, 'Rethinking the Methods of Dividing and Exercising, Powers in the EU: Reforming Subsidiarity and National Parliaments', Jean Monnet Working Paper No 9/02.

Bercusson, B, *European Labour Law* (London, Butterworths, 1996).
—— 'The Trade Union Movement and the European Union: Judgment Day' (2007) 13(3) *European Law Journal* 279.
Bernard, N, 'Between a Rock and a Soft Place: Internal Market v Open Coordination in EU Social Welfare Law' in M Dougan and E Spaventa (eds) *Social Welfare and EU Law* (Oxford, Hart Publishing, 2005), 261–87.
Bignami, F, 'Creating European Rights: National Values and Supranational Interests' (2005) 11 *Columbia Journal of European Law* 241.
—— 'Protecting Privacy against the Police in the European Union: The Data Retention Directive', Duke Law School Working Paper Series, Paper 76, 2007.
—— 'The Case for Tolerant Constitutional Patriotism: The Right to Privacy before the European Courts' (2008) 41 *Cornell International Law Journal* 211.
Biondi, A, 'Free Trade, a Mountain Road and the Right to Protest: European Economic Freedoms and Fundamental Individual Rights' (2004) 1 *European Human Rights Law Review* 52.
Blanke, T, 'Die Entscheidungen des EuGH in den Fällen Viking, Laval und Rueffert—Domestizierung des Streikrechts und europaweite Nivellierung der industriellen Bezieungen', Oldeburger Studien zur Europäisierung und zur transnationalen Regulierung Nr. 18/2008.
Boessen, S and Maarse, H, 'The Impact of the Treaty Basis on Health Policy Legislation in the European Union: A Case Study on the Tobacco Advertising Directive' (2008) 8(77) *BMC Health Services Research* 1.
Burri-Nenova, M, 'Cultural Diversity and the EC Audiovisual Media Services Directive: Beyond the Handsome Rhetoric', NCCR Trade Working Paper No 2009/9, April 2009.
Butler, I, 'Ensuring Compliance with the Charter of Fundamental Rights in Legislative Drafting: The Practice of the European Commission' (2012) 4 *European Law Review* 397.
Bygrave, LA, 'International Agreements to Protect Personal Data' in JB Rule and G Greenleaf (eds) *Global Privacy Protection—The First Generation* (Cheltenham, Edward Elgar, 2008) 15–49.
Campbell, T, 'Human Rights: A Culture of Controversy' (1999) 26(1) *Journal of Law and Society* 6.
Chalmers, D, Davies, G and Monti, G, *European Union Law* (Cambridge, Cambridge University Press, 2010).
Christensen, M, 'Contentious Terrain in EU Information Society Policies: Media Pluralism and Freedom of Expression' (2008) 45 *Mediekultur* 80.
Cnossen, S, 'Tobacco Taxation in the European Union' CESIFO Working Paper No 1718, May 2006.
Craig, P, 'Democracy and Rule-making Within the EC: An Empirical and Normative Assessment' (1997) 3 *European Law Journal* 105.
Craufurd Smith, R, *Broadcasting Law and Fundamental Rights*, (Oxford, Oxford University Press, 1997).
—— 'Media Convergence and the Regulation of Audiovisual Content: Is the European Community's Audiovisual Media Services Directive Fit for Purpose?' (2007) *Current Legal Problems* 238.
—— 'Rethinking European Union Competence in the Field of Media Ownership: The Internal Market, Fundamental Rights and European Citizenship' (2004) 29 *European Law Review* 652.
Crow, ME, 'Smokescreens and State Responsibility: Using Human Rights Strategies to Promote Global Tobacco Control' (2004) *Yale Journal for International Law* 209.
Däubler, W, 'Posted Workers and Freedom to Supply Services' (1998) 27 *Industrial Law Journal* 264.
Davies, ACL, 'One Step Forwards, Two Steps Back? The Viking and Laval Cases in the ECJ' (2008) 37(2) *Industrial Law Journal* 126.
Davies, P, 'Market Integration and Social Policy in the Court of Justice' (1995) 24(1) *Industrial Law Journal* 49.
—— 'Posted Workers: Single Market or Protection of National Labour Law Systems?' (1997) 34 *Common Market Law Review* 571.
—— 'Case Note on Rüffert' (2008) 37 *Industrial Law Journal* 384.

Davison, M, 'Plain Packaging and the TRIPS Agreement: A Response to Professor Gervais' (2013) 23 *Australian Intellectual Property Journal* 160.
Dawson, M, 'The Political Face of Judicial Activism: Europe's Law-Politics Imbalance', Maastricht Working Papers, Faculty of Law, 2012-1.
De Alwis, RS and Daynard, D, 'Reconceptualising Human Rights to Challenge Tobacco' (2008–09) 17 *Michigan State Journal of International Law* 291.
De Búrca, G, 'Convergence and Divergence in European Public Law: The Case of Human Rights' in P Beaumont, C Lyons and N Walker (eds), *Convergence And Divergence in European Public Law* (Oxford, Hart Publishing, 2002) 131–51.
—— 'New Modes of Governance and the Protection of Human Rights' in P Alston and O de Schutter (eds), *Monitoring Fundamental Rights in the EU—The Contribution of the Fundamental Rights Agency* (Oxford, Hart Publishing, 2005) 25–37.
De Goede, M, 'The Politics of Preemption and the War on Terror in Europe' (2008) 14 *European Journal of International Relations* 161.
De Herth, P and Gutwirth, S, 'Data Protection in the Case Law of Strasbourg and Luxemburg: Constitutionalisation in Action' in S Gutwirth, Y Poullet, P de Hert, J Nouwt and C Terwange, (eds), *Reinventing Data Protection?* (Dordrecht, Springer, 2009) 3–45.
De la Rosa, S, 'The Directive on Cross-border Healthcare or the Art of Codifying Complex Case Law' (2012) 49 *Common Market Law Review* 15.
De Schutter, O, 'Mainstreaming Human Rights in the Europea Union' in P Alston and O de Schutter (eds), *Monitoring Fundamental Rights in the EU—The Contribution of the Fundamental Rights Agency* (Oxford, Hart Publishing, 2005) 37–73.
—— Report for the 4th Round Table of European National Institutions for the Promotion and Protection of Human Rights and the Council of Europe Commissioner for Human Rights, 'When Can National Human Rights Institutions Successfully Intervene in the Process of Adopting Legislation?', CommDH/NHRI(2006)2 Original version.
—— 'The Two Europes of Human Rights: The Emerging Division of Tasks between the Council of Europe and the European Union in Promoting Human Rights in Europe' (2008) 14 *Columbia Journal of European Law* 509.
—— 'A New Direction for the Fundamental Rights Policy of the EU', Working Paper series: REFGOV-FR-33 (2010).
—— 'The Implementation of the Charter by the Institutions of the European Union' in S Peers, T Hervey, J Kenner and A Ward (eds), *The EU Charter of Fundamental Rights—A Commentary* (Oxford, Hart Publishing, 2014) 1627–55.
De Vries, K et al, 'The German Constitutional Court Judgment on Data Retention: Proportionality Overrides Unlimited Surveillance (Doesn't it?)' in S Gutwirth, Y Poullet, P de Hert and R Leenes (eds), *Computers, Privacy and Data Protection: An Element of Choice* (Dordrecht, Springer, 2011) 3–25.
De Vries, S, 'The Protection of Fundamental Rights within Europe's Internal Market after Lisbon—An Endeavour for More Harmony' in De Vries S A et al, *The Protection of Fundamental Rights in the EU After Lisbon* (Oxford, Hart Publishing, 2013) 59–97.
De Witte, B, 'The European Content Requirement in the EC Television Directive—Five Years after' (1995) 1 *Yearbook of Media and Entertainment Law* 101.
—— 'Setting the Scene: How Did Services Get to Bolkenstein and Why?', EUI Working Paper LAW No 2000/20.
—— 'Non-market Values in Internal Market Legislation' in N Shuibhne (ed), *Regulating the Internal Market* (Cheltenham, Edward Elgar, 2006) 61–87.
—— 'A Competence to Protect: The Pursuit of Non-market Aims through Internal Market Legislation' in P Syrpis (ed), *The Judiciary, the Legislature and the EU Internal Market* (Cambridge, Cambridge University Press, 2012) 25–48.

De Witte, B, Trechsel, A, Damjanović, D, Hellquist, E, Hien, J and Ponzano, P, 'Legislating after Lisbon—New Opprtunities for the European Parliament', EUDO study, Florence June 2010.

Dehousse, R, *The European Court of Justice: The Politics of Judicialisation* (Basingstoke, Macmillan, 1998).

Dommering, E, 'Part 1 Primary European Law' in O Castendyk, EJ Dommering and A Scheuer (eds), *European Media Law* (Alphen an den Rijn, Kluwer Law International, 2008) 35–245.

Doukas, D, 'The EU Media Market and the Interplay between the Legislature and the Judiciary' in P Syrpis (ed), *The Judiciary, the Legislature and the EU Internal Market* (Cambridge, Cambridge University Press, 2012) 147–76.

Doyle, G, 'From "Pluralism" to "Ownership": Europe's Emergent Policy on Media Concentrations Navigates the Doldrums' (1997) 3 *Journal of Information, Law and Technology* 1.

Dresler, C and Marks, S, 'The Emerging Human Right to Tobacco Control' (2006) 28 *Human Rights Quarterly* 599.

Dworkin, R, *Taking Rights Seriously* (Cambridge MA, Harvard University Press, 1977).

—— 'Constitutionalism and Democracy' (1995) 3 *European Journal of Philosophy* 4.

Edward, D, 'Guest Editorial: Will There Be Honey Still for Tea?' (2006) 43 *Common Market Law Review* 623.

Eeckhout, P, 'The EU Charter of Fundamental Rights and the Federal Question' (2002) 39 *Common Market Law Review* 945.

—— *External Relations of the European Union—Legal and Constitutional Foundations* (Oxford, Oxford University Press, 2004).

Eichhorst, W, 'European Social Policy between National and Supranational Regulation: Posted Workers in the Framework of Liberalised Services Provision', Max-Planck-Institut für Gesellshaftsforschung, Discussion Paper 98/6.

Eleftheriadis, P, 'A Right to Health Care' (2012) 40 *Journal of Law, Medicine & Ethics* 286.

Evans, S, 'Improving Human Rights Analyses in the Legislative and Policy Processes' (2005) 29 *Melbourne University Law Review* 665.

Ewing, KD and Hendy, J, QC, 'The Dramatic Implications of *Demir and Baykara*' (2010) 39(1) *Industrial Law Journal* 2.

Feintuck, M, 'Regulating the Media Revolution: In Search of the Public Interest' (1997) 3 *Journal of Information, Law and Technology* 1.

Frankel, S and Gervais, D, 'Plain Packaging and the Interpretation of the TRIPS Agreement' (2013) 46(5) *Vanderbilt Journal of Transnational Law* 1149.

Fuller, LL, 'The Forms and Limits of Adjudication' (1978) 92 *Harvard Law Review* 353.

Gearty, C, 'Against Judicial Enforcement' in *Debating Social Rights* (Oxford, Hart Publishing, 2011).

Giesen, R, 'Posting: Social Protection of Workers vs. Fundamental Freedoms?' (2003) 40 *Common Market Law Review* 143.

Gilmore, A and McKee, M, 'Tobacco Control Policy in the European Union: The Legal, Ethical and Policy Debates' in EA Feldman and R Bayer (eds), *Unfiltered: Conflicts over Tobacco Policy and Public Health* (Cambridge MA, Harvard University Press, 2004) 219–54.

Goerrens, P, 'Interplay between Relevant European Instruments—ECTT and TVwF Directive: Competition or Complementarity?' in IRIS Special, *Audiovisual Media Services without Frontiers, Implementing the Rules* (European Audiovisual Observatory, Strasbourg, 2006) 1–11.

Gounalakis, G and Zagouras, G, Publizistische Vielfaltsicherung—Eine Aufgabe für Europa?' (2008) 13 *Juristische Zeitung* 652.

Griller, S and Orator, A, 'Everything under Control? The "Way Forward" for European Agencies in the Footsteps of the Meroni Doctrine' (2010) 35 *European Law Review* 3.

Grossetête, F, 'Research and Development of Orphan Drugs: At Last a European Regulation' (2001) 3 *Pharmaceuticals Policy and Law* 7.

Groussot, X, 'Rock the KaZaA: Another Clash of Fundamental Rights' (2008) 45 *Common Market Law Review* 1745.

Harcourt, A, 'Engineering Europeanization: The Role of the European Institutions in Shaping National Broadcasting Regulation' (2002) 9(4) *Journal of European Public Policy* 736.

—— 'Introduction' in G Terzis (ed), *European Media Governance—The Brussels Dimension* (Bristol, Intellect, 2008) 13–23.

Harcourt, A and Radaelli, CM, 'Limits to EU Technocratic Regulation?' (1999) 35 *European Journal of Political Research* 107.

Harris, DJ and Darcy, J, *The European Social Charter* (Ardsley, NY, Transnational Publishers, 2001).

Harris, DJ, O'Boyle, M and Warbick, C, *Law of the European Convention on Human Rights* (Oxford, Oxford University Press, 1995).

Hatzopoulos, V, 'Health Law and Policy: The Impact of the EU' in G De Búrca (ed), *EU Law and the Welfare State: In Search of Solidarity* (Oxford, Oxford University Press, 2005) 123–60.

Hautamäki, V-P, 'Reasons for Saying No Thanks! Analysing the Discussion about the Necessity of a Constitutional Court in Sweden and Finland' (2006) 10(1) *Electronic Journal of Comparative Law* 1.

Heisenberg, D, *Negotiating Privacy: the European Union, the United States and Personal Data Protection*, (Boulder, CO, Lynne Rienner, 2005).

Hellsten, J, 'On the Social Dimension in Posting of Workers, Reasoning on Posted Workers Directive, Wage Liability, Minimum Wages and Right to Industrial Action' (2006) 301 *Publication of Labour Administration* 34.

Hendriks, A, 'The Right to Health in National and International Jurisprudence' (1998) 5 *European Journal of Health Law* 389.

Hervey, T, 'Up in Smoke? Community (Anti)Tobacco Law and Policy' (2001) 26(2) *European Law Review* 26.

—— 'The 'Right to Health' in EU Law' in T Hervey and J Kenner (eds), *Economic and Social Rights under the EU Charter of Fundamental Rights* (Oxford, Hart Publishing, 2003) 193–222.

—— 'We Don't See a Connection: The "Right to Health" in the EU Charter and European Social Charter' in G de Búrca and B de Witte (eds), *Social Rights in Europe* (Oxford, Oxford University Press, 2005) 305–35.

Hervey, T and McHale, J, *Health Law in the European Union* (Cambridge, Cambridge University Press, 2004).

—— 'Article 35—The Right to Health Care' in S Peers, T Hervey, J Kenner and A Ward (eds), *The EU Charter of Fundamental Rights* (Oxford, Hart Publishing, 2014).

Hiebert, J, 'Interpreting a Bill of Rights: The Importance of Legislative Rights Review' (2005) 35 *British Journal of Political* Science 235.

—— 'Parliament and the Human Rights Act: Can the JCHR Help Facilitate a Culture of Rights?' (2006) 4 *International Journal of Constitutional Law* 1.

Hins, W, 'The Freedom to Conduct a Business and the Right to Receive Information for Free: *Sky Österreich GmbH v. Österreichischer Rundfunk*' (2014) 51 *Common Market Law Review* 665.

Howells, G, Micklitz, H-W and Wilhelmson, T, *European Fair Trading Law—The Unfair Commercial Practices Directive* (Aldershot, Ashgate, 2006).

Hunt, P, 'The Health and Human Rights Movement: Progress and Obstacles' (2008) 15 *Journal of Law and Medicine* 714.

Hunt, P and Backmann, G, 'Health Systems and the Right to the Highest Attainable Standard of Health' (2008) 20(1) *Health and Human Rights* 81.

Hunt, P and MacNaughton, G, 'Impact Assessment, Poverty and Human Rights: A Case Study Using the Right to the Highest Attainable Standard of Health', Health and Human Rights Working Paper Series No 6.

Iosifides, P, 'Pluralism and Media Concentration Policy in the European Union' (1997) 4(1) *The Public* 85.

Jacobs, CL, 'Demystifying the Progressive Realisation of Socio-Economic Rights in South Africa', online paper presented to the Australia National University, October 2009.

Jacobson, PD and Banerjee, A, 'Social Movements and Human Rights Rhetoric in Tobacco Control' (2005) 14 *Tobacco Control* ii45.

Jacobson, PD and Soliman, S, 'Co-opting the Health and Human Rights Movement' (2002) 30 *Journal of Law, Medicine & Ethics* 705.

Jacobson, PD, Wasserman, J and Raube, KR, 'The Politics of Anti-smoking Legislation: Lessons from Six States' (1993) 18 *Journal of Health Politics, Policy and Law* 787.

Joerges, C and Roedl, F, 'Informal Politics, Formalised Law and "the Social Deficit" of European Integration: Reflections after the Judgments of the ECJ *Viking* and *Laval*' (2009) 15(1) *European Law Journal* 1.

Kennedy, D, 'The Critique of Rights in Critical Legal Studies' in W Brown and JE Halley (eds), *Left Legalism/Left Critique* (Durham NC, Duke University Press 2002) 178–229.

Kennedy, MS, 'Australia's Tobacco Plain Packaging Act: Convergence of Public Health and Global Trade' (2013) *North Carolina Journal of International Law & Commercial Regulation* 591.

Kenner, J, *EU Employment Law: From Rome to Amsterdam and Beyond* (Oxford, Hart Publishing, 2002).

Kilpatrick, C, 'The ECJ and Labour Law: A 2008 Perspective' (2009) 38(2) *Industrial Law Journal* 180.

Klimkiewicz, B, 'Is the Clash of Rationales Leading Nowhere? Media Pluralism in European Regulatory Policies' in A Czepek, M Hellwig and E Nowak (eds), *Press Freedom and Pluralism in Europe: Concepts and Conditions* (Bristol, Intellect, 2009) 45–74.

Klimkiewicz, B, 'Media Pluralism: European Regulatory Policies and the Case of Central Europe', EUI Working Paper, RSCAS, No 2005/19.

Knook, A, 'The Court, the Charter, and the Vertical Division of Powers in the European Union' (2005) 42 *Common Market Law Review* 367.

Komorek, E, 'Is Media Pluralism a Human Right? The European Court of Human Rights, the Council of Europe and the Issue of Media Pluralism' (2009) 3 *European Human Rights Law Review* 395.

Koplan, JP et al, 'Towards a Common Definition of Global Health' (2009) 373 *The Lancet* 1993.

Krzemińska, J, 'Freedom of Commercial Speech in Europe', Zentrum für Europäische Rechtspolitik Universität Bremen, online paper, 2005.

Kühling, J, 'Rückkehr des Rechts: Verpflichtung von "Google und Co." zu Datenschutz' (2014) 14 *Europäische Zeitschrift für Wirtschaftsrecht* 52.

Ladenburger, C, FIDE 2012—Session on Protection of Fundamental Rights Post-Lisbon—The Interaction between the Charter of Fundamental Rights, the European Convention of Human Rights and National Constitutions in J Laffrange (ed), *The Protection of Fundamental Rights Post-Lisbon, Reports of the XXV Fide Congress*, (Tallinn, Tartu University Press, 2012).

Lamping, W, 'European Integration and Health Policy—A Peculiar Relationship' in M Steffen (ed), *Health Governance in Europe. Issues, Challenges, Theories* (New York, Routledge, 2005) 18–48.

Laws, J, 'Is the High Court the Guardian of Fundamental Constitutional Rights?' [1993] *Public Law* 63.

LB/JHR, Editorial, 'The Relative Autonomy of the EU Human Rights Standard' (2008) 4 *European Constitutional Law Review* 199.

Lenaerts, K, 'The European Court of Justice and Process-Oriented Review', College of Europe, Research Paper in Law 01/2012.

Lenaerts, K and Gutiérrez-Fons, JA, 'The Constitutional Allocation of Powers and General Principles of EU Law' (2010) 47 *Common Market Law Review* 1629.

Lester, A, 'Parliamentary Scrutiny of Legislation under the Human Rights Act 1998' (2002) 4 *European Human Rights Law Review* 432.

London, L, 'What is a Human Rights-Based Approach to Health and Does it Matter?' (2008) 10(1) *Health and Human Rights* 65.

Long, WJ and Pang Quek, M, 'Personal Data Privacy Protection in an Age of Globalization": The US-EU Safe Harbor Compromise' (2002) 9(3) *Journal of European Public Policy* 325.

Maduro, MP, 'Europe's Social Self: "The Sickness unto Death"' in J Shaw (ed), *Social Law and Policy in an Evolving European Union* (Oxford, Hart Publishing, 2000) 325–50.

Majone, G, 'The European Community as a Regulatory State' in *Collected Courses of the Academy of European Law*, European Community Law, vol V, Book 1 (The Hague, Boston/London, Kluwer Law International/Martinus Nijhoff Publishers/Academy of European Law, 1994) 321–419.

Mantouvalou, V, 'In Support of Legalisation' in *Debating Social Rights* (Oxford, Hart Publishing, 2011) 85.

Martinez, V, 'Les péripéties du critère social dans l'attribution des marches publics' in G Clamour and M Ubaud-Bergeron (eds), *Contracts publics. Mélanges en l'honneur du professeur Michel Guibal*, vol II (Montpelier, Presses de la Faculté de droit de Montpellier, 2006) 251.

Mestre, B, 'The Ruling Laval un Partneri: Clarification and Innovation' (2008) 1 *European Law Reporter* 2.

Meuwese, ACM, *Impact Assessment in EU Lawmaking* (The Hague, Kluwer Law International, 2008).

Meyer, J (ed), *Kommentar zur Charta der Grundrechte der Europäischen Union* (Baden-Baden, Nomos, 2006).

Milburn, K, 'The Importance of Lay Theorising for Health Promotion Research and Practice' (1996) 11(1) *Health Promotion International* 41.

Morijn, J, 'Balancing Fundamental Rights and Common Market Freedoms in Union Law: Schmidberger and Omega in the Light of the European Constitution' (2006) 12 *European Law Journal* 15.

Mossialos, E, and McKee, M, *EU Law and the Social Character of Health Care* (Brussels, PIE-Peter Lang, 2002).

Müller, J-W, 'Three Objections to Constitutional Patriotism' (2007) 14 *Constellations* 197.

Newman, A, 'Innovating European Data Privacy Regulation: Unintended Pathways to Experimentalist Governance' in C Sabeland J Zeitlin (eds), *Experimentalist Governance in the European Union: Towards a New Architecture* (Oxford, Oxford University Press, 2010) 29–43.

Novitz, T, 'Labour Rights as Human Rights: Implications for Employers' Free Movement in an Enlarged European Union' (2006–07) 9 *Cambridge Yearbook of European Legal Studies* 358.

Nowak, M, 'The Agency and National Institutions for the Promotion and Protection of Human Rights' in P Alston and O de Schutter (eds), *Monitoring Fundamental Rights in the EU—The Contribution of the Fundamental Rights Agency* (Oxford, Hart Publishing, 2005) 91–111.

Nugter, ACM, *Transborder Flow of Personal Data within the EC* (Deventer/Boston, Kluwer Law and Taxation Publishers, 1990).

Orlandini, G, 'Right to Strike, Transnational Collective Action and European Law: Time to Move On?', Jean Monnet Working Paper 8/07.

Palm, W and Baeten, R, 'The Quality and Safety Paradox in the Patients' Rights Directive' (2011) 21(3) *European Journal of Public Health* 272.

Palmer, A et al, 'Does Ratification of Human-Rights Treaties Have Effects on Population Health?' (2009) 373(9679) *The Lancet* 1987.

Palzer, C and Hilger, C, 'Rechtliche Rundschau der europäischen audiovisuellen Informationsstelle' (2001) 8 *IRIS Plus* 1.

Poullet, Y and Gutwirth, S, 'The Contribution of the Article 29 Working Party to the Construction of a Harmonised European Data Protection System: An Illustration of Reflexive Governance' in O de Schutter and VM Lax (eds), *Human Rights in the Web of Governance—Towards a Learning-Based Fundamental Rights Policy for the European Union* (Brussels, Bruylant, 2010) 253–94.

Prah Ruger, J, 'Toward a Theory of a Right to Health: Capability and Incompletely Theorized Agreements' (2006) 18(2) *Yale Journal of Law & Humanities* 273.

Princen, S, 'Agenda-Setting Strategies in EU Policy Processes' (2011) 18(7) *Journal of European Public Policy* 927.

Rasanathan, K, Norenhag, J and Valentine, N, 'Realizing Human Rights-Based Approaches for Action on the Social Determinants of Health' (2010) 12(2) *Health and Human Rights: An International Journal* 1.

Reich, N, 'Free Movement v. Social Rights in an Enlarged Union—The Laval and Viking Cases before the ECJ' (2008) 2 *German Law Journal* 125.

Rosas, A, 'Finis Europae socialis?' in JC Piris et al (eds), *Chemins d'Europe, Mélanges en l'honneur de Jean-Paul Jacqué* (Paris, Dalloz, 2010) 591–607.

Russell, PH, 'The Political Purposes of the Canadian Charter of Rights and Freedoms' (1983) 61 *Canadian Bar Review* 30.

Ryle, M, 'Pre-legislative Scrutiny: A Prophylactic Approach to Protection of Human Rights' [1994] *Public Law* 192.

Sarikakis, K, *Powers in Media Policy: The Challenge of the European Parliament* (Oxford, Peter Lang International Publishers, 2004).

Sauter, W, The Proposed Patient Mobility Directive and the Reform of Cross-border Healthcare in the EU', TILEC Discussion Paper No 2008-034, September 2008.

Scharpf, F, *Governing in Europe: Effective and Democratic?* (Oxford, Oxford University Press, 1999).

Scharpf, F, 'Negative and Positive Integration in the Political Economy of European Welfare States' in G Marks (ed), *Governance in the European Union* (London, Sage, 1996) 15–39.

Scheinin, M, 'The Relationship between the Agency and the Network of Independent Experts' in P Alston and O de Schutter (eds), *Monitoring Fundamental Rights in the EU—The Contribution of the Fundamental Rights Agency* (Oxford, Hart Publishing, 2005) 73–91.

Schlachter, M, 'The Posting of Workers Directive—German Reactions and Perceptions', Formula Working Paper No 20, 2010.

Sciarra, S, 'Diritti sociali fondamentali' in A Bayls Grau, B Caruso, M D'Antona and S Sciarra (eds), *Dizionario di diritto del lavoro communitario,* (Bologna, Monduzzi, 1996) 71–90.

Shiner, RA, *Freedom of Commercial Expression* (Oxford, Oxford University Press, 2003).

Simitis, S, 'From the Market to the Polis: The EU Directive on the Protection of Personal Data' (1995) 80(3) *Iowa Law Review* 440.

—— 'Data Protection in the European Union—The Quest for Common Rules' in *Collected Courses of the Academy of European Law,* European Community Law, vol VIII, Book 1 (The Hague, Martinus Nijhoff Publishers/Academy of European Law, 1997) 95–141.

Skouris, V, 'Fundamental Rights and Fundamental Freedoms: The Challenge of Striking a Delicate Balance' (2006) 17 *European Business Law Review* 225.

Syrpis, P and Novitz, T, 'Economic and Social Rights in Conflict: Political and Judicial Approaches to their Reconciliation' (2008) 33 *European Law Review* 411.

Syrett, K, 'Of Sources, Rationality and Rights: Emerging Trends of Judicial Review in Allocative Decisions' (2001) 1 *Web JCLI* 1.

Tobler, C, 'Case C-236/09 Association belge des Consommateurs Test-Achats ASBL, Yann van Vugt, Charles Basselier v. Conseil des ministres, Judgment of the Court of Justice (Grand Chamber) of 1 March 2011' (2011) 48(6) *Common Market Law Review* 2041.

Toebes, B, *The Right to Health as a Human Right in International Law* (Antwerp, Intersentia, 1999).

Toggenburg, G, 'The EU Fundamental Rights Agency: Satellite or Guiding Star?' (2007) *SWP Comments* 5.

——'The Role of the New EU Fundamental Rights Agency: Debating the "Sex of Angels" or Improving Europe's Human Rights Performance?' (2008) 3 *European Law Review* 384.

—— 'Fundamental Rights and the European Union: How Does and How Should the EU Agency for Fundamental Rights Relate to the EU Charter of Fundamental Rights?', EUI Working Paper LAW 2013/13.

Trubek, L, Nance, M and Hervey, T, 'The Construction of Healthier Europe: Lessons from the Fight against Cancer' (2008) 26(3) *Wisconsin International Law Journal* 804.

Tuori, K, 'Combining Abstract *Ex Ante* and Concrete *Ex Post* Review: The Finnish Model', paper presented in the UNIDEM Seminar 'Definition and Implementation of Human Rights and Popular Sovereignty in Europe', Frankfurt am Main, 15–16 May 2009.

Usher, JA, 'Case Comment, Case C-378/9, *Germany v. Parliament and Council*, [2000] ECR I-8419' (2001) 38 *Common Market Law Review* 1519.

Valverde, JL, 'Editorial' (2001) 3 *Pharmaceuticals Policy and Law* 1.

Van Loon, A, 'EU Involvement in National Television Ownership and Control Policies and Practices' in European Audiovisual Observatory (ed), *Television and Media Concentration: Regulatory Models on the National and European Level* (Strasbourg, Council of Europe 2001) 63–74.

Vassiliou A, 'Patients' Rights in Cross-border Healthcare' in B Rangoni Machiavelli and F Velo (eds), *Healthcare Policy and Fundamental Rights in Europe—Conference Proceedings* (2008), 7–17.

Von Bogdandy, A, 'Europäischer Protektionismus im Medienbereich' (1992) 9 *Europäische Zeitschrift für Wirtschaftsrecht* 15.

—— 'The European Union as a Human Rights Organization? Human Rights and the Core of the European Union' (2000) 37 *Common Market Law Review* 1307.

Von Bogdandy, A and Von Bernstoff, J, 'The EU Fundamental Rights Agency within the European and International Human Rights Architecture: The Legal Framework and Some Unsettled Issues in a New Field of Administrative Law' (2009) 46 *Common Market Law Review* 1035.

Wagner, W, 'Positive and Negative Integration in EU Criminal Law Cooperation', paper prepared presented at the ECPR's 5th Pan-European Conference on EU Politics Porto, 24–26 June 2010.

Waldron, J, *Law and Disagreement* (Oxford, Oxford University Press, 1999).

Weatheril, S, 'The Internal Market' in S Peers and A Ward (eds), *The EU Charter of Fundamental Rights: Politics, Law and Policy* (Oxford, Hart Publishing, 2004).

—— 'The Limits of Legislative Harmonization Ten Years after *Tobacco Advertising*: How the Court's Case Law Has Become a "Drafting Guide"' (2011) 12(3) *German Law Journal* 827.

Weiler, JHH, 'The Transformation of Europe' (1991) 100 *Yale Law Journal* 2403.

—— 'Fundamental Rights and Fundamental Boundaries: On Standards and Values in the Protection of Human Rights' in NA Neuwahl and A Rosas (eds), *The European Union and Human Rights* (The Hague, Martinus Nijhoff Publishers, 1995) 51–76.

—— 'In Defence of the Status Quo: Europe's Constitutional Sonderweg' in JHH Weiler and M Wind (eds), *European Constitutionalism Beyond the State* (Cambridge, Cambridge University Press, 2003) 7–23.

Weiler, JHH and Fries, SC, 'A Human Rights Policy for the European Community and Union: The Question of Competences', Jean Monnet Working Paper 4/99.

Winslow, C, 'The Untilled Field of Public Health' (1920) 2 *Modern Medicine* 183.

Wolfson, M and Lievesley, D, 'Making Progress in Health and Healthcare', presentation at the OECD conference in Istanbul, June 2007.

Wong, R and Savirimuthu, J, 'All or Nothing: This is the Question? The Application of Art. 3(2) Data Protection Directive 95/46/EC to the Internet' (2008) 25(2) *The John Marshall Journal of Information Technology & Privacy Law* 241.

Woods, L, 'Freedom of Expression in the European Union' (2006) 12(3) *European Public Law* 371.

—— 'The Consumer and Advertising Regulation in the Television without Frontiers and Audiovisual Media Services Directive' (2008) 31 *Journal for Consumer Policy* 63.

Wright, RG, 'Content-Based and Content-Neutral Regulation of Speech: The Limitations of a Common Distinction' (2006) 60 *University of Miami Law Review* 333.

Young, KG, 'Securing Health through Rights' in T Pogge, M Rimmer and K Rubenstein (eds), *Incentives for Public Health: Patent Law and Access to Essential Medicines* (Cambridge, Cambridge University Press, 2010) 357–80.

Zellmer, SB, 'Saving Saving Clauses from Judicial Preemption' (29 August 2007), available at SSRN.

POLICY BRIEFS

Butler, I, 'How to Monitor the Rule of Law, Democracy and Fundamental Rights in the EU', Policy Brief, Open Society European Policy Institute, August 2013.

—— 'A Fundamental Rights Strategy for the European Union', Policy Brief, Open Society European Policy Institute, May 2014.

Ewing, KD, 'The Draft Monti II Regulation—An Inadequate Response to Viking and Laval', *IER Briefing*, 23 January 2012.

Toggenburg, G, 'Was soll die EU können dürfen, um die EU- Verfassungswerte und Rechtsstaatlichkeit der Mitgliedstaaten zu schützen? Ausblick auf eine neue Europäische Rechtsstaatshygiene', OEGfE Policy Brief, 9 September 2013.

REPORTS

International Organisations

Guidelines for implementation of Article 11 of the WHO Framework Convention on Tobacco Control (packaging and labelling of tobacco products).

International Labour Office, Report of the Committee of Experts on the Application of Conventions and Recommendations, Report III (Part 1a), International Labour Conference 99th Session (Geneva, ILO, 2010).

OECD report, 'Sustainability in Impact Assessments—A Review of Impact Assessment Systems in Selected OECD Countries and the European Commission', SG/SD(2011)6/FINAL (21 February 2012)7.

—— Working Party on Information Security and Privacy, 'The Evolving Privacy Landscape: 30 Years after the OECD Privacy Guidelines', DSTI/ICCP/REG(2010)6/FINAL (6 April 2011).

Office of the United Nations High Commissioner for Human Rights, Report of the Special Rapporteur on the Right of Everyone to the Enjoyment of the Highest Attainable Standard of Physical and Mental Health, A/HRC/4/28 (17 January 2007).

—— The World Health Report 2004 (Geneva, World Health Organization, 2004).

—— Report on the Global Tobacco Epidemic 2009—Implementing Smoke-Free Environments (Geneva, World Health Organization, 2009).

World Bank, Novotny, TE and Mamudu, HM, 'Progression of Tobacco Control Policies: Lessons from the United States and Implications for Global Action', Discussion Paper (Washington DC, World Bank, May 2008).

Research Institutions

The Centre for Media Pluralism and Media Freedom (CMPF), Robert Schuman Centre for Advanced Studies, 'European Union Competencies in Respect of Media Pluralism and Media Freedom', RSCAS Policy Papers 2013/01.

Comité des Sages, (Antonio Cassese, Catherine Lalumière, Peter Leuprecht and Mary Robinson), Leading by Example: A Human Rights Agenda for the European Union for the Year 2000 (Florence, European University Institute, 1998).

Study of the Center for Law and Democracy, 'Freedom of Expression and the Regulation of Television to Protect Children: Comparative Study of Brazil and Other Countries', March 2012.

Index

www.ingramcontent.com/pod-product-compliance
Lightning Source LLC
LaVergne TN
LVHW080016210926
848481LV00011B/3039
* 9 7 8 1 5 0 9 9 2 0 0 0 6 *